March 9–11, 2011
Newport Beach, California, USA

I0038165

Association for Computing Machinery

Advancing Computing as a Science & Profession

VEE'11

Proceedings of the 2011 ACM SIGPLAN/SIGOPS International Conference on
Virtual Execution Environments

Sponsored by:
ACM SIGPLAN & ACM SIGOPS

In cooperation with:
USENIX

Supported by:
VMware, Microsoft Research, Intel, IBM, & Google

**Association for
Computing Machinery**

Advancing Computing as a Science & Profession

The Association for Computing Machinery
2 Penn Plaza, Suite 701
New York, New York 10121-0701

Notice to Past Authors of ACM-Published Articles
ACM intends to create a complete electronic archive of all articles and/or other material previously published by ACM. If you have written a work that has been previously published by ACM in any journal or conference proceedings prior to 1978, or any SIG Newsletter at any time, and you do NOT want this work to appear in the ACM Digital Library, please inform permissions@acm.org, stating the title of the work, the author(s), and where and when published.

ISBN: 978-1-4503-1377-3

Additional copies may be ordered prepaid from:

ACM Order Department
PO Box 30777
New York, NY 10087-0777, USA

Phone: 1-800-342-6626 (USA and Canada)
+1-212-626-0500 (Global)
Fax: +1-212-944-1318
E-mail: acmhelp@acm.org
Hours of Operation: 8:30 am – 4:30 pm ET

Printed in the USA

Chairs' Welcome

It is our pleasure to welcome you to the 7th ACM SIGPLAN/SIGOPS Conference on Virtual Execution Environments (VEE'11).

As the leading conference for presentation of research results on all aspects of virtualization, VEE brings together researchers representing a diverse set of interests. This year, we received 84 abstracts, 68 full submissions, and selected 20 papers for presentation at the conference. In selecting papers, the program committee placed high priority on work that is broadly informative and applicable to both researchers and practitioners. We are confident these papers will make for an interesting conference and a valuable contribution to the study and practice of virtualization. Additionally, the program includes a keynote presentation by David Bacon on virtualizing new forms of devices such as FPGAs.

VEE'11 is again co-located with the International Conference on Architectural Support for Programming Languages and Operating Systems (ASPLOS). Our authors, program committee, sponsors, and supporters all span the boundaries between operating systems and programming language implementation, and reflect equally strong academic and industrial interests in the field.

Erez Petrank　　　　　　**Doug Lea**

VEE'11 General Chair　　　*VEE11 Program Chair*

The Technion, Israel　　　*SUNY Oswego, USA*

Table of Contents

Keynote

Session 1: Performance Monitoring

Session 2: Configuration

Session 3: Recovery

Session 4: Migration

VEE 2011 Conference Organization

General Chair: Erez Petrank *(The Technion, Israel)*

Program Chair: Doug Lea *(SUNY Oswego, USA)*

Steering Committee Chair: Chandra Krintz *(University of California, Santa Barbara, USA)*

Steering Committee: Vikram Adve *(University of Illinois, USA)*
David Bacon *(IBM Research, USA)*
Brian Bershad *(University of Washington, USA)*
Marc Fiuczynski *(Princeton, USA)*
David Gregg *(Trinity College Dublin, Ireland)*
Steve Hand *(Cambridge University, UK)*
Tony Hosking *(Purdue, USA)*
Orran Krieger *(VMWare, USA)*
Brian Noble *(University of Michigan, USA)*
David Tarditi *(Microsoft, USA)*
Andrew Warfield *(University of British Columbia, Canada)*

Program Committee: Muli Ben-Yehuda *(IBM Research, Israel)*
Michael Bond *(Ohio State University, USA)*
Trishul Chilimbi *(Microsoft Research, USA)*
Angela Demke Brown *(University of Toronto, Canada)*
Grzegorz Czajkowski *(Google, USA)*
Dave Dice *(Sun Labs at Oracle, USA)*
Alex Garthwaite *(VMWare, USA)*
Dan Grossman *(University of Washington, USA)*
Steve Hand *(University of Cambridge, UK)*
Chandra Krintz *(University of California, Santa Barbara, USA)*
Ross McIlroy *(Microsoft Research, UK)*
Ian Rogers *(Azul, USA)*
Dilma da Silva *(IBM Research, USA)*
Joe Sventek *(University of Glasgow, UK)*
Dan Tsafrir *(The Technion, Israel)*
Jan Vitek *(Purdue University, USA)*

Additional reviewers: Nadav Amit   Christopher Kruegel
                          Aart Bik   YongChul Kwon
                          Chris Bunch   Ely Levy
                          Navraj Chohan   Uri Lublin
                          Yoav Etsion   Fadi Meawad
                          Alexandra Federova   Kristi Morton
                          Daniel Fryer   Nagy Mostafa
                          Abel Gordon   Jelena Pjesivac-Grbovic
                          Nadav Har'El   Mark Silberstein
                          James Hendricks   Michal Wegiel
                          Ahmed Hussein   Wei Zhang
                          Nodira Khoussainova   Lei Zhao
                          Ilia Kravets

VEE 2011 Sponsors & Supporters

Sponsors:

In cooperation with:

Supporters:

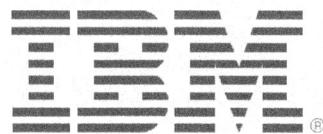

Virtualization in the Age of Heterogeneous Machines

David F. Bacon

IBM Research
dfb@us.ibm.com

Abstract

Since their invention over 40 years ago, virtual machines have been used to virtualize one or more von Neumann processors and their associated peripherals. System virtual machines provide the illusion that the user has their own instance of a physical machine with a given instruction set architecture (ISA). Process virtual machines provide the illusion of running on a synthetic architecture independent of the underlying ISA, generally for the purpose of supporting a high-level language.

To continue the historical trend of exponential increase in computational power in the face of limits on clock frequency scaling, we must find ways to harness the inherent parallelism of billions of transistors. I contend that multi-core chips are a fatally flawed approach - instead, maximum performance will be achieved by using heterogeneous chips and systems that combine customized and customizable computational substrates that achieve very high performance by closely matching the computational and communications structures of the application at hand.

Such chips might look like a mashup of a conventional multi-core, a GPU, an FPGA, some ASICs, and a DSP. But programming them with current technologies would be nightmarishly complex, portability would be lost, and innovation between chip generations would be severely limited.

The answer (of course) is virtualization, and at both the device level *and* the language level.

In this talk I will illustrate some challenges and potential solutions in the context of IBM's Liquid Metal project, in which we are designing a new high-level language (Lime) and compiler/runtime technology to virtualize the underlying computational devices by providing a uniform semantic model.

I will also discuss problems (and opportunities) that this raises at the operating system and data center levels, particularly with computational elements like FPGAs for which "context switching" is currently either extremely expensive or simply impossible.

Categories and Subject Descriptors   B.6.3 [*Design Aids*]: Hardware description languages;   D.3.2 [*Object-oriented languages*]

General Terms   Languages, Performance

Keywords   Virtual machine, heterogeneous hardware

Biography

David F. Bacon is a Research Staff Member at IBM's T.J. Watson Research Center. He led the Metronome project which which pioneered hard real-time garbage collection, opening the use of high-level languages like Java for time-critical systems in financial trading, aerospace, defense, video gaming, and telecommunications.

His recent work focuses on the creation of a language and associated compiler technology to allow fluid programming of software and reconfigurable hardware, to "JIT the hardware" – a project called Liquid Metal.

Dr. Bacon's algorithms are included in most compilers and run-time systems for modern object-oriented languages, and his work on Thin Locks was selected as one of the most influential contributions in the 20 years of the Programming Language Design and Implementation (PLDI) conference.

He received his Ph.D. in computer science from the University of California, Berkeley and his A.B. from Columbia University. He is a member of the IBM Academy of Technology, has served on the governing boards of ACM SIGPLAN and SIGBED, and is a Fellow of the ACM.

VEE'11,   March 9–11, 2011, Newport Beach, California, USA.
ACM 978-1-4503-0501-3/11/03.

Performance Profiling of Virtual Machines

Jiaqing Du

École Polytechnique Fédérale de
Lausanne (EPFL), Switzerland

jiaqing.du@epfl.ch

Nipun Sehrawat

University of Illinois at Urbana
Champaign, USA

sehrawa2@illinois.edu

Willy Zwaenepoel

École Polytechnique Fédérale de
Lausanne (EPFL), Switzerland

willy.zwaenepoel@epfl.ch

Abstract

Profilers based on hardware performance counters are indispensable for performance debugging of complex software systems. All modern processors feature hardware performance counters, but current virtual machine monitors (VMMs) do not properly expose them to the guest operating systems. Existing profiling tools require privileged access to the VMM to profile the guest and are only available for VMMs based on paravirtualization. Diagnosing performance problems of software running in a virtualized environment is therefore quite difficult.

This paper describes how to extend VMMs to support performance profiling. We present two types of profiling in a virtualized environment: *guest-wide profiling* and *system-wide profiling*. Guest-wide profiling shows the runtime behavior of a guest. The profiler runs in the guest and does not require privileged access to the VMM. System-wide profiling exposes the runtime behavior of both the VMM and any number of guests. It requires profilers both in the VMM and in those guests.

Not every VMM has the right architecture to support both types of profiling. We determine the requirements for each of them, and explore the possibilities for their implementation in virtual machines using hardware assistance, paravirtualization, and binary translation.

We implement both guest-wide and system-wide profiling for a VMM based on the x86 hardware virtualization extensions and system-wide profiling for a VMM based on binary translation. We demonstrate that these profilers provide good accuracy with only limited overhead.

Categories and Subject Descriptors D.4 [Operating Systems]: Performance; C.4 [Performance of Systems]: Performance Attributes

General Terms Performance, Design, Experimentation

Keywords Performance Profiling, Virtual Machine, Hardware-assisted Virtualization, Binary Translation, Paravirtualization

1. Introduction

Profilers based on the hardware performance counters of modern processors are indispensable for performance debugging of complex software systems [21, 4, 23]. Developers rely on profilers to understand the runtime behavior, identify potential bottlenecks, and tune the performance of a program.

Performance counters are part of the processor's performance monitoring unit (PMU). The PMU consists of a set of performance counters, a set of event selectors, and the digital logic to increase a counter after a hardware event specified by the event selector occurs. Typical events include clock cycles, instruction retirements, cache misses, TLB misses, etc. When a performance counter reaches a pre-defined threshold, a counter overflow interrupt is generated.

The profiler selects the event(s) to be monitored, and registers itself as the PMU counter overflow interrupt handler. When an interrupt occurs, it records the saved program counter (PC) and other relevant information. After the program is finished, it converts the sampled PC values to function names in the profiled program, and it generates a histogram that shows the frequency with which each function triggers the monitored hardware event. For instance, Table 1 shows a typical output of the widely used OProfile profiler [17] for Linux. The table presents the eight functions that consume the most cycles in a run of the profiled program.

PMU-based performance profiling in a native computing environment has been well studied. Mature profiling tools built upon PMUs exist in almost every popular operating system [17, 13]. They are extensively used by developers to tune software performance. This is, however, not the case in a virtualized environment, for the following two reasons.

On the one hand, running an existing PMU-based profiler in a guest does not result in useful output, because, as far as we know, none of the current VMMs properly expose the PMU programming interfaces to guests. Most VMMs simply filter out guest accesses to the PMU. It is possible to run a guest profiler in restricted timer interrupt mode, but doing so results in limited profiling results. As more and more applications run in a virtualized environment, it is necessary to provide full-featured profiling for virtual machines. In particular, as applications are moved to virtualization-based public clouds, the ability to profile applications in a virtual machine without the need for privileged access to the VMM allows users of public clouds to identify performance bottlenecks and to fully exploit the hardware resources they pay for.

On the other hand, while running a profiler in the VMM is possible, without the cooperation of the guest its sampled PC values cannot be converted to function names meaningful to the guest application developer. The data in Table 1 result from running a profiler in the VMM during the execution of a computation-intensive application in a guest. The first row shows that the CPU spends more than 98% of its cycles in the function vmx_vcpu_run(), which switches the CPU to run the guest. As the design of the profiler does not consider virtualization, all the CPU cycles consumed by the guest are accounted to this function in the VMM . Therefore, we cannot obtain detailed profiling data on the guest. Currently, only XenOprof [18] supports detailed profiling of virtual machines running in Xen [6], a VMM based on paravirtualization. For VMMs based on hardware assistance and binary translation, no such tools exist. Enabling profiling in the VMM provides users and developers of virtualization solutions with a full-scale view of the whole software stack and its interactions with the hardware, helping them to tune the performance of the VMM, the guest, and the applications running in the guest.

% CYCLE	Function	Module
98.5529	vmx_vcpu_run	kvm-intel.ko
0.2226	(no symbols)	libc.so
0.1034	hpet_cpuhp_notify	vmlinux
0.1034	native_patch	vmlinux
0.0557	(no symbols)	bash
0.0318	x86_decode_insn	kvm.ko
0.0318	vga_update_display	qemu
0.0318	get_call_destination	vmlinux

Table 1. A typical profiler output: the eight functions that consume the most cycles in a run of the profiled program.

In this paper we address the problem of performance profiling for three different virtualization techniques: hardware assistance, paravirtualization, and binary translation. We categorize profiling techniques in a virtualized environment into two types. *Guest-wide profiling* exposes the runtime characteristics of the guest kernel and all its active applications. It only requires a profiler running in the guest, similar to *native profiling*, i.e., profiling in a nonvirtualized environment. The VMM is responsible for virtualizing the PMU hardware, and the changes introduced to the VMM are transparent to the guest. *System-wide profiling* reveals the runtime behavior of both the VMM and any number of guests. It requires a profiler running in the VMM and in the profiled guests, and provides a full-scale view of the system.

The main contributions of this paper are:

1. We generalize the problem of performance profiling in a virtualized environment and propose two types of profiling: guest-wide profiling and system-wide profiling.

2. We analyze the challenges of achieving guest-wide and system-wide profiling for each of the three virtualization techniques. Synchronous virtual interrupt delivery to the guest is necessary for guest-wide profiling. The ability to convert samples belonging to a guest context into meaningful function names is required for system-wide profiling.

3. We present profiling solutions for virtualization based on hardware assistance and binary translation.

4. We demonstrate the feasibility and usefulness of virtual machine profiling by implementing both guest-wide and system-wide profiling for a VMM based on the x86 virtualization extensions and system-wide profiling for a VMM based on binary translation.

The rest of the paper is organized as follows. In Section 2 we review the structure and working principles of a profiler in a native environment. In Section 3 we analyze the challenges of supporting guest-wide and system-wide profiling for each of the three aforementioned virtualization techniques. In Section 4 we present the implementation of guest-wide and system-wide profiling in two VMMs, KVM and QEMU. We evaluate the accuracy, usefulness and performance of the resulting profilers in Section 5. In Section 6 we discuss some practical issues related to supporting virtual machine profiling in production environments. We describe related work in Section 7 and conclude in Section 8.

2. Native Profiling

Profiling is a widely used technique for dynamic program analysis. A profiler investigates the runtime behavior of a program as it executes. It determines how much of a hardware resource each function in a program consumes. A PMU-based profiler relies on performance counters to sample system states and figure out approximately how the profiled program behaves. Compared with other profiling techniques, such as code instrumentation [22, 12], PMU-based profiling provides a more accurate picture of the target program's execution as it is less intrusive and introduces fewer side effects.

The programming interface of a PMU is a set of performance counters and event selectors. When a performance counter reaches the pre-defined threshold, a counter overflow interrupt is generated by the interrupt controller and received by the CPU. Exploiting this hardware component for performance profiling, a PMU-based profiler generally consists of the following major components:

- *Sampling configuration.* The profiler registers itself as the counter overflow interrupt handler of the operating system, selects the monitored hardware events and sets the number of events after which an interrupt should occur. It programs the PMU hardware directly by writing to its registers.

- *Sample collection.* The profiler records the saved PC, the event type causing the interrupt, and the identifier of the interrupted process under the counter overflow interrupt context. The interrupt is handled by the profiler synchronously.

- *Sample interpretation.* The profiler converts the sampled PC values into function names of the profiled process by consulting its virtual memory layout and its binary file compiled with debugging information.

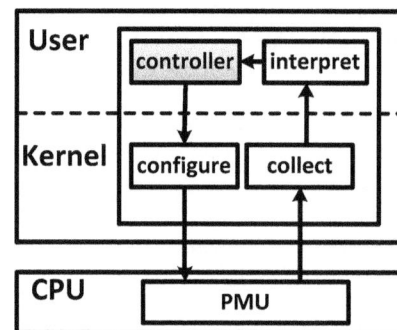

Figure 1. Block diagram of a native PMU-based profiler.

In a native environment, all three profiling components and their data structures reside in the operating system. They interact with each other through facilities provided by the operating system. Figure 1 shows a block diagram of a PMU-based profiler in a native environment.

In a virtualized environment, the VMM sits between the PMU hardware and the guests. The profiler's three components may be spread among the VMM and the guests. Their interactions may require communications between the VMM and the guests. In addition, the conditions for implementing these three components may not be satisfied in a virtualized environment. For instance, the sampling configuration component of a guest profiler may not be able to program the PMU hardware because of the interposition of the VMM. In the next section, we present a detailed discussion of the requirements for guest-wide and system-wide profiling for virtualization based on hardware extensions, paravirtualization and virtualization based on binary translation.

3. Virtual Machine Profiling

3.1 Guest-wide Profiling

Challenges By definition, guest-wide profiling runs a profiler in the guest and only monitors the guest. Although more information about the whole software stack can be obtained by employing system-wide profiling, sometimes guest-wide profiling is the only way to do performance profiling in a virtualized environment. As we explained before, users of a public cloud service are normally not granted the privilege to run a profiler in the VMM, which is necessary for conducting system-wide profiling. To achieve guest-wide profiling, the VMM needs to provide PMU multiplexing, i.e., saving and restoring PMU registers, and enable the implementation of the three profiling components in the guest. Since sample interpretation in guest-wide profiling is the same as in native profiling, we only present here the required facilities for sampling configuration and sample collection. We return to the topic of PMU multiplexing in Section 3.3.

To implement sampling configuration, the guest must be able to program the PMU registers, either directly or with the assistance of the VMM.

To achieve sample collection, the guest must be able to collect correct samples under interrupt contexts, which requires that the VMM supports synchronous interrupt delivery to the guest. This means that, if the VMM injects an interrupt into a guest, that injected interrupt is handled first when the guest resumes its execution. For performance profiling, when a performance counter overflows, an interrupt is generated and first handled by the VMM. If the interrupt is generated when the guest code is being executed, the counter overflow is considered to be contributed by the guest. The VMM injects a virtual interrupt into the guest, which drives the profiler to take a sample. If the guest handles the injected interrupt synchronously when it resumes execution, it collects correct samples as in native profiling. If not, at the time when the injected virtual interrupt is handled, the real interrupt context has already been destroyed and the profiler obtains wrong sampling information.

Hardware assistance The x86 virtualization extensions provide facilities that help implement guest-wide profiling. First, the guest can be configured with direct access to the PMU registers, which are model-specific registers (MSRs) in the x86. The save and restore of the relevant MSRs can also be done automatically by the CPU. Second, the guest can be configured to exit when interrupts occur. The hardware guarantees that event delivery to a guest is synchronous, so the VMM can forward to the guest all counter overflow interrupts contributed by it, and the guest profiler samples correct system states. We present our implementation of guest-wide profiling for virtualization based on the x86 hardware extensions in Section 4.1.

Paravirtualization The major obstacle of implementing guest-wide profiling for VMMs based on paravirtualization is synchronous interrupt delivery to the guest. At least for Xen, this facility is currently not available. External events are delivered to the guest asynchronously. Mechanisms similar to synchronous signal delivery in a conventional OS should be employed to add this capability to paravirtualization-based VMMs. For sampling configuration, as a paravirtualized guest runs in a deprivileged mode and cannot access the PMU hardware, the VMM must implement the necessary programming interfaces to allow the guest to program the PMU indirectly.

Binary translation For VMMs based on binary translation, sampling configuration can be achieved with the assistance of the VMM, which is able to identify instructions that access the PMU and rewrite them appropriately. Similar to paravirtualization, synchronous interrupt delivery to the guest is an engineering challenge. As far as we know, no VMMs based on binary translation support this feature.

3.2 System-wide Profiling

Challenges System-wide profiling reveals the runtime characteristics of both the VMM and the guests. It first requires that all three components of the profiler run in the VMM. Since the profiler resides in the VMM, it can program the PMU hardware directly and handle the counter overflow interrupts synchronously. The challenges for system-wide profiling come from the other two profiling components.

The first challenge for system-wide profiling comes from sample collection. If the counter overflow is triggered by a guest user process, the VMM profiler cannot obtain the identity of this process without the assistance of the guest operating system. This information is described by a global variable in the guest kernel, and the VMM does not know the internal memory layout of the guest. To solve this problem, the guest must share this piece of information with the VMM profiler.

The second challenge is interpreting samples belonging to the guests. Even if the VMM profiler is able to sample all the required information, sample interpretation is not possible because the VMM does not know the virtual memory layout of the guest processes or the guest kernel. This requires the guest to interpret its samples, which means that at least the sample interpretation component of a profiler should run in the guest.

One approach that addresses both the sample collection and the sample interpretation problem is to not let the VMM record samples corresponding to a guest, but to delegate this task to the guest. We call this approach *full-delegation*. It requires guest-wide profiling to be supported by the VMM. With this approach, during the profiling process, one profiler runs in the VMM and one runs in each guest. The VMM profiler is responsible for handling all counter overflow interrupts, but it only collects and interprets samples contributed by the VMM. For a sample not belonging to the VMM, a counter overflow interrupt is injected into the corresponding guest. The guest profiler is driven by the injected interrupts to collect and interpret samples contributed by the guest. Overall system-wide profiling results are obtained by merging the outputs of the VMM profiler and the guests.

An alternative solution is to let the VMM profiler collect all samples and to delegate the interpretation of guest samples to the corresponding guest [18]. We call this approach *interpretation-delegation*. With this solution, the guest makes the identity of the process to be run available to the VMM profiler. When a counter overflows, the VMM records the saved PC, the event type, and the identifier of the interrupted guest process, and sends it to the guest. After the guest receives the sample, it notifies the sample interpretation component of its profiler to convert the sample to a function name, in the same manner as a native profiler. After the profiling finishes, the results recorded in the guests are merged with those produced by the VMM profiler to obtain a system-wide view.

The interpretation-delegation approach for system-wide profiling requires explicit communication between the VMM and the guest. Their interaction rate approaches the rate of counter overflow interrupts, which can go up to thousands of times per second with a normal profiling configuration. Efficient communication methods should be used to avoid distortions in the profiling results. We choose to use a buffer shared among all the profiling participants for exchanging information. In addition, a guest should process samples collected for it in time. Otherwise, if a process terminates before the samples contributed by it are interpreted, there will be no way to interpret these samples because the sample interpretation component needs to consult the virtual memory layout of this process.

Similar to full-delegation, interpretation-delegation can also be implemented by running one profiler in the VMM and one in each guest. However, the guest profiler does not need to access the PMU hardware. It only processes samples in the shared buffer, which are collected for it by the VMM profiler, by running its sample interpretation component when handling a virtual interrupt injected by the VMM profiler.

The choice between full-delegation and interpretation-delegation to implement system-wide profiling depends on whether synchronous interrupt delivery is supported by the VMM. If so, full-delegation is the preferred approach. If not, one should either choose the interpretation-approach or add the support of synchronous interrupt delivery to the VMM. Full delegation requires less engineering effort and is transparent to the profiled guest. Implementing synchronous interrupt delivery to the guest in software is, however, not trivial, and current VMMs based on paravirtualization and binary translation do not support this feature. Therefore, we choose the full-delegation approach to implement system-wide profiling for a VMM based on hardware assistance and the interpretation-delegation approach for a VMM based on binary translation (see Section 4).

Hardware assistance For VMMs based on hardware extensions, since they have all the facilities to implement guest-wide profiling, the full-delegation approach can be employed to achieve system-wide profiling. This approach only requires minor changes to the VMM as our implementation of system-wide profiling for an open-source VMM in Section 4.1 shows. System-wide profiling can also be achieved by the interpretation-delegation approach. An efficient communication path between the guest and the VMM and extensions to the profilers running both in the VMM and in the guest require more engineering work than the full-delegation approach.

Paravirtualization For VMMs based on paravirtualization, system-wide profiling can be implemented by interpretation-delegation. XenOprof uses this approach to perform system-wide profiling in Xen. Its implementation requires less engineering effort than in VMMs based on hardware assistance or binary translation, because Xen provides the hypercall mechanism that facilitates interactions between the VMM and the guest. The full-delegation approach may also work if the VMM supports guest-wide profiling.

Binary Translation For VMMs based on binary translation, system-wide profiling can be achieved through the interpretation-delegation approach. If the VMM supports synchronous interrupt delivery to the guest, the full-delegation approach also works.

When using interpretation-delegation, VMMs based on binary translation need to solve the following additional problem. If the execution of a guest triggers a counter overflow, the PC value sampled by the VMM profiler points to a translated instruction in the translation cache, not to the original instruction. Additional work is required to map the sampled PC back to the guest address where the original instruction is located. This address translation problem can be solved by the following idea. During the translation of guest instructions, we save the mapping from the address(es) of one or more translated instructions to the address of the original guest instruction in the *address mapping cache*, a counterpart of the translation cache. For each memory address of

the translation cache, there is an entry in the address mapping cache, which points to the address holding the original guest instruction. For samples from a guest context, rather than storing the PC value itself, the VMM looks up the original instruction address in the address mapping cache and stores that address as part of the sample. This rewriting of the sampled PC value is transparent to the sample interpretation component in the guest.

3.3 PMU Multiplexing

Besides the requirements stated previously, another important question for both guest-wide and system-wide profiling is: what is the right time to save and restore PMU registers?

The first option is to save and restore these registers when the CPU switches between running guest code and running VMM code. We call this type of profiling *CPU switch*. Profiling results with CPU switch reflect the execution of the guest on the virtualized CPU, but not the guest's use of devices emulated by software. When the CPU switches to execute the VMM code that emulates the effects of a guest I/O operation, although the monitored hardware events are effectively being contributed by the guest, they are not accounted to it. In the case of guest-wide profiling, the PMU is turned off, and in the case of system-wide profiling the events are accounted to the VMM.

The second option is to save and restore relevant registers when the VMM switches execution from one guest to another. We call this *domain switch*. This method accounts to a guest all the hardware events triggered by its execution and by the execution of the VMM while emulating devices on its behalf. In other words, domain switch PMU multiplexing reflects the characteristics of the entire virtual environment, including both the virtualized hardware and the virtualization software.

Guest-wide and system-wide profiling can choose either of the two approaches for PMU multiplexing. Generally, domain switch provides a more realistic picture of the underlying virtual environment. We compare the profiling results of these two methods in Section 5.

4. Implementation

We describe the implementation of both guest-wide and system-wide profiling for the kernel-based virtual machine (KVM) [16], a VMM based on hardware assistance. We also present how system-wide profiling is implemented in QEMU [7], a VMM based on binary translation. As both KVM and QEMU are considered as hosted VMMs, we use the terms "VMM" and "host" interchangeably in this section.

Our implementation follows two principles. First, performance profiling should introduce as little as possible overhead to the execution of the guest. Otherwise, the monitoring results would be perturbed by monitoring overhead. Second, performance profiling should generate as little as possible performance overhead for the VMM. It should not slow down the whole system too much. To achieve these goals, we only introduce additional switches between the VMM and the guest when absolutely necessary. For all our implementations, except during the profiling initialization phase, only virtual interrupt injection into the guest causes additional context switches, but these are inevitable for PMU-based performance profiling.

4.1 Hardware Assistance

KVM is a Linux kernel infrastructure which leverages hardware virtualization extensions to add a virtual machine monitor capability to Linux. With KVM, the VMM is a kernel module in the host Linux, while each virtual machine resides in a normal user space process. Although KVM supports multiple hardware architectures, we choose the x86 with virtualization extensions to illustrate our implementation, because it has the most mature code.

The virtualization extensions augment x86 with two new operation modes: host mode and guest mode. KVM runs in host mode, and its guests run in guest mode. Host mode is compatible with conventional x86, while guest mode is very similar to it but deprivileged in certain ways. Guest mode supports all four privilege levels and allows direct execution of the guest code. A virtual machine control structure (VMCS) is introduced to control various behaviors of a virtual machine. Two transitions are also defined: a transition from host mode to guest mode called a VM-entry, and a transition from guest mode to host mode called a VM-exit. Regarding performance profiling, if a performance counter overflows when the CPU is in guest mode, the currently running guest is forced to exit, i.e., the CPU switches from guest mode to host mode. The VM-exit information filed in the VMCS indicates that the current VM-exit is caused by a non-maskable interrupt (NMI). By checking this field, KVM is able to decide whether a counter overflow is contributed by a guest. This approach assumes all NMIs are caused by counter overflows in a profiling session. To be more precise, KVM could also check the content of all performance counters to make sure that NMIs are really caused by counter overflows.

Our guest-wide profiling implementation requires no modifications to the guest and its profiler. The guest profiler reads and writes the physical PMU registers directly as it does in native profiling. KVM is responsible for virtualizing the PMU hardware and forwarding NMIs due to performance counter overflows to the guest. A user can launch the profiler from the guest and do performance profiling exactly as in a native environment.

We implement system-wide profiling by the full-delegation approach, since KVM is built upon hardware virtualization extensions and supports synchronous virtual interrupt delivery in the guest. In a profiling session, we run one unmodified profiler instance in the host and one in each guest. These profiling instances work and cooperate as we discussed in Section 3.2. The only changes to KVM are clearing the bit in an APIC register after each VM-exit (see below) and injecting NMIs into a guest that causes a performance counter overflow.

When CPU switch is enabled, KVM saves all the relevant MSRs when a VM-exit happens and restores them when the corresponding VM-resume occurs. By configuring certain fields in the VMCS, this is done automatically in hardware. When domain switch is enabled, we tag all (Linux kernel) threads belonging to a guest and group them into one domain. When the Linux kernel switches to a thread not belonging to the current domain, it saves and restores the relevant registers (in software).

In the process of implementing these two profiling techniques in KVM, we also observe the following two noteworthy facts. First, in the x86 architecture, there is one bit of a register in the Advanced Programmable Interrupt Controller (APIC) that specifies the delivery of NMIs due to performance counter overflows. Clearing this mask bit enables interrupt delivery and setting it inhibits delivery. After the APIC sends a counter overflow NMI to the CPU, it automatically sets this bit. To allow subsequent NMIs to be delivered, a profiler should clear this bit after it handles each NMI. In theory, exposing the register containing this bit to the guest would require the virtualization of the APIC. However, the current implementation of KVM does not virtualize the APIC, but emulates it in software. To bypass this problem, we simply clear the bit after each VM-exit, no matter whether the exit is caused by a performance counter overflow or not.

Second, for guest-wide profiling with CPU switch, we find that the CPU receives NMIs due to counter overflows in host mode, typically right after a VM-exit. For guest-wide profiling, however, performance monitoring is only enabled in guest mode, and NMIs due to performance counter overflows are not supposed to happen in host mode. We could not with 100% certainty determine the reason for this problem because of the lack of a hardware debugger. One plausible explanation is that the VM-exit operation is not "atomic". It consists of a number of sub-operations, including saving and restoring MSRs. A counter may overflow during the execution of VM-exit, but before performance monitoring is disabled. The corresponding NMI is not generated immediately, because the instruction executing when an NMI is received is completed before the NMI is generated [15]. The NMI due to a performance counter overflow in the middle of a VM-exit is thus generated after the VM-exit operation finishes, when the processor is in host mode. We solve this problem by registering an NMI handler in the host to catch those host counter overflows and inject the corresponding virtual NMIs into the guest.

4.2 Binary Translation

We present the implementation of system-wide profiling by the interpretation-delegation approach in QEMU, a VMM based on binary translation. In this environment, the guest profiler runs in the guest kernel space; the guest runs in QEMU; QEMU runs in the user space of the host; and the host profiler runs in the host kernel space. The implementation takes more engineering effort than that of the full-delegation approach in KVM. The implementation touches a number of major components in the whole software stack, including the host, the host profiler, the guest, and the guest profiler.

The conventional x86 is not virtualizable because some instructions do not trap when executed in the unprivileged mode. Dynamic binary translation solves this problem by rewriting those problematic instructions on the fly. A binary translator processes a basic block of instructions at a time. The translated code is stored in a buffer called the translation cache, which holds a recently used subset of all the translated code. Instead of the original guest code, the CPU actually executes the code in the translation cache.

Virtual interrupts injected to a guest are delivered asynchronously in QEMU. Once a virtual interrupt injection request is received, QEMU first unchains the translated basic block being executed and forces the control back to itself after this basic block finishes execution. It then sets a flag of the guest virtual CPU to indicate the reception of an interrupt. The injected interrupt is handled when the guest resumes execution.

To reduce the VM exit rate due to information exchange among the guest, QEMU, and the host, we design an efficient communication mechanism for interpretation-delegation. This is important because in a typical profiling session interactions among all these participants can occur at the rate of thousands of times per second. If each interaction involves one VM exit, the profiling results would be polluted and far from being accurate. The key data structure underlying this communication mechanism is a buffer shared among the three participants. All the critical information in a profiling session, such as the PCs and pointers to process descriptors, is exchanged through this buffer. Each profiling participant reads the buffer directly whenever it needs any information and no VM exits are triggered.

The shared buffer is allocated in the guest and shared through the following control channel. The guest exchanges information with QEMU through a customized virtual device added to QEMU and the corresponding device driver in the guest kernel. QEMU and the host kernel talk with each other through common user/kernel communication facilities provided by the host. After the address of the buffer is passed from the guest profiler to the host profiler, the guest profiler accesses the shared buffer by an address in the guest kernel space; QEMU uses this buffer through an address in its own address space; the host profiler accesses it with an address in the host kernel space.

In our implementation, QEMU is responsible for rewriting the PC value sampled by the host profiler into an address of the guest pointing to the original guest code. To reduce the overall overhead of PC value rewriting, the address mapping cache proposed in Section 3.2 does not map the host address of each instruction in the translation cache to its corresponding guest address. Instead, the cache only maintains one entry for one basic block. All the addresses of the instructions in a translated basic block are mapped to the starting address of the corresponding original basic block in the guest. This does not hurt the accuracy of performance profiling with functions as the interpretation granularity because of two reasons. First, a profiler always interprets any address pointing to the body of a function to the name of that function. Second, a basic block does not span across more than one function, because it terminates right after the first branch instruction.

Putting all the pieces together, the process of system-wide profiling for binary translation can be described as follows.

1. In the initialization phase, the host profiler is loaded to the host kernel, and the guest profiler is loaded to the guest kernel. A communication channel across all the profiling participants is established and a buffer is shared among them.

2. The user starts a profiling session by launching the host profiler. The host profiler sends a message to the guest to start the guest profiler.

3. When profiling is being conducted, the guest records the address pointing to the descriptor of each process right before it schedules the process to run. There is only one entry in the shared buffer for this address. The guest keeps overwriting this entry because it is only useful when the execution of the corresponding process triggers a performance counter overflow. When a counter overflows and if it is contributed by the guest, the host profiler copies the sampled PC value, the event type, and the address to the descriptor of the corresponding guest process to a sampling slot in the shared buffer. It then sends a signal to QEMU running in user space. After the counter overflow NMI is handled and QEMU is scheduled to run again, the signal from the host profiler is delivered first. The signal handler rewrites the sampled PC value, records the current privilege mode of the virtual CPU in the same sampling slot, and injects an NMI into the guest. Upon handling the injected NMI, the guest profiler processes all the available sampling slots one by one.

4. The user finishes the profiling session by stopping the host profiler. The host profiler sends a message to the guest to stop the guest profiler. The output of the host profiler and the guest profiler is merged together as the final profiling results.

Because the host knows little about the internals of a guest and the guest code is dynamically translated, the host profiler can only obtain limited runtime information about the guest under an NMI context. Both the guest and QEMU are required to help record or process sampling information on behalf of the host profiler. This leads to changes to all the participants involved in system-wide profiling based on interpretation-delegation[1].

5. Evaluation

We first verify the accuracy of our profilers by comparing the results of native profiling with profiling in various virtualized environments. We then show how guest-wide profiling can be used to profile two guests simultaneously. Next, by comparing the results of CPU switch and domain switch for guest-wide profiling, we show that domain switch sometimes provides considerably more information about the guest's execution. We also demonstrate the power of guest-wide profiling by using it on a couple of examples to explain why one virtualization technique performs better than the other. Finally, we quantify the overhead of our profilers by comparing the execution time of a computation-intensive program with and without profiling.

Our experiments involve two machines. The first one is a Dell OptiPlex 745 desktop with one dual-core Intel Core2 E6400 processor, 2GB DDR2 memory, and one Gigabit Ethernet NIC. The second machine is a Sun Fire x4600 M2 server with four quad-core AMD Opteron 8356 processors, 32GB DDR2 memory, and a dozen of Gigabit Ethernet NICs. Unless explicitly stated, all the experiments are conducted on the Intel machine.

For hardware-assisted virtualization, the VMM consists of the 2.6.32 Linux kernel with the KVM kernel module loaded and QEMU 0.11 in user space [7]. For virtualization based on binary translation, the VMM is QEMU 0.10.5 in user space, which runs on top of the 2.6.30 Linux kernel with virtualization extensions disabled. All guests are configured with one virtual CPU and run Linux with the 2.6.32 kernel. The profiler is OProfile 0.9.5.

For both guest-wide and system-wide profiling, CPU switch for KVM adds 170 lines of C code to the Linux kernel, while domain switch consists of 272 lines of C code. QEMU system-wide profiling with CPU switch introduces 1115 lines of C code to QEMU, the host kernel, and the guest kernel.

5.1 Computation-intensive Workload

To verify the accuracy of our profilers for computation-intensive workloads, we use the code given in Figure 2 as the profiled application, and we compare the output of native profiling with virtualized profiling. The program consists of an infinite loop executing two computation-intensive functions compute_a() and compute_b(), which perform floating point arithmetic and consume different number of CPU cycles. We run this program in two different processes, process1 and process2. We launch both processes at the same time and pin them to one CPU core.

```
int main(int argc, char *argv[])
{
    while (1) {
        compute_a();
        compute_b();
    }
}
```

Figure 2. Code used to verify the accuracy of VM profilers for computation-intensive programs.

Table 2 to Table 5 present the output of profiling runs of this program in which we measure the number of CPU cycles consumed, for native profiling (Table 2), guest-wide profiling in KVM (Table 3), system-wide profiling in KVM (Table 4), and system-wide profiling in QEMU (Table 5)[1]. The results for the

---

[1] For system-wide profiling, only CPU cycles consumed in the guest are counted in the percentages.

8

VM profilers are roughly the same as those for the native profiler. As expected, the two processes, `process1` and `process2`, consume roughly the same number of cycles, and the ratio between cycles consumed in `compute_a()` and in `compute_b()` is also roughly similar.

% CYCLE	Function	Module
40.3463	compute_a	process2
38.2010	compute_a	process1
10.6135	compute_b	process2
10.2371	compute_b	process1
0.1505	vsnprintf	vmlinux
0.1129	(no symbols)	bash
0.0376	(no symbols)	libc.so
0.0376	mem_cgroup_read	vmlinux

Table 2. % of cycles consumed in two processes running the program given in Figure 2, native profiling.

% CYCLE	Function	Module
38.8114	compute_a	process1
38.5913	compute_a	process2
10.3815	compute_b	process2
10.0880	compute_b	process1
0.5503	native_apic_mem_write	vmlinux
0.2201	(no symbols)	libc.so
0.2201	schedule	vmlinux
0.1101	(no symbols)	bash

Table 3. % of cycles consumed in two processes running the program given in Figure 2, KVM guest-wide profiling.

% CYCLE	Function	Module
39.9220	compute_a	process1
39.4209	compute_a	process2
10.3563	compute_b	process2
10.0223	compute_b	process1
0.0557	__switch_to	vmlinux
0.0557	ata_sff_check_status	vmlinux
0.0557	run_time_softirq	vmlinux
0.0557	update_wall_time	vmlinux

Table 4. % of cycles consumed in two processes running the program given in Figure 2, KVM system-wide profiling.

% CYCLE	Function	Module
40.0000	compute_a	process2
36.2963	compute_a	process1
9.2593	compute_b	process1
8.5185	compute_b	process2
0.7407	update_wall_time	vmlinux
0.3704	__schedule	vmlinux
0.3704	__tasklet_hi_schedule	vmlinux
0.3704	cleanup_workqueue_thread	vmlinux

Table 5. % of cycles consumed in two processes running the program given in Figure 2, QEMU system-wide profiling.

These results are further confirmed by Figure 3, which shows the average and the standard deviation of the percentage of CPU cycles consumed by `compute_a()` and `compute_b()` over 10 runs with all four profilers. Our profilers provide stable results, with standard deviations ranging from 0.44% to 2.87%. Native profiling has the smallest variance and system-wide profiling for QEMU has the largest.

Figure 4 shows the results of simultaneous guest-wide profiling of two KVM guests running the program described in Figure

2. The percentage of CPU cycles consumed by each function is the same in both guests, and similar to the percentage for each function for native profiling, indicating the accuracy of our profiler when used with multiple virtual machines.

Although the data in this experiment do not constitute "proof of correctness", they give us reasonable confidence that our design and implementation work reasonably well in terms of CPU cycles. We obtain similar results for instruction retirements.

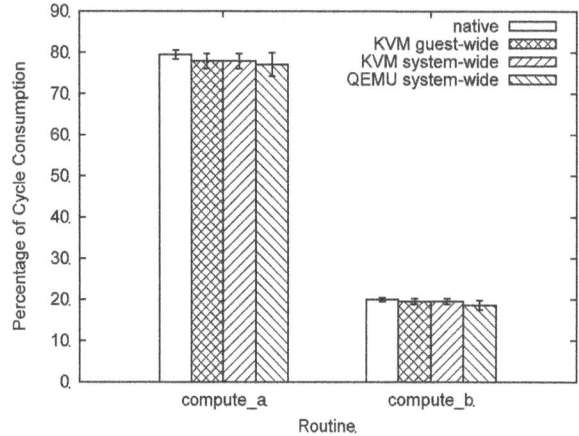

Figure 3. Average and standard deviation of the percentage of cycles consumed by `compute_a()` and `compute_b()`.

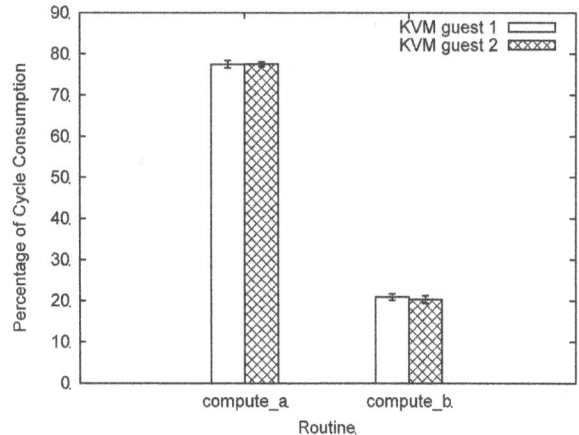

Figure 4. Average and standard deviation of the percentage of cycles consumed by `compute_a()` and `compute_b()` in two KVM guests, KVM guest-wide profiling.

5.2 Memory-intensive Workload

We use the program described in Figure 5 to demonstrate the operation of the KVM guest-wide profiling with memory-intensive programs. This program makes uniformly distributed random accesses to a fixed-size region of memory. We run this program with a working set of 512KB for which the entire execution fits in the L2 cache, and with a working set of 2048KB that causes many misses in the L2 cache.

Table 6 presents the profiling results for L2 cache misses for the 512KB working set, and Table 7 presents the results for the 2048KB working set. The results clearly reflect the higher number of L2 misses with the larger working set.

```
struct item {
    struct item *next;
    long pad[NUM_PAD];
}

void chase_pointer()
{
    struct item *p = NULL;
    p = &randomly_connected_items;
    while (p != null) p = p->next;
}
```

Figure 5. Code used to verify the accuracy of VM profilers for memory-intensive programs.

L2 Miss	Function	Module
1250	chase_pointer	cache_test
100	(no symbols)	bash
100	(no symbols)	ld.so
100	(no symbols)	libc.so
50	sync_buffer	oprofile.ko
50	do_notify_resume	vmlinux
50	do_wp_page	vmlinux
50	find_first_bit	vmlinux

Table 6. L2 cache misses (in thousands) for the program given in Figure 5 with a working set of 512KB, KVM guest-wide profiling.

L2 Miss	Function	Module
150750	chase_pointer	cache_test
2050	native_apic_mem_write	vmlinux
250	idle_cpu	vmlinux
250	run_posix_cpu_timers	vmlinux
200	account_user_time	vmlinux
200	unmap_vmas	vmlinux
200	update_curr	vmlinux
150	do_timer	vmlinux

Table 7. L2 cache misses (in thousands) for the program given in Figure 5 with a working set of 2048KB, KVM guest-wide profiling.

Figure 6 shows the average number of L2 cache misses triggered by one pointer access of our memory-intensive benchmark. We run the benchmark with different working set sizes in four different computing environments. For system-wide profiling of both KVM and QEMU, we only count the cache misses reported in the guest profiler. The number of cache misses per pointer access for native Linux, the KVM guests, and the QEMU guest follow a similar pattern. After the size of the working set exceeds a certain value, the amount of L2 cache available for the benchmark, the miss rate increases dramatically. For native Linux and KVM, the available L2 cache is about 1024 KB. For QEMU, it is 512 KB, because QEMU involves the execution of more software components, such as the binary translator and the MMU emulation code. The cache miss rate after these points grows linearly with the working set size.

5.3 CPU Switch vs. Domain Switch

For guest-wide profiling, there are two possible places to save and restore the registers related to profiling. CPU switch saves and restores the relevant registers when the CPU switches from running guest code to VMM code, or vice versa. Domain switch does

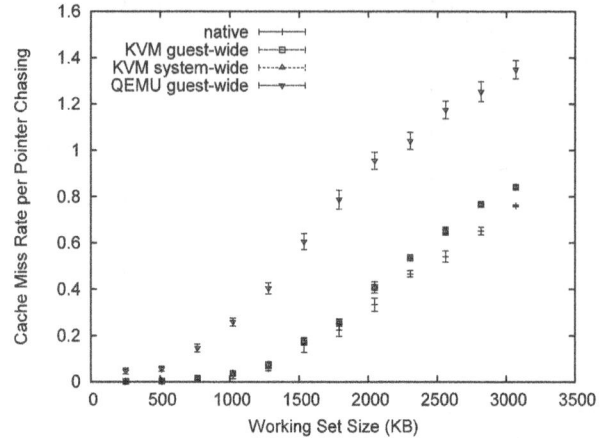

Figure 6. The number of L2 cache misses per pointer access for different working set sizes in four computing environments.

this when the VMM switches execution from one guest to another one.

To show the difference between CPU switch and domain switch, we use guest-wide profiling for KVM on a guest that receives TCP packets. In the experiment, as much TCP traffic as possible is pushed to the guest from a Gigabit NIC on a different machine. The virtual NIC used by the guest is RTL8139.

% INSTR	Function	Module
14.1047	csum_partial	vmlinux
8.9527	csum_partial_copy_generic	vmlinux
6.2500	copy_to_user	vmlinux
3.9696	ipt_do_table	ip_tables.ko
3.6318	tcp_v4_rc	vmlinux
3.2095	(no symbols)	libc.so
2.8716	ip_route_input	vmlinux
2.7027	tcp_rcv_established	vmlinux

Table 8. Instruction retirements for TCP receive in a KVM guest, guest-wide profiling with CPU switch.

% INSTR	Function	Module
31.0321	cp_interrupt	8139cp.ko
18.3365	cp_rx_poll	8139cp.ko
14.1916	cp_start_xmit	8139cp.ko
5.7782	native_apic_mem_write	vmlinux
5.1331	native_apic_mem_read	vmlinux
2.6215	csum_partial	vmlinux
1.4411	csum_partial_copy_generic	vmlinux
1.2901	copy_to_user	vmlinux

Table 9. Instruction retirements for TCP receive in a KVM guest, guest-wide profiling with domain switch.

Table 8 presents the eight functions with the largest number of instruction retirements with CPU switch, and Table 9 with domain switch. The total number of samples with CPU switch is 1184 vs. 7286 with domain switch. In other words, more than 80% of the retired instructions involved in receiving packets in the guest are spent outside the guest, inside the device emulation code of the VMM. The VMM spends a large number of instructions emulating the effects of the I/O operations in the virtual RTL8139 NIC and the virtual APIC. The top three functions in Table 9 are from the RTL8139 NIC driver, and the next two program the APIC.

Only below those five appear the three guest functions appearing at the top in Table 8.

This example clearly shows that domain switch can provide more complete information than CPU switch for I/O intensive programs.

5.4 The Power of Guest-wide Profiling

One of the advantages of guest-wide profiling is that it does not require access to the VMM. Nevertheless, it allows advanced performance debugging, as we demonstrate next with the following two examples.

We first profile the benchmark described in Figure 7 to show why hardware-supported nested paging [8] provides more efficient memory virtualization than shadow page tables [19]. This program is a familiar UNIX kernel micro-benchmark that stresses process creation and destruction.[2]

```
int main(int argc, char *argv[])
{
    for (int i = 0; i < 32000; i++) {
        int pid = fork();
        if (pid < 0) return -1;
        if (pid == 0) return 0;
        waitpid(pid);
    }
    return 0;
}
```

Figure 7. A micro-benchmark that stresses process creation and destruction [3].

CYCLE	Function	Module
1300	do_wp_page	vmlinux
1100	do_wait	vmlinux
750	page_fault	vmlinux
400	get_page_from_freelist	vmlinux
400	wait_consider_task	vmlinux
350	unmap_vmas	vmlinux
200	flush_tlb_page	vmlinux
200	native_flush_tlb_single	vmlinux

Table 10. Cycles (in millions) consumed in the program given in Figure 7 in a KVM guest with nested paging, KVM guest-wide profiling.

CYCLE	Function	Module
5450	native_set_pmd	vmlinux
5350	do_wp_pge	vmlinux
3500	native_flush_tlb_single	vmlinux
3050	get_page_from_freelist	vmlinux
2650	schedule	vmlinux
1100	native_flush_tlb	vmlinux
1050	do_wait	vmlinux
950	page_fault	vmlinux

Table 11. Cycles (in millions) consumed in the program given in Figure 7 in a KVM guest with shadow page tables, KVM guest-wide profiling.

Running natively, we measure 4.97 seconds to create and destroy 32000 processes. With nested paging, the guest takes 5.52

seconds, slightly slower than at native speed. When using shadow page tables, the execution time grows to 20.06 seconds. By profiling the benchmark in the guest, a developer can easily figure out which operations involved in process creation and destroying are expensive.

Table 10 presents the eight functions that consume the most CPU cycles with nested paging, and Table 11 presents the same results for shadow page tables. By comparing the profiling results presented in these two tables, we observe that operations related to page table manipulation, such as native_set_pmd() and do_wp_page(), become more expensive with shadow page tables. The shadow page table mechanism causes a large number of VM exits, including when loading and updating a page table in the guest, when accessing protected pages, and when performing privileged operations like TLB flushing. With nested paging, most of these operations do not cause a VM exit.

Our second example is again TCP receive, similar to the experiment described in Section 5.3. The difference in this experiment is that, instead of RTL8139, we use the E1000 virtual NIC and a virtual NIC based on VirtIO [20]. VirtIO is a paravirtualized I/O framework that provides good I/O performance for virtual machines.

% INSTR	Function	Module
25.2399	e1000_intr	e1000.ko
16.8906	e1000_irq_enable	e1000.ko
12.1881	e1000_xmit_frame	e1000.ko
4.6065	native_apic_mem_write	vmlinux
4.4146	csum_partial	vmlinux
3.3589	e1000_alloc_rx_buffers	e1000.ko
3.2630	native_apic_mem_read	vmlinux
3.0710	__copy_user_intel	vmlinux

Table 12. Instruction retirements for TCP receive in KVM guest with E1000 virtual NIC, guest-wide profiling with domain switch.

% INSTR	Function	Module
52.3312	native_safe_halt	vmlinux
7.7244	native_apic_mem_write	vmlinux
6.6806	csum_partial_copy_generic	vmlinux
1.8903	native_write_cr0	vmlinux
1.4614	ipt_do_table	ip_tables.ko
0.9047	(no symbols)	libc.so
0.9047	get_page_from_freelist	vmlinux
0.9047	schedule	vmlinux

Table 13. Instruction retirements for TCP receive in KVM guest with VirtIO virtual NIC, guest-wide profiling with domain switch.

Table 12 presents the profiling results of packet receive through the E1000 virtual NIC in a KVM guest. Similar to the results of RTL8139, interrupt handling functions retire more than 40% of all instructions, because of the high network I/O interrupt rate. Table 13 presents the results of the VirtIO-based NIC. The function native_safe_halt() retires more than half of all instructions, but this function actually executes the HLT instruction, which halts the CPU until the next external interrupt occurs. The frequent execution of this instruction in the guest shows that the guest is not saturated while handling 1Gbps TCP traffic. Compared with the data in Table 12, we do not find a single function related to interrupt handling, which indicates that the interrupt rate due to network I/O is low. Our profiling results validate the design of VirtIO, which improves virtualized I/O performance by batching I/O operations to reduce the number of VM exits.

Therefore, as these two experiments demonstrate, guest-wide profiling with domain switch helps developers understand the

---

[2] This experiment is conducted on our AMD machine, because KVM's modular implementation on AMD CPUs can easily be switched between shadow page tables and hardware-supported nested paging.

underlying virtualized environment without the need for accessing the VMM.

5.5 Profiling QEMU

With our system-wide profiling extensions for QEMU, we profile TCP receive of both the host and the guest. The experiment configuration is similar to the one described in Section 5.4. Instead of KVM, we use QEMU running in user space as the VMM. The virtual NIC is based on VirtIO. The observed TCP receive throughput is around 50MB/s. This amount of traffic saturates the physical CPU but does not keep the virtual CPU of the guest busy.

Table 14 presents the profiling results of the host part. Function `cpu_x86_exec()` retires a large portion of all the instructions. Its functionality is similar to `vmx_vcpu_run()` in KVM, which switches the CPU from the host context to the guest context.

Table 15 shows the results of the guest part, which is obtained by running a customized OProfile in the guest. The appearance of function `__schedule()` indicates that the virtual CPU is not saturated. The reason why function `strcat()` retires most instructions in the guest may be that the corresponding translated native code of this operation is expensive.

% INSTR	Function	Module
68.9548	cpu_x86_exec	qemu
6.0842	__ldl_mmu	qemu
4.2902	helper_cc_compute_c	qemu
1.7161	cpu_x86_handle_mmu_fault	qemu
1.7161	phys_page_find_alloc	qemu
1.4041	ld_phys	qemu
1.2480	tlb_set_page_exec	qemu
0.6240	helper_cc_compute_all	qemu

Table 14. Instruction retirements for TCP receive in QEMU host with VirtIO virtual NIC, system-wide profiling with CPU switch.

% INSTR	Function	Module
10.5178	strcat	vmlinux
3.8835	ipt_do_table	vmlinux
2.7508	olpc_ec_cmd	vmlinux
2.4272	__schedule	vmlinux
2.4272	__slab_alloc	vmlinux
2.2654	ip_route_input	vmlinux
2.2654	skb_gro_receive	vmlinux
1.9417	vring_add_buf	virtio_ring.ko

Table 15. Instruction retirements for TCP receive in QEMU guest with VirtIO virtual NIC, system-wide profiling with CPU switch.

5.6 Profiling Overhead

Profiling based on CPU performance counters inevitably slows down the profiled program, even in a native environment, because of the overhead of handling the counter overflow interrupts. In a virtualized environment, these interrupts need to be forwarded to the guest, adding more context switches between the host and the guest and therefore more overhead. In addition, the VMM needs to save and restore the performance counters on a VM switch.

We evaluate the overhead of our profiling extensions by comparing the execution time, with and without profiling, of the program in Figure 2, which is modified to execute a fixed number of iterations. The program runs in the guest, and we take a sample every 5 million CPU cycles (or about 400 times per second).

Table 16 presents the results for profiling overhead. In the native environment, the overhead of profiling is about 0.048%. For KVM guest-wide profiling, the overhead is about 0.386%. We

further breakdown the overhead into two parts: additional context switches due to interrupt injection account for about 80% of overall overhead and interrupt handling in the guest takes the remaining 20%. For KVM system-wide profiling, the overhead is 0.441%. This is roughly the sum of the overhead of native and KVM guest-wide profiling, because KVM system-wide profiling also runs a profiler in the host Linux. System-wide profiling for QEMU incurs more overhead, around 0.942%. The overhead comes from multiple sources. First, QEMU runs in user space, and forwarding an interrupt to the guest requires a change in CPU privilege level and a signal to the user space process. Second, QEMU needs to query the address mapping cache and rewrite the sampled address. Third, frequent context switches also hurt the performance of QEMU's binary translation engine.

Profiling environment	Execution time overhead
Native	$0.048\% \pm 0.0042\%$
KVM guest-wide	$0.386\% \pm 0.0450\%$
KVM system-wide	$0.441\% \pm 0.0435\%$
QEMU system-wide	$0.942\% \pm 0.0441\%$

Table 16. Profiling overhead. The sample rate of the profiler is about 400 times per second.

6. Discussion

Although both guest-wide and system-wide profiling are feasible and useful for diagnosing performance problems in a virtualized computing environment, there are still a number of issues that need to be considered before these techniques can be deployed in production use, as discussed next.

Virtual PMU interface Since the PMU is not a standardized hardware component of the x86 architecture, the programming interfaces for PMUs differ between hardware vendors and even between different models from the same hardware vendor. In addition, different processors may also support different profiling events. Therefore, for guest-wide profiling to be portable to different processors, a proper interface between the guest profiler and the virtualized PMU must be defined. There are two ways to expose PMU interfaces to the guests.

The first method is to rely on the `CPUID` instruction to return the physical CPU family and model identifier to the guest. This information tells the guest profiler how to program the PMU hardware directly. The burden on the VMM is minimal, but the solution breaks one fundamental principle of virtualization: decoupling software from hardware.

The second approach is to expose to the guest a standardized virtual PMU with a limited number of broadly used profiling events, such as CPU cycles, TLB and cache misses, etc. The guest profiler is extended to support this virtual PMU, and the VMM provides the mapping of operations between the virtual PMU and the underlying physical PMU. This approach decouples software from hardware, but imposes additional work on the VMM.

Profiling accuracy In addition to the statistical nature of sampling-based profiling, there are other factors that potentially affect profiling accuracy in virtualized environments.

The first problem is that the multiplexing of some hardware resources inevitably introduces noise into profiling results. For instance, TLBs are flushed when switching between the VMM and the guests. If TLB misses are being monitored, the profiling results in a guest are perturbed by the execution of the VMM and/or other guests. This problem also exists in native profiling. Although it can be mitigated by cache/TLB entry tagging, profiling results for these events are still not guaranteed to be entirely accurate.

The second problem is specific to profilers based on domain switch. If the VMM is interrupted to perform some action on behalf of another guest, the handling of this interrupt is incorrectly charged to the currently executing guest. The issue is similar to the resource accounting problem in a conventional operating system [5], and can possibly be solved by techniques such as early demultiplexing [10].

PMU emulation In addition to virtualizing the PMU, for VMMs based on binary translation and pure emulators, it is also possible to emulate the PMU hardware in software. In this case, the PMU of the physical CPU is not involved during the profiling process, and the entire functionality of the PMU is emulated in software. By emulating the PMU the VMM can support some events that are not implemented by the physical PMU. For instance, if the energy consumption of each CPU instruction is known, one could build an energy profiler in this way.

We use PMU emulation to count instruction retirements. When a basic block is translated, we count the number of guest instructions in the block and insert a few instructions at the beginning of the translated basic block. When the translated block is executed, these instructions increase the emulated performance counter. If the emulated counter reaches the predefined threshold, an NMI is injected into the virtual CPU. The difficulties of PMU emulation lie in supporting a large number of hardware events. Emulating these events may incur high overhead and emulating some of them may not even be possible for a binary translator or an instruction-level CPU emulator.

7. Related Work

The XenOprof profiler [18] is the first profiler for virtual machines. According to our definition, it does system-wide profiling. It is specifically designed for Xen, a VMM based on paravirtualization. A newer version of Xen, Xen HVM, supports hardware-assisted full virtualization. Xen HVM saves and restores MSRs when it performs domain switches, but it does not attribute samples from domain 0, in which all I/O device emulation is done, to any guest. VM exits in a domain that do not require the intervention of domain 0 are handled by Xen HVM under the context of that domain. As a result, guest-wide profiling in Xen HVM reflects neither the characteristic of the physical CPU nor that of the CPU plus the VMM.

Linux perf [2] is a new implementation of performance counter support for Linux. It runs in the Linux host and can profile a Linux guest running in KVM [1]. It obtains samples of the guest by observing its virtual CPU state. Because this is done outside the guest, only PC and CPU privilege mode can be recorded. The address of the descriptor of the current process is not known. As a result, Linux perf can only interpret samples that belong to the kernel of the Linux guest, and cannot handle samples contributed by user space applications. The binary image and the virtual memory layout of the guest kernel, necessary for sample interpretation, are obtained through an explicit communication channel.

VMware vmkperf [14] is a performance monitoring utility for VMware ESX. It runs in the VMM and only records how many hardware events happen in a given time interval. It does not handle counter overflow interrupts, and it does not attribute them to functions. It does not support the profiling mechanisms presented in this paper.

VTSS++ [9] demonstrates a profiling technique similar to guest-wide profiling. It requires the cooperation of a profiler running in the guest and a PMU sampling tool running in the VMM. It relies on sampling timestamps to attribute hardware events sampled in the host to the corresponding threads in the guest. Although it does not require modifications to the VMM, VTSS++ requires access to the VMM to run a sampling tool, and the accuracy of the profiling results is affected by the estimation algorithm it uses.

The work in this paper builds on our earlier work [11], which proposes some basic ideas of virtual machine profiling and only concentrates on guest-wide profiling for VMMs based on hardware-assisted virtualization. This paper extends the earlier work in several ways. We implement system-wide profiling for a VMM based on binary translation. We also evaluate our implementations through extensive experiments to demonstrate the feasibility and usefulness of virtual machine profiling.

8. Conclusions

Profilers based on CPU performance counters help developers debug performance problems in complex software systems, but they are not well supported in virtual machine environments, making performance debugging in such environments hard.

We define guest-wide profiling, which allows profiling of a guest without VMM access, and system-wide profiling, which allows profiling of the VMM and any number of guests. We study the requirements for each type of profiling. Guest-wide profiling requires synchronous interrupt delivery to the guest. System-wide profiling requires cooperation between the VMM and the guest to interpret samples belonging to the guest. We describe two approaches to implement this cooperation, full-delegation and interpretation-delegation.

We develop a guest-wide and a system-wide profiler for a VMM based on hardware-assisted virtualization (KVM), and a system-wide profiler for a VMM based on binary translation (QEMU). We demonstrate the accuracy and the power of these profilers, and show that their performance overhead is very small.

As more and more computing is migrated to virtualization-based cloud infrastructures, better profiling tools for virtual machines will facilitate performance debugging and improve resource utilization in the cloud.

Acknowledgements

We would like to thank Mihai Dobrescu, Simon Schubert and the anonymous reviewers for their valuable comments and help in improving this paper.

References

[1] Enhance perf to collect KVM guest os statistics from host side. 2010. http://lwn.net/Articles/378778.

[2] Performance Counters for Linux. 2010. http://lwn.net/Articles/-310176.

[3] K. Adams and O. Agesen. A comparison of software and hardware techniques for x86 virtualization. In *Proceedings of the 12th International Conference on Architectural Support for Programming Languages and Operating Systems*, 2006.

[4] J.M. Anderson, L.M. Berc, J. Dean, S. Ghemawat, M.R. Henzinger, S.T.A. Leung, R.L. Sites, M.T. Vandevoorde, C.A. Waldspurger, and W.E. Weihl. Continuous profiling: where have all the cycles gone? *Operating Systems Review*, 1997.

[5] G. Banga, P. Druschel, and J.C. Mogul. Resource containers: A new facility for resource management in server systems. *Operating Systems Review*, 1998.

[6] P. Barham, B. Dragovic, K. Fraser, S. Hand, T. Harris, A. Ho, R. Neugebauer, I. Pratt, and A. Warfield. Xen and the art of virtual-

ization. In *Proceedings of the 9th ACM Symposium on Operating Systems Principles*, 2003.

[7] F. Bellard. QEMU, a fast and portable dynamic translator. In *Proceedings of the USENIX 2005 Annual Technical Conference, FREENIX Track*, 2005.

[8] R. Bhargava, B. Serebrin, F. Spadini, and S. Manne. Accelerating two-dimensional page walks for virtualized systems. In *Proceedings of the 13th International Conference on Architectural Support for Programming Languages and Operating Systems*, 2008.

[9] Stanislav Bratanov, Roman Belenov, and Nikita Manovich. Virtual machines: a whole new world for performance analysis. *Operating Systems Review*, 2009.

[10] P. Druschel and G. Banga. Lazy receiver processing (LRP): A network subsystem architecture for server systems. *Operating Systems Review*, 1996.

[11] J. Du, N. Sehrawat, and W. Zwaenepoel. Performance profiling in a virtualized environment. In *Proceedings of the 2nd USENIX Workshop on Hot Topics in Cloud Computing*, 2010.

[12] S.L. Graham, P.B. Kessler, and M.K. Mckusick. Gprof: A call graph execution profiler. *ACM SIGPLAN Notices*, 1982.

[13] Intel Inc. Intel VTune Performance Analyser, 2010. http://software.intel.com/en-us/intel-vtune/.

[14] VMware Inc. Vmkperf for VMware ESX 4.0, 2010.

[15] Intel. *Intel 64 and IA-32 Architectures Software Developer's Manual Volume 3: System Programming Guide.*

[16] A. Kivity, Y. Kamay, D. Laor, U. Lublin, and A. Liguori. kvm: the Linux virtual machine monitor. In *Linux Symposium*, 2007.

[17] J. Levon and P. Elie. Oprofile: A system profiler for linux. 2010. http://oprofile.sourceforge.net.

[18] A. Menon, J.R. Santos, Y. Turner, G.J. Janakiraman, and W. Zwaenepoel. Diagnosing performance overheads in the Xen virtual machine environment. In *Proceedings of the 1st ACM/USENIX International Conference on Virtual Execution Environments*, 2005.

[19] M. Rosenblum and T. Garfinkel. Virtual machine monitors: Current technology and future trends. *Computer*, 2005.

[20] R. Russell. virtio: towards a de-facto standard for virtual I/O devices. *Operating Systems Review*, 2008.

[21] B. Sprunt. The basics of performance-monitoring hardware. *IEEE MICRO*, 2002.

[22] A. Srivastava and A. Eustace. ATOM: A system for building customized program analysis tools. In *Proceedings of the ACM SIGPLAN 1994 Conference on Programming Language Design and Implementation*, 1994.

[23] M. Zagha, B. Larson, S. Turner, and M. Itzkowitz. Performance analysis using the MIPS R10000 performance counters. In *Proceedings of the 1996 ACM/IEEE Conference on Supercomputing*, 1996.

Perfctr-Xen: A Framework for Performance Counter Virtualization

Ruslan Nikolaev   Godmar Back

Virginia Polytechnic Institute
Blacksburg
{rnikola,gback}@cs.vt.edu

Abstract

Virtualization is a powerful technique used for variety of application domains, including emerging cloud environments that provide access to virtual machines as a service. Because of the interaction of virtual machines with multiple underlying software and hardware layers, the analysis of the performance of applications running in virtualized environments has been difficult. Moreover, performance analysis tools commonly used in native environments were not available in virtualized environments, a gap which our work closes.

This paper discusses the challenges of performance monitoring inherent to virtualized environments and introduces a technique to virtualize access to low-level performance counters on a per-thread basis. The technique was implemented in perfctr-xen, a framework for the Xen hypervisor that provides an infrastructure for higher-level profilers. This framework supports both accumulative event counts and interrupt-driven event sampling. It is light-weight, providing direct user mode access to logical counter values. perfctr-xen supports multiple modes of virtualization, including paravirtualization and hardware-assisted virtualization. perfctr-xen applies guest kernel-hypervisor coordination techniques to reduce virtualization overhead. We present experimental results based on microbenchmarks and SPEC CPU2006 macrobenchmarks that show the accuracy and usability of the obtained measurements when compared to native execution.

Categories and Subject Descriptors   D.2.8 [*Software Engineering*]: Metrics—Performance measures; D.4.8 [*Operating Systems*]: Performance—Measurements

General Terms   Performance, Measurement

Keywords   Profilers, virtual machine monitors, perfctr, PAPI, HPCToolkit, Xen

1. Introduction

Virtualization allows multiple instances of an operating system to run on a single computer. The idea was first introduced for VM/370 [13] and has later been reincarnated for modern platforms as described in [11] and [24]. A *Hypervisor* or *VMM (virtual ma-*chine monitor) is a software layer that separates the virtual hardware an OS sees from the actual hardware and arbitrates access to physical resources such as CPU or memory. Among widely known VMMs are Xen [8] and KVM [18], [20]. Virtualization improves *isolation* and *reliability* because each OS runs independently from the others on its own virtual processor, increases *resource utilization* as the same hardware can be used for multiple purposes, and leads to better *productivity* as large pieces of software can be pre-configured and installed very easily.

Virtualization is widely used in several application domains. It allows the creation of "virtual appliances" [25], which are software bundles that contain their own specialized OS and run along with other virtual appliances and general purpose OS on a single machine. Commercial providers of infrastructure as a service (IaaS) solutions rely on virtualization to provide business solutions for server consolidation. Virtualization has also been proposed as a means of utilizing manycore platforms efficiently [7].

However, running performance-critical applications in virtualized systems is challenging because of virtualization overhead and the difficulty of making appropriate resource allocation and scheduling decisions. Commonly used performance evaluation frameworks extensively exploit profiling to allow systems and application developers to understand the performance of their applications. Such profiling frameworks rely heavily on hardware performance counters provided by modern CPUs. These counters provide information about hardware-related events such as cache misses, branch mispredictions, and many others.

Like any other resource, access to these hardware performance counters must be managed by both the hypervisor and the guest operating system kernel. However, current hypervisors are unable to provide efficient and virtualized access to performance counters. Our work closes this gap.

This paper presents perfctr-xen, an infrastructure to provide direct access to hardware performance counters in virtualized environments using the Xen hypervisor. Perfctr-xen relies on the cooperation of guest kernel and underlying hypervisor to provide profiling tools running in the guest with access to performance counters that is compatible with the APIs used in native, unvirtualized environments, notably PAPI [10]. Consequently, frameworks and libraries that rely on PAPI can now be used inside Xen, such as HPCToolkit [6] or TAU [26]. To accomplish this compatibility, we modified both the Xen hypervisor as well as the guest kernel running inside each virtual machine. Perfctr-xen supports both paravirtualized mode as well as hardware virtualization mode and exploits optimizations that avoid trap-and-emulate overhead. Although our implementation focuses on Xen, the techniques we use are applicable to other hypervisors.

Library/Framework	Type	Monitoring	Direct access	Interfaces Used
perf_events	low level	Per thread	Yes	ioctl, mmap, sysctl, prctl
perfctr	low level	Per thread	Yes	ioctl, mmap, dev
perfmon	high and low level	Per thread	No	syscalls, mmap, signals
PAPI	high level	Per thread	Yes (w/ perfctr)	perfctr, perf_events, perfmon
OProfile	profiler	System wide	N/A	oprofilefs
XenoProf	profiler	System wide	N/A	oprofilefs
TAU PerfExplorer	profiler	Per thread	N/A	PAPI
HPCToolkit	profiler	Per thread	N/A	PAPI

Table 1. Characteristics of Performance Monitoring Libraries and Frameworks

2. Background

This section introduces hardware event counters and existing libraries and frameworks that provide access to them. We further discuss the state of support for such counters in existing virtual machines.

2.1 Hardware Event Counters

Modern CPUs provide access to hardware event counters through programmable performance monitoring registers. Such registers can be programmed to count events of interest, such as cache accesses or misses or branch mispredictions. The registers may be read-only or read-write. System software controls whether registers are directly accessible to non-privileged user applications or whether accesses must be done in privileged mode from system code. The number of registers is typically smaller than the set of event types that can be counted, requiring that the user select a subset of events of interest. The set of event types is specific to a given microarchitecture and frequently changes as the microarchitecture evolves. Performance monitoring registers can be set up to trigger interrupts when they overflow. This mechanism is useful to perform statistical profiling using sampling intervals that contain a constant number of the events of interest in each interval.

2.2 Performance Monitoring Frameworks and Libraries

A cornucopia of performance monitoring frameworks and libraries exist. A representative set of examples is shown in Table 1. These frameworks and libraries differ in their functionality, level of abstraction, granularity of monitoring, and the interfaces upon which they rely.

At the bottom level, *low-level performance counter libraries* provide a thin layer over the facilities provided by the hardware, which does not hide architecture-specific event types from the user. These systems consist of kernel extensions and a corresponding user library. The kernel extensions implement operations that require privileged access, such as reprogramming counters or setting up interrupt handling and forwarding interrupt notifications to processes. The user library provides an API for accessing event counters.

Events may be counted globally (system-wide), or per thread. Most libraries support both modes, although some (e.g., OProfile [12]) provide only global counting. Global recording of events has the advantage that it can account for vertical interactions at all levels of the software stack as well as during horizontal interactions with other programs, such as local servers. On the other hand, global profiling makes it difficult to separate events of interest from unrelated system activities or noise.

Per-thread counting provides each thread with its own logical set of performance counters, just like each thread has its own logical set of machine registers. To implement per-thread accounting, the performance counter framework needs to maintain per-thread state which is updated on each context switch.

Some libraries (e.g., perfctr [22] and perf_events [2] [1]), allow a thread to directly read the physical performance monitoring register in user mode in order to obtain fine-grained and precise information about events during its execution, while other libraries (e.g., perfmon [17]) require a system call to obtain access to this information. Those systems that provide direct access must either maintain the thread's logical value in the physical register while the thread is scheduled, or they must place a correction (offset) value in an agreed-upon location (such as a memory-mapped area in the thread's address space) that allows a thread to compute its logical value based on the value read from the physical register.

High-level performance counter libraries such as PAPI [10] provide a layer that hides microarchitecture-specific event types behind a uniform, higher-level API. Performance profilers such as TAU [26] and HPCToolkit [6] in turn are built on top of higher-level performance counter APIs. These profilers statistically sample events and present cumulative statistics to the user that relates these events to instructions and functions in the user codes, with appropriate references to the source code if available.

The choice of framework influences the accuracy of measurements [27]. Bypassing high-level APIs in favor of low-level APIs typically reduces the measurement error, but depends on architecture-specific code. The accuracy depends also on which events should be counted (user mode only vs. user and kernel mode events [27]).

To compensate for the limited number of performance counter registers, some frameworks (perfmon, PAPI) support event multiplexing. This technique applies only a subset of the desired event sets during subsections of a program's execution, then scales the results to extrapolate their values for the entire program.

2.3 Virtualization Approaches

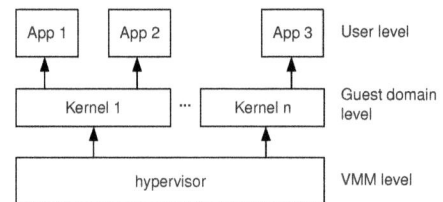

Figure 1. Architecture of a Type-I Virtual Machine Monitor

In this work, we consider Type I virtual machines [19] (see Figure 1) in which the hypervisor forms the lowest layer with direct access to the hardware and guest operating systems run on top of the hypervisor in separated domains.

Fully virtualized systems leave the guest OS entirely unaware that it is not running on physical hardware. As a result, an unchanged guest kernel (such as an off-the-shelf image of a commercial OS) can be executed. Such full virtualization can be accom-

---
[1] perf_events was previously known as perf_counter

16

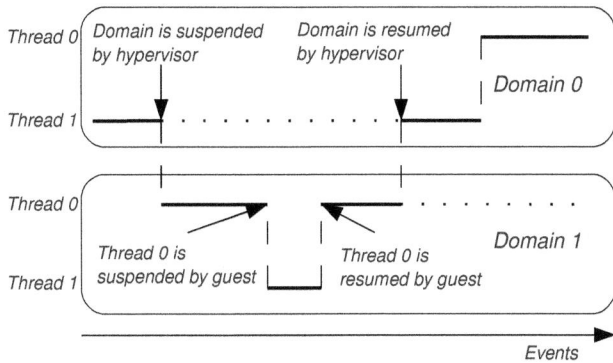

Figure 2. Context switching in a virtualized environment. The guest domains and the hypervisor are both unaware of when a domain or thread switch takes place.

plished either using hardware assist, or using binary translation. Hardware-assisted systems such as Intel VT or AMD-V run the kernel in a deprivileged mode, allowing the hypervisor to trap and emulate any instructions whose effect must be local to a given domain. Prior to the introduction of hardware assist, full virtualization of IA32-based systems required binary translation of the guest kernel code because the architecture lacked the ability to intercept all necessary instructions when executed in deprivileged mode [23].

For this reason, the Xen virtual machine monitor [8] introduced adaptations into the guest OS kernel code (a process known as paravirtualization), to reduce emulation and management costs and yield better performance. Beyond avoiding binary translation, the adaption of guest kernel code either in their core or through the use of special drivers has become common today for any virtual machine monitor.

2.4 Performance Counters in Virtual Machines

Support for performance event monitoring depends on the type of virtualization being used. There is limited support in Xen for selected microarchitectures when hardware-assisted virtualization (e.g., using Intel VT or AMD-V) is used. In this approach, accesses to performance monitoring registers are intercepted via traps. However, the set of architectures supported is far smaller than that supported by PAPI, and hardware-assisted virtualization is not always used.

The XenoProf [21] framework extends the OProfile [12] system-wide profiler to allow per-domain (e.g., per guest) profiling in Xen, even when hardware-assisted virtualization is not used. However, XenoProf does not allow independent and simultaneous profiling of different domains.

Aside from these approaches, most current virtual machines disallow access to the performance monitor registers by the guest operating systems, thus preventing widely used low-level libraries such as perfctr and perf_events from being used. Consequently, users cannot benefit from high-level performance profilers such as TAU PerfExplorer and HPCToolkit to diagnose the performance of their applications when executing on top of virtual machines.

3. Virtualizing Hardware Event Counters

The encapsulation of guest domains from the underlying hypervisor poses a difficulty for virtualizing performance counters, because these two components are mutually unaware of their scheduling policies. As shown in Figure 2, the guest kernel remains unaware if the hypervisor suspends its domain on the physical CPU on which it runs. Likewise, the hypervisor is unaware of when a

guest kernel switches to a different user task on its domain's virtual CPUs.

Both inter- and intra-domain context switches involve the performance monitoring framework and may require updating machine-specific (MSR) registers. First, PMU (Performance Monitoring Unit) configuration registers (e.g., event selectors) need to be re-programmed to reflect the desired event configuration of the thread to be resumed. Second, if the performance counter register contains the logical value of the thread to be resumed, it must be restored (and the value of the outgoing thread must be saved). Otherwise, its value must be sampled and recorded in the corresponding data structure for the thread or domain.

Since the guest domain kernel runs in a deprivileged environment, its access to the registers during intra-domain context switches must be managed by the hypervisor. For fully-virtualized domains, a trap-and-emulate approach can be used to intercept and emulate the corresponding privileged instructions that write to these registers. Although read accesses could be trapped as well, current architectures allow the hypervisor to grant direct read access to the MSR registers to guest domains. If the guest is adapted to use paravirtualization, the cost of trapping and emulating individual privileged instruction can be reduced by using hypercalls instead, which allows the batching of multiple updates. The guest can also cache previously activated configurations to avoid these hypercalls if possible, thus avoiding unnecessary writes to the MSR configuration registers.

Whereas the counter-related configuration information must be saved and restored on both inter- and intra-domain switches, the values of the registers containing the actual event counts require saving and restoring only if the register physically contains the thread's logical value during execution. Consequently, the cost of writing to these registers can be avoided when this is not required, which holds true in two cases. First, if a counter is used to obtain accumulated event counts (in 'a-mode'), a virtualization-aware guest domain can apply the necessary correction offsets to obtain the logical accumulated value from the physical value. Second, in the case of the timestamp counter (TSC) register, hardware-assisted virtualization via Intel VT or AMD-V allows for transparent, per-domain offsetting, which also avoids the cost of physically updating these registers on a context switch. In addition, on some architecture implementations, it is impossible to safely update the TSC register since it may be shared across cores. Avoiding the save-and-restore cost is beneficial because it can be expensive (66-93 CPU cycles per register; for Pentium 4 as much as 18 registers must be restored).

On the other hand, if a counter is used in interrupt mode ('i-mode'), the physical register contains a small negative value that will overflow, thus triggering an interrupt, after a desired number of events occurs. In this case, saving and restoring cannot be avoided. The interrupt is handled by the hypervisor, who must forward this interrupt to the affected domain via a virtual interrupt mechanism. Upon receipt of the virtual interrupt, the guest kernel notifies the user-level profiling components via a Unix signal. Previous work [21] claimed that such delivery needs to be synchronous, an assertion repeated in [15]. In Xen, the delivery of virtual interrupts to guest domains is not synchronous, but uses a software interrupt mechanism, thus making it possible that their delivery could be delayed by higher-priority interrupts. In Section 4.2.2, we argue that support for synchronous interrupt delivery is not required if the performance counter registers are restored before the guest domain is resumed, and if the guest domain verifies that a register in fact overflowed before delivering the notification to the user level.

Perfctr-xen supports performance counter virtualization in Xen in three configurations, which required different and separate implementations: (1) for paravirtualized guest kernels, which use hypercalls to communicate performance counter configuration changes from guest to hypervisor, and in which the guest and hypervisor cooperate to maintain information about the current thread context; (2) for fully-virtualized guest kernels, which use the save-and-restore approach for all registers; and (3) a hybrid approach in which a guest can run in a hardware-assisted, fully-virtualized domain but still enjoy the generality of and the optimizations developed for the paravirtualization case.

4. Implementation

Our implementation is based on, and compatible with, the existing *perfctr* [22] implementation. In this section, we describe *perfctr* in detail and outline how we adapted it to enable performance counter virtualization in Xen for paravirtualized and hybrid modes. Section 4.2.5 describes our virtualization strategy for fully virtualized domains.

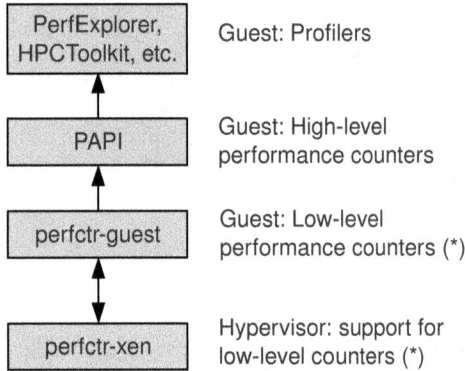

Figure 3. Software layers in perfctr-xen. Components marked with an asterisk (*) were adapted from *perfctr*.

4.1 The *perfctr* library

We chose *perfctr* because it is widely used and provides the foundation for higher-level libraries and frameworks such as PAPI, HPC-Toolkit, or PerfExplorer, as shown in Figure 3. It is efficient, lightweight and allows direct access to performance counters in user mode. *Perfctr* supports a wide range of x86 implementations spanning multiple generations and different vendors, whose hardware event counter implementation can differ significantly. In addition, *perfctr* works on non-x86 platforms such as PowerPC and ARM and can easily be integrated in any Linux distribution.

Perfctr consists of a kernel driver and a user-level library. The kernel driver maintains performance counter-related per-thread data structures, updates them on each context switch, and makes them available to the user-level library via a read-only mapping. Besides miscellaneous architecture-specific information, this per-thread data structure contains the following information:

- *Control State.* Information about which PMU data registers a thread is actively using, which events these registers count, and to which physical register address they are mapped. Similar information is kept with respect to the use of the time-stamp counter, which is also virtualized.

- *Counter State.* For each PMU data register, as well as the TSC register, two values are kept: Sum_{thread}, which reflects the thread's accumulated logical event count up to including the last suspension point; and $Start_{thread}$, which reflects the sampled value of the counter at the last resumption point.

Perfctr supports two types of counters: *a-mode* and *i-mode* counters. A-mode counters are used by threads to measure the

number of events occurring in some region of a program. User code explicitly reads the counter's value when needed. When a thread wants to access the logical value of a counter at time t, a user library function issues a RDTSC or RDPMC instruction to obtain the register's physical value $Phys(t)$ and computes the logical value $Log_{thread}(t)$ as

$$Log_{thread}(t) = Sum_{thread} + (Phys(t) - Start_{thread}) \quad (1)$$

On each context switch, the *perfctr* kernel driver updates the accumulated value of the outgoing thread as $Sum_{thread} \leftarrow Sum_{thread} + (Phys - Start_{thread})$ to account for the events during the last scheduling period. In addition, the $Start_{thread}$ value of the thread to be resumed is reset as $Start_{thread} \leftarrow Phys$. Note that the actual physical register value is not changed on a context switch for a-mode counters.

I-mode counters, which are used for sampling, trigger interrupts after a certain number of events has occurred, which represents the sampling period. Since the value at which an overflow interrupt is triggered is fixed at 0 and cannot be programmed, the physical register must be set to a small negative value whose absolute value represents the desired length of the sampling period. *I-mode* counters are treated differently during a context switch: their physical value is saved on suspend and restored on resume. The Sum_{thread} field maintains the counter's accumulated logical value as for a-mode counters. The $Start_{thread}$ field is used to record the physical value when a thread is suspended. Consequently, the logical value of an i-mode counter can also be obtained using equation (1).

When an overflow occurs, *perfctr* handles this interrupt, identifies the register(s) that have overflowed and updates Sum_{thread}, then disables further event counting for these registers. Using the OS's signal delivery mechanism, a signal is sent to the user process. The signal handler is then responsible for recording the sample based on the provided user process's state and it must re-enable event counting. Once re-enabled, the physical value of the register is reset to the sampling period, which is also recorded in the data structure maintained by *perfctr*.

4.2 The perfctr-xen framework

Perfctr-xen includes a hypervisor driver, a guest kernel driver, and a modified user-level library, whose functionality we describe in this section.

4.2.1 A-mode counters

The virtualization technique described in Section 4.1 requires that the underlying system perform two actions during a context switch: (1) update the counter state of the threads being suspended and resumed, and (2) activate the resumed thread's control state. As discussed in Section 3, in a virtualized environment, both intra-domain context switches between threads in a domain and inter-domain context switches between domains can occur. During intra-domain switches, the guest kernel can perform the state updates similar to the native implementation. For inter-domain context switches, the hypervisor must perform these updates.

We first considered having the hypervisor update each thread's counter state directly on the guest kernel's behalf. This approach has the advantage that no changes to the *perfctr* user library are required. However, it would create undesirable coupling between the hypervisor and the guest kernel implementations, because the hypervisor would need to traverse guest kernel data structures. Instead, we decided to split the control and counter state in two parts. At the guest kernel level, a per-thread data structure is maintained. At the hypervisor level, a per-VCPU data structure is maintained for each virtual CPU that is assigned to a guest domain. The hypervisor provides read-only access to this data structure to the guest

18

kernel, who in turn maps it into the address space of each thread using performance counters.

The per-VCPU data structure is modeled after the per-thread data structure used in the native version of *perfctr* (in fact, our implementation uses the same data structure declarations, as discussed in Section 4.2.4). For each PMU data register, as well as for the TSC register, the hypervisor maintains two values per VCPU: $Start_{vcpu}$ and Sum_{vcpu}. $Start_{vcpu}$ represents the sampled value of the counter at the most recent resumption point of the domain or thread (whichever happened last). If the hypervisor resumes a domain, it directly updates $Start_{vcpu}$ after sampling the counter. If the guest kernel resumes a thread, it requests via a hypercall that the hypervisor record the sampled value in $Start_{vcpu}$. The same hypercall is also used to activate this thread's counter-related control state.

The field Sum_{vcpu} represents the cumulative number of events incurred by this domain since the last intra-domain thread resumption point until the most recent domain suspension point. It is set to zero on each intra-domain switch during the hypercall that notifies the hypervisor that the guest kernel resumed a thread. On each inter-domain context switch, the perfctr-xen hypervisor driver updates the accumulated value of the outgoing VCPU as $Sum_{vcpu} \leftarrow Sum_{vcpu} + (Phys - Start_{vcpu})$ to account for the events incurred since the last intra- or inter-domain resumption point.

The perfctr-xen guest kernel driver maintains the value Sum_{thread} for each thread as in the native case, which represents the cumulative number of events up to the last thread suspension point. A counter's logical value at time t is computed as

$$Log_{thread}(t) = Sum_{thread} + (Phys^*(t) - Start^*_{thread}) \quad (2)$$

$Phys^*(t)$ represents the adjusted physical value that accounts for possible VCPU preemption, which is computed as

$$Phys^*(t) = Sum_{vcpu} + (Phys(t) - Start_{vcpu}) \quad (3)$$

Thus, the logical value represents the sum of the cumulative number of events until the last thread suspension point, plus the number of events encountered from there until the last domain resumption point while the domain was active, plus the events encountered since then until t, reduced by an adjusted start value $Start^*_{thread}$.

The adjusted thread start value $Start^*_{thread}$ compensates for the requirement that each intra-domain context switch includes a hypercall. Since this hypercall is introduced by our framework, we wish to exclude any events occurring during its execution. Right before resuming a guest thread, the guest kernel driver computes $Start^*_{thread} = Phys^*(t_r)$ after returning from the hypercall at time t_r.

$$Start^*_{thread} = Sum_{vcpu} + (Phys(t_r) - Start_{vcpu}) \quad (4)$$

This adjustment excludes any events incurred between when the hypervisor sampled the counter during the hypercall and t_r. The inclusion of the term Sum_{vcpu} ensures that all such events are excluded, even if the domain was suspended and resumed during the hypercall by the preemptive scheduler. Since $Start^*_{thread}$ takes the place of $Start_{thread}$ in equation (1), we store its value in the $Start_{thread}$ field of the per-thread structure.

The use of $Start^*_{thread}$ enables an additional optimization. In applications in which multiple threads count the same types of events, the hypercall accompanying the intra-domain context switch does not change any counter's control state. In this case, we skip this hypercall. Consequently, $Start_{vcpu}$ is not reset to the counter's current physical value and Sum_{vcpu} is not reset to 0. Since we still initialize $Start^*_{thread}$ using equation (4), we allow the thread being resumed to subtract events incurred by other threads within the same domain since $Start_{vcpu}$ was last initialized. This optimization reduces the frequency with which

$Start_{vcpu}$ is updated, which in turn increases the risk that an integer wrap-around leads to incorrect results when computing a thread's logical value. To reduce this risk, we expanded the width of the counters. Whereas *perfctr* uses 32 bits to represent only the lower 32 bits of all counters, our implementation uses their actual width (64 bits for the TSC register, and 48 bits for PMU data registers; 40 bits on older CPUs). We sign-extend based on the physical register width and store the extended values in 64-bit variables.

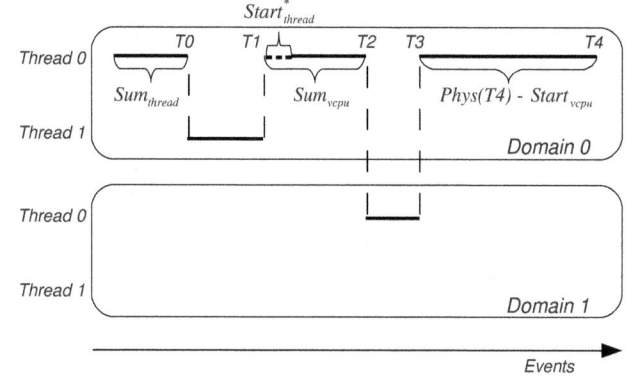

Figure 4. Example scenario for virtualized counters

Example Scenario. Figure 4 shows an example scenario to illustrate equations (2) and (3). Initially, thread 0 in domain 0 is running. At point T0, thread 0 is suspended by the guest kernel and its accumulated event count is recorded in Sum_{thread}. At T1, thread 0 is resumed. The hypervisor sets $Sum_{vcpu} \leftarrow 0$; upon return from the hypercall, the guest records $Start^*_{thread}$. At point T2, the domain is suspended; the hypervisor records the number of events elapsed in Sum_{vcpu} and later resumes the domain at point T3. At this point, the hypervisor samples $Start_{vcpu}$ as $Phys(T3)$. Finally, the logical value computed at time T4 reflects the sum of the three segments during which the thread was active, while excluding those time periods during which the thread or domain was suspended.

4.2.2 I-mode counters

As in the native *perfctr* implementation, i-mode counters require saving and restoring the physical register value on both intra- and inter-domain context switches. In addition, when a thread using i-mode counters is suspended by the guest, the PMU must be reprogrammed to stop triggering interrupts for this counter. Since writes to PMU registers can be performed only by the hypervisor, an additional hypercall is necessary when a guest thread is suspended. Our implementation uses the $Start_{vcpu}$ and Sum_{vcpu} fields in the VCPU structure to maintain the currently active thread's $Start_{thread}$ and Sum_{thread} values at the time the thread is resumed. While a thread is active, we set its per-thread $Start_{thread} \leftarrow 0$ and $Sum_{thread} \leftarrow 0$ in order to be able to use equation (2) to compute the logical value (if desired).

When an intra-domain context switch occurs, a guest invokes a suspension hypercall which will update Sum_{vcpu} and store the current physical value in $Start_{vcpu}$. These values are then preserved in the Sum_{thread} and $Start_{thread}$ fields of the outgoing thread. The guest then invokes a resumption hypercall which will restore Sum_{vcpu} and $Start_{vcpu}$ based on the previously saved Sum_{thread} and $Start_{thread}$ fields of the thread to be resumed. The $Start_{vcpu}$ value will be written to the corresponding physical register. When an inter-domain context switch occurs, the hypervisor updates Sum_{vcpu} to account for the events incurred by the domain and preserves the outgoing VCPU's value in its $Start_{vcpu}$ field before restoring the physical register value from the saved $Start_{vcpu}$ field of the VCPU to be scheduled.

When an overflow interrupt occurs, the hypervisor forwards this interrupt to the guest domain using a virtual interrupt we added for this purpose (VIRQ_PERFCTR). When the guest receives the virtual interrupt, it performs the same actions as in the native *perfctr* implementation, with three slight nuances: (1) When the guest receives the virtual interrupt, it suspends counting for the interrupted thread, and Sum_{vcpu} will be updated via the suspension hypercall. To prepare for the next sampling period, $Start_{thread}$ is reset with the negative sampling period. (2) When the user thread resumes counting, the resumption hypercall is executed, which restores $Start_{vcpu}$ from $Start_{thread}$ and sets the physical register value from $Start_{vcpu}$. (3) The guest does not need to re-program APIC controller, as it has been done already by the hypervisor.

The virtual interrupt is not delivered synchronously because a software interrupt mechanism is used. As such, it is possible that the delivery of the interrupt is delayed, for instance, because other, higher-priority interrupts are being handled first. This could have two consequences. First, it could affect the accuracy because the events incurred during those interrupts will be counted as being part of that thread's activity. However, it is already the case that interrupt-related guest kernel activities can perturb the currently running thread's event count. Second, it is possible that a higher-priority interrupt triggers a context switch in the guest. When the virtual interrupt is eventually handled, a different thread may be running on the VCPU. Since we save and restore each thread's counter state on intra-domain interrupts, we can check if the currently running thread indeed encountered an overflow (i.e., if any of its counters have a non-negative value), and prevent the delivery of the overflow notification if this is not the case. When a thread whose counters have overflowed is suspended before the interrupt has been delivered, we mark it by setting an 'interrupt pending' flag, which is checked when the thread is resumed so that the overflow notification is delivered in the correct context.

4.2.3 Memory Management

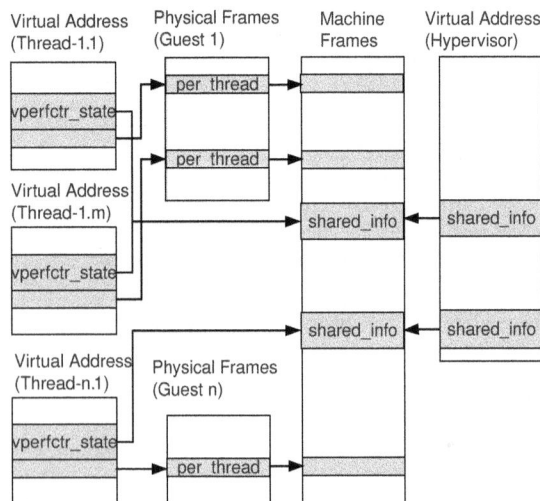

Figure 5. Page mappings in paravirtualized mode

The virtualization approach described in Sections 4.2.1 and 4.2.2 relies on sharing data structures between hypervisor and guest threads, as well as between guest kernel and guest threads. To expose the hypervisor's per-VCPU data structures, we extended the existing shared_info data structure in Xen. This addition increases the structure's size from 1 page to 8 pages; as a result, we needed to modify those places in the code where a single page size was assumed. The additional information, which is kept in 7 adjacent pages, is also made visible to user threads via a read-only mapping to facilitate the computation of the logical counter value. User threads also have read-only access to per-thread information which is mapped into their user space as in the original implementation.

The way in which the per-VCPU data mapping is established differs between paravirtualized and hardware-assisted mode. In paravirtualized mode, shown in Figure 5, the shared_info structure does not appear as physical memory to the guest kernel. Instead, it is allocated by the hypervisor in machine memory and appears at a fixed virtual address in the guest kernel's address space. The corresponding machine address is communicated to the guest kernel through the xen_start_info data structure. The guest kernel uses a Xen Guest API (xen_remap_domain_mfn_range) to create an additional mapping to these machine frames.

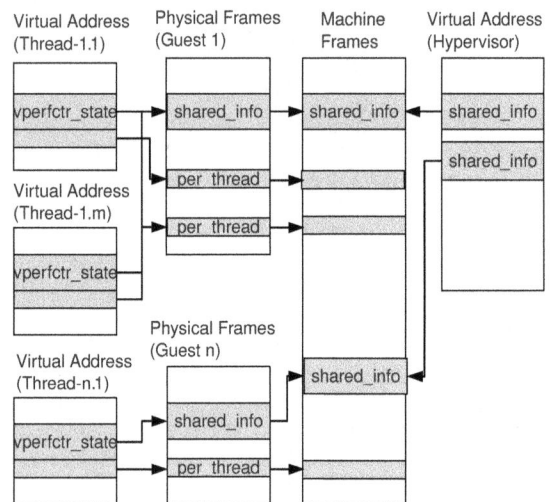

Figure 6. Page mappings in hybrid mode

In hardware-assisted mode, shown in Figure 6, the guest has full control over its physical address space. It can allocate the shared_info in any of its physical page frames. The chosen physical address is communicated from the guest kernel to the hypervisor. Since shared_info appears in the guest's physical memory map, Linux's standard mapping API (vm_insert_page) can be used to add read-only mappings into the user threads' address spaces.

A domain may use multiple VCPUs, and the guest kernel scheduler may migrate threads between VCPUs based on its scheduling policy. Consequently, we expose the per-VCPU data structures of *all* VCPUs to every user thread. We also added an additional field smp_id to the per-thread structure to record the VCPU on which the thread is resumed. The user-level library uses this field as an index to access the correct per-VCPU structure.

Care must be taken to handle thread or domain migrations that may occur while accessing those counters. We implemented an optimistic approach in which we check if the values of the $Start_{thread}$ and $Start_{vcpu}$ fields corresponding to the TSC counter changed between before and after the attempted access. Such a change indicates a domain and/or thread migration, in which case we retry the access until we succeed.

Component	Number of Lines	Details
perfctr	563	VCPU support, hypervisor communication, etc.
Linux	36	shared_info management, VIRQ_PERFCTR
Xen	3488	perfctr-xen, shared_info management, VIRQ_PERFCTR

Table 2. Added or modified code

4.2.4 Software Engineering Considerations

In addition to providing compatibility with *perfctr*, we aimed to reuse as much of its codebase as possible. We were able to reuse the architecture-dependent code portions almost entirely, which will allow us to add support for newer CPU families as soon as they are supported by *perfctr*. Both the guest kernel driver and the hypervisor driver are based on *perfctr*. For the guest kernel driver, we replaced the functions that assumed direct access to the hardware with the appropriate hypercalls. For the hypervisor driver, we needed to provide glue code so that it could function within the Xen hypervisor rather than the Linux kernel for which it was designed. This glue code was written in the form of preprocessor macros and inlined functions contained in a separate header file, allowing us to avoid changes to most of the *perfctr* code. Table 2 summarizes the total amount of added or modified lines of code in the Xen hypervisor, the Linux guest kernel and the imported *perfctr* code. We note that more than half of the number of lines of code added to Xen stems from the addition of the *perfctr* driver.

4.2.5 Counter Virtualization in Fully-Virtualized Domains

The implementation described in Sections 4.2.1 and 4.2.2 requires that the guest kernel includes our perfctr-xen implementation so that it can benefit from the optimizations we made to enable direct access to counter values, which avoids the cost associated with save-and-restore for a-mode counters. Fully-virtualized domains do not require any guest kernel changes.

For fully virtualized domains, Xen's VPMU driver already supports counter virtualization for PMU registers on some recent CPUs. This virtualization is achieved by using a save-and-restore mechanism for PMU registers on inter-domain context switches as well as a hardware-assisted trap-and-emulate mechanism for PMU configuration registers. (A similar approach was implemented for KVM in [15].) The hypervisor intercepts the privileged instructions a domain uses when writing to configuration registers. A hardware-supported access bitmap allows the hypervisor to provide exclusive access to dedicated PMU registers for a domain. These mechanisms allow the use of the native *perfctr* implementation in fully-virtualized environments for the PMU registers, but they fail to provide per-VCPU virtualization for the TSC register, which cannot be reliably written to.

Xen exploits the TSC offsetting feature provided in hardware-assisted virtualization, so that each domain can set its own virtual initial value. However, this per-VCPU offset δ is not adjusted during inter-domain switches, hence does not reflect just the cycles during which a particular VCPU was active. To address this problem, we modified the implementation in the following way. When a domain is suspended, we take a sample of the TSC value ($TSC_{last} \leftarrow Phys(t)$). When the domain resumes, we obtain the current value $TSC_{cur} \leftarrow Phys(t)$, and re-calculate the TSC offset as $\delta \leftarrow \delta - (TSC_{cur} - TSC_{last})$. The updated offset is recorded by the CPU and will be reflected when a guest executes the RDTSC instruction.

5. Experimental Results

Our perfctr-xen implementation was able to pass all *perfctr* and PAPI built-in tests. We verified that it functioned correctly with higher-level tools such as the HPCToolkit profiler. In this section, we discuss our experiments to validate the correctness of our implementation using microbenchmarks, we discuss test results obtained for the SPEC CPU2006 benchmarks, and show profiling results obtained using the HPCToolkit running on top of perfctr-xen. All experimental results were obtained for Xen 4.0.1, Linux 2.6.32.21-PvOps, perfctr 2.6.41 run on a Intel Xeon E5520 with 2x4 cores and 12 GB of RAM.

5.1 Validation of Correctness

To validate the correctness of our implementation, we compared the perfctr-xen implementation running in Xen with the original *perfctr* implementation running in native mode on the same hardware. For most counters, we expect to obtain the same value. For some counters (e.g., cache misses) we expect to see slight deviations because different domains running in parallel may compete for the same resource.

5.1.1 A-mode Counters

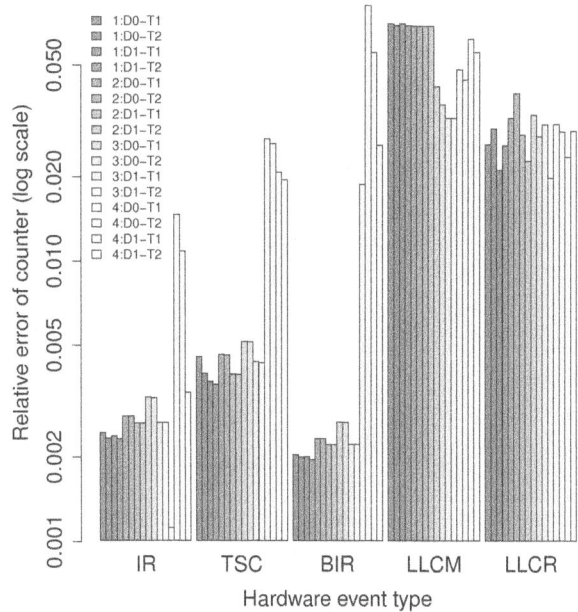

Figure 7. Microbenchmark result for a-mode counters

We first ran a specially developed 1-minute long microbenchmark. This synthetic microbenchmark heavily exercises branch instructions, memory accesses, and floating-point operations without performing a useful task. In Figure 7, the error relative to the native execution environment is shown for several test scenarios and event types. We considered two domains (Dom0 and Dom1) and two threads (Thread 1 and Thread 2) in each domain, running in parallel. Each test result is denoted as $N : D_x - T_y$, where N is the test case scenario, x is a guest domain and y is a thread. We considered the following test scenarios N, which represent different arrangements of CPU multiplexing: (1) Each domain runs on two dedicated physical cores (PCPUs), and each thread in every domain runs on a dedicated VCPU. (2) Each domain runs on a dedicated PCPU and all threads in every domain run on a shared VCPU. (3) Domains run on a shared PCPU and all threads in each domain run on a shared VCPU. (4) Like (1), except that threads are randomly migrated across VCPUs, and VCPUs are randomly migrated across different PCPUs. We used the Xen `xm` command to pin VCPUs to PCPUs, and we used the Linux `taskset` command to pin threads to VCPUs.

We considered the following counters: TSC (Time Stamp Counter), IR (Instructions Retired), BIR (Branch Instructions Retired), LLCM (L2 cache misses), and LLCR (L2 cache references). The results show some deviations, but the overall relative error (compared to native) remains very small. As expected, the per-thread values for the number of cycles spent, instructions and branch instructions retired match more closely the values obtained in native execution than the values corresponding to cache misses because those values are less affected by resource sharing. The results shown were obtained for paravirtualized domains; we obtained comparable results for hardware-assisted domains using our hybrid mode implementation.

5.1.2 I-mode Counters

To verify the functioning of our i-mode counter implementation, we used PAPI's included tests. We present the results for the *overflow_pthreads* test. The test is a synthetic benchmark that performs a set of floating point operations. We ran the test for 300 sampling periods, and recorded the logical counter values afterwards. The benchmark runs 4 threads for which it uses a random CPU (VCPU in our case) assignment. We present results for two scenarios: (1) Dom0 and Dom1 run on separate PCPUs. (2) Dom0 and Dom1 run on a shared PCPU. As Figure 8 shows, the error relative to the native mode for the number of retired floating-point instructions (PAPI_FP_INS) is negligible. Figure 9 shows the number of cycles as measured using the PAPI_TOT_CYC event type, which exhibit a larger relative error. This result is expected because we do not compensate for events occurring in the hypercall events at resumption points when using i-mode counters. The hypercalls consume cycles, but do not perform any floating point operations.

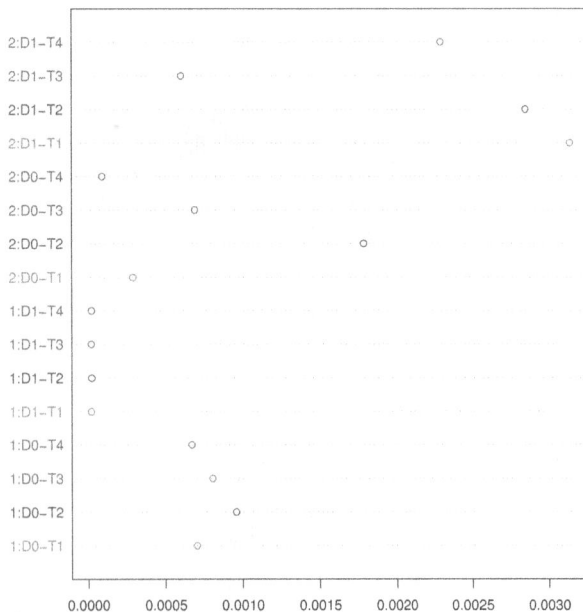

Figure 9. Relative error for i-mode counters (PAPI_TOT_CYC) for PAPI overflow test

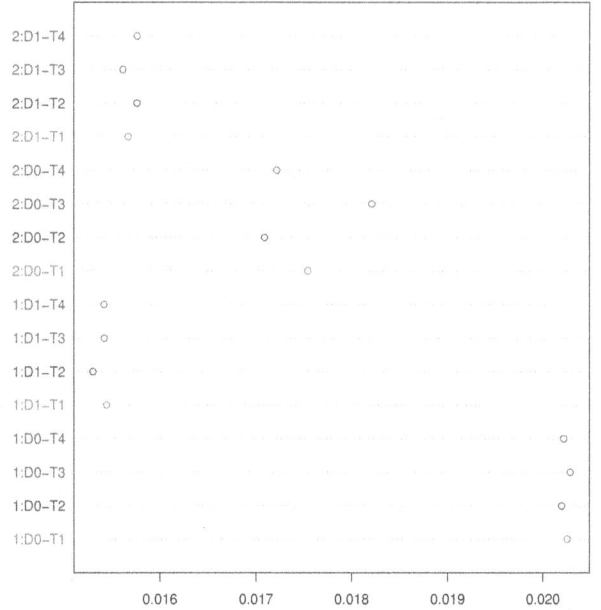

Figure 8. Relative error for i-mode counters (PAPI_FP_INS) for PAPI overflow test

5.2 SPEC CPU2006 benchmarks

We used the SPEC CPU2006 benchmarks as macrobenchmarks to show the correctness of our implementation and provide error esti-

mates for CPU and memory bounded workloads. Native mode execution is again used as reference point. Since Dom0 is a paravirtualized domain in Xen, we used the Dom1 and Dom2 domains for tests that include fully-virtualized domains. (To exclude any possible effect of Dom0, we pinned it to a dedicated core.) We considered 5 scenarios: (1) Native mode execution. (2) Fully-virtualized domains Dom1 and Dom2, each running on a dedicated core (DC). (3) Fully-virtualized domains Dom1 and Dom2 running on the same core (SC). (4) Paravirtualized domains Dom0 and Dom1, each running on a dedicated core (DC). (5) Paravirtualized domains Dom0 and Dom1 running on the same core (SC).

The official SPEC distribution contains a large set of different benchmarks. We ran all of them using the 'train' problem size and recorded the total number of events counted during their execution. Since some benchmarks were executed under different data sets, we calculated the cumulative event counter values for all data sets. We present results for a subset of benchmarks only, choosing those for which both a non-negligible number of events was counted and for which the difference between the scenarios was largest; these represent the relative weakest performance of our framework.

In Figure 10, the results for the cycle counts reported by the virtualized TSC are shown. If the benchmarks execution were unaffected by virtualization, and if our framework achieved the same accuracy as *perfctr* running natively, we would expect to obtain the same results for all test scenarios for a given benchmark. This is true for most benchmarks, although 3 benchmarks (*mcf*, *astar*, and *lbm*) show significant deviations for the fully virtualized configuration. When counting the number of instructions retired (Figure 11), we did not observe any significant differences.

Figures 12 and 13 display the number of L2 cache references and misses, respectively. Since these events are more strongly influenced by environmental factors inherent to the virtualized environment, they show slightly larger deviations, particularly for the number of cache misses. For example, *libquantum* shows a significant drop in the number of cache misses observed, although the number of cache references is roughly the same. These effect warrant further investigation to ascertain if they indeed reflect environmen-

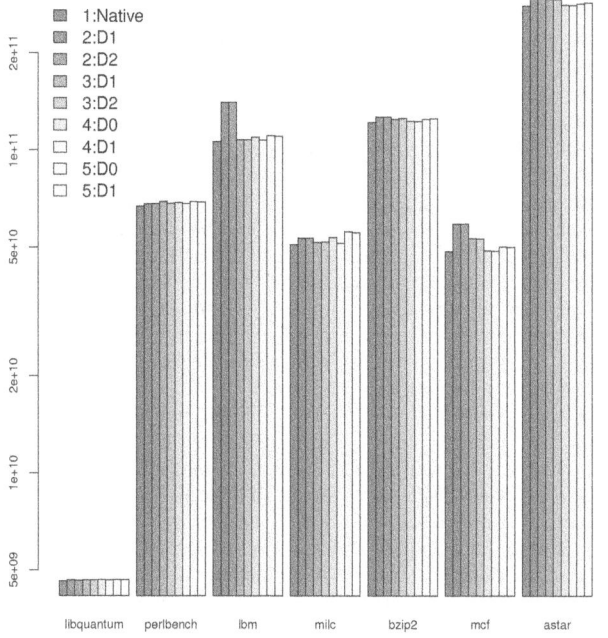

Figure 10. SPEC CPU2006, Time Stamp Counter (TSC)

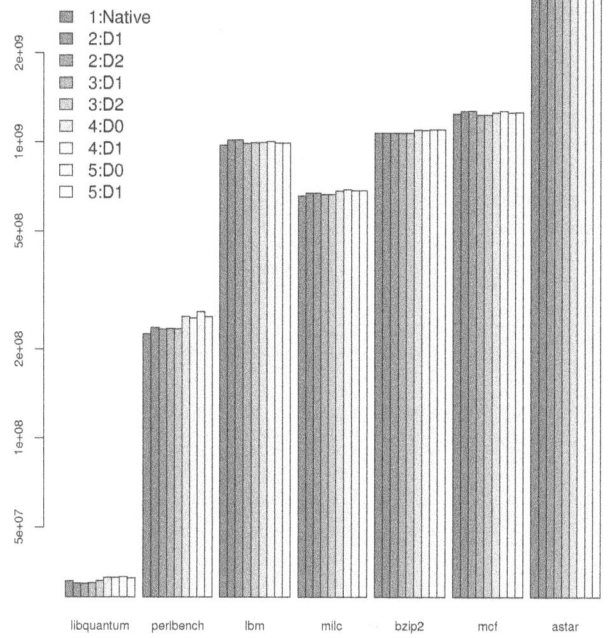

Figure 12. SPEC CPU2006, L2 Cache References

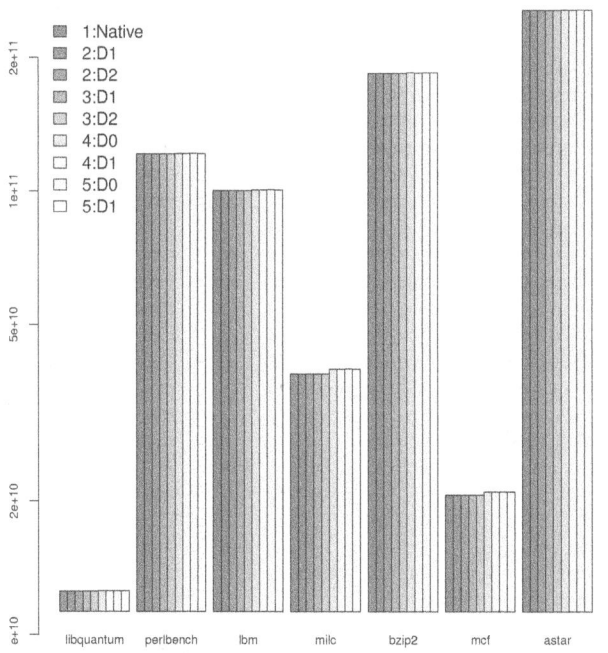

Figure 11. SPEC CPU2006, Instructions Retired

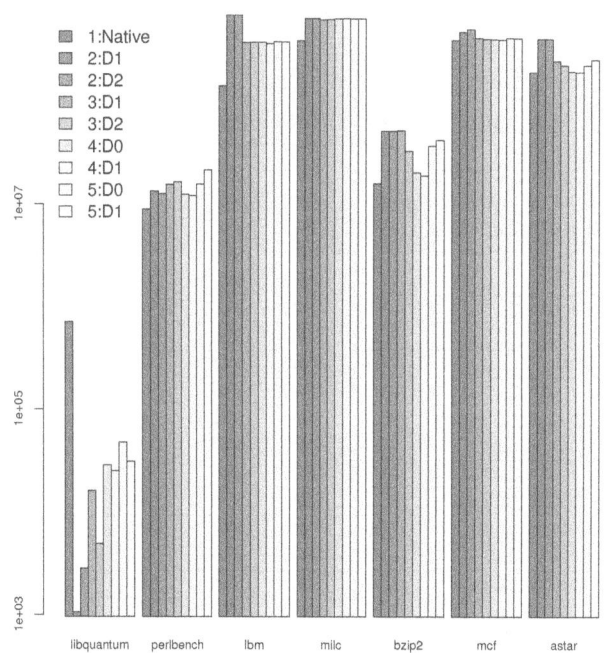

Figure 13. SPEC CPU2006, L2 Cache Misses

tal circumstances or are caused by inadvertent interactions with the measurement framework.

5.3 HPCToolkit Profiling

HPCToolkit's sampling mechanism is based on PAPI, which exploits the i-mode counter capabilities of our framework. As a profiler, HPCToolkit maps sample counts to individual functions. We tested HPCToolkit on the SPEC CPU2006 benchmarks. As an example, we selected the *429.mcf* benchmark, which performs combinatorial analysis. We considered PAPI_TOT_CYC (number of cy-

cles), PAPI_L2_TCM (L2 cache misses), and PAPI_BR_INS (number of branch instructions) events. We considered sampling periods of 40000, 1000, and 500 events, the overall event counts ranged from 10s to 100s of millions of events. Similar to our previous setup, we run 2 concurrent instances of HPCToolkit in two separate domains using the following scenarios that correspond to labels in Tables 3, 4, and 5. (1) Domains Dom0 and Dom1 run on the same PCPU. (2) Domains Dom0 and Dom1 run on different PCPUs. We present results for all top-level functions that accounted for at least 1% of the total number of samples, sorted by decreasing

Function	1:D0	1:D1	2:D0	2:D1
main	0.98	0.99	0.95	0.98
global_opt	0.98	1	0.95	0.98
price_out_impl	0.98	1.01	0.95	0.99
primal_net_simplex	0.98	0.98	0.94	0.96
primal_bea_mpp	0.99	0.99	0.97	0.98
replace_weaker_arc	0.9	0.97	0.88	0.94
refresh_potential	0.96	0.98	0.88	0.9
update_tree	0.96	0.97	0.9	0.93
primal_iminus	1.56	1.56	1.36	1.51
insert_new_arc	1.2	1.13	1.02	1.13
flow_cost	0.94	0.93	0.94	0.94
dual_feasible	0.95	0.95	0.95	0.93
suspend_impl	0.91	0.9	0.9	0.89

Table 3. HPCToolkit profiling results for 429.mcf, sample count ratio virtualized/native (PAPI_TOT_CYC)

Function	1:D0	1:D1	2:D0	2:D1
main	1.01	1.01	0.99	1.01
global_opt	1.01	1.01	0.99	1.01
price_out_impl	1	1.01	0.98	1.01
primal_net_simplex	1.03	1.02	1.01	1.01
primal_bea_mpp	1.04	1.04	1.07	1.05
replace_weaker_arc	0.97	0.97	1	0.96
refresh_potential	1.04	1.01	0.9	1.01
update_tree	0.83	0.72	0.53	0.61
primal_iminus	4.5	4.75	3.5	4.83
insert_new_arc	0.27	0.46	0.3	0.22
flow_cost	0.97	1.03	0.91	0.94
dual_feasible	0.95	0.95	1.05	1
suspend_impl	1	0.94	1	1.06

Table 4. HPCToolkit profiling results for 429.mcf, sample count ratio virtualized/native (PAPI_L2_TCM)

Function	1:D0	1:D1	2:D0	2:D1
main	1.01	1.01	0.98	1.01
global_opt	1.01	1.02	0.98	1.02
price_out_impl	1.02	1.04	0.99	1.03
primal_net_simplex	1	1	0.97	1
primal_bea_mpp	1	0.98	0.97	1
replace_weaker_arc	0.99	1.05	1.04	1.09
refresh_potential	1.02	1.28	1.03	1.04
update_tree	0.86	0.75	0.84	0.86
primal_iminus	1.53	1.47	1.23	1.27
insert_new_arc	0.99	0.87	0.95	0.96
flow_cost	0.97	0.97	0.97	0.97
dual_feasible	1.03	1	1	1
suspend_impl	1.07	1	1	1.07

Table 5. HPCToolkit profiling results for 429.mcf, sample count ratio virtualized/native (PAPI_BR_INS)

number of samples. The tables show the ratio of the sample counts reported under virtualized vs. native execution. For most functions, similar counts were reported, although one (primal_iminus) shows significant differences which will warrant further investigation. We note that the same set of functions was identified in both execution modes, making the use of **HPCToolkit** in a virtualized environment a viable tool for identifying bottleneck functions that account for the largest proportion of events.

6. Related Work

There has been a number of previous efforts to add support for hardware event counters to virtualized environments. Xeno-Prof [21], which is integrated in Xen, allows the use of event counters for system-wide monitoring and profiling. It is an extension of the OProfile Linux system-wide profiler. Each monitored domain runs an instance of OProfile with a Xen-specific driver, which communicates with XenoProf in the hypervisor. XenoProf collects PC samples and puts them into shared buffer. Then it notifies the corresponding domain via virtual interrupt, so that it can map the PC sample to a specific executable symbol. XenoProf does not support performance counter virtualization (i.e., the simultaneous monitoring of multiple domains), works only in paravirtualized mode, is specific to OProfile and cannot be easily adapted to work with other higher-level toolkits such as HPCToolkit.

Work concurrent with ours [15, 16] implemented performance counter virtualization for the hardware-assisted KVM virtual machine monitor that is included in recent versions of the Linux kernel. Like Xen's VPMU driver discussed in Section 4.2.5, their implementation uses a save-and-restore mechanism for PMU registers. During inter-domain context switches, the hypervisor saves and restores the PMU registers of a domain. The delivery of overflow interrupts to a domain relies on hardware support provided by architectural virtualization extensions. Such full virtualization approaches have the advantage that they do not require any accommodations to the guest kernel or user libraries, and thus allow the use of virtually any framework in the target domain, but they forgo the potential optimizations arising from guest kernel adaptation, such as the offsetting technique for a-mode counters discussed in Section 4.2.1. In addition, each instruction that changes a configuration register requires a separate trap to emulate its effect, whereas the use of hypercalls allows the batching of such changes by combining them into a single call. Finally, although hardware virtualization extensions are becoming increasingly common, some major IaaS cloud providers (e.g., Amazon EC2) still widely uses paravirtualized setups.

The VTSS++ system presented in [9] uses a system-wide global sampling mechanism that records time-stamped event counter values. The global TSC register is used to obtain these time stamps. In addition, the system records the time stamps of all intra- and inter-domain context switches. An off-line post-processing system then reconstructs the events produced by individual threads and domains. This method has the advantage that no guest kernel or user-level provisions are required, but its reliance on post-processing may make it unsuitable for some applications.

The vmkperf utility [4] used by VMWare ESX allows the counting of events occurring within given time intervals, similar to a-mode counters. vmkperf does not support the functionality of i-mode counters and therefore cannot easily be used to support high-level profiling toolkits.

The perf_events (previously known as perf_counter) framework [2] provides performance monitoring capabilities similar to those of *perfctr*. This framework has been integrated in recent versions of the Linux kernel. Like *perfctr*, it supports per-thread counters and direct user mode access. Higher-level frameworks such as PAPI include support for perf_events, although the recently added direct access feature [3] is not currently supported in PAPI. The techniques we presented in this paper are applicable to perf_events as well; a virtualization of perf_events is possible future work. The tight integration of perf_events with the Linux kernel may require a substantial amount of refactoring in order to create a hypervisor driver. This coupling may make it more difficult to exploit a single code base for the guest and hypervisor driver as done in our perfctr-xen implementation (see Section 4.2.4).

The perfmon framework [17] for Linux provides both low-level and high-level features. The framework supports per-thread monitoring and sampling, although it exclusively relies on system calls to access counter data. The Intel VTune performance analyzer [5] and AMD's Code Analyst [1, 14] are proprietary frameworks for precise, low-overhead event sampling. They consist of a kernel driver and high-level infrastructure that provides result analysis capabilities. Event counts can be viewed on per-thread or per-module basis. Our techniques could be applied to a possible virtualization of perfmon, VTune, and CodeAnalyst.

7. Conclusion

This paper presented perfctr-xen, a novel performance counter framework for the Xen hypervisor which we have developed. perfctr-xen extends the existing *perfctr* framework so it can be used in virtual machine environments running under the Xen hypervisor. perfctr-xen supports both paravirtualized guest and guests using hardware-based virtualization. It provides a hybrid mode in which paravirtualization techniques are applied to hardware-assisted guest virtual machine.

The technical contributions of this paper are the following: (1) application of an offsetting technique that allows direct access to logical per-thread counter values from user mode while avoiding the costs associated with saving and restoring physical PMU data registers; (2) the optimization of guest and hypervisor communication to minimize and amortize the costs associated with their coordination, while avoiding the costs of trapping and emulating counter-related instructions; (3) a technique for increasing the accuracy of performance monitoring by correcting for monitoring overhead.

Perfctr-xen enables the use of higher-level profiling frameworks such as PAPI or HPCToolkit in those environments, without requiring changes to them. As such, it addresses an urgent need in emerging IaaS cloud environments.

Acknowledgments

We thank the anonymous reviewers for their suggestions. This material is based upon work supported by the National Science Foundation (NSF) under Grant CSR–AES #0720673.

We released the code of our framework to the general public under an open source license. The latest version can be obtained at http://people.cs.vt.edu/~rnikola/.

References

[1] AMD CodeAnalyst. http://developer.amd.com/cpu/codeanalyst/, 2011.

[2] Performance counters for Linux. http://lwn.net/Articles/310176/, 2008.

[3] Perf_counter direct access support. http://lwn.net/Articles/323891/, 2009.

[4] Vmkperf utility for VMWare ESX 4.0, 2011.

[5] VTune amplifier profiler. http://software.intel.com/en-us/articles/intel-vtune-amplifier-xe/, 2011.

[6] L. Adhianto, S. Banerjee, M. Fagan, M. Krentel, G. Marin, J. Mellor-Crummey, and N. R. Tallent. HPCToolkit: Tools for performance analysis of optimized parallel programs. *Concurrency and Computation: Practice and Experience*, 22(6):685–701, 2010.

[7] G. Back and D. S. Nikolopoulos. Application-specific system customization on many-core platforms: The VT-ASOS framework. In *STMCS: Second Workshop on Software Tools for Multi-Core Systems (STMCS)*, San Jose, CA, Mar. 2007.

[8] P. Barham, B. Dragovic, K. Fraser, and et al. Xen and the art of virtualization. In *SOSP '03: Proceedings of the nineteenth ACM Symposium on Operating Systems Principles*, pages 164–177, New York, NY, USA, 2003. ISBN 1-58113-757-5.

[9] S. Bratanov, R. Belenov, and N. Manovich. Virtual machines: a whole new world for performance analysis. *SIGOPS Oper. Syst. Rev.*, 43: 46–55, April 2009.

[10] S. Browne, C. Deane, G. Ho, and P. Mucci. PAPI: A portable interface to hardware performance counters. In *Proceedings of Department of Defense HPCMP Users Group Conference*, June 1999.

[11] E. Bugnion, S. Devine, K. Govil, and M. Rosenblum. Disco: running commodity operating systems on scalable multiprocessors. *ACM Trans. Comput. Syst.*, 15(4):412–447, 1997. ISSN 0734-2071. doi: 10.1145/265924.265930.

[12] W. Cohen. Multiple architecture characterization of the build process with OProfile, Red Hat. http://people.redhat.com/wcohen/wwc2003/, 2003.

[13] R. Creasy. The origin of the VM/370 time-sharing system. *Softw. World (UK)*, 13(1):4 – 10, 1982. ISSN 0038-0652.

[14] P. Drongowski, L. Yu, F. Swehosky, S. Suthikulpanit, and R. Richter. Incorporating instruction-based sampling into AMD CodeAnalyst. In *IEEE International Symposium on Performance Analysis of Systems Software (ISPASS)*, pages 119 –120, Mar. 2010. doi: 10.1109/ISPASS.2010.5452049.

[15] J. Du, N. Sehrawat, and W. Zwaenepoel. Performance profiling in a virtualized environment. In *Proceedings of the 2nd USENIX conference on Hot topics in cloud computing*, HotCloud'10, Berkeley, CA, USA, 2010. USENIX Association.

[16] J. Du, N. Sehrawat, and W. Zwaenepoel. Performance profiling of virtual machines. In *Proceedings of the 7th ACM SIGPLAN/SIGOPS international conference on Virtual Execution Environments*, VEE '11, Newport Beach, CA, USA, 2011.

[17] S. Eranian. Perfmon2: A flexible performance monitoring interface for linux. In *Ottawa Linux Symposium*, pages 269–288, Ottawa, Canada, 2006.

[18] I. Habib. Virtualization with KVM. *Linux Journal*, 2008(166):8, 2008. ISSN 1075-3583.

[19] S. T. King, G. W. Dunlap, and P. M. Chen. Operating system support for virtual machines. In *ATEC '03: Proceedings of the annual conference on USENIX Annual Technical Conference*, pages 71–84, Berkeley, CA, USA, 2003. USENIX Association.

[20] A. Kivity. KVM: the Linux virtual machine monitor. In *OLS '07: The 2007 Ottawa Linux Symposium*, pages 225–230, July 2007.

[21] A. Menon, J. R. Santos, Y. Turner, G. J. Janakiraman, and W. Zwaenepoel. Diagnosing performance overheads in the Xen virtual machine environment. In *VEE '05: Proceedings of the 1st ACM/USENIX International Conference on Virtual Execution Environments*, pages 13–23, New York, NY, USA, 2005. ISBN 1-59593-047-7. doi: 10.1145/1064979.1064984.

[22] M. Pettersson. Perfctr library. http://user.it.uu.se/~mikpe/linux/perfctr/, 2011.

[23] J. S. Robin and C. E. Irvine. Analysis of the intel pentium's ability to support a secure virtual machine monitor. In *9th USENIX Security Symposium*, pages 129–144, 2000.

[24] M. Rosenblum. The reincarnation of virtual machines. *Queue*, 2(5): 34–40, 2004.

[25] C. Sapuntzakis, D. Brumley, R. Chandra, N. Zeldovich, J. Chow, M. S. Lam, and M. Rosenblum. Virtual appliances for deploying and maintaining software. In *LISA '03: Proceedings of the 17th USENIX conference on System administration*, pages 181–194, Berkeley, CA, USA, 2003. USENIX Association.

[26] S. Shende and A. D. Malony. TAU: The TAU parallel performance system. *International Journal of High Performance Computing Applications*, 20(2):287–311, 2006.

[27] D. Zaparanuks, M. Jovic, and M. Hauswirth. Accuracy of performance counter measurements. In *IEEE International Symposium on Performance Analysis of Systems and Software (ISPASS 2009)*., pages 23–32, Apr. 2009.

Dynamic Cache Contention Detection
in Multi-threaded Applications

Qin Zhao   David Koh   Syed Raza
Saman Amarasinghe

Computer Science and Artificial Intelligence Laboratory
Massachusetts Institute of Technology
Cambridge, MA, USA
{qin_zhao, dkoh, raza, saman}@csail.mit.edu

Derek Bruening

Google Inc
Mountain View
CA, USA
bruening@google.com

Weng-Fai Wong

School of Computing
National University of Singapore
Singapore
wongwf@comp.nus.edu.sg

Abstract

In today's multi-core systems, cache contention due to *true* and *false sharing* can cause unexpected and significant performance degradation. A detailed understanding of a given multi-threaded application's behavior is required to precisely identify such performance bottlenecks. Traditionally, however, such diagnostic information can only be obtained after lengthy simulation of the memory hierarchy.

In this paper, we present a novel approach that efficiently analyzes interactions between threads to determine thread correlation and detect true and false sharing. It is based on the following key insight: although the slowdown caused by cache contention depends on factors including the thread-to-core binding and parameters of the memory hierarchy, the amount of data sharing is primarily a function of the cache line size and application behavior. Using memory shadowing and dynamic instrumentation, we implemented a tool that obtains detailed sharing information between threads without simulating the full complexity of the memory hierarchy. The runtime overhead of our approach — a $5\times$ slowdown on average relative to native execution — is significantly less than that of detailed cache simulation. The information collected allows programmers to identify the degree of cache contention in an application, the correlation among its threads, and the sources of significant false sharing. Using our approach, we were able to improve the performance of some applications by up to a factor of $12\times$. For other contention-intensive applications, we were able to shed light on the obstacles that prevent their performance from scaling to many cores.

Categories and Subject Descriptors D.3.4 [*Programming Languages*]: Processors – Optimization, Run-time environments

General Terms Performance

Keywords False Sharing, Cache Contention, Shadow Memory, Dynamic Instrumentation

VEE'11, March 9–11, 2011, Newport Beach, California, USA.
Copyright © 2011 ACM 978-1-4503-0501-3/11/03...$10.00

```
int64 global_sum;
int64 local_sum[MAX_NUM_THREADS];
parallel_sum(int myid, int start, int end) {
  for (int i = start, i < end; i++)
    local_sum[myid] += buf[i];
  lock();
  global_sum += local_sum[myid];
  unlock();
}
```

Figure 1. Example code performing a parallel sum of elements in a buffer.

1. Introduction

One of the major success stories in modern computer architecture is the development of a memory hierarchy: the use of multiple levels of caches has helped bridge the large performance gap between processors and memory. A substantial body of work has focused on measuring and understanding cold, capacity, and conflict cache misses to better optimize applications for a given memory hierarchy. However, in the current multi-core era, additional cache misses can occur due to *true sharing* and *false sharing* in multi-threaded applications.

Threads:	1	2				
		Distinct cores			Same core	Padded
Time (s):	5.52	22.28	33.96	40.02	5.82	2.91

Table 1. Execution times of the parallel sum code from Figure 1 under different thread and core configurations.

Figure 1 shows a code fragment that computes the sum of elements in a buffer. Each thread adds up the elements in its assigned portion of the buffer, maintains the result in a private `local_sum` entry, and finally updates the `global_sum` atomically using its `local_sum`. Table 1 shows the execution times of this application on an eight-core (two quad-cores) machine under different configurations. When the application uses two threads running on separate cores, it is significantly *slower* than when it uses only a single thread or two threads on the same core. Furthermore, when the two threads run on different cores, the application has three possible execution times depending on how the threads are bound to different pairs of cores. These times range from $4\times$ *to* $7\times$ *slower* than the single-thread time. These results are quite surprising because the application has good parallelism and its threads only need to communicate at the end of their execution.

In this example, unexpected slowdowns are caused by false sharing, which occurs because two threads repeatedly update the same cache line holding their private `local_sum` entries. If we add padding between `local_sum` entries to place them in different cache lines, the performance of the application with two threads running on different cores is substantially improved, and the expected linear speed-up is achieved (final column in Table 1). In addition, the three distinct execution times when the two threads run on different cores reflect the varying performance penalty incurred by false sharing depending on which two cores compete for the same cache line: cache line exchanges cost less on cores with a shared L2 cache than on cores without one. Thus, if thread contention was unavoidable for some reason, we could still reduce slowdowns by scheduling threads that frequently access the same data on cores with lower communication cost.

Even in this contrived example, while the solution is simple, the real challenge lies in precisely identifying performance bottlenecks in the application. Usually, this requires an understanding of a multi-threaded application's behavior and its interactions with the underlying hardware. To the best of our knowledge, no existing tool provides accurate and detailed information to help programmers identify and solve performance problems caused by cache contention in an efficient manner. Previous work generally relies on full cache simulation with prohibitively high runtime overhead. For example, CMP$im [15] runs at only 4-10MIPS.

The key contribution of this paper is identifying the minimal information required for cache contention detection, cache line ownership, and realizing that a tool that focuses on that information can efficiently solve an important class of performance problems related to cache contention. We propose a novel approach to obtain detailed information about cache contention by tracking the ownership of each cache line via memory shadowing and dynamic instrumentation. This basic scheme for efficiently tracking cache line ownership allows us to bypass the full complexity of the memory hierarchy, do away with expensive cache simulation, and hence drastically reduce the cost of obtaining sharing information. Contention detection, thread correlation, and false sharing detection are three examples built on top of the basic scheme.

1.1 Memory shadowing

Memory shadowing is a powerful technique for tracking properties of an application's data. It has been successfully used by many dynamic program analysis tools that need to maintain meta-data about every byte of the application's memory, including tools for detecting race conditions [13, 23, 29, 30], tracking dynamic information flow propagation [8, 22, 25], detecting memory usage errors [28, 31], and many others [5, 19, 20, 40]. General frameworks like Umbra [38] have been developed to help users build customized memory shadowing tools. In this paper, we propose a new application of memory shadowing. By using shadow memory and dynamic instrumentation to track ownership of application memory at the granularity of cache lines, we are able to efficiently determine an application's sharing profile. Using appropriate meta-data, we can collect several types of information about thread interactions, and help programmers to identify and solve cache contention problems.

1.2 Contributions

This paper's contributions include:

- We present a novel scheme that, to the best of our knowledge, is the first scheme that can efficiently account for cache misses and invalidations caused by cache contention without resorting to expensive full cache simulation.

- We propose a novel use of shadow memory to track ownership of cache lines in application memory for cache contention analysis.

- We introduce a set of analysis tools that can determine the cache contention in applications, discover thread correlation, and detect true and false sharing, with an average overhead of $5\times$ slowdown compared to native execution.

- We were able to identify significant false sharing in 4 out of 18 real benchmark applications, and were able to improve the performance of 2 applications by up to a factor of $12\times$.

- We discovered thread communication patterns and thread correlation in real applications via cache contention analysis.

- We showed that two benchmarks benefited from scheduling threads based on the memory hierarchy and their thread correlation, achieving up to a $2.4\times$ performance improvement.

1.3 Paper Layout

The rest of the paper is organized as follows: Section 2 provides an overview of inter-thread cache contention and describes our detection scheme. Section 3 discusses the details of our implementation. Section 4 presents experimental results from using our approach, Section 5 discusses related work, and Section 6 concludes the paper.

2. Overview

In multi-core systems, each individual core typically has a private L1 data cache for its own use. These private caches are the source of cache contention. When threads running on different cores access the same data or data within the same cache line, multiple copies of the cache line are created in the private caches of those cores. A hardware cache coherency mechanism is required to guarantee consistency between these copies. If a thread attempts to update a cache line that has been replicated in other cores' private caches, the hardware must invalidate all the other copies before the core can proceed with the write operation. A cache invalidation is an expensive operation as it causes memory operations to stall and wastes memory bandwidth. Moreover, cache invalidations can cause cache misses later when other cores access the same cache line again. Cache invalidations and misses can occur when cores compete to access the same data (*true sharing*) or different data items that happen to reside in the same cache line (*false sharing*). If cache invalidations and cache misses occur frequently, the performance of the application can suffer severely. It is therefore important for developers to be aware of sharing-induced slowdowns in order to scale their applications.

Traditionally, developers have had to resort to full cache simulation to obtain detailed cache behavior when studying capacity and conflict misses. Cache behavior can also vary significantly depending on the configuration of the memory hierarchy. However, we observe that the true/false sharing is only related to the size of a cache line and the application's behavior, and is independent of the other memory hierarchy parameters. This insight allows us to efficiently simulate cache contention behavior without running detailed cache simulations. Our approach dynamically tracks changes in ownership of application memory at the granularity of individual cache lines. This allows us to identify instructions that are responsible for the bulk of the cache misses and cache invalidations, threads that communicate frequently with each other, and interleaved accesses between different cores that cause cache contention.

2.1 Basic Scheme

We assume that our target application is running on a machine that has enough computational cores that each thread can run on

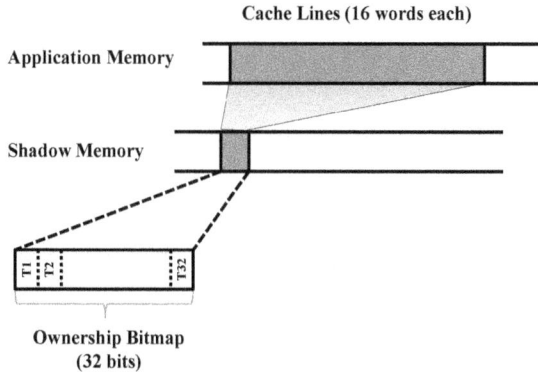

Figure 2. The shadow memory data structure used for our base contention detection scheme. Application memory is shadowed at cache line granularity with a bitmap indicating which cores contain a copy of that data.

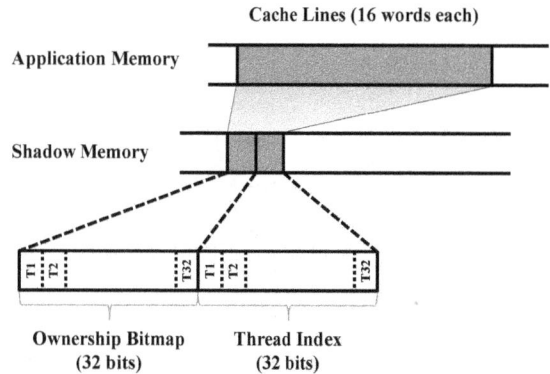

Figure 3. The shadow memory data structure used for determining thread correlation. A thread index is used to track which thread last updated the cache line.

its own dedicated core. This way, we can refer to threads and cores interchangeably, and report the *worst-case* results caused by contention. In this section we describe a design that assumes there are no more than 32 threads/cores simultaneously active in an application; Section 3 explains how our implementation scales to more threads.

We further assume that each core has a private L1 cache, and that data is never evicted from this private cache except through cache invalidations. This assumption allows us to avoid expensive cache simulation, ignore capacity and conflict misses, and isolate the inter-thread communication patterns that are sufficient for detecting cache contention. This assumption may also introduce inaccuracy due to not faithfully simulating the actual cache behavior, which will be discussed later in Section 3.5.

As shown in Figure 2, we use an *ownership bitmap* in shadow memory to track the distribution of each application memory cache line's copies. Each bit in the bitmap represents one core or thread. If it is set, it means that particular core has a copy of the associated cache line in its private cache, or that the core *owns* the cache line.

The bitmaps in the shadow memory are maintained by dynamically inserting instrumentation code for every application memory reference. When a thread reads a data object, it creates a copy of the cache line containing that data object in its own cache. We simulate this by setting the thread's bit in the cache line's ownership bitmap, indicating that the thread owns the cache line. When a thread updates an object, it invalidates all copies of the entire cache line in other cores' private caches, and updates the copy in its own cache. This is simulated by setting the current thread's bit and simultaneously clearing all other bits in the cache line's bitmap, thereby indicating the thread's exclusive ownership of this cache line.

Using this approach, we can simply examine ownership bitmaps at any time to observe the status of the cache lines. In addition to tracking cache line ownership, we often want to collect more information about an application in order to understand thread contention. In particular, we may wish to determine the degree of cache contention in the application, identify *delinquent instructions* that cause most of the cache contention events, determine the communication patterns and hence the correlation between threads, and compute the frequency of true/false sharing. In order to obtain such information, we need to add more instrumentation code and maintain additional information in shadow memory.

2.2 Contention Detection

The first step in performance debugging is to check whether an application does indeed suffer from cache contention. Therefore,

we may wish to determine the frequency of cache contention events (cache misses or cache invalidations) during program execution. To do so, we need to detect and count the total number of cache contention events, which can be easily done using the ownership bitmap of Figure 2.

A cache miss occurs when a core attempts to read a cache line that it does not own. In our scheme, this can be discovered by checking whether the current thread's bit is set in the corresponding ownership bitmap in shadow memory on a memory read. A cache invalidation happens when a core wants to update a cache line that it does not exclusively own. We can discover this by checking whether any bit other than the current thread's bit is set in the ownership bitmap. By checking the ownership of the target cache line on every memory reference, we can count the total number of cache contention events.

In addition, we can also track the behavior of individual memory access instructions. We associate each instruction with two thread-private counters that count the number of cache misses and invalidations it causes, respectively. By checking these counters after execution, we can easily identify the *delinquent access* instructions that are responsible for most of the cache misses and/or invalidations. Pinpointing such instructions is an important step in trying to reverse any performance losses due to cache contention.

2.3 Determining Thread Correlation

An effective optimization strategy is to identify groups of threads that communicate frequently with each other, and reduce the performance penalties of cache contention by scheduling them on cores with lower communication costs, e.g., cores with shared L2 caches.

We can extend our scheme to determine *thread correlation*. Two threads are *strongly correlated* if they communicate frequently with each other during the course of program execution. For instance, two threads may have a producer/consumer relationship and may need to communicate at fine granularity. To obtain thread correlation information, we allocate an array of counters for each thread to record its interaction frequency with other threads. We also add a field in the shadow memory unit to record the last thread that updated a data item, as shown in Figure 3. When a thread accesses a data item in a cache line, we identify which thread previously updated the cache line and increment the corresponding counter. We only update a counter when a cache miss or a cache invalidation occurs, so our correlation statistics only capture thread interactions that contribute to performance slowdowns. If there are two accesses to a piece of data and only one of the accesses causes a cache miss or invalidation, the counter is incremented only once. At the end of

Cache Lines (16 words each)

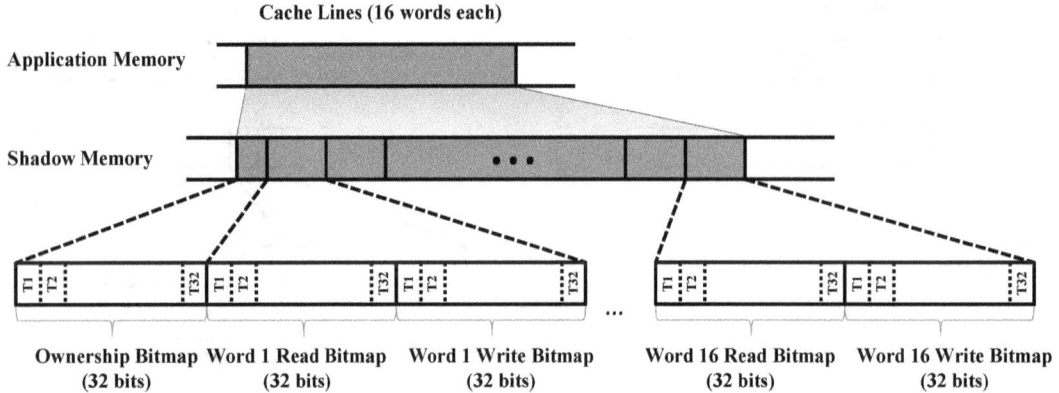

Figure 4. The shadow memory data structure used for false sharing detection. We track which threads read and wrote to each word in each cache line.

2.4 False Sharing Detection

Because cache lines are often larger than the data objects they contain, a single cache line often holds multiple data objects. Cache contention can arise due to true or false sharing of the cache line.

Definitions of false sharing are often imprecise or impractical for real-time detection [3, 18]. Here, we identify false sharing based on the following intuition: if a cache miss or cache invalidation could have been avoided had the target data been moved to another cache line, we consider the cache miss or invalidation to be caused by false sharing. More specifically, on a cache miss or invalidation, if the target location is also accessed by other threads, then it is a result of true sharing, and is unavoidable. Otherwise, it is result of false sharing.

In order to detect true/false sharing, we must maintain more information in the shadow memory for each cache line. As shown in Figure 4, we record the access history for each word within a cache line in the shadow memory. Specifically, we maintain a bitmap for each word within a cache line. Each thread has two bits in this bitmap to indicate whether it read and/or wrote the corresponding word. For every memory access, code is inserted to set the current thread's read or write bit in the bitmap for the specific word that was accessed.

During a delinquent access, we can determine if the cache miss or invalidation was caused by true or false sharing by examining the shadow memory of the corresponding cache line. On a cache miss, we can identify which threads updated this word by examining the bitmap associated with the word: the miss is due to false sharing if no other thread's write bit is set. Otherwise, it is due to true sharing. On a cache invalidation caused by a write, we check whether the target word was read or written by another thread by examining its bitmap once again. The invalidation is due to true sharing if some other thread's read or write bit is set. Otherwise, it is caused by false sharing. For a store, we clear all the bitmaps for the entire cache line in the shadow memory, and only mark the write bit of the current thread in the target word's bitmap. This is to capture the fact that the thread has exclusive ownership of the cache line, and to detect subsequent false or true sharing.

2.5 Further Extensions

Being architecture-independent, our approach can easily be applied to collect arbitrary information for a wide class of problems. Be-

yond the features described above, there are many other possible ways to extend the instrumentation for different purposes. For instance, we could add fields in the shadow memory to record which cache lines caused most of the cache invalidations, and report these problematic data locations to the user. It is also possible to add time stamps in the shadow memory to keep track of access times so that even more complex temporal relationships can be derived. Adding a field in shadow memory for storing call-stack context information is another possible extension to help programmers identify delinquent accesses with more context information.

Using a software-based approach lends our tool flexibility. First, it enables our tool to run on a wide range of commodity hardware. Second, our tool can change its parameters to analyze contention behavior over various thread and cache configurations that are different from the actual machine where the application is run. Finally, we can target different levels of the memory hierarchy; e.g., we can study not only private caches but also caches shared by a subset of cores by simply assigning the same thread bit to multiple threads.

3. Implementation

We implemented our detector on top of the shadow memory framework Umbra [38], which is an efficient memory shadowing framework that uses a novel mapping scheme [37] to translate application memory addresses to shadow memory addresses. Umbra is integrated with DynamoRIO [1, 4] and provides a simple API for client applications to easily add instrumentation to manipulate shadow memory without knowing the details of the underlying memory mapping scheme.

3.1 Base Framework

As described in Section 2, we associate each cache line (64 bytes) with a shadow memory unit in which a bitmap is used to represent which cores own the cache line. Using a 32-bit bitmap, we can track up to 32 threads or cores. We use Umbra's API to add instrumentation to update the shadow memory for every application memory reference. We instrument both reads and writes to keep track of cache line ownership changes in the bitmap. For each memory read, we set the bit for the current thread in the shadow memory bitmap corresponding to the cache line using an OR operation. For each memory write, we use a MOV instruction to set the bit corresponding to the current thread and clear all other bits at the same time.

Our implementation faced three main challenges. The first challenge is performance. The simple instrumentation described above

execution, using these counters, we can report the degree of correlation between threads, enabling the developer to act on the information and achieve better performance.

could cause high runtime overhead. Because we must update the shadow memory on every memory access, a significant amount of bandwidth may be used by the shadow memory updates which will cause system bus congestion and stall execution. Moreover, the updates to the shadow memory itself will introduce high cache contention among threads. To avoid such problems, we optimized our instrumentation by adding checks and updating the shadow memory only when necessary (we call this approach *racy test and set*). In the common case, if multiple threads read but do not write the same cache line, only each thread's first read will cause a shadow memory update. In contrast, blindly writing the shadow memory (we call this approach *set*) even when no updates are necessary would cause different cores to compete on the cache line holding the shadow memory unit, incurring much higher runtime overhead. In addition, to minimize cache contention caused by accessing shadow memory, we ensure shadow memory units are cacheline-sized (64 bytes) or larger even though the actual meta-data in the shadow memory might be as small as 32 bits.

The second challenge is handling concurrent accesses to the bitmap. When multiple threads access the same cache line simultaneously, the corresponding instrumented code will simultaneously update the same bitmap. We could assign a lock to each bitmap and require any access to the bitmap to first acquire the lock (we call this approach *atomic test and set*). This guarantees that the bitmap check and update operations are atomic, but the runtime overhead is high. This is because the lock operation, an XCHG instruction in our implementation, is a very expensive operation that stalls the system in order to ensure atomic operation. In contrast, if we allow racy accesses, we may miss a few cache miss or cache invalidation events, but we will still catch most of them, which is sufficient for our analysis purposes. Our implementation uses racy accesses without locks (*racy test and set*).

The third challenge is scalability of design when more threads are added. Our current design uses one bit per thread in a 32-bit bitmap and is limited to 32 threads. One simple method is to recycle thread bits: e.g., represent thread 0 and thread 32 with the same bit. Bit recycling can lose precision and miscalculate cache misses or invalidations, because we cannot determine actual behavior when two threads represented by the same bit access the same cache line. Another method is to use a multi-word bitmap to track more threads. However, this approach incurs higher runtime overhead for its multi-word checks and updates. More importantly, using more words cannot scale up to a high number of threads. In real-world applications, some programs first create a group of threads to perform one task, destroy them, and then create another group of threads to perform the next task in sequence. Such programs can create hundreds of threads over the application lifetime, although only a few of them are simultaneously active. For such programs bit recycling works better than a multi-word bitmap scheme. It is possible to combine the two approaches to achieve both better precision and better scalability. In the prototype we implemented, we used bit recycling on a 32-bit bitmap.

3.2 Contention Detection

We extend the basic framework implementation described above to discover cache contention in an application. We associate two thread-private counters with each application memory reference instruction to count the cache misses and cache invalidations it causes in each thread, respectively. By doing so, we not only know the total number of cache misses and invalidations, but can also easily identify delinquent instructions, i.e., memory access instructions that cause most of the cache contention events.

For a memory read, we use a TEST instruction [1] to check whether the current thread has a copy of the referenced cache line (i.e., whether it owns the cache line). If the thread does indeed have a copy, no additional work is necessary. Otherwise, we can infer that there is a cache miss. Therefore, we update the cache miss counter and set the thread's bit in the shadow memory bitmap for that cache line using an OR instruction.

For a memory write, we use a CMP instruction to check if the only bit set in the bitmap for the cache line belongs to the current thread, i.e., whether it has exclusive ownership of the cache line. Again, if this is the case, no additional work is necessary. Otherwise, the inserted code will increment the cache invalidation counter and update the bitmap to reflect the thread's exclusive ownership with a MOV instruction.

When a cache invalidation occurs, we could determine whether the data has not been accessed by any other thread yet (a cold miss indicated by an all-0 bitmap), or whether there is at least one copy of the cache line in some other core (indicating a likely prior cache invalidation). However, this would increase the runtime overhead of our dynamic instrumentation. Because our focus is on inter-thread sharing contention rather than full cache simulation, each cache line can at most experience one cold miss in our model. Hence, we are trading off some accuracy for better performance. Similarly, for a memory read, the cache miss counter actually includes cache misses due to both cold misses and cache invalidations. It is possible to tell the difference between these two forms of misses by maintaining more information in the shadow memory. We make the same accuracy versus performance trade-off as before.

We also insert code to record the total number of instructions executed for each thread. When a thread terminates, we scan the two counters kept for each memory reference instruction to obtain the total number of cache misses and invalidations, and compare that against the total number of instructions executed by the thread to understand the extent of its cache contention. In addition, we can determine the delinquent instructions that contributed most to cache misses and cache invalidations for that thread. Where debug information is present, these instructions can be easily mapped back to the application's source code.

3.3 Determining Thread Correlation

To compute thread correlation, we allocate an array T_i of counters for each thread i. Counter $T_i[j]$ of the array corresponds to thread j. The first entry in the array is reserved for counting first-time accesses.

We also add a field in our shadow memory for each cache line that stores the index of T_i corresponding to the thread that performed the latest update to that cache line. On a cache miss or cache invalidation, we obtain the latest thread index from the shadow memory, and update the corresponding counter accordingly.

The stored counters can indicate a producer-consumer relationship. It is possible to separate cache misses from cache invalidations when updating these counters, so that producers can be distinguished from consumers. However, for our purposes, details about these relationships are not important, so we simply use one counter.

Because the memory is shadowed at the granularity of a cache line, our thread correlation actually reflects architectural-level correlation, which may or may not be equivalent to semantic correlation within the application. For example, if one thread updates one part of a cache line while another thread reads a different part of that cache line, our correlation counter is updated. This correlation is caused by false sharing, but it also affects performance, so reporting it is necessary.

---

[1] The TEST instruction performs an AND operation, updates the condition flags accordingly, and then discards the result.

In essence, our counters hold the frequency of a thread's interaction with every other thread. At the end of the application's execution, this correlation information is output to the user who may then use the information to understand the interaction among threads and schedule groups of correlated threads accordingly for better performance.

3.4 False Sharing Detection

In order to detect false sharing, we extend our shadow memory to record which threads have read and written to each word in a cache line.

Ideally, we should use 132 bytes of shadow memory for each 64-byte cache line to track 32 threads: 4 shadow bytes for recording cache line ownership, and 16 pairs of 4-byte bitmaps to track which of the 32 threads has read or written to each word in the cache line. However, Umbra does not currently support such a mapping scheme. Because we perform our experiments on an 8-core system, our prototype uses a compacted shadow memory data structure to track 8 threads using the configuration described below.

For each 64-byte cache line of the application, we maintain a data structure of the same size in the shadow memory, which is divided into 16 four-byte entries corresponding to the 16 application words in the cache line. The first byte of the first entry is used as the bitmap for tracking the ownership of the entire cache line as before. The last two bytes of each entry are used as the read and write bitmaps to track access history for 8 threads for the associated word in the cache line. The second byte of each entry is not used. We use bit recycling to handle applications that need to create more than 8 threads.

We check whether there is a cache miss or invalidation using the ownership bitmap as described before. In addition, we set the bit corresponding to the word that was accessed by the current thread using an OR operation. We again use a test and set scheme to avoid unnecessary memory updates for better performance. On a cache miss, we check whether the word being accessed has write bits set by other threads. If not, a false sharing instance is reported. On a cache invalidation, we check whether any other thread had accessed the word by checking its bitmap. If there were no previous accesses, false sharing is reported. For a store, we clear the whole shadow memory unit for the cache line and set the cache line bitmap and the word bitmap with the write bit for the current thread. This approach limits multi-word updates to only cache invalidation events.

Our use of word granularity in false sharing detection may cause inaccuracy as some applications may have false sharing at the level of individual bytes. It is possible to implement byte granularity in our scheme, but we chose to use words instead, for two reasons. First, a byte granularity implementation incurs higher overhead.

Second, while the compiler often arranges for two unrelated data fields to lie in the same cache line unbeknownst to the programmer, and such fields can be difficult for the programmer to identify, two fields that occupy the same word are rarer and usually easier to locate: e.g., an array of characters or several consecutive sub-word struct fields. The compiler often generates padding to expand unrelated adjacent sub-word fields to have word alignment. Thus, we choose to use word granularity.

3.5 Accuracy Discussion

There are several potential sources of inaccuracy in our design and implementations. One source of inaccuracy is our assumption that data is only evicted from a core's private cache through invalidations. This may cause our profiling results to differ from the actual behavior of the application when executing on a particular hardware configuration, i.e., a particular private cache size and replacement scheme. However, our approach separates application behavior from the actual hardware configuration, which provides users with an insightful view of application behavior independent of any particular hardware features or configurations except the cache line size. We believe that this is more important than accurately reporting behavior on a particular execution instance, which may change when the application runs in a different environment.

In fact, the accuracy of cache contention analysis is difficult to evaluate. It depends on many factors, especially the interleaved order of memory accesses by different threads, which may change from run to run. Although full cache simulation can simulate detailed cache behavior, the input, i.e., the memory access trace, does not always reflect actual execution; thus, the simulation results are often artificial. For example, Cachegrind, a cache simulation tool built on Valgrind [21], serializes multithreaded execution, resulting in a memory reference sequence that would almost never happen in actual execution on a multi-core system. Even full cache simulation can report accurate results for one particular execution instance only and may not accurately reflect application behavior in other runs with different interleavings.

Other sources of inaccuracy, including the number of threads exceeding the number of bits in our bitmap, using word rather than byte granularity in false sharing detection, and not being able to separate cold misses from cache misses due to cache contention, have been discussed above.

4. Experimental Results

We conducted a series of experiments to evaluate our approach.

4.1 Experimental Setup

Our tool is implemented on top of Umbra for Linux. We used applications from two parallel, shared-memory benchmark suites for our experiments: the SPLASH2 [36] and Phoenix [27] suites. Three benchmarks from SPLASH2, namely volrend, water-spatial, and cholesky, were not included in our experiments because they complete in very short times (< 0.5 seconds). All benchmarks were compiled as 64-bit executables using gcc 4.3.2 with the -O2 optimization flag. The hardware platform we used has two quad-core Intel Xeon processors with 3.16GHz clock rate and 8GB total RAM running 64-bit Debian GNU/Linux 5.0. Each core has its own private 32KB L1 data cache, whose cache line size is 64 bytes. The four cores in each quad-core die are arranged into two groups of two cores each that share a 6MB L2 cache. Thus, the fastest a given core can acquire a copy of a missing cache line is from the other core that shares its L2 cache, followed by one of the other cores on the same die. Fetching a cache line from the other die is even slower, followed by the case when a cache line must be loaded from memory.

4.2 Performance Evaluation

We first evaluate the performance of our base framework that tracks cache line ownership implemented using different instrumentation schemes: set only, test and set, and atomic test and set, which we discussed in Section 3. Table 2 shows the performance of the two benchmark suites with these different instrumentation schemes. It is clear that test and set has much lower runtime overhead. The reasons have been discussed in Section 3.1. The atomic test and set is much slower than the simple set scheme, primarily because of the high cost of the XCHG instruction.

We next compare the performance of our three contention detectors. Figure 5 presents the results. It shows that contention detection and thread correlation have similar performance overhead. This is easily understood: they both check for changes in shadow memory bitmaps, and update counters accordingly (see Section 3). Thread correlation is slightly slower than contention detection because it also needs to record the thread that last updated the cache

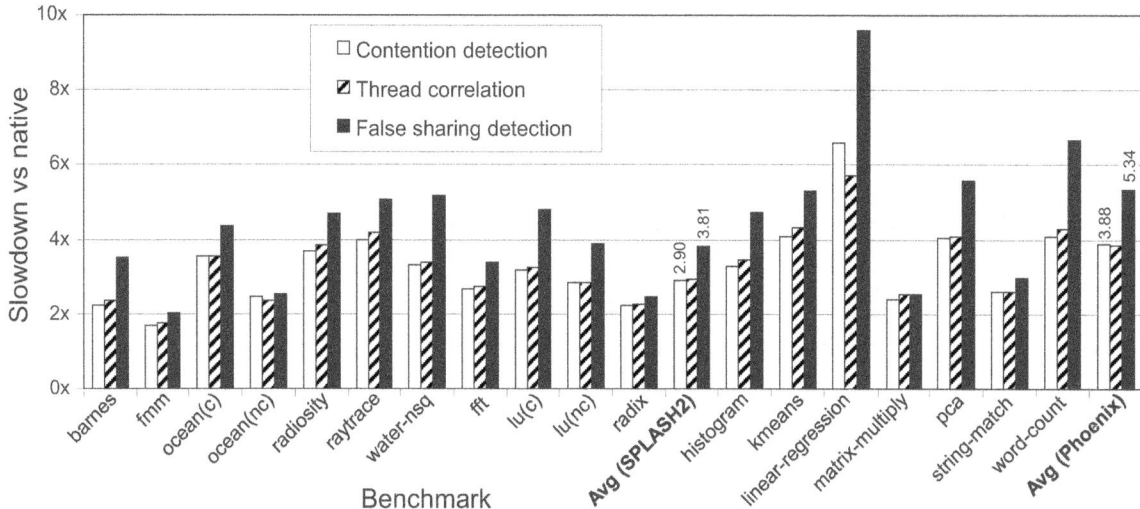

Figure 5. Performance evaluation of contention detection, thread correlation, and false sharing detection. Performance is normalized to 8-thread native execution time. Arithmetic average is used.

Benchmarks	Set	Racy test & set	Atomic test & set
SPLASH2	31.83×	2.68×	50.82×
Phoenix	50.64×	3.61×	95.88×

Table 2. Performance of our base framework with different instrumentation schemes for tracking 8 threads, normalized to native execution (i.e., without any instrumentation) and averaged across each benchmark suite.

line for each memory access. False sharing detection is the slowest. This is due mainly to the more complex instrumentation code needed to update the access positions within each cache line. On average, our tool causes a 3× to 5× slowdown when compared to native execution.

Benchmark	Misses	Invalidation
barnes	0.15%	0.10%
fmm	20.52%	1.36%
ocean (c)	0.15%	0.13%
ocean (nc)	0.92%	0.55%
radiosity	10.94%	16.89%
raytrace	16.78%	22.06%
water-nsq	1.78%	2.54%
fft	0.00%	0.00%
lu (c)	0.23%	0.01%
lu (nc)	0.11%	0.02%
radix	0.00%	0.00%
histogram	0.00%	3.04%
kmeans	0.00%	0.00%
linear_reg	54.65%	69.91%
matrix_mul	0.13%	0.04%
pca	0.10%	0.67%
string_match	0.00%	2.82%
word_count	0.93%	0.17%

Table 3. Relative error between using racy versus atomic operations for counter updates.

4.3 Accuracy of Racy Updates

Racy shadow memory checks and updates have much better performance than using atomic test and set in the instrumentation scheme on the shadow memory. However, races could result in loss of accuracy. Table 3 shows the relative errors (in percentages) of the miss and invalidation counts obtained using racy test and set versus atomic test and set instrumentation. We found that there are negligible differences between the two results for most benchmarks. For four of the 18 benchmarks, the error exceeded 10%. In our analysis, it is the relative magnitude rather than the absolute counts that matters. As such, we regard the trade-off between performance and accuracy of the final counts a worthwhile one to make.

Apart from the obvious reason that racy updates can cause inaccuracies, there is another possible cause for the differences: the slowdown may change how threads interleave their accesses, usually causing more interleaved accesses due to fewer references in each interval. An example is linear_reg: the atomic update causes higher runtime overhead, so more interleaved references happen, and more cache misses and invalidations occur and are detected. We believe this is the cause for the 50% variant of linear_reg in Table 3, not errors due to racy updates.

4.4 Benchmark Analysis

In this section, we describe some interesting benchmark results, and the insights they yielded. The way we analyzed the results also reflects how we believe a developer would use our tool to discover and fix inter-thread sharing contention problems.

4.4.1 Contention Detection

Contention detection can help programmers identify whether their multi-threaded programs suffer from cache contention due to data sharing, and pinpoint the most problematic instructions if there are any. The *contention rate* is the total number of cache misses and cache invalidations divided by the total number of instructions executed by all threads. Table 4 lists the speedups of our benchmarks due to parallelization using eight threads as well as their contention rates. Benchmarks with higher contention rates usually benefit little from parallelization. In other words, they are not scalable. The converse, however, is not true: a benchmark showing little speedup, as the number of threads and cores are scaled, does not necessarily have a high contention rate. There are many possible causes of limited scalability in an application, including an unbalanced workload, expensive communication, or excessive synchronization. The rest of this paper focuses on those benchmarks that have high contention rates (i.e., a contention rate of more than 10^{-3}). These are the benchmarks ocean (nc), fft, histogram, radix, and linear_regression.

Benchmark	8-Thread Speedup	Contention rate
barnes	6.59	1.61×10^{-4}
fmm	6.42	8.36×10^{-5}
ocean (c)	4.26	6.12×10^{-4}
ocean (nc)	2.85	1.82×10^{-3}
radiosity	5.30	2.87×10^{-4}
raytrace	7.27	6.72×10^{-5}
water-nsq	5.87	2.34×10^{-5}
fft	2.07	2.28×10^{-3}
lu (c)	3.00	2.63×10^{-4}
lu (nc)	3.39	2.27×10^{-4}
radix	5.69	2.18×10^{-3}
histogram	3.18	4.26×10^{-3}
kmeans	3.96	1.09×10^{-5}
linear_regression	0.56	3.68×10^{-2}
matrix_multiply	1.02	6.85×10^{-5}
string_match	5.01	2.60×10^{-4}
word_count	7.24	1.32×10^{-4}

Table 4. The correlation between parallelization speedup and contention rate. The speedup is the native running time of a single thread divided by the total number of application instructions executed.

For the benchmarks with high contention rates, we examined the instructions causing the contention. There are four common reasons for their behavior:

1. Initialization. Some of the problematic instructions are found in initialization functions, especially in the first thread of the benchmark, which usually reads data from input files and causes cold misses. Because cold misses are treated as contention-causing misses for performance reasons in our implementation (Section 3.2), such instructions are identified as delinquent accesses. For example, there are three instructions in histogram that are responsible for more than 99% of the cache misses, and all of them are from an initialization function that reads data.

2. Global data update. In some benchmarks, such as radiosity, threads update global data from time to time, which is often a source of cache contention.

3. False sharing. The linear_regression benchmark contains good examples of false sharing that resulted in many cache invalidations. It has 8 instructions that together are responsible for more than 99% of the total cache misses and invalidations. They all access data that resides in the same cache line from multiple threads. This will be discussed later in detail.

4. Communication. In some benchmarks, threads communicate with each other after each phase. fft is a typical benchmark that performs a lot of communication, thereby causing a high amount of contention.

4.4.2 Determining Thread Correlation

We next present results for our thread correlation algorithm. As expected, different benchmarks showed different communication

Benchmark	No binding	Worst case	Best case
ocean (nc)	1.95s	1.99s	0.79s
linear_regression	2.31s	3.08s	1.66s

Table 5. Performance impact of scheduling different threads on different cores for two of our benchmarks. All times are in seconds. 'No binding' lets the operating system decide the scheduling. The other two columns show the extremes of performance when scheduling on different cores. ocean's 'No binding' time averaged 1.95s but varied significantly.

patterns. The most common pattern we see is that all other threads have strong correlation with thread 0, the master thread. Benchmarks likes barnes, radiosity, lu, and water-nsquared have such patterns. In these benchmarks, the master thread will first initialize the data and then each thread works on its own tasks.

Some benchmark threads simply read data in parallel, and have little communication with each other. Most of the benchmarks from Phoenix fit this pattern. This is not surprising, since this set of benchmarks was designed to evaluate the performance of mapreduce, and so the benchmarks are mostly embarrassingly parallel.

We also tested the performance impact of scheduling different threads on different cores. In our platform, we have two quad cores on two different dies. Communication between two cores from different dies is much more expensive than communication between two cores on the same die. Based on the observed correlations, we cluster threads into two groups using two different methods. One method minimizes communication between the two groups while the other maximizes the communication. We considered the performance difference between these two methods on benchmarks with high contention rates based on thread correlations. histogram's correlation array shows that all threads interact most with the first entry, which indicates most misses are cold misses for first-time accesses. So it was not very interesting. fft and radix have almost identical correlation values among threads, revealing no optimization opportunities. ocean (nc) and linear_regression, on the other hand, showed interesting correlation patterns. ocean (nc) has a paired communication pattern: every two threads communicate significantly with each other but very little with the other threads. linear_regression, in contrast, forms a chain of communication. Each thread talks very frequently with its neighbors. As shown in Table 5, scheduling threads on different cores has a profound impact on the execution time for these two benchmarks. For ocean (nc), we observe a significant performance difference. The 'worst case', i.e., when threads were clustered to maximize communication, runs $2.4\times$ slower than the 'best case' where communication is minimized. The 'normal case', in which we left it to the operating system to decide the scheduling, is closer to the worst case. We see a smaller improvement in linear_regression, because it does not have a regular pattern that perfectly matches the core configuration as was the case in ocean (nc).

4.4.3 False Sharing Detection

Because software, including our benchmarks, is usually performance-tuned before release, many applications have already inserted padding on their own to avoid false sharing. It is therefore difficult to find a mature program with significant performance problems. However, we did find several benchmarks with large amounts of false sharing. Table 6 shows the false sharing rate of the benchmarks that suffer from high contention rates. The *false sharing rate* is defined as the total number of false sharing misses divided by the total number of instructions executed. Our results show that these benchmarks also experience high rates of false sharing. The misses

Benchmark	Contention rate	False sharing rate
`ocean (nc)`	1.82×10^{-3}	1.57×10^{-3}
`fft`	2.28×10^{-3}	7.50×10^{-4}
`radix`	2.18×10^{-3}	1.16×10^{-3}
`histogram`	4.26×10^{-3}	4.26×10^{-3}
`linear_regression`	4.33×10^{-2}	4.33×10^{-2}

Table 6. False sharing rates of benchmarks with high contention rates. The false sharing rate is the number of false sharing instances divided by the total number of application instructions executed.

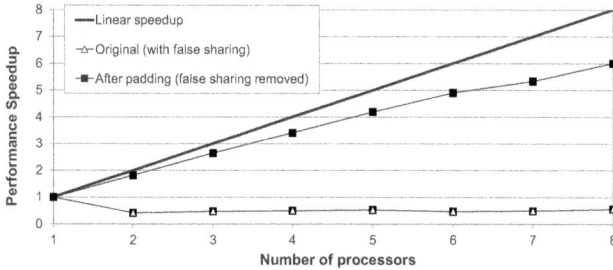

Figure 6. Speedup with and without false sharing. To eliminate false sharing we added padding to the data structures identified by our tool.

in `histogram` are mostly cold cache misses, which are identified as false sharing in our algorithm. It is possible to differentiate the cold misses from the real false sharing, but this requires extra instrumentation and shadow data fields. Note that the contention rate for `linear_regression` is different from the value in Table 4. This is because false sharing detection causes more runtime overhead than contention detection, and leads to more interleaved accesses on the same cache line by different threads, and thus higher contention rates.

By studying the source code of `linear_regression`, we found that it allocates an array, passes one entry to each thread, and each thread then updates the entry simultaneously. This is a common programming practice that causes false sharing. Because several entries share a cache line, a large amount of false sharing happens when multiple threads update neighboring entries. By adding pads into the data structure, we achieved a significant improvement ($12\times$ for 8 cores) for this benchmark, as shown in Figure 6.

We also find that the benchmark `radix` from SPLASH2 [36] has a significant amount of false sharing. `radix` is a benchmark that implements a parallel radix sort that sorts an array one digit at a time. In every round, it copies entries from the array into another array of the same size ordered by that round's digit. Multiple threads fill in the array, causing false sharing. However, this is behavior that we cannot change without drastically changing the algorithm. We tried to add padding between the data but the runtime actually increased because of lost cache locality. In fact, `radix` has a relatively good speed up, as shown in Table 4. This is because it sorts over 50 million integers, using two 400MB chunks of memory. Its working set is much larger than the available amount of caches in all eight cores. So there is a good chance that the data may already be evicted before invalidations or misses can happen.

`ocean (nc)` also exhibited significant false sharing as well and has algorithmic issues. In `ocean (nc)`, different threads update different columns of a 2D array. Because the array is stored in row-major order, a lot of false sharing occurs during this updating process. Our data shows that almost every instruction that accesses the array experiences false sharing. Due to the large size of the array, padding does not work well. However, as we showed in the previous section, we can still improve the overall performance by judiciously scheduling the threads so as to reduce communication cost. `fft`, in contrast, has an all-to-all communication pattern, so the majority of contention is actually caused by true sharing, and it has no easy way to optimize it due to its communication pattern.

An artifact of our implementation is that false sharing detection can precisely track up to 8 threads, while contention detection can track upto 32 threads. There are two benchmarks `pca` and `kmeans` that use more than 8 threads. They create 8 threads in every phases or iteration. In total, `pca` and `kmeans` used 16 and 1,317 threads respectively. Table 4.4.3 lists the data obtained from contention detection and false sharing detection. False sharing detection reported less cache misses and invalidations because fewer number of bits were used in thread tracking. How to precisely and efficiently track a large number of threads (hundreds or thousands) simultaneously is still an unresolved issue.

Benchmarks	Contention detection		False sharing detection	
	# misses	# inv	# misses	# inv
`kmeans`	3.23×10^{6}	1.53×10^{6}	4.25×10^{5}	4.25×10^{5}
`pca`	5.63×10^{6}	4.37×10^{6}	1.16×10^{6}	1.16×10^{6}

Table 7. The number of cache misses and invalidations observed during contention detection and false sharing detection for benchmarks that created more than 8 threads.

Our experiments showed that the novel analysis made possible by our tool can help programmers discover intense thread contention, determine thread correlation, and detect false sharing. This helps programmers better understand their applications and make better choices, for example, in the implementation of the data structures, or the scheduling decisions, so as to improve performance.

5. Related Work

We discuss related work in the areas of false sharing detection and thread correlation.

5.1 False Sharing

False sharing can be difficult to define precisely [3, 18, 35]. For instance, false sharing can be defined as the additional cache misses incurred by a program running with a given cache line size compared to the same program running with one-word cache lines. This may seem like a good definition because using one-word cache lines minimizes the amount of data transferred between processors. However, since programs cannot exploit spatial locality with word-sized cache lines, the number of coherence operations needed between processors may still increase. Thus, this definition can result in a negative amount of false sharing if the loss in spatial locality eclipses any savings due to reduced false sharing. In this paper, we chose an intuitive definition of false sharing that can be practically used for dynamic detection.

Before the proliferation of multi-core systems, false sharing emerged as a significant performance problem for distributed shared memory (DSM) systems. However, because cache coherency protocols in DSM systems operate at the granularity of individual memory pages, DSM false sharing is much more likely to occur than cache line false sharing in multi-core machines. Many approaches developed to dynamically control DSM false sharing [7, 11] used relaxed memory consistency models and version vectors with smaller granularity than memory pages.

Intel's Performance Tuning Utility (PTU) [14] provides hints that can be used by developers to identify false sharing: for each cache line, it collects the thread ID and offset of sampled accesses. Also, the Precise Event Based Sampling (PEBS) support on Intel processors can provide reports of coherency events and identify addresses of the corresponding memory accesses. However, because both of these approaches are sampling-based, they only aggregate memory access statistics without recording the order of interleaved memory accesses. Thus, these approaches cannot distinguish between false and true sharing and can greatly overstate the incidence of false sharing. Hardware approaches [9] for reducing false sharing include protocols that perform invalidations on a word basis or postpone invalidations at the sender/receiver or both. However, such approaches rely on special hardware support.

Compiler optimizations for reducing both DSM and cache line false sharing have also been proposed in the past. Static analysis can be used to approximate program memory-access patterns and apply data layout transformations to improve memory locality [16]. Other proposed approaches reorganize control structures (e.g., loop distribution) along with shared data to reduce false sharing [17, 24]. These approaches rely on the regularity of code and data layout to approximate the memory reference behavior of programs, which greatly limits their usage and accuracy.

Memory managers such as Hoard [2] try to *prevent* false sharing caused by concurrent requests by ensuring that data allocated for separate threads does not lie on the same cache line. Unfortunately, these allocators have no control over inter-thread contention inadvertently caused by developers in real-world applications because of poor data layout or thread scheduling. Diagnostic tools are invariably required to help developers reduce false sharing and thread contention.

A full architecture simulation for detecting false sharing is employed by CacheIn [34]. The runtime overhead for the full simulation is not mentioned but we can reasonably expect it to be very high. Furthermore, the false sharing detection algorithm works by creating a serial trace of all memory references and comparing the address of shared writes to subsequent shared reads. This approach is not efficient in terms of the sheer amount of data generated during program execution and the likely post-processing overhead. Furthermore, the machine model of this simulation only uses the latencies of a few instructions. Traditional full simulations [15] can be used to obtain detailed information about cache behavior, but at the cost of orders of magnitude of slowdown. Our method is an order of magnitude faster.

Pluto [12] tries to detect cache false sharing via dynamic binary instrumentation. However, it simply aggregates information about the number of threads that access a given cache block (and the corresponding access offsets), without retaining any information about the timing of these accesses. While Pluto uses heuristics about thread offsets (just like PEBS) to account for true sharing, it cannot accurately differentiate between true or false sharing, and its results can be very inaccurate. It cannot accurately provide the cache invalidation or false sharing statistics for each instruction. Furthermore, Pluto's reported performance overhead can be as high as two orders of magnitude on target applications.

5.2 Thread Correlation

Most thread libraries allow programmers to specify thread relationships, execution priorities, and scheduling policies. For instance, programmers can statically bind threads to specific processors on most operating systems. Some frameworks allow programmers to declare groups of related threads (e.g., via RTIDs [26]) so that thread schedulers can run these related threads accordingly to avoid performance penalties due to thread communication.

Real-world applications are often developed in different phases, utilize modules from many libraries, and are coded by many programmers. Therefore, it may not be easy for application developers to specify the scheduling of threads or their processor bindings. In the absence of programmer directives, many frameworks track the cache behavior of threads at runtime to make scheduling decisions that improve performance. For instance, cache-aware schedulers can dynamically identify threads that reference shared data [6, 10, 32, 33] so that they can be scheduled accordingly or migrated to specific processors. Such optimizations can reduce overhead due to poor thread scheduling, but they often use hardware sampling of cache misses or other hardware facilities, which makes their approaches inaccurate and platform specific. As a result, these approaches often cannot help developers identify the exact threads and instructions in an application that communicate excessively with each other. With such diagnostic information, developers would be able to take more aggressive, application-specific steps to overcome thread correlation penalties. To the best of our knowledge, no existing dynamic instrumentation tool provides thread correlation analysis for diagnosis without incurring prohibitive performance overheads.

6. Conclusion

Merely porting an application to use multiple threads is insufficient to guarantee good performance on today's multi-core systems. In this paper, we focused on reducing unexpected performance degradation in multi-threaded applications that can arise from inter-thread cache contention and sub-optimal placement of correlated threads across multiple cores. In particular, we outlined a novel approach for identifying delinquent accesses, measuring thread correlation, and detecting true/false sharing. Our tool is based on the insight that the rate of true/false sharing in an application primarily depends on application behavior and cache line size, and can be accurately determined without considering the full complexity of the actual memory hierarchy. We outlined a novel use of shadow memory and dynamic instrumentation that tracks ownership of cache lines in application memory to detect true/false sharing. Our approach is more accurate than static analysis or the use of hardware counters, because we use the exact sequence of memory references in an executing application to detect both true and false sharing, and to differentiate between them. We show that our approach incurs an average of $3\times$ to $5\times$ slowdown relative to native execution, and thus is much more efficient than cache simulations.

We used our tool to analyze 18 shared memory benchmarks. We showed how the information obtained by our tool can be used to significantly improve application performance. We first performed contention detection to identify benchmarks that suffer from contention issues. We then examined thread correlation to derive the communication patterns of problematic applications. In one instance, namely ocean, we attained a $2.4\times$ performance improvement by optimally scheduling the threads of the application. Next, we illustrated that applications with high contention rates consistently exhibit high degrees of false sharing. For one benchmark, namely linear_regression, we removed false sharing by means of padding and turned slowdowns originally experienced by the application into near-linear speedups: we turned a $2\times$ slowdown into a $6\times$ speedup relative to native execution on 8 cores. For other applications, the information that our tool provided was used to explain why no performance improvement was possible without drastic restructuring of the underlying algorithms.

In the future, we would like to explore how we can further speed up our approach through the use of *sampling*. If this turns out to be feasible, it may be possible to extend our tool into a runtime framework that interacts directly with the thread scheduler, allowing for tuning of multi-threaded applications as they execute through their various program phases, and dynamic load-balancing of the system. Alternatively, we could integrate our tool with micro-simulations [39] to obtain even greater detail about the application's and/or the platform's behavior.

References

[1] DynamoRIO dynamic instrumentation tool platform, Feb. 2009. http://dynamorio.org/.

[2] E. Berger, K. McKinley, R. Blumofe, and P. Wilson. Hoard: A scalable memory allocator for multithreaded applications. *ACM SIGPLAN Notices*, 35(11):117–128, 2000.

[3] P. W. Bolosky, W. J. Bolosky, and M. L. Scott. False sharing and its effect on shared memory. In *In Proceedings of the USENIX Symposium on Experiences with Distributed and Multiprocessor Systems (SEDMS IV)*, pages 57–71, 1993.

[4] D. Bruening. *Efficient, Transparent, and Comprehensive Runtime Code Manipulation*. PhD thesis, M.I.T., Sept. 2004.

[5] M. Burrows, S. N. Freund, and J. L. Wiener. Run-time type checking for binary programs. In *Proc. of the 12th International Conference on Compiler Construction (CC '03)*, pages 90–105, 2003.

[6] J. M. Calandrino and J. H. Anderson. On the design and implementation of a cache-aware multicore real-time scheduler. *Real-Time Systems, Euromicro Conference on*, 0:194–204, 2009.

[7] J. Carter, J. Bennett, and W. Zwaenepoel. Implementation and performance of Munin. In *Proceedings of the thirteenth ACM symposium on Operating systems principles*, page 164. ACM, 1991.

[8] W. Cheng, Q. Zhao, B. Yu, and S. Hiroshige. Tainttrace: Efficient flow tracing with dynamic binary rewriting. In *Proc. of the Proceedings of the 11th IEEE Symposium on Computers and Communications (ISCC '06)*, pages 749–754, 2006.

[9] M. Dubois, J. Skeppstedt, L. Ricciulli, K. Ramamurthy, and P. Stenstrom. The detection and elimination of useless misses in multiprocessors. *ACM SIGARCH Computer Architecture News*, 21(2):88–97, 1993.

[10] A. Fedorova. *Operating system scheduling for chip multithreaded processors*. PhD thesis, Harvard University, Cambridge, MA, USA, 2006.

[11] V. W. Freeh. Dynamically controlling false sharing in distributed shared memory. *International Symposium on High-Performance Distributed Computing*, 0:403, 1996.

[12] S. Gunther and J. Weidendorfer. Assessing cache false sharing effects by dynamic binary instrumentation. In *Proceedings of the Workshop on Binary Instrumentation and Applications*, pages 26–33. ACM, 2009.

[13] J. J. Harrow. Runtime checking of multithreaded applications with visual threads. In *Proc. of the 7th International SPIN Workshop on SPIN Model Checking and Software Verification*, pages 331–342, 2000.

[14] Intel-Corporation. Intel Performance Tuning Utility 3.2. *User Guide, Chapter 7.4.6.5*, 2008.

[15] A. Jaleel, R. S. Cohn, C.-K. Luk, and B. Jacob. CMP$im: A Pin-based on-the-fly multi-core cache simulator. In *Proc. of the The Fourth Annual Workshop on Modeling, Benchmarking and Simulation (MoBS)*, pages 28–36, Beijing, China, Jun 2008.

[16] T. Jeremiassen and S. Eggers. Reducing false sharing on shared memory multiprocessors through compile time data transformations. *ACM SIGPLAN Notices*, 30(8):179–188, 1995.

[17] Y. Ju and H. Dietz. Reduction of cache coherence overhead by compiler data layout and loop transformation. *Languages and Compilers for Parallel Computing*, pages 344–358, 1992.

[18] V. Khera, P. R. LaRowe, Jr., and S. C. Ellis. An architecture-independent analysis of false sharing. Technical Report DUKE-TR-1993-13, Duke University, Durham, NC, USA, 1993.

[19] S. Narayanasamy, C. Pereira, H. Patil, R. Cohn, and B. Calder. Automatic logging of operating system effects to guide application-level architecture simulation. In *Proc. of the Joint International Conference on Measurement and Modeling of Computer Systems (SIGMETRICS '06/Performance '06)*, pages 216–227, 2006.

[20] N. Nethercote and A. Mycroft. Redux: A dynamic dataflow tracer. In *Electronic Notes in Theoretical Computer Science*, volume 89, 2003.

[21] N. Nethercote and J. Seward. Valgrind: A framework for heavyweight dynamic binary instrumentation. In *Proc. of the ACM SIGPLAN Conference on Programming Language Design and Implementation (PLDI '07)*, pages 89–100, June 2007.

[22] J. Newsome. Dynamic taint analysis for automatic detection, analysis, and signature generation of exploits on commodity software. In *Proc. of the Network and Distributed System Security Symposium (NDSS 2005)*, 2005.

[23] OpenWorks LLP. Helgrind: A data race detector, 2007. http://valgrind.org/docs/manual/hg-manual.html/.

[24] J. Peir and R. Cytron. Minimum distance: A method for partitioning recurrences for multiprocessors. *IEEE Transactions on Computers*, 38(8):1203–1211, 1989.

[25] F. Qin, C. Wang, Z. Li, H.-s. Kim, Y. Zhou, and Y. Wu. Lift: A low-overhead practical information flow tracking system for detecting security attacks. In *Proc. of the 39th International Symposium on Microarchitecture (MICRO 39)*, pages 135–148, 2006.

[26] M. Rajagopalan, B. Lewis, and T. Anderson. Thread scheduling for multi-core platforms. In *Proceedings of the 11th USENIX workshop on Hot topics in operating systems*, pages 1–6. USENIX Association, 2007.

[27] C. Ranger, R. Raghuraman, A. Penmetsa, G. Bradski, and C. Kozyrakis. Evaluating mapreduce for multi-core and multiprocessor systems. In *Proceedings of the 2007 IEEE 13th International Symposium on High Performance Computer Architecture*, pages 13–24, 2007.

[28] Rational Software. Purify: Fast detection of memory leaks and access errors, 2000. http://www.rationalsoftware.com/products/whitepapers/319.jsp.

[29] M. Ronsse, B. Stougie, J. Maebe, F. Cornelis, and K. D. Bosschere. An efficient data race detector backend for DIOTA. In *Parallel Computing: Software Technology, Algorithms, Architectures & Applications*, volume 13, pages 39–46. Elsevier, 2 2004.

[30] S. Savage, M. Burrows, G. Nelson, P. Sobalvarro, and T. Anderson. Eraser: a dynamic data race detector for multithreaded programs. *ACM Trans. Comput. Syst.*, 15(4):391–411, 1997.

[31] J. Seward and N. Nethercote. Using Valgrind to detect undefined value errors with bit-precision. In *Proc. of the USENIX Annual Technical Conference*, pages 2–2, 2005.

[32] S. Sridharan, B. Keck, R. Murphy, S. Chandra, and P. Kogge. Thread migration to improve synchronization performance. In *Workshop on Operating System Interference in High Performance Applications*, 2006.

[33] D. Tam, R. Azimi, and M. Stumm. Thread clustering: sharing-aware scheduling on smp-cmp-smt multiprocessors. In *EuroSys '07: Proceedings of the 2nd ACM SIGOPS/EuroSys European Conference on Computer Systems 2007*, pages 47–58, New York, NY, USA, 2007. ACM.

[34] J. Tao and W. Karl. CacheIn: A Toolset for Comprehensive Cache Inspection. *Computational Science–ICCS 2005*, pages 174–181, 2005.

[35] J. Weidendorfer, M. Ott, T. Klug, and C. Trinitis. Latencies of conflicting writes on contemporary multicore architectures. *Parallel Computing Technologies*, pages 318–327, 2007.

[36] S. C. Woo, M. Ohara, E. Torrie, J. P. Singh, and A. Gupta. The SPLASH-2 programs: characterization and methodological considerations. In *Proc. of the 22nd International Symposium on Computer Architecture (ISCA '95)*, pages 24–36, 1995.

[37] Q. Zhao, D. Bruening, and S. Amarasinghe. Efficient memory shadowing for 64-bit architectures. In *Proc. of the The International Symposium on Memory Management (ISMM '10)*, Toronto, Canada, Jun 2010.

[38] Q. Zhao, D. Bruening, and S. Amarasinghe. Umbra: Efficient and scalable memory shadowing. In *Proc. of the International Symposium on Code Generation and Optimization (CGO '10)*, Apr. 2010.

[39] Q. Zhao, R. Rabbah, S. Amarasinghe, L. Rudolph, and W.-F. Wong. Ubiquitous memory introspection. In *International Symposium on Code Generation and Optimization*, San Jose, CA, Mar 2007.

[40] Q. Zhao, R. M. Rabbah, S. P. Amarasinghe, L. Rudolph, and W.-F. Wong. How to do a million watchpoints: Efficient debugging using dynamic instrumentation. In *Proc. of the 17th International Conference on Compiler Construction (CC '08)*, pages 147–162, 2008.

Rethink the Virtual Machine Template

Kun Wang, Jia Rao, Cheng-Zhong Xu

Department of Electrical & Computer Engineering
Wayne State University, Detroit, Michigan 48202
{kwang,jrao,czxu}@wayne.edu

Abstract

Server virtualization technology facilitates the creation of an elastic computing infrastructure on demand. There are cloud applications like server-based computing and virtual desktop that concern startup latency and require impromptu requests for VM creation in a real-time manner. Conventional template-based VM creation is a time consuming process and lacks flexibility for the deployment of statefull VMs. In this paper, we present an abstraction of VM substrate to represent generic VM instances in miniature. Unlike templates that are stored as an image file in disk, VM substrates are docked in memory in a designated VM pool. They can be activated into statefull VMs without machine booting and application initialization. The abstraction leverages an arrange of techniques, including VM miniaturization, generalization, clone and migration, storage copy-on-write, and on-the-fly resource configuration, for rapid deployment of VMs and VM clusters on demand. We implement a prototype on a Xen platform and show that a server with typical configuration of TB disk and GB memory can accommodate more substrates in memory than templates in disk and statefull VMs can be created from the same or different substrates and deployed on to the same or different physical hosts in a cluster without causing any configuration conflicts. Experimental results show that general purpose VMs or a VM cluster for parallel computing can be deployed in a few seconds. We demonstrate the usage of VM substrates in a mobile gaming application.

Categories and Subject Descriptors D.4.7 [*Operating Systems*]: Organization and Design,Distributed Systems

General Terms Management, Measurement, Performance

Keywords Virtual machine deployment, Data center, Virtual machine template, Cloud computing

1. Introduction

Cloud computing in its original form offers virtualized resources, and infrastructure in general, as a service over the Internet. A key requirement is resource provisioning on-demand in a real-time manner. In the model of infrastructure-as-a-service, applications are often run in virtual machines (VMs) and their performance relies on effective management of the VMs in the whole life-cycle from creation, deployment, execution, to termination. Because of the nature of on-demand computing, VM startup latency is a crucial performance factor in application responsiveness, in particular for those that interactive, impromptu, and short-lived computing [10].

An example of such applications is server-based computing (SBC) [12], in which resource-constrained client applications offload compute- or data-intensive tasks to VMs running in a data center, e.g., through computation offloading or wrapping mobile OS to VMs running in the cloud can significantly extends the computing capability of mobile devices as well as saves the scarce battery resource. [3]. In such case, the VMs may need to be created and deployed on the fly during the execution time of the applications. Another example is virtual desktop infrastructure (VDI) [25], in which clients would launch their VMs associated with their personalized working environments and data on a remote client device upon request. In addition, in virtualized parallel computing, the size of a VM cluster varies with the workload which requires new VMs worker can be created instantaneously. Startup latency is pivotal to the success of all these cloud computing usage cases.

VM creation from scratch requires to create a virtual hard drive image, configure virtualized resources, install OS and initialize application services. This process would take tens of minutes. To reduce the startup latency, in practice, public IaaS providers like Amazon Web Services provide users an option to create VMs from template. A VM template [20, 26] is a reusable image created from a clean VM and stored in disk as a file. Although a VM can be created by booting from a template in tens of second, the template become non-reusable by others. VM cloning from a template would retain the reusability of the template but at the cost of expensive disk copy of large image files. In either approach, there is no time-efficient way to create multiple VMs simultaneously from the sample template, although such parallel deployment is crucial to parallel computing and server clustering.

There were recent studies on reducing the startup latency and supporting parallel deployment of homogeneous VMs; see Potemkin [27] and Snowflock [11] for examples. Potemkin proposed a delta virtualization technique for flash VM cloning. It relies a copy-on-write optimization technique to have multiple VMs share memory pages as much as possible. Snowflock proposed a process-fork like API to fork VMs for parallel processing during the execution of a program. The VMs created inherit the software stack from their parent VMs and can not exist without the presence of their parents.

In this paper, we propose an abstraction of VM substrate as an alternative to VM template for rapid deployment and parallel deployment of VMs. VMs created from substrates have the same life cycle as template-based VMs and the VMs are of independent by origin and can be deployed across different physical hosts. Unlike templates that are stateless and stored in disk as an image file, substrates is a generic VM instance in miniature that docked in memory of a designated machine in an inactive state. They can be present with or without application footprints and ready to be

VEE'11, March 9–11, 2011, Newport Beach, California, USA.
Copyright © 2011 ACM 978-1-4503-0501-3/11/03...$10.00

Template Size	2G	5G	10G	20G
cp(local disk)	36.06s	58.75s	547.45s	1228.69s
cp(nfs)	46.16s	78.21s	640.28s	1412.42s
scp	43.31s	114.66s	749.97s	1589.35s
dd(single disk)	3.07s	45.55s	195.71s	515.17s

Table 1. Cost of creating VM from templates.

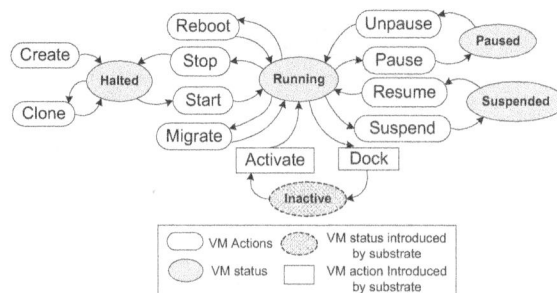

Figure 1. VM State Transition.

powered on upon request. Creation of VMs from substrates saves time from time-consuming disk-based booting and deployment. The substrate mechanism leverages an array of techniques, including VM miniaturization, generalization, clone and migration, page copy-on-write, and on-the-fly resource configuration, to save memory space, generalize substrate usages, and resolve resource configuration conflicts on VMs to be created. The mechanism facilitates parallel VM deployment via multicast.

We have implemented a prototype on a Xen/Linux server cluster and tested the system in two scenarios: on-demand deployment of VMs for cloud-assisted gaming and parallel deployment of heterogeneous VM clusters like LAMP (Linux/Apache/MySQL/PHP). Experimental results showed the mechanism capable of creating VMs in subsecond, while retaining the flexibility of VM resource configuration. The experiment results also show that the substrate mechanism makes it possible to deploy a VM cluster in a few second or a speedup of more than 50 times in comparison with default VM deployment from template.

The rest of this paper is organized as follows. Section 2 gives background information about VM lifecycle and in particular the cost sources of VM creation. Section 3 presents the concept of substrate, substrate pool, and revised VM life cycle due to the use of substrate. Section 4 presents implementation details and results from micro-benchmark testing of key implementation issues. Evaluation results of the system as a whole are discussed in Section 5. Section 6 discusses related work. Section 7 concludes this paper with remarks about future work.

2. Background

Deployment of a VM in a data center involves a number of steps: (1) VM creation with virtual hard disk; (2) Installation of OS images and applications; (3) Deployment with configuration (networking, etc) on selected host/cluster; (4) VM startup.

New VMs can be created either from scratch or from template. As the process of VM creation from scratch takes tens of minutes, it is rarely used in cloud. On the other hand, deploying a VM from templates, which removes the process of OS and software installation, is widely used in practice. VM creation from templates involves two steps: (1) create a copy of the template's virtual disk image and (2) customize the VM configuration as needed. Configuration customization includes parameter settings for boot option, host name and network. VMs can be created from templates through either cloning or conversion. VM templates are usually created for a specific purpose such as a web server or a database server. Once booted, the VM which originates from a template can be further extended by deploying more applications or run-time libraries. In the following, we first discuss the cost of VM creation and then examine the state transition of a VM. Next, we present the challenges of fast VM deployment.

2.1 Cost of VM creation

The cost of template-based VM creation comes from different sources. First, depending on the storage environment and VM template image size, the cost of VM disk duplication varies. In order to support VM live migration [4], VM disk images are usually stored in centralized storage servers. NFS and iSCSI are two popular choices for the deployment of VM virtual disks. In either case, the duplication of the template's disk image is necessary for a new VM creation. Table 1 shows the cost of disk duplication with different disk sizes and different methods. Regardless the underlying storage organization and duplication methods, the cost increases significantly with the VM disk size. A 5GB VM disk requires more than one minute to be copied. The latency incurred by disk duplication is not acceptable to interactive applications. Besides, according to the table, to clone a new VM from a template on remote host (*scp*) takes tens of seconds or even a few minutes, consuming a significant amount of network bandwidth in the data center. Note that although create a blank disk image on local disks (*dd*) takes less time, but deploying root filesystem takes even more time than directly duplicate a disk VM with root filesystem as a whole. Second, the booting process of a VM includes booting the kernel and starting default services. Kernel booting usually takes sub-seconds while starting different services is both error-prone and costly. The general purpose OS installation activates many services by default. RightScale [22] templates and Oracle VM templates [20] disable most of the application unrelated services to minimize the cost. Third, traditional JeOS templates are usually extended by installing more applications to generate new application specific templates. The cost of maintaining various VM templates increases with the diversity of application oriented templates. All these costs together makes template based VM creation impractical for interactive applications.

2.2 VM state transition

Starting from a template, a VM experiences multiple states in its life cycle. Figure 1 shows state transition diagram for a VM. Each VM is initially halted after being created from scratch or cloned from templates. Although each halted VM is a static instance only consuming disk space, it still can be edited or customized by installing new applications or changing the associated configuration. A VM is changed to a running state when it is started and A VM can be paused or suspended on local host or migrated to another host. We added one additional state and two new actions to the conventional VM state diagram [20]. A new substrate is generated from a running VM through docking. Docking can be done by converting or checkpointing. Converting puts the running VM to an inactive state, while checkpointing keeps the VM running. The tradeoff between these two solutions are discussed in substrate design section. Note that an inactive state is different from a halted state. An inactive VM consumes memory and maintains running status, but a halted VM only consumes disk space.

2.3 Challenges of rapid VM deployment

Rapid VM deployment calls for minimal costs in each step of VM creation. However, as discussed above, virtual disk image duplication is time-consuming. It leads to a large startup latency.

Moreover, if multiple VMs need to be created at the same time, disk duplication is the key impediment to fast VM deployment. In addition, the automatic resource reconfiguration of new VMs is also challenging, especially in a heterogeneous virtualized cluster of VMs with interactive applications.

Stateless VM creation has limited usage cases due to the fact that it creates brand new VM every time without preserving run-time environment or intermediate result. A brand new VM with necessary applications pre-installed is how the general VM template is used. This is insufficient for many of the cloud applications like parallel computing or mobile computation offloading. Thus the fast creation of statefull VMs is necessary.

Rapid VM deployment also requires that the creating process should be transparent to users and applications. Because creating a new VM always takes time, in the cases of user interactive applications or other request-driven VM creation, startup latency caused by creating a new VM must be small enough so as to make the creating process transparent to application. If the cost of creating process is negligible, from applications' perspective, VMs are always ready for use.

3. Design of VM substrate

Modern applications and libraries consume a considerable amount of disk space, which makes the size of templates usually large. To address these limitations, a few questions need to be answered. First, can image file be stored in memory instead of disk? Although, solid-state-disk(SSD) attempts to increase the efficiency of data transfer between disk and memory, it is still not fast enough to meet the requirement of duplicating disk image on demand. Moreover, the size of traditional templates can easily go beyond the limitation of the memory of a server or a common SSD. Thus it is impractical to maintain templates in memory and only a limited number of templates can be saved on SSD. Second, is it possible to avoid the booting process while still maintaining previous running states when starting a VM? An AMI [6] or oracle VM contains a minimal Linux installation with only essential Linux services, leaving the installation of additional applications to package management tools. Thus the images are much smaller than default Linux OS installation. However, it is a brand new OS with only a limited number of services installed. Third, is it possible to deploy a VM in a real-time manner? Real-time VM deployment allows VMs to be created on demand and only be activated when in use. In the remaining section, we elaborate the design of VM substrate and compare VM substrate with alternative approaches.

3.1 VM substrate and pool

The design of VM substrate aims to leverage existing virtualization techniques to provide an agile cloud computing environment which allows users to create VMs or VM clusters on demand. A VM substrate is a static reusable instance that can be duplicated or reactivated for later use. VM substrates are categorized into three types. Public substrates contain minimal clean JeOS and generic configuration. Restricted substrates are the extensions of public substrates with specific applications and run-time environment. Alternatively, private substrates include users' personal data which can only be reused under strict sharing policy. These types of substrates are designed for different use cases, but they follow the same docking and reactivating process.

Saving the running states of VMs into in-memory VM substrates has many advantages over having VMs always run in full capacity. If a VM in full capacity is paused or suspended to the local machine, the resulted memory footprint which contains the VM's running state is usually quite large, in proportion to the VM's original capacity. If the saved state is stored in local machine's memory, the restarting of the paused/suspended VM is instant but at

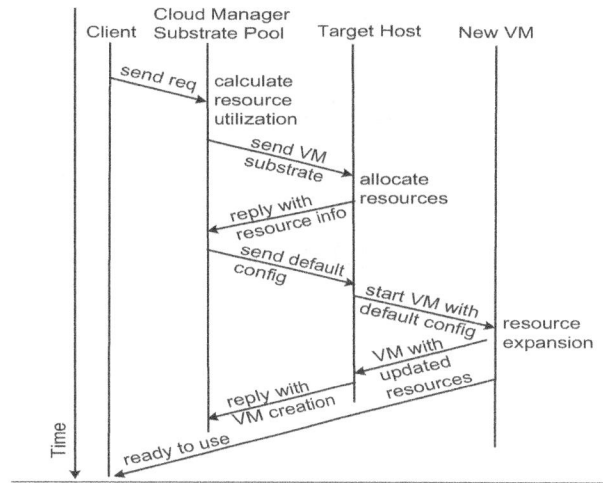

Figure 2. Create VM from substrate.

a cost of wasted memory resources which can be otherwise used by other running VMs. If the state is saved on local hard disk, the time required to resume the VM is unacceptable. For example, it takes approximately 40 second to restore a VM with 2 GB memory from a 7200RPM SATA disk. In VM substrates, we first trim the VM to its minimal capacity (minimal CPU and memory, detached block and network devices) that preserve essential running states, and then temporarily dock the VM to memory other than disk. After the final compression, the resulted memory footprint which usually in a size of tens of megabytes is transferred and consolidated to a dedicated substrate pool. Upon resuming, the corresponding VM's substrate is activated by expanding to its real capacity. The restoration latency is comparable to the local in-memory restore but with a much less memory cost on each local host.

A substrate pool is a centralized repository where all the substrates are maintained. Unlike traditional VM template pool, The substrate pool stays mainly in memory and the backup substrates are stored on disk. The size of a substrate pool is dynamically reconfigurable without affecting the existing substrates. Our preliminary experiment results show that a substrate with minimal programming environment can be as small as 16MB. With the similar substrate, we successfully hosted several hundreds of substrates on a physical machine with a 4GB memory. However, the sizes of the substrates depend on the running status of the hosted application. In order to maintain a statefull substrate with manageable cost, we aim to embed only necessary data into a substrate.

VM substrate is proposed to be an alternative effective VM administration solution not only applicable to instant parallel workers creation, but also applicable to standalone VM deployment, also taking the reusability and scalability into consideration. Different from VM Descriptors proposed by Snowflock [11], VM substrate doesn't have heavy dependancy on any parent VM and has many varieties. VM Descriptors contain only the minimal critical metadata needed to start execution and use *Memory-On-Demand* mechanism lazily fetch portions of VM sate over network as it is accessed. In contrast, VM substrates are static VM abstraction resides in a pool in memory. Activation, resource expansion and remapping are the typical three steps to create a new VM from a substrate. In theory, it is possible to maintain a pool of template parent VM and then fork child VMs on demand. However, this solution can hardly get rid of the limitation of dependancy and hard to meet the requirement of VM creation for long standing services. Moreover, due to the size of the parent VM, the cost of maintaining template parent VMs is much higher than maintaining a substrate pool. In addition, if the application is CPU intensive and requires minimal updates to disk or the intermediate results can be discarded, an alternative way to VM fork is to start multiple VMs on different hosts with the same disk image located on a centralized server. But this solution has very limited usage cases.

The abstraction of VM substrate introduces two VM state transfer actions in the life-cycle of a VM which are docking and activating. A VM substrate is constructed by docking a running VM maintaining applications' running status. There are two ways of docking: intrusive converting of a running VM and live checkpointing of a VM. In contrast, VM substrate activating includes dispatching substrate, launching substrate and reconfiguring substrate's resources. A new VM is created after the activating process.

3.2 VM clone from substrate

We employ four steps to address the challenges in on-the-fly VM creation. First, VM miniaturization and generalization. Before generating new VM substrate, the parent VM is shrunk to a miniature state. A VM substrate has minimal memory footprint, single vCPU core, detached network interface and reference to virtual disk. Since the memory size is a major factor of the final size of a VM substrate, the memory size needs to be shrunk to the greatest degree through either intrusive shrinking or live checkpointing. In either case, the data in the system cache is synchronized to disk first. Through predictive calculation, we reconfigure VM's memory to a size that only contains data necessary for the restoration. VM configuration generalization assures the VM specific configuration of public or restricted VM. Configurations such as host name, networking parameters are reset to the default value. The resources of a private VM substrate is minimized while still maintaining its original configuration. Second, raw VM substrate is generated right after the VM's resource shrinking. A snapshot of the minimal running VM is created and stored in local memory. Third, raw substrates are compressed to be the final VM substrates before they are moved to a substrate pool. Compression reduces the substrates to a size as small as tens of megabytes which can be transfered over WAN. Fourth, the minimal VM substrate on local memory is transfered to a centralized pool. Figure 3 illustrates the steps of docking a running VM to a substrate.

When a substrate is selected to create a new VM, as shown in Figure 2, it is duplicated to other physical hosts simultaneously via multicast. Each physical host then decompresses the VM substrate and activates it from memory. Through reconfiguration, newly created VMs on each host will be allocated more memory and vCPU resources depending on application needs. New network interface with predefined parameters is attached to the VM and the configuration takes effect immediately. Depending on the type of a substrate, root disk is remapped and user's personal disk partitions can be attached to the VM.

3.3 VM substrate generation

Converting a VM to a substrate starts with reconfiguring a running VM's resource to minimal memory footprint and vCPU number, detaching the network card and saving the disk states. The initial VM from which a substrate is constructed can be a VM template or any VM with applications running. Intrusive conversion can be initiated in the application level by administrators whenever the VM has no scheduled work and is ready to be docked.

A VM substrate can also be created through live checkpointing in system level. VM checkpointing has been widely used for various purpose like high availability [5], VM migration [2, 4, 16, 28],fault-tolerant [15] or debugging [8]. We also leverage checkpointing to create VM substrates without interrupting the running services. Most of existing VM level checkpointing techniques tend to save the entire running states(*cpu,memory,disk*) in a core dump

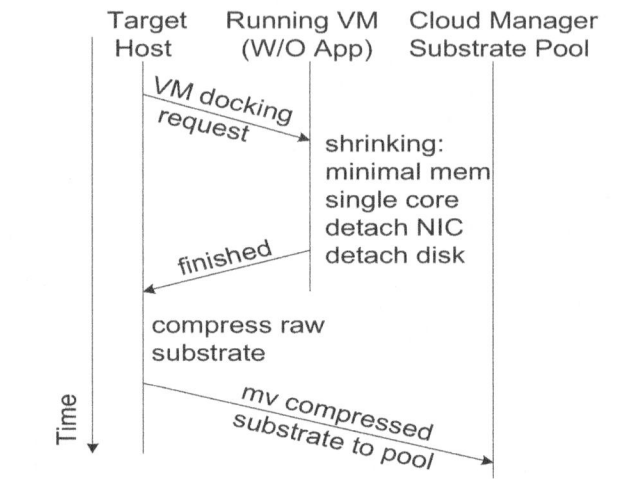

Figure 3. VM dock to substrate.

where the resulted checkpoint size is the VM's memory size, and the checkpointing time is closely related to memory page dirty rate. We employ two techniques to ensure that a VM can be correctly restored from a substrate and the size of the resulted substrate is minimized. First is selective memory checkpointing, through which only reusable memory pages are saved to substrates, discarding the reconstructable or zero pages. Selective checkpointing memory is able to reduce the size of raw substrates considerably. Second is the generalization of VM configuration, which set all VM specific resource identifiers like*vmid* or *uuid* to default values in a VM substrate. By using these two techniques, a checkpointing substrate of existing running VM instance can be created any time without conflicting with the original VM.

Compared with intrusive conversion, live checkpointing is able to create VM substrate without interrupting user applications, but it requires the modification of the VMM for selective memory dumping. In contrast, application level substrate conversion is independent on the underlying VMM. It only requires that virtual hardware resources of a guest VM can be configured dynamically without a restart.

3.4 VM fork

We note that VM fork has been recently proved to be an efficient way to clone a parent VM to multiple copies swiftly[11, 27]. Similar to process level fork, VM fork allows a child VM to inherit all the states originated from its parent VM prior to forking, enabling creating statefull computing instance rapidly. However, different from process fork, VM fork is capable of creating VM clones across a set of physical hosts. It can also work in a parallel manner where a single API call launches multiple VMs. Each child VM has its own independent copy of resources and runs independently from the parent VM. Once forked, and the changes made to each cloned VM are maintained separately. We analyze the advantages and the disadvantages of VM fork and compare it with VM dock and reactivate in the remaining of this section.

VM fork is capable of creating transient VMs whose virtual resources are discarded once they exit. The intermediate states or values generated by the applications in a child VM are lost unless being explicitly synchronized to the parent VM. Due to the characteristic of a fork operation, VM fork has a few limitations. First, VM fork is applicable to computation intensive applications with limited or disposable intermediate results. Existing VM fork leverages disk Copy-On-Write(COW) techniques to offer each child VM a COW slice of disk and all the disk updates or intermediate values are preserved on the COW disk. The child VMs share the running environment of the parent VM and the coordination between the parent and the children is mainly limited to computation. In the case of IO intensive applications, each child VM needs to make changes to their own disks which are actually COW slices. When the tasks in children VMs finish the updates on each child may need to be synchronized back to the parent. The integration of the updated data to the base disk incurs significant cost. It is challenging to achieve consistent synchronization once several VMs changed the same data. Second, sharing the same base disk partition between parent and children VMs limits the scalability of VM multiplexing. With IO intensive applications, the disk bandwidth of the base partition can easily become the performance bottleneck. Although *multicast* can be used to render memory pages concurrently to all the children VMs and memory page prefetching can possibly speed up on-demand paging, VMMs like Xen only grants the privileged domain direct access to the devices and does not allow the guest domains to access them directly [7, 19]. If the number of child VMs that request missing pages is large, the parent VM would receive a considerably amount of page requests from network interface. The parent VM can possibly become a hot-spot. Third, current VM fork implementation remains at application level focusing on parallel applications which need to re-spawn additional temporary workers. However, VM fork is not ideally suitable for deploying longstanding independent VMs at cloud administration level. Server applications such as web hosting and database warehousing usually run in loose coupled virtual clusters with minimal correlation. Such applications often require persistent data storage for each virtual node. Another drawback of the VM fork mechanism is its inability to create a heterogeneous VM cluster at a time. The VM substrate approach proposed here tries to create a cluster of heterogeneous VMs in a real time manner.

4. Implementation

We have implemented our VM substrate pool mechanism on the Xen platform. Xen is capable of running two leading approaches for virtualization: para-virtualization(PV) and full virtualization(FV). FV is designed to provide total abstraction of the underlying physical system, in which guest OS or applications are not aware of the virtualized environment. However, it incurs much performance overhead and can not be reconfigured on the fly without reboot of the VM. In contrast, PV presents each VM an abstraction of the hardware and requires modification of OS, allowing near-native performance. The memory size and the number of vCPUs of a PV guest VM can be reconfigured without restarting the VM. Thus, we select PV VMs in our prototype implementation. Our implementation includes modifications to the hypervisor, the `libxc` library, and the `xend` management daemon. In the remaining of this section, we elaborate the implementation details and compare them with alternative approaches. We also present microbenchmark results to show the feasibility and effectiveness of the VM substrate.

4.1 Resource shrinking and expanding

vCPU: vCPUs are what the guest sees as CPUs on which the guest OS schedules applications processes or thread. The final size of a VM substrate is not affected by the number of vCPU configured in a VM. In order to make each substrate be more generic and with minimal resources, each VM substrate has an default configuration of a single vCPU core. In practice, vCPUs are usually pined to specific physical CPUs for predictable performance. VM substrate is designed to be a generic mechanism that does not assume any physical host information. Thus, CPU affinity information is not maintained in the substrate. In a heterogeneous cluster, a VM substrate with a single vCPU is able to be deployed on any physical

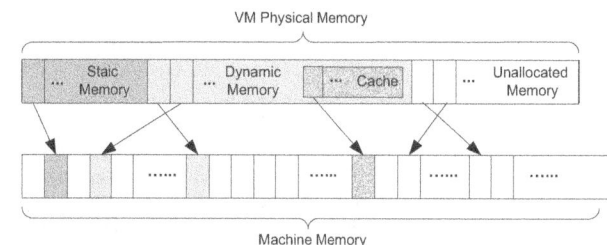

Figure 4. VM's memory footprint.

machine. Since Xen VMM does not allow the actual vCPU number to exceed the maximal number of vCPU specified in the guest's configuration file, we set the default maximal number of vCPU to be the total number of physical CPU cores for each substrate. Any newly created VM initially has single CPU core by default. More vCPUs can be allocated at a step of one vCPU.

Memory: Xen VMM is responsible for managing the allocation of physical memory to guest domains and maintaining a triple indirection model(*virtual memory, pseudo physical memory and machine memory*). Each VM runs in an illusory flat, continuous address space. Xen reserves the top 64M of the virtual address space for every domain. The remaining physical memory is available for allocation at a granularity of one physical page. Xen maintains a globally readable mapping table between PFN(Pseudo-physical Frame Number) and MFN(Machine Frame Number). The OS running in a VM maintains the mapping between virtual memory and pseudo physical memory. As shown in Figure 4, each VM's physical memory is part of the machine memory and can be divided to several parts including used pages and unallocated free memory. The used pages can be further divided into static memory pages and dynamic memory pages. The later one also includes disk cache. Note that although the used pages are not available for reallocation, it is still possible that some of those pages are zero pages either because they are set to zero by programs or they are used as heap initialized by compiler. Traditional VM save `xen save` writes the VM's entire memory including zero pages, cache pages and free pages to a checkpoint file. Including free and zero pages in the checkpoint file is likely to be a waste because those pages store no information of the checkpointed states. In order to minimize the size of a VM substrate, we only keep the reusable and minimal memory footprint while still maintaining the integrity of a VM's state.

A VM substrate which excludes free pages does not harm the correctness of VM when it is relaunched because those free pages can be easily reconstructed by manipulating the mapping table of MFN and PFN. Zero pages are still included in a VM substrate for the following reasons: First, there is no more efficient way to extract zero pages other than doing a bit by bit comparision. The cost rises as the size of VM memory increases. Second, each VM substrate is compressed before going to a substrate pool, the compression algorithm is capable of compressing the zero pages with a large compression ratio which reduces the size of the substrates considerably. Note that disk cache is used for performance optimization where recently accessed data can be retrieved from memory without incurring disk IO. Before creating a public or a restricted VM substrate, disk cached pages are synchronized to the disk which yeilds more free pages and the final substrate size can be further reduced.

Most of existing Linux distributions enable many optional services by default even for a base installation. Rightscale[22] uses bash scripts to disable those optional services before building a template. In addition to kicking off disk cache pages, we also release part of the memory occupied by killing user applications that are not relavent to the main purpose of the substrate. For example, in a substrate dedicated for web hosting applications, optional services like *sendmail, nfs* can be removed. We customize the application level services before docking a VM.

Memory ballooning is used by VMMs like Xen to achieve memory over-commitment. It provides the ability for the sum of the physical memory allocated to all active domains to exceed the total actually physically available memory on the system. Recent dynamic memory balancing work [29] proposed mathematical models to forecast memory needs and dynamically adjust the memory for VMs. The objective of these two memory adjustment approaches is to improve memory utilization. The later one also considers applications' throughput and performance. It is possible to instrument Xen to track memory accesses with each VM through the use of shadow page table. Shadow page tables are enabled during Xen's VM migration to determine which pages are dirtied during the migration. However, trapping each memory access results in a significant application slowdown and is only acceptable during migration [4, 23].

After a new VM is created from a VM substrate, it will start running at the initial state with minimal memory. It later expands to a larger size according to the setting in the configuration file. Each VM has a maximum and current memory size. Current memory size can be adjusted up to the maximum size. We configure the maximum memory of each substrate to be the physical memory size. The total memory size is extended dynamically. We implement an application level memory shrinking mechanism which is used to convert a VM to a substrate based on simple speculation in our prototype. We use the Linux /proc interface (in particular `/proc/meminfo`) to analyze the memory usage. Before docking a VM, we first kick all the cached data back to disk and consider the remaining memory size being actively used. Then we determine the minimal amount of memory the VM needs by adding a safe margin preventing Out-of-Memory crashes when the VM is restarted from substrate. The VM is set to the resulted memory size. The memory footprint of a guest VM will directly influence the final size of the VM substrate. The effect will be evaluated at the end of this subsection.

Network: The privileged domain in Xen VMM implements the network interface driver and all other guest domains access the driver via virtual device abstractions. Each domain is attached one or more virtual interfaces. Due to the fact that virtual interfaces are not necessary for booting a VM, their configurations can be postponed until rest of the guest OS ready to work. Conventional migration keeps network connection status by maintaining all protocol states and keeping IP addresses and MAC addresses in a record. Existing solutions used to manage network configuration during migration are to generate an unsolicited ARP reply form the migrated host, which lets the switch and other hosts know that the MAC is connected a new port [4]. However, even if the switch is configured not to block ARP broadcast, conflicts still exist if multiple VMs are created from the same substrate because all the network configurations of the new VMs are originated from the same substrate. In order to avoid the conflicts, We detached the network interface before docking a VM and VMs created from substrates do not have network interfaces initially.

The network parameters are configured when a new network interface is attached to a VM. In our prototype implementation, we also developed a mechanism to isolate the network in order to prevent interference between unrelated VMs. First, the networking mode (NAT,bridge or routing) can be dynamically configured with an interface in a physical host. Besides, the IP, MAC addresses and even the network mode can be determined within a physical host and transfered to guests as parameters. We implemented guest network configuration mechanism based on `Xenstore` to provide

agile and immediate configurations. Depending on the purpose of newly created VMs. Especially when a virtual cluster is created, they are deployed with private network addresses and only guests within the same subnet are visible to each other.

A VM substrate is the snapshot of an original VM, and the memory and process running status are preserved in the substrate. This may result in some conflicts if new VMs are created based on one VM substrate because they share the same running environment. It is possible that multiple processes in different VMs may need to connect to the same socket or open the same file. In our prototype implementation, docking VM can be done at administrative level when one phase of computation is finished or before the application starts to run. Another solution is to create a substrate directly from a running template.

Disk: Disk image files are commonly used as virtual disks by guest VMs. Because the disk image files, which are usually in a size of tens of Gigabytes, stores the application specific data, costly disk duplication is often unavoidable if new VMs are to be created. Existing template-based VM creation simply distributes the virtual disk image in a copy-and-paste manner to reconstruct the same VM without reinstalling OS or applications. Thus any two VMs from the same template are independent from each other, guaranteeing the isolation of VMs. However, the time spent on copying virtual disks is unacceptable provided that the disk size is usually large. Disk copy-on-write is often used to avoid unnecessary disk space waste. Multiple COW slices can share the same read-only base image file and all the updates are directed to those COW slices. Wide-area VM migration used disk COW to transfer VM disk state over low bandwidth and high-latency links [9, 23]. To reduce the startup latency of new VMs, disk COW is also used recently by Snowflock [11] and Potemkin [27] to generate temporary disk slices for newly created VMs.

There are two different types of disk COW. Frist, a *blocktap* driver combined with a *qcow* slice, which is supported by Xen VMM. Second, LVM supports creating writable snapshots of logical volumes quickly and each snapshot can be used as a COW disk slice by guest VMs. However, both of these two approaches have their limitations. Traditional *qcow* based COW has a limit on the total number of slices created and also has to make the tradeoff between the size of the COW disk and the depth of the COW disk hierarchy. Deeper hierarchy leads to bigger image files. Figure 5(a) and Figure 5(b) illustrate two typical ways to create a COW disk partition. The linear COW approach in Figure 5(b) applies incremental COW slices onto existing disk partitions. The existing disk partition can be an initial base partition or a partition already having COW slices on it. The vertical hierarchy as shown in Figure 5(a) dedicates a VM to a single purpose with fewer applications installed, thus it is able to limit the resulted partition size to a certain extent. In order to avoid the high The root COW disk is the initial image file and usually installed with the JeOS, then multiple child COW disks are created afterwards with each taking the previously created root COW as its parent and install with different kind of application. Due to the IO scheduling of virtualized disks, more COW slices result in higher dependency and the more degradation of the performance in either mode. Moreover, it is very challenging to merge multiple COW slices to the base image because the order of updating disk file is usually not preserved. On the other hand, LVM snapshots usually apprear as a physical partition and requires using tools like ATA over ethernet(AoE) or iSCSI[14] to export COW slices when VMs need to be deployed across multiple hosts. Each new slice requires an update to the running AoE or iSCSI service to export a new disk partition. In addition, only recent LVM version supports merging a COW back to the base and it also needs to use the latest Linux kernel. In conclusion, disk COW slice is only applicable to temporary VM creation.

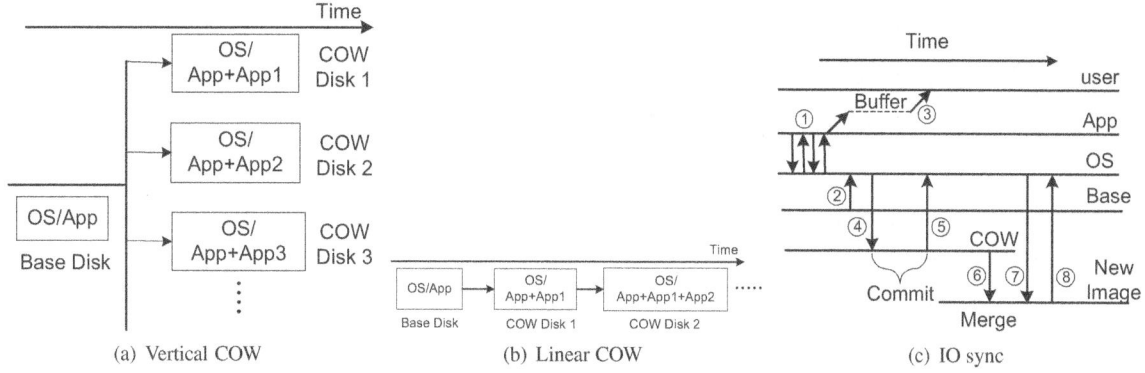

Figure 5. Cow disk hierarchy and IO flow.

Xen disk block device supports split driver model and the VMM provides a mechanism for device discovery and data movement between domains. The device drivers are split across Domain 0 and guest domains which are also called back-end and front-end respectively. Domain 0 is responsible for supporting hardware, running back-end devices drivers and providing the administrative interface to Xen. This VM disk model allows that a VM's disk can be reconfigured. We leverage COW techniques for substrate-based VM deployment with some modifications to the existing COW mechanism. The objective of real time VM creation are two folds. First, in the long run, VM substrate-based VM creation should guarantee the correctness and should generate consistent application result compared to the VMs created from templates. Second, from the users' perspective, a VM can be created on the fly in a real time manner with small latency. Inspired by [17], We create a temporary COW slices and remap it to a newly created VM from substrate, giving users near realtime responses to the VM creation requests. The temporary COW slices work as the root partitions in order to speed up the booting process. At the same time, we duplicate the base image in the background. Once duplication of the base image finishes, instead of merging COW slice back to the original base, we merge the COW slice to the duplication of the base, removing the dependencies between the parent's base image and children's COW slices. We changed existing *qcow* to work as a buffer of disk updates supporting dynamically merging to any duplicated copy of its original base. Thus, the time-consuming disk duplication can be hidden as a background job. An externally synchronous file system has been proposed by Edmund et al. [17] to amortize modifications across a single commit where only external output will trigger file modifications to be committed. Similarly, our COW slice can be regarded as the buffer of modifications, the commit will be triggered when the duplication of base image is done. Figure 5(c) shows the synchronization of disk IOs when a new VM is created from a substrate. Each VM is assigned a COW slice initially, but will have its own independent disk partition in the long run. Step 1 groups multiple modifications before committing the changes to the disk. Step 2 and step 4 represent retrieving data from the base image and the COW slice respectively. Step 3 and Step 5 show that disk changes are synchronized to the COW slice. When a request of creating a new VM is received by a cloud manager, the duplication of the base image file is started as a background job. Other than synchronizing the COW slice to original base image, we synchronize the changes to new base image which is shown in step 6. After merging COW slices to the new base image. VM starts to read and write data directly from and to the new image as shown in step 7 and step 8. After step 8, the VM creation process finishes and the VM works just as the VMs created from a static templates. Note that the

VMs created from substrates are online whenever the COW slices are ready (step 1), which gives almost real time responses to users' requests. In practice, the intermediate COW slices turn to be very small after merging, thus can be discarded with minimal cost. The original base image still remains reusable.

Evaluation. To understand the impact of shrinking degree on generating VM substrates and reactivating substrates, we shrunk a VM's memory from different sizes. We experimented with various memory sizes from 128M to 2GB and verified the time spent on preparing raw VM substrates and the time reactivating them. All the cached data was synchronized back to disk before docking. As shown in Figure 6, the sizes of a raw substrate are slightly larger than the memory footprint. If VM's memory can be shrunk to around 128M, the docking or reactivating can be done within 0.875 seconds. In our test, a VM with some applications like Webserver, MySQL database or program development environment installed could further be compressed, leading to a final VM substrate as small as 16MB.

4.2 Substrate multicast and compression

In our prototype implementation, we use multicast to dispatch VM substrates in parallel to other physical hosts. Traditional point-to-point communication has the drawback of inefficiency if a substrate needs to be sent to multiple hosts simultaneously. The transferring of VM substrates consumes considerable network bandwidth. In order to make sure that all the VM substrates are only transfered within the data center, we set the time-to-live (TTL) value of all multicast packets to be 1. Since the size of VM substrates can be as small as 16MB, the multicast packets can be encapsulated into the payload of TCP packets and can be sent quickly to another node in a LAN environment. Due to the small footprint of the substrates, our current implementation can alse be extended to a WAN environment connecting different data centers.

The raw VM substrates are compressed before moved to a pool. The objective of the compression is to make each VM substrate as small as possible. In our prototype implementation, we used the gzip algorithm to compress raw VM substrates. In order to reduce the cost of compression, the compression is done in memory and the resulted compressed substrates are also stored in memory temporarily before they are moved to the substrate pool. In our experiment, a VM with a development environment installed leads to a size of 16MB after compression. Compression of a substrate is more costly than decompression. Decompression usually takes less than half of the time than compression. The small cost incurred by decompression further speed up the launching process of a VM from the substrate pool.

45

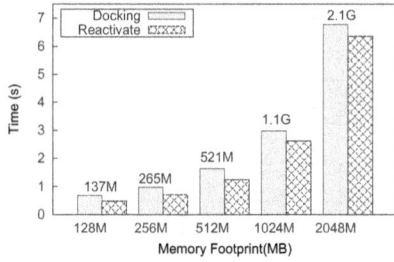

Figure 6. Impact of shrinking degree.

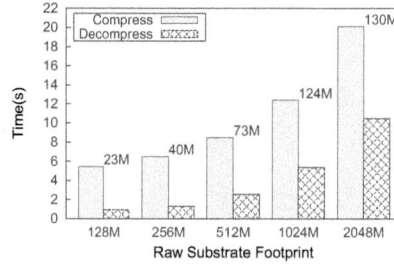

Figure 7. Compression cost.

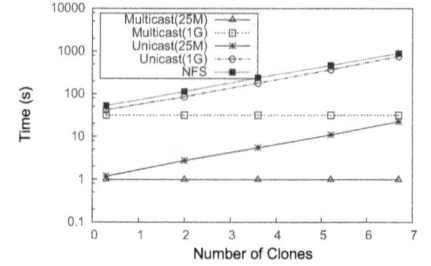

Figure 8. Effectiveness of multicast.

Evaluation. To evaluate the effectiveness of multicast, we compared the time spent on deploying multiple VMs from the same VM substrate. Figure 8 shows the strength of multicast, especially when the number of clones increases. In this experiment, we sent two different substrates with sizes of 25MB and 1GB to different physical hosts in order to create a group of new VMs. As shown in Figure 8, multicasting a 25MB substrate to different hosts took less than 1 second while sending the 1GB substrate took around 30 seconds. These are two extreme cases. In the more general case, VM's memory should be able to be shrunk to between 128MB and 1GB, most VMs with barely application environment installed could be shrunk to less than 200MB memory. Thus, the total time on multicast is in the magnitude of several seconds. On the other hand, in the case of unicast without using multicast, the total time of sending the substrates to the others would increase with the number of required clones. Figure 8 also plots the time of propagating the VM substrate by duplicating the saved state in a networked file system (NFS).

We also evaluated the cost of compression and decompression on the VM startup latency. We compared the time spent on conversion between raw substrate and final substrate when the size of raw substrate varied from 128MB to 2048MB. As shown in Figure 7, compression is more costly than decompression. The final size of each raw substrate is shown in the figure. For a raw substrate of 256M, which is the size for a typical VM after selective memory dumping, the decompression only took about one second. The startup latency incurred by the decompression algorithm does not significantly affect the users' experiences. Although compression is time consuming especially for large size of raw substrates, the compression is usually done before docking to prepare new VM substrate for future use which does not affect VMs' startup.

5. Evaluation

In this section, we examine the overhead and design a set of experiments to verify the effectiveness of VM substrate. We begin by examining the overhead of using a substrate to create new VMs, and then go on to explore one typical usage case of offloading mobile computation to a cloud environment. At the end of this section, we compare the cost of launching a VM with different methods.

The machines used in the experiments consist of a server dedicated to the VM pool and a client machine. All the experiments were conducted in a LAN environment connected by a Gigabit Ethernet switch. The physical hosts for the VM pool is a Dell PowerEdge 1950 server with two quad-core Intel Xeon CPU and 8GB memory. The client machine is a PC with dual CPU cores. We used Xen version 3.4.1 as our virtualization platform. Both dom0 and the guest VMs were running CentOS Linux 5.3 with kernel 2.6.18.

5.1 Overhead

We began our evaluation by examining the overhead of VM substrate. We study the latency of preparing a VM or VM cluster on demand. Figure 9 draws the time needed to create different number of VMs through VM substrate pool. In this experiment, we prepared several different VM substrates for each type of applications. Whenever a new VM is needed, in order to minimize the time spent on preparing virtual disks, we created a new VM using a temporary COW slice. The root partition of each VM is 4GB and the partition which is used to store the modification is set to 1GB.

In this experiment, we created different numbers of VMs from the same VM substrate and evaluated the absolute cost. The memory size of a raw substrate in this experiment was shrunk to 118MB, leading to the final compressed substrate of 16MB. This is the smallest size we can achieve with minimal installation of the guest OS and necessary running environment. We intend to answer the following questions in this experiment: (a) What is the optimal speedup VM substrate can achieve? (b) Where is the time spent on VM creation? (c) What is the scalability of the VM substrate approach?

Figure 9 shows the time for creating new VMs on demand from the VM substrate pool. The time is broken down into four parts: preparing the disk, multicasting substrate over local network, decompressing VM substrate, and activating VM. From this figure, we can see that the total time of creating a single VM from substrate is as small as 2.5 seconds. This time does not contain the time to generate VM substrates. It assumes that the substrate is always available in the pool. This figure shows VM substrate pool is capable of providing prompt response to laterncy sensitive VM creation requests. When the number of VMs to be created increases, the total latency of the VM creation does not increases significantly. This is due to the use of multicast, which does not incur proportional overhead when the scale increases. Similarly, the cost of transferring substrates to more than one physical host is almost the same as transferring to a single host. However, the cost of disk creation increases with the number of VMs. Note that the absolute creation time for a single disk is less than a second, given enough storage bandwidth, the disk creation part is not the limiting factor of the scalability of our VM substrate approach.

5.2 Case Study: Mobile Application Offloading

In this experiment, we analyze the effectiveness of VM substrate from the standpoint of cloud users. We implemented a usage case to create new VM on demand to offload the computation from mobile devices. We selected a mobile version of the chess game as the source of computation to be offloaded. It is representative because the user interface is simple and lightweight but the backend computation of the piece movement is computation intensive for mobile devices like smart phones. The chess game allows human players to play with a computer. We implemented an AI component on the server side to calculate each move for the computer side. This AI component is not only CPU intensive, but also consumes considerable amount of memory to record the game status of both players. For the computer side, It can make decisions for current

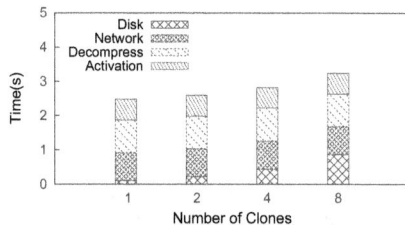

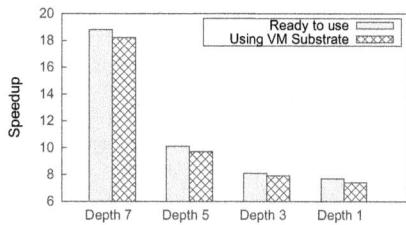

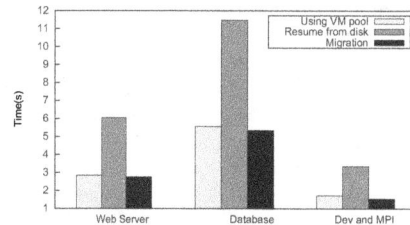

Figure 9. Time breakdown of VM creation.　**Figure 10.** Delay time of offloading checker.　**Figure 11.** Startup time comparison.

move based on different number of steps looking into the future. More computation and resources are required if the computer side looks into the future with a large number of steps. Mobile devices are limited in terms of memory, computation power and energy reserves. If the mobile device is running an AI opponent which is configured with large resource requirement, the user would have to wait noticeable amounts of time for the opponent to make its move. The battery of the mobile device can also burn out quickly. In fact, if the computer side is configured to be intelligent enough, some early mobile phones may not even be able to run the chess game successfully. One solution is to offload the computation to a VM in cloud. Although offloading itself has some limitations because it requires computation of an application can be separated from the ches game itself and be executed on a remote VM server, it is still a viable workaround for many applications with simple frontend graphics interface and relatively loosely coupled backend. All the local mobile device needs to do is to collect and display the results. In our experiment, the chess game is one of the applications that can take advantage of on-demand prompt VM creation. Because the human player may have non-deterministic think time between two moves, we choose to dock the offloading VM after it finishes the computation for one move. When the human player initiate another move, the docked VM is restarted upon the human's move. In this setting, the latency incurred by VM startup from substrate directly affect human players' experience.

We compare the performance speedup of the chess game when the computation is offloaded to a VM with full capacity (i.e. "ready to use") with the performance when the computation is offloaded to a newly created VM from substrates (i.e. "using VM substrate"). The baseline performance was obtained from a cell phone running the android OS which has a 1Ghz CPU and 512MB memory. The speedup was calculated as the ratio of the processing time on the VM server over the time on the phone. Figure 10 shows very similar speedup between offloading to on-demand VMs from substrates and offloading to static VMs. It suggests that on-demand creation of VMs from substrate incurs minimal latency and thus can provide instant responses to users' request.

5.3 Performance Comparison

In practice, there are a few different options to start a new VM. These options includes suspend and resume [24], migrating VM from other hosts [4], creating VM from scratch and our VM creation from VM substrate Among these options, creating VM from scratch involves the whole OS installation process and takes a significant amount of time, which is not considered for comparison.

In this experiment, we created three new VMs containing a web server, a database server and a VM with development environment respectively in the above three different ways. Figure 11 draws the the startup time of these methods. The startup time is the time between the creation , migration or resume request is received and the time the VM is ready. A VM is considered ready when it is responsive to user's other request like launching a program. Technically, it is when all the virtual CPUs are back online, memory

is ballooned back and network interfaces are attached. As shown in Figure 11, VM creation from substrate is almost as fast as VM migration. Note that VM migration need to maintain the VM running in its full capacity, which consumes a significant amount of resources limiting the scalability. In contrast, VM substrate maintains a large pool of substrates with minimal footprints. In our testbed with 8GB memory, we were able to host as many as 230 substrates. As expected, the suspend and resume approach incurred considerable startup time because the resume process needs to load a large state file from hard disk.

6. Related work

VM templates are widely used to create new VMs in the majority of system virtualization platforms. Through preparing reusable templates, which are usually configured to include a standardized set of hardware and software configuration settings, the efficiency of deploying VM infrastructure could be significantly increased due to the fact that many repetitive installation and configuration tasks are avoided. A base VM template contains the essentials of server image so called Just-Enough-OS(JeOS) and the base template can be extended by installing software application(s) in order to generate new template. VM templates[20] can be either converted to virtual machines and powered on without deploying them. The conversion will either turn the original template into VMs which means the template doesn't exist anymore or clone the templates to VMs through replication which involves time consuming disk copy. Moreover, starting a new VM created from a VM template needs error prone booting process.

The Amazon Elastic Compute Cloud (EC2) [6] is a widely used cloud computing platform. EC2 allows users to create an Amazon Machine Image (AMI) containing their applications, libraries, data and associated configuration settings or use pre-configured, template images to get up and running immediately. Amazon's EC2 claims to instantiate multiple VMs in "minutes" is still not enough to meet requirement of some real time VM creation requests. RightScale [22] also provides scripts to create and configure a basic VM from scratch. Although the installation and configuration are done automatically, it is often not applicable to on-demand VM creation due to the time consuming installation.

Some recent research work explores the idea of process fork to VM level where a running VM spawns child VMs that are clones of itself. The Potemkin project [27] realized a VM fork scheme that creates lightweight VMs from a static template locally within a single machine. Through aggressive memory sharing and COW techniques, Potemkin allows quick VM forking by deferring the duplication of memory pages until the contents of pages actually differ between VMs. It can support potentially hundreds of short-lived VMs on physical honeyfarm servers. However, Potemkin does not have the flexibility to create multiple VMs onto different hosts and does not offer runtime statefull cloning. Snowflock [11] extends the concept of VM fork in a distributed manner, enabling cloning a VM into multiple statefull replicas running in a cluster of machines. Snowflock leverages the same COW technique used by Potemkin and takes advantage of the high correlation of the children VM, providing a immutable image of the parent VM and a demand-paging mechanism to let children retrieve missing pages. Similar to process fork, VM fork is able to efficiently share parent's resources and swiftly create interim VM clones that run simultaneously in a real time manner. However, current VM fork implementations do not aim to deploy longstanding independent VMs. VM substrate is different from Potemkin or Snowflock in their purposes. Potemkin and Snowflock aim to provide on-demand virtual clusters with "identical" and "temporary" VM children forked from a single parent. VM substrate's objective is to preserve and restore customized user working space (VM's with different running states) with minimal cost. The VMs in question are heterogeneous and not necessarily belong to the same user.

The idea of a pool structure is widely used in the design of computer systems. Most of early works focused on thread and process level pools [1, 13, 18, 21], or processor level pool [30]. The popular Apache web server [1] uses a thread pool to handle incoming request, but there is no resource reconfiguration for each thread. Iran Pyarali et al. [21] proposed an optimization to improve the quality of thread pools in real-time systems. They described the key patterns underlying common strategies for implementing RT-CORBA thread pools and evaluated each thread pool strategy from various aspects. In [13], Ling et al. characterized several system resource costs associated with thread pool size and analytically determined the optimal thread pool size to maximize the expected gain of using a thread and minimize the overhead of run-time memory allocation and deallocation while creating and destroying a thread. In [30], the authors proposed a class of scheduling algorithms based on a processor level pool which is used to organize and manage a large number of processors to improve performance.

7. Future Work and Conclusions

In this section, we briefly discuss a number of directions that we intend to explore in the future to improve and extend our VM substrate framework. As we have discussed in the previous sections, VM substrate based VM deployment is able to deploy diverse VM within seconds. The idea is preliminary and we plan to further investigate the following areas.

VM streaming. Our current implementation decompress the VM substrate to get the raw substrate and then start new VMs from the raw substrate. Although from Figure 7, we can see that decompression takes less time than compression, it is still costly to decompress the substrate when the memory footprint is large. Thus, a mechanism that allows a VM to boot while the decompression is in process will further reduce the startup latency.

Dynamically linked storage. Because VMs' resources such as vCPU number, memory size and network bandwidth are configurable, it makes the charge of VM resources in pay-as-you-go manner possible. However, storage is not so easily reconfigured as other resources. First, the change of disk size can not take effect without reboot even when LVM is used. Second, running VM's root disk is unable to be altered. Both of these two factors affect the agility of deploying VMs. On the other hand, if each VM can use dynamically linked storage, the actual physical disk partition can be dynamically changed.

Improved memory metering. As discussed in the previous sections, memory footprint is closely related to the final size of VM substrate. The smaller the memory footprint, the smaller the substrate. Our current implementation leverages the `proc` interface under Linux to get the memory utilization. Only the used memory pages need to be dumped in the VM substrate. Identification of unused memory pages or calculation of the memory utilization of a running VM is not trivial. Different from free pages, unused pages refer to those that once touched but not actively being accessed by the system. It can be calculated as the total memory minus the system working set. One possible direction is to integrate more accurate memory metering in VMM level.

In closing, we introduce the primitive of retrofitting VM deployment by using VM substrate and present the design, implementation, and evaluation of a novel approach to manage VMs in agile virtualized environment. Our VM substrate-based VM shrinking and expansion management allows VM creating, reconfiguration in a way that is transparent to users and enables the instantiation of statefull VMs or VM clusters with sub-seconds latency. Our VM pool architecture is effective in reducing the latency of preparing new VMs and increasing the reusability of VM substrates. It incurs small overhead on the creation of a single or a cluster of VMs. Experiment results on the computation offloading from mobile devices show that the pool of VM substrates is able to provide instantaneous response to user request in an interactive job.

Acknowledgments

We would like to thank the anonymous reviewers for their constructive comments. This work was supported in part by U.S. NSF grants CNS-0702488, CRI-0708232, CNS-0914330, and CCF-1016966.

References

[1] Apache thread pool. http://commons.apache.org/sandbox/threadpool.

[2] R. Bradford, E. Kotsovinos, A. Feldmann, and H. Schiöberg. Live wide-area migration of virtual machines including local persistent state. In *VEE*, 2007.

[3] B.-G. Chun and P. Maniatis. Augmented smartphone applications through clone cloud execution. In *HotOS*, 2009.

[4] C. Clark, K. Fraser, S. Hand, J. G. Hansen, E. Jul, C. Limpach, I. Pratt, and A. Warfield. Live migration of virtual machines. In *NSDI*, 2005.

[5] B. Cully, G. Lefebvre, D. Meyer, M. Feeley, N. Hutchinson, and A. Warfield. Remus: high availability via asynchronous virtual machine replication. In *NSDI*, 2008.

[6] EC2. http://aws.amazon.com/ec2.

[7] S. Govindan, J. Choi, A. R. Nath, A. Das, B. Urgaonkar, and A. Sivasubramaniam. Xen and co.: Communication-aware cpu management in consolidated xen-based hosting platforms. Jan 2009.

[8] S. T. King, G. W. Dunlap, and P. M. Chen. Debugging operating systems with time-traveling virtual machines. pages 1–15, 2005.

[9] H. A. Lagar-Cavilla, N. Tolia, E. de Lara, M. Satyanarayanan, and D. O'Hallaron. Interactive resource-intensive applications made easy. In *Middleware '07: Proceedings of the ACM/IFIP/USENIX 2007 International Conference on Middleware*, pages 143–163, New York, NY, USA, 2007. Springer-Verlag New York, Inc.

[10] H. A. Lagar-Cavilla, J. Whitney, A. Scannell, S. M. Rumble, E. de Lara, M. Brudno, and M. Satyanarayanan. Impromptu clusters for near-interactive cloud-based services. Technical Report CSRG-TR578, Department of Computer Science, University of Toronto, 2008.

[11] H. A. Lagar-Cavilla, J. Whitney, A. Scannell, P. Patchin, S. M. Rumble, E. de Lara, M. Brudno, and M. Satyanarayanan. Snowflock: Rapid virtual machine cloning for cloud computing. In *Eurosys*, 2009.

[12] F. Li and J. Nieh. Optimal linear interpolation coding for server-based computing. In *ICC*, 2002.

[13] Y. Ling, T. Mullen, and X. Lin. Analysis of optimal thread pool size. *SIGOPS Operating System Review*, 2000.

[14] K. Z. Meth and J. Satran. Design of the iscsi protocol. In *MSS*, 2003.

[15] A. B. Nagarajan and F. Mueller. Proactive fault tolerance for hpc with xen virtualization. In *In Proceedings of the 21st Annual International Conference on Supercomputing (ICS'07*, pages 23–32. ACM Press, 2007.

[16] M. Nelson, B.-H. Lim, and G. Hutchins. Fast transparent migration for virtual machines. In *USENIX Annual Technical Conference*, 2005.

[17] E. B. Nightingale, K. Veeraraghavan, P. M. Chen, and J. Flinn. Rethink the sync. In *In Proc. OSDI*, pages 1–14, 2006.

[18] S. Oaks and H. Wong. *Java Threads*. O'Reilly Media, Inc., 2004.

[19] D. Ongaro, A. L. Cox, and S. Rixner. Scheduling i/o in virtual machine monitors. In *VEE '08: Proceedings of the fourth ACM SIGPLAN/SIGOPS international conference on Virtual execution environments*, pages 1–10, New York, NY, USA, 2008. ACM. ISBN 978-1-59593-796-4. doi: http://doi.acm.org/10.1145/1346256.1346258.

[20] Oracle VM Templates. http://www.oracle.com/technology/products/vm/templates/index.html.

[21] I. Pyarali, M. Spivak, R. Cytron, and D. C. Schmidt. Evaluating and optimizing thread pool strategies for real-time corba. In *LCTES*, 2001.

[22] RightScale VM Templates. http://blog.rightscale.com/2010/03/22/rightscale-servertemplates-explained.

[23] C. P. Sapuntzakis, R. Chandra, B. Pfaff, J. Chow, M. S. Lam, and M. Rosenblum. Optimizing the migration of virtual computers. *SIGOPS Operating System Review*, 2002.

[24] M. Satyanarayanan, B. Gilbert, M. Toups, N. Tolia, A. Surie, D. R. O'Hallaron, A. Wolbach, J. Harkes, A. Perrig, D. J. Farber, M. A. Kozuch, C. J. Helfrich, P. Nath, and H. A. Lagar-Cavilla. Pervasive personal computing in an internet suspend/resume system. In *IEEE Internet Computing*, 2007.

[25] Virtual desktop infrastructure. http://www.vmware.com/pdf/virtual-desktop-infrastructure-wp.pdf.

[26] VMware. http://www.vmware.com/pdf/vc_2_templates_usage_best_practices_wp.pdf.

[27] M. Vrable, J. Ma, J. Chen, D. Moore, E. Vandekieft, A. C. Snoeren, G. M. Voelker, and S. Savage. Scalability, fidelity, and containment in the potemkin virtual honeyfarm. In *SOSP*, 2005.

[28] C. Wang, F. Mueller, C. Engelmann, and S. L. Scott. Proactive process-level live migration in hpc environments. In *SC*, 2008.

[29] W. Zhao and Z. Wang. Dynamic memory balancing for virtual machines. In *VEE*, 2009.

[30] S. Zhou and T. Brecht. Processor-pool-based scheduling for large-scale numa multiprocessors. In *SIGMETRICS*, 1991.

Dolly: Virtualization-driven
Database Provisioning for the Cloud

Emmanuel Cecchet, Rahul Singh, Upendra Sharma, Prashant Shenoy

University of Massachusetts, Amherst, USA
{cecchet,rahul,upendra,shenoy}@cs.umass.edu

Abstract

Cloud computing platforms are becoming increasingly popular for e-commerce applications that can be scaled on-demand in a very cost effective way. Dynamic provisioning is used to autonomously add capacity in multi-tier cloud-based applications that see workload increases. While many solutions exist to provision tiers with little or no state in applications, the database tier remains problematic for dynamic provisioning due to the need to replicate its large disk state.

In this paper, we explore virtual machine (VM) cloning techniques to spawn database replicas and address the challenges of provisioning shared-nothing replicated databases in the cloud. We argue that being able to determine state replication time is crucial for provisioning databases and show that VM cloning provides this property. We propose Dolly, a database provisioning system based on VM cloning and cost models to adapt the provisioning policy to the cloud infrastructure specifics and application requirements. We present an implementation of Dolly in a commercial-grade replication middleware and evaluate database provisioning strategies for a TPC-W workload on a private cloud and on Amazon EC2. By being aware of VM-based state replication cost, Dolly can solve the challenge of automated provisioning for replicated databases on cloud platforms.

Categories and Subject Descriptors D.2.9 [**Software Engineering**]: Management.

General Terms Algorithms, Management, Measurement, Performance, Design, Experimentation.

Keywords Database, Autonomic Provisioning, Virtualization.

1. Introduction

Online applications have become popular in a variety of domains such as e-retail, banking, finance, news, and social networking. Typically such web-based applications are hosted in data-centers or on cloud computing platforms, which provide storage and computing resources to these applications. Numerous studies have shown that the workloads seen by these web-based cloud applications are highly dynamic and exhibit variations at different time-scales [21], [22]. For instance, an application may see a rapid increase in its popularity, causing its workload to grow sharply over a period of days or weeks. At shorter time-scales, a flash crowd can cause the application workload to surge within minutes. Applications can also see seasonal trends such as higher workloads during particular periods, e.g., during Black Friday, marketing campaigns, or a new product launch.

One possible approach for handling workload fluctuations is to employ dynamic provisioning of server capacity. Dynamic provisioning involves increasing or decreasing the number of servers (and server capacity) allocated to an application in response to workload changes. Dynamic provisioning is especially well-suited to web-based cloud applications for two reasons. First, it is often difficult to estimate the peak workload of an Internet application, making it challenging to a priori provision for the peak demand. Second, today's cloud platforms support on-demand allocation of servers and employ a pay-as-you-go service model. These features are attractive from an application provider's perspective, since servers can be requested only when a workload spike arrives or is anticipated, and charging is based only on the duration of the workload surge. Cloud platforms employ virtualization to support these features—upon a customer request for a new (virtual) server, a new virtual machine (VM) is created on a physical server with idle capacity, and the specified virtual disk image is copied to the server, upon which the server is ready for use. In fact, cloud platforms such as Amazon's EC2 platform already support dynamic provisioning (aka "auto scaling") where such VMs are automatically started when a threshold on a user-specified metric such as CPU utilization is exceeded in the current application [1].

Much of the prior work on dynamic provisioning [20], [21], [22], [4] has assumed that web applications have a multi-tier architecture and focus on dynamic provisioning of the front web tier or the middle application tier. Provisioning of these front and middle tiers is simple since these tiers have little or no application state and provisioning merely involves dynamic startup (or shutdown) of VMs in response to workload fluctuations. This prior work assumes that the backend database tier, where much of the application state is stored, is over-provisioned and thus does not require dynamic provisioning. However, in scenarios where the database tier is the bottleneck (e.g., due to compute-intensive query workloads), this simplifying assumption has meant that our inability to a priori estimate the peak workload for Internet applications will cause the database tier to become overloaded and drop user requests. Further it prevents the web application from fully exploiting the benefits of the pay-as-you-go and on-demand server allocation in the cloud for the backend tier. Dynamic provisioning of the back-end database tier has not been considered in the prior literature since it is harder to implement—replication and synchronization of the associated disk state of the database needs to be handled, in addition to the 'simpler' problem of starting up new database VM replicas.

In this paper, we consider the problem of dynamic provisioning of the database tier of online web applications. We use virtualization as a key building block of our dynamic provisioning system, in particular by leveraging VM snapshots and cloning as the basis for replicating database state in a platform-independent manner. In addition, we devise intelligent state replication strategies to reduce the latency of starting up new database replicas in virtualized public and private clouds.

1.1 Why is database provisioning hard?

Dynamic provisioning of server capacity typically involves two problems: *when* to trigger a capacity increase (or decrease), and *how* to achieve the desired capacity addition or reduction. Both the "when" and the "how" questions are simpler in case of the web and application tiers than the database tier.

Typically the decision of *when* to trigger provisioning is made in a *lazy* fashion for the web and the application tiers—upon an actual significant workload change, or an anticipation of one in the near future. Such lazy triggers are appropriate for these tiers since front-end provisioning schemes assume that new capacity can be added immediately whenever needed and that the only latency is that incurred for VM startup. In contrast, provisioning of a new database replica involves (i) extracting database content from an existing replica, if not already available, and (ii) copying and restoring that content on a new replica. These operations can take minutes or hours depending on the database size.

In fact, traditional "just-in-time" cloud provisioning techniques, including Amazon Auto Scaling [1], are similarly based on lazy triggers and/or thresholds and do not take into account the time to replicate the database state. If this state replication and synchronization overhead is ignored, the newly provisioned capacity comes online far too late to handle the workload increase and the capacity requirements will not be met in a timely fashion.

Similarly the "how" to achieve the desired capacity increase must be handled differently in case of dynamic database provisioning. Typically this part involves (i) a capacity determination model to estimate how many replicas to provision for a given workload, and (ii) the actual system steps necessary in starting up and configuring those replicas for use. Capacity determination models predict the future workload using historical data or dynamic predictors [11] and then use queuing techniques to estimate the number of replicas needed to service the predicted workload [9]. This aspect of provisioning is similar for both the front-end web and the back-end database tier. In fact, one of the few papers to address dynamic provisioning of the database tier [8] proposed an analytical model for databases to determine capacity needed to service a given workload. However, this work did not address the important systems issues of "when" to trigger provisioning based on state replication overheads, nor did it address the many system challenges involved in dynamically starting up database replicas. Specifically, in database provisioning, even after a VM replica starts up, there is an additional overhead of synchronizing the state of the new replica with the current state of all other replicas to preserve data integrity. No such overheads are incurred when provisioning "stateless" web and application tier replicas.

Thus, database provisioning differs significantly from traditional web server provisioning because databases are stateful and their state can be very large (and this state must be replicated before a new database replica can be spawned). To provision database replicas in a timely fashion, it is necessary to know how much time will be required to replicate/synchronize this disk state and bring the replicas online. These times vary greatly with the database size, schema complexity, backup/restore tool options, database artifacts (e.g., storage engine configuration). Moreover, there are many tradeoffs on how and when to snapshot the database state to minimize replica resynchronization time. It is therefore non-trivial to estimate the exact time needed to spawn a new replica.

1.2 Research Contributions

In this paper, we present Dolly[1], a system for dynamically provisioning database replicas in cloud platforms. Dolly is database platform-agnostic and uses virtualization-based replication mechanisms for efficiently spawning database replicas.

The key insight in Dolly is to intelligently use VM snapshots and cloning as the basis for dynamic database provisioning. In Dolly, each database replica runs in a separate virtual machine. Instead of relying on the traditional database mechanisms to create a new replica, Dolly clones the entire virtual machine (VM) of an existing replica, including the operating environment, the database engine with all its configuration, settings and the database itself. The cloned VM is started on a new physical server, resulting in a new replica, which then synchronizes state with other replicas prior to processing user requests.

Our work on Dolly has led to the following contributions:

- *When to provision:* Dolly takes the long latency of spawning database replicas into account when triggering "eager" provisioning decisions. To do so, Dolly incorporates a model to estimate the latency to spawn a replica, based on the VM snapshot size and the database resynchronization latency, and uses this model to trigger the replica spawning process well in advance of the anticipated workload increase.

- *How to provision:* Dolly incorporates an intelligent scheduling technique that can determine whether it is cheaper to take a new VM snapshot or use an older snapshot when spawning a new replica. In addition, the technique can proactively trigger VM snapshots to reduce the future latency of spawning database replicas. These mechanisms are implemented in a new provisioning algorithm, with user-defined cost functions to characterize database provisioning policies on cloud platforms. This allows the system administrator to tune the provisioning decisions to optimize resource usage of her cloud infrastructure.

- *Prototype implementation:* We have developed a prototype of Dolly using Sequoia [16], a commercial-grade open-

---

[1] Inspired by the sheep Dolly, the first mammal to be cloned successfully.

source database clustering middleware, and have combined it with the OpenNebula [14] cloud manager to address provisioning in both private and public clouds. We demonstrate the efficacy of Dolly in provisioning *Mysql*-based database tiers.

- *Evaluation on public and private clouds:* We conduct an experimental evaluation of Dolly on Amazon's EC2 public cloud and on a laboratory-based Xen private cloud. Our experiments with a TPC-W [19] e-commerce workload show the ability of Dolly to properly schedule provisioning decisions to meet capacity requirements in a timely fashion while optimizing resource usage in private clouds and minimizing cost in public clouds.

The remainder of this paper is organized as follows. Section 2 introduces the necessary background on database replication and replica spawning. Section 3 discusses the core techniques for database provisioning in the cloud and *when* to provision, while section 4 addresses *how* to provision. Section 5 presents Dolly's implementation. We perform an experimental evaluation on private and public clouds in Section 6. Finally, Section 7 discusses related work before concluding in Section 8.

2. Background

In this section, we present background on virtualized cloud platforms and database replication and also formulate the problem of dynamic database provisioning.

2.1 Virtualized Cloud Platforms

Our work assumes a virtualized cloud platform that runs distributed web-based applications. The cloud platform is essentially a data center that provides compute and storage resource to its applications. Each physical server in the data center is assumed to run a virtual machine monitor (aka hypervisor) and one or more virtual machines that encapsulate application components. The cloud platform, whether public or private, is assumed to support on-demand allocation of virtual machines—applications can request one or more virtual machines at any time, upon which the requested VMs are created, placed on to physical servers with idle capacity and started up. We assume that application components are preconfigured as virtual disk images that are available to the cloud platform, enabling automated VM allocation and startup. Such on-demand VM allocation is a prerequisite for our dynamic provisioning techniques. Our work targets both public cloud platforms such as Amazon EC2 as well as private Linux-based clouds constructed using Xen/KVM virtualization platforms. In case of public clouds, where servers and storage is charged based on a pay-as-you-use model, we assume that the pricing model is known a priori and can be taken into account when making provisioning decisions.

2.2 Problem Formulation

We assume that cloud platforms run distributed web applications. Each application is assumed to employ a multi-tier architecture consisting of a front-end web tier, a middle application (e.g., J2EE) tier, and a backend database tier. Each tier is assumed to be dynamically replicable. That is, each tier is assumed to comprise one or more VM replicas, and it is assumed that the number of replicas at each tier can be varied based on changing workload demands at that tier. We assume that each tier also assumes a

dispatcher/load-balancer that is responsible for distributing requests to various replicas.

Our work focuses on the database tier. In contrast to prior work that has typically assumed a static number of (over-provisioned) replicas at the database tier, we assume that this tier can also be dynamically provisioned like the other tiers. The dynamic provisioning problem for the database tier can then be stated as two sub-tasks: (i) *when* to trigger a capacity change based on current and future workload trends, and (ii) *how* to startup or shutdown the desired number of VM replicas. As discussed above, both tasks raise new challenges when dynamically provisioning databases. Our goal is to design a database provisioning platform that (i) given future workload forecasts, will estimate the time to start up a new database replica and will use this latency to trigger a provisioning change sufficiently in advance of the anticipated change, and (ii) uses an intelligent algorithm that takes user-specified cost functions to optimize the overheads of starting up (or terminating) the desired number of replicas.

2.3 Database Replication

Before presenting our provisioning technique, we present brief background on database replication. Dynamic database provisioning assumes that the underlying database platform is replicable and clusterable. In general, there are two primary architectures for implementing database replication: *shared-disk* and *shared-nothing*. In the *shared-disk* architecture, there is a single copy of the data on a shared disk (SAN or NAS) that is accessed by all replicas. Typically shared-disk database platforms such as Oracle RAC [13] require specific hardware (in the form of shared disk systems) that may not be available in commodity cloud platforms.

In the *shared-nothing* architecture, there are multiple database server processes that run on different machines, and each replica has a copy of the database content on its local disk. Consistency is maintained across replicas using LAN communications. Dolly currently assumes a shared-nothing architecture since they are well suited for today's cloud platforms and also commonly used in multi-tier web applications.

Within shared-nothing systems, there are two main replication strategies: master-slave and multi-master. In *master-slave*, updates are sent to a single master node and lazily replicated to slave nodes. Data on slave nodes might be stale and it is the responsibility of the application to check for data freshness when accessing a slave node. *Multi-master* replication enforces a serializable execution order of transactions between all replicas so that each of them applies update transactions in the same order. This way, any replica can serve any read or write request.

Further, replication can be implemented inside the database engine, also known as *in-core* replication, or externally to the database, commonly called *middleware-based* replication. The technique to add a new replica is similar in both environments. In both architectures, transactions are balanced among the replicas and are stored in a transactional log (also called recovery log). The middleware design usually keeps a separate transactional log for replication, whereas the in-core approach stores the information in each database's replica transactional log.

Figure 1 shows the steps to spawn a replica in a middleware-based replication environment. First, a command to add a new replica is issued from the management console to the replication middleware. A checkpoint is then created in the transactional log (step 2) and a replica is temporarily taken out of the cluster to take a snapshot (also called database dump) of the database content (step 3 via DB_2). As soon as the snapshot has been taken, this replica is resynchronized by replaying the transactions written in the transactional log since the checkpoint (step 4) and it rejoins the cluster. A new replica is then started on a separate node, and the snapshot is seeded to this new replica using a restore operation (step 5). Finally, the updates that have occurred since the snapshot was taken are replayed from the transactional log (step 6) to resynchronize the new replica and bring it up-to-date with all other replicas in the system.

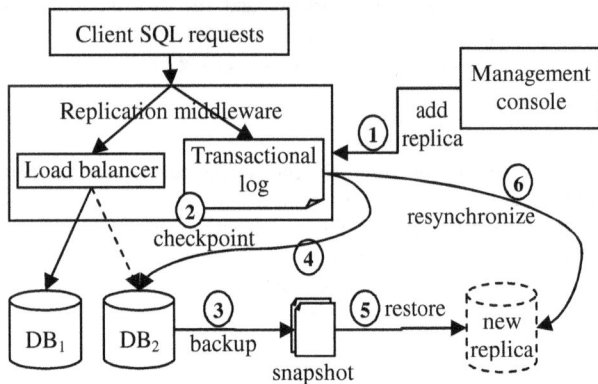

Figure 1. Procedure to spawn a replica.

Conceptually, the above steps for replica creation can be classified into three key phases: (i) the *backup* phase, where database content is extracted from an existing replica and moved to a new node, (ii) the *restore* phase, where a new replica is seeded with this snapshot, and (iii) the *replay* phase, where the replica is resynchronized with others by replaying new updates from the transactional log.

As we will see in the Dolly design, the use of virtualization simplifies these steps. Dolly employs VM snapshots to implement the backup phase and uses VM cloning to restore the snapshot onto a new replica. By doing so, Dolly is *database-platform agnostic*, since it relies on the virtualization platform, rather than native platform-specific tools, to implement provisioning via backup/restore. VM cloning is independent of the database schema complexity and eliminates common backup issues of database specific extensions and configurations [7].

Further, the Dolly design is general and can accommodate both master-slave and multi-master shared-nothing architectures; our current implementation, however, is based on a multi-master middleware-based replication and is implemented on Sequoia, a commercial-grade database clustering middleware [16].

3. Dolly: When to Provision

In this section, we first describe the high-level approach used in Dolly to provision database replicas via VM snapshot and cloning and then present a model to estimate the latency of these operations when provisioning a new replica.

3.1 Replica Spawning via VM Cloning

Dolly uses the ability to make VM snapshots and clone VMs to efficiently replicate database state and start new replicas. Figure 2 illustrates the high-level approach to spawn 2 new replicas in a private cloud. First, the virtual machine (VM) running a database replica is stopped on machine 1 and cloned to be stored on a backup server (machine B). Two new replicas are then spawned by cloning the VM from the backup server and starting these new VMs. Dolly minimizes the downtime of the existing replica that is being cloned by exploiting VM or file-system-level snapshots. A file-system or VM-level snapshot [5] is a point-in-time copy of the virtual disk image; snapshots can be made efficiently, after which the original VM replica can be resumed immediately and the snapshot image can be copied to the other machine(s) in the background.

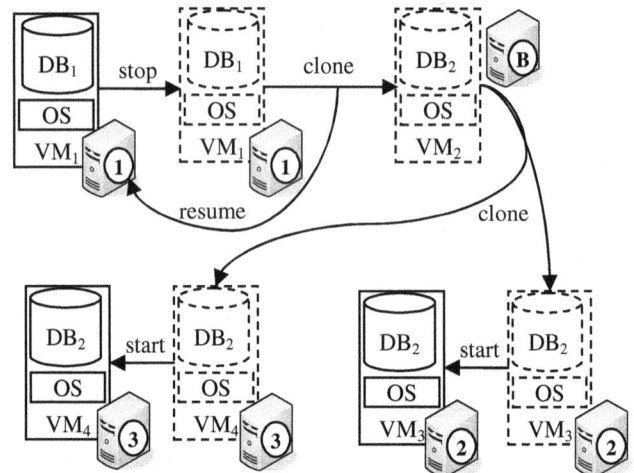

Figure 2. Replica spawning in a private cloud.

Figure 3 shows how spawning 2 replicas works in a public cloud such as Amazon EC2 that provides a Network Attached Storage (NAS) service called Amazon Elastic Block Storage (or EBS). Note that EBS volumes cannot be shared by multiple instances and are therefore different from a SAN or shared disk approach.

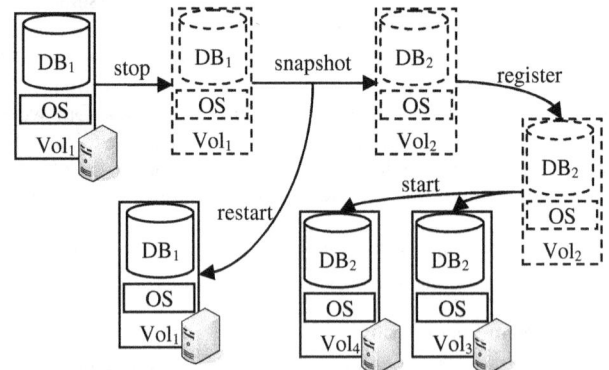

Figure 3. Replica spawning in a public cloud.

The VM disk image is stored on an EBS volume and the VM boots from this image. When the VM is stopped, the volume is detached from its running server. EBS allows snapshots of the volume to be created; doing so asynchronously replicates the volume. The volume snapshot must then be registered in EC2 in order to create new VMs. This is equivalent to storing the image to a backup server in a private cloud. When a new VM is created from an EBS snapshot, a clone of that volume is created and dedicated to the newly started instance. In our case, we assume that the database server disk state (configuration file and data within the database) are stored on the EBS volume; thus snapshots and booting a new VM from the snapshot is an effective mechanism to replicate the shared-nothing database content and start up a new database replica.

3.2 Determining replica spawning time

Dolly must accurately estimate the overheads of the above VM snapshot and cloning operations in order to intelligently trigger the spawning of new replica(s). We now present a simple model to estimate this latency.

In general, there is a tradeoff between the time to snapshot/clone a database/VM, the size of the transactional log and the amount of update transactions in the workload. For example, a new replica can be seeded with an old snapshot (e.g., a snapshot that was taken to seed a different replica), which eliminates the backup phase overhead. However, use of an older snapshot forces the system to keep a larger transactional log and also increases the time to replay updates from this log during the *replay* phase. On the other hand, taking a new snapshot for each new replica may incur significant overheads during the *backup* phase, especially if the database is large. By analyzing the overheads of these operations, Dolly can choose the option with the lower latency.

The replica spawning overhead can be analyzed using the five variables defined in Table 1.

Table 1. Replica spawning time variables.

b_i	backup time to generate VM snapshot i
r_i	time to restore/clone snapshot i on a new replica
$replay_i$	time to replay update transactions logged since snapshot i
w_t	average update transaction throughput observed at the time the new replica spawning command is issued
w_{max}	maximum update transaction throughput of the replica

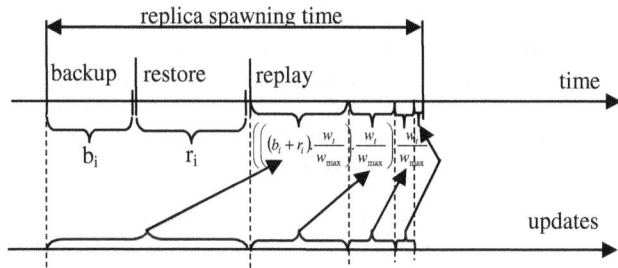

Figure 4. Decomposition of the replica spawning time with a new snapshot.

When no snapshot is available, it is necessary to perform a new backup and restore, yielding an overhead of $(b_i + r_i)$ as shown on Figure 4. The replay phase then replays all updates that have occurred during this period. We can estimate the replay time by observing the current rate of update transactions and assume that it will remain a valid approximation during the replay time. The new replica will be able to replay the requests at w_{max} speed since

it does not have to execute any other transaction. Therefore, the time to replay the updates that occurred during backup/restore is $(b_i + r_i)w_t / w_{max}$. Since new updates will occur during this replay, it will take an additional $((b_i + r_i)w_t / w_{max})w_t / w_{max}$ to replay them. This is the geometric series with: $p = \dfrac{w_t}{w_{max}}, w_t < w_{max} \cdot \sum_{k=0}^{\infty} p^i = \dfrac{1}{1-p}$

If the system is under peak load, $w_t = w_{max}$, the replica will never be able to catch up and it will have a lag of $b_i + r_i$.

Table 2. Replica spawning time formulas

Replica spawning time when no snapshot is available	$(b_i + r_i)\dfrac{w_{max}}{w_{max} - w_t}$
Replica spawning time from an existing snapshot i	$(r_i + replay_i)\dfrac{w_{max}}{w_{max} - w_t}$

We find the equations in Table 2 and conclude that: *it is faster to take a new snapshot j to spawn a new replica if $b_j + r_j < r_i + replay_i$.* Any dynamic provisioning technique for replicating the database tier of the application needs to consider this key tradeoff. The VM cloning mechanism used by Dolly provides a predictable backup/restore time independent of the database size and schema complexity as shown in Table 8. Cloning only depends on the VM image size that is known and its snapshotting time can be easily predicted. *replay_i* can be accurately predicted by recording the execution times of each update transaction and adding them up.

Since *replay_i* can be accurately predicted, having a constant b_j and r_j, that are independent of the database size or complexity, allows Dolly to decide if $b_j < replay_i$ in which case it is faster to take a new snapshot than to use an existing one to spawn a new replica.

4. Dolly: How to Provision

Our Dolly provisioning system has four main components: capacity provisioning engine, snapshot scheduler, paused pool cleaner and actuator. Typically, the provisioning engine will employ a workload predictor (Section 4.1) that observes the behavior of the system. To provision a certain capacity by a given deadline, it is necessary to schedule *capacity provisioning* actions according to the time it takes to replicate the database state (Section 4.2). As replicas have to be spawned from a database snapshot, the *snapshot scheduler* decides when new database snapshots (VM clones) have to be taken (Section 4.3). Some stopped or paused VMs become obsolete over time and need to be purged by the *paused pool cleaner* (Section 4.4). The *actuator* orchestrates and executes the orders of all the other components.

Whenever new workload predictions become available, the capacity provisioning algorithm is invoked to compute a new schedule to meet capacity demands. Then the snapshot scheduler runs to check if new snapshots could be generated (possibly from paused VMs) to make future spawning operations cheaper. If new VM snapshots are generated, we re-run the capacity provisioning algorithm to generate a new schedule. In the end, we obtain a schedule of snapshot and capacity provisioning actions (adding, pausing, resuming replicas) that are executed by the actuator. Dolly also regularly triggers the paused pool cleaner to free old paused VMs and snapshots that are no longer needed. A more detailed description of the algorithms is available in [6].

To adapt provisioning policies to the target cloud platform, Dolly uses cost functions to allow the administrator to define which option is best if multiple strategies are available. The cost can model any metric like time, resource usage or actual resource cost as we will show in the next sections. Table 3 lists the seven cost functions used by Dolly and the definitions for each.

Table 3. Cloud platform specific cost functions used by Dolly.

Cost function name	Definition
`pause_cost(VM, t)`	cost of pausing VM at time t
`spawn_cost(s, t, d)`	cost to spawn a replica from snapshot s at time t to meet deadline d
`spawn_cost(VM, t, d)`	cost to spawn a replica from a paused VM at time t to meet deadline d
`running_cost(VM,t1,t2)`	cost to run a VM from time t1 to time t2
`pause_resume_cost(VM, t1, t2)`	cost to pause a VM at time t1 and resume it at time t2
`backup_paused_cost(VM)`	cost to backup a paused VM
`backup_live_cost(VM, t)`	cost to backup an active VM at time t

Table 4 summarizes the variables used to measure the time used by the different operations used by the algorithms described in this section.

Table 4. Variables used to measure replica spawning operations.

rr	Time to restore and replay from the latest snapshot
br	Time to spawn from a new snapshot (backup+restore)
rs_{VM_i}	Time to resume paused VM i
psr	Time to pause/snapshot/resume a VM
pw	Prediction window

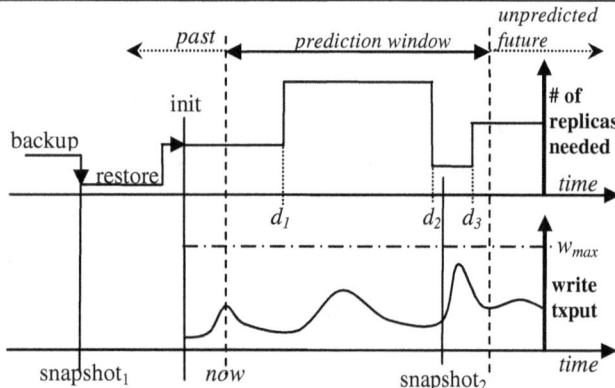

Figure 5. Example of a capacity and write workload prediction over time. Dolly provision replicas based on the forecast available in the prediction window.

4.1 Capacity and workload predictors

Previous work has established how to predict replicated database capacity based on a standalone node measurement [9]. This allows forecasting performance scalability and identifying potential bottlenecks. Many models exist for workload prediction [11], [20]. Dolly does not assume any particular workload predictor or capacity model; it can use any existing approach and can be a platform to test new predictors or improve existing ones.

Depending on the capacity and workload predictors used, the forecast will have a limited visibility in the future. Web sites with stable workloads might have accurate static weekly predictions possibly adjusted by administrators for seasonal peaks. More

dynamically changing workloads can be less predictable and only sketch the demand for the next hour or so. We call *prediction window* the time between now and the latest time in the future for which the load and capacity demand can be predicted.

Figure 5 shows an example of capacity demand and write throughput of a replicated database. The prediction window slides as time goes on. Prediction windows are not necessarily of a fixed size since a predictor can dynamically change the technique it uses to forecast the load thus increasing or decreasing the prediction window size. Dolly has to schedule provisioning decisions for deadlines d_1, d_2 and d_3, where the capacity demand changes in the prediction window.

4.2 Provisioning replicas

The provisioning algorithm scans the prediction window and looks for deadlines where changes in workload require additional capacity (such as time d_1 and d_3 on Figure 5) or less capacity (such as time d_2 on Figure 5). The algorithm handles all deadlines in sequence. In Figure 5, d_1 is handled first. Once a schedule has been found for d_1, it moves to d_2 and so on. The algorithm works in two phases for each deadline: 1) list all possible options for replica spawning or releasing and 2) sort these options according to a cost function.

4.2.1 Decreasing capacity

When the capacity requirements decrease, replicas that are no longer needed are paused. The replication engine keeps track of the state of each stopped virtual machine replica so that it knows exactly what has to be replayed when the VM is resumed. A similar state is saved in the slave nodes for master/slave replication.

When a VM is stopped in a private cloud, its image still resides on the machine's local disk. As we might want to resume that image later, we do not return the machine to the free server pool but it is put it in a special *paused server pool*. The machine can be shutdown as long as it is in the paused pool. A machine can be reclaimed from the paused server pool by the private cloud infrastructure if the free pool is empty and additional capacity is required for other databases or tiers. In a public cloud like EC2, the computing instance is simply detached from the storage and can be re-attached later to any other instance.

The platform specific cost function, `pause_cost(VM, d)` determines the cost of pausing *VM* at time *d*. For example, in EC2 where server time is billed by the hour, if at time *d* VM_1 has just started a new billed hour and VM_2 is toward the end of its billed hour, we would have pause_cost(VM_1, d)>pause_cost(VM_2, d). On a private cloud, the administrator might prefer to switch off the hottest machines to improve cooling. If the capacity has to be reduced by r replicas at time d, the algorithm schedules the r replicas that have the lowest `pause_cost` for pausing.

4.2.2 Increasing capacity

When an increase in capacity is predicted at deadline d, the algorithm explores all replica spawning options from snapshots and paused VMs.

In our system, the replicated database always has at least one snapshot available for creating new replicas. The first snapshot is created when initializing the system as shown on Figure 5, and snapshots are updated regularly when needed, as will be explained in section 4.3. When new replicas are spawned from a snapshot, we can predict the time it takes to bring the replica online using the formula described in section 3.2.

Dolly looks at all available snapshots that can spawn replicas in time to meet deadline d, as well as all paused VMs that can be resumed and resynchronized in time. Each option has its own cost defined by the `spawn_cost` function. For example, on a private cloud, options using the latest start times allow unused nodes to remain switched off longer and save energy. On a public cloud such as EC2, the cost can be defined by the price the user is going to pay for the compute hours of the instance, the IOs on EBS and the monthly cost for data storage.

The cheapest options are selected to be executed. Note that if there are not enough options to provision all replicas, this means that it is not possible to spawn all replicas in time for the deadline given the current workload. We address this scenario in the next section.

4.2.3 Admission control

If a capacity deadline cannot be met in time with the current forecast, it is possible to perform admission control on the system in multiple ways. Note that this scenario can only happen if the predictor drastically changes its predictions for the current prediction window (such as an unpredicted flash crowd).

First we assume that no writes will update the system from now on and compute the time it takes to restore and replay from the latest snapshot (rr), to take a new snapshot and spawn a replica from it (br=backup+restore) or resume from paused VMs (rs_{VM_i}). If we find that $now + min(rr, br, rs_{VM_i}, rs_{VM_j}) \leq d$, this implies that

there is enough time to create replicas but the write throughput is too high or too close to w_{max} for replicas to catch up in time. Doing admission control on the write throughput w_t can be used to meet the deadline as long as:

$$w_t \leq w_{max} - \frac{min(rr, br, rs_{VM_i}, rs_{VM_j}).w_{max}}{d - now}$$

Note that doing admission control on writes (*write throttling*), means that update transactions are going to be delayed. Depending on timeout settings, this might translate into transactions being aborted. The minimum acceptable write throughput can be set by the administrator.

If replicas cannot be spawned in time even with write throttling, it is necessary to perform admission control on the incoming workload to prevent the system from crashing due to overload. Admission control can be performed by the replication engine by allowing only a fixed number of transactions in the system at any given time. It can also be achieved at another tier in front of the database (e.g. web tier admission control). A workload matching the current capacity has to be maintained until additional capacity becomes available at time:

$$d - now + min(rr, br, rs_{VM_i}, rs_{VM_j}) \frac{w_{max}}{w_{max} - w_t}$$

The administrator can set a minimum acceptable w_t and let Dolly perform admission control and schedule spawning operations accordingly.

4.3 Scheduling new database snapshots

In addition to provisioning new replicas or pausing existing ones, Dolly must deal with the problem of periodically creating new database snapshots by cloning VMs. A newer snapshot reduces the cost of spawning a new replica in the future (since it has a more recent version of the database and will incur a lower synchronization overhead). However, creating a snapshot incurs an overhead, and Dolly must intelligently schedule their creation to balance the cost and the benefit.

Two problems have to be solved to schedule new database snapshots: *how* and *when*. *How* can either be from an already paused VM or by pausing an active VM for the time of the snapshot (see section 4.3.1). A new snapshot must be ready *when* the time to restore and replay from the previously available snapshot is greater than the prediction window (see section 4.3.2).

4.3.1 How to snapshot?

An opportunistic method to create a new snapshot is to clone VMs that have been paused. While a paused VM only captures the database state until the time it was paused, it might still be a significant improvement over the last snapshot available.

The only other option requires taking an existing replica offline for the time of the pause/snapshot/resume (psr) operation and replaying of updates that happened since the VM was paused. This means that the capacity of the system is going to be reduced by 1 replica from t_{backup} to $t_{backup} + \left(psr + replay_{t_{backup}}\right)\frac{w_{max}}{w_{max} - w_t}$.

If the workload prediction does not allow a replica to be temporarily disabled during that time interval, an additional replica has to be provisioned at time t_{backup} to allow taking a new snapshot. This new deadline can be added to the current capacity prediction and the capacity provisioning algorithm described in section 4.2 has to be re-executed to provision this additional replica in time.

4.3.2 When to snapshot?

If we want to provision additional replicas in time, the time to restore and replay from the latest available snapshot should never exceed the prediction window. Otherwise, when the predictor forecasts a new capacity demand increase at the end of the prediction window, there would not be enough time to spawn new replicas. This means that a new snapshot must be ready to be fully restored at time t_{switch} defined by: $r_{backup_i} + replay_{backup_i, switch} = pw$

where pw is the prediction window and $replay_{backup_i, switch} = \sum_{t=t_{backup_i}}^{t_{switch}} \frac{w_t}{w_{max}}$

To make sure that additional replicas can be provisioned at t_{switch} using the new snapshot, the backup operation must be started prior to time $t_{backup_{i+1}}$ so that there is enough time to backup, restore and replay a new replica at time t_{switch}. This translates to:

$$b_{backup_{i+1}} + r_{backup_{i+1}} + replay_{backup_{i+1}, switch} \leq t_{switch} - t_{backup_{i+1}}$$

To guarantee that a new snapshot can be ready in time, the prediction window must be long enough so that:

$$pw \geq t_{switch} - t_{backup_{i+1}} \geq b_{backup_{i+1}} + r_{backup_{i+1}} + replay_{backup_{i+1}, switch}$$

If the prediction window is too short or write throughput is too high, admission control can be used to make sure that new snapshots can be prepared in time within the prediction window.

The algorithm then scans the prediction window and look at each deadline where new replicas have to spawned (adding capacity only). For each deadline, it calculates the cost to spawn new replicas for 3 strategies:

1) The cost to spawn replicas from a snapshot given by `spawn_cost` (defined in section 4.2.2) for all snapshots that can be restored and replayed by the deadline.

2) For each paused VM (step 3) that can be snapshotted, restored and replayed by the deadline, the cost to take the backup from the paused VM is given by the cost function `backup_paused_cost` to which we add the cost of spawning replicas from this backup.

3) The cost of creating a backup from a live replica is given by the `backup_live_cost` function to which we add the cost of spawning replicas from this backup and the eventual cost of bringing a replica online if no idle replica is available.

Next, the algorithm keeps the option that has the minimal cost for each deadline and schedules the operations accordingly. If no option is available to spawn a replica in time for a given deadline, the algorithm computes at what time a snapshot should be taken and modifies the capacity requirements to ask for one replica to be ready by that time. The capacity provisioning is then invoked to provision that replica, eventually using admission control if needed.

The capacity provisioning algorithm is re-run every time new snapshots have been scheduled to check if a better replica spawning schedule is available. If this is the case, the old schedule is replaced by the new schedule.

4.4 Relinquishing resources

Over time, some paused VMs become obsolete and are not cost effective to be resumed. The same applies to old VM snapshots that need to be erased. The *paused pool cleaner* has the responsibility of releasing these resources. It is invoked at regular time intervals that can be set by the administrator (from every hour, to every day or every week). It scans each paused VM and checks the cost of resuming that VM ($spawn\_cost(VM, now, pw_{end})$) and compares it to the cost of spawning a replica from the latest available snapshot ($spawn\_cost(b_i, now, pw_{end})$). If the cost of resuming the VM is higher, it means that this VM will not be used anymore and it can be released.

A similar approach can be used for snapshots. All snapshots that are older than the current latest available snapshot can be released. However, the administrator might want to keep multiple older backups for recovery purposes. On a public cloud like EC2, since storage is paid for on a monthly basis, a better policy may be to retain old volumes until the end of the billing cycle.

4.5 Current limitations

Dolly assumes that all the components of the cloning operation (backup, restore, snapshot...) have a constant time which is correct for homogeneous setups with LAN interconnections. This might not be the case with heterogeneous resources or resources in different EC2 regions or clouds using WAN interconnections. The worst case scenario measurement could be taken to ensure safe scheduling, but specific optimizations for such environments are left to future work. Additional optimizations such as virtual machine migration can also be considered in these environments.

When synchronizing slave nodes in a master/slave setup, the synchronization process uses master node resources and potentially impacts its performance. We have not currently

modeled this performance impact but we did not find it noticeable in our early experiments.

5. Dolly Implementation

We have implemented the concepts of Dolly in the Sequoia 4.0 [16] database clustering middleware and integrated it with the OpenNebula cloud infrastructure manager v1.4 [14]. OpenNebula works with both private and public cloud resources and offers a single API to manipulate VMs independently of the target platform. Figure 6 shows an overview of the integration of Dolly with Sequoia and OpenNebula in the context of the TPC-W benchmark.

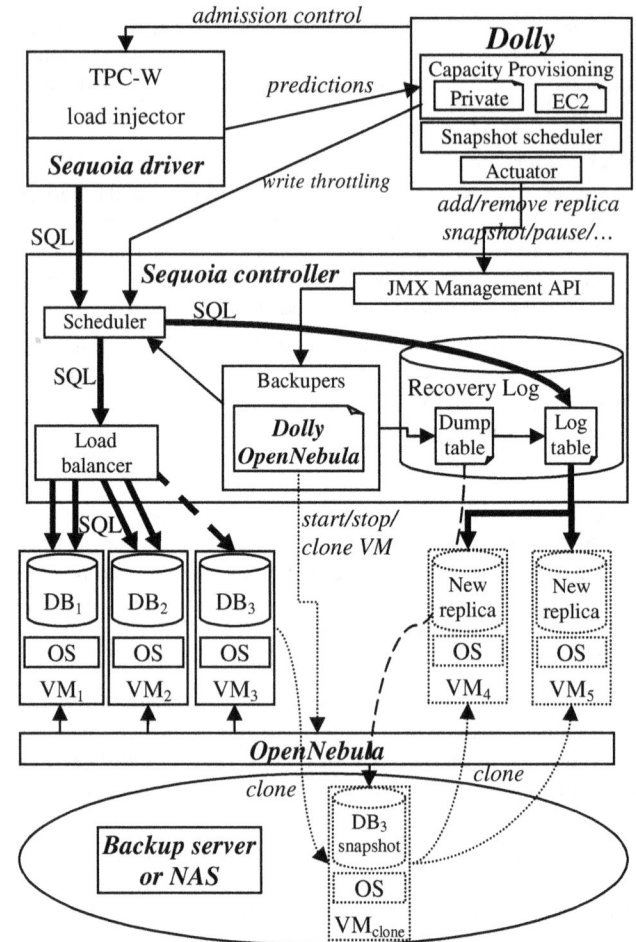

Figure 6. Overview of Dolly integration in Sequoia and OpenNebula running the TPC-W benchmark.

Client applications send SQL requests to the Sequoia controller that forwards them to the underlying databases to perform replication. The SQL commands of update transactions are recorded with their execution time in a transactional log called *recovery log*. The log itself is stored in an embedded database running within the Sequoia controller. The recovery log can be replayed to synchronize new or failed replicas. Additionally, Sequoia has a replica spawning infrastructure with a pluggable *backuper* interface that interacts with the recovery log and allows for database specific implementations of backup and restore operations. We have implemented a Dolly/OpenNebula backuper that interacts with OpenNebula to start/stop and clone/snapshot virtual machines to implement the backup and restore functionality. When a new backup is triggered, a pointer to the current state of the recovery log is stored with the dump metadata. When a restore operation is launched, the dump is first restored and dedicated threads then replay the recovery log (i.e. re-execute the SQL commands) from the point that was saved in the metadata. Updates are applied in a serializable order to bring the new replica in a consistent state with other replicas. The time to replay is computed by summing the recorded execution time of all queries to replay. More information about Sequoia internals and its recovery log can be found in the Sequoia documentation [16].

Dolly takes predictions directly from the TPC-W load injectors that act as oracles with perfect information. A tunable prediction window can be used from 1 minute to the entire length of the benchmark run. The provisioning actions are directly sent to the Sequoia controller through its administration interface. Dolly performs admission control directly on the load injectors but it would typically do this at the web tier level in a multi-tier setup. The write throttling is achieved by interacting with the Sequoia scheduler. We have implemented different cost functions to model our private cloud platform and the Amazon EC2 public cloud.

The private cloud cost functions detailed in pseudo-code in Table 5 optimize the time the resources are used. The longer the resources are used, the more power they use and the higher the cost. When the algorithm has to decide which VM to pause, it selects the hottest machine at that time.

Table 5. Cost function implementation for our private cloud.

Cost function name	Implementation
`pause_cost(VM, t)`	`return 1/VM->machine->temp`
`spawn_cost(s, t, d)`	`return d-t`
`spawn_cost(VM, t, d)`	`return d-t`
`running_cost(VM,t1,t2)`	`return 1`
`pause_resume_cost(VM, t1, t2)`	`if (t2-t1>VM->pause+VM->resume) return 0 else return 2`
`backup_paused_cost(VM)`	`return backup_time`
`backup_live_cost(VM, t)`	`return VM->pause + backup_time + VM->resume`

Table 6 models the cost functions as the real cost the user would pay for EC2 resource usage. It includes both the compute time for server instances (charged by the hour at the *hour$* rate) and the IO cost (charged monthly per GB of storage (*EBS_storage$*) and IOs are charged per million (*EBS_io$*)). EBS snapshots are stored on S3 and are charged monthly per GB of storage (*S3_storage$*).

Table 6. Cost function implementation for Amazon EC2.

Cost function name	Implementation
`pause_cost(VM, t)`	`return 60-((t-VM->start)%60)`
`spawn_cost(s, t, d)`	`comp$=(d-t)/60*hour$` `io$=EBS_storage$*s->size +` `  EBS_io$*` `  (s->restore_io+s->replay_io)` `return comp$+io$`
`spawn_cost(VM, t, d)`	`comp$=(d-t)/60*hour$` `io$= EBS_io$*` `  (s->resume_io+s->replay_io)` `return comp$+io$`
`running_cost(VM,t1,t2)`	`(t2-t1)/60*hour$;`
`pause_resume_cost(VM, t1, t2)`	`io$= EBS_io$*` `  (VM->pause_io+VM->resume_io)` `comp$=(60-(VM->stop-VM->start)` `  %60)/60*hour$` `return io$+ comp$`
`backup_paused_cost(VM)`	`return S3_storage$*s->size`
`backup_live_cost(VM, t)`	`return pause_cost(VM, t)$+` `S3_storage$*s->size +` `(VM->stop_io+VM->start_io)*` `  EBS_io$`

6. Experimental Evaluation

This section first introduces the cloud platforms used for our experiments. We then present our performance evaluation.

6.1 Cloud Platforms

We conduct experiments on private and public clouds. We use a private cloud composed of a cluster of Pentium 4 2.8GHz machines. Each machine is running a CentOS 5.4 Linux distribution with a Linux kernel version 2.6.18-128.1.10.el5xen, the Xen 3.3 hypervisor, Java runtime version 1.6.0_04-b12and MySQL v5.0.45. All machines are interconnected by a Gigabit Ethernet network.

We use Amazon EC2 as our public cloud. EC2 instances are created from EBS volumes. We use standard large on-demand EC2 instances in our experiments. Each EC2 instance has CloudWatch running on it to monitor the number of writes. The price of our EC2 instance with CloudWatch is $0.355 per hour. The price of an EBS volume is $0.10 per allocated GB of data per month. The cost of doing I/O requests to an EBS volume is $0.10 per million I/O requests. There is a cost of $0.15 per GB per month associated with the storage of EBS volume snapshots.

Table 7. Operation timings in seconds for a TPC-W benchmark virtual machine on our private cloud and EC2.

Operation	Private Cloud	Public Cloud (EC2)
start VM	42s	220s
pause VM	26s	30s
resume VM	42s	30s
backup (stop/clone)	150s	320s
restore (clone/start)	165s	220s
w_{max}	149 writes/sec	197 writes/sec
Avg IOs per write	15	13

We build a 4GB VM image of the TPC-W benchmark for both cloud platforms. We report our measurements of the various VM management and cloning operations in Table 7. We measure the maximum write throughput of a single replica (w_{max}) obtained by running only write transactions of the TPC-W workload on a standalone database. The average number of IOs per write transaction is calculated by running iostat before and after the w_{max} run.

6.2 VM Cloning vs Database Backup/Restore

VM cloning is an alternative mechanism for replicating content when compared to the traditional database-specific backup-restore mechanism. In this section, we compare the copy overheads of the two approaches.

Table 8 shows the time to copy various databases using the database native backup/restore tool (e.g. mysqldump, pg_dump) versus VM cloning. The RUBiS benchmark database [3] is tested with 3 configurations on MySQL using the InnoDB engine: without constraint or index (-c-i), with integrity constraints and basic indexes (+c+bi) and with constraints and full text indexes (+c+fi). TPC-W and TPC-H [19] databases are stored in a PostgreSQL RDBMS. We also experiment with two virtual machine image sizes (4 and 16GB) where we store both the operating system and the database within its content.

Indexes significantly increase the database footprint on disk. We observe from the RUBiS results that integrity constraints checks as well as index building can increase database backup/restore time by a factor of more than 7 for the exact same database content. Not only do the database schema and backup tool configurations affect timings, different database engines yield very different results for databases with a similar size on disk as shown on Figure 7. We observe that large or complex databases can take more than 1 hour to replicate.

Table 8. Backup/restore and VM cloning time in seconds for various standard benchmark databases.

Database	DB size on disk	DB Backup Restore	Dolly 4GB VM cloning	Dolly 16GB VM cloning
RUBiS −c−i	1022MB	843s	281s	899s
RUBiS +c+bi	1.4GB	5761s	282s	900s
RUBiS +c+fi	1.5GB	6017s	280s	900s
TPC-W	684MB	288s	275s	905s
TPC-H 1GB	1.8GB	1477s	271s	918s
TPC-H 10GB	12GB	5573s	n/a	911s

In contrast, VM cloning performs a filesystem level copy without interpreting database objects, thus it offers a constant time regardless of the database complexity or engine used. The time only depends on the VM image size on disk (280s for a 4GB image and about 900s for a 16GB image). Consequently, since the VM disk size is fixed a priori, VM cloning makes it easy to predict database backup/restore time incurred when spawning a new replica—a crucial pre-requisite for database provisioning. Additionally VM cloning captures the entire OS/database configuration and settings preventing any error in reproducing these settings on the new replica machine.

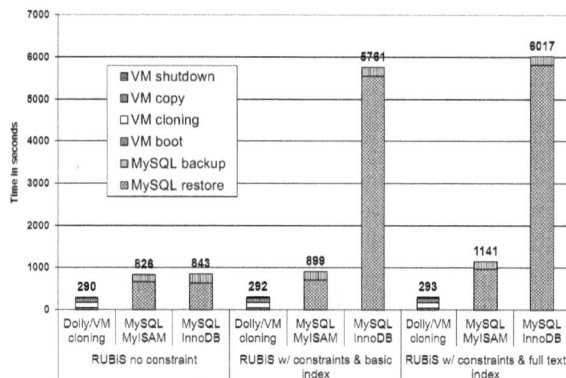

Figure 7. Time breakdown for cloning a database with Dolly and MySQL backup/restore tools with the MyISAM and InnoDB engines using the RUBiS benchmark database with various constraints and indices.

6.3 Provisioning Evaluation

We experiment with TPC-W, an eCommerce benchmark from the Transaction Processing Council [19] that emulates an online bookstore. We use the ObjectWeb implementation of the TPC-W benchmark [17]. The setup is similar to the one depicted in Figure 6 with load injectors providing a 2 hour prediction window. The web tier (not shown on Figure 6) is statically provisioned with enough servers for the length of the experiment.

We compare the provisioning decisions of Dolly for the private and public clouds with traditional provisioning techniques given the workload and initial conditions defined in section 6.3.1.

6.3.1 Workload Description

We have generated a custom mix of interactions to create the workload depicted at the top of Figure 8. We generate a read-only request mix by using the TPC-W browsing mix workload and removing its few write interactions. We use httperf to create the desired number of clients that send these read-only interactions. The write interactions are generated using the customer registration servlet of TPCW. Another set of httperf clients generate these write-only interactions.

We use the model described in [9] to determine the capacity requirements shown in Figure 8. The initial capacity demand at t=0 is 4 replicas (middle graph) and the write throughput is 20% of the maximum write throughput (bottom graph). A snapshot s_0 is also available at time t_0. After 10 minutes the number of replicas needed decreases from 4 to 3. We denote this deadline by d_1. The number of replicas needed decreases further from 3 to 2 at $d_2=20$ minutes. The capacity demand increases sharply from 2 to 5 replicas at $d_3=80$ minutes, then drops to 2 at $d_4=90$ minutes and increases up to 6 replicas at $d_5=100$ minutes. The number of writes remains constant to 0.2 times the maximum write throughput for one hour with a 10 minute read-only workload starting at d_2. After that hour, the write throughput is 0 until d_3 with a write surge at 50% of the maximum write throughput. The write peak continues for 10 minutes and the write throughput drops to 0 at d_4.

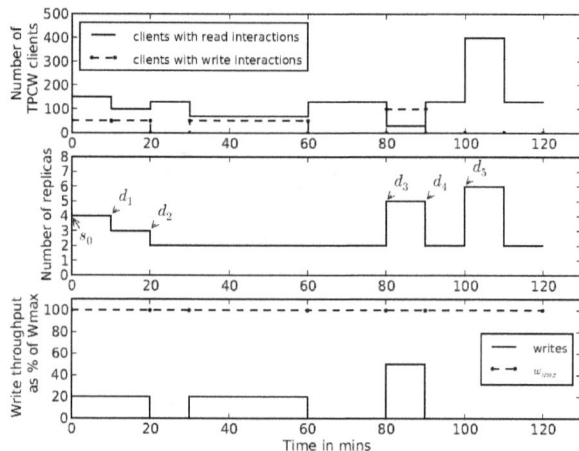

Figure 8. TPC-W workload, predicted capacity requirements and write workload.

6.3.2 Provisioning results

We compare Dolly's performance with two traditional provisioning techniques: *reactive provisioning* and *overprovisioning*. These techniques behave similarly on the private and public clouds.

Reactive provisioning does not use any prediction and just reacts to the current capacity demand. When reactive provisioning is used, database snapshots are generated at fixed time intervals. We use intervals of 15 minutes (Reactive15m), 1 hour (Reactive1h) and 2 hours (Reactive2h), generating 7, 1 and 0 snapshots respectively during the experiment.

The overprovisioning configuration (Overpro6) uses a constant set of 6 nodes. As for reactive provisioning, snapshots are generated periodically. We choose to only generate 1 snapshot during the experiment.

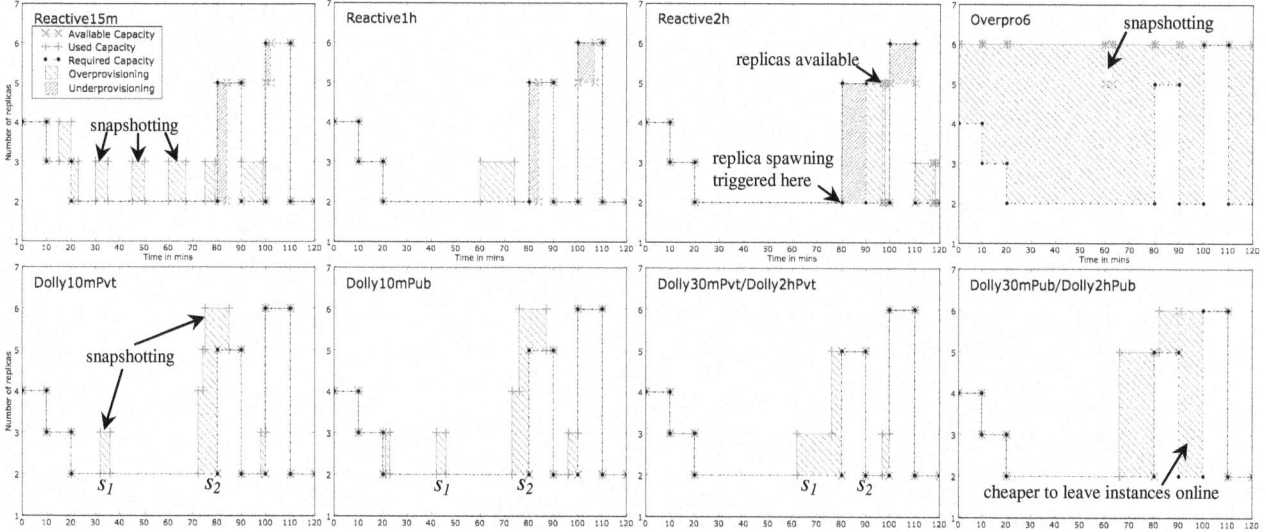

Figure 9. Capacity made available by each provisioning algorithm compared to the required capacity and the total capacity actually used.

We run Dolly with three prediction windows of 10 minutes, 30 minutes and 2 hours. Dolly uses the cost functions presented in section 5 for the private and public clouds. The performance of the different algorithms is summarized in Table 9. The cost for the private cloud represents the cumulative machine uptime (6 machines up for 5 minutes accounts for 30 minutes). The cost for the public cloud (Amazon EC2) is the real cost in $USD. The second metric used is *missing replica minute* (MRM) that measures capacity underprovisioning (i.e. SLA violations). 1 MRM corresponds to a missing capacity of 1 replica for 1 minute (5 replicas missing for 2 minutes accounts for 10MRM).

Table 9. Provisioning algorithm performance for private and public clouds in terms of cost and missing replica minute (MRM).

Provisioning algorithm	Private Cloud		Public Cloud (EC2)	
	Cost (time)	MRM	Cost ($)	MRM
Reactive15m	381m42s	17.5	18.29	27.2
Reactive1h	360m30s	25.8	5.00	33.7
Reactive2h	410m	42.1	4.61	41.5
Overpro6	720m	0	8.39	0
Dolly10m	381m54s	0	7.16	0
Dolly30m	352m	0	3.73	0
Dolly2h	352m	0	3.73	0

The results show that reactive provisioning is not able to properly provision the system with missing capacity ranging from 23.2 to 44.2 missing replica minute. Snapshotting more often reduces the time to spawn new replicas by restore and replay but capacity is missing during the spawning operations.

Overprovisioning (Overpro6) always provides an adequate capacity but at a significantly larger cost on each cloud platform. In contrast, Dolly uses much less resources while still providing the required capacity. A 10 minute prediction window (Dolly10m) requires more snapshots to be able to react to any new capacity demand at the end of the short prediction window. A 30 minute prediction window (Dolly30m) is enough to provide an optimal

provisioning using less than half of the resources of the overprovisioned configuration.

Figure 9 shows in more detail the behavior of each algorithm. When reactive provisioning is used, additional capacity is used to spawn a new replica from the latest snapshot so that a new snapshot can be generated. When capacity needs to be increased, the system remains underprovisioned during the time replicas are spawned. The older the snapshot the longer it takes to spawn new replicas. In the Reactive2h case, replicas spawning starting at t=80 completes only 17 minutes later, leaving the system with only 2 available replicas to serve requests during the first peak period.

The Overpro6 configuration constantly provides 6 replicas except for when the snapshot is generated where a node is briefly paused. The large shaded area shows the amount of wasted resources.

Dolly with a 10 minute prediction window (Dolly10m) behaves similarly on both cloud platforms. As the prevision window slides the time to restore and replay from the latest snapshot exceeds the prediction window size. This is why Dolly spawns new replicas to generate new snapshots at deadlines s_1 and s_2. While new replicas are spawned from s_1 during the first capacity increase, the write spike quickly triggers an additional replica to generate s_2. Four replicas are paused at the end of the first peak and resumed for the second peak (no replay time since no write occurred during that paused time). An additional replica is quickly spawned from s_2.

With a 30 minute or longer prevision window (Dolly30m and Dolly2h), decisions change between the private and the public cloud according to the cost functions. While less machine time is used on the private cloud by generating new snapshots from an additional replica online (s_1) or from a paused replica (s_2), the storage cost of a new snapshot dominates the IO cost of replay for EC2. Therefore all replicas are always spawned from the original s_0 snapshot in the public cloud. Instances are also not stopped between the two peaks as instances are paid for a full hour, pausing and restarting them 10 minutes later costs more than letting them run.

In summary, we have shown that Dolly with a prediction window as short as 30 minutes is able to provide optimal resource utilization (according to administrator defined cost functions) while always providing the required capacity.

7. Related Work

Much of the prior work on dynamic provisioning [20], [21], [22], [4] has focused on dynamic provisioning of the front tiers of web applications. In this work we focus on the database tier that differs from other tiers due to its large dynamic state. Commercial solutions such as Oracle RAC [13] use a shared disk approach to avoid the state replication problem. The use of in-memory databases on top of a shared storage has also been considered [12]. Our work focuses on cloud environments where a shared disk approach cannot typically be deployed.

Amazon Relational Database Service (RDS) [2] works with Amazon Auto Scaling [1] to provide reactive provisioning of asynchronously replicated (i.e. master/slave) MySQL databases based on static thresholds. Microsoft in its Azure PaaS (Platform as a Service) cloud offering provides built-in replication in the lower layer of its platform but hides it to the user [15]. Provisioning could be enhanced on both platform using Dolly.

The few papers related to dynamic provisioning of databases usually focus on workload prediction without modeling the time to spawn new replicas [8]. Dolly can work with any load predictor and provisions database replicas accordingly by predicting VM cloning and replica resynchronization time. The problem of re-synchronizing database replicas in a shared nothing environment has been described in [17]. However, the proposed technique only relies on log replay and does not exploit snapshotting as a way to bring up new replicas. Even in a more recent work [10], state synchronization time is based on fixed estimates for replay. We have shown that using virtualization, we are able to snapshot databases via VM cloning and predict state replication time accurately.

8. Conclusion

Database provisioning is a challenging problem due to the need to replicate and synchronize disk state. Since modern data centers and cloud platforms employ a virtualized architecture, we proposed a new database replica spawning technique that leverages virtual machine cloning. We argued that VM cloning offers a replication time that depends solely on the VM disk size and is independent of the database size, schema complexity and database engine. We proposed models to accurately estimate replica spawning time and analyzed the tradeoffs between capacity provisioning and database state snapshotting. To the best of our knowledge, Dolly is the first database provisioning system that can be adapted to the specifics of various cloud platforms via administrator-defined cost functions.

We implemented Dolly and integrated it with a commercial-grade open source database clustering middleware. We proposed different cost functions to optimize resource usage in a private cloud and to minimize cost for the Amazon EC2 public cloud. We evaluated our prototype with a TPC-W e-commerce workload and demonstrated the benefits of an automated database provisioning system for the cloud, with optimized solutions adapted to different cloud platform specifics. We plan to release Dolly as open source software and hope that it will facilitate replicated database deployments in virtualized environments such as clouds.

Acknowledgement

We would like to thank Steve Dropsho for early contributions to this work. This research was supported in part by NSF grants CNS-0834243, CNS-0720616, CNS-0916972, CNS-0855128, and a gift from NEC.

9. References

[1] Amazon Auto Scaling - http://aws.amazon.com/autoscaling/

[2] Amazon RDS - http://aws.amazon.com/rds/

[3] C. Amza, E. Cecchet, Anupam Chanda, Alan L. Cox, S. Elnikety, R. Gil, J. Marguerite, K. Rajamani, and W. Zwaenepoel – *Specification and implementation of dynamic Web site benchmarks* – WWC, 2002.

[4] M. N. Bennani and D. A. Menasce – *Resource allocation for autonomic data centers using analytic performance models* – ICAC '05, Washington, DC, USA, 2005.

[5] J. Blancet – *Snapshots in Xen* – Online FAQ, https://zagnut.storeit offsite.com/home/jim.blancet/FAQ/Snapshots%20in%20xen

[6] E. Cecchet, R. Singh, U. Sharma and P. Shenoy – *Dolly: Virtualization-driven Database Provisioning for the Cloud* – UMass Technical Report UM-CS-2010-006.

[7] E. Cecchet, G. Candea and A. Ailamaki – *Middleware-based Database Replication: The Gaps between Theory and Practice.* – ACM SIGMOD, June 10-12, 2008

[8] J. Chen, G.Soundararajan, C.Amza – *Autonomic Provisioning of Backend Databases in Dynamic Content Web Servers* – ICAC '06, June 2006.

[9] S. Elnikety, S. Dropsho, E. Cecchet and W. Zwaenepoel – *Predicting Replicated Database Scalability from Standalone Database Profiling* – EuroSys, April 2009.

[10] S. Ghanbari, G. Soundararajan, J. Chen, and C. Amza – *Adaptive Learning of Metric Correlations for Temperature-Aware Database Provisioning* – ICAC, June 2007.

[11] J. Hellerstein, F. Zhang, and P. Shahabuddin – *An Approach to Predictive Detection for Service Management* – Proceedings of the 12th Conference on Systems and Network Management, 1999.

[12] K. Manassiev and C. Amza – *Scaling and Continuous Availability in Database Server Clusters through Multiversion Replication* – DSN 2007, June 2007.

[13] Oracle – Oracle Real Application Clusters 11g – Oracle Technical White Paper, April 2007.

[14] OpenNebula project. http://opennebula.org/

[15] M. Otey – *SQL Server vs. SQL Azure: Where SQL Azure is Limited* - SQL Server Magazine, August 2010.

[16] Sequoia Project. http://sourceforge.net/projects/sequoiadb/

[17] G. Soundararajan and C. Amza – *Online data migration for autonomic provisioning of databases in dynamic content web servers* – 2005 Conference of the Centre For Advanced Studies on Collaborative Research, Toronto, October 2005.

[18] TPC-W Benchmark, ObjectWeb implementation, http://jmob.objectweb.org/tpcw.html.

[19] Transaction Processing Council. http://www.tpc.org/.

[20] B. Urgaonkar, P. Shenoy, A. Chandra, and P. Goyal – *Dynamic Provisioning for Multi-tier Internet Applications* – ICAC-05, Seattle, June 2005.

[21] D. Villela, P. Pradhan, and D. Rubenstein – *Provisioning Servers in the Application Tier for E-commerce Systems* – IWQOS 2004, June 2004.

[22] Q. Zhang, L. Cherkasova, and E. Smirni – *A regression based analytic model for dynamic resource provisioning of multi-tier applications* – ICAC '07, Washington, DC, 2007.

ReHype: Enabling VM Survival Across Hypervisor Failures

Michael Le   Yuval Tamir

Concurrent Systems Laboratory
UCLA Computer Science Department
{mvle,tamir}@cs.ucla.edu

Abstract

With existing virtualized systems, hypervisor failures lead to overall system failure and the loss of all the work in progress of virtual machines (VMs) running on the system. We introduce ReHype, a mechanism for recovery from hypervisor failures by booting a new instance of the hypervisor while preserving the state of running VMs. VMs are stalled during the hypervisor reboot and resume normal execution once the new hypervisor instance is running. Hypervisor failures can lead to arbitrary state corruption and inconsistencies throughout the system. ReHype deals with the challenge of protecting the recovered hypervisor instance from such corrupted state and resolving inconsistencies between different parts of hypervisor state as well as between the hypervisor and VMs and between the hypervisor and the hardware. We have implemented ReHype for the Xen hypervisor. The implementation was done incrementally, using results from fault injection experiments to identify the sources of dangerous state corruption and inconsistencies. The implementation of ReHype involved only 880 LOC added or modified in Xen. The memory space overhead of ReHype is only 2.1MB for a pristine copy of the hypervisor code and static data plus a small reserved memory area. The fault injection campaigns used to evaluate the effectiveness of ReHype involved a system with multiple VMs running I/O and hypercall-intensive benchmarks. Our experimental results show that the ReHype prototype can successfully recover from over 90% of detected hypervisor failures.

Categories and Subject Descriptions

D.4.5 [Operating Systems]: Reliability - Fault-tolerance

General Terms

Reliability, Experimentation, Performance

Keywords

Virtualization, Reliability, Recovery, VMM, Microreboot, Xen

1. Introduction

System virtualization[19] enables server consolidation by allowing multiple virtual machines (VMs) to run on a single physical host while providing workload isolation and flexible resource management. The hypervisor manages the access of the VMs to physical resources and is critical to the operation of the entire system. Failure of the hypervisor due to software bugs or transient hardware faults generally results in the failure of *all* the system's VMs. Recovery from such a failure typically involves rebooting the entire system, resulting in loss of the work in progress in all the VMs. This problem can be mitigated through the use of periodic checkpointing of all the VMs and restoration of all the VMs to their last checkpoint upon reboot. However, this involves performance overhead for checkpointing during normal operation as well as loss upon recovery of work done since the last checkpoint.

This paper introduces and evaluates a mechanism for recovery from hypervisor failures called *ReHype*. To the best of our knowledge, ReHype is the first mechanism that allows VMs to survive hypervisor failure without any loss of work in progress and without any performance overhead during normal operation. Upon hypervisor failure, ReHype boots a new hypervisor instance while preserving the state of running VMs. VMs are stalled for a short duration during the hypervisor reboot. After a new hypervisor is booted, ReHype integrates the preserved VM states with the new hypervisor to allow the VMs to continue normal execution.

Hypervisor failure almost always involves state corruption. Corruptions can occur in the hypervisor state as well as in VM state. Hence, no recovery mechanism that relies on system state at the time a failure is detected can be 100% guaranteed to restore all system components to valid states. Furthermore, since ReHype involves reinitializing part of the hypervisor state while preserving the rest of the state, the result of recovery may include inconsistencies in the hypervisor state, between hypervisor and VM states, and between the hypervisor and hardware states. For example, hypervisor failure can occur in the middle of handling a hypercall from a VM or before acknowledging an interrupt from a device controller.

A key contribution of our work is to identify the specific sources of state corruptions and inconsistencies, determine which of those are most likely to prevent successful recovery, and devise mechanisms to overcome these problems. We have implemented and tested ReHype with the Xen[2] hypervisor and VMs running Linux. We use the results of fault injection to incrementally enhance[17] an initial basic version of ReHype. These incremental steps improve the rate of successful recovery from an initial 5.6% of detected faults to over 90% of detected faults. Our evaluation of the final scheme points to ways in which the success rate can be further improved.

ReHype builds upon the Otherworld[4] mechanism for microrebooting the Linux kernel while preserving process states and the RootHammer[12] mechanism for rejuvenation of the Xen hypervisor through a reboot while maintaining VM state without the overhead of saving VM memory images to persistent storage. Compared to Otherworld, the memory overhead for ReHype is significantly lower. Furthermore, while ReHype does not involve any changes to the VMs or the applications in the VMs, Otherworld requires modifications for system call retries and, in many cases, application-level "crash procedures" that are invoked upon recovery. Finally, we design and evaluate enhancements to the basic recovery mechanism in the context of a hypervisor, while Otherworld is focused on microrebooting of an OS kernel. RootHammer does deal with the Xen hypervisor and provides proactive rejuvenation. However, proactive rejuvenation is simpler since it does not address recovery from failure and thus does not deal with possible arbitrary corruptions and inconsistencies throughout the system.

The following section discusses the requirements and approaches to recover from a failed hypervisor. Section 3, describes the implementation of a version of ReHype that provides basic transparent hypervisor recovery but does not deal with many problems caused by state corruptions and inconsistencies. Incremental improvements to ReHype, based on fault injection results, are described in Section 4. The details of the experimental setup are presented in Section 5. Section 6 presents an analysis of the results for the final version of ReHype. Related work is discussed in Section 7.

2. Tolerating VMM Failure

Hardware faults or software bugs in the virtual machine monitor (VMM†) can cause the corruption of VMM state or the state of VMs. As a result, the VMM or individual VMs may crash, hang, or perform erroneous actions. The safest way to recover the system is to reboot the VMM and also reboot each of the VMs. However, this requires a lengthy recovery process and involves loss of the work in progress of applications running in the VMs. Periodic checkpointing of VMs can reduce the amount of lost work upon recovery but the work done since the last checkpoint is lost and there is performance overhead during normal operation for checkpointing. Alternative mechanisms involve less overhead and lost work but may result in recovery of only parts of the system or even a complete failure to recover a working system. This section discusses the basic design alternatives for mechanisms that can recover from VMM failure.

Virtualization is often used to consolidate the workloads of multiple physical servers on a single physical host. With multiple physical servers, a single software or transient hardware fault may cause the failure of one of the servers. An aggressive reliability goal for a virtualized system is to do no worse than a cluster of physical servers. Hence, if a transient hardware fault or a software fault in any component (including the VMM) affects only one VM running applications, the goal is met. Recovery from VMM failure that avoids losing work in progress in the VMs necessarily relies on utilizing the VM states at the time of failure detection. One or more of those VM states may be corrupted,

---

† The terms *hypervisor* and *VMM* are used interchangeably.

resulting in the failure of those VMs even if the rest of the system is restored to correct operation. Based on the reliability goal above, we define recovery from VMM failure to be successful if no more than one of the existing VMs running applications fails *and* the recovered VMM maintains its ability to host the other existing VMs as well as create and host new VMs.

Successfully "tolerating" VMM failure requires detection of such failures and successfully recovering from them, as defined above. To accomplish this goal, mechanisms must exist to: (1) detect VMM failure, (2) repair VMM corruption, and (3) resolve inconsistencies within the VMM, between the VMM and VMs, and between the VMM and the hardware. Detecting VMM failure boils down to being able to detect a VMM crash, hang, or silent data corruption, as described in Subsection 2.1. Subsection 2.2 discusses different approaches to repairing VMM corruption and the tradeoffs among them in terms of implementation complexity and expected success rates. Inconsistencies among the states of different components following recovery may be resolved entirely in the VMM or may require VM modifications. Details of the sources of inconsistencies and techniques for resolving inconsistencies are described in Subsection 2.3.

2.1. Detection

VMM failures can be manifested as VMM crashes, hangs, or silent corruption (arbitrary incorrect actions). Crashes can be detected using existing VMM panic and exception handlers. If the VMM panics, then a crash has occurred. Detecting VMM hangs requires external hardware. A typical hang detector, such as the one implemented in the Xen VMM, uses a watchdog timer that sends periodic interrupts to the VMM. The interrupt handler checks whether the VMM has performed certain actions since the last time the handler was invoked. If it has not, the handler signals a hang.

Silent VMM corruption is more difficult to detect. Detection mechanisms involve redundant (e.g., replicated) data structures and redundant computations (e.g., performing sanity checks). Fortunately, our fault injection results (Section 6) indicate that the majority of VMM failures (80%) are manifested as crashes and hangs and are thus detectable using the simple mechanisms discussed above. More extensive fault injection campaigns in the Linux kernel[7, 8] indicate that the fraction of VMM failures manifested as crashes or hangs is likely to be significantly higher.

2.2. Repairing VMM Corruption

Repair is initiated when the detection mechanism invokes a failure handler. Corrupted VMM state can then be repaired by either identifying and fixing the specific parts of the VMM state that are corrupted or simply booting a new VMM instance. A major difficulty with the first alternative is the requirement to identify which parts of the state are erroneous. This is likely to require significant overhead for maintaining redundant data structures. Furthermore, complex repair operations performed in the context of a failed VMM can increase the chance of failed recoveries[20]. Hence, we focus on the latter alternative.

Normally, a system reboot would cause the loss of all VM states. The simplest approach to preserve all VM states across a reboot is to checkpoint the VMs to stable storage in the failure handler. Once a fresh system boots up, the VMs can be restored. However, checkpointing VM state in the context of a failed VMM can increase the chance of failed recoveries since the VMM must perform I/O and access possibly corrupted structures that hold VM state. In addition, the space and time overhead of checkpointing can be large as the state of all VMs must be copied to stable storage.

An alternative approach to a system-wide reboot, is to microreboot[3] the VMM. In this approach, VM states are preserved in memory across the reboot. This avoids the space and time overhead of checkpointing VM states to stable storage. Once the new VMM has been booted, it must be re-integrated with the preserved VMs. This re-integration can be done by either recreating the VMM structures used to manage the VMs or reusing VMM structures preserved from the old VMM. Either way, some amount of VMM data needs to be preserved across a VMM reboot for the re-integration process.

Variations of the microreboot approach can be categorized based on whether the new VMM is rebooted in place or in a reserved memory area, and, regarding VMM structures for managing VMs, whether to reuse these structures from the old VMM instance or create new instances of these structures. The following paragraphs discuss these variations, their effect on the ability to successfully recover a VMM, and the implementation complexity involved.

The choices of whether to reboot the VMM in place or in a reserved memory area affects the operations that must be done in the failure handler. This, in turn, can affect the chances of a successful recovery. When the new VMM is booted in place, the failure handler must perform two operations: 1) preserve VMM state (data structures) needed for re-integration by copying it to a reserved memory location, and 2) overwrite the existing VMM image in memory with a new image. These two operations do not have to be performed if the new VMM is booted into a reserved memory area. There is no VMM state to copy since the new VMM is confined to the reserved memory area on boot so no old VMM memory state is lost. In addition, the new VMM image can be preloaded into the reserved memory area without affecting the operation of the current VMM. Performing fewer operations in the failure handler, as is the case when rebooting into a reserved area, can increase the chance of a successful recovery. However, as discussed below, the choice of booting the new VMM instance in a reserved memory area requires complex operations for the re-integration of the new VMM instance with the preserved VMs.

Since the state of the old VMM instance may be corrupted, the ability to successfully recover is directly related to the amount of data reused from the old VMM instance. In some cases, data structures in the new VMM instance can be re-initialized to static values (e.g., clearing all locks) or reconstructed from sources that are unlikely to be corrupted (e.g., obtaining the CPUID of a core from the hardware). However, some data structures are dynamically updated based on the activity of the system and cannot be re-initialized with static or "safe" values. For example, a corrupted VM page table can allow a VM access to the VMM or another VM's memory space.

Re-integrating the new VMM state with preserved VM states involves creating VMM structures that can manage the VMs.

This can be done by either directly reusing the preserved VMM structures from the old VMM instance or creating new instances of the structures and populating them with values from the old VMM instance. The first alternative is simpler to implement as only pointers to the preserved structures need to be restored in the new VMM instance. Implementation of the second alternative is more complex, as it requires deep copy of all the required structures from the old VMM and updating all pointers within those structures. With either of these alternatives there is a possibility of ending up with corrupted values in the new VMM's data structures. However, if the preserved structures are reused, there is a greater risk of also introducing into the new VMM instance corrupted pointers, which may lead to further corruption.

There is no perfect solution to the problem of ending up with corrupted values in the new VMM's data structures. As discussed above, some structures can be initialized with static or "safe" values. In other cases, data structures may be populated based on other data structures from the failed VMM instance, at least ensuring consistency (see Section 2.3). In general, the recovery process needs to ensure that all values that will be used by the new VMM instance are safe — will not lead to subsequent VMM failure. This may involve performing integrity checks, possibly requiring maintaining redundant information, such as logs, during normal operation.

Given the tradeoffs presented in this subsection, ReHype uses the microreboot approach and opts for a simple implementation that does not require major modifications to the VMM. Hence, ReHype preserves and reuses almost all of the VMM's dynamic memory but updates a few key data structures with "safe" values, as described in sections 3 and 4. The benefit of reusing most of the VMM's data structures is that it allowed ReHype to be easily integrated into a VMM (Xen in our case) with minor (880 LOC added/modified) modifications. Despite the reuse of old VMM data in ReHype, fault injection results show a high rate of successful recoveries (Section 6).

2.3. Resolving Inconsistencies

By design, the VMM is assumed to be reliable by the VMs and hardware. Typically, the VMM itself is, for the most part, implemented with the assumption that there are no hardware faults and no software faults in the VMM code. These assumptions are violated when the VMM fails. Thus, after recovery from a failed VMM, even if none of the states of the system components are corrupted, these states may be *inconsistent*, preventing the system from operating correctly.

The VMM executes some operations in critical sections to ensure atomicity, e.g. update a VM grant table. Atomicity can be violated when a VMM failure occurs in the middle of such critical sections. In such cases, some data structures may be partially updated, leading to inconsistencies within the VMM (VMM/VMM). The VMs expect the VMM to provide a monotonically increasing system time, handle hypercalls, and deliver interrupts. The hardware expects the VMM to acknowledge all interrupts it receives. When a VMM failure occurs, the assumption of a reliable VMM is violated and this can lead to inconsistencies between the VMM and VMs (VMM/VM) and between the VMM and hardware (VMM/hardware). The recovery process must resolve these inconsistencies so that the virtualized system can continue to operate correctly. The following paragraphs discuss in more detail these inconsistencies and the techniques for resolving them.

Sources of VMM/VMM inconsistencies include partially updated structures, unreleased locks, and memory leaks. The options for resolving these inconsistencies are, essentially, special cases of the options for dealing with state corruption, discussed in the previous subsection. Resolving inconsistencies caused by partially updated structures requires either reconstructing the data structures using information from the failed VMM or using redundant information logged prior to failure to fix the new VMM's state. A scheduler's run queue is an example of a data structure for which the former technique can be used. Inconsistency can occur if a VCPU becomes runnable but the VMM fails before inserting it into the run queue. Resolving this inconsistency requires re-initializing the run queue to empty upon bootup and re-inserting all runnable VCPUs (obtained from the failed VMM) into the run queue. For other data structures, such as the ones that track memory page usage information, reconstruction is more difficult so the latter technique may be preferable. For instance, an inconsistency can occur if a failure happens right when a page use counter has been updated but before that page has been added to a page table. Resolving this inconsistency by traversing all page table entries to count the actual mappings to that page can be done but is complex and slow. Instead, the entire mapping operation can be made atomic with respect to failure using *write-ahead logging*, involving a small overhead during normal operation and simple, fast correction of any inconsistencies upon recovery.

Locks and semaphores that are acquired prior to VMM failure must be released (re-initialized to a static value) upon recovery to allow the system to reacquire them when needed. In order to do so, all locks and semaphores must be tracked and re-initialized in data structures that are reused or copied from the failed VMM.

A memory leak can occur if a failure happens between allocation and freeing of a memory region in the VMM. Such a memory leak is benign if the leaked region is small. After VMM recovery, the system can be scheduled to be rebooted to reclaim leaked memory. Alternatively, leveraging work by Kourai and Chiba[13], after recovery, the virtualized system can be quickly rejuvenated to get rid of any memory leaks.

Sources of VMM/VM inconsistency include non-monotonically increasing system time, partially executed hypercalls, and undelivered virtual interrupts. The correct operation of many VMs depends on a monotonically increasing system time. In a virtualized system, the VMs' source of time is the VMM. When a VMM is rebooted, its time keeping structures are reset, potentially resulting in a time source for VMs that is not monotonically increasing. In addition, such a reset can result in timer events set using time relative to the VMM's system time prior to recovery to be delayed. One technique for resolving this inconsistency is to simply save the VMM time structures upon failure and restore those structures after the VMM reboot and before the VMs are scheduled to run. This allows time to continue moving forward with no interruption visible by the VMs.

When the VMM recovers from a failure, partially executed hypercalls must be re-executed. Our experimental results show that, at least for the hypercalls that were exercised by our target system, simply retrying hypercalls does work most of the time and allows VMs to continue to operate. In general, hypercalls that are not idempotent may fail on a retry, in which case the VM executing the hypercall may also fail.

Hypercall retry can be implemented by modifying the VM to add a "wrapper" around hypercall invocation that will re-invoke the hypercall if a retry value is returned by the VMM. The VMM must also be modified to return a retry value indicating a partially executed hypercall. This approach allows the VMs more control over which hypercalls to retry and allows the VMs to gracefully fail if a hypercall retry is unsuccessful.

Hypercall retry can be implemented without modifying the VMs. To force re-execution of a hypercall after recovery, the VMM adjusts the VM's instruction pointer to point back to the hypercall instruction (usually a trapping instruction). When the VM is scheduled to run, the very next instruction it executes will be the hypercall. This mechanism is already used in the Xen [2] VMM to allow the preemption of long running hypercalls transparently to the VMs.

The VMM is responsible for delivering interrupts from hardware and event signals from other VMs as virtual interrupts to the destination VM. These virtual interrupts may be lost if the VMM fails. Some inconsistencies of this type can be resolved without any modifications to the system by relying on existing timeout mechanisms that are implemented in the kernels and device drivers of the VMs. A timeout handler can resend commands to a device or resignal another VM if an expected interrupt does not arrive within a specified period of time. We have verified that timeout mechanisms exist for the Linux SCSI block driver (used for SATA disks) and the Intel E1000 NIC driver, representing the most important devices for servers (storage and network controllers). Obviously, such timeout mechanisms do not deal with lost interrupts from unsolicited sources, such as packet reception from a network device. However, at least for network devices, the problem is ultimately resolved by existing higher-level end-to-end protocols (e.g., TCP).

A source of VMM/hardware inconsistency is unacknowledged interrupts. Interrupt controllers will block an interrupt source until the previous interrupt from that source has been acknowledged by the processor. Since VMM failure can occur at any time, pending interrupts may never get acknowledged, thus blocking the interrupt source indefinitely. If VMM recovery is done without performing a hardware reset, a mechanism is needed to either reset the I/O controller or to acknowledge all pending interrupts during recovery. In the case of acknowledging pending interrupts, the interrupt source must be blocked at the interrupt controller before the interrupt is acknowledged to prevent another interrupt from slipping by before the VMM is ready to handle the interrupt.

3. Transparent VMM Microreboot

We have implemented a ReHype prototype for version 3.3.0 of the Xen [2] VMM. This section describes the implementation of a version of ReHype that provides the basic capability to microreboot the VMM while preserving the running VMs and allowing them to resume normal execution following the microreboot. Improvements to the basic scheme that enhance recovery success rates are discussed in Section 4. So far, ReHype has been evaluated and validated only with paravirtualized VMs. However, based on preliminary experimentation, we expect the current ReHype implementation, with few or no modifications, to operate successfully with fully-virtualized VMs.

To microreboot the VMM, ReHype uses the existing Xen port of the Kdump[6] tool. Kdump is a kernel debugging tool that provides facilities to allow a crashed system to load a pristine kernel image, in this case the VMM image, on top of the existing image and directly transfer control to it. The Kdump tool by itself, however, does not provide any facilities to preserve parts of memory, such as those holding VM states. The burden of memory preservation is on the kernel or VMM being booted.

A VMM microreboot is differentiated from a normal VMM boot by the value of a global flag added to the initialized data segment of Xen. The flag is clear in the original VMM image on disk but is set after loading the recovery image to memory using the Kdump tool upon initial system boot. All the modifications to the bootup process described henceforth refer to actions performed when the flag is set (the microreboot path).

On boot, the stock Xen VMM initializes the entire system memory and allocates memory for its own use. The modifications for ReHype must ensure that, upon recovery, the new VMM instance preserves the memory used by VMs and memory that was used by the previous VMM instance to hold state needed for managing the VMs. Hence, as described in Subsection 3.1, the ReHype version of the Xen VMM allocates "around" the preserved memory regions during a VMM microreboot. When the new VMM instance is booted and initialized, it does not contain information about the running VMs, and thus has no way to run and manage them. Subsection 3.2 describes how the VMM and VM states preserved during VMM recovery are re-integrated with the new VMM instance.

3.1. Preserving VMM and VM States

The state that must be preserved across a VMM microreboot includes information in the VMM's static data segments, the VMM's heap, the structure in the VMM that holds information about each machine page, and special segments that are normally used only during VMM bootup.

VMM microreboot involves overwriting the existing VMM image (code, initialized data, and bss) with a pristine image. The VMM's static data segments (initialized data and bss) contain critical information needed for the operation of the system following bootup of the new VMM instance. For example, this includes interrupt descriptors and pointers to structures on the Xen heap, such as Domain 0's VM structure and the list of domains. Hence, some of the information in the old static data segments must be preserved. While it is only necessary to preserve a subset of the static data segments, since they are relatively small, we reduce the implementation complexity by preserving the segments in their entirety.

Figure 1 shows the memory layout for Xen, as modified for ReHype. In particular, the bss segment is extended by approximately 1MB — sufficient space to hold complete copies of the original bss and initialized data segments. This is done by

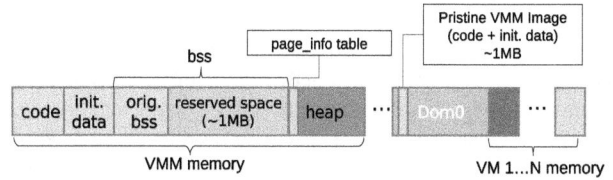

Figure 1: Layout of system memory for ReHype.

changing the linker script used for creation of the Xen image. Since the area reserved is in the bss segment, no extra disk space is taken up for the new VMM image. The bss segment only takes up space when it is loaded into memory. Upon failure detection, before initiating a VMM microreboot, the failure handler copies the initialized data and (unextended) bss segments to this new reserved memory.

As discussed above, for each VM, the state that must be preserved includes both the VM's memory image and parts of the VMM state used to manage the VM. Since this information is maintained on the VMM's heap, the VMM's heap must be preserved. Preserving the VMM's heap requires modifications of the VMM's bootup code. During VMM initialization, before the heap is created, the old heap (from the previous VMM instance) is walked to identify all the free pages. When the new heap is created and populated with free pages, only pages that are free in the old heap are added to the new heap. This ensures that the new VMM will not allocate (overwrite) any pages that are still in use. To access the old heap, the page table from the old VMM must be restored. This requires copying the old page directory from the old bss segment, preserved as discussed above, to the new bss segment.

The Xen VMM maintains a structure (page_info) that holds information about each machine page, such as the page ownership and use count. For all the pages that are preserved across a VMM microreboot, the information in this structure must be preserved. This structure is allocated in a special memory area, between the bss segment and the heap. The VMM bootup code was modified to avoid initializing the page_info entries for pages that are not free.

The stock Xen VMM image includes two static segments (init.text and init.data) that are normally used during bootup and then freed to the heap so that they can be used for other purposes. Hence, with stock Xen, a microreboot would overwrite these segments, potentially corrupting data in pages that had been reallocated. To prevent this problem, the bootup code (normal and microreboot) has been modified to avoid freeing these pages. This results is an extra 100KB memory overhead.

Preserving the heap and static data segments of a failed VMM is unsafe — it can result in recovery failure if those preserved values are corrupted by the failed VMM. Section 4 will discuss mechanisms that dramatically improve the chances of successful recoveries despite re-using the preserved heap and static data segments.

3.2. Re-integrating VMM and VM States

Following a VMM microreboot, the VMM does not have the information required to resume execution and manage the VMs that were running at the time of failure. The missing system state includes the list of VMs it was managing, the system time that was provided to the VMs, information for interrupt routing (to processors) and forwarding (to VMs), and timer events that were scheduled by the VMs. To allow the virtualized system to continue running, these components of the system state must be restored. As discussed in the previous subsection, all the required state is preserved across a VMM microreboot. Hence, all that is needed is to re-integrate the preserved information with the new VMM instance. This re-integration is accomplished by copying a few key values from the old static data segments to the new static data segments. The restoration is done before the VMs can be scheduled to run. The following structures must be restored:

• Pointer to xmalloc free list: prevent memory leaks.
• Pointers to the domain list and hash table: allow Xen to access the state of the running VMs.
• Pointer to the Domain 0 descriptor: since Domain 0 is not rebooted as part of recovery, the pointer to it must be restored to allow Xen access to the Domain 0 structure.
• Pointers to timer event objects: restore pending timer events on the old timer heap to the new timer heap.
• Pointer to the machine-to-physical (m2p) mapping table: make available mapping of machine frame numbers to physical frame numbers.
• System time variables: maintain monotonically increasing time. The time-stamp counter (TSC) must not be reset.
• IRQ descriptor table and IO-APIC entries, including correct IRQ routing affinity and mask: allow VMs to continue to receive interrupts from their devices.
• Structures for tracking the mappings of pages shared between VMs and the VMM: prevents overwriting mappings that are still in use.

There are two additional differences between the VMM microreboot path and a normal VMM boot: Domain 0 is not created and VMs are re-associated with the scheduler. The bootup code has been modified to skip Domain 0 creation and to restore the Domain 0's global pointer so that the new Xen can access Domain 0's state. VMs are re-associated with the VMM's scheduler by invoking the scheduling initialization routines for each VM and inserting runnable VCPUs into the new run queue.

Some of the structures needed by the VMM are re-created during a microreboot. These include the idle domain as well as structures holding hardware information such as the model and type of the CPU and the amount of memory available. For structures that are re-created on the heap, ReHype prevents a memory leak by first freeing the old structures.

4. Improving Recovery

The scheme presented in the previous section provides basic capabilities for VMM microreboot. However, as explained below, with this basic mechanism the probability of successful recovery is very low. The section starts with the basic scheme and incrementally improves on that scheme to achieve higher recovery success rates. Table 1 shows the mechanisms used to improve the basic recovery scheme. As in [17], the choice of improvements is guided by results from fault injection experiments.

We used software-implemented fault injection to introduce errors into CPU registers when the VMM is executing. The goal of the injection was to cause arbitrary failures in the VMM and

Table 1. Improvements over the basic ReHype recovery.

Mechanism	Description
NMI IPI	Use NMI IPIs in failure handler. Avoid IPI blocking by failed VMM.
Acknowledge interrupts	Acknowledges all pending interrupts in all processors to avoid blocked interrupts after recovery.
Hypercall retry	All partially executed hypercalls are retried transparently to the VMs.
FixSP	Stack pointer set to "safe" value in failure handler.
NMI "ack"	Execute iret to "ack" NMI when hang detected on non-CPU0.
Reinitialize locks	Dynamically allocated spin locks and non-spin locks are unlocked.
Reset page counter	Reset page use counter based on page validation bit.

evaluate the effectiveness of different recovery mechanisms. Two system setups were used: 1AppVM and 3AppVM. The 1AppVM setup was comprised of two VMs: Domain 0, the *Privileged VM* (PrivVM), and an Application VM (AppVM) running a disk I/O (block) benchmark. This setup was used to quickly identify major short comings with the recovery mechanisms. The more complex 3AppVM system setup, shown in Figure 2, was used to further stress the virtualized system, once the majority of sources of failed recoveries had been fixed. In this setup, AppVM2 is designed to boot after VMM recovery. This is a check of whether the recovered virtualized system maintains the ability to create new VMs.

Table 2. Injection outcomes.

Outcome	Description
Detected VMM failure	Crash: VMM panics due to unrecoverable exceptions Hang: VMM no longer makes observable progress
Silent failure	Undetected failure: No VMM crash/hang detected but applications in one or more VMs fail to complete successfully
Non-manifested	No errors observed

Table 2 summarizes the possible outcomes from an injected fault (injection experiment). Only detected VMM failures lead to VMM recoveries. With the 1AppVM setup, a recovery is considered successful if the benchmark in the AppVM completes correctly. With the 3AppVM setup, following the explanation in Section 2, a recovery is considered successful if either AppVM0 or AppVM1 completes its benchmark correctly and AppVM2 is able to boot and run its benchmark to completion without errors. Silent failures, discussed in Section 6, do not trigger VMM recovery and are thus excluded from further discussion in this section. Details of the experimental setup, fault injection campaign, and failure detection mechanisms are in Section 5.

In the rest of this section, each version of the recovery

Table 3. Fault injection results for 1AppVM system setup. Percentage of successful recoveries out of detected VMM failures (VMM crash/hang).

Mechanism	Successful Recovery Rate
Basic	5.6%
+ NMI IPI	17.6%
+ Ack interrupts	48.6%
+ Hypercall retry	62.6%
+ FixSP+NMI "ack"	77.0%
+ Reinitialize locks	95.8%

scheme is described, and fault injection results are presented. This is followed by an analysis of the main cause of failed recoveries, motivating the next version of the recovery scheme. At each step, only the problem that leads to the plurality of failed recoveries is analyzed and fixed. Table 3 summarizes the rate of successful recoveries with the basic ReHype scheme and the various incremental improvements that are made.

Basic: As shown in Table 3, with the Basic recovery scheme (Section 3), the successful recovery rate is only 5.6%. A large fraction of recovery failures (44%) occur because the failure handler is unable to initiate the VMM microreboot. Normally, the failure handler relies on interprocessor interrupts (IPIs) to force all processors to save VM CPU state and halt execution before microrebooting the VMM. Microrebooting the VMM cannot proceed until all processors execute the IPI handler. Therefore, the failure handler is stuck if a processor is unable to execute the IPI handler due to a blocked IPI or memory corruption.

NMI IPI: To get around the above problem, NMI IPIs can be used. In addition, a spin lock protecting a structure used to set up an IPI function call must be busted to prevent the failure handler from getting stuck.

Table 3 shows an increase in recovery success rate to 17.6% when these fixes are used. Only 8.2% of the failures are now caused by an inability to initiate the VMM microreboot. The plurality of the remaining failures (45%) are due to interrupts from the block device not getting delivered to the PrivVM. This causes the block device driver in the PrivVM to time out, thus leading to the failure of block requests from the AppVM.

The block device uses level-triggered interrupts. For such interrupts, the I/O controller blocks further interrupts until an acknowledgment from the processor arrives. If the VMM fails before acknowledging pending interrupts, those level-triggered interrupts remain blocked after recovery.

Acknowledge interrupts: To prevent level-triggered interrupts from being blocked, the failure handler must acknowledge all pending interrupts on all processors. This must be done in the failure handler since information about pending interrupts are cleared after a CPU reset during a VMM reboot.

Table 3 shows that when this mechanism is added, the successful recovery rate jumps to 48.6%. Of the remaining unsuccessful recoveries, 52.8% are caused by a crashed AppVM or PrivVM after recovery. The crashes are caused by bad return values from hypercalls. Since VMM failures can occur in the middle of a hypercall, it is necessary to be able to transparently continue the hypercall after recovery. Without mechanisms to do

this, after recovery, the VM starts executing right after the hypercall, using whatever is currently in the EAX register as the return value.

Hypercall retry: The ability to restart a hypercall is already provided in Xen. The mechanism involves changing the program counter (PC) of the VCPU to the address of the instruction that invokes the hypercall. For each VM, the VMM determines whether a hypercall retry is needed after the VMM microreboot, before loading the VM state. Specifically, for each VCPU, the VMM checks if the VCPU's PC is within the VM's hypercall page. If so, the VMM updates the VCPU's PC. Arguments to the hypercall are already preserved in the VM VCPU state.

Table 3 shows that, with hypercall retry, the successful recovery rate is 62.6%. Out of the remaining unsuccessful recoveries, 41% are caused by the same symptom encountered and partially solved with the Basic scheme — the inability of the failure handler to initiate the VMM microreboot. With the improved recovery rate, the causes of this symptom not previously resolved are now responsible for the plurality of failed recoveries.

The experimental results show two causes for the symptom above: 1) NMI IPIs sent to the wrong destination CPU due to stack pointer corruption and 2) NMIs are blocked due to NMI-based watchdog hang detection. Problem (1) occurs because a corrupted stack pointer is used to obtain the CPUID of the currently running processor. The obtained CPUID is incorrect and is, in turn, used to create a CPU destination mask for the NMI IPI. This mask can end up containing the sending processor as one of the destination CPUs. The result of this is that an IPI is incorrectly sent to the sending processor. This IPI is dropped and the sender waits forever for the completion of the IPI handling.

Problem (2) is due to the fact that NMI delivery is blocked if a CPU is in the middle of handling a previous NMI — an *iret* instruction matching a previous NMI has not been executed [10]. The Xen hang detector is based on periodic NMIs from a watchdog timer. If a hang is detected on a processor, that processor immediately executes the panic handler and never executes an *iret* instruction. This prevents the processor from getting an NMI IPI from the boot processor to initiate recovery.

FixSP+NMI "ack": Problem (1) above can be fixed by not relying on the stack pointer to obtain the CPUID during failure handling. Instead the CPUID can be obtained by first reading the APICID from the CPU and then converting the APICID to CPUID by using an existing APICID to CPUID mapping structure stored in the static data segment of Xen. With this technique, the VMM has a chance to continue with the recovery despite a corrupted stack pointer. However, the corrupted stack pointer can cause critical problems that are unrelated to the CPUID. Specifically, the handler invoked when VMM failure is detected must save VCPU registers (located on the stack) into preserved VMM state. A corrupted stack pointer leads to saving the contents of a random region in memory as the saved VCPU register values. This can cause the VMM to crash after recovery when trying to restore the corrupted (incorrect) values to VCPU registers. Specifically, when attempting to load the saved VCPU registers after recovery, the VMM may try to restore a corrupted value as the VCPU code segment register. This may cause the VMM to continue executing with VMM privilege using corrupted (incorrect) register values.

ReHype implements a solution to Problem (1) above that avoids the deficiency described in the previous paragraph. Specifically, the failure handler, invoked upon VMM failure, sets the stack pointer to a "safe" value. This can be done based on the observation that the failure handler never returns, and therefore, the stack pointer can be reset to any valid stack location. The address of the bottom of the stack is kept by Xen in a static data area. The stack pointer is set to that value minus sufficient space for local variables used by the failure handler.

Problem (2) above is resolved by forcing the execution of *iret* in the failure handler. The stack is manipulated so that the *iret* instruction returns directly to the failure handler code.

With the two improvements above, the rate of successful recoveries is 77.0%. The majority of the increase is due to fixing the stack pointer. Since hangs are responsible for only a small fraction (7.1%) of detected VMM failures, the impact of fixing problem (2) on the overall recovery success rate is small. However, with this fix, there was successful recovery from all hangs detected in this experiment.

Out of the remaining unsuccessful recoveries, 82.8% are due to spin locks being held after recovery. Spin locks that are statically allocated are re-initialized on boot but locks that are on the heap are not. This causes the VMM to hang immediately after recovery.

Reinitialize locks: Re-initializing dynamically-allocated spin locks requires tracking the allocation and de-allocation of these locks. All locks that are still allocated upon recovery are initialized to unlocked state. This tracking of spin locks is the only extra work that ReHype must perform during normal operation. The associated performance overhead is negligible since the allocation and de-allocation of spin locks is normally done only as part of VM creation and destruction. Furthermore, there are only about 20 spin locks that are tracked per VM.

Locking mechanisms that are not spin locks must also be re-initialized to their free states. A key example of this are the page lock bits used to protect access to bookkeeping information of pages. With the previous version of the recovery scheme, not initializing these bits resulted in 10% of unsuccessful recoveries.

As shown in Table 3, re-initializing locks increases successful recovery rate to 95.8%. For the remaining recovery failures there is not one dominant cause.

While the 1AppVM system setup is useful for uncovering the main problems with the Basic ReHype recovery, it is very simple, thus potentially hiding important additional problems. To better stress the virtualized system, the rest of the experiments in this section use the 3AppVM setup. The results with this setup are summarized in Table 4.

As shown in Table 4, with the 3AppVM setup, the reinitialize locks mechanism results in a recovery success rate of 90.2%. Hence, there is a small decrease in the success rate compared to the 1AppVM setup. Out of the remaining recovery failures, 25% are due to the VMM hanging immediately after recovery. This problem is caused by a data inconsistency resulting from a VMM failure while in the middle of handling a page table update hypercall. This hypercall promotes an unused VM page frame into a page table type by incrementing a page type use counter and performing validity check on the page frame. After the

Table 4. Fault injection results using 3AppVM system setup. Percentage of successful recoveries out of detected VMM failures (VMM crash/hang).

Mechanisms	Successful Recovery Rate
Reinitialize locks	90.2%
+ Reset page counter	94.3%

validity check, a validity bit is set to indicate that the page can be used as a page table for the VM. Inconsistency arises when a VMM failure occurs before the validity check is completed but after the page type use counter has been incremented. When the hypercall is retried after recovery, since the page use counter is not zero and the validity bit is not set, it assumes validation is in progress and waits by spinning. Of course, there is no validation taking place, and the CPU is declared hung by the hang detector.

Reset page counter: To fix the above problem, code is added during VMM bootup to check the consistency between the validity bit and page use counter. If the page use counter is non-zero but the validity bit is not set, then the page use counter is set to zero.

With the page counter fix employed, recovery success rate improves to 94.3% The remaining causes of failed recoveries vary widely and are discussed in more detail in Section 6.

5. Experimental Setup

This section presents the experimental setup used to evaluate the ReHype prototype. It discusses details of the target virtualized system, the benchmarks running in the Application VMs (AppVMs), the VMM failure detection mechanisms (that trigger recovery), and the fault injection campaign.

The evaluation of ReHype was done on a system comprising of the Xen VMM, augmented with ReHype, hosting multiple paravirtualized VMs. To simplify the setup for software-implemented fault injection, the target system was run inside a fully-virtualized (FV) VM [14]. This made it easy to restart the target system and refresh its disk images after each injection run to isolate the effects of faults injected in different runs.

As mentioned in Section 4, two system configurations were used: 1AppVM and 3AppVM. With the 1AppVM configuration, the system hosts two VMs: a PrivVM (Domain 0) and a single AppVM. The AppVM runs the *blkbench* benchmark, described below, which continuously performs disk I/O (block) operations. The PrivVM hosts the block backend for the AppVM. Each of the VMs consists of one virtual CPU (VCPU) that is pinned to its own physical CPU (PCPU).

The 3AppVM configuration is shown in Figure 2. In this configuration, the PrivVM's root filesystem is in memory and the PrivVM does not access any devices. A separate Driver VM (DVM)[15] has direct access to the network and SCSI controllers and serves as the network backend for AppVM0 and block backend for AppVM2. AppVM1 has direct access to the IDE controller, and thus does not rely on the DVM for any device access. Each VM consists of one VCPU which is pinned to its own PCPU. To check whether the recovered system maintains its

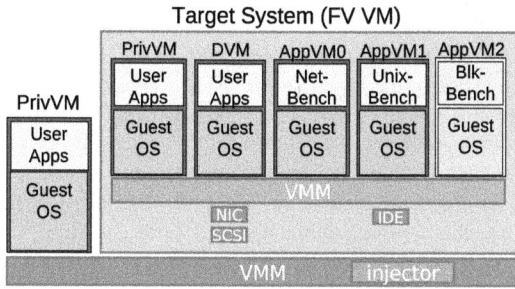

Figure 2: System configuration for 3AppVM. AppVM2 created after recovery.

ability to create new VMs, AppVM2 is designed to boot up after a possible VMM recovery and run the *blkbench* benchmark.

Three application benchmarks are used in our experiments: *netbench*, *blkbench*, and *UnixBench*. *Netbench* is a user-level *ping* program that exercises the interface to the network. It consists of two processes: one running inside an AppVM (the *receiving host*), and another running on a separate physical machine (the *sending host*). Every 1ms the sending host transmits a UDP packet to the receiving host, which, upon receiving this packet, transmits UDP packet back to the sending host. Unsuccessful application completion occurs when the packet reception rate on the *sending host* drops below a threshold (450 packets per second).

Blkbench stresses the interface to the block device (disk) by creating directories and creating, removing, and copying 1MB files. To ensure block activity, this benchmark prevents caching of block and filesystem data inside the AppVM's OS. Unsuccessful application completion occurs when the application reports an error (failed system call) or the resulting disk image when the benchmark completes differs from a reference image.

The third benchmark (*UnixBench*) is a subset of the set of programs in UnixBench [1] with minor modifications to improve logging and failure detection. The selected programs were chosen for their abilities to stress the VMM's handling of hypercalls such as virtual memory management and process scheduling. Unsuccessful application completion occurs when one or more programs in UnixBench terminate prematurely due to failed system calls or the resulting program output differs from a reference output.

As summarized in Table 2, the outcome of each injection run is classified as: detected (VMM crash/hang), silent (undetected failure), or non-manifested. A crash occurs when the VMM panics due to unrecoverable exceptions. Hangs are detected using a watchdog mechanism built into Xen. Specifically, Xen maintains a watchdog counter that is supposed to be incremented by a normal timer event every 500ms. A watchdog NMI is generated every 500ms of unhalted CPU cycles. If the watchdog NMI handler detects that the watchdog counter has not been incremented for 2s, the system is declared hung.

A silent VMM failure occurs when no VMM hang or crash is detected but the applications (benchmarks) in one or more AppVMs fail to complete successfully. What constitutes unsuccessful completion is application specific and is discussed above. Non-manifested means that no errors are observed.

We used the UCLA *Gigan* fault injector [14, 9] to evaluate

ReHype. Gigan can reside in the VMM and inject many types of faults into the VMs and the VMM. Injection into VMs can be done without any modifications to the VMs. With the ReHype evaluation setup, the entire target system is in an FV VM so the injection does not require any modifications (intrusion) of the target system. Single bit-flip faults were injected into the registers of the processors during the execution of VMM code. While these injected faults do not accurately represent all possible faults, they are a good choice since transient hardware faults in CPU logic and memory are likely to be manifested as erroneous values in registers. Furthermore, these faults can cause arbitrary corruptions in the entire system. Hence, this limited fault injection satisfies the main goal of the evaluation, which is to "stress" the recovery mechanisms in order to identify problem areas. There is a possibility that some problem areas remain and will be uncovered only by a more comprehensive fault injection campaign. This will be investigated in future work.

A fault injection campaign consists of many fault injection runs. A single fault injection run that uses the 1AppVM system configuration consists of first booting the VMM along with the PrivVM and AppVM. The AppVM begins running the blkbench benchmark and a fault is injected into the VMM. The injection campaign infrastructure allows the target system sufficient time for the VMM to recover and for the benchmark to complete. If the benchmark does not complete, a timeout mechanism identifies system failure. At the end of each run, fault injection logs and benchmark output are retrieved and stored for analysis.

An injection run using the 3AppVM configuration is similar to the 1AppVM configuration except that an injection is performed only after the VMM, PrivVM, DVM, AppVM0, and AppVM1 have been booted and the two AppVMs have started running their respective benchmarks. 9s after the two AppVMs begin running their benchmarks, AppVM2 is booted to run its own benchmark. The injection run ends when all three AppVMs complete their benchmark runs or a timeout occurs.

An injection is triggered after a random time period between 500ms to 6.5s after the AppVMs begin running their benchmarks. To ensure that the injection occurs only when the VMM is executing, a fault is only injected after the designated time has elapsed and 0 to 20,000 VMM instructions, chosen at random, have been executed. The injection is a single bit-flip into a randomly selected bit of a randomly selected register. The target registers include general purpose registers, instruction and stack pointer registers, and the system flags register. Each injection selects randomly among the VCPUS of the target system.

6. Analysis

This section analyzes fault injection results for the final version of ReHype, with all the recovery improvements from Section 4. We discuss: I) the impact of the distribution of injections across CPUs, II) the causes of AppVM failure in the successful VMM recoveries that result in single AppVM failure, and III) the causes of VMM recovery failures and silent system failures.

It is expected that faults in a CPU that rarely executes VMM code are less likely to lead to VMM failures than faults in a CPU that executes a larger fraction of VMM code. Due to different activities on different VMs, the execution time of VMM code is not evenly distributed across the CPUs hosting these VMs. However, for the fault injection results presented so far, injections were uniformly distributed across CPUs. Hence, it is critical to evaluate whether the results are qualitatively different if the distribution of fault injections is adjusted to match the fraction of time each CPU spends executing VMM code.

We use the Xenoprof profiler [16] to measure the distribution of Xen execution time across CPUs when running the 3AppVM setup. As explained in Section 5, each VM is pinned to a CPU. The results are as follows: 7.5% PrivVM CPU, 11.7% DVM CPU, 5.1% AppVM0 (NetBench) CPU, and 75.6% AppVM1 (UnixBench) CPU. The AppVM2 CPU is not included in the profile because it is created after the injection.

Table 5. Fault injection results for the final version of ReHype with injections distributed across CPUs uniformly or weighted by VMM execution time. Percentage of successful recoveries are out of detected VMM failures. Percentage of silent failures are out of manifested faults.

Distribution of Injections Across CPUs	Manifested		
	Detected	Silent	Silent
	Successful Recovery Rate	Single AppVM Failure	System Failure
Uniform	94.3%	6.0%	14.0%
Weighted	94.5%	6.6%	11.3%

Table 5 shows the injection results using the uniform distribution across CPUs and when injection distribution is weighted VMM execution time. The results are very similar. This is due to a combination of two factors. First, the fraction of injected faults leading to detected VMM failures is approximately the same across the four CPUs (24%-27%). Second, under uniform distribution of injections, 5.7% of detected VMM failures result in unsuccessful recoveries. Considering only injections into AppVM1, the corresponding number is almost the same — 5.2%. Hence, with the weighted distribution of injections, most of the injections are applied to a CPU whose behavior with respect to injection closely matches the behavior of the overall system under uniform distribution of injections. Since results from the two injection distributions are very similar, the rest of the analysis in this section is based on the uniform distribution results.

As explained in Section 2, VMM recovery that leads to the failure of only a single AppVM is considered successful. However, it is clearly preferable for none of the AppVMs to fail. In our experiments, a single AppVM fails to correctly execute its application in 32.6% of successful recoveries. The vast majority of such cases are due to the failure of netbench in AppVM0. The failure of netbench is caused by blocked network interrupts at the I/O controller after recovery, preventing netbench from receiving additional packets from the sender host. Unfortunately, the *acknowledge interrupts* mechanism discussed in Section 4 cannot be used to solve this problem. To acknowledge an interrupt, the CPU must be currently servicing that interrupt. However, a VMM failure can occur after an I/O controller delivers an interrupt to the CPU but before the CPU begins servicing the interrupt. Thus, upon recovery, the CPU cannot acknowledge the interrupt, leaving

the interrupt blocked at the I/O controller. To resolve this problem, there needs to be a way to clear pending interrupt states in the I/O controller without performing a full hardware reset. Based on code in the Linux kernel and Xen, there is a way to do this (simulating an interrupt acknowledgment by setting the interrupt trigger mode to edge then back to level). However, this has not worked with our experimental setup, where the entire target system is running in an FV VM. We plan to further investigate this approach in future work.

ReHype failed to recover the VMM in only 5.7% of detected failures. Approximately 50% of failed recoveries are caused by three problems: (1) failure of the PrivVM or DVM, preventing successful completion of applications in more than one AppVM, (2) a triple fault exception generated during the execution of the failure handler triggering a hardware system reset, and (3) a combination of problems causing the failure of both the unixbench and netbench to complete successfully. The following paragraphs discuss these three problems in more detail.

Failures of the PrivVM and DVM in problem (1) are due to kernel panics in the VMs caused by state corruption and error return values from hypercalls. Problem (1) can be partly resolved by providing mechanisms to recover a PrivVM or DVM from failures. DVM recovery has been previously explored in non-VMM failure context [5, 15, 11]. A simple DVM recovery scheme would include destroying the failed DVM, booting a new DVM in its place, and restoring device access to the AppVMs. PrivVM recovery can potentially be done in a similar way. However, unlike DVM recovery, recovering the PrivVM would require preserving configurations of running VMs to allow the PrivVM the ability to continue managing the VMs after recovery.

A double fault exception is generated if a fault is triggered while trying to invoke an exception handler. A triple fault exception is generated if a fault is triggered while trying to invoke the double fault handler. Problem (2) above prevents the failure handler from completing because a triple fault exception is generated. Normally, this causes the hardware to perform a system reset. With our setup, the VMM hosting our target system in an FV VM performs an FV VM reset. This problem may be caused by corruption of VMM state while executing the failure handler. Corruptions can affect the interrupt descriptor table or the page directory, which can lead to a triple fault exception. There is evidence that the frequency of this problem could be reduced by simplifying the failure handler, possibly including the elimination of output of debugging information.

Problem (3) is caused by two independent problems that prevented AppVM0 (netbench) and AppVM1 (unixbench) from finishing their respective applications. The first problem is caused by the blocking of network interrupts at the I/O controller after recovery, preventing the netbench from continuing correctly. This is the same problem described above with respect to successful recoveries resulting in one failed AppVM. The second problem is caused by a panic in AppVM1's kernel after receiving an error return value from a hypercall, preventing the unixbench from completing correctly. The error return value may be caused by inconsistencies within the VMM, and as discussed in Subsection 2.3, may require maintaining redundant information during normal operations to resolve. Fixing either problem should improve overall successful recoveries.

The remaining recovery failures are caused by various VMM corruptions and inconsistencies. Some of the causes of these failures include: (1) corruption of VM's VCPU registers causing the new VMM to crash after recovery when restoring the VCPU, (2) corruption of the timer heap which leads to a page fault in the VMM when the old timer heap is walked to restore timer events, and (3) page table corruption that causes the new VMM to page fault early in the boot code. These problems require mechanisms to check and ensure these data are "safe" to use as discussed in Subsection 2.2. Checks are needed to ensure that critical VCPU register values are consistent, e.g. code segment contains the correct privilege, pointers in the timer heap are valid, and page tables contain well formed entries before using or restoring them.

VMM corruptions can lead to failures that are not detectable by simple crash and hang detectors. These silent failures can manifest as failures of one or more VMs and/or failure of the VMM to host additional VMs. As discussed in Section 2, the reliability goal of ReHype is met if no more than one AppVM fails due to a fault and the VMM can still host existing VMs and create new VMs. In the case of a silent single AppVM failure, the reliability goal is met. However, silent system failures, which are silent VMM failures that result in more than one VM failure and/or the failure of the VMM to host additional VMs, reduce the reliability of the virtualized system. Hence, the rest of this section discusses the causes of these failures.

In our experiments, silent VMM failures are roughly 20% of all manifested failures. However, only 14% cause system failures (Table 5). The remaining 6% cause a benchmark (netbench or unixbench) in a single AppVM to complete incorrectly. This can be caused by a failed hypercall causing a VM kernel panic or a blocked interrupt. Roughly 60% of silent system failures are caused by a hardware system reset due to a triple fault exception. Unlike the triple fault exceptions discussed above that occurred during the execution of the failure handler, in these cases, there are no clear indications whether the failure handler ever executed. Simplifying the failure handler, as described above, should allow for a better understanding of this problem.

35% of silent system failures may be artifacts of the fault injection setup. Specifically, in 20% of failures the host VMM crashes the FV VM running the target system. This can happen if the VMM attempts to access invalid state in the FV VM while performing some operations on its behalf. For example, as part of handling paging mode updates (writes to CR4 register) from an FV VM using hardware-assisted paging, the VMM may map in the page pointed to by the FV VM's CR3 register. If the mapping fails (no valid page) due to a corrupted CR3, the VMM will crash the FV VM. With ReHype running directly on hardware, such a scenario would likely result in a detected VMM failures, allowing recovery to be attempted. 15% of silent system failures are caused by communication failures (dropped event signals) between the fault injection campaign on the host VMM and campaign coordination code in the target system. In these cases, the host campaign times out and records a target system failure when it fails to receive a signal from the target system after an injection. In an actual deployment of ReHype, the same fault may not be manifested or may be manifested in a different way, possibly allowing recovery to be attempted.

The remaining 5% of silent system failures are cases in which the kernel in the PrivVM or DVM crashed because of memory corruption or hypercalls returning errors. This caused more than one AppVM to fail completing its benchmark. Mechanisms to recover the PrivVM and DVM should reduce this type silent system failures.

7. Related Work

Many researchers have proposed rebooting subcomponents in application software systems, operating systems, and virtualized systems to increase system reliability and availability [3, 21, 11, 15]. These works, however, have not addressed how to preserve the subcomponents while rebooting the underlying system. The two works that are most closely related to ReHype are RootHammer [13] and Otherworld [4].

RootHammer reduces the time to reboot (rejuvenate) a virtualized system by rebooting the Xen VMM and Domain 0 while preserving in memory the states of VMs and their configurations. During rejuvenation, Domain 0 is properly shut down and the VMs suspend themselves cleanly. Kexec [18] is used to quickly reboot the Xen VMM and Domain 0, similar to ReHype. After a reboot, Domain 0 must re-instantiate and resume all the VMs. This requires modifications to tools in Domain 0 to access VM configurations and state already resident in memory.

RootHammer operates within a healthy and functioning virtualized system. Hence, there is no concern for the safety of the VMM due to corrupted VM states during VM re-integration or the need to resolve inconsistencies, such as acquired locks and interrupted hypercalls. On the other hand, ReHype aims to recover a failed VMM that can be corrupted and may have inconsistencies within the VMM state, between the VMM and VMs, and between the VMM and hardware.

Unlike RootHammer, ReHype preserves Domain 0 and management structures for VMs across a VMM failure. As discussed in Subsection 2.2, this can be unsafe as states can become corrupted. However, preserving Domain 0 allows recovery to occur without any modifications to the VMs as is needed with RootHammer. In addition, without tying Domain 0 recovery to the VMM recovery, recovery latency can be reduced as VMs can continue to operate as soon as the VMM is booted without having to also wait for Domain 0 to boot. A possible extension of ReHype is to follow the microreboot of the VMM with a subsequent proactive rejuvenation, scheduled at a convenient time, involving recovery of Domain 0 and re-creation of the VM structures in the VMM.

Otherworld [4] allows a Linux kernel to be recovered from failures while preserving the state of the running processes. KDump [6] is used to load and boot a new kernel. The new kernel boots within a reserved memory space. Hence, the memory contents of the failed system are preserved. In ReHype, the VMM is booted with access to the entire system memory and does not need a large preserved memory region (64MB used in Otherworld). With Otherworld, processes are restored by recreating the process descriptors and copying the process memory from the old memory region. ReHype reuses the VM descriptors and does not need to copy the VM memory. Both approaches require mechanisms to ensure the safety of the reused data (see Section 2.2).

With Otherworld, restoration of kernel components requires traversing many complex data structures in a possibly corrupted kernel. This increases the chance of failed recoveries. ReHype benefits from the simplicity of the state that the VMM keeps for the VMs, enabling a simpler recovery process and increasing the chance of a successful recovery. Specifically, the number of components that must be restored in a VMM for each VM is small, as discussed in Section 3.

Otherworld must individually restore kernel resources that are used by the processes, such as open files, signal handlers, and shared memory IPC. The network stack and pipes cannot yet be restored. Applications that use such kernel resources need to have custom crash procedures to perform application specific recovery tasks, such as re-opening sockets or restarting the application. With ReHype, all the states of the applications are maintained within the VM. Hence, application failure handlers or any other application modifications are not needed. VM failure handlers could be useful for performing data integrity checks in the VM using VM-specific knowledge. Since there are fewer types of VMs than there are applications, if VM failure handlers are needed, fewer have to be written.

8. Conclusions and Future Work

We have developed the ReHype mechanism that recovers from hypervisor failure, using microreboot, while preserving the state of running VMs. The basic version of ReHype recovered successfully from only 5.6% of detected hypervisor failures. We used fault injection results to guide incremental improvements of ReHype, leading to a success rate of over 90%. The incremental improvements involved a combination of mechanisms to repair VMM corruption and resolve inconsistencies within the VMM, between the VMM and VMs, and between the VMM and the hardware. Our results indicate that almost half of the remaining failed recoveries (3% of detected failures) may be resolved by performing PrivVM or DVM recovery, simplifying the failure handler, and clearing pending interrupts in the I/O controller. 14% of manifested faults lead to undetected VMM failures that result in system failures. 60% of these failures are caused by a single problem — triple fault exception leading to a system reset.

In future work, we will add PrivVM and DVM recovery to enhance overall system reliability. We also plan to evaluate ReHype on bare hardware to check whether any of our results are significantly skewed by our current experimental setup, where the target system is in an FV VM. Additional areas of interest are: evaluation and optimization of recovery latency, preserving FV VMs across a VMM microreboot, and additional stressing of ReHype using, for example, injected software errors.

Acknowledgments

This work was supported, in part, by a donation from the Xerox Foundation University Affairs Committee.

References

[1] "UnixBench," *www.tux.org/pub/tux/benchmarks/System/unixbench*.

[2] P. Barham, B. Dragovic, K. Fraser, S. Hand, T. Harris, A. Ho, R. Neugebauer, I. Pratt, and A. Warfield, "Xen and the Art of Virtualization," *Nineteenth ACM Symposium on Operating Systems Principles*, Bolton Landing, NY, pp. 164-177 (October 2003).

[3] G. Candea, S. Kawamoto, Y. Fujiki, G. Friedman, and A. Fox, "Microreboot - A Technique for Cheap Recovery," *6th Symposium on Operating Systems Design and Implementation*, San Francisco, CA, pp. 31-44 (December 2004).

[4] A. Depoutovitch and M. Stumm, "Otherworld - Giving Applications a Chance to Survive OS Kernel Crashes," *5th ACM European Conference on Computer Systems*, Paris, France, pp. 181-194 (April 2010).

[5] K. Fraser, S. Hand, R. Neugebauer, I. Pratt, A. Warfield, and M. Williamson, "Safe Hardware Access with the Xen Virtual Machine Monitor," *1st Workshop on Operating System and Architectural Support for the on demand IT InfraStructure (OASIS) (ASPLOS)* (October 2004).

[6] V. Goyal, E. Biederman, and H. Nellitheertha, "Kdump, A Kexec-based Kernel Crash Dumping Mechanism," *lse.sourceforge.net/kdump/documentation/ols2oo5-kdump-paper.pdf* (2005).

[7] W. Gu, Z. Kalbarczyk, R. K. Iyer, and Z. Yang, "Characterization of Linux Kernel Behavior Under Errors," *International Conference on Dependable Systems and Networks*, San Francisco, CA, pp. 459-468 (June 2003).

[8] W. Gu, Z. Kalbarczyk, and R. K. Iyer, "Error Sensitivity of the Linux Kernel Executing on PowerPC G4 and Pentium 4 Processors," *International Conference on Dependable Systems and Networks*, Florence, Italy, pp. 887-896 (June 2004).

[9] I. Hsu, A. Gallagher, M. Le, and Y. Tamir, "Using Virtualization to Validate Fault-Tolerant Distributed Systems," *International Conference on Parallel and Distributed Computing and Systems*, Marina del Rey, CA, pp. 210-217 (November 2010).

[10] Intel Corporation, *Intel 64 and IA-32 Architectures Software Developer's Manual: Volume 3A*, 2010.

[11] H. Jo, H. Kim, J.-W. Jang, J. Lee, and S. Maeng, "Transparent Fault Tolerance of Device Drivers for Virtual Machines," *IEEE Transactions on Computers* **59**(11), pp. 1466-1479 (November 2010).

[12] K. Kourai and S. Chiba, "A Fast Rejuvenation Technique for Server Consolidation with Virtual Machines," *International Conference on Dependable Systems and Networks*, Edinburgh, UK, pp. 245-255 (June 2007).

[13] K. Kourai and S. Chiba, "Fast Software Rejuvenation of Virtual Machine Monitors," *IEEE Transactions on Dependable and Secure Computing* (May 2010).

[14] M. Le, A. Gallagher, and Y. Tamir, "Challenges and Opportunities with Fault Injection in Virtualized Systems," *First International Workshop on Virtualization Performance: Analysis, Characterization, and Tools*, Austin, TX (April 2008).

[15] M. Le, A. Gallagher, Y. Tamir, and Y. Turner, "Maintaining Network QoS Across NIC Device Driver Failures Using Virtualization," *8th IEEE International Symposium on Network Computing and Applications*, Cambridge, MA, pp. 195-202 (July 2009).

[16] A. Menon, J. R. Santos, Y. Turner, G. J. Janakiraman, and W. Zwaenepoel, "Diagnosing Performance Overheads in the Xen Virtual Machine Environment," *First ACM/USENIX Conference on Virtual Execution Environments*, Chicago, IL, pp. 13-23 (June 2005).

[17] W. T. Ng and P. M. Chen, "The Systematic Improvement of Fault Tolerance in the Rio File Cache," *29th Fault Tolerant Computing Symposium*, Madison, WI, USA, pp. 76-83 (June 1999).

[18] A. Pfiffer, "Reducing System Reboot Time With kexec," *devresources.linuxfoundation.org/andyp/kexec/whitepaper/kexec.pdf* (April 2003).

[19] M. Rosenblum and T. Garfinkel, "Virtual Machine Monitors: Current Technology and Future Trends," *IEEE Computer* **38**(5), pp. 39-47 (May 2005).

[20] M. Sullivan and R. Chillarege, "Software Defects and their Impact on System Availability: A Study of Field Failures in Operating Systems," *21st Fault-Tolerant Computing Symposium*, Montreal, Quebec, Canada, pp. 2-9 (June 1991).

[21] M. M. Swift, B. N. Bershad, and H. M. Levy, "Improving the Reliability of Commodity Operating Systems," *ACM Transactions on Computer Systems* **23**(1), pp. 77-110 (February 2005).

Fast and Space-Efficient Virtual Machine Checkpointing *

Eunbyung Park, Bernhard Egger, and Jaejin Lee

School of Computer Science and Engineering, Seoul National University, Seoul 151-744, Korea
eunbyung@aces.snu.ac.kr, bernhard@aces.snu.ac.kr, jlee@cse.snu.ac.kr
http://aces.snu.ac.kr

Abstract

Checkpointing, i.e., recording the volatile state of a virtual machine (VM) running as a guest in a virtual machine monitor (VMM) for later restoration, includes storing the memory available to the VM. Typically, a full image of the VM's memory along with processor and device states are recorded. With guest memory sizes of up to several gigabytes, the size of the checkpoint images becomes more and more of a concern.

In this work we present a technique for fast and space-efficient checkpointing of virtual machines. In contrast to existing methods, our technique eliminates redundant data and stores only a subset of the VM's memory pages. Our technique transparently tracks I/O operations of the guest to external storage and maintains a list of memory pages whose contents are duplicated on non-volatile storage. At a checkpoint, these pages are excluded from the checkpoint image.

We have implemented the proposed technique for paravirtualized as well as fully-virtualized guests in the Xen VMM. Our experiments with a paravirtualized guest (Linux) and two fully-virtualized guests (Linux, Windows) show a significant reduction in the size of the checkpoint image as well as the time required to complete the checkpoint. Compared to the current Xen implementation, we achieve, on average, an 81% reduction in the stored data and a 74% reduction in the time required to take a checkpoint for the paravirtualized Linux guest. In a fully-virtualized environment running Windows and Linux guests, we achieve a 64% reduction of the image size along with a 62% reduction in checkpointing time.

Categories and Subject Descriptors D.4 [*Operating Systems*]: Organization and Design; D.4.7 [*Reliability*]: Checkpoint/Restart; D.4.2 [*Storage Management*]: Virtual Memory

General Terms Design, Measurement, Performance, Reliability

Keywords Virtual Machine, Checkpointing

* This work was supported by grant 2009-0081569 (Creative Research Initiatives: Center for Manycore Programming) and the BK21 project from the National Research Foundation of Korea funded by the Korean government (Ministry of Education, Science and Technology). ICT at Seoul National University provided research facilities for this study.

1. Introduction

Virtualization technology continues to gain importance in server, desktop, and embedded systems. Its applications are numerous. Data center and cluster computing providers use virtualization technology to run many OS instances concurrently on a single, physical machine with high performance, thereby providing custom-tailored environments, better use of physical resources, higher availability through live migration and security [5, 8, 11, 13, 31, 32, 34].

A useful feature of virtualization technology is virtual machine (VM) checkpointing; the ability to save and restore the state of a virtual machine. VM checkpoints (also called *snapshots*) are useful in many situations: for simply stopping a VM and later resuming work on a desktop computer; for migrating a VM to another host in a data center; or for performing intrusion analysis of commodity operating systems by continuously taking snapshots of the system under attack.

To completely record the state of a virtual machine, the virtual machine monitor (VMM) must store the virtual CPU's state, the current state of all emulated devices, and the contents of the virtual machine's memory to non-volatile memory. An identical copy of the VM's memory contents stored to disk, therefore, the size of the snapshot is typically dominated by the amount of the guest's memory.

With the rapid growth of memory in virtual machines, the size of snapshots is becoming more and more of a concern, especially in situations where a multitude of snapshots is taken over a certain period of time, such as, for example, in intrusion detection. The prevalent technique to alleviate this problem is incremental checkpointing [1, 23, 26, 27]. In incremental checkpointing, the first snapshot contains a complete image of the VM's memory. Subsequent snapshots only store pages that have been modified since the previous snapshot. Initially all memory pages are marked read-only. Whenever the guest modifies a page, that page is remapped read-write. When the subsequent snapshots are taken, only pages that are mapped read-write are included in the image.

In this paper, we propose a fast and space-efficient virtual machine checkpointing method for memory. With this technique, the size of the snapshot image is reduced considerably. Furthermore, compared to existing methods, significantly less time is needed to take a snapshot. The basic observation is that it is unnecessary for the VMM to store the full contents of the VM's memory because a large part of the data is already present on external storage. Modern operating systems allocate most of the memory that is not currently in use by either the kernel or the running processes to a cache commonly known as *page cache* [7]. The page cache contains data that has been recently read from (or is to be written to) block devices in order to reduce the long access latency incurred when accessing external devices. In situations where it is unnecessary to restore the contents of memory not currently allocated by the guest, such pages do not need to be included in the snapshot.

In a VM environment, all I/O operations to devices go through the VMM. In the proposed technique, the VMM keeps track of I/O operations to block devices and maintains data structures that map the blocks of non-volatile storage (a virtual disk or a partition) to the VM's memory pages. At a checkpoint, memory pages that are known to be identical copies of disk blocks are excluded from the VM memory image.

We have implemented the proposed technique both in Xen's paravirtualized and fully-virtualized VMM. In both cases, the VMM keeps transparently track of I/O operations. In a paravirtualized environment, the guest VM informs the VMM about the contents of its page cache and free memory pages when it is about to be checkpointed. The VMM uses this information to filter out pages that have been modified after their contents have been read from/written to disk. Additionally, the VMM also discards free memory pages from the memory image. In a fully-virtualized environment, the unmodified guests do not provide any information to the VMM. To maintain consistency, the VMM must intercept all possible actions that can invalidate the contents of a memory page that is known to contain data from external storage. This is accomplished by marking the guest's memory pages as read-only in the shadow page tables of the VMM and updating the internal data structures on a write fault.

The contributions of this paper are as follows:

- We introduce a fast and space-efficient checkpointing technique for virtual machines. By ignoring memory pages whose contents are available on non-volatile storage, we are able to reduce the time and the space required to take a checkpoint.

- We have implemented the proposed technique in Xen's paravirtualized environment and modified the Linux guest running in it. We identify and correctly handle all scenarios that could lead to a corruption of the VMM's disk-to-memory mapping data structures which would result in a corrupted memory image.

- We have implemented the proposed technique in Xen's fully-virtualized VMM and ran the benchmarks on Microsoft Windows and Linux guest operating systems.

- We compare the performance of the unmodified Xen VMM with the paravirtualized and fully-virtualized approach, both for individual checkpoints as well as incremental checkpoints. Compared to the unmodified VMM, we achieve an 81% and 64% reduction in disk space plus a 74% and 62% reduction in time required to complete a snapshot in paravirtualized and fully-virtualized environments, respectively. The proposed method also outperforms incremental checkpointing with a 57% reduction in disk space and a 26% reduction in time needed to take a checkpoint.

The rest of this work is organized as follows: Section 2 discusses related work; Section 3 contains an overview of VM checkpointing; and Section 4 outlines our method. In Section 5, we discuss the implementation of the proposed technique. The experimental setup is described in Section 6 and Section 7 presents the results. Finally, Section 8 concludes the paper.

2. Related Work

Since the emergence of virtualization technology, physical memory allocation to VMs and related functionality such as checkpointing, live migration, fault tolerance, and logging with replay have received a lot of attention in the research community.

While the available CPUs and I/O bandwidth on a physical machine can be fairly time-shared or multiplexed, allocating or dynamically reclaiming memory is not easy due to the fact that memory has an inherent weakness as a shared resource. Reclaiming memory from a running VM, without seriously affecting its performance, is not easy because the VMM has limited knowledge over the contents memory and thus its importance to the VM. A common technique is Ballooning [32]: the VMM communicates with the ballooning driver running inside the VM. This driver requests non-shared memory from the guest operating system. Since that memory cannot be used by any guest application, the VMM can reuse this memory and allocate it to another VM. Most major VMMs, such as KVM [14], VMware [4], VirtualBox [3], and Xen [6], make use of the ballooning technique to reclaim memory from a running VM. Transcendent memory [2, 22] is another approach to efficient memory management between multiple VMs, and in terms of dealing with free memory it resembles our approach. It maintains a system-wide global memory pool that contains memory not allocated to any VM. Paravirtualized guests can access that memory indirectly through an API. Based on paravirtualization, several approaches have been proposed such as efficient memory provisioning [29], memory sharing between multiple VMs [9, 24], and hot spot migration [33].

VM live migration [10, 25] builds on checkpointing techniques to migrate a running VM from one physical machine to another without stopping the execution of the VM being migrated. Both studies take a pre-copy approach in which memory pages are iteratively copied. In the first iteration, the VM's memory as a whole is transferred to the target machine while the guest keeps running on the source machine. In the following iterations, only modified pages are copied repeatedly until either a fixed number of iterations is reached or the number of dirty pages drops below a certain threshold. The VM is then stopped on the source machine and the VM's state, as well as with the remaining dirty pages, is sent to the target machine where the VM is restarted. Post-copy approaches have also been studied [15].

Remus [11] and Kemari [30] achieve high availability of VMs based on continuous live migration. A backup of the running VM on a physically different host is maintained by repeatedly transferring the state of the running VM. In case of a hardware failure, the backup starts running on behalf of the original VM. Frequent checkpointing is used to keep the amount of modified pages low. In case of a write-intensive VM, even frequent checkpoints cannot guarantee a sufficiently low number of modified pages. In such situations, a copy-on-write (CoW) approach [15] can be taken. All memory pages are marked read-only and transferred immediately to the backup on a write fault.

The studies most relevant to the proposed page cache tracking mechanism are Geiger [16] and VM memory access tracing with an exclusive cache in the VMM [21]. Both approaches focus on the working set size (WSS) estimation of a VM in order to allot the exact amount of memory needed by the VM. The page miss ratio curve [35] used to estimate the WSS is based on the reuse distance [16]. The reuse distance is tracked by detecting promotion and eviction of pages to the page cache. While external requests from or to secondary storage can be traced transparently in the VMM, the eviction of a page from the page cache is hidden from the VMM. Geiger uses heuristics to detect that pages have been evicted from the page cache, whereas in the VM memory access tracking approach the guest is modified to notify the VMM of any page evictions from the page cache.

Both operating system debugging, through the use of a VM [18], and intrusion analysis, via logging and replay [12], benefit from efficient VM checkpoints. The Potemkin virtual honeyfarm [31], used to gather intelligence on network honeypots, and Snowflock [19], a system which enables rapid construction of VM cluster computing systems, also profit from efficient checkpointing.

3. VM Checkpointing

VM checkpointing refers to the process of saving the state of a virtual machine to non-volatile storage so that it can be completely stopped and restored in its exact state at a later time. Checkpoints (also referred to as *snapshots*) can be taken of running as well as stopped VMs. A snapshot of a running VM includes the VM's memory contents and the state of its devices including the CPU(s). A checkpoint of a stopped VM is usually limited to creating a snapshot of the current state of the external storage. In this work, we focus on improving the process of checkpointing a running system.

A snapshot of a running system comprises the context of the virtual CPUs (VCPU), virtual devices connected to the VM (such as network adapters, keyboard, and the display), and a copy of the memory allocated to the VM. Typically, it is assumed that the external storage connected to the guest (i.e., its virtual disk) should not be modified until the guest is restored. This is a reasonable assumption since modifying the contents of the disk while the guest is not running will most likely make it impossible to resume the guest. Modern operating systems often cache disk blocks in memory, and modifying the disk behind the guest's back would lead to inconsistencies in the cache.

VMMs provide a paravirtualized or a fully-virtualized execution environment. In a paravirtualized environment, the VMM exposes certain APIs to the VM. The VM communicates with the VMM through this *para-API*. The weakness of this approach is that the guest operating system needs to be modified in order to take advantage of the para-API. Nevertheless, paravirtualization is a pervasive virtualization technology supported by most major VMMs due to its benefits, such as improved I/O performance [20, 28], better memory management [9, 24, 29], and load balancing [33]. Full virtualization, on the other hand, provides a complete emulation of the underlying hardware and does not require guest modification. This approach is more difficult to implement, and emulating certain functionality may lead to reduced performance in the guest. It is still the prevalent emulation method because guest operating systems that cannot be modified easily (such as Microsoft Windows) can be supported as well.

Recent versions of the open source Xen Hypervisor [6] offer a paravirtualized environment as well as full virtualization. The following paragraphs describe the differences in context of checkpointing for both the paravirtualized and the fully-virtualized Xen implementation.

Paravirtualized environment. When the VMM checkpoints a VM, the paravirtualized guest is first notified through the para-API. The guest itself then carries out several tasks including disconnecting devices, disabling interrupts, or marking page tables. After finishing the preparation work, the guest transfers control to the VMM. The VMM uses the privileged *dom0* domain to save the state of the VM to persistent storage. In addition to the contents of the VM's volatile memory, the state of the virtual devices owned by the guest, such as network adapters, the keyboard, the display and the number and context of the processors (*vcpus*) are stored as well. Special care needs to be taken when saving the page tables of the guest as they contain physical machine addresses of memory allocated to the guest at checkpoint time. The physical addresses are changed to pseudo-physical addresses that simplify restoration as well as migration to another host.

Restoring a guest running in a VM is the exact opposite process. The *dom0* first creates a new user domain, allocates the necessary amount of memory, assigns and restores the context of the *vcpus* and the virtual devices. The pseudo-physical addresses in the guest's page tables are modified to match the actual physical addresses of the memory allocated to the VM. Control is then transferred to the guest which reconnects the devices to its event queue,

	Total Memory Size	
	512 MB	1024 MB
Linux	466 MB (91%)	966 MB (93%)
Windows	353 MB (84%)	860 MB (84%)

Table 1. Data duplication between memory and disk.

VMM	Snapshot Size (MB)	Remarks
VMware	1057	
VirtualBox	450	compressed
Xen	1025	

Table 2. Size of a snapshot of a VM with 1 GB of memory.

re-enables interrupts and then continues executing where it left-off before the checkpoint.

Fully-virtualized environment. In a fully-virtualized environment, the guest is not aware that it is being checkpointed. The VMM stops the guest, and saves the state of all virtual devices owned by the guest as well as the contents of the VM's volatile memory to disk. The guests page tables can be saved as-is since they do not contain physical machine addresses (the VMM uses *shadow page tables* to fully virtualize memory accesses. See Section 5.3). Restoring a fully-virtualized guest is similar to restoring a paravirtualized one. In a fully-virtualized environment, however, the VMM has to re-initialize the devices itself since the guest expects the devices to operate as if it had never been checkpointed.

Live migration [10, 25] and VM replication systems, such as Remus [11], build on top of checkpointing/restoration functionality. In both cases, frequent and continuous checkpointing functionality is required. Under such circumstances, *incremental checkpointing*, i.e., saving only the differences since the last checkpoint, is more efficient than saving the whole state of the VM. Incremental checkpointing can also be beneficial for guests that are not write-intensive.

4. Motivation

Memory sizes of several gigabytes are not uncommon these days, even for virtual machines. The operating system and the running applications often occupy only a small fraction of the total available memory, leaving most of the memory unused. Modern operating systems use this unused memory to cache recently read data as well as data yet to be written to disk, thereby hiding the long access latency to external storage. Depending on the usage scenario and the size of the memory, the memory allocated to this *page cache* may easily exceed 90% of the physically available memory.

Table 1 shows the extent to which memory contents are duplicated on disk. To extract this data, we have saved the guest's memory after booting-up the system and copying some large files. We then compared the memory contents to the disk on a 4096-byte page level. While copying around large files provokes a big page cache and may not be a very realistic scenario, it shows the amount of duplication between memory and disk in an extreme case.

Up to this day, VMMs typically store a one-to-one image of the guest's memory in the snapshot. Table 2 lists the size of the VM snapshot (memory image plus device state) for major VMMs such as VirtualBox [3], VMware [4], and Xen [6]. The snapshots for VMware and Xen are both a bit larger than the VM's memory size. VirtualBox compresses snapshots, but nevertheless stores all of the memory allocated to the VM.

From Tables 1 and 2 it follows that there exists a big potential to reduce the size of VM snapshots. Instead of storing the redundant data in the VM snapshot, a simple reference to the external storage medium, along with an offset, suffices. This will not only reduce

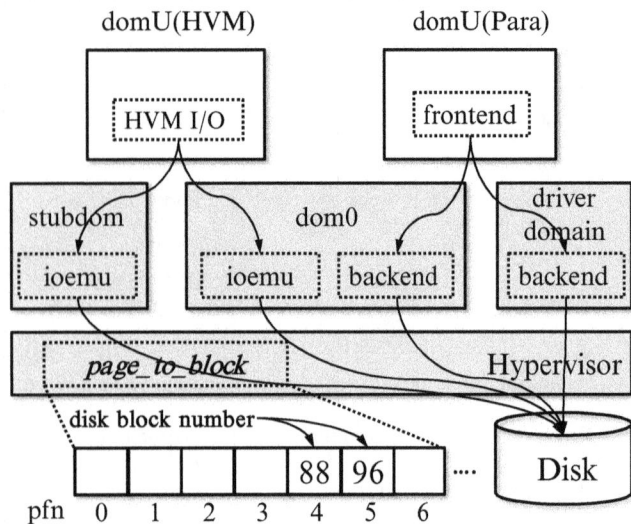

Figure 1. Disk I/O flow in the Xen VMM and the page-to-block map.

the size, but also shorten the time required to take a snapshot. This reduction comes at the expense of slightly increasing the time to restore a snapshot since reading a contiguous file into memory is faster than fetching single blocks from a disk image.

There exist other opportunities to further reduce the size of snapshots, such as free memory pages and memory that is not mapped into the guest's address space. The former can only be exploited in a paravirtualized environment since VMM has no knowledge of which mapped memory pages the guest is currently using and which represent free pages. The latter can be excluded from the snapshot both in paravirtualized and fully-virtualized environments because the VMM can inspect the guest's page tables to check what pages are actually mapped.

5. Implementation

To achieve space as well as time efficient checkpointing, the proposed method minimizes duplication of pages in the checkpoint file that are also available on the disk of the VM. The key idea is to detect promotion of memory pages into the guest's page cache by transparently intercepting I/O requests to external storage by the guest.

5.1 Transparent I/O Interception

In virtualized environments, the VMM (or *hypervisor*) virtualizes some hardware resources in order to make them visible to guests running in VMs as if they were dedicated. For some types of hardware resources such as network interface cards (NIC) or disks, concurrent accesses to these hardware resources by multiple VMs need to be arbitrated by the VMM. While accesses to physical memory are implicitly multiplexed by the memory controller or the hardware, bus arbitration is not visible to the software and simultaneous requests to the physical disk or NIC without mediation of software can cause unknown behavior or even device crashes. For this reason, I/O operations to secondary storage without hardware virtualization support are always under control by the VMM. We can thus intercept all I/O requests transparently.

Figure 1 shows the flow of disk I/O requests in the Xen VMM for both a paravirtualized and a fully-virtualized guest. An I/O request from a paravirtualized guest running in the user domain,

domU (Figure 1 on the right), is either forwarded directly to the VMM's domain zero, *dom0*, or handled by a specialized driver domain. Any I/O request to the physical disk can therefore be intercepted in the driver backend either in the VMM's privileged domain zero or the driver domain for the disk. For fully-virtualized guests (Figure 1 on the left), I/O requests go through *ioemu* located either in *dom0* or a stub domain *stubdom*. Here, we can intercept all I/O activity in *ioemu*.

Mapping page frames to disk blocks. We associate the VM's memory contents with physical disk blocks by transparently tracking all read and write requests from the guest to external storage. The gathered information is stored in a memory page-to-disk block map (*page_to_block* map) that is maintained for every running VM. Since the number of memory pages is typically much smaller than the number of disk blocks, the map is indexed by the guest's memory page index, the so-called *page frame number* (*PFN*). The data stored in the map is the 8-byte disk block number. The *page_to_block* map is updated whenever the guest issues an I/O request. Both the space and runtime overhead of maintaining the *page_to_block* map are relatively small. For a VM with 1 GB of allocated memory, the *page_to_block* map requires 2 MB of memory. I/O operations are costly operations by themselves; the table update does not noticeably increase the I/O latency (Section 7).

Figure 1 shows the contents of the *page_to_block* after the guest reads the disk blocks number 88 and 96 into its memory pages at index 4 and 5, respectively.

The VMM can track all disk I/O operations of the guest transparently and maintain a mapping of memory pages to disk blocks. Once in the guest's memory, however, modifications to cached pages through memory writes are hidden from the VMM. One could compare the contents of both the memory page and the associated disk blocks when the checkpoint is taken. This, however, would impose an unacceptable computational overhead. In order to efficiently store only those memory pages whose contents are not duplicated on the guest's disk, the memory-to-disk mapping represented by the *page_to_block* map must be up-to-date at checkpoint time. To maintain an up-to-date *page_to_block* map, modifications to memory pages in the map must be tracked. This is where the paravirtualized and fully-virtualized implementation diverge. The following sections describe the implementation issues for the paravirtualized environment (Section 5.2) and the fully-virtualized approach (Section 5.3).

5.2 Paravirtualized Environment

In a paravirtualized environment, there exist two type of pages that do not need to be included in a snapshot: (a) unmodified pages in the page cache, and (b) free pages.

5.2.1 The Page Cache

The page cache, also referred to as disk cache or buffer cache, is designed to offset the performance gap between the main memory (RAM) and block devices by keeping the most frequently used data of block devices in main memory. In modern operating systems such as Microsoft Windows, Linux, Solaris, and many more, the biggest part of the available memory (i.e., memory available to the operating system and not in use by the kernel or any active application) is allocated to the page cache.

The page cache caches pages for an indefinite period of time. As long as the system has sufficient memory to satisfy all currently running processes and no additional memory requests occur, pages are not dropped from the page cache. That is, data in the page cache is not expelled unless it is replaced by more recent data or by the kernel reclaiming pages from the page cache to serve memory allocation requests.

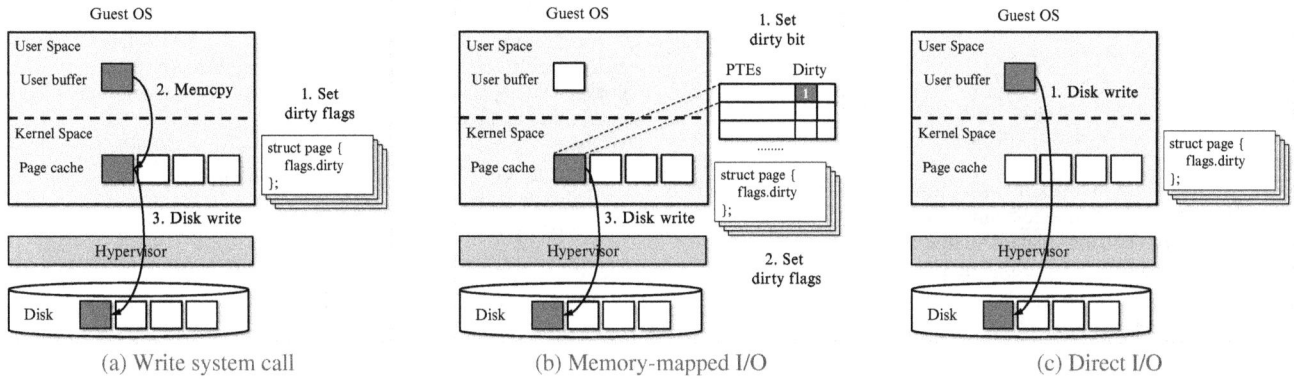

Figure 2. Write operations : write system call, memory-mapped I/O, and direct I/O.

Write operations to the disk are also cached by the page cache. The page cache typically operates in *write-back* mode, i.e., dirty pages are not written to disk immediately, but rather marked dirty and flushed periodically by a background thread.

Note that a reverse mapping from disk blocks to memory pages is not necessary because the OS guarantees that a disk block is not cached more than once by the page cache.

5.2.2 Maintaining Consistency

The operating system maintains consistency between the page cache and the disk by periodically flushing dirty pages (i.e., pages whose contents have been modified) to disk. However, at the moment of the checkpoint dirty pages may exist in the page cache. There are four distinct operations that can render a page in the page cache dirty: write system calls, memory mapped I/O, direct I/O, and I/O at a sub-page granularity. The following paragraphs describe these operations in detail and show how to identify dirty pages so that the VMM can include them in the memory image of the checkpoint.

The *write* system call. When a process issues a write system call, the file descriptor, the user buffer and the size of the write operation are passed as parameters. The file descriptor points to a specific file, and the user buffer is normally located in the user heap or global buffer memory (Figure 2a). If a page cache hit occurs, the kernel marks the affected pages as dirty in its internal data structures and then performs a simple memory copy from the user buffer to the pages in the page cache. If the pages are not present in the page cache the kernel first allocates pages to the page cache, marks them as dirty, and then performs the memory copy operation. The interpretation of a page's dirty flag is thus that the contents of the page differ from the data on disk. For the VMM, it is not possible to detect changes to the internal data structures of a guest, hence it is not aware of the fact that some pages in the page cache are dirty.

In the paravirtualized Xen environment, the guest performs preparatory work prior to being checkpointed. We insert an additional phase that scans the dirty bit of the kernel's page cache data structures and adds them to a list of pages to be saved by the VMM.

Memory mapped I/O. The memory pages involved in memory mapped I/O are part of the kernel's page cache, that is, there is no user space buffer involved (Figure 2b). As a consequence, the kernel itself is not immediately aware of modifications to pages used for memory mapped I/O. To detect write operations to memory mapped pages in the page cache, the kernel periodically scans the dirty bit of the corresponding page table entries (PTE) and sets the *dirty* flag in the page cache data structures accordingly.

It is possible that some dirty bits in the PTEs have not yet been propagated to the corresponding dirty flags in the page cache at the moment a guest is checkpointed. The VMM knows which memory pages contain the guest's page tables and scans the user address space for *dirty* bits. The corresponding pages in the *page_to_block* map are included in the memory checkpoint. It would be possible to let the guest scan the PTEs as part of the preparatory work, however, we chose to perform this task in the VMM in order to keep the necessary changes to the guest OS to a minimum.

Note that the kernel often maps memory pages into its own address space. The Linux kernel maps the whole kernel address space with the *dirty* bit set. We therefore do not consider the PTEs of kernel memory as candidates for PTE scanning. Since most modern operating systems including Microsoft Windows and Linux use separate address spaces for user and kernel processes, it is not difficult to distinguish the PTEs of kernel memory pages.

Direct I/O. Direct I/O refers to file system I/O operations that bypass the OS-level page cache (Figure 2c). When a self-caching application, such as Oracle's DBMS, opens a file with the O_DIRECT flag, pages that have already been cached for that file are dropped from the page cache. The user process is responsible to provide buffers for direct I/O. These buffers are located in the user's address space, and the application is responsible for maintaining consistency between the data in memory and on disk.

The proposed method transparently traces all I/O operations, hence the memory pages used as buffers in direct I/O are also recorded in the *page_to_block* map. However, these user mode buffers are not part of the page cache and have thus not been added to the file-backed page list. We conservatively assume that all pages used for direct I/O are dirty and include them in the snapshot image.

Sub-page I/O granularity. In many modern operating systems, including Linux, the majority of disk I/O operations are performed at memory page granularity (typically 4 KB) as opposed to the smaller granularity of disk blocks. There are several reasons for this, the most compelling being the ever increasing trend towards page-based file systems, more efficient manageability of the memory and compatibility for other kernel components, such as virtual memory management. However, depending on the type of the file system or the underlying block device, finer-grained block-based I/O operations (typically 512 or 1024 bytes) may be necessary to handle file system metadata (e.g., superblocks, meta data, journal data, and so on). To cache I/O operations performed at block granularity, a page is logically divided into several subpages that are managed separately. We could also track these types of I/O operations, however, because of the small number of such blocks and for the sake of simplicity, we do not consider such pages for exclusion from the memory checkpoint.

In the Linux kernel, subpages are managed with an additional data structure in the form of a linked buffer list pointed to by the *buffer_head* on top of the page cache data structure. For block-based I/O requests, the kernel adds a new element to the buffer list and links it to a page in the page cache. Every element in the buffer list thus points to a specific part of a page that is logically split into several blocks. For compatibility reasons, some elements of the buffer list may point to an entire page, however, such elements are easily recognized by their size being equal to the size of the page. We scan the *buffer_head* data structure and remove all logically split pages from the *page_to_block* map.

5.2.3 Free Pages

Pages that are not in use by the guest at checkpoint time do not need to be saved. Ignoring free pages does not hamper correctness because no assumptions on the contents of free pages can be made. For security reasons or when allocating the *BSS* (i.e., zero-filled) segment of an executable image, memory pages may be requested to be *zero-filled-on-demand* (ZFOD). However, ZFOD pages are not handled by the low-level memory manager that is in charge of managing the free pages, hence we can safely ignore this issue.

In the Linux kernel, a system-wide memory manager, the *buddy allocator*, is responsible for satisfying memory requests and managing free pages at the lowest level. The buddy allocator manages free pages in chunks. A chunk consists of physically continuous free pages. The size of a chunk (i.e., the number of consecutive free pages) is a power of 2, and the buddy allocator maintains several free lists for the different chunk sizes. We have modified the guest OS to inform the VMM of all physical frame numbers of free pages in the context of the preparatory work carried out by the guest before a checkpoint. These pages are then excluded from the memory checkpoint.

5.3 Fully-virtualized Environments

In a fully-virtualized environment, the VMM cannot obtain any information about pages in the page cache directly from the guest. Instead, the VMM itself must track all operations that might lead to an inconsistency between the memory page and the VMM's *page_to_block* map.

5.3.1 Double Mappings and Unaligned I/O

Unlike in paravirtualized environments, a reverse mapping from disk blocks to memory pages is required with full virtualization. Assuming that the guest OS has issued two read operations $read(pfn : 1, block : 16, size : 4K)$ and $read(pfn : 3, block : 16, size : 4K)$, the *page_to_block* map contains two references to block #16 in indices 1 and 3. A subsequent write operation to block #16, i.e., $write(pfn : 2, block : 16, size : 4K)$ must invalidate the entries at positions 1 and 3, plus add a new reference to block #16 at index 2 of the *page_to_block* map.

To implement this invalidation efficiently, the VMM maintains a hash map that provides a reverse mapping from disk blocks to memory pages. The hash key is the disk block number, and the data is a linked list containing the indices of all associated memory pages.

The reverse page-to-block map is also used to keep track of unaligned I/O requests. In the paravirtualized environment, page cache-related I/O operations are aligned at 8-block boundaries (assuming 512 byte disk blocks, this is equal to the size of a memory page; 4 KB). However, a fully-virtualized guest may issue I/O requests to arbitrary disk block numbers. The offset to the next lower 8-block boundary is thus also recorded in the reverse page-to-block map. This allows us to track I/O requests that span several entries in the *page_to_block* map and correctly invalidate them if necessary.

5.3.2 Maintaining Consistency

Similarly to the paravirtualized scenario, the VMM has to follow modifications to memory pages that are currently tracked in the *page_to_block* map. In a fully-virtualized environment, the VMM maintains shadow page tables to provide the guest with the illusion of virtual memory. Our technique builds on top of this mechanism to detect modifications to tracked memory pages.

Shadow page tables. In a fully-virtualized environment, the guest does not control the hardware page tables; instead it maintains guest page tables, and the VMM manages the hardware page tables. The VMM reflects changes made by the guest to its page tables into the hardware page tables. These tables are commonly referred to as *shadow page tables* (SPTs). Initially, VMM identifies the guest's page tables by following the (guest's) page table base register and walking the page tables. It then marks these pages read-only to provoke a write fault exception whenever the guest modifies one of its page tables. When running on real hardware, page tables contain physical addresses. For the guest, the VMM uses pseudo-physical addresses (PFNs) in its page tables, and the VMM uses machine physical addresses (MFNs) in the shadow page tables. Keeping the shadow page tables in sync with the guest's tables and validating and translating PFNs to MFNs are important, performance-critical operations in a fully-virtualized environment. There are many subtleties associated with shadowing page tables; these are, however, not important for our work and outside the scope of this paper.

To intercept write accesses to pages tracked in the *page_to_block* map, we mark all entries in the shadow page that point to such pages as read-only. This happens whenever we update the *page_to_block* map due to an I/O operation. Similarly, whenever the guest OS maps a page into its address space, we check if it is present in the *page_to_block* map and, if so, mark it read-only. As soon as the guest tries to write to a write-protected page, a write fault exception is raised. The VMM detects that the guest is about to modify a page in the *page_to_block* map, deletes the relevant entry from the map, re-maps the page as read-write, and finally restarts the aborted write operation.

Memory pages can be mapped into the virtual address space more than once. Since it would be too time-consuming to scan all shadow page tables for possible double mappings, we maintain a reverse map that maps MFNs to shadow page table entries. The reverse map does not need to track all pages, only pages in the *page_to_block* map that have been re-mapped read-write need to be stored in the reverse shadow page table.

On modern hardware, shadow page tables are no longer necessary thanks to hardware-assisted virtualized memory translation (extended page tables (EPT, Intel) and nested page tables (NPT, AMD), respectively). With EPT/NPT, a global physical-to-machine table is available per domain (and not per process), so flipping one entry in that table is sufficient to mark a page read-only, thereby eliminating the need for a reverse map.

5.4 Incremental Checkpointing

With incremental checkpointing, only the changes since the previous checkpoint are recorded. Several studies on VM live migration [10, 25] employ incremental checkpointing for their purposes. When migrating a VM from one machine to another, the memory contents are copied to the target machine iteratively. In the first iteration, the entire memory contents are transferred. At each successive iteration, only the pages that have been modified while the previous iteration was running are transferred until a threshold is reached.

The Xen VMM uses shadow page tables (SPT, see Section 5.3) and a dirty map to track pages that have been changed. As a first step, the dirty map is cleared and SPT mode is enabled. Write operations cause the dirty bit in the SPT to be set from where

Dirty page
at intervals

	0			1		1			1
	0			1		1			3
	0			1		1			1
	0			0		0			0
	0			0		2			3
	0			0		2			2

Time

0   1   2   3

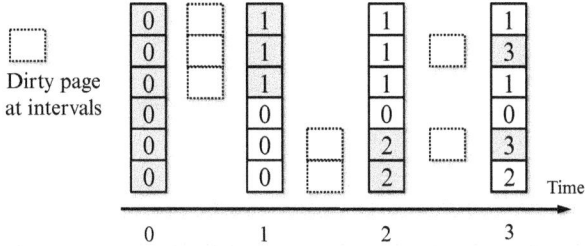

Figure 3. Incremental checkpointing

it is propagated to the dirty map by a periodically running scan. In the proposed method, we leverage this feature to implement incremental checkpointing of memory. At every checkpoint, we collect the dirty pages by inspecting the dirty map and clearing the dirty bits in the SPTs. Then, SPT mode is enabled to track modifications to memory pages ending at the next checkpoint. In order to restore a guest to one of the incremental checkpoints, it is necessary to maintain a history of which pages have been recorded in which checkpoint file. Figure 3 shows the history for three incremental checkpoints.

Incremental checkpoints are especially effective for guests that are not write intensive or in situations where frequent checkpoints are required, otherwise the advantage is lost. As shown in the next section, compared to the technique presented in this paper, incremental checkpointing outperforms our basic method only if the number of modified pages between checkpoint internals is sufficiently small.

Our proposed method of minimizing duplication between the memory checkpoint and the guest's virtual disk can be combined with incremental checkpointing. At each checkpoint, pages that have already been flushed to disk or added to the free page list are removed from the set of pages that have been modified since the previous checkpoint and do not need to be saved. The combined method outperforms incremental checkpointing in all situations (see Section 7).

6. Experimental Setup

We have conducted a series of experiments with several benchmark applications representing various usage patterns. The following measures are of interest to us: (1) compared to the current Xen implementation, how does the proposed method perform in terms of disk space and runtime? (2) compared to incremental checkpointing of the entire guest memory, how does the proposed method, with and without incremental checkpointing, perform in terms of disk space and runtime? (3) how big is the runtime overhead incurred by transparently tracking I/O accesses and the additional bookkeeping? and finally, (4) what is the effect on checkpoint restoration time?

We have implemented the proposed technique for fast and space-efficient checkpointing for paravirtualized and fully-virtualized environments in the 3.4.2 Xen VMM, the 2.6.31.6 dom0 pvops Linux kernel, and the 2.6.32.10 domU Linux kernel; the official release versions at the time development started. The experiments have been conducted on a host machine with an Intel Core Duo T2300 running at 1.66 GHz with 2 GB of RAM. The guest operating systems ran in a domU environment with one virtual CPU and 1 GB of RAM.

Lacking a standard benchmark suite for virtualized environments, we have chosen several general benchmark scenarios that are similar to what has been used in related work [11, 18]. Table 3 lists the benchmarks. *Make* compiles the current Linux ker-

Benchmark	Description
Postmark	file system benchmark (file size 4K-10MB; 128 files; 1000 transactions)
Desktop	Firefox with two windows and 3 tabs each; OpenOffice Writer and Presentation
Software Installation	installation of OpenOffice and Firefox
Gzip	compress an Apache access log file of 1.4 GB
Make	compilation of the Linux kernel tree (make bzImage; make modules; make modules_install)

Table 3. Benchmark Scenarios

nel tree by executing the commands *make bzImage; make modules; make modules_install. Gzip* compresses a 1.4 GB log file of an Apache web server. *Make* and *Gzip* represent CPU-intensive benchmarks with moderate memory and disk I/O bandwidth. The *postmark* benchmark [17] is designed to measure file system performance. We have chosen Postmark as a representative for an I/O intensive application. Postmark was configured to run 1000 transactions on 128 files ranging in size from 4 KB to 10 MB. The *Desktop* benchmark represents a user session with several applications running at the same time. In the guest VM, we run two Firefox web browsers with three open tabs each, as well as OpenOffice Writer and OpenOffice Presentation. Checkpointing is often used before and after performing software updates in order to revert to the last known working and clean configuration, respectively. This scenario is represented by *Software installation* in which the installation of several widely-used packages are performed.

7. Results

We have conducted two sets of experiments: in the first, for both paravirtualized and fully-virtualized guests, a single checkpoint was taken after each benchmark application was run to completion. In the second, only for a paravirtualized guest, a series of checkpoints were taken at fixed interval while the benchmark applications were still running.

7.1 Single Checkpointing in Paravirtualized Environments

Table 4 presents results for a single checkpoint taken after each benchmark ran to completion using the paravirtualized technique presented in this paper. Columns two to five contain the break down of the memory contents into different memory categories recognized by our technique. Column two, *Free pages*, shows the amount of free memory at the time of checkpointing. *Page cache*, in column three, displays the size of the clean pages in the page cache that do not need to be included in the snapshot image. The fourth column, *Dirty pages*, shows the total size, in megabytes, of the dirty pages in the page cache, i.e., pages that need to be saved because they had been modified but have not yet been written to disk. Column five, labeled *Others*, shows the amount of memory in use for other purposes, such as the heap or the stack. With the proposed method, only the amounts listed in columns four and five, *Dirty pages* and *Others*, need to be saved to disk; not the entire 1 GB of memory. The sum of columns two and three, *Free pages* and *Page cache*, represents the amount of memory that does not need to be saved in the checkpoint file and is equal to the improvement over the default Xen checkpointing method. Column 5, *Space*, shows the total amount of memory, in megabytes and as a percentage, that was saved to disk. The last column, *Time*, shows both the total time required to take the checkpoint and the speedup compared to the unmodified Xen checkpointing.

The results show that the ratio of dirty pages to clean pages in the page cache is very low. This is not surprising because with the default settings for the page cache, Linux flushes dirty pages back to disk every 5 seconds and allows, at most, 10% of dirty pages. Except for *Desktop*, the majority of available memory was

Benchmark	Free pages [MB]	Page cache [MB]	Dirty pages [MB]	Others [MB]	Space [MB]	Ratio [%]	Time [sec]	Speedup
Postmark	49.2	704.6	2.6	267.6	270.2	26.4	12.86	3.0
Desktop	489.5	257.1	6.4	271.0	277.4	27.0	12.47	3.1
Software update	151.0	739.5	16.6	116.7	133.3	13.0	9.72	4.0
Gzip	19.5	883.6	3.5	117.4	120.9	11.8	8.87	4.3
Make	141.1	713.7	5.0	164.2	169.2	16.5	8.53	4.5
Average	170.6	659.7	6.8	247.4	194.2	18.9	10.49	3.8

Table 4. Results of checkpointing paravirtualized guests.

OS	Benchmark	Space [MB]	Ratio [%]	Time [sec]	Speedup	Reverse Map Average
Linux	Postmark	363.7	35.3	16.17	2.4	0.440
	Desktop	809.1	78.7	30.77	1.3	0.364
	Software Installation	263.5	25.6	13.95	2.8	0.349
	Gzip	157.8	15.3	10.48	3.7	0.810
	Make	178.9	17.4	10.55	3.6	0.472
Windows	Postmark	231.1	22.5	14.19	2.7	0.202
	Desktop	759.5	73.8	32.00	1.2	0.315
	Software Installation	357.5	34.7	15.80	2.4	0.203
	Gzip	237.9	23.1	12.70	3.0	0.220
	Average	373.2	36.3	17.40	2.6	0.375

Table 5. Results of checkpointing fully-virtualized guests.

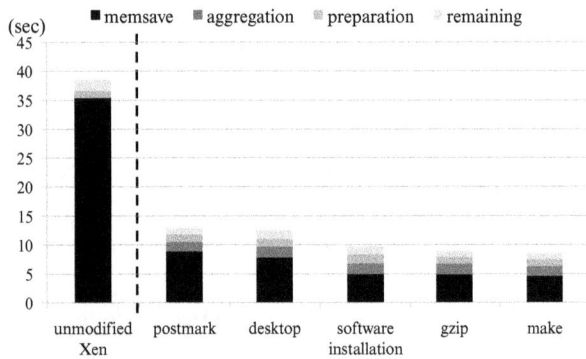

Figure 4. Breakdown of the checkpoint time.

allocated to the page cache and did not have to be saved to disk. *Desktop* and *Postmark* display a relatively large amount of memory in the *Others* column. *Desktop* runs several big applications that use large amounts of heap memory, and *Postmark* consumes a lot of memory for user-level buffers due to frequent *write* system calls. *Desktop* is not a very I/O intensive benchmark, hence the amount of memory committed to the page cache is relatively small, and, as a consequence, the amount of free memory is rather large.

Compared to the default Xen implementation that saves the entire 1 GB of memory, our method achieves a reduction of 89% in the amount of disk space consumed in a paravirtualized environment, at a 3.5-fold speedup in runtime. The time required to write a checkpoint image to external storage is dominated by the I/O latency, hence the reduction of disk I/O is directly reflected in the speedup.

Runtime overhead. To analyze the runtime overhead of the proposed technique, we have divided the time required to save a checkpoint into different phases: *Memsave* indicates the time required to write the memory contents to disk. *Aggregation* represents the time needed to combine the *page_to_block* map with the information obtained from the guest and perform the scan for dirty bits in the page tables. *Preparation* shows the time consumed by the guest to execute the preparation work and includes the time required to transfer information about free and dirty pages to the

VMM. *Remaining* is the time consumed to record the device states and finalize the checkpoint.

Figure 4 shows the breakdown of the checkpoint time for the different benchmarks using the proposed technique and the standard Xen implementation. Including the additional work required for our technique, *preparation* takes only 0.2s on average and does not significantly contribute to the total checkpointing time. The *aggregation* phase does not appear in the standard Xen implementation. Using the proposed technique, it consumes an average of 1.7 seconds. This is not insignificant, however, the benefits of reduced I/O time, as shown by the *memsave* phase, by far outweigh the cost introduced by the *aggregation* phase.

Transparently tracking I/O requests and keeping the *page_to_block* map up-to-date does incur a small runtime overhead. To measure that overhead, we ran the I/O-intensive *Postmark* benchmark in an unmodified Xen environment and under our modified conditions. The results show no statistically significant difference. In other words, the overhead incurred by tracking I/O requests is not noticeable.

Restoration Time. With the presented technique, we have measured restoration times of up to 50% slower than those obtained in an unmodified Xen environment. This degradation is due to the increased seek activity caused by reading a small number of disk blocks spread all over the guest's virtual disk. Currently, we read the disk blocks one-by-one in no particular order which may lead to an excessive seek overhead. This overhead can be reduced by sorting the disk blocks in ascending order (assuming that the disk image itself is not heavily fragmented on the physical disk). We are saving this optimization for future work.

7.2 Single Checkpointing in Fully-virtualized Environments

Table 5 presents the results of our method in a fully-virtualized environment. Except for *Make*, we ran all benchmarks on both Ubuntu Linux and Microsoft Windows XP. Column three shows the amount of data, in megabytes and as a percentage, that was saved to disk. Column four shows the total time that was required to take the checkpoint and the speedup compared to an unmodified Xen environment. The last column, labeled *Reverse Map Average*, shows the average degree of reverse mapping per page. A value of 1 indicates that all guest pages have been mapped one time.

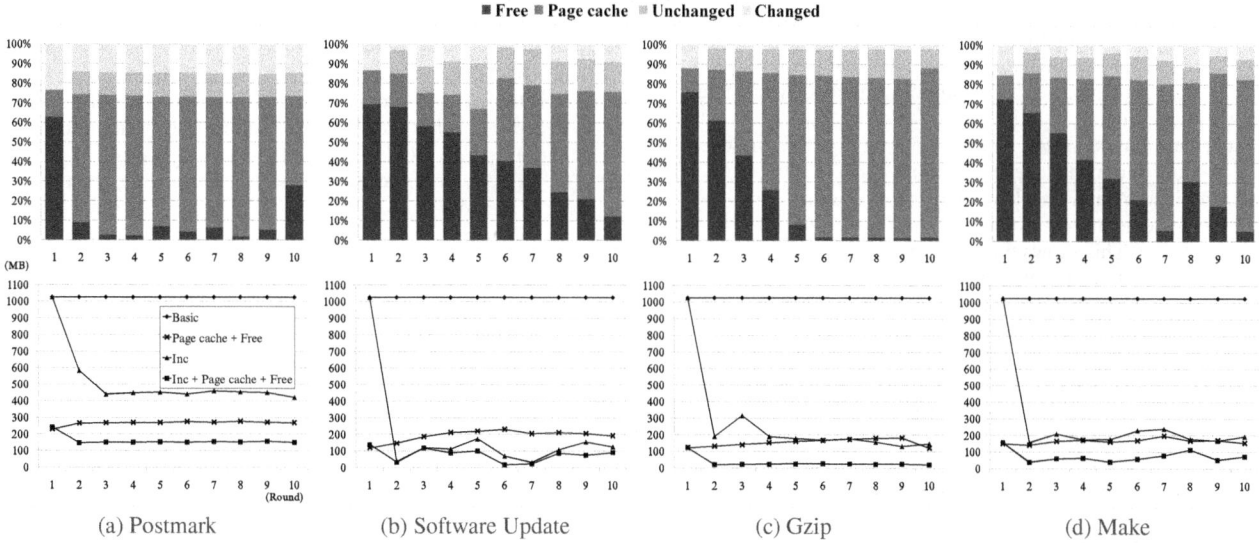

■ Free ■ Page cache ▪ Unchanged ░ Changed

| (a) Postmark | (b) Software Update | (c) Gzip | (d) Make |

Figure 5. Variations of space overhead and memory usage.

Benchmark	Unmodified		Page cache + Free		Incremental		Incremental + Page cache + Free	
	Time[sec]	Space[MB]	Time[sec]	Space[MB]	Time[sec]	Space[MB]	Time[sec]	Space[MB]
Postmark	-	-	12.48	269.8	17.59	460.8	8.41	151.4
Software update	-	-	9.80	200.1	5.26	103.4	6.32	70.7
Gzip	-	-	8.53	156.3	8.12	183.2	5.18	24.3
Make	-	-	8.67	166.2	7.87	191.3	5.91	64.6
Average	38.50	1025	9.9	198.1	9.71	234.7	6.5	77.6

Table 6. Results of periodic checkpointing.

In a fully-virtualized environment, our approach saves 64% of disk space at a 2.6-fold speedup in runtime compared to the default Xen implementation. A comparison of the results obtained for a fully-virtualized guest with the paravirtualized environment shows that the latter performs significantly better. This is because in a fully-virtualized environment, free pages cannot be detected, however, in the paravirtualized case free pages are excluded from the snapshot. *Desktop* shows that in the paravirtualized environment, a total of 490 MB of free pages and 257 MB of page cache data were excluded, resulting in a snapshot image of only 277 MB. A snapshot in the fully-virtualized environment, however, is a sizable 809 MB. This corresponds almost exactly to the savings that can be achieved from the page cache in the paravirtualized environment.

The numbers for *Reverse Map Average* deserve some more analysis. Since we maintain the reverse map only for read-write SPTEs (and ignore read-only mapped entries), the average reverse mapping degree is very low. Most modern OSes use a copy-on-write approach for multi-mappings, hence mappings are typically read-only. In other words, the space overhead of the reverse map is moderate even if the guest OS re-maps the same physical memory page several times.

Runtime overhead. The runtime overhead caused by transparently tracking I/O requests, maintaining the reverse map and handling the extra write fault exception is most pronounced for benchmarks with a high write activity such as *Postmark*. Compared to the unmodified Xen VMM, the experiments show a moderate 1.5% runtime performance degradation for the *Postmark* benchmark.

7.3 Periodic checkpointing

Exploiting free pages and unmodified pages in the page cache allow us to save a significant amount of space and time, however, we can further optimize the proposed method for periodic checkpoints by combining it with incremental checkpointing. To understand the effects of incremental checkpointing, we run the benchmark applications (Table 3) while taking periodic checkpoints. The *Desktop* benchmark is excluded from these experiments since it is not a good candidate for periodic checkpoints because the system is idle once all applications have been started. For each of the remaining four benchmarks, we have taken ten checkpoints over the course of each benchmark. The checkpointing interval differs for each benchmark as their execution times differ as well: for *Make*, the checkpointing interval was 360 seconds, for *Postmark* 25, *Software update* 10, and *Gzip* 5 seconds.

Figure 5 shows the results of periodic checkpointing. For each benchmark, the upper-hand graph shows the breakdown of the memory contents at each checkpoint. Here, *free* represents the amount of free memory. *Page cache* shows the amount of unmodified pages in the page cache. *Unchanged* stands for the amount of unmodified pages. None of these three classes of pages need to be saved to disk. *Changed*, finally, shows the amount of pages that have been modified since the last checkpoint and therefore need to be included in the incremental checkpoint image. To show the correlation between the page cache and the free pages more precisely, *changed* includes dirty pages from the page cache, heap, and stack, whereas *unchanged* only contains pages from the heap and the stack. Unmodified pages from the page cache are shown in *page cache*. The lower-hand graph shows the total amount of memory saved at each checkpoint for *unmodified*, the unmodified Xen checkpointing method; *page cache + Free*, the proposed method without incremental checkpointing; *inc*, incremental checkpointing implemented on top of *unmodified*; and, finally, *inc + page cache + free*, which represents the proposed method with incremental checkpointing.

For the benchmarks *Make*, *Postmark*, and *Gzip*, the proposed method without incremental checkpointing (*page cache + free*) outperforms incremental checkpointing (*inc*), whereas for *Desktop*, simple incremental checkpointing, *inc*, performs better than *page cache + free*. This shows the inherent weakness of incremental checkpointing in write-intensive situations. In addition good performance can be achieved by not saving pages from the page cache that are consistent with the data on disk. Another observation that can be made from the graphs in Figure 5 is that the proposed method does perform well and does not fluctuate regardless of the checkpointing interval or the I/O intensity of the application. Our technique directly benefits from the observation that the guest OS itself maintains consistency between dirty pages in the page cache and the disk while keeping the ratio of dirty pages at a minimum. In addition to that, the proposed technique benefits from incremental checkpointing as well. Our results show that *inc + page cache + free* outperforms all other methods independent of the I/O activity or the checkpointing interval.

Note that pure incremental checkpointing, as represented by *inc*, still needs to save the full contents of the guest's memory at the first checkpoint, whereas the proposed method, with or without incremental checkpointing, is able to reduce the size of the first checkpoint to a small fraction of the guest's memory.

The upper-hand graph of the *Make* benchmark (Figure 5 (d)) shows the correlation between the page cache and free pages. As more and more files get compiled, the number of pages allocated to the page cache increases and consequently the number of free pages decreases. At the 7th checkpoint, there are almost no free pages left, and the OS starts reclaiming pages from the page cache to satisfy memory requests. As a result, the amount of pages in the page cache has shrunk by the amount of pages reclaimed as free pages. This can be observed in the memory breakdown graph for the 8th checkpoint. This is a typical phenomenon in modern operating systems and can be observed in the other benchmarks as well.

Table 6 shows the average time required to save a checkpoint and the average size of the memory checkpoint files for an unmodified Xen implementation (*unmodified*, column two), the proposed method without incremental checkpointing (*page cache + free*, column three), the standard Xen implementation with incremental checkpointing (*incremental*, column five), and finally, the proposed method with incremental checkpointing (*incremental + page cache + free*, last column). Each of the result columns is broken down into the time required to take a checkpoint and the amount of disk space consumed. In the case of *unmodified*, the full memory contents are saved at every checkpoint independent of the benchmark. When computing the average, we do not consider the first checkpoint since incremental checkpointing (*incremental*) needs to save the full memory contents at the first iteration. Comparing our method with incremental checkpointing (*incremental + page cache + free*) to the *unmodified* approach, we achieve a 92% reduction in disk space and an 83% reduction in the time consumed to save the checkpoint. It also outperforms incremental checkpointing (*incremental*) by 67% for disk space and 33% for checkpointing time. Finally, we observe that our method, without incremental checkpointing (*page cache + free*), requires more time on average (9.9 sec compared to 9.71 sec) than the incremental approach (*incremental*) despite a smaller amount of saved data (198.7 MB compared to 234.7 MB). The reason for this is the aggregation time (Section 7.1) that is not present in *incremental*.

8. Conclusion and Future Work

In this work, we have presented a technique for fast and space-efficient checkpointing of virtual machines. Modern operating systems (OS) use the better part of the available memory for a page cache that caches data recently read from or written to disk. Through transparent I/O interception at the virtual machine monitor (VMM) level, we track I/O requests and maintain an up-to-date mapping of memory pages to disk blocks in our *page_to_block* map. At checkpoint time, we exclude those pages from the memory images written to disk, thereby saving a considerable amount of disk space and time. Several operations in the OS, such as removing pages from the page cache or writing to pages without flushing them to disk, are invisible to the VMM and would invalidate the *page_to_block* map. We have identified all these operations and notify the VMM in order to keep the mapping consistent.

We have implemented the proposed technique into the current Xen VMM, both for paravirtualized and fully-virtualized guests. Our experiments show that, on average, we achieve an 81% reduction in the stored data and a 74% reduction in the time required to take a single checkpoint in a paravirtualized environment.

For future work, we plan to integrate the presented technique into a framework for live migration of virtual machines with the goal of improving both the migration time as well as the downtime of the running guest.

References

[1] Red Hat, Inc. LVM architectural overview. http://www.redhat.com/docs/manuals/enterprise/RHEL-5-manual/Cluster_Logical_Volume_Manager/LVM_definition.html.

[2] Transcendent Memory Project. http://oss.oracle.com/projects/tmem.

[3] VirtualBox. http://www.virtualbox.org.

[4] VMware Workstation. http://www.vmware.com/products/workstation.

[5] M. Armbrust, A. Fox, R. Griffith, A. D. Joseph, R. H. Katz, A. Konwinski, G. Lee, D. A. Patterson, A. Rabkin, I. Stoica, and M. Zaharia. Above the clouds: A berkeley view of cloud computing. Technical Report UCB/EECS-2009-28, EECS Department, University of California, Berkeley, Feb 2009. URL http://www.eecs.berkeley.edu/Pubs/TechRpts/2009/EECS-2009-28.html.

[6] P. Barham, B. Dragovic, K. Fraser, S. Hand, T. Harris, A. Ho, R. Neugebauer, I. Pratt, and A. Warfield. Xen and the art of virtualization. In *SOSP '03: Proceedings of the nineteenth ACM symposium on Operating systems principles*, pages 164–177, New York, NY, USA, 2003. ACM. ISBN 1-58113-757-5. doi: http://doi.acm.org/10.1145/945445.945462.

[7] D. Bovet and M. Cesati. *Understanding the Linux Kernel, 3rd Edition*. Oreilly & Associates, 2005.

[8] T. C. Bressoud and F. B. Schneider. Hypervisor-based fault tolerance. *ACM Trans. Comput. Syst.*, 14(1):80–107, 1996. ISSN 0734-2071. doi: http://doi.acm.org/10.1145/225535.225538.

[9] E. Bugnion, S. Devine, K. Govil, and M. Rosenblum. Disco: running commodity operating systems on scalable multiprocessors. *ACM Trans. Comput. Syst.*, 15(4):412–447, 1997. ISSN 0734-2071. doi: http://doi.acm.org/10.1145/265924.265930.

[10] C. Clark, K. Fraser, S. Hand, J. G. Hansen, E. Jul, C. Limpach, I. Pratt, and A. Warfield. Live migration of virtual machines. In *NSDI'05: Proceedings of the 2nd conference on Symposium on Networked Systems Design & Implementation*, pages 273–286, Berkeley, CA, USA, 2005. USENIX Association.

[11] B. Cully, G. Lefebvre, D. Meyer, M. Feeley, N. Hutchinson, and A. Warfield. Remus: high availability via asynchronous virtual machine replication. In *NSDI'08: Proceedings of the 5th USENIX Symposium on Networked Systems Design and Implementation*, pages 161–

174, Berkeley, CA, USA, 2008. USENIX Association. ISBN 111-999-5555-22-1.

[12] G. W. Dunlap, S. T. King, S. Cinar, M. A. Basrai, and P. M. Chen. Revirt: enabling intrusion analysis through virtual-machine logging and replay. In *OSDI '02: Proceedings of the 5th symposium on Operating systems design and implementation*, pages 211–224, New York, NY, USA, 2002. ACM. ISBN 978-1-4503-0111-4. doi: http://doi.acm.org/10.1145/1060289.1060309.

[13] D. Gupta, S. Lee, M. Vrable, S. Savage, A. C. Snoeren, G. Varghese, G. M. Voelker, and A. Vahdat. Difference engine: Harnessing memory redundancy in virtual machines. In *OSDI '08: Proceedings of the 8th symposium on Operating systems design and implementation*, 2008.

[14] I. Habib. Virtualization with kvm. *Linux J.*, 2008, February 2008. ISSN 1075-3583. URL http://portal.acm.org/citation.cfm?id=1344209.1344217.

[15] M. R. Hines and K. Gopalan. Post-copy based live virtual machine migration using adaptive pre-paging and dynamic self-ballooning. In *VEE '09: Proceedings of the 2009 ACM SIGPLAN/SIGOPS international conference on Virtual execution environments*, pages 51–60, New York, NY, USA, 2009. ACM. ISBN 978-1-60558-375-4. doi: http://doi.acm.org/10.1145/1508293.1508301.

[16] S. T. Jones, A. C. Arpaci-Dusseau, and R. H. Arpaci-Dusseau. Geiger: monitoring the buffer cache in a virtual machine environment. In *ASPLOS-XII: Proceedings of the 12th international conference on Architectural support for programming languages and operating systems*, pages 14–24, New York, NY, USA, 2006. ACM. ISBN 1-59593-451-0. doi: http://doi.acm.org/10.1145/1168857.1168861.

[17] J. Katcher. PostMark: A New File System Benchmark. Technical Report Technical Report TR3022, Network Appliance, October 1997.

[18] S. T. King, G. W. Dunlap, and P. M. Chen. Debugging operating systems with time-traveling virtual machines. In *ATC '05: Proceedings of the annual conference on USENIX Annual Technical Conference*, pages 1–1, Berkeley, CA, USA, 2005. USENIX Association.

[19] H. A. Lagar-Cavilla, J. A. Whitney, A. M. Scannell, P. Patchin, S. M. Rumble, E. de Lara, M. Brudno, and M. Satyanarayanan. Snowflock: rapid virtual machine cloning for cloud computing. In *EuroSys '09: Proceedings of the 4th ACM European conference on Computer systems*, pages 1–12, New York, NY, USA, 2009. ACM. ISBN 978-1-60558-482-9. doi: http://doi.acm.org/10.1145/1519065.1519067.

[20] J. Liu, W. Huang, B. Abali, and D. K. Panda. High performance vmm-bypass i/o in virtual machines. In *ATEC '06: Proceedings of the annual conference on USENIX '06 Annual Technical Conference*, pages 3–3, Berkeley, CA, USA, 2006. USENIX Association.

[21] P. Lu and K. Shen. Virtual machine memory access tracing with hypervisor exclusive cache. In *ATC'07: 2007 USENIX Annual Technical Conference on Proceedings of the USENIX Annual Technical Conference*, pages 1–15, Berkeley, CA, USA, 2007. USENIX Association. ISBN 999-8888-77-6.

[22] D. Magenheimer, C. Mason, D. McCracken, and K. Hackel. Transcendent memory and linux. In *Proceedings of the Linux Symposium*, pages 191–200, Montreal, Quebec Canada, 2009.

[23] D. T. Meyer, G. Aggarwal, B. Cully, G. Lefebvre, M. J. Feeley, N. C. Hutchinson, and A. Warfield. Parallax: virtual disks for virtual machines. In *Eurosys '08: Proceedings of the 3rd ACM SIGOPS/EuroSys European Conference on Computer Systems 2008*, pages 41–54, New York, NY, USA, 2008. ACM. ISBN 978-1-60558-013-5. doi: http://doi.acm.org/10.1145/1352592.1352598.

[24] G. Milos, D. G. Murray, S. Hand, and M. A. Fetterman. Satori: Enlightened page sharing. In *ATC'09: 2009 USENIX Annual Technical Conference on Proceedings of the USENIX Annual Technical Conference*, Berkeley, CA, USA, 2009. USENIX Association.

[25] M. Nelson, B.-H. Lim, and G. Hutchins. Fast transparent migration for virtual machines. In *ATEC '05: Proceedings of the annual conference on USENIX Annual Technical Conference*, pages 25–25, Berkeley, CA, USA, 2005. USENIX Association.

[26] J. S. Plank, M. Beck, G. Kingsley, and K. Li. Libckpt: transparent checkpointing under unix. In *TCON'95: Proceedings of the USENIX 1995 Technical Conference Proceedings on USENIX 1995 Technical Conference Proceedings*, pages 18–18, Berkeley, CA, USA, 1995. USENIX Association.

[27] J. S. Plank, Y. Chen, K. Li, M. Beck, and G. Kingsley. Memory exclusion: optimizing the performance of checkpointing systems. *Softw. Pract. Exper.*, 29(2):125–142, 1999. ISSN 0038-0644. doi: http://dx.doi.org/10.1002/(SICI)1097-024X(199902)29:2⟨125::AID-SPE224⟩3.0.CO;2-7.

[28] J. R. Santos, Y. Turner, G. Janakiraman, and I. Pratt. Bridging the gap between software and hardware techniques for i/o virtualization. In *ATC'08: USENIX 2008 Annual Technical Conference on Annual Technical Conference*, pages 29–42, Berkeley, CA, USA, 2008. USENIX Association.

[29] M. Schwidefsky, H. Franke, R. Mansell, H. Raj, D. Osisek, and J. Choi. Collaborative memory management in hosted linux environments. In *Proceedings of the Linux Symposium*, pages 313–328, Ottawa, Ontario, Canada, 2006.

[30] Y. Tamura. Kemari: Virtual machine synchronization for fault tolerance using domt. In *Xen Summit*, 2008.

[31] M. Vrable, J. Ma, J. Chen, D. Moore, E. Vandekieft, A. C. Snoeren, G. M. Voelker, and S. Savage. Scalability, fidelity, and containment in the potemkin virtual honeyfarm. In *SOSP '05: Proceedings of the twentieth ACM symposium on Operating systems principles*, pages 148–162, New York, NY, USA, 2005. ACM. ISBN 1-59593-079-5. doi: http://doi.acm.org/10.1145/1095810.1095825.

[32] C. A. Waldspurger. Memory resource management in vmware esx server. In *OSDI '02: Proceedings of the 5th symposium on Operating systems design and implementation*, pages 181–194, New York, NY, USA, 2002. ACM. ISBN 978-1-4503-0111-4. doi: http://doi.acm.org/10.1145/1060289.1060307.

[33] T. Wood, P. Shenoy, A. Venkataramani, and M. Yousif. Black-box and gray-box strategies for virtual machine migration. In *NSDI'07: Proceedings of the 5th USENIX Symposium on Networked Systems Design and Implementation*, Berkeley, CA, USA, 2007. USENIX Association.

[34] W. Zhao and Z. Wang. Dynamic memory balancing for virtual machines. In *VEE '09: Proceedings of the 2009 ACM SIGPLAN/SIGOPS international conference on Virtual execution environments*, pages 21–30, New York, NY, USA, 2009. ACM. ISBN 978-1-60558-375-4. doi: http://doi.acm.org/10.1145/1508293.1508297.

[35] P. Zhou, V. Pandey, J. Sundaresan, A. Raghuraman, Y. Zhou, and S. Kumar. Dynamic tracking of page miss ratio curve for memory management. In *ASPLOS-XI: Proceedings of the 11th international conference on Architectural support for programming languages and operating systems*, pages 177–188, New York, NY, USA, 2004. ACM. ISBN 1-58113-804-0. doi: http://doi.acm.org/10.1145/1024393.1024415.

Fast Restore of Checkpointed Memory using Working Set Estimation

Irene Zhang   Alex Garthwaite   Yury Baskakov   Kenneth C. Barr

VMware, Inc.

{izhang, alextg, ybaskako, kbarr}@vmware.com

Irene Zhang   Alex Garthwaite   Yury Baskakov   Kenneth C. Barr

VMware, Inc.

{izhang, alextg, ybaskako, kbarr}@vmware.com

Abstract

In order to make save and restore features practical, saved virtual machines (VMs) must be able to quickly restore to normal operation. Unfortunately, fetching a saved memory image from persistent storage can be slow, especially as VMs grow in memory size. One possible solution for reducing this time is to lazily restore memory after the VM starts. However, accesses to unrestored memory after the VM starts can degrade performance, sometimes rendering the VM unusable for even longer. Existing performance metrics do not account for performance degradation after the VM starts, making it difficult to compare lazily restoring memory against other approaches. In this paper, we propose both a better metric for evaluating the performance of different restore techniques and a better scheme for restoring saved VMs.

Existing performance metrics do not reflect what is really important to the user—the time until the VM returns to normal operation. We introduce the time-to-responsiveness metric, which better characterizes user experience while restoring a saved VM by measuring the time until there is no longer a noticeable performance impact on the restoring VM. We propose a new lazy restore technique, called working set restore, that minimizes performance degradation after the VM starts by prefetching the working set. We also introduce a novel working set estimator based on memory tracing that we use to test working set restore, along with an estimator that uses access-bit scanning. We show that working set restore can improve the performance of restoring a saved VM by more than 89% for some workloads.

Categories and Subject Descriptors D.4.5 [*Reliability*]: Checkpoint/restart

General Terms Measurement, Performance

Keywords Checkpoint/restore, Performance

1. Overview

Virtual machines (VMs) have become one of the primary computing environments in the cloud. One benefit of virtualization is the ability to save and restore the state of a running VM. This ability enables users to *suspend* an idle VM, pausing its execution, which can free up data center resources and reduce power usage. It also al-

lows users to *checkpoint* a VM, freezing the VM at a single point in time, which is used for backup and fault tolerance. Outside of the cloud, VMs have become ubiquitous on desktops and laptops as well. These users save VMs for similar reasons, suspending VMs to allow them to easily return to previous work while freeing up resources for other applications, and checkpointing VMs to save their operating system and applications in a known good state.

In order to make suspending and checkpointing VMs practical, the hypervisor must be able to quickly restart the VM from a saved state. Users are more inclined to suspend an idle VM if it takes seconds to resume rather than minutes. The ability to restore quickly from a saved image can also enable many other useful features. For example, cloud service providers would like to be able to quickly boot stateless VMs, allowing them to dynamically allocate VMs as needed. This quick-boot feature could be simulated by restoring to a checkpoint taken right after boot if the restore process is very fast.

It is challenging to restore a saved VM quickly because the VM's saved state must be retrieved from slow persistent storage. This state includes some CPU and device state, and the contents of the VM's memory. Restoring the saved memory image, which is generally an order of magnitude or two larger than device state, takes the bulk of the time. The time to restore a VM continues to grow as the memory requirements of virtual machines increase while the speed of storage does not keep pace. Reflecting the growth in memory size for PCs, VMs 10 years ago typically had less than 256 MB of memory, while today 1 GB VMs are common on laptops and PCs and even larger VMs are used in datacenters.

The simplest approach to resuming a VM's execution is to restore all memory contents at once, along with the device state. We call this method *eager restore* because the hypervisor eagerly retrieves and sets up all guest memory before starting the guest. The time to restore a VM this way increases linearly with the size of the VM. This method worked well when VMs used relatively small amounts of memory, but cannot be sustained as the size of VM memory grows. It takes tens of seconds to retrieve a few hundred megabytes of saved memory contents from disk, but this time increases to minutes as the saved memory image becomes larger than a gigabyte.

An alternate approach is to load only the CPU and device state before starting execution, and restore memory contents in the background while the VM runs. Any time the VM touches memory that has not yet been restored, the hypervisor pauses the execution of the VM and retrieves that memory from disk. Because the memory contents are retrieved when the VM accesses that memory, we call this approach *lazy restore*. This approach is appealing because the VM starts much faster, after retrieving only a small amount of device state, and the cost does not grow with the VM's memory size. However, whenever the VM accesses a page of memory that has not yet been restored, the contents of that page must be faulted in from

VEE'11, March 9–11, 2011, Newport Beach, California, USA.
Copyright © 2011 ACM 978-1-4503-0501-3/11/03...$10.00

disk on-demand, and the execution of the VM cannot be resumed until the page has been retrieved.

Handling these on-demand page faults can have a significant performance impact. Previous research has shown that users notice if the response time to a user action exceeds 100 milliseconds, and become frustrated if it exceeds 1 second [17, 23]. With disk seek times on the order of 10 milliseconds, this allows only around 10 accesses to unrestored memory before the user notices performance degradation and around 100 accesses before the user becomes frustrated. Unfortunately, even simple user actions like moving the mouse can require hundreds of memory accesses, giving some idea of the performance impact if all of those accesses cause a page fault. Our experiments and previous user reports reflect this—even though the VM is running during the lazy restore, it is so slow that it is essentially unusable. In fact, we found that the VM's performance can be impacted severely for so long during a lazy restore that eager restore can actually seem to perform better from the user's point of view. [1]

Neither the eager approach nor the lazy approach to restoring a saved VM offer ideal performance for the user. Instead, we propose using a hybrid approach that prefetches the working set of the VM's memory, then starts the VM and restores the rest of memory lazily. We call this approach *working set restore*. By prefetching the working set, we minimize the performance degradation after the VM starts because most of the memory that the VM accesses will have already been restored. Working set prefetching is commonly used for applications [11]; our contribution is to apply it to the problem of optimizing the restore of a saved VM.

The success of working set restore depends on the accuracy of the working set estimator. We discuss two estimators in this paper. The first is a working set estimator that uses access-bit scanning. While the access-bit scanning technique is simple, it still does a good job of finding the working set. Our experiments show that, for some workloads, the access-bit working set estimator was able to predict up to 98.6% of the VM's accesses while the VM is being restored. We also implemented a novel technique for checkpointed VMs that traces memory access during checkpointing to gather the working set. Our insight is that when a checkpointed VM is restored, it returns back to the point where checkpointing began. If the VM is deterministic, it should re-execute in the same way after it restores as when it was checkpointed. This means that we can almost perfectly predict the memory accesses of the VM after it starts by tracing memory accesses during the checkpointing. Our experiments show this to be true; we found that we could predict up to 99.2% of memory accesses using this technique.

It is difficult to measure the performance benefit of working set restore using existing metrics because they do not account for performance degradation after the VM starts. The two most commonly used metrics are the total time to restore the VM and the time until the VM starts. The total time to restore the VM does not account for the fact that, during a lazy restore, the VM starts (and the user may be able to use the VM) long before the entire VM is restored. Using the total time until the VM starts avoids this problem, but does not account for the fact that the VM might not be usable after it starts. This paper presents a new metric, called *time-to-responsiveness* (TTR), that better measures the time until the VM appears restored to the user (i.e. the time until the VM returns to normal operation). Time-to-responsiveness builds on the idea of a minimum mutator utilization (MMU) [3, 4, 14], a metric previously used to measure the ongoing overhead of a service like garbage-collection techniques. We extend MMU to give us the time

until the overhead of the restore process has fallen to an acceptable level for the VM to appear restored.

The rest of this paper is organized as follows. In Section 2 we examine the problem with the two existing metrics for comparing restore techniques and explain our new time-to-responsiveness metric. Section 3 gives background on the checkpoint and suspend mechanism in VMware Workstation that working set restore is built on. In Section 4, we present the design and implementation of working set restore for VMware Workstation. This section also details our simple working set estimator using access-bit scanning and our new working set estimator that uses memory tracing. Section 5 evaluates the performance benefit of working set restore and how the accuracy of the working set estimator affects performance using our time-to-responsiveness metric. Section 6 discusses related work, and Section 7 concludes.

2. Measuring Restore Performance

One reason designing a better restore scheme is difficult is that there are no effective metrics to compare the performance of different restore schemes. Using the total time to restore or the time until the VM starts to measure performance can make eager restore or lazy restore appear optimal. However, neither metric reflects what is really important to the user, which is the time until the VM and its applications return to normal performance. With this observation, we propose a new time-to-responsiveness metric that better characterizes the user experience while restoring a saved VM.

2.1 Common Metrics

There are two commonly used metrics for measuring restore performance: the total time to restore the VM and the time until the VM starts. Both are appealing metrics because they are easy to measure and understand. The total time to restore the VM measures the amount of time it takes for all of the VM's memory to be copied from persistent storage to host memory. For eager restore, the total time to restore depends on the size of the saved VM and the speed of the persistent store. The performance of eager restore using this metric scales linearly with the size of the VM's memory. For this metric, eager restore is optimal because it allows memory to be linearly fetched from the disk as fast as possible, maximizing disk throughput. Lazy restore can take quite some time to completely finish because memory is restored only when it is accessed by a VM or touched by a slow-running background thread. Therefore, the performance is bounded by the memory size of the saved VM and the speed at which the background thread retrieves memory. If the VM is not using most of its memory, the background process could take a long time to restore all of memory because it is not important to quickly restore memory that is not being used. However, this metric does not account for the fact that the VM has started and the user might be able to use the VM long before the lazy restore completely finishes.

The time until the VM starts measures the time until the VM is able to begin execution of the guest. This metric better accounts for the fact that the VM might start before it is completely restored. For eager restore, this metric is the same as the total time to restore the VM because the VM does not start until it is completely restored. The performance of a lazy restore using this metric depends on the size of the device state of the saved VM and disk speed. Unlike eager restore, the performance of lazy restore for this metric does not decrease with the size of memory. Using this metric, it appears that lazy restore is optimal because the device state is the minimal state that must be restored before the VM can start, so the VM starts as soon as possible. However, we observed that the VM is not immediately usable during a lazy restore because of performance degradation caused by accesses to unrestored memory. Depending on the severity of the performance degradation, the user cannot

---

[1] For this reason, VMware Workstation 7.0 switched from lazy restore back to eager restore.

necessarily use the VM and its applications although the VM has started. While the time until the VM starts better accounts for restore performance than the total time to restore, it still does not measure when the VM becomes responsive to the user.

2.2 Mutator Utilization

Instead of measuring the total time to restore or start the VM, a better metric for restore performance should measure the time until the VM *appears* to be restored, which is when the performance degradation is no longer apparent to the user. In order to pinpoint that time, we must be able to measure the performance degradation of different restore schemes after the VM starts.

Measuring the performance degradation of a service has been well studied. In particular, work on the impact of pause times caused by garbage-collection makes use of the notion of a *minimum mutator utilization* (MMU) to evaluate and compare different garbage-collection techniques [3, 4, 14]. Pause times are periods in which an application—the *mutator*—is inactive while the garbage collector (GC) performs some amount of work. In the context of restore, the VM and its applications can be considered the mutator and the pauses caused by accesses to unrestored memory can be considered similar to pause times. The MMU is the lowest utilization achieved by the application during its execution for some application-specific window of time; the window reflects both the scheduling needs of the application and the fact that GC pauses may not be uniformly distributed or of equal duration.

Unlike a service like garbage collection that is on-going, a restore is limited by the size of the VM's memory. When the VM first starts it may access a lot of unrestored memory, but as more of its memory is restored, either by accesses from the VM or by the background thread, the accesses to unrestored memory will slow and eventually stop. It is important to measure this change over time, so a single minimum mutator utilization is not sufficient. But we can apply the idea of a mutator utilization as a way of measuring performance degradation over time. We can track the performance degradation caused by the ongoing restore process by measuring how much time was spent restoring memory and how much time was available to the guest OS and other "normal" processes, the mutator, during a particular window of time after the VM starts. For that window, if most of the time is spent restoring memory, then the VM's performance must suffer. If most of that window was spent running the guest OS or doing other normal work, then the VM must be running normally.

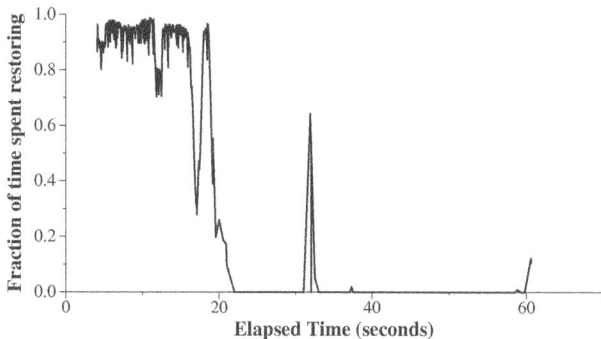

Figure 1. Fraction of each second restoring pages accessed by the VM during the lazy restore of a 1 GB VM running Red Hat Enterprise Linux 4. For the first 20 seconds, almost 0% of the time is available to the VM, which will lead to severe performance degradation. After the first 20 seconds, the VM will see minimal overhead from memory being lazily restored except for a few spikes, causing small lags.

As an example, Figure 1 shows the fraction of time spent restoring memory during the lazy restore of a typical Linux VM. It is clear from Figure 1 that there must be significant performance degradation for the first 20 seconds, as nearly all time is devoted to restoring memory. After the first 20 seconds, the VM is probably running normally because there is very little overhead (other than a few spikes) imposed by restoring memory and most of the time is spent doing normal work in the guest or elsewhere.

2.3 Time-to-responsiveness (TTR)

The utilization graph shows how the restore process affects the VM after it starts. In order to pinpoint the time when the performance degradation of the restore process is no longer apparent to the user, we extend the notion of MMU to calculate the time-to-responsiveness (TTR) metric for restoring a saved VM. We define TTR as:

$$\text{TTR}(w, u) = \min\{t | \text{MMU}_{\forall t' \geq t}(w) \geq u\}$$

where the time-window w and desired utilization u are application-specific parameters. TTR is the earliest time such that from that point forward in the execution of the VM, we achieve a minimum level of utilization for the VM. The level of performance is entirely application-dependent because some applications can tolerate more performance degradation than others, so we look at TTR as a curve instead of a single number. In general, we choose to fix w and then plot TTR as minimum utilization over time, which shows, for each point in time t, the minimum mutator utilization from t until the end of the restore. To find the actual time until the performance degradation is no longer apparent from such a graph, we need to determine the minimum utilization that the VM can tolerate. For example, for VMs and applications that can operate normally with at least 90% of the execution time each second, the minimum utilization for TTR would be 90% with a one second window.

Figure 2 shows the TTR graph for the example from Figure 1 with window sizes of 0.1 seconds, 1 second and 10 seconds. From such a graph, one can choose a suitable level of performance and identify the earliest point in the restore process where the minimum utilization is achieved. Such a point is the TTR for the corresponding level of performance. One can see that when the minimum utilization is 0, the TTR is also 0, so a VM that can tolerate any degree of performance degradation and still operate normally can be considered restored right away. When the level is 100%, the TTR is the time that the last page was restored on-demand. VMs that require all of the system time (i.e. cannot tolerate any performance degradation) cannot be considered fully restored until there are no more pages to be restored on-demand. Section 5 discusses how the TTR metric correlates to actual application performance.

To compare restore schemes using TTR, we can compare TTR for each scheme for a particular window and minimum utilization. Alternatively, we could plot the TTR curves for each scheme, giving a comparison over a range of applications. The TTR for an eager restore is always the same for all window sizes and minimum utilizations because eager restore does not impact the performance of a VM after it starts. We show the TTR of a lazy restore in Figure 2; the TTR of eager restore for the same VM is 32 seconds. Using TTR to compare, it becomes less obvious whether eager restore or lazy restore are optimal. For the example VM, the TTR of both eager and lazy restore is about 32 seconds, if the VM can tolerate a minimum utilization of 80% for a window size of 1 second. With TTR, one can see that both eager and lazy restore are optimal for certain classes of applications. In this example, if the VM requires a minimum utilization of more than 80% for a window size of 0.1 seconds, which would indicate that it is running a very time-sensitive application, then eager restore would be the better choice. If the VM can tolerate a minimum utilization of 80% for a window

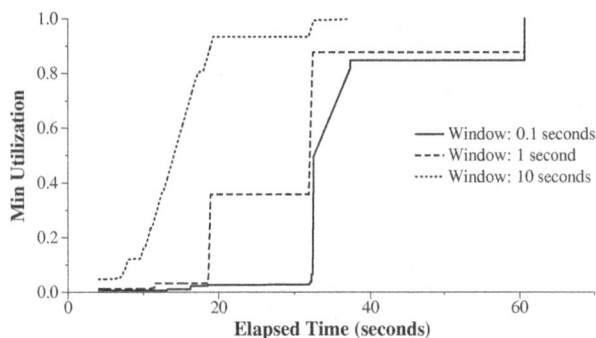

Figure 2. Minimum utilization of an idle RHEL VM during a lazy restore as shown in Figure 1. For each level of performance, the x-axis shows the corresponding TTR. Ideally, the percentage rises to 1 as quickly as possible, returning the system to 100% utilization.

size of 10 seconds, then lazy restore would be the better solution. This conclusion makes sense intuitively: lazy restore is better for applications that can tolerate more performance degradation and eager restore is better for applications that cannot.

3. Saving and Restoring in VMware Workstation

We implemented a prototype of working set restore using the suspend and checkpoint features in VMware Workstation. Workstation is a hosted hypervisor that runs guest OSes on top of a host OS, in contrast to a native hypervisor, which runs directly on hardware [22]. This section describes how Workstation saves and restores VM memory for suspend and checkpoint, providing context for the design of working set restore discussed in the next section. Both suspend and checkpoint use the same mechanism, so working set restore improves the performance of both.

3.1 Memory Model

In a hosted hypervisor, the hypervisor must depend on the host to allocate memory for the VM. Workstation backs guest memory using a memory-mapped file, called the paging file. In addition to being used for backing guest memory, Workstation directly uses the paging file as the VM's saved memory image for a suspend. Workstation uses a copy of the paging file as the saved memory image for a checkpoint to keep the format of the memory image identical for suspended and checkpointed VMs, so that one restore mechanism can be used for restoring both.

Workstation uses the memory pages allocated by the host for the paging file to store pages of guest memory. Workstation sets up page tables to allow the guest to directly access this memory. The paging file is a raw data file and stores the VM's memory sequentially by guest physical address. For example, the first 4096 bytes of the paging file are the first page of guest physical memory and so on. The advantage of keeping the paging file unformatted and memory-mapped is that the host OS can do almost all of the work in managing the memory pages backing guest memory; the hypervisor only needs to manage memory mappings for the guest.

3.2 Suspend and Checkpoint Mechanisms

Workstation supports both suspending and checkpointing VMs. An important difference between the two features is that a checkpointed VM continues to run after the checkpoint. We will discuss the process of suspending a VM first as it is simpler. Since the VM stops running after the suspend, Workstation can directly use the VM's current paging file as the saved memory image. This makes the process of saving a VM's memory for suspend relatively easy.

Workstation just unmaps the paging file, being sure to mark pages that are dirty. The host OS will handle writing dirty pages to disk.

Checkpointing a VM is more complicated because Workstation must make a copy of the paging file. Workstation cannot directly use the VM's paging file in this case because the VM continues running and using its paging file after the checkpoint. To minimize the impact on the running VM, Workstation stops the VM, saves the device state, and then restarts the VM and copies the paging file lazily while the VM continues running. A background thread linearly scans pages of memory, copying them to the saved paging file. Since the VM continues to modify memory, Workstation must ensure that no memory is overwritten before the background thread copies it to the saved paging file. It does this by using memory *write traces*. Write traces notify the hypervisor before the guest OS writes to a traced page. For checkpointing, Workstation puts write traces on all guest memory pages. When the guest tries to write to one of those pages, the write trace will trigger. Workstation will copy the page to the saved paging file and remove the write trace on the page, then allow the guest to write to the page. The background thread removes write traces as it scans through memory because the guest is free to write any page that the background thread has already copied.

3.3 Restore Mechanisms

VMware Workstation can restore suspended and checkpointed VMs. Workstation must preserve the state of a checkpointed VM when restoring it, so that the VM can be restored back to that checkpoint again, which is not necessary with a suspended VM. Since we do not have to worry about preserving the state of a suspended VM, we can directly use the saved paging file as the paging file for the running VM. The paging file is memory-mapped into the hypervisor's address space and used to back guest memory. Workstation touches each page of the paging file to force the host to allocate a page and bring the memory contents off of disk, and to set up meta-data for the page. Again, because the file is memory-mapped, the host will take care of allocating memory and reading the file from disk.

Workstation cannot directly use the saved paging file as the paging file for a checkpointed VM, so it must first make a copy of the old paging file. Workstation allocates a memory-mapped file, then copies the saved paging file into that file. This process has the same effect as touching each page when restoring a suspended VM; it causes the host to allocate a page, then Workstation copies the page from the old paging file into the page and sets up the meta-data for the page. At this point, Workstation can start execution of the VM.

The process just described is eager restore for suspended or checkpointed VMs. Workstation also supports lazy restore for both suspended and checkpointed VMs. Instead of touching or copying each page of the paging file before starting the VM, Workstation starts the VM first. While the VM runs, Workstation executes a separate thread in the background that touches, and copies if necessary, the pages of the paging file. To keep track of which pages have been touched, Workstation keeps a bitmap of restored pages. When the guest accesses an unallocated page, the hypervisor checks if the page is unrestored. If so, the hypervisor restores the page on-demand by touching it, which causes the host OS to allocate a page and fetch the contents from disk, and copying the page if necessary.

4. Working Set Restore

Working set restore is built on the features of VMware Workstation discussed in the last section. First, we discuss techniques for estimating the working set of the VM. Then, we explain the details of implementing working set restore.

4.1 Working Set Estimation

We implemented two working set estimators: one using access-bit scanning and another using memory traces to track memory accesses. Estimating the working set by access-bit scanning works for both suspend and checkpoint, while estimating the working set using memory tracing only works for checkpoint. Using access-bit scanning is more general-purpose, but imposes a constant overhead while the VM runs. Our implementation requires a hardware MMU [2], which most modern machines support. Access-bit scanning can also be done with a software MMU, but it imposes a greater overhead and misses some accesses. Using memory tracing only works for checkpoints, but it only imposes an overhead during the checkpointing process, which has an overhead anyway. Our experiments found using memory tracing to be more accurate at estimating the working set.

4.1.1 Access-bit Scanning

Our implementation of working set estimation using access-bit scanning works like a simplified CLOCK algorithm [8]. We use the flags in the page table entries to monitor the access patterns of the guest OS. We constantly loop over the page tables, scanning and clearing access-bits in the background while the VM is running. Any page whose access-bit has been set during the scan loop is marked as being part of the working set. The speed at which the scanner runs depends on the time it takes to restore the VM. In particular, we would like to scan memory at about the same speed at which it is restored by the background thread. This is simple because the speed of the background thread is set by a configuration option, so the speed of the scanner can be set using the same configuration option. By making the two rates equal, the working set we get is approximately the number of pages that the guest OS touches during the amount of time that it takes for a restore. If the page scanning rate is too fast or slow, then we will underestimate or overestimate the number of pages that we need to prefetch. We would like to avoid overestimating because a larger working set takes longer to copy when saving the VM and prefetch when the VM is being restored. Underestimating the working set, even by a small amount, can degrade performance during the lazy restore, as we show in Section 5.4.2.

4.1.2 Memory Tracing

The insight that motivates using memory traces for working set estimation is that when a checkpointed VM is restored, it returns to the point where lazy checkpointing of memory began. Thus, if the VM is deterministic, it will re-execute the same code that it executed during the lazy checkpoint period. Most VMs are not perfectly deterministic, as timing can change, so the prediction will not be perfect. However, our experiments show that this working set estimator comes close to having an oracle predict the memory accesses of the VM during the lazy restore.

To capture the memory accesses during the lazy checkpointing process, we add read traces to the write traces that Workstation uses already. Like write traces, read traces notify the hypervisor before the guest reads a page of memory. When notified of a read or a write during the lazy checkpoint, we note that the guest accessed that page and add it to our working set. If it is a write trace that triggered, we copy the page as usual and remove both traces. There is no need to leave the traces in place once the page has been added to the working set, so we remove them to reduce the performance overhead. If it is a read trace that triggered, we add the page to our working set and remove the read trace, leaving the write trace. It is not necessary to copy the page for reads, so we do not. This reduces the cost of handling a read trace since reads are more common than writes. We need to leave the write trace intact because the guest might still write to the page, at which point we would have to copy the page. For pages that are copied by the background thread, we leave the read and write traces in place. Leaving both traces in place ensures that we do not miss any page accesses, but adds some overhead to the lazy checkpointing process. However, the overhead is minimal because we only need to set a bit when those traces trigger, rather than copying a page to disk.

4.2 Saving and Restoring the Working Set

For a checkpoint or suspend, the working set must be saved with the VM after it is collected. Depending on the working set estimator, the working set is either collected continuously, for the access-bit scanning estimator, or during the checkpointing process, for the memory tracing estimator. After the working set has been collected, the pages in the working set are copied to a separate file, so that they are stored sequentially on disk. This copying incurs some cost when saving the VM. We save the working set separately from the memory image because the saved memory image shares the same format as the paging file. It is possible to avoid the cost of copying the working set by reorganizing the saved memory image to group the pages in the working set together, but that would negate the advantages of keeping the format of the paging file and the saved memory image of a checkpointed VM the same. We also save a bitmap of which pages in memory are in the working set, which is an efficient way of saving the guest physical address of each page in the working set.

Working set restore depends on both lazy and eager restore mechanisms in VMware Workstation. Working set restore first pre-restores the working set by copying pages from the saved working set file into the paging file before starting the VM. It marks those pages as restored in the bitmap that tracks restored pages. Workstation then starts the VM and restores the rest of memory in the background while the VM runs. Like lazy restore, if the VM accesses unrestored memory, it causes a page fault and Workstation restores (by either touching or copying) the page on-demand.

5. Evaluation

This section evaluates the performance of working set restore. We answer the following questions:

- Does working set restore improve overall performance?
- Does time-to-responsiveness correlate to user experience?
- How do eager restore, lazy restore and working set restore compare using TTR?
- Does working set size affect TTR for different restore techniques?
- How accurate are our working set estimators?
- Does the accuracy of the working set estimator affect the performance of working set restore?

5.1 Test Setup

We evaluated the performance of working set restore using a mechanical hard disk. All of the experiments in this paper were run with dual 2.3 GHz AMD Opteron 2376 Quad-Core processors, 4 GB of memory, and a Seagate model ST3750330AS hard disk with the specifications shown in Table 1. The AMD Shanghai processor supports hardware virtualization, allowing us to use hardware page tables for access-bit scanning. The host OS was 64-bit Ubuntu 9.10.

In general, our testing procedure consisted of the following steps:

1. Run the VM until the VM achieves steady state. Since the steady state is different for each workload, we define the steady state separately for each experiment in the following sections.

Table 1. Disk Specifications for Seagate ST3750330AS [20]

Interface	SATA 3.0 Gb/s
Capacity	750 GB
RPM	7200 RPM
Cache	32 MB
Average Latency	4.16 ms
Random read seek	< 8.5 ms
Random write seek	< 9.5 ms

2. Save the VM along with the working set.

3. Ensure that none of the saved VM state is cached on the host by clearing out the host buffer cache using `sync` and `echo 3 > /proc/sys/vm/drop_caches` to drop all file caches.

4. Restore the saved VM image with one of the restore techniques.

To ensure fair comparisons between restore techniques, we restored the same checkpointed VM for each technique. The simple eager and lazy schemes ignored the working set information saved in the checkpoint. We saved the working set as estimated by both access-bit scanning and memory tracing for each checkpoint, so that we can compare the two techniques with the same checkpointed VM. Working set restore also works for suspended VMs, but we use checkpointed VMs because the experiments are easier to replicate with a checkpoint. The performance for restoring both are similar because they share the same restore mechanism.

For all of the experiments, we fix the window size for TTR at 1 second and only draw the minimum utilization curve for that window size. We believe that 1 second is an appropriate window size for the applications that we use and is a small enough window to provide good user responsiveness.

Since the performance of eager restore is always about 32 seconds for our 1 GB VM, we do not include it the graphs. For our application tests, we plot lazy restore against working set restore using memory tracing estimator. The performance of working set restore using both estimators that we implemented is similar, so we do not include both in our graphs. Section 5.4.1 compares the two working set estimators that we implemented and shows the effects of the accuracy of the working set estimator on working set restore.

5.2 Simple Linux Test

First, we revisit the motivating example from Section 2. The VM in Figure 1 was running 32-bit Red Hat Enterprise Linux 4 Update 4 (Linux 2.6.9-42.0.3ELsmp). We consider the VM to have reached steady state 20 minutes after booting without any applications running, so we save the VM after running for 20 mins. In this experiment, the working set was about 3% of the 1 GB of memory. The `free` command reported 36 MB used and 230 MB used for buffer caches.

We compared the performance of lazy restore and working set restore by restoring the same saved VM image using both methods. Figure 3 shows the location in the guest's physical address space of prefetched pages and pages restored on-demand. For lazy restore, there were a large number of accesses to unrestored memory after the VM starts. There is some locality to the accesses. The cluster of accesses in the very low physical address space is from the kernel. The cluster of accesses in the higher physical address space is from applications. The locality of application accesses is mostly because the VM is newly booted and has not run many applications yet, so the physical address space is not yet fragmented.

Working set restore prefetches exactly those regions of memory where most of the accesses to unrestored memory were during the lazy restore. Once the VM starts, there are less accesses to unrestored memory for working set restore compared to lazy restore.

The next section shows how this reduction in accesses to unrestored memory leads to less performance degradation after the VM starts.

5.3 Application Testing

We evaluated the end-to-end application performance of working set restore using two sample applications: SPECjbb and MPlayer. Our goal was to determine the performance improvement of working set restore for applications and show how TTR correlates with application performance. We selected these applications because they are representative of a range of workloads and have a metric that clearly shows the effects of performance degradation during a restore. We are interested in MPlayer because it has a small, active working set (primarily its frame buffer) and it cannot tolerate lag. SPECjbb is interesting because it has a larger working set, with some parts of the working set being more active than others, and its performance is not time-sensitive.

Application performance was measured as the instantaneous performance of the application over time for a relevant metric. We found the steady state for the application by running the application by itself in a VM until the chosen metric stabilized. To determine when the application returned to normal operation on restore, we measured the time between the start of the restore and when instantaneous application performance reverted to one standard deviation of the steady state.

5.3.1 SPECjbb Setup

The Standard Performance Evaluation Corporation's Java Business Benchmark (SPECjbb®2005) implements a Java application server in a simulated three-tier system [21]. We ran the benchmark in a virtual machine with 1 GB of memory and 1 virtual CPU. The guest operating system was a 32-bit Ubuntu 8.10 Server (Linux 2.6.27-11-server) running a Java virtual machine (Sun's JVM 1.5.0_17) configured with a 768 MB heap. We chose this benchmark because it exhibits little spatial locality, making it a challenge for simplistic working set estimators and a good stress of working set restore.

The standard implementation of SPECjbb runs for a fixed amount of time (several minutes) and outputs the number of *business operations* achieved during that amount of time as BOPS: business operations per second. To capture the instantaneous performance of SPECjbb, we measured the number of business operations completed during each second of the test and plotted the BOPS over time.

When running in a VM, the BOPS metric is relative to guest time. Unfortunately, such performance metrics can be inaccurate because of different timing behavior in virtualized environments [24]; these timing effects are exacerbated while the VM is being restored. Thus, we modified the benchmark to respond to periodic requests from an external monitoring computer. That computer sent a periodic, timestamped status request to the virtual machine over a UDP channel. The modified workload replied with the number of elapsed business operations. This allowed us to monitor the performance of SPECjbb in the VM over time using wallclock time.

We instantiate two warehouses, the recommended set up for a single CPU VM, which have a working set of 190 MB. The steady state number of BOPS per second for SPECjbb depends on the speed of the host machine running the VM. In this case, the steady state performance was around 8307 BOPS, with a standard deviation of 440 BOPS.

5.3.2 MPlayer Setup

Enjoyment of multimedia playback relies on good interrupt service latency and low jitter. Thus, we chose a video playback benchmark as another stress test of working set restore; any slowdown during

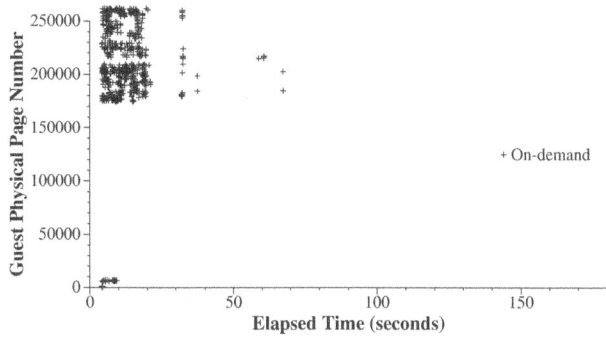

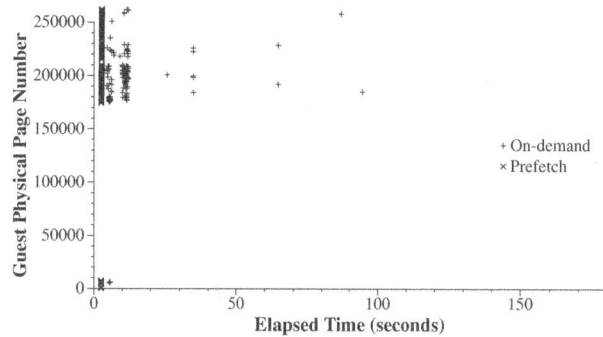

Figure 3. Comparison of location of page requests for a lazy restore (left) and working set restore (right). On-demand pages are unrestored pages accessed by the VM after it starts. Prefetch pages are pages in the working set that were prefetched by working set restore. Working set restore prefetches the pages that were restored on-demand during the lazy restore, reducing the number of accesses to unrestored memory after the VM starts.

the restore will be evident in the frames-per-second metric. We used MPlayer version 1.0rc2-4.2.4 in a 64b Ubuntu 8.04.3 LTS virtual machine (Linux 2.6.24-24-generic SMP). We played a 320x240 24bpp video clip encoded with AVC1 at 29.970 frames-per-second (fps). Thus, the steady state is ~30 fps.

MPlayer was modified to augment its existing continuous progress report with timestamps. After each frame was decoded, the program logged the current time and the number of decoded video frames. This allowed us to compute a continuous fps metric. When playback drops below ~30 fps, we consider the performance to be degraded.

5.3.3 Performance Evaluation

We first discuss the end-to-end performance impact of working set restore for our two applications. Figure 4 shows the instantaneous throughput of SPECjbb during a lazy restore and a working set restore. For the lazy restore, the throughput dropped to almost zero for the first 12 seconds of the restore. It does not return to steady state performance until 20 seconds after execution begins. For working set restore, the throughput returns to steady state performance within 3 seconds. However, the graph does not include the time required to prefetch the working set, which must be taken into account to compare with lazy restore. Working set restore estimates the working set to be 192MB, which takes 6 seconds to prefetch. Altogether, working set restore returns the application to steady state performance in 9 seconds. In comparison, eagerly restoring the VM would have taken 32 seconds, so both lazy and working set restore are faster than eager in this case, but working set restore is the fastest of the three.

Figure 5 shows the number of frames rendered by MPlayer during a restore. The VM was saved after 410 seconds of video playback. Performance drops for both restore methods simply because the VM stops in the middle of playback. With working set restore, playback recovers after 3 seconds and MPlayer returns to rendering 30 fps. With lazy restore, MPlayer is completely stopped for the first 20 seconds and only recovers after 35 seconds. Like the previous experiment, these graphs do not include the time to prefetch the working set. The working set size of MPlayer is fairly small because it mostly consists of the video buffer cache; working set restore only prefetched 41 MB of memory, requiring 1 second of prefetching. In this experiment, 1 second of prefetching saved 32 seconds of performance degradation after the VM starts, clearly showing the benefit of working set restore for workloads with a small working set. When we account for both prefetching time and performance degradation, working set restore takes 4 seconds to restore MPlayer back to steady state performance. Using eager restore, MPlayer would have resumed with no performance degrada-

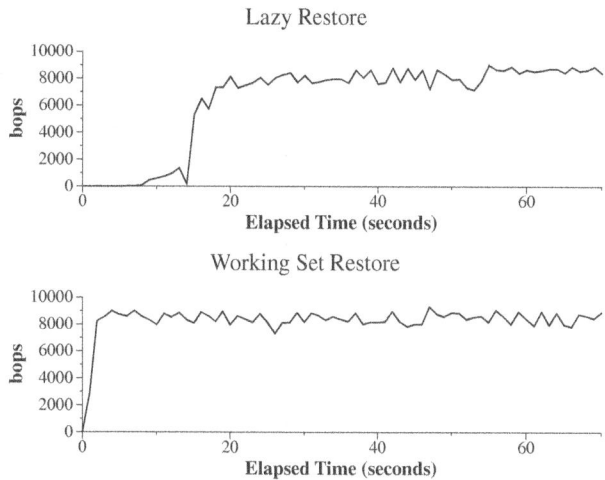

Figure 4. Comparison of instantaneous throughput of SPECjbb during a lazy restore and working set restore. The BOPS drops below steady state performance for the first 20 seconds of the lazy restore, but only for the first 3 seconds of working set restore. Working set restore takes an additional 6 seconds to prefetch the working set, which is 192 MB, so altogether working set restore improves performance by 11 seconds over lazy restore. Eager restore takes 32 seconds, so working set restore reduces restore time by 23 seconds when compared to eager restore.

tion after 32 seconds. In this case, lazy restore performed worse than eager restore, but working set restore offers much better performance than either eager or lazy restore.

5.3.4 TTR Evaluation

Next, we'll discuss the time-to-responsiveness of MPlayer and SPECjbb and how TTR correlates with the application performance shown in the last section. Figure 6 shows TTR for the SPECjbb application and Figure 7 shows TTR for the MPlayer application. Unlike the previous section, both graphs in this section begin when Workstation starts and include the time to restore the device state and prefetch the working set.

It is easy to see the advantage of working set restore from the TTR graph. Comparing Figure 6 and Figure 4 from the previous section shows that a minimum utilization for SPECjbb of 70% is required. For the SPECjbb workload, it takes lazy restore 22.8 seconds to gain 70% minimum utilization, which is close to the 20 seconds that it takes SPECjbb to return to steady state performance

Lazy Restore

Working Set Restore

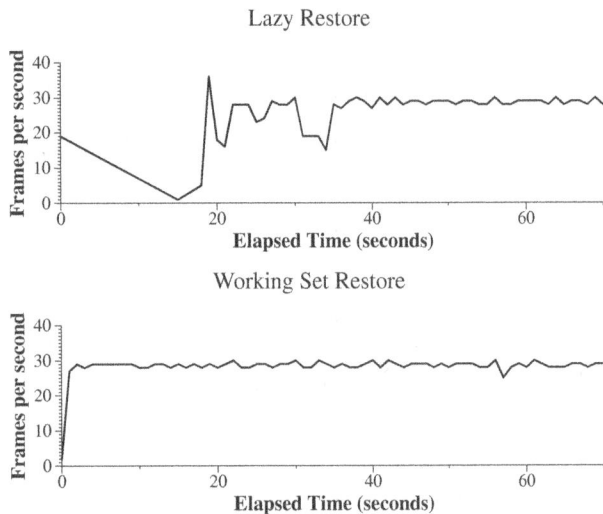

Figure 5. Comparison of the MPlayer frame rate during a lazy restore and a working set restore. During the lazy restore, the frame rate is impacted for 35 seconds. Working set restore only takes 1 second to restore the 41 MB working set. Using working set restore, the frame rate only slows for 3 seconds, giving a 31 second improvement in overall performance.

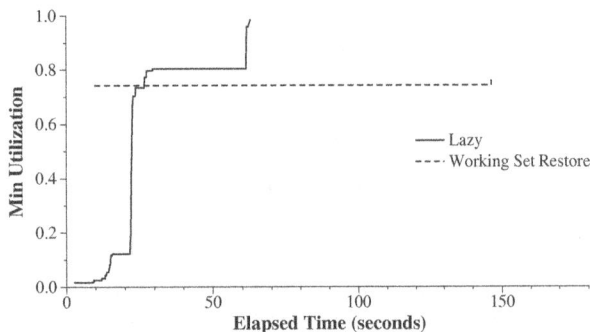

Figure 6. TTR for the SPECjbb application using lazy restore and working set restore. With working set restore, the TTR reaches 70% in 9.8 seconds seconds, including 6 seconds of prefetching. With lazy restore, there is no prefetching, but the TTR does not reach 70% until 22.8 seconds after the VM starts. Comparing with Figure 4 shows that a required minimum utilization of 70% correlates well with performance impact on throughput for SPECjbb.

during a lazy restore. In contrast, working set restore achieves this level of minimum utilization 9.8 seconds after starting. Working set restore impacts performance for 9 seconds total in the previous experiment, including the time to prefetch the working set.

Figure 7 shows the time-to-responsiveness for the MPlayer application. Again, this graph starts from when the hypervisor starts, so it includes the time to restore the device state and prefetch the working set. The MPlayer VM has a 128 MB SVGA frame buffer. The SVGA frame buffer is part of the virtual graphics driver, so it must be restored along with the other devices before the VM starts. This adds around 5 seconds to the time until the VM starts for both lazy and working set restore. Altogether, the total time until the VM starts is 7.4 seconds for lazy restore and 9.3 seconds for working set restore.

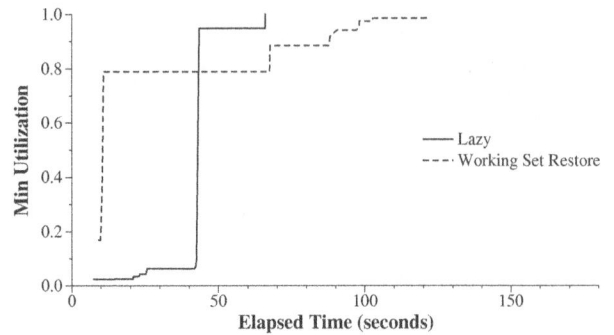

Figure 7. TTR for the MPlayer application using lazy restore and working set restore. By looking at Figure 5, MPlayer seems to require a min utilization of around 80% to maintain its base frame rate. The TTR for MPlayer does not correlate as well with the application metric as SPECjbb.

Comparing the TTR with Figure 5 shows that MPlayer requires a minimum utilization of around 80%. Lazy restore achieves this level of utilization after 43.3 seconds, which is 35.9 seconds after the VM starts. Working set restore gains a minimum utilization of 80% after 11 seconds, which is 1.7 seconds after the VM starts. The TTR for MPlayer does not correlate as well with our chosen performance metric of frames per second as SPECjbb. We speculate that there is less of a direct correlation between TTR and FPS because of buffer effects caused by the frame buffer and MPlayer adjusting its playback in real-time in response to performance degradation.

Using these two example workloads, we have shown how TTR might be used to compare the performance of restore techniques. The window and minimum utilization can be determined experimentally by using an end-to-end metric like throughput, but it does not always correlate directly to end-to-end performance. Nevertheless, TTR better reflects user experience than either total time to restore or total time until the VM starts. In the following sections, we use TTR to compare several aspects of working set restore.

5.4 Working Set Estimation

This section compares the accuracy of the two working set estimators that we implemented and analyzes the impact of imperfect working set estimators on working set restore.

5.4.1 Estimator Comparison

We compared the accuracy of the access-bit estimator and the memory tracing estimator for different workloads by taking several measurements during the restore. We measured the number of prefetched pages to find the size of the estimated working set. We counted the number of accesses to prefetched pages and unrestored pages after the VM starts. These two numbers give some idea of the accuracy of the working set estimator. The number of pages accessed that were prefetched is the number of pages where the restore *avoided* demand-paging. The number of pages accessed that were unrestored represents the number of pages restored *on-demand*. These two numbers also give some sense of whether each working set estimator overestimates, underestimates or completely misses the working set. Table 2 gives a comparison for the MPlayer benchmark, and Table 3 gives a comparison of the two estimators for the SPECjbb benchmark.

Since MPlayer has a well-defined active working set, both estimators do well. The memory trace estimator does slightly better by avoiding the most accesses to unrestored memory, but the access-bit estimator still reduces accesses by 80%, while only prefetching 4% of memory. While MPlayer is very predictable, the working set

Table 2. Measure of the effectiveness of the working set estimator for MPlayer in reducing demand-paging. Both access-bit scanning and trace-based working set estimation reduce the number of accesses to unrestored memory, reducing performance degradation.

MPlayer	Prefetched Pages	Avoided Accesses	On-demand Pages
Lazy	0	0	1,548
A-bit	10,114	8,617	343
Trace	10,113	10,084	84
Eager	262,144	0	0

Table 3. Measure of effectiveness of working set estimators for SPECjbb in reducing demand-paging. The access-bit working set estimator does not perform as well as the memory trace estimator for SPECjbb. SPECjbb is a deterministic workload, so memory tracing is effective, reducing the number of on-demand pages by more than 97%.

SPECjbb	Prefetched Pages	Avoided Accesses	On-demand Pages
Lazy	0	0	1,623
A-bit	83,471	30,501	442
Trace	47,082	47,082	47
Eager	262,144	0	0

of SPECjbb is more difficult to predict for a simple working set estimator. It is larger and not accessed as consistently as the MPlayer frame buffer. It is clear that the access-bit estimator does not work as well. Working set restore with the access-bit estimator prefetches almost twice as much memory as working set restore with the memory trace estimator (83,471 vs. 47,082) but uses less of it (30,501 vs. 47,082). However, SPECjbb is a deterministic workload, so memory tracing works very well, reducing the number of accesses to unrestored memory by more than 97%. Working set restore using the memory tracing estimator only prefetches 193 MB, which is close to the size that we estimated the working set of SPECjbb to be.

5.4.2 Estimator Accuracy

The performance of working set restore is dependent on the accuracy of the working set estimator. With an oracle, working set restore would be optimal, but no estimation techniques are perfect. The goal of this experiment was to measure the decrease in performance of working set restore as the accuracy of the working set estimator decreases. We tested this by restoring the same saved VM several times with a fraction of the working set retained. We randomly dropped a percentage of the pages in the working set for each experiment. Since the pages removed from the working set are randomly chosen, there is some variation in the experiments. We did not test the performance of a working set estimator that overestimates the working set because overestimating does not lead to performance degradation after the VM starts, it simply increases the time to prefetch the working set. If our working set estimators are very accurate and only include the minimal set of pages accessed by the VM after staring in the working set, then the performance of working set restore should drop as soon as some of the working set is not prefetched.

Figure 8 shows the TTR for different percentages of the working set dropped and the TTR for lazy restore for the MPlayer experiment. The more pages missing from the working set estimate, the more pages must be faulted in on-demand. When we drop even 5% of the working set, the performance begins to look like lazy restore. This sharp decrease reflects the cost of paging content from a relatively slow medium like a disk. This decrease also reflects well

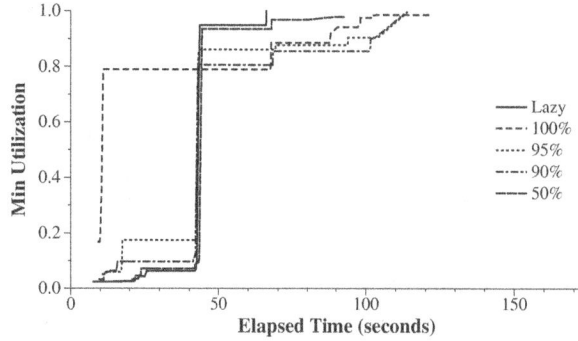

Figure 8. TTR for lazy restore and working set restore with partial working sets. We started with the memory trace estimator, which only missed 84 pages of the working set (see Table 2). We retain a random portion of the working set for each percentage line. Note that the performance drops quickly, meaning that the original working set was already the minimum set of pages that needed to be prefetched to guarantee good performance.

on our original working set estimate because it shows that our original working set was already the minimal set of pages that must be prefetched to guarantee good performance after the VM starts.

5.5 Working Set Size Microbenchmark

This benchmark artificially generates working sets of differing sizes by allocating a percentage of guest memory, then touching pages at random. The pages are chosen completely randomly, so there is no guarantee that all pages are touched or that all pages are touched once before being touched again. This benchmark runs on top of the basic RHEL VM presented in Section 5.2.

As the working set size becomes a larger fraction of total memory, the performance of both lazy restore and working set restore will decrease. Lazy restore has increased performance degradation because there will be more accesses to unrestored memory, so the VM will be unusable for longer. If the VM is actively using most of its memory then the working set will be almost all of the memory. Working set restore will have to prefetch most of memory, and its performance will approach the performance of eager restore.

Figure 9 shows the performance of lazy restore for a working set that occupies 20% to 80% of memory. As expected, the performance degrades as the VM accesses more memory actively because the VM will touch more unrestored memory during the restore. The performance for all sizes of working sets is worse than eager restore, which takes around 32 seconds, showing that lazy restore is only the better choice if the VM is actively using very little of its memory.

Figure 10 shows the performance with working set restore. The performance of working set restore also suffers as the size of the working set increases. As the benchmark is accessing memory randomly, it is difficult for the working set estimator to capture all of the working set. As the size of the working set grows, it becomes more likely that the working set estimator will miss part of the working set because it was just not accessed before the checkpoint was taken. However, working set restore still offers better performance than lazy restore for all sizes of working sets. For a minimum utilization of 60%, working set restore does well, staying below 35 seconds for all working set sizes except for when the working set is 80% of the memory size.

5.6 Working Set Restore Overhead

Using working set estimation for working set restore imposes an overhead on the VM. The amount of performance impact from

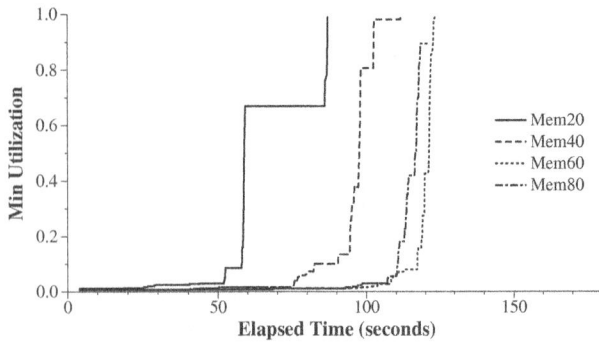

Figure 9. TTR for lazy restore of varying working set sizes. The time to reach 80% minimum utilization degrades quickly with lazy restore. There is more disk thrashing as the size of the working set increases because the microbenchmark is randomly accessing a larger region of memory.

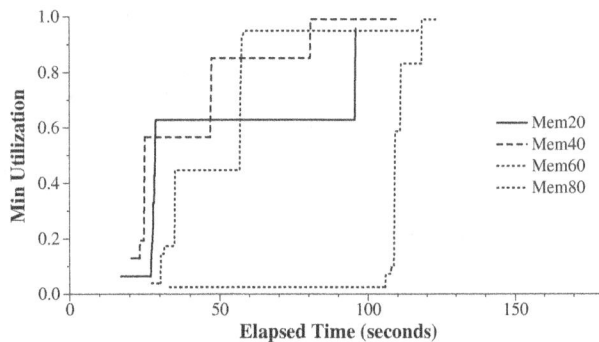

Figure 10. TTR for working set restore of varying working set sizes. Because the microbenchmark is random, the working set estimation techniques are not as successful, but working set restore still performs better than lazy restore for all memory sizes.

working set estimation depends on the estimator and the application. These experiments give the overhead for our two working set estimators for our benchmark applications, MPlayer and SPECjbb.

The overhead of the access-bit scanning estimator is ongoing because the scanning process always runs while the VM is running. However, the overhead is small because we are only scanning 4,096 pages every second. We ran each VM for 10 mins and measured the number of cycles for each scan. The overhead varies slightly for each workload depending on how much memory the application is using and how much memory is mapped in the guest OS. The access-bit scanner is optimized to first scan page directory entries and not scan the page table entries if the page directory entry does not exist or has not been accessed.

Table 4 shows the average number of cycles required to scan the access-bits for 4,096 pages each second and the percentage overhead based on the total number of cycles between scans. For SPECjbb, the access-bit scanning process takes 76,040 cycles on average every second to scan 4,096 pages. This translates to less than a fifth of a percent of overhead for the SPECjbb VM. The MPlayer VM is using less memory, so the access-bit scanner spends even less time scanning page tables on average, only 57,372 cycles on average. This gives only slightly more than a tenth of a percent of overhead for the MPlayer VM.

The memory tracing estimator only imposes an overhead on the VM while the VM is being checkpointed. The estimator requires

Table 4. Average number of cycles spent scanning access-bits each second and the estimated percentage overhead for access-bit scanning. The overhead for the access-bit scanning estimator is ongoing because it must constantly scan pages to estimate the working set, but the amount of overhead is small.

	Avg. Cycles	% Overhead
SPECjbb	76,040	.0016%
MPlayer	57,372	.0012%

read traces in addition to write traces and the traces can only be removed once the page has been added to the working set, so more traces are triggered. The overhead imposed by the additional traces depends on the workload because some workloads read from memory more than others.

Each trace causes a page fault, so the VM must pause while the hypervisor handles the trace. It is somewhat difficult to measure the overhead of a page fault because the switch between the VM and the hypervisor pollutes caches as well as using cycles. This experiment attempts to show both the end-to-end and low level effects of additional traces. We measured the increase in the total time to checkpoint as well as the total increase in number of traces triggered. Table 5 shows the results for the SPECjbb workload and Table 6 shows the results for the MPlayer workload.

For SPECjbb, read traces add 30.9% to the number of traces triggered over the lazy checkpoint period, so SPECjbb probably reads and writes many of the same pages. In contrast, we see a 76.8% increase in triggered traces with MPlayer, showing that MPlayer reads more pages that it does not write than SPECjbb. However, an increase in traces does not lead to a significant change in the time to save the VM for either workload. Despite working set restore spending 7.5 seconds copying the working set for SPECjbb, the total time to save increases by 7 seconds. The increase in triggered traces actually decreases the time to lazily save the VM's memory slightly. The lazy save proceeds faster because more pages are being saved when the VM accesses them and fewer are being saved by the slow-running background thread. Similarly, the total time to checkpoint the VM increases by 0.9 seconds for MPlayer, but 5.9 seconds are spent copying the working set. There is also an increase in the total time to checkpoint or suspend a VM for the access-bit scanning estimator, but it simply adds to the total time based on the size of the estimated working set.

Table 5. Overhead of memory tracing for SPECjbb. With the addition of read traces, the number of traces triggered during the checkpointing process increases by 30.9%. The total time to checkpoint the VM increased by 7 seconds, with 7.5 seconds spent copying the working set. The slight decrease in the time to lazily save is caused by more pages being saved when the VM accesses them and fewer pages being saved by the slow-running background thread.

SPECjbb	Traces Triggered	Time to Save
Baseline	42,849	91.7 s
Working Set Restore	56,087	98.7 s

Table 6. Overhead of memory tracing for MPlayer. There was a 76.8% increase in the number of traces triggered with working set restore. The total time to save the VM increased by 0.9 seconds, with 5.9 seconds spent copying the working set.

MPlayer	Traces Triggered	Time to Save
Baseline	5,811	101.7 s
Working Set Restore	10,272	102.6 s

6. Related Work

The time-to-responsiveness performance metric for restoring saved VMs and the working set restore technique build on related work from several different areas of research. We built on work from the HCI and garbage collection communities for evaluating the responsiveness of a VM and work from the OS community on techniques for working set estimation and prefetching.

6.1 Restore and Prefetching Techniques

There is not much previous research in improving the performance of restoring saved VMs, but one related area where there has been more work is improving the performance of restarting an operating system from hibernation. Operating systems cannot take advantage of lazy fetching of memory as easily as the hypervisor because the operating system would have to fetch its own pages lazily, which would be much more complex. Accordingly, most operating systems eagerly fetch saved memory before restarting. Both Linux and Windows use compression to speed up the process of reading saved data from disk [1, 15]. We found that compression is not very effective for saved VMs, unless there is a lot of unused memory that is zeroed. Unless the guest was recently booted, there is generally not much unused memory, as the guest OS will always try to use any unused memory for buffer cache.

Unlike a hypervisor, the operating system does not have to save or restore all of memory; it can dump memory that it knows is not necessary to save, such as the buffer cache. Dumping the buffer cache can hurt performance after the OS restarts, but it also saves a lot of time when hibernating and restarting the OS. In contrast, the hypervisor cannot throw away any of the VM's memory because it does not know what memory the VM is using. We could ask the guest to drop its buffer cache, which only requires a single command in Linux for example, but we would have to paravirtualize the guest to figure out which pages are part of the buffer cache because dropping the buffer cache does not zero those pages. Using working set estimation is a better solution because it gives us an idea of the active memory of the VM without requiring modifications to the guest.

Working set prefetching has been explored for applications. Windows uses a system called SuperFetch [11] that prefetches frequently used files and binaries for commonly used applications. SuperFetch also traces the boot process to predict what files will be needed for the next boot and reorganizes files on disk in the order that they will be needed during the boot process. Some of the ideas are similar to working set restore (i.e. reorganizing data on disk based on when it is needed), but Windows has more information about accesses and dependencies. In contrast, we treat the VM as a black box, so we assume that all accesses are unrelated. A single action in the operating system can look like a series of random memory accesses as different levels of the operating system are accessed, such as the application or the file system stack. Working set estimation works well with this kind of view because it predicts the set of active memory using only memory accesses and does not require additional information.

VM migration faces some of the same problems as restoring a saved VM. In particular, the pull model of migration, where the VM starts at the destination and lazily pulls memory over from the source, is similar in implementation to a lazy restore. One key difference between migration and restore is that the memory comes over the network and is in memory on the source. So, while there is a latency for fetching a page during lazy migration, there is no penalty for random access versus linear access.

Similar to our findings on the performance degradation of lazy restore, the latency of the network makes lazy migration difficult. Sapuntzakis[19] and Clark[7] both dismiss lazy migration due to the performance overhead. Hines[10] propose a scheme simi-

lar to working set restore for migration, although they choose all pages that are not dirty, rather than using working set estimation. They propose a "bubbling scheme" for the background restore process where the background thread chooses pages located around the most recent access of unrestored memory. Such a bubbling scheme is not really practical for pulling memory off a mechanical disk where there is a penalty for random access. Recently, the SnowFlock system [16] for VMfork, where a running VM is copied and started on another host, used lazy restore of memory. They use a purely lazy scheme, but paravirtualize the guest to avoid restoring pages that will only be re-allocated. They argue that with this optimization, the performance degradation is minimal because newly forked VMs generally allocate new memory and do not request much memory from the parent VM. We chose not to paravirtualize because running unmodified guests is more general and we cannot expect the VM to allocate new memory when restoring from a suspend or checkpoint.

6.2 Performance Metrics

The HCI community has defined what constitutes good responsiveness for an application. Miller [17] set a general standard for response time more than 30 years ago. A response time of less than 100 milliseconds appears instantaneous to the user, a response time of greater than 1 second requires user feedback, and a response time of greater than 10 seconds will cause the user's attention to wander. Using this standard, we can calculate a rough upper bound for how many times the restore process can go to disk and fetch a page before the VM appears to lag. For each user action, there can only be 10 accesses to unrestored memory. This limit gives us insight into why lazy restore causes such noticeable performance degradation. We found there to be more than a thousand accesses to unrestored memory during a lazy restore, so each user action causes tens or hundreds of disk accesses, causing the VM to slow down, sometimes so much that the user would consider the VM to be unusable during the entire restore process.

In order to compare the performance degradation of various restore schemes, we introduced the time-to-responsiveness metric. TTR quantifies acceptable overhead for a particular service: the restoring of a VM. It answers the question of when the VM is suitably responsive, or alternatively, when it is no longer overly taxed by the process of being restored. Other services have also investigated how one reasons about and reports their overhead. On-going services such as garbage-collection [14] have examined the concept of *minimum mutator utilization* [6] or MMU: given an appropriate time interval or window, it is the least amount of time not consumed by collection activity and so available to the application. Unlike the MMU, time-to-responsiveness differs in that the restoring of a VM is not an on-going activity and we are interested in knowing at which point in time its overhead is sufficiently small.

6.3 Working Set Estimation

The idea of estimating working sets attempts to capture an important notion about locality of accesses [9]. Uses proposed by Denning [9] include not only determining what memory to page out but also what memory to page in. In one sense, restoring a VM is an extreme version of this where the state capturing the working-set for the VM must persist with the saved state. Unlike the working set described by Denning, our working set is simply defined by the set of pages accessed by the VM during a restore, since those are the pages that cause disk accesses during the restore process.

There is much work on improved methods for identifying pages in a working set [5, 12, 13, 18]. This previous work extends the CLOCK algorithm [8] to be resilient to incidental or transient accesses such as those that occur when memory is scanned. Our working set estimators are geared towards predicting accesses during a very specific period of time, which makes them simpler than more general working set estimators. For example, our estimators do not need to ignore transient accesses, since even transient accesses to unrestored memory cause performance degradation. In addition, the rate of our access-bit scanner can be set by the speed of the background restore process and our memory trace estimator only captures accesses to memory during the checkpointing process.

7. Conclusion

We examined existing metrics for comparing techniques for restoring VMs and found that they do not reflect what is most important to the user—when the VM and its applications return to normal performance. We proposed both a better metric and a better restore technique for user experience. Our new time-to-responsiveness metric takes into account the time until the VM starts and the performance degradation of the VM after it starts. Working set restore starts the VM as soon as possible, while minimizing performance degradation after the VM starts. Working set restore accomplishes this by estimating the working set of the VM before the checkpoint, saving the working set along with the checkpointed state and prefetching it before starting the VM. We showed that working set restore works well even with a simple working set estimator that scans access-bits. We introduced a new working set estimator that uses memory tracing during lazy checkpointing to more accurately capture the VM's working set. We found that with the memory tracing estimator, working set restore can anticipate 99% of the VM's memory accesses after starting, avoiding most of the performance degradation of lazy restore with just a few seconds of prefetching.

Working set restore is a predictive technique, so it works best with predictable workloads. The behavior of the VM does not have to be exactly the same before and after the checkpoint, but the VM must use the same set of active memory after it restarts as it did before it was saved. We found that with a random workload working set restore does better than lazy restore, but slightly worse than eager restore. Improving the performance of lazy restore for an unpredictable workload is extremely difficult. Using the guidelines from the HCI community, the VM and its applications must respond to any user action within 100 milliseconds, limiting the VM to around 10 accesses to unrestored memory. Without the ability to use previous memory accesses to predict future accesses, it would be extremely difficult to keep the number of accesses to unrestored memory under that limit and keep the VM responsive. If the VM's workload is truly random, then the technique that is optimal for user experience is not using lazy restore at all, but eagerly restoring the VM's memory image. Fortunately, many applications are predictable because they actively use a limited set of memory pages allocated to them by the OS, so predictive techniques like working set restore can still offer significant performance improvements.

Acknowledgments

Thanks to Dong Ye for modifications to MPlayer and to Lenin Singaravelu for modifications to SPECjbb®2005. Thanks to Kevin Christopher and Jesse Pool for many discussions of ideas and experiences about checkpointing and restore. Thanks to Dan Ports and Karen Zee for their feedback on the many drafts of this paper.

References

[1] μswsusp. http://suspend.sourceforge.net/.

[2] AMD64 virtualization codenamed "pacifica" technology: Secure virtual machine architecture reference manual, May 2005. http://enterprise.amd.com/downloadables/Pacifica_Spec.pdf.

[3] D. F. Bacon, P. Cheng, and V. Rajan. A real-time garbage collector with low overhead and consistent utilization. In *Proc. POPL '03*, New Orleans, LA, USA, Jan. 2003.

[4] D. F. Bacon, P. Cheng, and V. Rajan. The Metronome, a simpler approach to garbage collection in real-time systems. In *Proc. OTM 2003 Workshops*, 2003.

[5] S. Bansal and D. S. Modha. CAR: Clock with adaptive replacement. In *Proc. FAST '04*, 2004.

[6] G. E. Blelloch and P. Cheng. On bounding time and space for multiprocessor garbage collection. In *Proc. PLDI '99*, Atlanta, GA, USA, May 1999.

[7] C. Clark, K. Fraser, S. Hand, J. G. Hansen, E. Jul, C. Limpach, I. Pratt, and A. Warfield. Live migration of virtual machines. In *Proc. NSDI '05*, 2005.

[8] F. J. Corbato. A paging experiment with the Multics system. Technical report, MIT Project MAC, May 1969.

[9] P. J. Denning. The working set model for program behaviour. *Commun. ACM*, 11(5), 1968.

[10] M. R. Hines and K. Gopalan. Post-copy based live virtual machine migration using adaptive pre-paging and dynamic self-ballooning. In *Proc. VEE 2009*, Washington, DC, USA, 2009.

[11] T. Holwerda. SuperFetch: How it works & myths, May 2009. http://www.osnews.com/story/21471/SuperFetch_How_it_Works_Myths.

[12] S. Jiang and X. Zhang. LIRS: an efficient low inter-reference recency set replacement policy to improve buffer cache performance. In *Proc. SIGMETRICS '02*, Marina del Rey, California, USA, 2002.

[13] S. Jiang, F. Chen, and X. Zhang. CLOCK-Pro: An effective improvement of the CLOCK replacement. In *Proc. USENIX '05*, 2005.

[14] R. E. Jones. *Garbage Collection: Algorithms for Automatic Dynamic Memory Management*. Wiley, Chichester, July 1996. URL http://www.cs.ukc.ac.uk/people/staff/rej/gcbook/gcbook.html.

[15] kernel-enhancements-xp. Kernel enhancements for Windows XP, jan 2003. http://www.microsoft.com/whdc/archive/XP_kernel.mspx.

[16] H. A. Lagar-Cavilla, J. A. Whitney, A. M. Scannell, P. Patchin, S. M. Rumble, E. de Lara, M. Brudno, and M. Satyanarayanan. SnowFlock: rapid virtual machine cloning for cloud computing. In *Proc. Eurosys '09*, Nuremberg, Germany, 2009.

[17] R. B. Miller. Response time in man-computer conversational transactions. In *Proceedings of the fall joint computer conference, part I*, AFIPS '68 (Fall, part I), pages 267–277, New York, NY, USA, 1968. ACM.

[18] E. J. O'Neil, P. E. O'Neil, and G. Weikum. The LRU-K page replacement algorithm for database disk buffering. In P. Buneman and S. Jajodia, editors, *Proc. SIGMOD '93*, 1993.

[19] C. P. Sapuntzakis, R. Chandra, B. Pfaff, J. Chow, M. S. Lam, and M. Rosenblum. Optimizing the migration of virtual computers. *SIGOPS Operating Systems Review*, 36, 2002.

[20] Seagate. Product Manual. Barracuda 7200.11 Serial ATA. http://www.seagate.com/staticfiles/support/disc/manuals/desktop/Barracuda7200.11/100452348g.pdf, Jan. 2009.

[21] Standard Performance Evaluation Corporation. SPECjbb2005 User's Guide. http://www.spec.org/jbb2005/docs/UserGuide.html, April 2006.

[22] J. Sugerman, G. Venkitachalam, and B.-H. Lim. Virtualizing I/O devices on VMware Workstation's hosted virtual machine monitor. In *Proceedings of the 2001 USENIX Annual Technical Conference*, Boston, MA, USA, June 2001.

[23] N. Tolia, D. G. Andersen, and M. Satyanarayanan. Quantifying interactive user experience on thin clients. *IEEE Computer*, 39(3), Mar. 2006.

[24] VMware. Timekeeping in VMware virtual machines. http://www.vmware.com/vmtn/resources/238, Aug. 2008.

Fast and Correct Performance Recovery of Operating Systems Using a Virtual Machine Monitor

Kenichi Kourai

Kyushu Institute of Technology
kourai@ci.kyutech.ac.jp

Abstract

Rebooting an operating system is a final but effective recovery technique. However, the system performance largely degrades just after the reboot due to the page cache being lost in the main memory. For fast performance recovery, we propose a new reboot mechanism called the *warm-cache reboot*. The warm-cache reboot preserves the page cache during the reboot and enables an operating system to restore it after the reboot, with the help of a virtual machine monitor (VMM). To perform correct recovery, the VMM guarantees that the reused page cache is consistent with the corresponding files on disks. We have implemented the warm-cache reboot mechanism in the Xen VMM and the Linux operating system. Our experimental results showed that the warm-cache reboot decreased performance degradation just after the reboot. In addition, we confirmed that the file cache corrupted by faults was not reused. The overheads for maintaining cache consistency were not usually large.

Categories and Subject Descriptors D.4.2 [*Operating Systems*]: Storage Management

General Terms Design, Performance, Reliability

Keywords Reboot, Page Cache, Performance Degradation, Cache Consistency

1. Introduction

Operating systems are frequently rebooted to recover the whole system. When an operating system crashes due to Mandelbugs [8], it can usually recover from the crash after being rebooted. Since the causes of Mandelbugs are very complex, the rebooted operating system rarely crashes again. The reboot is also used as a simple method for software rejuvenation [7, 10]. Software rejuvenation is a proactive technique to counteract software aging, which is the phenomenon that the state of running software degrades with time. Even if an operating system slows down due to aging-related bugs [8] such as memory leaks, the rebooted operating system can easily restore its normal state.

However, the system performance largely degrades just after the reboot of an operating system. The primary cause is to lose the page cache, namely, disk cache. An operating system stores file contents in the main memory as the page cache to speed up file accesses. When an operating system is rebooted, the contents of the main memory are erased and the page cache is lost. Without the page cache, an operating system has to read files from slow disks. Worse, if the operating system runs in a virtual machine (VM), such cache misses may greatly affect the whole system performance because disks are shared between VMs. The conflicts of disk accesses degrade the performance of not only the rebooted VM but also the other VMs.

Thus, recovery by the reboot is not complete until the system performance is recovered. When an operating system is booted and all the applications on top of it are started, the system can start providing the same services as before the reboot. To make this reboot procedure faster, many techniques have been proposed [2, 12, 20]. However, the system does not restore the same performance at that time. For example, server processes can accept new connections, but they may not return quick responses due to performance degradation caused by frequent cache misses. Such performance degradation lasts until the page cache is re-filled. The size of the page cache tends to increase as the main memory becomes larger.

For fast performance recovery, we propose a new reboot mechanism with the help of a virtual machine monitor (VMM), which is called the *warm-cache reboot*. The warm-cache reboot preserves the page cache in the main memory during the reboot and enables an operating system to restore it after the reboot. This mechanism prevents performance degradation caused by frequent cache misses. To maintain the consistency of the page cache after the reboot, our VMM makes sure that the contents of the page cache are the same as those of corresponding files on disks. A software layer like a VMM is necessary to preserve the page cache in an operating system through its reboot and to reuse only consistent pages even after the crashes of an operating system.

We have developed *CacheMind* on the basis of Xen [3] and implemented the warm-cache reboot mechanism in the VMM and the Linux operating system running on top of it. CacheMind preserves memory allocation to rebooted VMs, manages the page cache through the reboot of operating systems, and maintains the consistency of the page cache. It protects the page cache to prevent operating systems from reusing the corrupted one and reduces the overhead of unprotecting the page cache on file writes by *double caching*. To maintain the cache consistency even for writes to memory-mapped files, we introduced the *unprotect-on-write* bit in page table entries.

From our experimental results, the performance degradation just after the warm-cache reboot was 0 % to 39 % while that just after a normal reboot was 39 % to 90 %. The performance just after the warm-cache reboot was 8.7 times higher at maximum. The overheads for enabling the warm-cache reboot were usually less than 5.5 % for accesses to regular files and less than 13 % for those to memory-mapped files. In worst cases, however, they were 33 % for writes to regular files and 25 % for those to memory-mapped files. In addition, our fault-injection test showed that a part of the page cache could be corrupted by faults but it was not reused by the consistency mechanism of the warm-cache reboot.

The rest of this paper is organized as follows. Section 2 describes problems of recovering the system performance after the reboot of an operating system. Section 3 presents the warm-cache reboot. Section 4 explains our implementation based on Xen and Section 5 shows our experimental results. Section 6 examines related work, and Section 7 concludes the paper.

2. Performance Recovery

After the reboot of an operating system, the system performance is largely degraded for a while. The primary cause is various caches being lost in an operating system. Particularly, losing the page cache largely affects the performance. An operating system stores file contents in the main memory as the page cache when it reads them from disks. Since disks are much slower than the main memory, an operating system can speed up file accesses by using the page cache in memory. When an operating system is rebooted, the contents of main memory are erased and the page cache managed by the operating system is lost. Just after the reboot of an operating system, the execution performance of applications running on top of it degrades due to frequent cache misses.

It takes a long time to recover the same performance as before the reboot. To regain the same performance, an operating system has to re-fill the page cache. However, modern operating systems use most of free memory as the page cache to improve performance. The amount of the page cache is almost equivalent to that of free memory, which tends to be larger because the size of memory installable on one machine is increasing due to cheaper memory modules. In addition, widespread 64-bit processors enable an operating system to deal with more than 4 GB of memory. Until the page cache is re-filled, an operating system has to read necessary files from slow disks and cannot recover the performance.

In a VM environment, the performance recovery needs a longer time after an operating system in a VM is rebooted. Recently, server consolidation is performed with VMs for cost efficiency. In such an environment, physical disks are often shared among VMs. Although a different physical disk may be allocated to each VM exclusively, this is usually difficult due to physical constraints or cost. In other words, one VM cannot occupy the whole disk bandwidth. Worse, disk bandwidth allocated to each VM may be limited for fairness. Since this disk sharing degrades the throughput of disk accesses, it takes a longer time to re-fill the page cache by reading files from disks.

Frequent disk accesses affect not only a rebooted VM but also all the other VMs. The conflicts of disk accesses degrade the performance of all the VMs. Just after an operating system in a VM is rebooted, it frequently accesses a physical disk. Increasing disk accesses in one VM affects the performance of the disk access by the other VMs. From the same reason, prefetching does not work well in a VM environment. Prefetching is a common technique for hiding the initial cache misses particularly when the system is booted. Files are read from disks in advance before they are accessed. Prefetching issues too many requests for disk accesses during a short period because it is batch processing, not on-demand. This influences the performance of the other VMs worse.

3. Warm-cache Reboot

To quickly recover the system performance after the reboot of an operating system, we propose a new reboot mechanism called the warm-cache reboot. The warm-cache reboot is achieved by combining an operating system and the underlying VMM. To use the VMM, operating systems run on VMs created by the VMM.

A VMM is a useful software layer underlying operating systems to preserve the page cache through the reboot and maintain its consistency.

3.1 Preserving the Page Cache

The basic idea of the warm-cache reboot is to preserve the page cache in memory during the reboot and enable an operating system to restore it after the reboot. We believe that the page cache does not need to be discarded at a reboot. The purpose of a reboot is to initialize the internal state in an operating system or to update its components such as its kernel. Even if the data structures in an operating system are changed by its update, the contents of the page cache are reusable because they are just the copies of file blocks on disks. However, an operating system should not reuse corrupted page cache. Rather, it should read file blocks from disks. The warm-cache reboot discards only corrupted page cache by the consistency mechanism described in Section 3.2.

By reusing the page cache, the warm-cache reboot prevents performance degradation caused by cache misses just after the reboot. In other words, it recovers the system performance as well as the functionality. After the reboot, most of files accessed are expected to exist on the page cache as long as a working set is within the size of the page cache. The workload does not largely change after the reboot because the time needed for the reboot is not very long. Normally, the files accessed during the reboot are not included in the working set just before the reboot. However, the access would just replace a very small part of the page cache in many cases.

While an operating system in a VM is rebooted by using the warm-cache reboot mechanism, the VMM preserves the contents of the memory allocated to the VM. The VMM allocates the same physical memory as before the reboot to the VM. The memory layout is the same as well. Without the VMM, it is not guaranteed that the contents of physical memory are preserved because of a hardware reset. A hardware reset may corrupt a part of memory, depending on hardware [18] and temperature [9]. When the VMM reallocates physical memory, it leaves the contents of the memory as it is. Normally, when the VMM allocates memory pages to VMs, it erases the contents for security. The memory pages may include sensitive information used by another operating system. At the warm-cache reboot, reusing memory pages without erasing the contents is secure. Those pages are necessarily reused for the same operating system.

A rebooted operating system reserves all the pages that have been cached in the page cache before the reboot. We call such memory pages *cache pages*. This reservation is performed at the early stage of booting the kernel, that is, before the kernel starts dynamic memory allocation. This prevents the cache pages from being used for other purposes and corrupted. Since the cache management in an operating system is initialized by the reboot, the VMM manages information to reuse the page cache of an operating system. When an operating system allocates a cache page, it registers the page to the VMM, with the information on the corresponding file block. When an operating system uses that page for other purposes, it unregisters the page. When an operating system is rebooted, it obtains the information on the page cache from the VMM.

3.2 Maintaining Cache Consistency

The warm-cache reboot reuses a cache page only when the page is guaranteed to be consistent. We assume that a cache page is consistent when the contents of the page are the same as those of the corresponding file block on a disk. When a file block is read from a disk to a cache page, the page is consistent. After the page is modified by file writes or destroyed by faults, it becomes

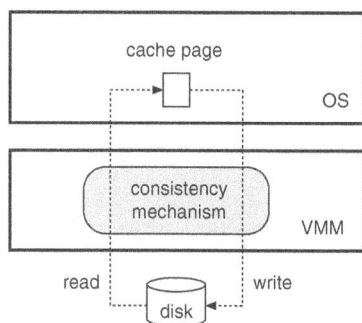

Figure 1. Tracking the consistency of cache pages.

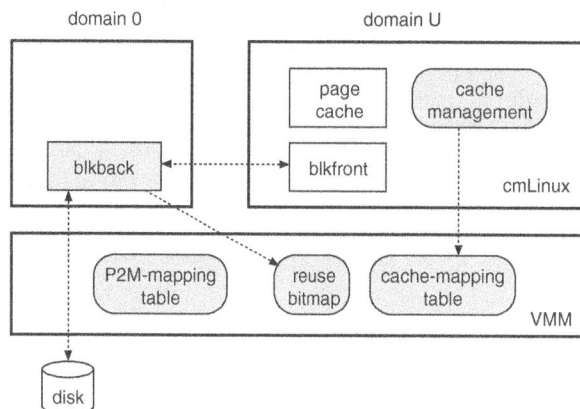

Figure 2. The system architecture of CacheMind.

inconsistent. When the cache page is written back to a disk, it becomes consistent again.

The VMM maintains the consistency of each cache page. In a VM environment, device accesses in an operating system running on a VM are performed via the VMM. The VMM reads data on a disk into a cache page passed from an operating system or writes data in a cache page into a disk, as illustrated in Figure 1. When disk reads or writes complete, the VMM makes the cache page reusable because the contents of the cache page are guaranteed to be the same as those of a file block on a disk. We assume that the VMM works as intended and disk reads and writes are performed correctly.

To track the cache consistency, the VMM protects cache pages in a read-only manner. When the VMM reads a file block into a cache page, it protects the page *before* that file has read so that it can detect the modification to the cache page. While a cache page is protected, it is reusable because the cache page is guaranteed to be consistent. This memory protection also prevents a cache page from being corrupted by faults. When an operating system modifies the protected cache page to write data into a file, the VMM changes its protection mode to writable before that write so that an operating system can modify the cache page freely. In this state, the cache page is not reusable because the page is not consistent. When the VMM writes back the contents of the cache page into a disk, it protects the page again before that file write. Thus the cache page becomes reusable again.

The help of the VMM is indispensable to guarantee this cache consistency. Without the VMM, an operating system cannot read a file block on disk into protected cache pages because it cannot write data in protected memory pages. Therefore, the contents of cache pages may be corrupted *during* disk reads because an operating system has to protect cache pages *after* disk reads. If faults make an operating system unstable, the operating system may not protect the cache page correctly. Even if the page is protected correctly, the protection mode may be changed to writable by corrupting the page table. Although an operating system has to manage the reusability of cache pages, such management information may be corrupted accidentally. If that information were wrong, the warm-cache reboot would reuse inconsistent cache pages.

Our assumption for the cache consistency is strong but reasonable. When the page cache is not corrupted, it could be reused even if the contents have not been written back to disk. This enables an operating system to use the latest updates to files after it is rebooted. However, it is difficult to distinguish correct modification from corruption because the correctness of modification depends on semantics. To avoid this semantic problem, we reuse a cache page only after the modification to the page is written back to a disk. Since the modification becomes persistent at that time, the cache page becomes reusable even if its contents are corrupted. In this situ-

ation, applications always use the corrupted file even without the page cache. The administrator should recover corrupted files, for example, from the backup.

4. Implementation

We have developed *CacheMind* on the basis of Xen 3.0.0 [3]. Figure 2 shows the system architecture. Xen provides the VMM and VMs running on top of it. A VM is called a *domain* in Xen. Specifically, the privileged VM that manages VMs and handles I/O is called *domain 0* and the other VMs are called *domain Us*. Domain 0 is often considered a part of the VMM. Our modified Linux operating system in domain U is called *cmLinux*. When cmLinux in domain U accesses a virtual disk, its device driver called *blkfront* sends requests to the *blkback driver* in domain 0. The blkback driver accesses a physical disk drive and returns the results to the blkfront driver.

To achieve the warm-cache reboot, our VMM manages a P2M-mapping table, cache-mapping tables, and reuse bitmaps. A *P2M-mapping table* is used for preserving the contents of the memory of domain U even through its reboot. A cache-mapping table and a reuse bitmap are created for each domain U. A *cache-mapping table* is used for restoring the page cache after the reboot. A *reuse bitmap* is used for maintaining the cache consistency.

4.1 Memory Management

In Xen, the VMM distinguishes machine memory and pseudo-physical memory to virtualize memory resources. Machine memory is physical memory installed in the machine and consists of a set of machine page frames. For each machine page frame, a machine frame number (MFN) is consecutively numbered from 0. Pseudo-physical memory is the memory allocated to domains and gives the illusion of contiguous physical memory to domains. For each physical page frame in each domain, a physical frame number (PFN) is consecutively numbered from 0.

A P2M-mapping table is a one-dimensional array that records mapping from PFN to MFN for each domain. In the 64-bit architecture, the table is 2 MB for 1 GB of pseudo-physical memory. A new mapping is created in this table when a new machine page frame is allocated to a domain. When a machine page frame is deallocated, an existing entry is removed. In the current implementation, we do not assume memory overcommitment.

Our VMM preserves the mappings in the P2M-mapping table while a domain is rebooted. In Xen, rebooting a domain destroys the domain and re-creates a new one from scratch. Moreover, if an operating system in a domain crashes, the user has to re-create a

101

new domain by hand because the original domain is destroyed with the crash. Even when a domain is destroyed, our VMM does not release machine page frames for the domain. If a new domain is re-created with the same domain ID, the VMM allocates the same machine page frames to pseudo-physical page frames in accordance with the P2M-mapping table. The same domain ID is automatically assigned when a domain is rebooted. When a domain crashes, its ID has to be specified by the user to use the same memory mapping. For normally terminated domains, the user can remove all the entries in the table by specifying its ID to release unnecessary memory.

4.2 Cache Management

A cache-mapping table is a hash table whose keys are a tuple of a device number, an i-node number, and a file offset. The value is a PFN assigned to a cache page. When cmLinux accesses files, it first searches its page cache. If no cache page exists in the page cache, cmLinux searches the cache-mapping table in the VMM. If a cache page exists, cmLinux adds a new entry to its page cache so that it can find the cache page quickly the next time. If no cache pages exist in either, cmLinux reads a file block from a disk to a new cache page and adds it to the page cache and the cache-mapping table.

For consistently modifying the cache-mapping table, the VMM provides new hypercalls for cmLinux. After cmLinux reads a file block to a cache page, it adds a new entry to the cache-mapping table by issuing the add_cache hypercall. When it stops using a cache page as the page cache, it removes the corresponding entry from the table by the remove_cache hypercall. These hypercalls perform the sanity check of a request and modify the cache-mapping table consistently. Even if faults make cmLinux unstable, it cannot directly corrupt the table inside the VMM. In addition, such a narrow interface of hypercalls reduces the possibility of incorrectly modifying the cache-mapping table, compared to that of directly corrupting the table without protection by the VMM. Since the VMM updates the table atomically by using the hypercalls, the data structure of the table is preserved correctly. Once the hypercall is issued, it is completed even if cmLinux crashes.

For efficiency, cmLinux can map the cache-mapping table into its kernel address space in a read-only manner. This allows cmLinux to refer to the table directly. If such memory mapping were not performed, cmLinux would have to issue a hypercall even for searching the entries in the table. Such read-only memory mapping eliminates the cost of issuing a hypercall. Since the table is still protected against writes, cmLinux cannot corrupt the table directly. Also, it cannot change its protection mode to writable because the VMM prohibits cmLinux from modifying the page table entries (PTEs) for that memory-mapped table. The VMM can intercept all modifications to the page table by cmLinux.

When cmLinux is rebooted, the VMM first checks its reuse bitmap and removes entries that cannot be reused from the cache-mapping table. Then cmLinux reserves reused cache pages on the basis of the cache-mapping table. The physical address of the table is obtained from the *start_info* page in Xen, which is allocated at the fixed memory location. After cmLinux sets up its page table, it protects reused cache pages on the basis of the table. We assume that no cache pages are corrupted until cmLinux completes the protection. If cmLinux requires new pages but cannot find any free pages due to the reservation of cache pages, it randomly releases the reserved but unused cache pages.

4.3 Reusability Management

A reuse bitmap is a bitmap for maintaining the reusability of cache pages for each domain. Each bit in this bitmap represents whether the corresponding pseudo-physical memory page is reusable as the page cache. A reuse bit is set if the page is used as the page cache and if the contents of the page are guaranteed to be the same as those of a file block on a disk.

4.3.1 Access to Disks

When the blkback driver in domain 0 reads a file block from a disk to a page used as the page cache of cmLinux or writes back a cache page to a disk, it issues the set_reuse_bit hypercall to set a reuse bit for the cache page. This hypercall can be issued only by domain 0. The hypercall sets a reuse bit only if the contents of a cache page are not corrupted during disk I/O. To guarantee this, the page must not be mapped in domain U in a writable manner. If it is, its contents may be corrupted while the blkback driver performs disk I/O. In the current implementation, cmLinux itself protects the cache page just before it sends a request to the blkback driver.

To check that a cache page is not mapped anywhere in a writable manner, our VMM examines the number of writable mapping, which is tracked by the VMM. The VMM assigns a type to each page (such as writable, page table, and so on) and counts that reference. When a page type is writable, the reference count indicates the number of writable mapping. The count is incremented by one whenever a page is mapped in a writable manner in domain U, domain 0, or the VMM. It is decremented by one whenever a writable page is unmapped. The reference count is more than one when there is writable mapping for the page. The count may be more than the actual number of writable mapping because the VMM temporarily increments the value while it manages the page. However, this does not lower the safety.

In addition, the blkback driver checks that a cache page has not been mapped in a writable manner during I/O even temporarily. To do this, the blkback driver issues the set_canary hypercall before starting disk I/O. The hypercall sets a *canary* bit for a specified page if the page is not mapped anywhere in a writable manner. The canary bit shows that the corresponding page has not been mapped in a writable manner. It is cleared once the page is mapped in a writable manner. It is not set again even if the page is unmapped or remapped in a read-only manner. Only domain 0 and the VMM can set the bit. After disk I/O completes, the blkback driver issues the check_canary hypercall to check the canary bit. If the bit is still set, the hypercall sets a reuse bit for a specified page. This guarantees that the page has not been mapped in a writable manner during disk I/O.

4.3.2 Access to Memory-mapped Files

The mmap system call maps cache pages to the address space of a process so that the process can access a file via virtual memory. When a process accesses a memory region where a file is mapped at the first time, a page fault occurs and the kernel maps the corresponding cache page into the region. If no cache page exists, the kernel reads the corresponding file block from a disk. When the mmap system call is issued with the PROT_READ flag, a cache page is mapped in a read-only manner on a page fault caused by the first read access. The VMM does not change the reuse bit for the page because the read-only mapping does not affect the reusability.

On the other hand, when the mmap system call is issued with the PROT_WRITE flag, we have to consider a reuse bit because cache pages can be modified. In the original implementation of Linux, even when a page fault is caused by a read access, the kernel maps the corresponding cache page in a writable manner because the page is permitted to be written. At that time, the VMM clears the reuse bit for the page because its contents may be corrupted. In this implementation, the kernel cannot reuse even cache pages that have not been written. The VMM has no chance to set the reuse bit once a cache page is mapped in a writable manner.

To solve this problem, cmLinux maps a cache page in a read-only manner when a page fault is caused by a read access. At that time, the VMM does not change the reuse bit like the case in which the mmap system call is issued with only the PROT_READ flag. Such a page can be reused safely because the page is guaranteed not to be corrupted. When the page in this state is written, a page fault occurs again and the page is remapped in a writable manner. At the same time, the VMM clears its reuse bit. We call this mechanism *unprotect-on-write*. This is similar to the copy-on-write mechanism, but unprotect-on-write does not copy the contents of the original page to a new page when the page is written. To distinguish unprotect-on-write from copy-on-write, cmLinux sets the unprotect-on-write (UOW) bit in a PTE. For the bit, we used a bit available to operating systems in the x86 architecture.

A cache page modified via a mapped memory region is written back to a disk after the munmap system call is issued to unmap a file. When the blkback driver in domain 0 writes back a cache page, the VMM sets the corresponding reuse bit if possible. The munmap system call does not write back cache pages immediately, but it traverses PTEs and sets a dirty flag to a cache page if a dirty bit is set in the corresponding PTE. A dirty bit in a PTE is set by a write access to the corresponding cache page. Cache pages with a dirty flag are written back periodically or by system calls such as sync.

The other method for writing back modified cache pages is to issue the msync system call explicitly. Like the munmap system call, this system call sets dirty flags to modified cache pages. If the MS_SYNC flag is specified, the system call waits until dirty cache pages are written back. If the MS_ASYNC flag is specified, dirty cache pages are not written back synchronously. To set reuse bits for the cache pages, cmLinux remaps the pages in a read-only manner. If cache pages were mapped in a writable manner, domain 0 could not set their reuse bits. To make the state of these pages unprotect-on-write, cmLinux sets UOW bits for the corresponding PTEs. Since cache pages are protected, a page fault occurs when the first write access is performed to these pages after the msync system call.

Since the mmap system call maps cache pages directly, a process can write data to the region that exceeds the file size. If the file size is not multiples of the page size, the cache page for the end of a file has such a region. To prevent data in such a region from being written back to a disk, the original Linux always fills that extra region with zero when it writes back a modified cache page to a disk. To do this in cmLinux, the kernel has to unprotect the page because the page is not mapped in a writable manner in the kernel address space. To reduce this overhead, cmLinux does not fill the extra region with zero if all the bytes in the region are already zero. This is a normal case because the extra region is zero as long as a process does not modify the region wrongly.

4.3.3 Modification of Page Tables

When the protection mode of a cache page is changed to writable by cmLinux, the VMM clears a reuse bit for the page. Changing a protection mode means modifying a PTE. To virtualize a page table, our VMM supports two mechanisms: the direct page table and the writable page table. If the *direct page table* is used, the VMM can recognize the modification of PTEs by the issues of hypercalls. cmLinux has to issue hypercalls such as mmu_update and update_va_mapping to modify PTEs.

If the *writable page table* is used, the VMM can trap the modification of PTEs. cmLinux can modify PTEs of the writable page table as it directly modifies the table. When it attempts to modify a PTE, a page fault occurs against a page including the PTE because the page table is protected by the VMM. The VMM saves all the PTEs in the page and maps it in a writable manner to the kernel

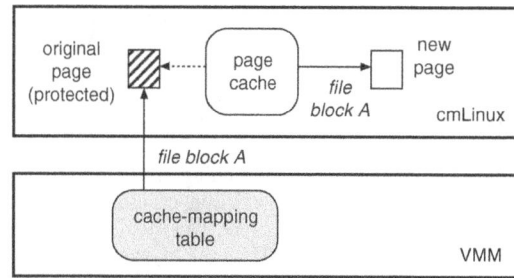

Figure 3. Double caching for reducing write overheads.

address space. At the same time, the page is disconnected from a page directory entry so that the modification to PTEs in the page is not immediately reflected to the actual page table. The page including modified PTEs is connected to the original page directory entry again after it is revalidated. In the revalidation process, the VMM also clears the corresponding reuse bit if the protection mode of each page is changed to writable.

4.3.4 Out-of-control Pages

When domain 0 maps a cache page passed from domain U in a writable manner, the VMM clears the reuse bit for the page. For example, let us consider that the netfront driver in domain U erroneously passes a cache page as a buffer to the netback driver in domain 0 for receiving network packets. Like the blkfront and blkback drivers, the netfront and netback drivers communicate with each other to process network packets. If the netback driver overwrites the contents of the cache page with received packets, the corrupted cache page may be reused.

When cmLinux returns a part of memory to the VMM, the VMM clears the reuse bits for the pages. For example, cmLinux returns memory when it receives requests for memory ballooning from the VMM via the balloon driver [23]. It returns several pages and obtains new ones again when it needs contiguous machine memory for DMA. Returning a memory page means that a pseudo-physical page frame does not correspond to any machine page frame. Such returned pages cannot be reused.

4.4 Write Optimization

The write system call is a heavyweight operation in cmLinux because cmLinux has to first unprotect the target cache page if the page is protected. Unlike file reads, the overhead of unprotecting the page is not hidden by a disk access. When cmLinux reads a file block whose cache does not exist in memory, it has to protect a newly allocated cache page, but the overhead of the protection is much smaller than a disk access. However, the write system call without the O_SYNC flag just modifies the page cache in memory and does not require any disk accesses. A disk access is performed later when the dirty cache page is written back. Therefore, the overhead of unprotecting a cache page occupies a large portion of the execution of the write system call.

To eliminate the overhead of unprotecting a cache page during the execution of the write system call, cmLinux temporarily performs *double caching* as in Figure 3. When the write system call is issued, cmLinux allocates a new cache page if the original cache page is protected. It then copies the memory region that will not be modified in the original page to the new one. Finally, it writes data specified by the system call into the new page. At the same time, it replaces the original page in the page cache with the new one. Note that the cache-mapping table is not changed yet. The successive writes to the same file block are performed to that new cache page without unprotecting it. When the dirty cache page is written back to a disk, cmLinux changes the cache-mapping table, unprotects the original page, and releases it. The overhead of unprotecting the original page is hidden by that disk write. As a side effect, the original cache page is reusable even before the modification to the new page is written back to a disk.

cmLinux performs this double caching only when the written size is bigger than a threshold. The double caching needs memory to be copied from the original cache page to the new one. At worst, cmLinux has to copy 4097 bytes of memory when only one byte is written to a protected cache page. In such a case, the cost of unprotecting a cache page may be less than that of copying a necessary memory region. Since the threshold depends on the MMU performance and memory bandwidth, we can configure the value experimentally.

The double caching does not completely eliminate the overhead in the write system call. First, it still needs extra memory copy. Second, it consumes double the amount of memory used for writes. This memory pressure may cause earlier writeback of dirty pages. To reduce this memory pressure, cmLinux can release the original cache pages before writeback. Third, the double caching cannot be performed when the cache page is already mapped in the address space of a process. To make the double caching consistent, cmLinux also changes memory mapping of the process so that the process refers to a new page. Such an operation, however, is costly.

5. Experiments

We performed experiments to show that the warm-cache reboot is effective. For a server machine, we used a PC with two Dual-Core Opteron processors Model 280, 12 GB of PC3200 DDR SDRAM memory, a 36.7 GB of 15,000 rpm SCSI disk (Ultra 320), and Gigabit Ethernet NICs. We used our VMM and cmLinux based on Linux 2.6.12. For comparison, we used the original Xen 3.0.0 for a normal reboot. We used one physical partition of a disk for a virtual disk of domain U except for experiments in Section 5.4. The Linux ext3 file system was mounted with the ordered mode. We configured several thresholds for writeback so that Linux does not write back dirty cache pages until we issue system calls for writeback, except for experiments in Section 5.5, 5.6, and 5.7. We used the 64-bit execution environment except for experiments in Section 5.7. For a client machine, we used a PC with dual Core 2 Quad processors, 4 GB of memory, and Gigabit Ethernet NICs. The operating system was Linux 2.6.18.

5.1 Effects of Double Caching

We performed an experiment to determine the threshold of the double caching, which we described in Section 4.4. The effects of the double caching depend on the size of the first write to a cache page because cmLinux copies from the original a memory region that will not be written in. In this experiment, we wrote various sizes of data per page and measured the throughputs of the write accesses when we used the double caching and when we unprotected cache pages without using the double caching. Figure 4 shows the throughputs and the performance improvement by using the double caching. The maximum improvement was 37%. The performance improves as the size of written data increases. As an exception, the improvement is not linear when 4096 bytes are written. This is because it is not necessary to issue the lseek system call for moving the file offset to the next 4096-byte block.

However, when the size of written data is less than 1536 bytes, the performance is not improved. In other words, unprotecting a cache page is better than the double caching. Therefore, we used 1536 bytes as the threshold for enabling the double caching in our experiments. If the first write to a cache page is less than 1536

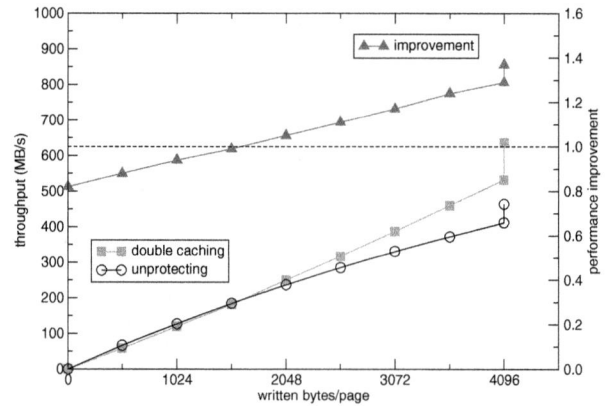

Figure 4. The performance improvement by the double caching for various write sizes.

bytes, cmLinux unprotects the cache page and writes data to it directly.

5.2 Effects of the Warm-cache Reboot

To examine the performance improvement just after the warm-cache reboot, we measured the throughput of file accesses before and after the reboot of an operating system. We accessed one 1-GB file six times and rebooted between the third and fourth accesses. We allocated 4 GB of memory to one domain U and 4 GB to domain 0. In this experiment, all the file blocks were cached in memory. We performed experiments for the warm-cache reboot and the normal reboot.

First, we measured the throughput of file read accesses, changing the block size for file reads. Figure 5 shows the results. For the 4-KB file block, the throughput just after the normal reboot was degraded by 90 % compared with that just before the reboot. The time needed for performance recovery was 8.9 seconds for a 1-GB file. On the other hand, when we used the warm-cache reboot, the throughput just after the reboot was degraded only by 16 %. The throughput is 8.7 times of that just after the normal reboot. The time for performance recovery was only 1.0 second. For the 512-byte block size, the performance degraded by 5.7 %. This improvement was achieved by there being no cache misses in the page cache even when a file was accessed at the first time after the reboot. The remaining performance degradation is caused by misses of other caches in the operating system such as i-node cache.

After the normal reboot, the throughput always becomes worse than that after the warm-cache reboot. The cause is the change of memory allocation to the VM. After the warm-cache reboot, the same memory allocation is preserved by the VMM. However, after the normal reboot, a new VM is created and different ranges of memory are allocated. Since Opteron processors we used adopt non-uniform memory architecture (NUMA), the latency of memory access became large due to this change. Also, the third and fifth accesses are better than the second and sixth, respectively. This is because Linux moves a cache page from the inactive list to the active one.

Second, we measured the throughput of file write accesses. We prepared a 1-GB file in advance and rewrote it repeatedly. Figure 6 shows the results when we changed the block size for file writes. For the block sizes less than 4 KB, the throughput just after the reboot was improved when we used the warm-cache reboot. When the block size is 2 KB, the performance degradation is 92 % in the normal reboot but 37 % in the warm-cache reboot. In this case, the time needed for performance recovery was 31 and 3.8 seconds in

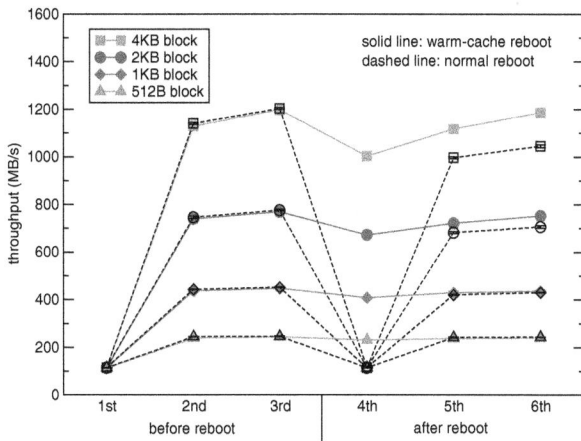

Figure 5. The throughput of file reads through the reboot.

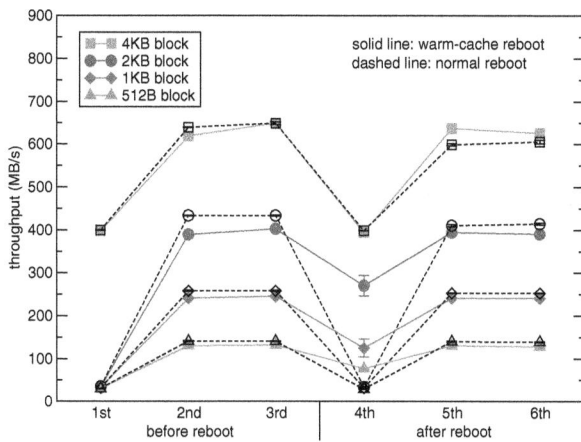

Figure 6. The throughput of file writes through the reboot.

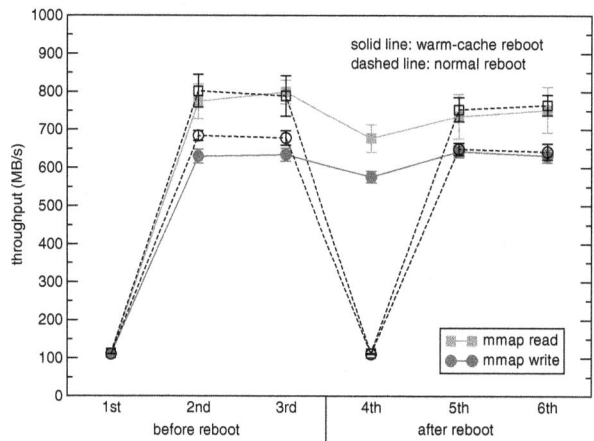

Figure 7. The throughput of accesses to a memory-mapped file through the reboot.

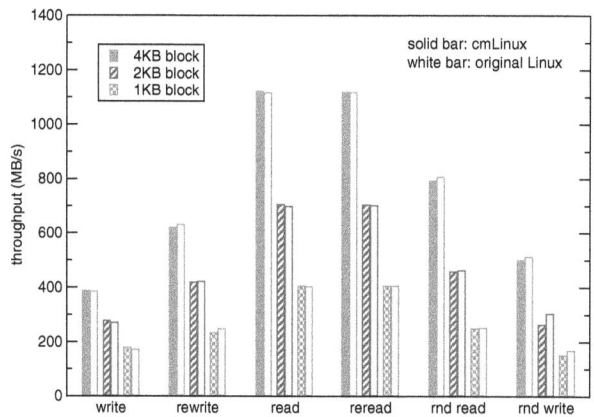

Figure 8. The results of IOzone.

the normal reboot and in the warm-cache reboot, respectively. This performance improvement is caused by a file read before the first write to a new cache page. In the normal reboot, the file read is done from the disk. The warm-cache reboot can reuse the cache page in memory. For the 4-KB block size, on the other hand, both throughputs are almost the same and the degradation is 39 %. Since the block size is the same as the page size, file reads after the reboot are not performed.

Third, we measured the throughput of the accesses to a memory-mapped file. For reads, we mapped a 1-GB file into the memory and read it sequentially. For writes, we mapped a prepared 1-GB file into the memory and rewrote it sequentially. The block size was 4 KB because it did not greatly affect the throughput. Figure 7 shows that the warm-cache reboot can decrease the performance degradation just after the reboot. In case of the normal reboot, the throughputs of reads and writes are degraded by 86 % and 83 % and the recovery times are 9.0 and 9.2 seconds, respectively. For the warm-cache reboot, the throughputs are degraded only by 15 % and 9.1 % and the recovery times are only 1.5 and 1.8 seconds, respectively.

5.3 Overheads

To examine the overheads for enabling the warm-cache reboot, we first executed the IOzone 3.347 benchmark [19] in cmLinux and

the original Linux. We specified 512 MB as its file size. We executed sequential write, rewrite, read, and reread and then executed random read and write. We allocated 4 GB to domain U and all the file blocks created temporarily were cached in memory. Figure 8 shows the results when IOzone uses file I/O system calls. The overheads for file reads are negligible. On the other hand, file writes involve overheads. The worst throughput degradation among sequential writes is 5.5% with the 1-KB block size. For random writes, the overheads are 2.3 % to 13 %. Figure 9 shows the results when IOzone uses the mmap system call. The throughput of all accesses is degraded and the overheads are 2.9 % to 8.9 %.

Second, we examined the relationship between the overhead of file writes and the write size per cache page. We changed the write size for each 4-KB file block and measured the throughput of file writes. Figure 10 shows the throughputs in cmLinux and the original Linux and the overhead in cmLinux. For 1-byte write per page, the overheads are 33% and quite large. This is due to unprotecting a cache page for only 1-byte write. However, the overhead decreases as the write size per page increases.

Third, we examined the overhead of unprotect-on-write for a memory-mapped file. We mapped a file to the memory with the PROT_READ and PROT_WRITE flags, read the memory, and then wrote it. In cmLinux, a page fault occurs at the first write after reads to achieve unprotect-on-write. We measured the throughput

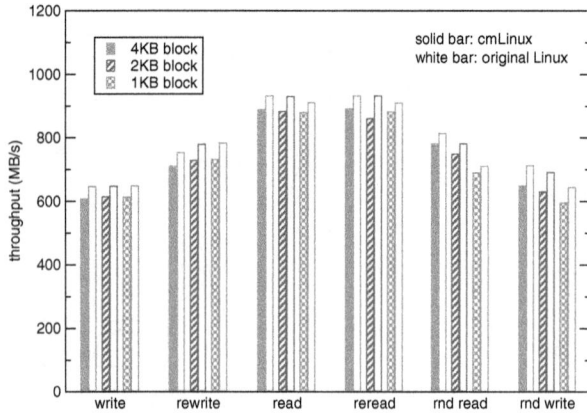

Figure 9. The results of IOzone with mmap.

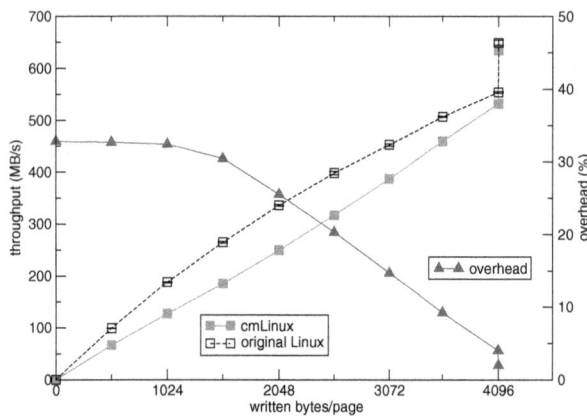

Figure 10. The throughput of partial writes for each cache page.

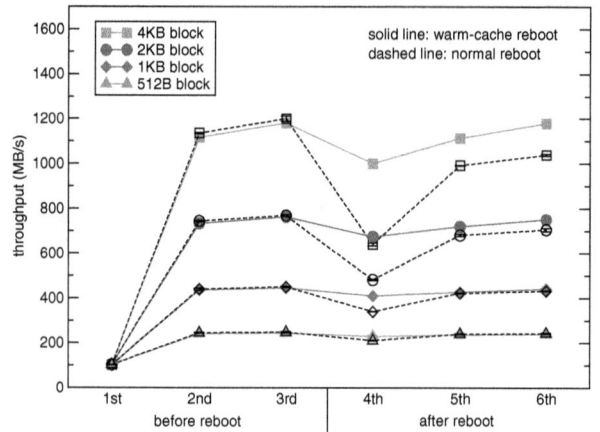

Figure 11. The throughput of file reads from a file-backed virtual disk through the reboot.

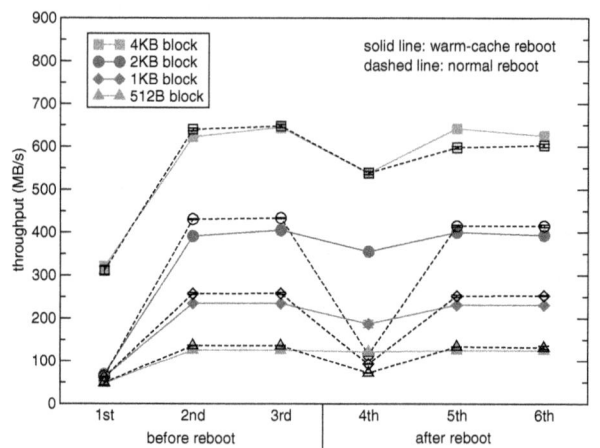

Figure 12. The throughput of file writes from a file-backed virtual disk through the reboot.

of a set of read and write after the file blocks are cached in memory. The throughputs in cmLinux and the original Linux were 344 and 459 MB/s, respectively. Compared with the original Linux, the throughput in cmLinux degraded by 25%.

Finally, we measured the time needed for the writeback in cm-Linux and compared it with that in the original Linux. When cm-Linux writes back a dirty cache page to a disk, it performs heavy-weight operations. It has to protect the page before the writeback. If the double caching is performed, cmLinux also has to modify the cache-mapping table by issuing a hypercall and unprotect the original page. We wrote 1-GB data and wrote back all of the dirty cache pages. To make cmLinux write back dirty cache pages, we issued the fsync system call when we wrote data by using the write system call. For writes to a memory-mapped file, we issued the msync system call for the writeback. The times needed for fsync were 11.0 and 10.9 seconds for cmLinux and the original Linux, respectively. Those for msync were 12.2 and 12.0 seconds, respectively. As a result, the overheads of the writeback are only 0.4% and 1.6% for fsync and msync, respectively. This means that the overheads are hidden by disk accesses.

5.4 Effects of the Page Cache in Domain 0

To examine the effects of the page cache in domain 0, we used a file-backed virtual disk for domain U. In the experiments of previous sections, we used a partition-based virtual disk. In this configuration, the blkback driver in domain 0 directly reads the

physical partition without the interference with any file systems of the operating system in domain 0. On the other hand, when the domain U reads a file block in a file-backed virtual disk, the blkback driver in domain 0 reads the corresponding file block from the image file for a virtual disk. At that time, the operating system in domain 0 also caches the file block. Even if the domain U is rebooted, the file block is still cached in domain 0. When domain U reads a file after the reboot, the blkback driver in domain 0 returns data in the page cache without accessing a physical disk.

Since we allocated 4 GB to domain 0 and domain U for each, all the file blocks were cached in the page cache of both domain 0 and domain U. Figures 11 and 12 show the throughputs of file reads and writes, respectively. When we used the normal reboot, the throughput of file reads degraded by 47 % for the 4-KB file block and that of file writes by 73 % for the 2-KB file block. Compared with when we used a partition-based virtual disk, the performance improved because of the page cache in domain 0. However, the performance degradation was larger than when we used the warm-cache reboot. The blkfront driver had to communicate with the blkback driver in domain 0 and copy file blocks from domain 0 to domain U.

	before reboot		after reboot	
	1st	2nd	3rd	4th
normal reboot	499	168	502	168
warm-cache reboot	509	168	168	167

Table 1. The time for the power test in the DBT-3 benchmark (sec).

Next, we changed the memory size of domain 0 from 4 GB to 1 GB. When we access a 1-GB file in domain U, all the file blocks cannot be cached in the page cache in domain 0. As a result, the throughput degradation of file reads increased from 47 % to 90 %. That of file writes also increased from 73 % to 89 %. These degradation levels are almost the same as when we use a partition-based virtual disk.

By comparing the results in Figure 11 with those in Figure 5, reusing metadata in file systems is found to not improve the performance just after the reboot. When we use a file-backed virtual disk, not only file data but also metadata in the disk image is cached in domain 0. However, the throughput just after the reboot is almost the same as when we use a partition-based virtual disk.

5.5 DBT-3

To examine the performance of more realistic applications, we measured the time needed for the power test with the scale factor of one in the DBT-3 benchmark 1.9 [24] before and after the reboot. DBT-3 tests database performance in a decision support system and it is a simplified implementation of the TPC-H benchmark [22]. Its power test measures the performance of the read access to databases. We used PostgreSQL 8.2.4 as a database. We measured the performance four times and rebooted between the second and third tests. We allocated 11 GB of memory to one domain U and 512 MB to domain 0. All the file blocks were cached in memory in this experiment. We performed this experiment for the warm-cache reboot and a normal reboot.

Table 1 shows the results when the data size was 1 GB. When we used the normal reboot, the performance just after the reboot degraded by 67 % compared with that just before the reboot. On the other hand, when we used the warm-cache reboot, the performance did not degrade at all.

5.6 Web Server

We measured the changes of the throughput of a web server before and after the reboot of an operating system. The Apache web server 2.0.54 [1] served 4000 files of 1 MB, and httperf 0.8 [17] in a client host sent requests to the server one by one. Since we allocated 11 GB of memory to one domain U, all the files served by the web server were cached in memory. We allocated 512 MB of memory to domain 0.

Figure 13 shows the changes of the throughput of a web server when we used the normal reboot and the warm-cache reboot. We executed the reboot command in domain U in 30 seconds. When we used the warm-cache reboot, the throughput was degraded only by 5 % after the reboot. In 60 seconds after the web server restarts its service, the throughput is recovered completely. On the other hand, when we used a normal reboot, the throughput was degraded by 41 % on average. The performance degradation lasts for 90 seconds after the web server restarts its service. During this period, the web server loses the benefit to be gained of about 3300 requests, compared with before the reboot.

5.7 Fault Injection

We injected faults into an operating system in domain U and examined the consistency of reused cache pages. We ported the fault injection tool used in the Nooks [21] project to the Linux 2.6 kernel.

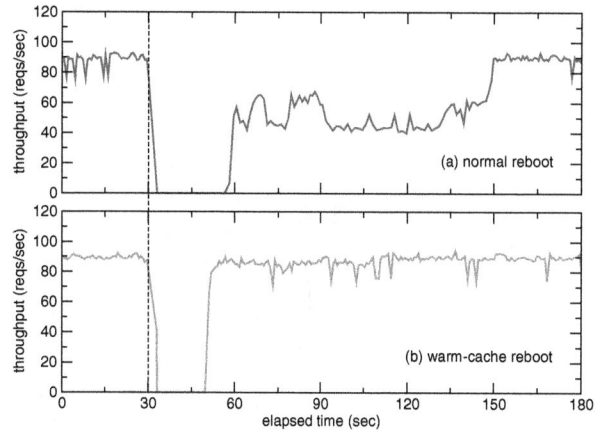

Figure 13. The changes of the throughput of a web server when an operating system is rebooted.

Originally, the tool was developed for the Rio file cache [5] project. Since the tool developed by the Nooks project strongly depends on Intel 32-bit architecture, we used the 32-bit execution environment.

Faults injected by this tool are categorized into three types. The first category is programming errors. *Destination faults* flip a random bit of the destination of an instruction to emulate assignment errors. *Pointer faults* flip a random bit of the address for memory reference to emulate incorrect pointer calculations. *Initialization faults* delete an instruction that initializes a local variable on the kernel stack to emulate the usage of uninitialized local variables. *Interface faults* delete an instruction that reads a function parameter to emulate bad parameters. *Branch faults* delete a branch instruction or a repeat prefix to emulate bugs in control flow. *Loop faults* invert the termination condition for a repeat prefix or a branch instruction. *Panic faults* cause a kernel panic.

The second category is memory management errors. *Allocation faults* return NULL at the kmalloc function to emulate memory exhaustion. *Free faults* release a memory region that is still used. *Memory leak faults* do not release a memory region at the kfree function. *Bcopy faults* overrun the length of memory copy by one byte to four pages.

The third category is memory corruption errors. *Text faults* flip a random bit of a random instruction in the kernel. *Stack faults* flip a random bit in a stack of a random process. *NOP faults* delete a random instruction in the kernel.

We examined the consistency of the page cache after we injected faults into an operating system and rebooted it using the warm-cache reboot. First, we booted an operating system in domain U and waited until the page cache is filled by sending HTTP requests. We allocated 1 GB of memory to domain U and sent requests for 768 MB of files. Then we injected ten faults of the same type into the kernel and waited for 60 seconds. Finally we rebooted the operating system and checked the consistency of the page cache by comparing it with files on a disk. We repeated this fault injection 50 times for each fault type.

Figure 14 shows the ratio at which the page cache was inconsistent when the consistency mechanism was disabled. The VMM did not manage the page cache. Instead, an operating system managed a cache-mapping table and a reuse bitmap without the help of the VMM. For most of fault types, the page cache was inconsistent at a high ratio. This figure also shows the breakdown of the results of this fault injection when the page cache was inconsistent. Although fault injection did not always cause a crash, the page cache became inconsistent.

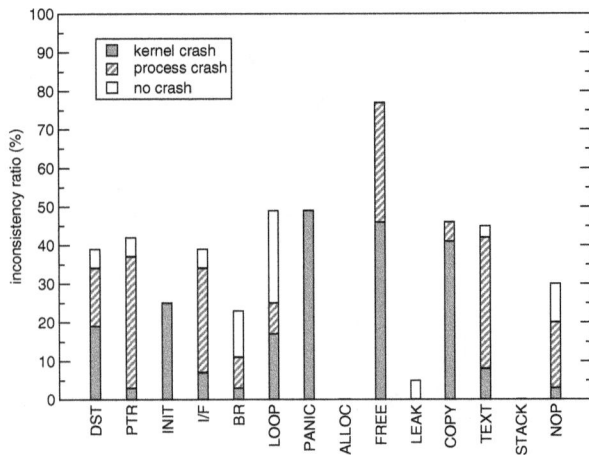

Figure 14. The ratio of cache inconsistency when the consistency mechanism was disabled.

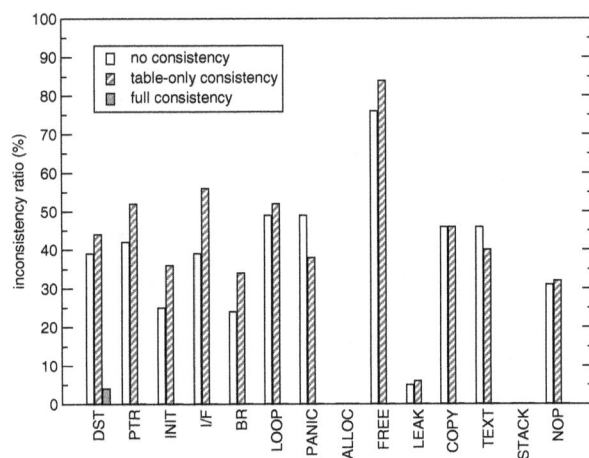

Figure 15. The ratios of cache inconsistency when the consistency mechanism was enabled at various levels.

Figure 15 shows the ratios at which the page cache was inconsistent: (1) when the consistency mechanism was disabled, (2) when the consistency mechanism was enabled only for a cache-mapping table, not for a reuse bitmap, and (3) the consistency mechanism was fully enabled. When only a cache-mapping table was managed by the VMM, the ratio did not decrease. This means that a cache-mapping table is unlikely to be corrupted by faults. When the full consistency mechanism was enabled, the page cache was consistent for all fault types except destination faults (DST). According to our deep inspection, some faults were injected into the ext3 file system in this exceptional case. Then the file system failed to write back cache pages to a disk. This resulted in the inconsistency between the page cache and files on the disk. However, the contents of the page cache were correct while those of files on the disk were incorrect. Therefore, reusing the page cache is correct although the consistency is not maintained.

6. Related work

The Rio file cache [5] enables dirty file cache to survive crashes of an operating system. When an operating system crashes, Rio saves dirty cache pages to a disk and prevents the reboot from losing any modification to files. The biggest difference between Rio and CacheMind is that Rio is designed for reliability while CacheMind is for high performance. When an operating system is rebooted, Rio discards non-dirty file cache because saving it is not necessary for improving reliability. To the contrary, CacheMind reuses non-dirty page cache but discards dirty ones because dirty pages are inconsistent with disks. In addition, because Rio has to read saved file cache from a slow disk, the performance degrades just after the reboot. CacheMind prevents such performance degradation by reusing the page cache preserved in memory.

The other big difference is that Rio relies only on an operating system (and hardware) while CacheMind relies on the VMM. For example, Rio provides two mechanisms to save the file cache to a disk on a crash. One is to perform a warm reboot, which preserves memory contents during the reboot, and save dirty file cache after the reboot [5]. The other is to save the file cache using a BIOS routine before a reboot [18]. The former depends on hardware and is not generally supported in PCs. The latter might fail because Rio cannot always execute the BIOS routine after a crash. In Cache-Mind, an operating system in a VM can perform a warm reboot, independently of hardware, because the VMM guarantees to preserve memory contents during the reboot of the VM.

Besides, Rio uses memory protection to prevent the file cache from being corrupted by crashes of an operating system. Rio protects the file cache by using functions in an operating system while CacheMind protects it by the VMM. In Rio, if the page table is corrupted by a crash of an operating system, memory protection might be ineffective. In CacheMind, although the page table may be corrupted, the VMM tracks any modification and maintains the reusability of the page cache. Also, Rio cannot atomically modify its registry for cache management because the registry is also managed by an operating system. Therefore, the consistency of the registry is not guaranteed when an operating system crashes. CacheMind manages a cache-mapping table for cache management with the VMM. The modification of the table can be atomically performed by the VMM.

As described in Section 5.4, when a file-backed virtual disk is used in Xen, the page cache in domain 0 helps performance recovery just after the reboot of an operating system in domain U. Even in type-II VMMs such as Linux Kernel-based Virtual Machine (KVM) [13], the page cache in its host operating system is helpful as well. However, the performance still degrades due to the memory copy from the page cache in domain 0 to that in domain U. Another drawback is that domain 0 needs larger memory to cache file blocks for all domain Us. It is not efficient to store the same file blocks both in domain 0 and domain U.

Non-volatile disk cache such as Microsoft hybrid hard drive (HHD) and Intel Turbo Memory are also useful for fast performance recovery. HHD includes non-volatile memory inside a disk drive while Turbo Memory is attached to a motherboard. They enable an operating system to read file blocks from fast non-volatile memory even if the page cache in memory is lost after the reboot. Furthermore, a solid-state drive (SSD) speeds up the whole disk accesses by using flash memory. However, file blocks from non-volatile memory must be copied to the page cache in the main memory. CacheMind does not need any memory copies because it preserves the page cache on the main memory through the reboot.

Geiger [11] maintains the mapping between disk blocks and the page cache only by the VMM without the knowledge of operating systems. Since it infers the mapping using several heuristics, it can miss the detection of cache-page eviction by operating systems. This is critical in our context because such cache pages are reused for other purposes and do not contain valid contents for associated files. Similarly, the time lag between actual page eviction and its detection is also critical. To address this problem, hypervisor exclusive cache [16] modifies operating systems so as to notify the VMM of page eviction.

Otherworld [6] quickly recovers applications by using the microreboot technique [4]. When the kernel crashes, Otherworld starts another kernel called the crash kernel and restores the state of applications and the operating system, including dirty file cache. The correctness of the recovery mainly depends on the assumption that the probability of the data corruption necessary for recovery is low. CacheMind protects the file cache by using the VMM because the amount of reused non-dirty file cache is large and the probability of cache corruption is high, as shown in Section 5.7.

Recovery Box [2] preserves the state of an operating system and applications on non-volatile memory for fast recovery. It restores the state quickly after rebooting an operating system. The state stored in that memory is protected by checksum. In addition, Recovery Box speeds up a reboot by reusing the kernel image left on memory. This is less effective recently because recent disks are fast enough to read the small file for the kernel image.

RootHammer [14, 15] enables only the VMM to be quickly rebooted by leaving VM images in memory. It uses the fact that VM images can be reused after the reboot of the VMM. Similarly, CacheMind uses the fact that the page cache can be reused after the reboot of an operating system. In addition, CacheMind reuses only consistent page cache with the help of the VMM.

7. Conclusion

In this paper, we proposed a new reboot mechanism, called the *warm-cache reboot*, for fast and correct performance recovery. The warm-cache reboot preserves the page cache on main memory during the reboot and restores it quickly after the reboot. The VMM guarantees that the page cache reused after the reboot is consistent with the corresponding files on disks by maintaining reuse bitmaps. We have implemented the warm-cache reboot mechanism in Xen. According to our experimental results, the performance just after the reboot became 8.7 times higher at most when we used the warm-cache reboot. The overheads for enabling the warm-cache reboot were usually not large. In addition, it was shown that faults did not corrupt the reused page cache. One of our future work will be to reuse other caches in an operating system such as i-node cache to improve the performance just after the reboot.

Acknowledgments

This research was supported in part by JST, CREST.

References

[1] Apache Software Foundation. Apache HTTP Server Project. http://httpd.apache.org/.

[2] M. Baker and M. Sullivan. The Recovery Box: Using Fast Recovery to Provide High Availability in the UNIX Environment. In *Proceedings of the Summer USENIX Conference*, pages 31–44, 1992.

[3] P. Barham, B. Dragovic, K. Fraser, S. Hand, T. Harris, A. Ho, R. Neugebauer, I. Pratt, and A. Warfield. Xen and the Art of Virtualization. In *Proceedings of the 19th Symposium on Operating Systems Principles*, pages 164–177, 2003.

[4] G. Candea, S. Kawamoto, Y. Fujiki, G. Friedman, and A. Fox. Microreboot – A Technique for Cheap Recovery. In *Proceedings of the 6th Symposium on Operating Systems Design and Implementation*, pages 31–44, 2004.

[5] P. Chen, W. Ng, S. Chandra, C. Aycock, G. Rajamani, and D. Lowell. The Rio File Cache: Surviving Operating System Crashes. In *Proceedings of the 7th International Conference on Architectural Support for Programming Languages and Operating Systems*, pages 74–83, 1996.

[6] A. Depoutovitch and M. Stumm. Otherworld - Giving Applications a Chance to Survive OS Kernel Crashes. In *Proceedings of the 5th European Conference on Computer Systems*, pages 181–194, 2010.

[7] S. Garg, A. Puliafito, M. Telek, and K. Trivedi. Analysis of Preventive Maintenance in Transactions Based Software Systems. *IEEE Transactions on Computers*, 47(1):96–107, 1998.

[8] M. Grottke and K. Trivedi. Fighting Bugs: Remove, Retry, Replicate, and Rejuvenate. *IEEE Computer*, 40(2):107–109, 2007.

[9] J. Halderman, S. Schoen, N. Heninger, W. Clarkson, W. Paul, J. Calandrino, A. Feldman, J. Appelbaum, and E. Felten. Lest We Remember: Cold Boot Attacks on Encryption Keys. In *Proceedings of the USENIX Security Symposium*, pages 45–60, 2008.

[10] Y. Huang, C. Kintala, N. Kolettis, and N. Fulton. Software Rejuvenation: Analysis, module and Applications. In *Proceedings of the 25th International Symposium on Fault-Tolerant Computing*, pages 381–391, 1995.

[11] S. Jones, , A. Arpaci-Dusseau, and R. Arpaci-Dusseau. Geiger: Monitoring the Buffer Cache in a Virtual Machine Environment. In *Proceedings of the 12th International Conference on Architectural Support for Programming Languages and Operating Systems*, pages 14–24, 2006.

[12] H. Kaminaga. Improving Linux Startup Time Using Software Resume (and Other Techniques). In *Proceedings of the Linux Symposium*, pages 25–34, 2006.

[13] A. Kivity, Y. Kamay, and D. Laor. KVM: The Linux Virtual Machine Monitor. In *Proceedings of the Linux Symposium*, pages 225–230, 2007.

[14] K. Kourai and S. Chiba. A Fast Rejuvenation Technique for Server Consolidation with Virtual Machines. In *Proceedings of the 37th International Conference on Dependable Systems and Networks*, pages 245–254, 2007.

[15] K. Kourai and S. Chiba. Fast Software Rejuvenation of Virtual Machine Monitors. *IEEE Transactions on Dependable and Secure Computing*, 2010.

[16] P. Lu and K. Shen. Virtual Machine Memory Access Tracing with Hypervisor Exclusive Cache. In *Proceedings of the USENIX Annual Technical Conference*, pages 1–15, 2007.

[17] D. Mosberger and T. Jin. httperf: A Tool for Measuring Web Server Performance. *Performance Evaluation Review*, 26(3):31–37, 1998.

[18] W. Ng and P. Chen. The Design and Verification of the Rio File Cache. *IEEE Transactions on Computers*, 50(4):322–337, 2001.

[19] W. Norcott and D. Capps. IOzone Filesystem Benchmark.

[20] A. Pfiffer. Reducing System Reboot Time with kexec. http://www.osdl.org/.

[21] M. Swift, B. Bershad, and H. Levy. Improving the Reliability of Commodity Operating Systems. In *Proceedings of the 19th Symposium on Operating Systems Principles*, pages 207–222, 2003.

[22] Transaction Processing Performance Council. TPC Benchmark H Standard Specification Revision 2.9.0. http://www.tpc.org/, 2009.

[23] C. Waldspurger. Memory Resource Management in VMware ESX Server. In *Proceedings of the 5th Symposium on Operating Systems Design and Implementation*, pages 181–194, 2002.

[24] J. Zhang and M. Wong. Database Test Suite. http://osdldbt.sourceforge.net/.

Evaluation of Delta Compression Techniques for Efficient Live Migration of Large Virtual Machines

Petter Svärd
Umeå University
petters@cs.umu.se

Benoit Hudzia
SAP Research CEC Belfast
benoit.hudzia@sap.com

Johan Tordsson
Umeå University
tordsson@cs.umu.se

Erik Elmroth
Umeå University
elmroth@cs.umu.se

Abstract

Despite the widespread support for live migration of Virtual Machines (VMs) in current hypervisors, these have significant shortcomings when it comes to migration of certain types of VMs. More specifically, with existing algorithms, there is a high risk of service interruption when migrating VMs with high workloads and/or over low-bandwidth networks. In these cases, VM memory pages are dirtied faster than they can be transferred over the network, which leads to extended migration downtime. In this contribution, we study the application of delta compression during the transfer of memory pages in order to increase migration throughput and thus reduce downtime. The delta compression live migration algorithm is implemented as a modification to the KVM hypervisor. Its performance is evaluated by migrating VMs running different type of workloads and the evaluation demonstrates a significant decrease in migration downtime in all test cases. In a benchmark scenario the downtime is reduced by a factor of 100. In another scenario a streaming video server is live migrated with no perceivable downtime to the clients while the picture is frozen for eight seconds using standard approaches. Finally, in an enterprise application scenario, the delta compression algorithm successfully live migrates a very large system that fails after migration using the standard algorithm. Finally, we discuss some general effects of delta compression on live migration and analyze when it is beneficial to use this technique.

Categories and Subject Descriptors D.4.1 [*Operating Systems*]: Process Management; D.4.8 [*Operating Systems*]: Performance

General Terms Design, Measurement, Performance

Keywords Virtualization, Live migration, Compression, Performance evaluation

1. Introduction

Virtualization is an abstraction of computer hardware as a software implementation of a machine, a virtual machine (VM) that can execute programs just as a physical machine. By using a hypervisor, several VMs can share the same underlying hardware with neglectable overhead [2]. Virtualization thus allows multiple operating system instances to run concurrently on a single physical machine. This enables more efficient usage of hardware resources by use of techniques such as server consolidation. Virtualization also makes it easier to achieve isolation of services since each service can run on a dedicated virtual server. Other benefits of virtualization are dynamic allocation of resources (i.e., resizing of VMs) to meet deviations in workload as well as simplified provisioning, monitoring, and administration of servers.

In addition, it is possible to move (migrate) a VM from one host to another without shutting it down, increasing flexibility in VM provisioning. Live migration techniques for VMs [6] focus on capturing and transferring the run time, in memory, state of a VM over a network. Live migration enables administrators to reconfigure virtual machine hardware and move running virtual machines from one host to another while maintaining near continuous service availability. This ability to migrate applications encapsulated within VMs without perceivable downtime is becoming increasingly important in order to provide continuous operation and availability of services in the face of outages, whether planned or unplanned. Live migration also increases efficiency as it is possible to manage varying demands in an organization with fewer physical servers and less human effort by enabling on-the-fly server consolidation.

So far, live migration research has focused on transferring the run-time in-memory state of VMs with relative limited memory size in Local Area Networks (LANs). The usability of current live migration techniques is limited when large VMs or VMs with high memory loads such as VMs running large enterprise applications have to be migrated, or when migration is performed over slow networks. The reason for this shortcoming is that the hypervisor is unable to transfer the VM memory in the same rate as it is dirtied by the VM. This limitation can easily neutralize the advantages of live migration.

This work extends on an idea by Hacking et al. [7], who propose a live migration algorithm where the VM in-memory state is compressed during transfer. In this contribution, we modify the KVM hypervisor by implementing a delta compression live migration algorithm where changes to memory pages are transferred instead of the full page contents. We evaluate the performance of this approach by analyzing the effects of compression on migration downtime and total migration time. The evaluation is based on experiments with migration of VMs running three different workloads, a synthetic benchmark and a transcoding video server over 100 Mbit/s network (Fast Ethernet), and an enterprise application over a 1000 Mbit/s network (Gigabit Ethernet). The results demonstrate significantly reduced migration downtimes in all cases. We also discuss some general principles regarding the effects of delta compression on live migration performance and analyze when the use of such techniques is beneficial.

2. Background and related work

In order to migrate a VM, its state has to be transferred. A VM's state consists of its memory contents and local file system. However, the transfer of the local file system can be avoided by keeping it on a network file system storage volume accessible to both the source and the destination. To migrate a VM, it is first suspended, its state is then transferred, and the VM is finally resumed on its new host. While the VM is suspended it is unreachable and service is thus interrupted.

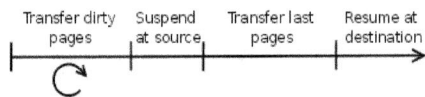

Figure 1. Overview of a typical live migration process.

Live migration aims to solve the problem of migrating a VM without service interruption by keeping the VM running on the source while transferring the state in the background to the destination, an approach first demonstrated by Clark et al. [6]. Although various versions of this algorithm exist, including usage of push and pull techniques for page transfers, on-demand paging, etc., the typical live migration algorithm is as follows. First, all pages are marked as dirty. Then, a number of iterations are performed. In each iteration, the memory pages dirtied in the host during the previous iteration are retransferred. Notably, all memory pages are transferred in the first iteration. Once the number of dirty pages in the source is below a certain threshold, typically set based on the network bandwidth and the desired maximum downtime, the VM is suspended at the source and the last few pages are transferred. Finally, the VM is resumed on the destination. This typical live migration process is outlined in Figure 1. The rationale behind this scheme is that as most of the state already is transferred when the VM is suspended, the downtime before the VM is resumed at the destination can be significantly shortened. If the suspension time is short enough, network connections can be kept alive and service is thus not interrupted. Live migration does not significantly degrade the performance experienced by users (the perceived downtime) of services running in the VM, Furthermore, the migration process is completely transparent as services running in the migrated VM do not need to be migration-aware in any way.

Most virtual machine hypervisors, such as Xen [5], KVM [11], and VMWare [20] support live migration [6, 21] that involve extremely short downtimes ranging from tens of milliseconds to a second. Usually, these techniques assume that migration is performed over a Local Area Network (LAN). However live Wide Area Network (WAN) migration has been demonstrated by several researchers [4, 8, 16, 19], achieved by use of novel techniques based on, e.g., IP tunneling, Mobile IP, and light path reservation.

Bradford et al. [4] propose a solution to live migration of VMs over WANs that uses pre-copying and write throttling. The latter is a dynamic VM rate limiting technique where the amount of hardware resources allocated to the migration is increased at the ex-

pense of the performance of the VM. Bradford et al. use a combination of dynamic DNS and IP tunneling to ensure that network connections in the VMs are kept alive during migration. In a contribution by Harney et al. [8], Mobile IPv6 is used to ensure continuous network connectivity without the use of virtual networks. This approach is evaluated in scenarios with and without shared storage. Sapuntzakis et al. [18] present several techniques to improve VM migration, including the use of memory ballooning where a VM can dynamically change its memory usage by evicting unused memory during runtime to make its memory state more compressible. Other techniques used by Sapuntzakis et al. include demand paging of VM disks and content-based block sharing across disk state. Zhao et al. analyze how performance degradation varies with various migration strategies [23]. So far, most of the experiments concerning live migration has focused on small to medium sized VMs typically running web server workloads. Notably, Anedda et al. propose a method for migrating virtual clusters for data-driven HPC applications using delta compression techniques [1]. Their work is however restricted to non-live migration.

3. The problem of Live Migration

While a VM is running, its memory is dirtied at a specific rate, the *dirtying rate*. If this rate is higher than the network throughput, the number of dirty pages to re-transfer increases for each iteration of page transfers (see Figure 1). The hypervisor's migration algorithm can thus not complete the dirty page transfer phase of the migration and the VM has to be prematurely suspended in order to be migrated. The *migration downtime* is the time period from when the VM is suspended in the source host until it is resumed and responding to requests at the destination host. If the memory block that is left untransferred when the VM is suspended is large, this downtime can be long.

This drawback of the current live migration approaches can lead to extensive migration downtime when migrating VMs with high workloads, and/or large RAM sizes such as VMs running large enterprise applications, or when migrating over slow networks. Liu et al. show that the total migration time and the migration downtime do not only depend on the amount of VM memory to transfer but also on the workload type [12]. They illustrate that even for a small VM with a mere 156 MB of RAM, a migration downtime of three seconds and a total migration time of ten seconds may be necessary even over a Gigabit Ethernet network.

3.1 Effects of extended migration downtime

Extended migration downtime can lead to several problems, including issues related to service interruption, consistency problems and unpredictable performance.

3.1.1 Service interruption

Most server applications rely on TCP connections and the connectivity of these must be guaranteed during live migration of the VMs in which they are running. To achieve reliable transmission, TCP packages are resent unless acknowledgements are achieved. The amount of time between retries is determined by the Smoothed Round Trip Time (SRTT). The SRTT varies with the network speed and latency as TCP tunes itself to each network connection for retransmissions. Over Fast Ethernet, TCP connections are aborted after around eight seconds while over Gigabit Ethernet, which is recommended for nearly every implementation of live migration, the timeout occurs even faster, after around five seconds. In effect, this means that all TCP connections are dropped if a VM is suspended with more than 500 MB of memory left to transfer over a Gigabit Ethernet network. Considering that many of today's applications use more than 16 GB of RAM and have large workloads, TCP timeouts are not uncommon.

3.1.2 Consistency and transparency problems

A direct consequence of migration downtime is the difficulty to maintain consistency and transparency. Online transaction processing systems such as Enterprise Resource Planning (ERP) software are very sensitive to variations in delay. Such a system relies heavily on precise scheduling capabilities, triggers, timers, and on the underlying database systems to perform various operations efficiently and with desired properties, i.e., that these ensure Atomicity, Consistency, Isolation and Durability (ACID). If the VM is suspended for too long during a critical execution phase of the system, the downtime often results in data corruption and/or a crash due to missed timers, unscheduled or delayed events, clock drift, etc. For the enterprise application used in the evaluation of our work, downtimes as low as half a second are known to result in unrecoverable problems of this kind.

3.1.3 Unpredictability and rigidity

In their current state, live migration operations tend to be unpredictable as to how much time they need in order to complete. This is because it is difficult to assess the number of iterations required in the dirty page retransfer phase of the typical live migration algorithm. This in turn depends on the page dirtying rate that is unique to each application [6] and cannot be determined by the amount of resources allocated to the VM (CPUs, amount of RAM), etc. As a result, the use of current live migration algorithms is infeasible when timely migrations are needed.

3.2 Existing solutions

To shorten migration downtime, current hypervisors use various methods such as dynamic rate-limiting [4, 6] where the migration traffic bandwidth limit is dynamically increased during migration. There is however a risk of networking resource outage for the VM unless a dedicated network card is used for live migration operations since migration traffic tend to have a higher priority. Because of this, dynamic rate-limiting gradually degrades performance of the VM and to a certain extent the performance of any co-located VMs. Another approach is rogue processes stunning, where processes that write too much in memory are stunned or frozen. Rouge process stunning can be highly disruptive and dangerous with applications that use transactions. Both dynamic rate-limiting and rogue process stunning might significantly degrade the performance of the running VM which is in conflict with the goals of live migration.

These drawbacks are worsened when live migration is done over unreliable or slow connections such as WANs and the Internet. In such environments, it is quite often as efficient and recommended to simply shut-down the VM before migrating it rather than performing the migration live.

4. A Delta Compression approach

Current live migration algorithms normally starts by marking all RAM memory pages as dirty on the source host. Then, a typical algorithm iteratively transfers pages that have been dirtied since the last round of transfers. The longer time an iteration takes, the more memory is dirtied during the process and has to be re-transferred. When the estimated remaining transfer time is below a certain threshold, the VM is suspended to stop further memory writes and allow the remaining pages to be transferred. The remaining transfer time is calculated as $t_r = m_d/b$, where m_d is the amount of dirty RAM remaining and b is the available bandwidth. The main bottleneck in this algorithm is the transfer of memory pages over the network, as even Gigabit Ethernet is several orders of magnitude slower than RAM or disk access. If the VM dirtying rate is higher than the migration throughput, the migration downtime

can be long and service interruption may occur. In order to improve the performance and shorten the migration downtime, either the dirtying rate has to be reduced or the network throughput increased.

As discussed earlier, reducing the dirtying rate by stunning or freezing processes leads to performance degradation and possibly also service interruption. Increasing network throughput thus seems like a more promising approach.

4.1 Run Length Encoding Delta Compression

By compressing the memory pages before transfer, the amount of data to transfer is reduced and the migration throughput is thus increased. This allows the live migration algorithm to better keep up with the VM's dirtying rate. It is important to note that as the type of data in the VM's memory varies depending on which workload the VM runs, the compression algorithm must be able to efficiently compress any type of data. In many applications, the same set of memory pages are written to over and over again, i.e. a specific part of the VM's RAM is constantly dirtied which means that delta compression is a promising candidate to compress the memory pages.

Delta compression is a method for storing data in the form of changes between versions instead of the full data sets. The technique is relatively old and its origins comes from the problem of finding the minimum number of edit operations necessary to transform one string into another [22]. One early application of delta compression was to manage revision control systems in order to save large amounts of storage by storing changes to files rather than the files themselves. Another well known use of binary delta compression is by Microsoft to reduce the download size of software update packages [14]. Delta compression is already used to improve VM operation but its usage is mainly focused on compressing I/O buffers for VMs or storage [10].

The VM memory pages that needs to be compressed are in binary form and it is thus easy to compute the delta page by applying XOR on the current and previous version of a page. To compose the new page at the destination, this process is simply reversed to produce a copy of the source's current version from the previous version and the delta page. The delta page is the same size as the original memory page and as our goal is to reduce the amount of transferred data during migration, the delta page must be compressed. The data must be compressed efficiently enough to significantly reduce transfer time and the compression algorithm should consume a minimum of CPU resources in order not to slow down the migration process or hurt the VM's performance. Fortunately, in many cases when a page is dirtied, only a couple of words are changed. This means that the delta pages can be efficiently compressed by binary Run Length Encoding (RLE) [15] which is a well-known, fast, and efficient compression algorithm.

Another approach is to use domain-specific compression algorithms and select the most suitable one according to the nature of the workload on the VM to be migrated. However, even if the memory contents of a VM running for example a streaming video server would probably compress better using video compression techniques this would come at the expense of VM performance. The live migration algorithm runs in parallel with the VM and each CPU cycle added affects the performance of the VM as well as the live migration and most domain-specific compression techniques tend to be CPU intensive. In addition, many domain-specific compression techniques are destructive and, as a bit-for-bit replica of the memory contents is needed, such techniques cannot be used. Finally, a choice would have to be made as to which compression technique to use for a specific application, making the live migration process less transparent. We therefore believe that it is best to use a lean and efficient general compression technique and, in our evaluation, we opted to use a a straight-forward word-wise RLE algorithm.

4.1.1 Caching

In order to compute a delta page, the previous version of the page is needed. On the destination side this is not a problem since the source's previous version of a page is the destination's current version. However, on the source side the memory contents are continuously overwritten and a copy of the previously sent version of the page must be kept. It is not feasible to store a copy of every page in memory since this would double the VMs memory usage and render the caching approach unusable for CPU intensive VMs with large memory, which are the ones most likely to benefit from this technique. Hence, only a subset of the VM's memory pages should be stored which means that a caching scheme must be used.

As discussed eariler, it is often the case that a set of memory pages is being constantly dirtied, this set is called the VM's *hot pages set*. For large VMs or VMs running heavy workloads, the hot pages set can be large and the page cache needs to be large enough to hold a significant part of the hot pages or cache churn might occur, i.e., the contents of the cache is constantly replaced and migration performance is thus decreased. In addition, the cache lookup time should remain constant when the cache size increases as not to decrease migration performance when using larger cache sizes. Finally, the algorithm should consume a minimum of CPU resources, both for cache hits and cache misses to not slow down the migration process or disrupt the performance of the VM.

Various caching schemes like LRU and ARC [13] were evaluated, but failed to fulfill these requirements. Finally, a 2-way set associative caching scheme, commonly used in high performance CPU caches [9], was chosen. In this scheme, the cache maps memory addresses to cache buckets, each bucket holding maximum two memory pages, see Figure 2. If a bucket is full, the oldest entry is evicted and replaced with the new entry. This sort of cache is suitable in our case as it is very lean and the time to locate an element is constant even as the cache size grows.

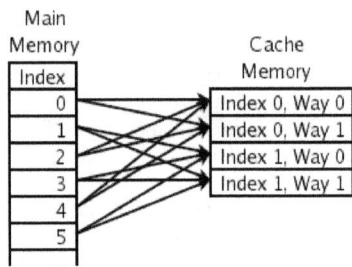

Figure 2. 2-way set associative cache.

4.2 Delta Compression Algorithm Overview

In our evaluation, we use a XOR binary RLE (XBRLE) live migration algorithm in order to increase migration throughput and thus reduce downtime. When transferring a page, the source checks if a previous version of the page exists in the cache. If this is the case, a delta page between the new version and the cached version is created using XOR. The delta page is compressed using XBRLE and a delta compression flag is set in the page header. Finally, the cache is updated and the compressed page is transferred. On the destination side, if the delta compression flag is set for a page, the delta page is decompressed and the new version of the page is reconstructed from the delta page and the destination's previous version of the page using XOR. A schematic overview of the delta compression scheme on the source and destination side respectively can be found in Figures 3 and 4. The algorithm is implemented as modification to the user space code of the qemu-kvm [11] hypervisor.

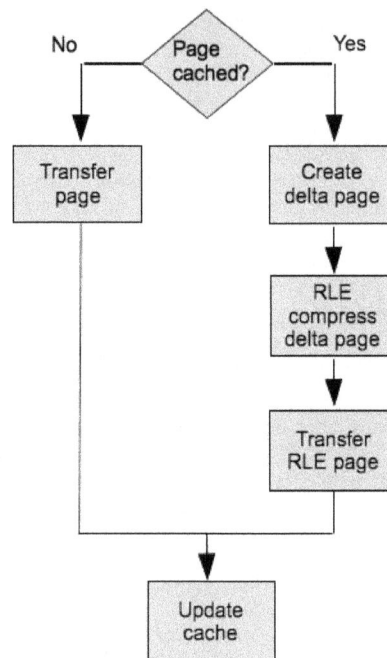

Figure 3. Source side delta compression scheme.

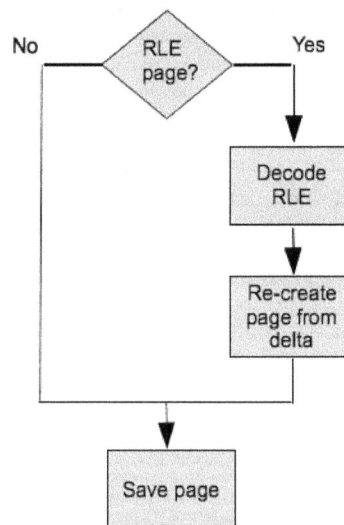

Figure 4. Destination side delta compression scheme.

5. Evaluation

To evaluate the performance of the XBRLE live migration algorithm, a number of VMs were live migrated. In order to test the algorithm under various conditions we investigated three live migration scenarios using VMs running different workloads. The workloads where selected to range from ideal conditions (high dirtying rate, data suitable for delta compression, limited bandwidth) to less ideal cases (data not so suitable for delta compression, high bandwidth).

The algorithm's performance is highly dependent on the cache size. A too small cache will most likely result in cache churn and no performance gain. A large cache size does not hurt the performance but is wasteful with the host's system resources. In the three scenarios, the cache size was chosen to match the size of the hot pages set of the VM. The size of the hot pages set was estimated by studying the memory usage of the running processes.

5.1 Experimental Scenarios

As described in the previous section, three scenarios were considered in the performance evaluation. For the "ideal" scenario, a synthetic benchmark was used. In the second scenario, a real-world application which produces a high dirtying rate was used, namely a VLC server. Finally, a SAP ERP system was chosen as it is a well-known, widely used business application that puts a high load on the system and is sensitive to network timeouts.

The characteristics of the three scenarios are as follows:

Fast Ethernet (benchmark): 1 GB RAM, 1 vcpu VM running two instances of the LMbench memory write benchmark of 256 MB each.

Fast Ethernet (HD video transcoding): 1 GB RAM, 1 vcpu VM running a VLC transcoding video server streaming 720p video.

Gigabit Ethernet (ERP system): 8 GB RAM, 4 vcpus VM running a SAP CI ERP system with 100 concurrent users.

In the first two scenarios, the tests were performed on two Intel 2.66 GHz core2quad servers with 16 GB of RAM running Ubuntu 9. The servers were connected to fast Ethernet using separate network adapters for the host and the VM networks. The VM images were stored on a NFS share on the source machine. The size of the 2-way set associative cache was 512MB.

In the last scenario, the test was performed on two Intel 3 GHz 4 x Dual Core Xeon servers with 32 GB of RAM running Ubuntu 10.4. The servers were connected to a Gigabit Ethernet network using a shared network adapter for the host and the VM networks. The VM images were stored on a 16 TB Raid 5, 4 x quad core Xeon NFS server with 16 GB of RAM and a 6 Gbit/s trunked Ethernet card. In this scenario, the size of the set associative cache was 1GB.

Each test was run twice, the first time using the standard qemu-kvm migration algorithm, henceforth referred to as *vanilla*, and a second time using the XBRLE algorithm. The version of qemu-kvm used in the evaluation is 0.11.5. The modified version of qemu-kvm used for the evaluation is built from the qemu-kvm 0.11.5 source with the delta compression modifications described above.

5.2 Experimental Results

In this section, the results from the three test scenarios are presented. The performance evaluation demonstrate that migration downtime, both VM suspension time and perceived downtime, is reduced in all of the studied scenarios when using XBRLE compression. The difference in the first two cases is significant and promises improved live migration of memory-intensive VMs with large working sets and migration over slower networks without service interruption. In the last scenario, the difference in migration downtime is less significant, but large large enough for the migration to succeed in the XBRLE case whereas it failed using the vanilla algorithm.

5.2.1 Fast Ethernet (benchmark) scenario

In the first scenario a synthetic benchmark which gives a high dirtying rate was run. The total migration time, the suspension time, and the migration downtime for the benchmark test is shown in minutes, seconds, and milliseconds in Figure 5. The total migration time was decreased from 65 s to 48 s and the suspension time

dropped from 32 s to 0.297 s using the XBRLE algorithm. The migration throughput in MB/s, shown in Figure 7, was increased by around 80%. The ping downtime, i.e., the time when the VM is unresponsive to ICMP ping requests, dropped from 32 s to 1 s. However, as the ping resolution used was 1 s, it is likely that the downtime in the XBRLE case was even shorter.

The synthetic benchmark used in the evaluation, the LMbench [3] memory write benchmark, is part of the LMbench suite of performance benchmarks for UNIX. The *bw_mem_wr* benchmark allocates a specified amount of memory, zeros it, and then coordinates the writing of that memory as a series of four byte integer stores and increments. This benchmark causes a very high dirtying rate within the allocated memory block since the memory contents are constantly overwritten. This type of workload is also known as a *diabolic workload*. As the dirtying rate is higher than the network throughput, the standard migration algorithm cannot keep up and has to suspend the VM with around half of the working set untransferred (256 MB), which causes the extended downtime that can be seen in Figure 5. As the data consists mostly of zeros, it is very suitable for RLE encoding. The hypervisor thus manages to transfer almost all of the working set before suspending the VM in the XBRLE case. To conclude, the results from the benchmark test demonstrate the benefits of the XBRLE live migration algorithm under near ideal conditions.

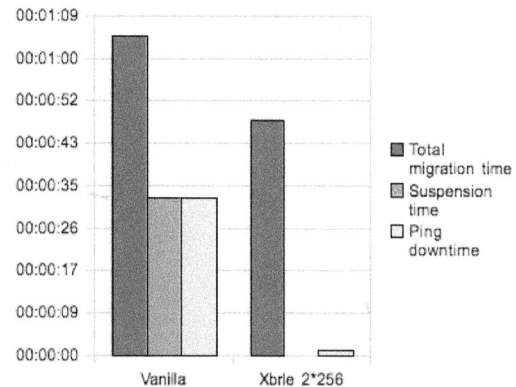

Figure 5. Migration time (LMbench).

5.2.2 Fast Ethernet (HD video transcoding) scenario

In the first real-world application scenario, a VLC transcoding video server was migrated over a LAN. The total migration time, which can be seen in Figure 6, was two seconds longer in the XBRLE case (28 s vs 26 s) but the suspension time was much shorter (0.028 s vs 2 s). The *UDP downtime*, which is the time when no UDP packets are received at the client, was decreased from 8 s to 2 s and the migration throughput was increased from 11.39MB/s to 12.38 MB/s.

Streaming video is an example of a service that is widely available over the Internet and, as in the benchmarking case, this type of application causes a high dirtying rate, especially when, as in our case, the video stream is transcoded. However, the data is not very compressible as the content of the streaming buffer changes constantly and the difference between subsequent video frames can be large. Because of this, many pages could not be compressed as the data stream had changed too much since the last iteration of the dirty pages transfer. This explains that, in the test, the increase in throughput was lower than in the benchmark case. However, the shortened suspension leads to a shorter UDP downtime which means that the gap in the video stream is reduced. This difference is clearly visible in Figure 8 and Figure 9, which show the amount of UDP packages sent from the video transcoding server to the client during migration of the VM that runs the streaming server. Notably, the spikes in these graphs that appear after migration is caused by the post-migration decrease in I/O bandwidth that results from keeping the VM file system on a NFS share on the source host. Because of the difference in downtime, when migrating using the vanilla algorithm, the video on the client was frozen for eight seconds and choppy for some additional time. When using the XBRLE algorithm, the migration was unnoticeable since the gap in the data stream was short enough to fit in the client side streaming buffer. These results demonstrate that also applications that have a high page dirtying rate and working set data not suitable for RLE compression can be migrated with good results using the XBRLE algorithm.

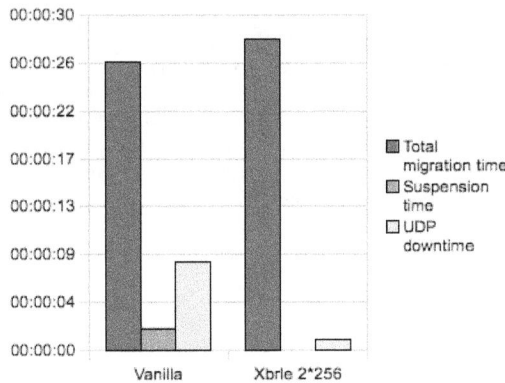

Figure 6. Migration time (HD video).

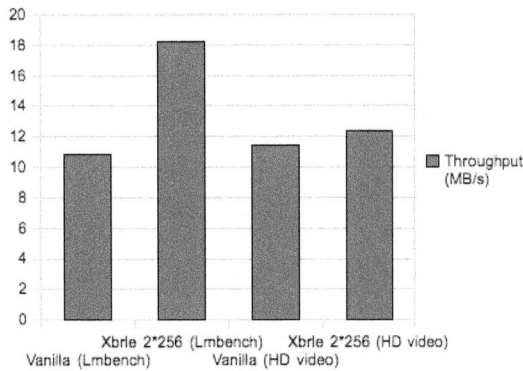

Figure 7. Migration throughput for LMBench and HD video (100 Mbit/s Ethernet).

5.2.3 Gigabit Ethernet (ERP system) scenario

In the final test, a VM running a SAP Central Instance ERP system was migrated over Gigabit Ethernet. With XBRLE, the total migration time was reduced from 235 s to 139 s, the suspension time was reduced from 3 s to 0.2 s, and the ping downtime from 5 s to 1 s, all illustrated in Figure 10.

SAP is one of the most commonly used business intelligence applications. It puts a high load on the CPU and it is considered notoriously hard to migrate these kind of systems live because of their dependency on transactions and time-out sensitive network connections. According to our experience with the SAP ERP system, fatal timing problems can occur already for migration downtimes as low as half a second. In our test, the total migration time was reduced

with around 40% but as the system is very complex, the migration time can vary greatly depending on actual load during migration, etc. It is thus hard to draw any definitive conclusions regarding total migration time. More importantly, the migration downtime usually does not vary as much and even if the difference in downtime was not as dramatic as in the two other scenarios, it was still reduced from 3 s to 0.2 s with the XBRLE algorithm. The smaller decrease in downtime compared to the earlier cases can partly be explained by the fact that the network is not as much of a bottleneck as in previous two cases.

Notably, in our test, the vanilla migration did not succeed. In this case, the system was resumed after migration but, as shown in Figure 11, application CPU usage (the dark line) rose to 100% and the system was in an unstable state, probably due to timing errors. Also shown in Figure 11 is the system CPU usage (bright line), of which the KVM hypervisor constitutes the greater part. This value was around 10% during the page transfer iterations, fluctuated substantially as the VM was shut down and resumed, and dropped almost to zero post migration. The third line in Figure 11 shows I/O wait, i.e., processes waiting for network or disk I/O. The I/O wait showed a similar pattern as the system CPU usage.

In contrast, the XBRLE algorithm successfully migrated the ERP system, even at a higher load (70% application CPU) than where the vanilla algorithm failed (20% application CPU). The application CPU usage during migration is shown as the upper dark line in Figure 12. This value fluctuated a bit as the VM was suspended and resumed, but returned to the 70% level after migration. As for system CPU usage (the bright line in Figure 12), this value varied between 5% and 10% during the page transfer iterations. The spikes in this value can be attributed to the rather CPU-intensive compression of delta pages that are part of each iteration. These spikes got higher when more pages were compressed in later iterations, as the reduced amount of VM RAM remaining to transfer resulted in a higher cache hit ratio. The dark line in the lower part of Figure 12 denotes I/O wait, which was low for the XBRLE algorithm, except for a spike during the final shutdown and resume of the VM.

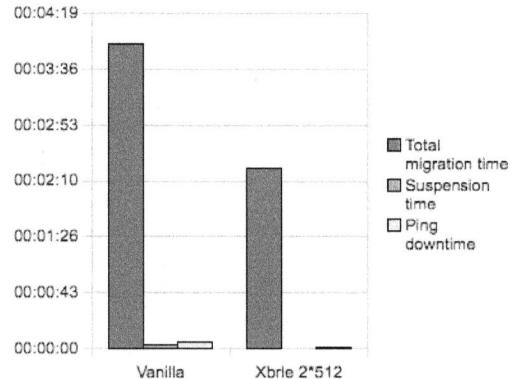

Figure 10. Migration time (ERP).

As the system CPU utilization on the VM was level at around 10% during migration in both cases, we conclude that the XBRLE migration algorithm had about the same impact on VM performance as the vanilla algorithm.

6. Analysis of the General effects of delta compression on Live Migration

In this section, we analyze in which cases delta compression is beneficial by use of a simple model. We also discuss the impact

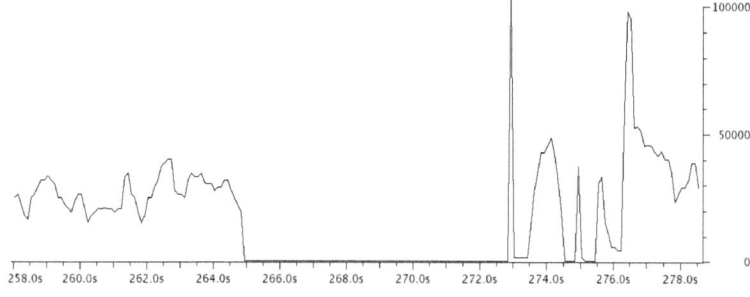

Figure 8. UDP traffic, HD video (vanilla).

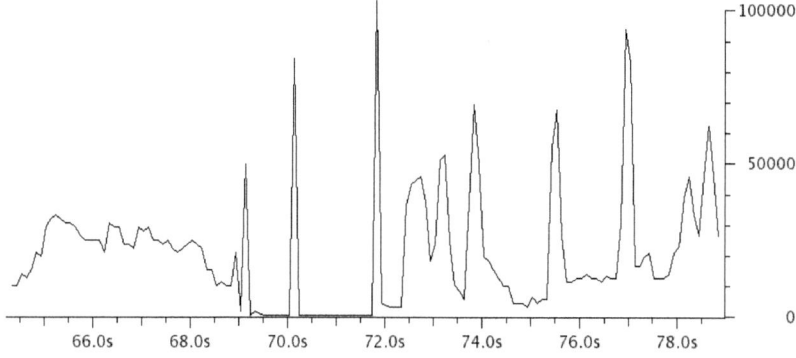

Figure 9. UDP traffic, HD video (XBRLE).

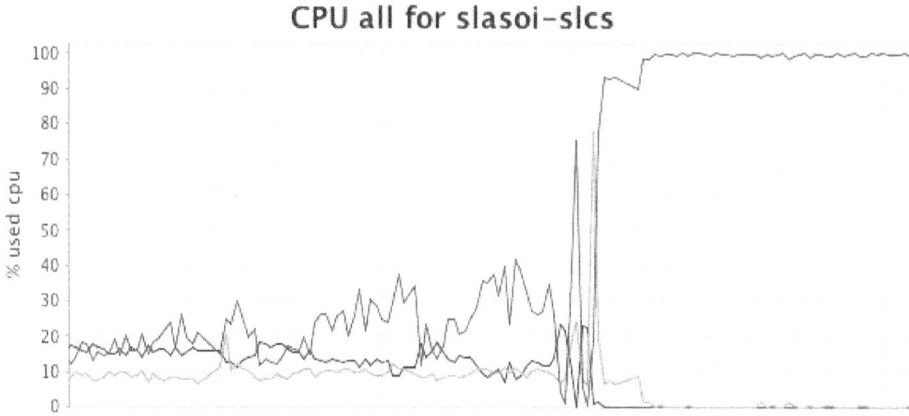

Figure 11. CPU utilization (ERP vanilla).

of cache size on migration performance. When studying the use of delta compression in live migration algorithms there are several parameters that must be considered. As our goal is to reduce migration downtime, the per page migration time is central. In the standard non-compression live migration algorithm, this time can be described as:

$$t_{nc} = t_{tr}, \tag{1}$$

where t_{tr} is the transfer time. When using the delta compression approach evaluated in this paper there are two cases, the first being cache hit:

$$t_h = t_c + t_{cp} + t_{trh} + t_d, \tag{2}$$

where t_c is the cache time, t_{cp} is the compression time, t_{trh} is the cache hit transmission time, and t_d is the decompression time. The

second case is cache miss, where:

$$t_m = t_c + t_{tr}. \tag{3}$$

From this follows that the total migration time using the no compression approach can be expressed as:

$$t = \sum_1^n P t_{nc}, \tag{4}$$

where P is the total number of pages and n is the number of iterations. The total migration time using the delta compression method is:

$$t = \sum_1^n P_h t_h + \sum_1^n P_m t_m, \tag{5}$$

117

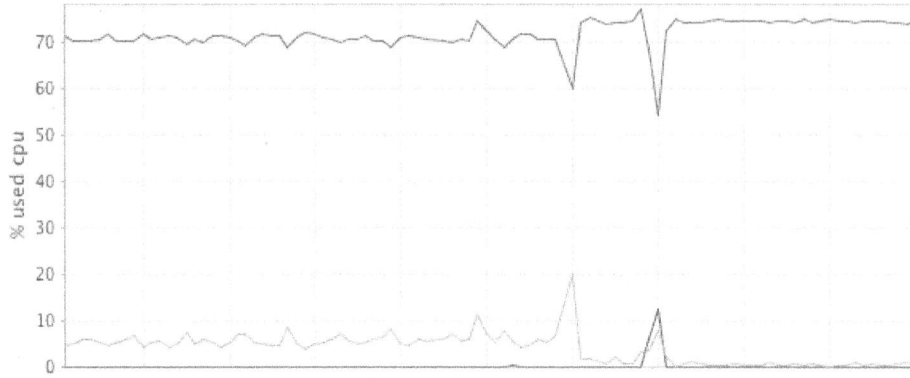

Figure 12. CPU utilization (ERP XBRLE).

where P_h is the number of cache hit pages and P_m is the number of cache miss pages. The total migration time, can also be expressed as:

$$t = n(ht_h + (1-h)t_m), \qquad (6)$$

where n is the number of page transfer iterations and h is the cache hit ratio.

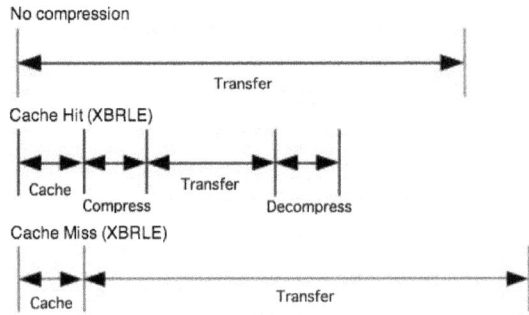

Figure 13. Page transfer times compared.

As illustrated in Figure 13, if the time to cache, compress and decompress a page exceeds the difference in transfer time between the uncompressed and compressed case, the compression case performs worse than the uncompressed. However, using an efficient caching and compression scheme, the shorter transfer time for the cache hit pages makes the total time to process and transfer a page significantly shorter as the time to cache, compress, and decompress the page is short compared to the time gained by transferring less data.

From equations 1 and 3 as well as figure 13 it can be seen that the time it takes to transfer a cache miss page is longer than the time it takes to transfer the same page without compression. From this follows that the cache hit ratio needs to be large enough for the algorithm to be efficient. The potential time gain can be expressed as:

$$t_g = (1-h)(t_m - t_{nc}) - h(t_{nc} - t_h). \qquad (7)$$

If the cache hit time, cache miss time, and no compression time can be measured, it seems that the needed cache hit ratio in order for the delta compression algorithm to be faster than the no compression case can be calculated. However, this is an oversimplification. Because the delta compression algorithm is faster at catching up with the VM dirtying memory, the downtime can be reduced even if the total migration time might be longer than using the standard

algorithm. This behavior was observed in the streaming video scenario. The reason for this is that during the initial iterations, there is a high number of cache misses but after a couple of iterations, the cache hit ratio increases and the algorithm begins to catch up with the VM. In subsequent iterations, the cache hit ratio increases even more until it reaches a stable value. At this point, the VM dirties memory pages in the source at the same rate as the (compressed) pages can be transferred to the destination. The dirty pages set does thus not decrease in size and the VM has to be suspended for the migration to proceed. In comparison, the vanilla algorithm reaches this point with more memory remaining to transfer since it has no possibility to catch up when the VM dirtying rate is as fast as the algorithm can transfer pages over the network.

In order to achieve this increase in cache hit ratio and the associated reduction in number of pages to transfer in the next iteration, a large enough cache must be used. With a too small cache, the cache hit ratio typically never increases over the iterations and the behavior of the XBRLE migration algorithm becomes very similar to that of the vanilla one. Exactly how large cache is required to achieve the desired performance is difficult to determine analytically as this depends on the page dirtying rate, size of the hot pages set, page compression ratio, network bandwidth, etc. In our evaluation, the cache size was set to match the memory usage of the most active process in the VM which is an estimation of the VM's hot pages set. In the three scenarios investigated, a 512 MB cache was used for migration of the benchmark and HD video VMs, both with 1 GB RAM. For the ERP scenario, a 1 GB cache was used to ensure successful migration of the 8 GB VM running the SAP application.

Figure 14 gives a conceptual illustration of the relationship between the cache hit ratio, amount of dirty pages, number of iterations, and iteration length. In this figure, the height of each block denotes the amount of dirty VM memory remaining to transfer in each iteration. The width of the block is the transfer time. Notable, both the amount of memory remaining and the transfer time are reduced for each iteration, until the steady state is reached. The solid line in Figure 14 shows the cache hit ratio. For the initial iterations, this value is low (zero for the very first iteration), but it then increases rapidly and converges towards a value associated with the steady state where the number of dirty pages is constant between two subsequent iterations.

Another performance metric can be given by the the migration throughput, which can be expressed as:

$$t = P_t * B_p/t_{tr}, \qquad (8)$$

118

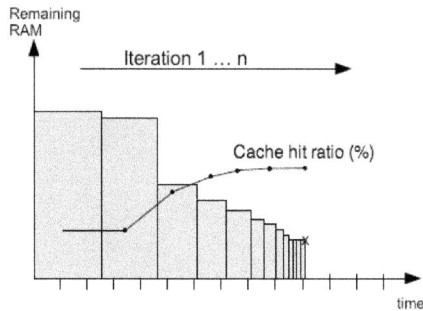

Figure 14. Illustration of how cache hit ratio, number of dirty pages, and transfer time evolve with each iteration of page transfers.

where P_t is the number of transferred pages, B_p is the page size in bytes and t_{tr} is the transfer time. A large increase in throughput compared to the vanilla algorithm is an indication of an efficient compression algorithm and a large number of cache hits. However, it might also be the case that the hot pages set is only a little bit too large for the hypervisor to be able to suspend the VM with an acceptable downtime using the vanilla algorithm. In this case, not that many pages need to be compressed to reach the point where the VM can be suspended and this results in only a small increase in migration throughput. This means that while the throughput sometimes is a good measure of the algorithms performance, this is not always the case.

7. Conclusion and future work

Improved live migration performance is important since it allows for a broader usage of live migration technologies, for example by cloud infrastructure providers in provisioning and relocating of VMs in or between data centers [17]. In this paper, we demonstrate that using delta compression when live migrating large VMs or VMs with heavy load can shorten migration time, migration downtime, and enable live migration with a reduced risk of service interruption. We investigate three test cases migrating VMs that run different workloads, spanning from a synthetic benchmark to an ERP application. For these, we observe a reduced migration downtime of a factor 100 for the benchmark (the ideal scenario), a drop in user-perceived downtime from 8 s to zero for transcoded streaming video, and a reduction of migration downtime from 3 to 0.2 s for an ERP application. Although the improvement was less significant in the ERP scenario, it made, due to the rigid timing requirements of this application, the difference between successful and failed migration.

In summary, our evaluation indicates that using XBRLE compression is particularly beneficial for live migration of:

- VMs running workloads with a highly compressible working set,

- VMs running heavy workloads with large working sets,

- and/or over slow networks (i.e., WANs).

To further improve the performance of live migration, we plan to investigate the use of a better strategy for selection of which memory pages to transfer and in what order to transfer them. The overall idea is to transfer the busiest pages last, as these pages are the ones most likely to be dirtied again. We believe that this method can reduce the number of page re-transfers and thus shorten migration time as well as migration downtime. We also plan to investigate dynamic adjustment of the cache size during migration. As it is very difficult to determine a suitable cache size analytically, this method

can be used both to improve migration performance, should the allocated page cache be too small, and reduce the amount of memory allocated to the migration when a too large cache is chosen. Another benefit of dynamic cache size adjustment is that, due to the fact that as the VM working set size changes with each iteration of page copying, the optimal cache size varies accordingly.

Acknowledgments

We acknowledge Stuart Hacking for his contributions to the foundation of this work and Tomas Ögren for installing and configuring the experimental environment. We also thank Eliezer Levy who has been instrumental in setting up this research collaboration. Financial support has been provided by the European Commission's Seventh Framework Programme ([FP7/2001-2013]) under grant agreements no. 215605 (RESERVOIR) and 257115 (OPTIMIS) as well as by UMIT research lab and the Swedish Governments strategic research project eSSENCE.

References

[1] P. Anedda. Suspending, migrating and resuming HPC virtual clusters. *Future Generation Computer Systems*, 26(8):1063 – 1072, 2010.

[2] P. Barham, B. Dragovic, K. Fraser, S. Hand, T. Harris, A. Ho, R. Neugebauer, I. Pratt, and A. Warfield. Xen and the art of virtualization. In *SOSP '03: Proceedings of the nineteenth ACM symposium on Operating systems principles*, pages 164–177. ACM, October 2003.

[3] Bitmover. Lmbench, 2010. http://www.bitmover.com/lmbench/, visisted June 2010.

[4] R. Bradford, E. Kotsovinos, A. Feldmann, and H. Schiöberg. Live wide-area migration of virtual machines including local persistent state. In *VEE '07: Proceedings of the 3rd international conference on Virtual execution environments*, pages 169–179. ACM, June 2007.

[5] Citrix Systems. Xen. http://www.xen.org, visited October 2010.

[6] C. Clark, K. Fraser, S. Hand, J. G. Hansen, E. Jul, C. Limpach, I. Pratt, and A. Warfield. Live migration of virtual machines. In *Proceedings of the 2nd ACM/USENIX Symposium on Networked Systems Design and Implementation (NSDI)*, pages 273–286. ACM, May 2005.

[7] S. Hacking and B. Hudzia. Improving the live migration process of large enterprise applications. In *VTDC '09: Proceedings of the 3rd international workshop on Virtualization technologies in distributed computing*, pages 51–58. ACM, June 2009.

[8] E. Harney, S. Goasguen, J. Martin, M. Murphy, and M. Westall. The efficacy of live virtual machine migrations over the internet. In *VTDC '07: Proceedings of the 3rd international workshop on Virtualization technology in distributed computing*, pages 1–7. ACM, November 2007.

[9] M. D. Hill. *Aspects of cache memory and instruction buffer performance*. PhD thesis, University of California, Berkeley, 1987.

[10] W. Huang, Q. Gao, J. Liu, and D. K. Panda. High performance virtual machine migration with RDMA over modern interconnects. Technical report, IBM T. J. Watson Research Center, 2007.

[11] Kernel Based Virtual Machine. KVM - kernel-based virtualization machine white paper, 2006. http://kvm.qumranet.com/kvmwiki, visited October 2010.

[12] P. Liu, Z. Yang, X. Song, Y. Zhou, H. Chen, and B. Zang. Heterogeneous live migration of virtual machines. Technical report, Parallel Processing Institute, Fudan University, 2009.

[13] N. Megiddo and D. S. Modha. ARC: A self-tuning, low overhead replacement cache. In *FAST '03: Proceedings of the 2nd USENIX Conference on File and Storage Technologies*, pages 115–130. USENIX Association, March 2003.

[14] S. Potter. Using binary delta compression (BDC) technology to update Windows XP and Windows Server 2003, October 2005. http://www.microsoft.com/downloads/details.aspx?FamilyID=4789196c-d60a-497c-ae89-101a3754bad6, visited October 2010.

119

[15] D. Pountain. Run-length encoding. *Byte*, 12(6):317–319, 1987.

[16] K. K. Ramakrishnan, P. Shenoy, and J. Van der Merwe. Live data center migration across WANs: a robust cooperative context aware approach. In *INM '07: Proceedings of the 2007 SIGCOMM workshop on Internet network management*, pages 262–267. ACM, August 2007.

[17] B. Rochwerger, D. Breitgand, E. Levy, A. Galis, K. Nagin, I. Llorente, R. Montero, Y. Wolfsthal, E. Elmroth, J. Caceres, M. Ben-Yehuda, W. Emmerich, and F. Galan. The RESERVOIR model and architecture for open federated cloud computing. *IBM Journal of Research and Development*, 53(4):1–11, 2009.

[18] C. P. Sapuntzaki, R. Chandra, B. Pfaff, J. Chow, M. S. Lam, and M. Rosenblum. Optimizing the migration of virtual computers. *SIGOPS Oper. Syst. Rev.*, 36(SI):377–390, 2002.

[19] F. Travostino. Seamless live migration of virtual machines over the MAN/WAN. In *SC '06: Proceedings of the 2006 ACM/IEEE conference on Supercomputing*, page 290. ACM, November 2006.

[20] VMWare. VMWare. http://www.vmware.com, visited October 2010.

[21] VMWARE. VMware VMotion: Live migration of virtual machines without service interruption datasheet, 2007. http://www.vmware.com/files/pdf/VMware-VMotion-DS-EN.pdf, visited October 2010.

[22] R. A. Wagner and M. J. Fischer. The string-to-string correction problem. *J. ACM*, 21(1):168–173, 1974.

[23] M. Zhao and R. J. Figueiredo. Experimental study of virtual machine migration in support of reservation of cluster resources. In *VTDC '07: Proceedings of the 3rd international workshop on Virtualization technology in distributed computing*, pages 1–8. ACM, June 2007.

CloudNet: Dynamic Pooling of Cloud Resources by Live WAN Migration of Virtual Machines

Timothy Wood   Prashant Shenoy

University of Massachusetts Amherst
{twood,shenoy}@cs.umass.edu

K.K. Ramakrishnan   Jacobus Van der Merwe

AT&T Labs - Research
{kkrama,kobus}@research.att.com

Abstract

Virtual machine technology and the ease with which VMs can be migrated within the LAN, has changed the scope of resource management from allocating resources on a single server to manipulating pools of resources within a data center. We expect WAN migration of virtual machines to likewise transform the scope of provisioning compute resources from a single data center to multiple data centers spread across the country or around the world. In this paper we present the CloudNet architecure as a cloud framework consisting of cloud computing platforms linked with a VPN based network infrastructure to provide seamless and secure connectivity between enterprise and cloud data center sites. To realize our vision of efficiently pooling geographically distributed data center resources, CloudNet provides optimized support for live WAN migration of virtual machines. Specifically, we present a set of optimizations that minimize the cost of transferring storage and virtual machine memory during migrations over low bandwidth and high latency Internet links. We evaluate our system on an operational cloud platform distributed across the continental US. During simultaneous migrations of four VMs between data centers in Texas and Illinois, CloudNet's optimizations reduce memory migration time by 65% and lower bandwidth consumption for the storage and memory transfer by 19GB, a 50% reduction.

Categories and Subject Descriptors   C.2.4 [*Computer Communication Networks*]: Distributed Systems

General Terms   Design, Performance

Keywords   WAN migration, Virtualization, Cloud Computing

1. Introduction

Today's enterprises run their server applications in data centers, which provide them with computational and storage resources. Cloud computing platforms, both public and private, provide a new avenue for both small and large enterprises to host their applications by renting resources on-demand and paying based on actual usage. Thus, a typical enterprise's IT services will be spread across the corporation's data centers as well as dynamically allocated resources in cloud data centers.

From an IT perspective, it would be ideal if both in-house data centers and private and public clouds could be considered as a flexible pool of computing and storage resources that are seamlessly connected to overcome their geographical separation. The management of such a pool of resources requires the ability to flexibly map applications to different sites as well as the ability to move applications and their data across and within pools. The agility with which such decisions can be made and implemented determines the responsiveness with which enterprise IT can meet changing business needs.

Virtualization is a key technology that has enabled such agility *within* a data center. Hardware virtualization provides a logical separation between applications and the underlying physical server resources, thereby enabling a flexible mapping of virtual machines to servers in a data center. Further, virtual machine platforms support resizing of VM containers to accommodate changing workloads as well as the ability to live-migrate virtual machines from one server to another without incurring application down-times. This same flexibility is also desirable *across* geographically distributed data centers. Such cross data center management requires efficient migration of both memory and disk state between such data centers, overcoming constraints imposed by the WAN connectivity between them. Consider the following use cases that illustrate this need:

Cloud bursting: Cloud bursting is a technique where an enterprise normally employs local servers to run applications and dynamically harnesses cloud servers to enhance capacity during periods of workload stress. The stress on local IT servers can be mitigated by temporarily migrating a few overloaded applications to the cloud or by instantiating new application replicas in the cloud to absorb some of the workload increase. These cloud resources are deallocated once the workload peak has ebbed. Cloud bursting eliminates the need to pre-provision for the peak workload locally, since cloud resources can be provisioned dynamically when needed, yielding cost savings due to the cloud's pay-as-you go model. Current cloud bursting approaches adopt the strategy of spawning new replicas of the application. This limits the range of enterprise applications that may use cloud bursting to stateless applications or those that include elaborate consistency mechanisms. Live migration permits *any* application to exploit cloud bursting while experiencing minimal downtime.

Enterprise IT Consolidation: Many enterprises with multiple data centers have attempted to deal with data center "sprawl" and cut costs by consolidating multiple smaller sites into a few large data centers. Such consolidation requires applications and data to be moved from one site to another over a WAN; a subset of these applications may also be moved to cloud platforms if doing so is more cost-effective than hosting locally. Typically such transformation projects have incurred application down-times, often spread over multiple days. Hence, the ability to implement these moves with minimal or no down-time is attractive due to the corresponding reduction in the disruption seen by a business.

Follow the sun: "Follow the sun" is a new IT strategy that is designed for project teams that span multiple continents. The scenario assumes multiple groups spanning different geographies that are collaborating on a common project and that each group requires low-latency access to the project applications and data during normal business hours. One approach is to replicate content at each site—e.g., a data center on each continent—and keep the replicas consistent. While this approach may suffice for content repositories or replicable applications, it is often unsuitable for applications that are not amenable to replication. In such a scenario, it may be simpler to migrate one or more VM containers with applications and project data from one site to another every evening; the migration overhead can be reduced by transferring only incremental state and applying it to the snapshot from the previous day to recreate the current state of the application.

These scenarios represent the spectrum from pre-planned to reactive migrations across data centers. Although the abstraction of treating resources that span data centers and cloud providers as a single unified pool of resources is attractive, the reality of these resources being distributed across significant geographic distances and interconnected via static wide area network links (WANs) conspire to make the realization of this vision difficult. Several challenges need to be addressed to realize the above use-cases:

Minimize downtime: Migration of application VMs and their data may involve copying tens of gigabytes of state or more. It is desirable to mask the latency of this data copying overhead by minimizing application downtimes during the migration. One possible solution is to support live migration of virtual machines over a WAN, where data copying is done in the background while the application continues to run, followed by a quick switch-over to the new location. While live migration techniques over LAN are well known, WAN migration raises new challenges, such as the need to migrate disk state in addition to memory state.

Minimize network reconfigurations: Whereas VM migration over a LAN can be performed transparently from a network perspective (IP addresses remains unchanged, TCP connections move over, etc), doing so transparently is a major challenge over a WAN. Different data centers and cloud sites support different IP address spaces, so additional network support is necessary if WAN migration is to remain transparent from a user and application perspective.

Handle WAN links: Migration of virtual machines over a LAN is relatively simple since data center LANs are provisioned using high-speed low-latency links. In contrast, WAN links interconnecting data centers of an enterprise and the connection to cloud sites may be bandwidth-constrained and speed-of-light contraints dictate that inter-data center latencies are significantly higher than in a LAN environment. Even when data centers are inter-connected using well provisioned links, it may not be possible to dedicate hundreds of megabits/s of bandwidth to a *single* VM transfer from one site to another. Further, cloud sites charge for network usage based on the total network I/O from and to cloud servers. Consequently WAN migration techniques must be designed to operate efficiently over low bandwidth links and must optimize the data transfer volume to reduce the migration latency and cost.

In this paper we propose a platform called *CloudNet* to achieve the vision of seamlessly connected resource pools that permit flexible placement and live migration of applications and their data across sites. The design and implementation of CloudNet has resulted in the following contributions.

Network virtualization and Virtual Cloud Pools: We propose a Virtual Cloud Pool (VCP) abstraction which allows CloudNet to seamlessly connect geographically separate servers and provide the illusion of a single logical pool of resources connected over a LAN. VCPs can be thought of as a form of network virtualization where the network identity of a VM can be dynamically (re)bound to a server at any physical site. This minimizes the need for network reconfiguration during WAN migration. CloudNet uses existing VPN technologies to provide this infrastructure, but we present a new signaling protocol that allows endpoint reconfiguration actions that currently take hours or days, to be performed in tens of seconds. This capability is crucial, since scenarios such as Cloud Bursting require rapid reconfiguration of the VCP topology in order to offload local applications to newly instantiated cloud servers.

Live Migration over WANs: CloudNet supports live migration of virtual machines over WANs. There are two key differences between LAN-based live migration and WAN-based migration. First, live migration over LAN only moves memory state, since disk state is assumed to be stored on a storage area network. In contrast, WAN migration may need to move both memory and disk state of an application if the Storage Area Network (SAN) does not span multiple data center sites. Second, LAN VM migration is transparent to an application from a network standpoint. In contrast, WAN-based VM migration must coordinate with the network routers to implement a similar level of transparency. CloudNet includes a storage migration mechanism and leverages its dynamic VCP abstraction to support transparent VM migration over WANs.

WAN Optimizations: CloudNet implements several WAN optimizations to enable migration over low-bandwidth links. It implements an adaptive live migration algorithm that dynamically tailors the migration of memory state based on application behavior. It also implements mechanisms such as content-based redundancy elimination and page deltas into the hypervisor to reduce the data volume sent during the migration process. Collectively these optimizations minimize total migration time, application downtime, and volume of data transferred.

Prototyping and Experimentation across multiple data centers: We implement a prototype of Cloudnet using the Xen platform and a commercial layer-2 VPN implementation. We perform an extensive evaluation using three data centers spread across the continental United States. Our results show CloudNet's optimizations decreasing memory migration and pause time by 30 to 70% in typical link capacity scenarios; in a set of VM migrations over a distance of 1200km, CloudNet saves 20GB of bandwidth, a 50% reduction. We also evaluate application performance during migrations to show that CloudNet's optimizations reduce the window of decreased performance compared to existing techniques.

2. Cloudnet Overview

In this section, we present an overview of the key abstractions and design building blocks in CloudNet.

2.1 Resource Pooling: Virtual Cloud Pools

At the heart of CloudNet is a Virtual Cloud Pool (VCP) abstraction that enables server resources across data centers and cloud providers to be logically grouped into a single server pool as shown in Figure 1. The notion of a Virtual Cloud Pool is similar to that of a Virtual Private Cloud, which is used by Amazon's EC2 platform and was also proposed in our previous research [30]. Despite the similarity, the design motivations are different. In our case, we are concerned with grouping server pools across data centers, while Amazon's product seeks to provide the abstraction of a private cloud that is hosted on a public cloud. Both abstractions use virtual private networks (VPNs) as their underlying interconnec-

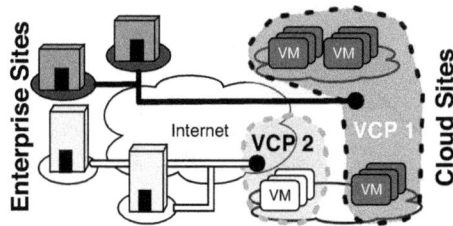

Figure 1. Two VCPs isolate resources within the cloud sites and securely link them to the enterprise networks.

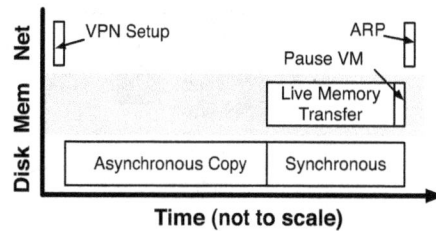

Figure 2. The phases of a migration for non-shared disk, memory, and the network in CloudNet .

tion technology—we employ Layer 2 VPNs to implement a form of network virtualization/transparency, while Amazon's VPC uses layer 3 VPNs to provide control over the network addressing of VM services.

The VCPs provided by CloudNet allow cloud resources to be connected to as securely and seamlessly as if they were contained within the enterprise itself. Further, the cloud to enterprise mappings can be adjusted dynamically, allowing cross data center resource pools to grow and change depending on an enterprise's needs. In the following sections we discuss the benefits of these abstractions for enterprise applications and discuss how this dynamic infrastructure facilitates VM migration between data centers.

2.2 Dynamic, Seamless Cloud Connections

CloudNet uses Multi-Protocol Label Switching (MPLS) based VPNs to create the abstraction of a private network and address space shared by multiple data centers. Since addresses are specific to a VPN, the cloud operator can allow customers to use any IP address ranges that they prefer without concern for conflicts between cloud customers. CloudNet makes the level of abstraction even greater by using *Virtual Private LAN Services (VPLS)* that bridge multiple MPLS endpoints onto a single LAN segment. This allows cloud resources to appear *indistinguishable* from existing IT infrastructure already on the enterprise's own LAN. VPLS provides transparent, secure, and resource guaranteed layer-2 connectivity without requiring sophisticated network configuration by end users. This simplifies the network reconfiguration that must be performed when migrating VMs between data centers.

VPNs are already used by many large enterprises, and cloud sites can be easily added as new secure endpoints within these existing networks. VCPs use VPNs to provide secure communication channels via the creation of "virtually dedicated" paths in the provider network. The VPNs protects traffic between the edge routers at each enterprise and cloud site. Within a cloud site, the traffic for a given enterprise is restricted to a particular VLAN. This provides a secure end-to-end path from the enterprise to the cloud and eliminates the need to configure complex firewall rules between the cloud and the enterprise, as all sites can be connected via a private network inaccessible from the public Internet.

As enterprises deploy and move resources between cloud data centers, it is necessary to adjust the topology of the client's VCP. In typical networks, connecting a new data center to a VPN endpoint can take hours or days, but these delays are administrative rather than fundamental to the network operations required. CloudNet utilizes a VPN Controller to automate the process of VPN reconfiguration, allowing resources at a new cloud data center to be connected to a VPN within seconds.

2.3 Efficient WAN Migration

Currently, moving an application to the cloud or another data center can require substantial downtime while application state is copied and networks are reconfigured before the application can resume

operation. Alternatively, some applications can be easily replicated into the cloud while the original continues running; however, this only applies to a small class of applications (e.g. stateless web servers or MapReduce style data processing jobs). These approaches are insufficient for the majority of enterprise applications which have not been designed for ease of replication. Further, many legacy applications can require significant reconfiguration to deal with the changed network configuration required by current approaches. In contrast, the live VM migration supported by CloudNet provides a much more attractive mechanism for moving applications between data centers because it is completely application independent and can be done with only minimal downtime.

Most recent virtualization platforms support efficient migration of VMs within a local network [9, 21]. By virtue of presenting WAN resources as LAN resources, CloudNet's VCP abstraction allows these live migration mechanisms to function unmodified across data centers separated by a WAN. However, the lower bandwidth and higher latencies over WAN links result in poor migration performance. In fact, VMWare's preliminary support for WAN VM migration requires at least 622 Mbps of bandwidth dedicated to the transfer, and is designed for links with less than 5 msec latency [29]. Despite being interconnected using "fat" gigabit pipes, data centers will typically be unable to dedicate such high bandwidth for a *single* application transfer and enterprises will want the ability to migrate a group of related VMs concurrently. CloudNet uses a set of optimizations to conserve bandwidth and reduce WAN migration's impact on application performance.

Current LAN-based VM migration techniques assume the presence of a shared file system which enables them to migrate only memory data and avoid moving disk state. A shared file system may not always be available across a WAN or the performance of the application may suffer if it has to perform I/O over a WAN. Therefore, CloudNet coordinates the hypervisor's memory migration with a disk replication system so that the entire VM state can be transferred if needed.

Current LAN-based live migration techniques must be optimized for WAN environments, and cloud computing network infrastructure must be enhanced to support dynamic relocation of resources between cloud and enterprise sites; these challenges are the primary focus of this paper.

3. WAN VM Migration

Consider an organization which desires to move one or more applications (and possibly their data) between two data centers. Each application is assumed to be run in a VM, and we wish to live migrate those virtual machines across the WAN.

CloudNet uses these steps to live migrate each VM:
Step 1: Establish virtual connectivity between VCP endpoints.
Step 2: If storage is not shared, transfer all disk state.
Step 3: Transfer the memory state of the VM to a server in the destination data center as it continues running without interruption.
Step 4: Once the disk and memory state have been transferred,

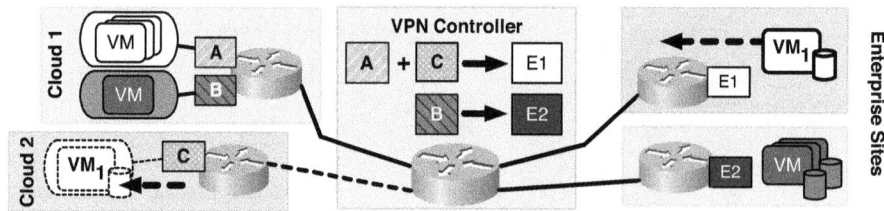

Figure 3. The VPN Controller remaps the route targets (A,B,C) advertised by each cloud data center to match the proper enterprise VPN (E1 or E2). To migrate VM_1 to Cloud Site 2, the VPN controller redefines E1's VPN to include route target A and C, then performs the disk and memory migration.

briefly pause the VM for the final transition of memory and processor state to the destination host. This process must not disrupt any active network connections between the application and its clients.

While these steps, illustrated in Figure 2, are well understood in LAN environments, migration over the WAN poses new challenges. The constraints on bandwidth and the high latency found in WAN links makes steps 2 and 3 more difficult since they involve large data transfers. The IP address space in step 4 would typically be different when the VM moves between routers at different sites. Potentially, application, system, router and firewall configurations would need to be updated to reflect this change, making it difficult or impossible to seamlessly transfer active network connections. CloudNet avoids this problem by virtualizing the network connectivity so that the VM appears to be on the same virtual LAN. We achieve this using VPLS VPN technology in step 1, and CloudNet utilizes a set of migration optimizations to improve performance in the other steps.

3.1 Migrating Networks, Disk, and Memory

Here we discuss the techniques used in CloudNet to transfer disk and memory, and to maintain network connectivity throughout the migration. We discuss further optimizations to these approaches in Section 3.2.

3.1.1 Dynamic VPN Connectivity to the Cloud

A straightforward implementation of VM migration between IP networks results in significant network management and configuration complexity [14]. As a result, *virtualizing network connectivity is key in CloudNet for achieving the task of WAN migration seamlessly relative to applications.* However, reconfiguring the VPNs that CloudNet can take advantage of to provide this abstraction has typically taken a long time because of manual (or nearly manual) provisioning and configuration. CloudNet explicitly recognizes the need to set up new VPN endpoints quickly, and exploits the capability of BGP route servers [28] to achieve this.

In many cases, the destination data center will already be a part of the customer's virtual cloud pool because other VMs owned by the enterprise are already running there. However, if this is the first VM being moved to the site, then a new VPLS endpoint must be created to extend the VCP into the new data center.

Creating a new VPLS endpoint involves configuration changes on the data center routers, a process that can be readily automated on modern routers [8, 20]. A traditional, but naive, approach would require modifying the router configurations at each site in the VCP so they all advertise and accept the proper *route targets*. A route target is an ID used to determine which endpoints share connectivity. An alternative to adjusting the router configurations directly, is to dynamically adjust the routes advertised by each site within the network itself. CloudNet takes this approach by having data center routers announce their routes to a centralized VPN Controller. The VPN Controller acts as an intelligent route server and is connected via BGP sessions to each of the cloud and enterprise data

centers. The controller maintains a ruleset indicating which endpoints should have connectivity; as all route control messages pass through this VPN Controller, it is able to rewrite the route targets in these messages, which in turn control how the tunnels forming each VPLS are created. Figure 3 illustrates an example where VM_1 is to be migrated from enterprise site E1 to Cloud Site 2. The VPN Controller must extend E1's VPLS to include route targets A and C, while Enterprise 2's VPLS only includes route target B. Once the change is made by the VPN Controller, it is propagated to the other endpoints via BGP. This ensures that each customer's resources are isolated within their own private network, providing CloudNet's virtual cloud pool abstraction. Likewise, the VPN Controller is able to set and distribute fine grained access control rules via BGP using technologies such as Flowspec (RFC 5575).

Our approach allows for fast VCP reconfiguration since changes only need to be made at a central location and then propagated via BGP to all other sites. This provides simpler connectivity management compared to making changes individually at each site, and allows a centralized management scheme that can set connectivity and access control rules for all sites.

In our vision for the service, the VPN Controller is operated by the network service provider. As the VPLS network in CloudNet spans both the enterprise sites and cloud data centers, the cloud platform must have a means of communicating with the enterprise's network operator. The cloud platform needs to expose an interface that would inform the network service provider of the ID for the VLAN used within the cloud data center so that it can be connected to the appropriate VPN endpoint. Before the VPN Controller enables the new endpoint, it must authenticate with the cloud provider to ensure that the enterprise customer has authorized the new resources to be added to its VPN. These security details are orthogonal to our main work, and in CloudNet we assume that there is a trusted relationship between the enterprise, the network provider, and the cloud platform.

3.1.2 Disk State Migration

LAN based live migration assumes a shared file system for VM disks, eliminating the need to migrate disk state between hosts. As this may not be true in a WAN environment, CloudNet supports either shared disk state or a replicated system that allows storage to be migrated with the VM.

If we have a "shared nothing" architecture where VM storage must be migrated along with the VM memory state, CloudNet uses the DRBD disk replication system to migrate storage to the destination data center [11]. In Figure 3, once connectivity is established to Cloud 2, the replication system must copy VM_1's disk to the remote host, and must continue to synchronize the remote disk with any subsequent writes made at the primary. In order to reduce the performance impact of this synchronization, CloudNet uses DRBD's *asynchronous* replication mode during this stage. Once the remote disk has been brought to a consistent state, CloudNet switches to a *synchronous* replication scheme and the live migration of the VM's memory state is initiated. During the VM migration, disk updates are synchronously propagated to the remote disk to ensure consistency when the memory transfer completes. When the migration completes, the new host's disk becomes the primary, and the origin's disk is disabled.

Migrating disk state typically represents the largest component of the overall migration time as the disk state may be in the tens or hundreds of gigabytes. Fortunately, disk replication can be enabled well in advance of a planned migration. Since the disk state for many applications changes only over very long time scales, this can allow the majority of the disk to be transferred with relatively little wasted resources (e.g., network bandwidth). For unplanned migrations such as a cloud burst in response to a flash crowd, storage may need to be migrated on demand. CloudNet's use of asynchronous replication during bulk disk transfer minimizes the impact on application performance.

3.1.3 Transferring Memory State

Most VM migration techniques use a "pre-copy" mechanism to iteratively copy the memory contents of a live VM to the destination machine, with only the modified pages being sent during each iteration [9, 21]. At a certain point, the VM is paused to copy the final memory state. WAN migration can be accomplished by similar means, but the limited bandwidth and higher latencies can lead to decreased performance–particularly much higher VM downtimes–since the final iteration where the VM is paused can last much longer. CloudNet augments the existing migration code from the Xen virtualization platform with a set of optimizations that improve performance, as described in Section 3.2.

The amount of time required to transfer a VM's memory depends on its RAM allocation, working set size and write rate, and available bandwidth. These factors impact both the total time of the migration, and the application-experienced downtime caused by pausing the VM during the final iteration. With WAN migration, it is desirable to minimize both these times as well as the bandwidth costs for transferring data. While pause time may have the most direct impact on application performance, the use of synchronous disk replication throughout the memory migration means that it is also important to minimize the total time to migrate memory state, particularly in high latency environments.

As bandwidth reduces, the total time and pause time incurred by a migration can rise dramatically. Figure 4(a) shows the pause time of VMs running several different applications, as the available bandwidth is varied (assumes shared storage and a constant 10 msec round trip latency). Note that performance decreases nonlinearly; migrating a VM running the SPECjbb benchmark on a gigabit link incurs a pause time of 0.04 seconds, but rises to 7.7 seconds on a 100 Mbps connection. This nearly 200X increase is unacceptable for most applications, and happens because a migration across a slower link causes each iteration to last longer, increasing the chance that additional pages will be modified and thus need to be resent. This is particularly the case in the final iteration. This result illustrates the importance of optimizing VM migration algorithms to better handle low bandwidth connections.

Migrations over the WAN may also have a greater chance of being disrupted due to network failures between the source and destination hosts. Because the switch-over to the second site is performed only after the migration is complete, CloudNet will suffer no ill effects from this type of failure because the application will continue running on the origin site, unaffected. In contrast, some pull or "post-copy" based migration approaches start running the application at the destination prior to receiving all data, which could lead to the VM crashing if there is a network disconnection.

3.1.4 Maintaining Network Connections

Once disk and memory state have been migrated, CloudNet must ensure that VM_1's active network connections are redirected to Cloud 2. In LAN migration, this is achieved by having the destination host transmit an unsolicited ARP message that advertises the VM's MAC and IP address. This causes the local Ethernet switch to adjust the mapping for the VM's MAC address to its new switch port [9]. Over a WAN, this is not normally a feasible solution because the source and destination are not connected to the same switch. Fortunately, CloudNet's use of VPLS bridges the VLANs at Cloud 2 and E1, causing the ARP message to be forwarded over the Internet to update the Ethernet switch mappings at both sites. This allows open network connections to be seamlessly redirected to the VM's new location.

In the Xen virtualization platform, this ARP is triggered by the VM itself after the migration has completed. In CloudNet, we optimize this procedure by having the destination host preemptively send the ARP message immediately after the VM is paused for the final iteration of the memory transfer. This can reduce the downtime experienced by the VM by allowing the ARP to propagate through the network in parallel with the data sent during the final iteration. However, on our evaluation platform this does not appear to influence the downtime, although it could be useful with other router hardware since some implementations can cache MAC mappings rather than immediately updating them when an ARP arrives.

3.2 Optimizing WAN VM Migration

In this section we propose a set of optimizations to improve the performance of VM migration over the WAN. The changes are made within the virtualization hypervisor; while we use the Xen virtualization platform in our work [9], they would be equally useful for other platforms such as VMWare which uses a similar migration mechanism [21].

3.2.1 Smart Stop and Copy

The Xen migration algorithm typically iterates until either a very small number of pages remain to be sent or a limit of 30 iterations is reached. At that point, the VM is paused, and all remaining pages are sent. However, our results indicate that this tends to cause the migration algorithm to run through many unnecessary iterations, increasing both the total time for the migration and the amount of data transferred.

Figure 4(b) shows the number of pages remaining to be sent at the end of each iteration during a migration of a VM running a kernel compilation over a link with 622 Mbps bandwidth and 5 msec latency. After the fourth iteration there is no significant drop in the number of pages remaining to be sent. This indicates that (i) a large number of iterations only extends the total migration time and increases the data transferred, and (ii) the migration algorithm could intelligently pick when to stop iterating in order to decrease both total and pause time. For the migration shown, picking the optimal point to stop the migration would reduce pause time by 40% compared to the worst stopping point.

CloudNet uses a *Smart Stop and Copy* optimization to reduce the number of unnecessary iterations and to pick a stopping point that minimizes pause time. Unfortunately, these two goals are potentially conflicting. Stopping after only a few iterations would reduce *total time*, but running for an extra few rounds may result in a lower *pause time*, which can potentially have a larger impact on application performance. The Smart Stop algorithm is designed to balance this trade-off by minimizing pause time without significantly increasing total time.

We note that in most cases (e.g. Figure 4(b)), after about five iterations the migration reaches a point of diminishing returns, where in a given iteration, approximately the same amount of data

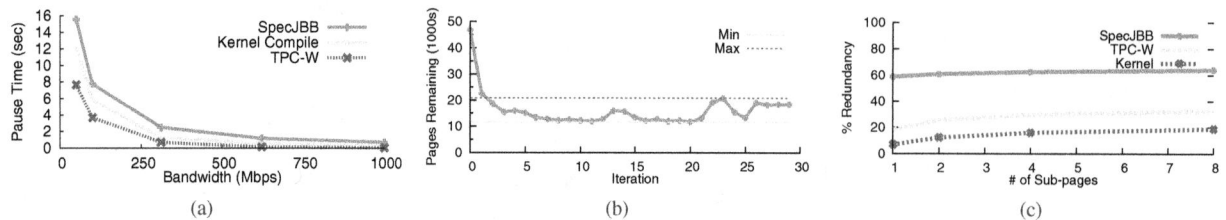

Figure 4. (a) Low bandwidth links can significantly increase the downtime experienced during migration. (b) The number of pages to be sent quickly levels off. Intelligently deciding when to stop a migration eliminates wasteful transfers and can lower pause time. (c) Each application has a different level of redundancy. Using finer granularity finds more redundancy, but has diminishing returns.

is dirtied as is sent. To detect this point, the first stage of Smart Stop monitors the number of pages sent and dirtied until they become equal. Prior to this point there was a clear gain from going through another iteration because more data was sent than dirtied, lowering the potential pause time.

While it is possible to stop the migration immediately at the point where as many pages are dirtied as sent, we have found that often the random fluctuations in how pages are written to can mean that waiting a few more iterations can result in a lower pause time with only a marginal increase in total time. Based on this observation, Smart Stop switches mode once it detects this crossover, and begins to search for a local minimum in the number of pages remaining to be sent. If at the start of an iteration, the number of pages to be sent is less than any previous iteration in a sliding window, Smart Stop pauses the VM to prevent any more memory writes and sends the final iteration of memory data.

3.2.2 Content Based Redundancy

Content based redundancy (CBR) elimination techniques have been used to save bandwidth between network routers [2], and we use a similar approach to eliminate the redundant data while transferring VM memory and disk state.[1] Disks can have large amounts of redundant data caused by either empty blocks or similar files. Likewise, a single virtual machine can often have redundant pages in memory from similar applications or duplicated libraries.

There are a variety of mechanisms that can be used to eliminate redundancy in a network transfer, and a good comparison of techniques is found in [1]. CloudNet can support any type of redundancy elimination algorithm; for efficiency, we use a block based approach that detects identical, fixed size regions in either a memory page or disk block. We have also tested a Rabin Fingerprint based redundancy elimination algorithm, but found it to be slower without substantially improving the redundancy detection rate.

CloudNet's block based CBR approach splits each memory page or disk block into fixed sized blocks and generates hashes based on their content using the Super Fast Hash Algorithm [16]. If a hash matches an entry in fixed size, FIFO caches maintained at the source and destination hosts, then a block with the same contents was sent previously. After verifying the pages match (in case of hash collisions), the migration algorithm can simply send a 32bit index to the cache entry instead of the full block (e.g. 4KB for a full memory page).

Dividing a memory page into smaller blocks allows redundant data to be found with finer granularity. Figure 4(c) shows the amount of memory redundancy found in several applications

during migrations over a 100 Mbps link as the number of blocks per page was varied. Increasing the number of sub-pages raises the level of redundancy that is found, but it can incur greater overhead since each block requires a hash table lookup. In CloudNet we divide each page into four sub-pages since this provides a good trade-off of detection rate versus overhead.

Disk transfers can also contain large amounts of redundant data. Our redundancy elimination code is not yet fully integrated with DRBD, however, we are able to evaluate the potential benefit of this optimization by analyzing disk images with an offline CBR elimination tool.

We currently only detect redundancy within a single VM's memory or disk. Previous work has demonstrated that different virtual machines often have some identical pages in memory, e.g. for common system libraries [13, 31]. Likewise, different virtual machines often have large amounts of identical data on disk due to overlap in the operating system and installed applications. Some of this redundancy could be found by using a network based appliance to detect redundancy across the migration traffic of multiple virtual machines. However, a network based approach can only find a redundant disk or memory block if it matches a packet sent during a previous migration. In order to find redundancy in the disks or memories of VMs which are not being moved, such an approach could be complemented with a distributed, content addressable cache run across the hosts at each site [22]. Fortunately, the single VM redundancy detection technique used in CloudNet is still able to save a significant amount of bandwidth without this added complexity.

3.2.3 Using Page Deltas

After the first iteration, most of the pages transferred are ones which were sent previously, but have since been modified. Since an application may be modifying only portions of pages, another approach to reduce bandwidth consumption is to keep a cache of previously transmitted pages, and then only send the difference between the cached and current page if it is retransmitted. This technique has been demonstrated in the Remus high availability system to reduce the bandwidth required for VM synchronization [10] in a LAN. We enhance this type of communicating deltas in a unique manner by complementing it with our CBR optimization. This combination helps overcome the performance limitations that would otherwise constrain the adoption of WAN migration

We have modified the Xen migration code so that if a page, or sub page block, does not match an entry in the cache using the CBR technique described previously, then the page address is used as a secondary index into the cache. If the page was sent previously, then only the difference between the current version and the stored version of the page is sent. This delta is calculated by XOR'ing the current and cached pages, and run length encoding the result.

Figure 5 shows histograms of delta sizes calculated during migrations of two applications. A smaller delta means less data needs

---

[1] Commercial products such as those from RiverBed Technologies can also perform CBR using a transparent network appliance. Such products may not be suitable in our case since memory and/or disk migration data is likely to use encryption to avoid interception of application state. In such cases, end-host based redundancy elimination has been proposed as an alternative [1]—an approach we use here also.

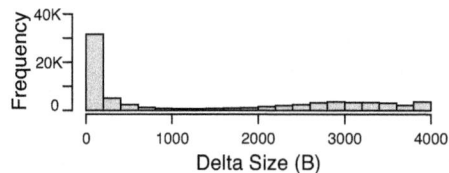

(a) Kernel Compile

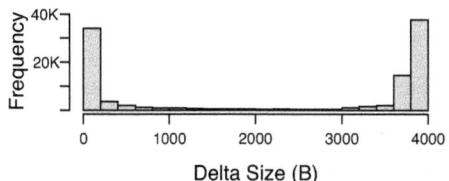

(b) TPC-W

Figure 5. During a kernel compile, most pages only experience very small modifications. TPC-W has some pages with small modifications, but other pages are almost completely changed.

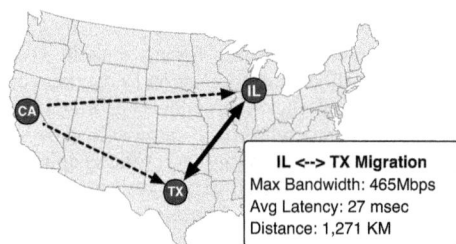

IL <--> TX Migration
Max Bandwidth: 465Mbps
Avg Latency: 27 msec
Distance: 1,271 KM

Figure 6. Our CloudNet testbed is deployed across three data centers. Migrations are performed between the data centers in IL and TX, with application clients running in CA.

to be sent; both applications have a large number of pages with only small modifications, but TPC-W also has a collection of pages that have been completely modified. This result suggests that page deltas can reduce the amount of data to be transferred by sending only the small updates, but that care must be taken to avoid sending deltas of pages which have been heavily modified.

While it is possible to perform some WAN optimizations such as redundancy elimination in network middleboxes [2], the Page Delta optimization relies on memory page address information that can only be obtained from the hypervisor. As a result, we make all of our modifications within the virtualization and storage layers. This requires no extra support from the network infrastructure and allows a single cache to be used for both redundancy elimination and deltas. Further, VM migrations are typically encrypted to prevent eavesdroppers from learning the memory contents of the VM being migrated, and network level CBR generally does not work over encrypted streams [1]. Finally, we believe our optimization code will be a valuable contribution back to the Xen community.

4. Evaluation

This section evaluates the benefits of each of our optimizations and studies the performance of several different application types during migrations between data center sites under a variety of network conditions. We also study migration under the three use case scenarios described in the introduction: Section 4.4 illustrates a cloud burst, Section 4.8 studies multiple simultaneous migrations as part of a data center consolidation effort, and Section 4.9 looks at the cost of disk synchronization in a follow-the-sun scenario.

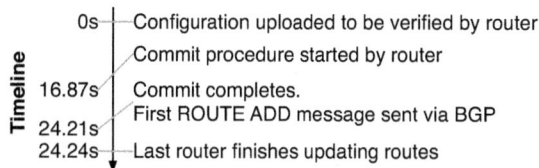

Figure 7. Timeline of operations to add a new endpoint.

4.1 Testbed Setup

We have evaluated our techniques between three data center sites spread across the United States, and interconnected via an operational network, as well as on a laboratory testbed that uses a network emulator to mimic a WAN environment.

Data Center Prototype: We have deployed CloudNet across three data centers in Illinois, Texas, and California as shown in Figure 6. Our prototype is run on top of the ShadowNet infrastructure which is used by CloudNet to configure a set of logical routers located at each site [7]. At each site we have Sun servers with dual quad-core Xeon CPUs and 32GB of RAM. We use Juniper M7i routers to create VPLS connectivity between all sites. We use the California site to run application clients, and migrate VMs between Texas and Illinois. Network characteristics between sites are variable since the data centers are connected via the Internet; we measured an average round trip latency of 27 msec and a max throughput of 465 Mbps between the sites used for migrations.

Lab Testbed: Our lab testbed consists of multiple server/router pairs linked by a VPLS connection. The routers are connected through gigabit ethernet to a PacketSphere Network Emulator capable of adjusting the bandwidth, latency, and packet loss experienced on the link. We use this testbed to evaluate WAN migrations under a variety of controlled network conditions.

4.2 Applications and Workloads

Our evaluation studies three types of business applications. We run each application within a Xen VM and allow it to warm up for at least twenty minutes prior to migration.

SPECjbb 2005 is a Java server benchmark that emulates a client/server business application [24]. The majority of the computation performed is for the business logic performed at the application's middle tier. SPECjbb maintains all application data in memory and only minimal disk activity is performed during the benchmark.

Kernel Compile represents a development workload. We compile the Linux 2.6.31 kernel along with all modules. This workload involves moderate disk reads and writes, and memory is mainly used by the page cache. In our simultaneous migration experiment we run a compilation cluster using *distcc* to distribute compilation activities across several VMs that are all migrated together.

TPC-W is a web benchmark that emulates an Amazon.com like retail site [26]. We run TPC-W in a two tier setup using Tomcat 5.5 and MySQL 5.0.45. Both tiers are run within a single VM. Additional servers are used to run the client workload generators, emulating 600 simultaneous users accessing the site using the "shopping" workload that performs a mix of read and write operations. The TPC-W benchmark allows us to analyze the client perceived application performance during the migration, as well as verify that active TCP sessions do not reset during the migration.

4.3 VPN Endpoint Manipulation

Before a migration can begin, the destination site may need to be added to the customer's VPN. This experiment measures the time required for CloudNet's VPN Controller to add the third data center site to our Internet-based prototype by manipulating route targets.

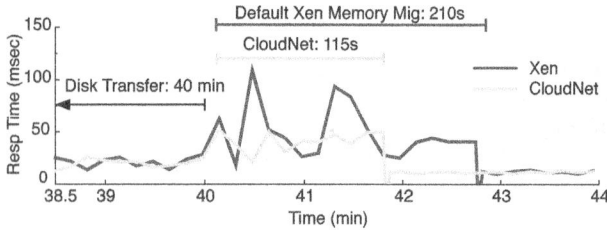

Figure 8. Response times rise to an average of 52 msec during the memory migration, but CloudNet shortens this period of reduced performance by 45%. Response time drops to 10msec once the VM reaches its destination and can be granted additional resources.

Figure 7 shows a timeline of the steps performed by the VPN Controller to reconfigure its intelligent route server. The controller sends a series of configuration commands followed by a commit operation to the router, taking a total of 24.21s to be processed on our Juniper M7i routers; these steps are manufacturer dependent and may vary depending on the hardware. As the intelligent route server does not function as a general purpose router, it would be possible to further optimize this process if reduction in VPN reconfiguration time is required.

Once the new configuration has been applied to the router maintained by the VPN controller, the updated information must be propagated to the other routers in the network. The information is sent in parallel via BGP. On our network where three sites need to have their routes updated, the process completes in only 30 milliseconds, which is just over one round trip time. While propagating routes may take longer in larger networks, the initial intelligent route server configuration steps will still dominate the total cost of the operation.

4.4 Cloud Burst: Application Performance

Cloud Bursting allows an enterprise to offload computational jobs from its own data centers into the cloud. Current cloud bursting techniques require applications to be shut down in the local site and then restarted in the cloud; the live WAN migration supported by CloudNet allows applications to be seamlessly moved from an enterprise data center into the cloud.

We consider a cloud bursting scenario where a live TPC-W web application must be moved from an overloaded data center in Illinois to one in Texas without disrupting its active clients; we migrate the VM to a more powerful server and increase its processor allocation from one to four cores once it arrives at the new data center location. In a real deployment a single VM migration would not have access to the full capacity of the link between the data centers, so we limit the bandwidth available for the migration to 85Mbps; the VM is allocated 1.7GB of RAM and has a 10GB disk. We assume that CloudNet has already configured the VPN endpoint in Texas as described in the previous section. After this completes, the DRBD subsystem begins the initial bulk transfer of the virtual machine disk using asynchronous replication; we discuss the disk migration performance details in Section 4.5 and focus on the application performance during the memory migration here.

The full disk transfer period takes forty minutes and is then followed by the memory migration. Figure 8 shows how the response time of the TPC-W web site is affected during the final 1.5 minutes of the storage transfer and during the subsequent memory migration when using both default Xen and CloudNet with all optimizations enabled. During the disk transfer period, the asynchronous replication imposes negligible overhead; average response time is 22 msec compared to 20 msec prior to the transfer. During the VM migration itself, response times become highly variable, and the average rises 2.5X to 52 msec in the default Xen case. This overhead is pri-

	Data Tx (GB)	Total Time (s)	Pause Time (s)
TPC-W	$1.5 \rightarrow 0.9$	$135 \rightarrow 78$	$3.7 \rightarrow 2.3$
Kernel	$1.5 \rightarrow 1.1$	$133 \rightarrow 101$	$5.9 \rightarrow 3.5$
SPECjbb	$1.2 \rightarrow 0.4$	$112 \rightarrow 35$	$7.8 \rightarrow 6.5$

Table 1. CloudNet reduces bandwidth, total time, and pause time during migrations over a 100Mbps link with shared disk.

marily caused by the switch to synchronous disk replication—any web request which involves a write to the database will see its response time increased by at least the round trip latency (27 msec) incurred during the synchronous write. As a result, it is very important to minimize the length of time for the memory migration in order to reduce this period of lower performance. After the migration completes, the response time drops to an average of 10 msec in both cases due to the increased capacity available for the VM.

While both default Xen and CloudNet migrations do suffer a performance penalty during the migration, CloudNet's optimizations reduce the memory migration time from 210 to 115 seconds, a 45% reduction. CloudNet also lowers the downtime by half, from 2.2 to 1 second. Throughout the migration, CloudNet's memory and disk optimizations conserve bandwidth. Using a 100MB cache, CloudNet reduces the memory state transfer from 2.2GB to 1.5GB. Further, the seamless network connectivity provided by the Cloud-Net infrastructure prevents the need for any complicated network reconfiguration, and allows the application to continue communicating with all connected clients throughout the migration. This is a significant improvement compared to current cloud bursting techniques which typically cause lengthy downtime as applications are shutdown, replicated to the second site, and then rebooted in their new location.

4.5 Disk Synchronization

Storage migration can be the dominant cost during a migration in terms of both time and bandwidth consumption. The DRBD system used by CloudNet transfers disk blocks to the migration destination by reading through the source disk at a constant rate (4MB/s) and transmitting the non-empty blocks. This means that while the TPC-W application in the previous experiment was allocated a 10GB disk, only 6.6GB of data is transferred during the migration.

The amount of storage data sent during a migration can be further reduced by employing redundancy elimination on the disk blocks being transferred. Using a small 100MB redundancy elimination cache can reduce the transfer to 4.9GB, and a larger 1GB cache can lower the bandwidth consumption to only 3.6GB. Since the transfer rate is limited by the disk read speed, disk migration takes the same amount of time with and without CloudNet's optimizations; however, the use of content based redundancy significantly reduces bandwidth costs during the transfer.

4.6 Memory Transfer

Here we discuss the benefits provided by each of our optimizations for transferring memory state. To understand each optimization's contribution, we analyze migration performance using VMs allocated 1GB of RAM running each of our three test applications; we create the VMs on a shared storage device and perform the migrations over a 100 Mbps link with 20 msec RTT in our local testbed.

Figure 9 shows each of CloudNet's optimizations enabled individually and in combination. We report the average improvement in total time, pause time, and data transferred over four repeated migrations for each optimization. Overall, the combination of all optimizations provides a 30 to 70 percent reduction in the amount of data transferred and total migration time, plus up to a 50% reduction in pause time. Table 1 lists the absolute performance of migrations with the default Xen code and with CloudNet's optimizations.

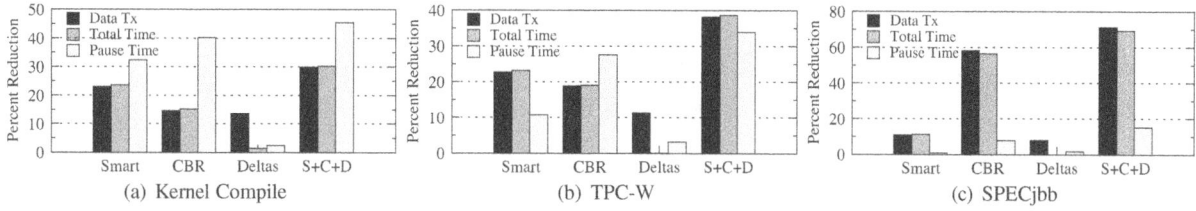

(a) Kernel Compile (b) TPC-W (c) SPECjbb

Figure 9. CloudNet's optimizations affect different classes of application differently depending on the nature of their memory accesses. Combining all optimizations greatly reduces bandwidth consumption and time for all applications.

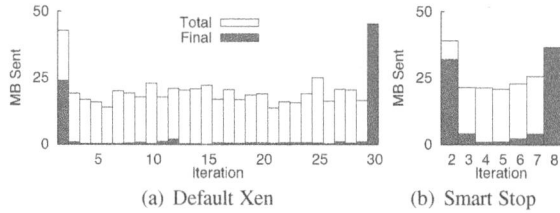

(a) Default Xen (b) Smart Stop

Figure 10. Smart Stop reduces the iterations in a migration, significantly lowering the number of "useless" page transfers that end up needing to be retransmitted in the default case.

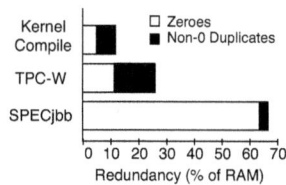

Figure 11. Different applications have different levels of redundancy, in some cases mostly from empty zero pages.

Smart Stop: The Smart Stop optimization can reduce the data transferred and total time by over 20% (Figure 9). Using Smart Stop lowers the number of iterations from 30 to an average of 9, 7, and 10 iterations for Kernel Compile, TPC-W, and SPECjbb respectively. By eliminating the unnecessary iterations, Smart Stop saves bandwidth and time.

Smart Stop is most effective for applications which have a large working set in memory. In TPC-W, memory writes are spread across a database, and thus it sees a large benefit from the optimization. In contrast, SPECjbb repeatedly updates a smaller region of memory, and these updates occur fast enough that the migration algorithm defers those pages until the final iteration. As a result, only a small number of pages would have been sent during the intermediate iterations that Smart Stop eliminates.

Figure 10 shows the total number of pages sent in each iteration, as well as how much of the data is *final*–meaning it does not need to be retransmitted in a later iteration–during a TPC-W migration. After the second iteration, TPC-W sends over 20MB per iteration, but only a small fraction of the total data sent is final–the rest is resent in later iterations when pages are modified again. Smart Stop eliminates these long and unnecessary iterations to reduce the total data sent and migration time.

Smart Stop is also able to reduce the pause time of the kernel compile by over 30% (Figure 9(a)). This is because the compilation exhibits a variance in the rate at which memory is modified (Figure 4(b)). The algorithm is thus able to pick a more intelligent iteration to conclude the migration, minimizing the amount of data that needs to be sent in the final iteration.

	Data Transfer (MB)		Page Delta
	Iter 1	Iters 2-30	Savings (MB)
TPC-W	954	315	172
Kernel	877	394	187
SPECjbb	932	163	127

Table 2. The Page Delta optimization cannot be used during the first iteration, but it provides substantial savings during the remaining rounds.

Redundancy Elimination: Figure 11 shows the amount of memory redundancy found in each applications during migrations over a 100 Mbps link when each memory page is split into four blocks. SPECjbb exhibits the largest level of redundancy; however, the majority of the redundant data is from empty "zero" pages. In contrast, a kernel compilation has about 13% redundancy, of which less than half is zero pages. The CBR optimization eliminates this redundancy, providing substantial reductions in the total data transferred and migration time (Figure 9). Since CBR can eliminate redundancy in portions of a page, it also can significantly lower the pause time since pages sent in the final iteration often have only small modifications, allowing the remainder of the page to match the CBR cache. This particularly helps the kernel compile and TPC-W migrations which see a 40 and 26 percent reduction in pause time respectively. SPECjbb does not see a large pause time reduction because most of the redundancy in its memory is in unused zero pages which are almost all transferred during the migration's first iteration.

Page Deltas: The first iteration of a migration makes up a large portion of the total data sent since during this iteration the majority of a VM's memory–containing less frequently touched pages–is transferred. Since the Page Delta optimization relies on detecting memory addresses that have already been sent, it can only be used from the second iteration onward, and thus provides a smaller overall benefit, as seen in Figure 9.

Table 2 shows the amount of memory data transferred during the first and remaining iterations during migrations of each application. While the majority of data is sent in the first round, during iterations 2 to 30 the Page Delta optimization still significantly reduces the amount of data that needs to be sent. For example, TPC-W sees a reduction from 487MB to 315MB, a 36 percent improvement.

Currently, the Page Delta optimization does not reduce migration time as much as it reduces data transferred due to inefficiencies in the code. With further optimization, the Page Delta technique could save both bandwidth and time.

Results Summary: The combination of all optimizations improves the migration performance more than any single technique. While the Page Delta technique only comes into effect after the first iteration, it can provide significant reductions in the amount of data sent during the remainder of the migration. The CBR based approach, however, can substantially reduce the time of the first iteration during which many empty or mostly empty pages are transferred. Finally, Smart Stop eliminates many unnecessary iterations

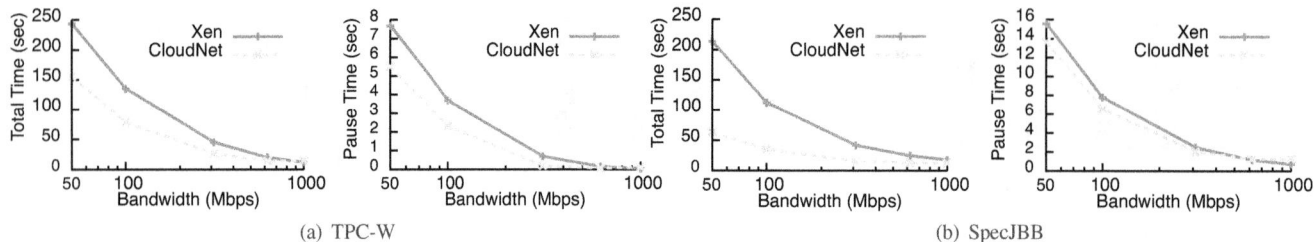

(a) TPC-W (b) SpecJBB

Figure 12. Decreased bandwidth has a large impact on migration time, but CloudNet's optimizations reduce the effects in low bandwidth scenarios.

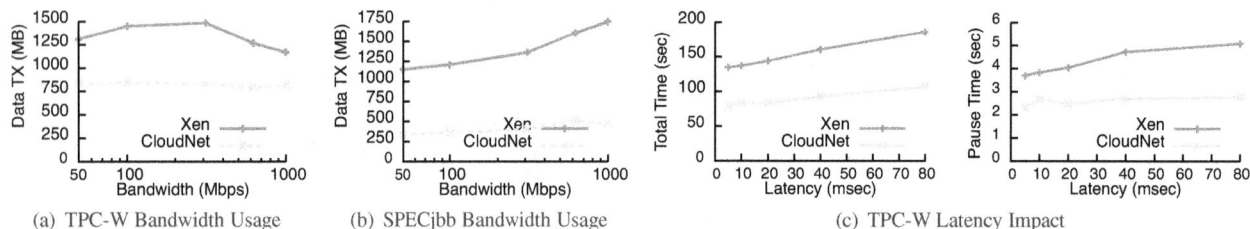

(a) TPC-W Bandwidth Usage (b) SPECjbb Bandwidth Usage (c) TPC-W Latency Impact

Figure 13. (a-b) CloudNet's optimizations significantly reduce bandwidth consumption. (c) Increased latency has only a minor impact on the migration process, but may impact application performance due to synchronous disk replication.

and combines with both the CBR and Page Delta techniques to minimize the pause time during the final iteration.

4.7 Impact of Network Conditions

We next use the network emulator testbed to evaluate the impact of latency and bandwidth on migration performance.

Bandwidth: Many data centers are now connected by gigabit links. However, this is shared by thousands of servers, so the bandwidth that can be dedicated to the migration of a single application is much lower. In this experiment we evaluate the impact of bandwidth on migrations when using a shared storage system. We vary the link bandwidth from 50 to 1000 Mbps, and maintain a constant 10 msec round trip delay between sites.

Figure 12 compares the performance of default Xen to Cloud-Net's optimized migration system. We present data for TPC-W and SPECjbb; the kernel compile performs similar to TPC-W. Decreased bandwidth increases migration time for both applications, but our optimizations provide significant benefits, particularly in low bandwidth scenarios. CloudNet also substantially reduces the amount of data that needs to be transferred during the migration because of redundancy elimination, page delta optimization and the lower number of iterations, as seen in Figure 13(a-b).

CloudNet's code presently does not operate at linespeed when the transfer rate is very high (e.g. about 1Gbps or higher *per VM transfer*). Thus in high bandwidth scenarios, CloudNet reduces the data transferred, but does not significantly affect the total migration or pause time compared to default Xen. We expect that further optimizing the CloudNet code will improve performance in these areas, allowing the optimizations to benefit even LAN migrations.

Latency: Latency between distant data centers is inevitable due to speed of light delays. This experiment tests how latency impacts migration performance as we adjust the delay introduced by the network emulator over a 100Mbps link. Even with TCP settings optimized for WAN environments, slow start causes performance to decrease some as latency rises. CloudNet's optimizations still provide a consistent improvement regardless of link latency as shown in Figure 13(c). While latency has only a minor impact on total migration and pause time, it can degrade application performance due to the synchronous disk replication required during the VM

migration. Fortunately, CloudNet's optimizations can significantly reduce this period of lowered performance.

Results Summary: CloudNet's optimized migrations perform well even in low bandwidth (50 to 100Mbps) and high latency scenarios, requiring substantially less data to be transferred and reducing migration times compared to default Xen. In contrast to commercial products that require 622 Mbps per VM transfer, CloudNet enables efficient VM migrations in much lower bandwidth and higher latency scenarios.

4.8 Consolidation: Simultaneous Migrations

We next mimic an enterprise consolidation where four VMs running a distributed development environment must be transitioned from the data center in Texas to the data center in Illinois. Each of the VMs has a 10GB disk (of which 6GB is in use) and is allocated 1.7GB of RAM and one CPU, similar to a "small" VM instance on Amazon EC2[2]. The load on the cluster is created by repeatedly running a distributed kernel compilation across the four VMs. The maximum bandwidth available between the two sites was measured as 465Mbps with a 27 msec round trip latency; note that bandwidth must be *shared* by the four simultaneous migrations.

We first run a baseline experiment using the default DRBD and Xen systems. During the disk synchronization period a total of 24.1 GB of data is sent after skipping the empty disk blocks. The disk transfers take a total of 36 minutes. We then run the VM memory migrations using the default Xen code, incurring an additional 245 second delay as the four VMs are transferred.

Next, we repeat this experiment using CloudNet's optimized migration code and a 1GB CBR cache for the disk transfer. Our optimizations reduce the memory migration time to only 87 seconds, and halves the average pause time from 6.1 to 3.1 seconds. Figure 14 compares the bandwidth consumption of each approach. CloudNet reduces the data sent during the disk transfers by 10GB and lowers the memory migrations from 13GB to 4GB. In total, the

---

[2] Small EC2 instances have a single CPU, 1.7GB RAM, a 10GB root disk, plus an additional 150GB disk. Transferring this larger disk would increase the storage migration time, but could typically be scheduled well in advance.

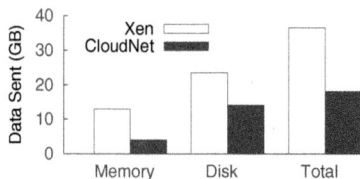

Figure 14. CloudNet saves nearly 20GB of bandwidth when simultaneously migrating four VMs.

data transferred to move the memory and storage for all four VMs falls from 37.4GB in the default Xen case to 18.5GB when using CloudNet's optimizations.

Results Summary: CloudNet's optimizations reduce pause time by a factor of 2, and lower memory migration time–when application performance is impacted most–by nearly 3X. The combination of eliminating redundant memory state and disk blocks can reduce the total data transferred during the migration by over 50%, saving nearly 20GB worth of network transfers.

4.9 Follow-the-Sun: Disk Synchronization

In a follow-the-sun scenario, one or more applications are moved between geographic locations in order to be co-located with the workforce currently using the application. In this experiment we consider moving an application with a large amount of state back and forth between two locations. We focus on the disk migration cost and demonstrate the benefits of using incremental state updates when moving back to a location which already has a snapshot from the previous day.

We use the TPC-W web application, but configure it with a much larger 45GB database. The initial migration of this disk takes 3.6 hours and transfers 51GB of data to move the database and root operating system partitions. We then run a TCP-W workload which lasts for 12 hours to represent a full workday at the site. After the workload finishes, we migrate the application back to its original site. In this case, only 723MB of storage data needs to be transferred since the snapshot from the previous day is used as a base image. This reduces the migration time to under five minutes, and the disk and memory migrations can be performed transparently while workers from either site are accessing the application. This illustrates that many applications with large state sizes typically only modify relatively small portions of their data over the course of a day. Using live migration and incremental snapshots allows applications to be seamlessly moved from site to site for relatively little cost and only minimal downtime.

5. Related Work

Cloud Computing: Armbrust et al provide a thorough overview of the challenges and opportunities in cloud computing [3]. There are several types of cloud platforms, but we focus on Infrastructure as a Service (IaaS) platforms which rent virtual machine and storage resources to customers. InterCloud explores the potential for federated cloud platforms to provide highly scalable services [6]; CloudNet seeks to build a similar environment and uses WAN migration to move resources between clouds and businesses.

Private Clouds & Virtual Networks: The VIOLIN and Virtuoso projects use overlay networks to create private groups of VMs across multiple grid computing sites [23, 25]. VIOLIN also supports WAN migrations over well provisioned links, but does not have a mechanism for migrating disk state. Overlay network approaches require additional software to be run on each host to create network tunnels. CloudNet places this responsibility on the routers at each site, reducing the configuration required on end hosts.

Our vision for Virtual Private Clouds was initially proposed in [30]. Subsequently, Amazon EC2 launched a new service also called "Virtual Private Clouds" which similarly uses VPNs to securely link enterprise and cloud resources. However, Amazon uses IPSec based VPNs that operate at layer-3 by creating software tunnels between end hosts or IPSec routers. In contrast, CloudNet focuses on VPNs provided by a network operator. Network based VPNs are typically realized and enabled by multiprotocol label switching (MPLS) provider networks, following the "hose model" [12] and are commonly used by enterprises. Provider based VPNs can be either layer-3 VPNs following RFC 2547, or layer-2 virtual private LAN Service (VPLS) VPNs according to RFC 4761. CloudNet relies on network based VPLS as it simplifies WAN migration, has lower overheads, and can provide additional functionality from the network provider, such as resource reservation.

LAN Migration: Live migration is essentially transparent to any applications running inside the VM, and is supported by most major virtualization platforms [9, 18, 21]. Work has been done to optimize migration within the LAN by exploiting fast interconnects that support remote memory access technology [17]. Jin et al. have proposed using memory compression algorithms to optimize migrations [19]. Breitgand et al. have developed a model based approach to determine when to stop iterating during a memory migration [5], similar to Smart Stop. Their approach can allow them to more precisely predict the best time to stop, but it requires knowledge of the VM's memory behavior, and it is not clear how the model would perform if this behavior changes over time. CloudNet's CBR and Page Delta optimizations are simple forms of compression, and more advanced compression techniques could provide further benefits in low bandwidth WAN scenarios, although at the expense of increased CPU overhead. The Remus project uses a constantly running version of Xen's live migration code to build an asynchronous high availability system [10]. Remus obtains a large benefit from an optimization similar to CloudNet's Page Delta technique because it runs a form of continuous migration where pages see only small updates between iterations.

WAN Migration: VMware has announced limited support for WAN migration, but only under very constrained conditions: 622 MBps link bandwidth and less than 5 msec network delay [29]. CloudNet seeks to lower these requirements so that WAN migration can become an efficient tool for dynamic provisioning of resources across data centers. Past research investigating migration of VMs over the WAN has focused on either storage or network concerns. Bradford et al. describe a WAN migration system focusing on efficiently synchronizing disk state during the migration; they modify the Xen block driver to support storage migration, and can throttle VM disk accesses if writes are occurring faster than what the network supports [4]. Shrinker uses content based addressing to detect redundancy across *multiple* hosts at the destination site during VM migrations [22]. This could allow it to reduce bandwidth costs compared to CloudNet, but exposes it to security concerns due to hash collisions, although the likelihood of this can be bounded. The VM Turntable Demonstrator showed a VM migration over intercontinental distances with latencies of nearly 200 msec; they utilize gigabit lightpath links, and like us, find that the increased latency has less impact on performance than bandwidth [27]. Harney et al. propose the use of Mobile IPv6 to reroute packets to the VM after it is moved to a new destination [15]; this provides the benefit of supporting layer-3 connections between the VM and clients, but the authors report a minimum downtime of several seconds due to the Mobile IP switchover, and the downtime increases further with network latency. In this work, we leverage existing mechanisms to simplify storage migration and network reconfiguration, and propose a set of optimizations to reduce the cost of migrations in low bandwidth and high latency environments.

131

6. Conclusions

The scale of cloud computing is growing as business applications are increasingly being deployed across multiple global data centers. We have built CloudNet, a prototype cloud computing platform that coordinates with the underlying network provider to create seamless connectivity between enterprise and data center sites, as well as supporting live WAN migration of virtual machines. CloudNet supports a holistic view of WAN migration that handles persistent storage, network connections, and memory state with minimal downtime even in low bandwidth, high latency settings.

While existing migration techniques can wastefully send empty or redundant memory pages and disk blocks, CloudNet is optimized to minimize the amount of data transferred and lowers both total migration time and application-experienced downtime. Reducing this downtime is critical for preventing application disruptions during WAN migrations. CloudNet's use of both asynchronous and synchronous disk replication further minimizes the impact of WAN latency on application performance during migrations. We have demonstrated CloudNet's performance on both a prototype deployed across three data centers separated by over 1,200km and a local testbed. During simultaneous migrations of four VMs between operational data centers, CloudNet's optimizations reduced memory transfer time by 65%, and saved 20GB in bandwidth for storage and memory migration.

Acknowledgements: This work was supported in part by NSF grants CNS-0916972, CNS-0720616, CNS-0855128, and a VURI award from AT&T.

References

[1] B. Aggarwal, A. Akella, A. Anand, P. Chitnis, C. Muthukrishnan, A. Nair, R. Ramjee, and G. Varghese. EndRE: An end-system redundancy elimination service for enterprises. In *Proceedings of NSDI*, 2010.

[2] A. Anand, V. Sekar, and A. Akella. SmartRE: an architecture for coordinated network-wide redundancy elimination. *SIGCOMM Comput. Commun. Rev.*, 39(4):87–98, 2009.

[3] M. Armbrust, A. Fox, R. Griffith, A. D. Joseph, R. H. Katz, A. Konwinski, G. Lee, D. A. Patterson, A. Rabkin, I. Stoica, and M. Zaharia. Above the clouds: A Berkeley view of cloud computing. Technical Report UCB/EECS-2009-28, EECS Department, University of California, Berkeley, Feb 2009.

[4] R. Bradford, E. Kotsovinos, A. Feldmann, and H. Schiöberg. Live wide-area migration of virtual machines including local persistent state. In *Proceedings of the 3rd international conference on Virtual execution environments*, pages 169–179, San Diego, California, USA, 2007. ACM.

[5] D. Breitgand, G. Kutiel, and D. Raz. Cost-aware live migration of services in the cloud. In *Proceedings of the 3rd Annual Haifa Experimental Systems Conference*, SYSTOR '10, New York, NY, USA, 2010. ACM.

[6] R. Buyya, R. Ranjan, and R. N. Calheiros. Intercloud: Utility-oriented federation of cloud computing environments for scaling of application services. In *International Conference on Algorithms and Architectures for Parallel Processing*, 2010.

[7] X. Chen, Z. M. Mao, and J. Van der Merwe. ShadowNet: a platform for rapid and safe network evolution. In *USENIX Annual Technical Conference*, 2009.

[8] Cisco Active Network Abstraction. http://www.cisco.com.

[9] C. Clark, K. Fraser, S. Hand, J. Hansen, E. Jul, C. Limpach, I. Pratt, and A. Warfield. Live migration of virtual machines. In *Proceedings of NSDI*, May 2005.

[10] B. Cully, G. Lefebvre, D. Meyer, M. Feeley, N. Hutchinson, and A. Warfield. Remus: High availability via asynchronous virtual machine replication. In *NSDI*, 2008.

[11] Drbd. http://www.drbd.org/.

[12] N. G. Duffield, P. Goyal, A. Greenberg, P. Mishra, K. K. Ramakrishnan, and J. E. Van der Merwe. Resource management with hoses: point-to-cloud services for virtual private networks. *IEEE/ACM Transactions on Networking*, 10(5), 2002.

[13] D. Gupta, S. Lee, M. Vrable, S. Savage, A. C. Snoeren, G. Varghese, G. M. Voelker, and A. Vahdat. Difference engine: harnessing memory redundancy in virtual machines. *Commun. ACM*, 53(10):85–93, 2010.

[14] M. Hajjat, X. Sun, Y. Sung, D. Maltz, S. Rao, K. Sripanidkulchai, and M. Tawarmalani. Cloudward bound: Planning for beneficial migration of enterprise applications to the cloud. In *Proceedings of SIGCOMM*, 2010.

[15] E. Harney, S. Goasguen, J. Martin, M. Murphy, and M. Westall. The efficacy of live virtual machine migrations over the internet. In *Proceedings of the 3rd VTDC*, 2007.

[16] Hsieh. hash functions. http://www.azillionmonkeys.com/qed/hash.html.

[17] W. Huang, Q. Gao, J. Liu, and D. K. Panda. High performance virtual machine migration with RDMA over modern interconnects. In *Proceedings of the 2007 IEEE International Conference on Cluster Computing*, pages 11–20. IEEE Computer Society, 2007.

[18] Microsoft Hyper-V Server. www.microsoft.com/hyper-v-server.

[19] H. Jin, L. Deng, S. Wu, X. Shi, and X. Pan. Live virtual machine migration with adaptive memory compression. In *Cluster*, 2009.

[20] Juniper Networks, Configuration and Diagnostic Automation Guide. http://www.juniper.net.

[21] M. Nelson, B.-H. Lim, and G. Hutchins. Fast transparent migration for virtual machines. In *ATEC '05: Proceedings of the annual conference on USENIX Annual Technical Conference*, 2005.

[22] P. Riteau, C. Morin, and T. Priol. Shrinker: Efficient Wide-Area Live Virtual Machine Migration using Distributed Content-Based Addressing. Research Report RR-7198, INRIA, 02 2010.

[23] P. Ruth, J. Rhee, D. Xu, R. Kennell, and S. Goasguen. Autonomic live adaptation of virtual computational environments in a multi-domain infrastructure. In *Proceedings of ICAC*, 2006.

[24] The SPEC java server benchmark. http://spec.org/jbb2005/.

[25] A. I. Sundararaj and P. A. Dinda. Towards virtual networks for virtual machine grid computing. In *VM'04: Proceedings of the 3rd conference on Virtual Machine Research And Technology Symposium*, 2004.

[26] TPC. the tpcw benchmark. Website. http://www.tpc.org/tpcw/.

[27] F. Travostino, P. Daspit, L. Gommans, C. Jog, C. de Laat, J. Mambretti, I. Monga, B. van Oudenaarde, S. Raghunath, and P. Y. Wang. Seamless live migration of virtual machines over the MAN/WAN. *Future Generation Computer Systems*, Oct. 2006.

[28] J. Van der Merwe, A. Cepleanu, K. D'Souza, B. Freeman, A. Greenberg, D. Knight, R. McMillan, D. Moloney, J. Mulligan, H. Nguyen, M. Nguyen, A. Ramarajan, S. Saad, M. Satterlee, T. Spencer, D. Toll, and S. Zelingher. Dynamic connectivity management with an intelligent route service control point. In *Proceedings of the 2006 SIGCOMM workshop on Internet network management*.

[29] Virtual machine mobility with VMware VMotion and Cisco Data Center Interconnect Technologies. http://www.cisco.com/en/US/solutions/collateral/ns340/ns517/ns224/ns836/white_paper_c11-557822.pdf, Sept. 2009.

[30] T. Wood, A. Gerber, K. Ramakrishnan, J. Van der Merwe, and P. Shenoy. The case for enterprise ready virtual private clouds. In *Proceedings of the Usenix Workshop on Hot Topics in Cloud Computing (HotCloud), San Diego, CA*, June 2009.

[31] T. Wood, G. Tarasuk-Levin, P. Shenoy, P. Desnoyers, E. Cecchet, and M. Corner. Memory buddies: Exploiting page sharing for smart colocation in virtualized data centers. In *2009 ACM SIGPLAN/SIGOPS International Conference on Virtual Execution Environments (VEE 2009)*, Washington, DC, USA, March 2009.

Workload-Aware Live Storage Migration for Clouds *

Jie Zheng   T. S. Eugene Ng

Rice University

Kunwadee Sripanidkulchai

NECTEC, Thailand

Abstract

The emerging open cloud computing model will provide users with great freedom to dynamically migrate virtualized computing services to, from, and between clouds over the wide-area. While this freedom leads to many potential benefits, the running services must be minimally disrupted by the migration. Unfortunately, current solutions for wide-area migration incur too much disruption as they will significantly slow down storage I/O operations during migration. The resulting increase in service latency could be very costly to a business. This paper presents a novel storage migration scheduling algorithm that can greatly improve storage I/O performance during wide-area migration. Our algorithm is unique in that it considers individual virtual machine's storage I/O workload such as temporal locality, spatial locality and popularity characteristics to compute an efficient data transfer schedule. Using a fully implemented system on KVM and a trace-driven framework, we show that our algorithm provides large performance benefits across a wide range of popular virtual machine workloads.

Categories and Subject Descriptors   D.4.0 [*Operating Systems*]: General

General Terms   Algorithms, Design, Experimentation, Performance

Keywords   Live Storage Migration, Virtual Machine, Workload-aware, Scheduling, Cloud Computing

1. Introduction

Cloud computing has recently attracted significant attention from both industry and academia for its ability to deliver IT services at a lower barrier to entry in terms of cost, risk, and expertise, with higher flexibility and better scaling on-demand. While many cloud users' early successes have been realized using a single cloud provider [4, 8], using multiple clouds to deliver services and having

---

* This research was sponsored by NSF CAREER Award CNS-0448546, NeTS FIND CNS-0721990, NeTS CNS-1018807, by an IBM Faculty Award, an Alfred P. Sloan Research Fellowship, and by Microsoft Corp. Jie Zheng is additionally supported by an IBM Scholarship. Views and conclusions contained in this document are those of the authors and should not be interpreted as representing the official policies, either expressed or implied, of NSF, IBM Corp., Microsoft Corp., the Alfred P. Sloan Foundation, or the U.S. government.

the flexibility to move freely among different providers is an emerging requirement [1]. The Open Cloud Manifesto is an example of how users and vendors are coming together to support and establish principles in opening up choices in cloud computing [16]. A key barrier to cloud adoption identified in the manifesto is data and application portability. Users who implement their applications using one cloud provider ought to have the capability and flexibility to migrate their applications back in-house or to other cloud providers in order to have control over business continuity and avoid fate-sharing with specific providers.

In addition to avoiding single-provider lock-in, there are other availability and economic reasons driving the requirement for migration across clouds. To maintain high performance and availability, virtual machines (VMs) could be migrated from one cloud to another cloud to leverage better resource availability, to avoid hardware or network maintenance down-times, or to avoid power limitations in the source cloud. Furthermore, cloud users may want to move work to clouds that provide lower-cost. The current practice for migration causes significant transitional down time. In order for users to realize the benefits of migration between clouds, we need both open interfaces and mechanisms to enable such migration while the services are running with as minimal service disruption as possible. While providers are working towards open interfaces, in this paper we look at the enabling mechanisms without which migrations would remain a costly effort.

Live migration provides the capability to move VMs from one physical location to another while still running without any perceived degradation. Many hypervisors support live migration within the LAN [6, 10, 13, 17, 20, 25]. However, migrating across the wide area presents more challenges specifically because of the large amount of data that needs to be migrated over limited network bandwidth. In order to enable live migration over the wide area, three capabilities are needed: (i) the running state of the VM must be migrated (i.e., memory migration), (ii) the storage or virtual disks used by the VM must be migrated, and (iii) existing client connections must be migrated while new client connections are directed to the new location. Memory migration and network connection migration for the wide area have been demonstrated to work well [5, 24]. However, storage migration inherently faces significant performance challenges because of its much larger size compared to memory.

In this paper, we improve the efficiency of migrating storage across the wide area. Our approach differs from the existing work in storage migration that treats storage as one large chunk that needs to be transferred from beginning to end. We introduce *storage migration scheduling* to transfer storage blocks according to a deliberately computed order. We develop a workload-aware storage migration scheduling algorithm that takes advantage of temporal locality, spatial locality, and access popularity – patterns commonly found in a wide range of I/O workloads – at the properly chosen granularity to optimize the data transfer. We show that our scheduling algorithm can be leveraged by previous work in storage migration

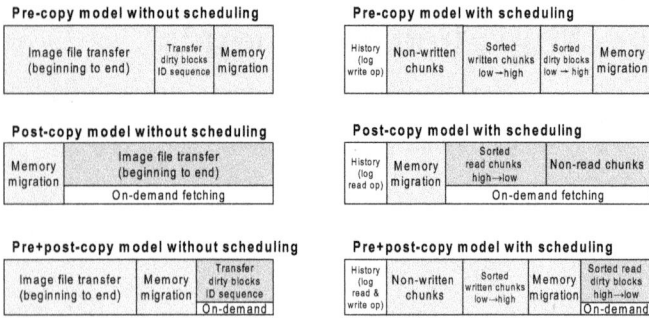

Figure 1. Models of live storage migration.

to greatly improve storage I/O performance during migration across a wide variety of VM workloads.

In the next section, we provide an overview of the existing storage migration technologies and the challenges that they face. Section 3 quantifies the locality and popularity characteristics we found in VM storage workload traces. Motivated by these characteristics, we present in Section 4 a novel storage migration scheduling algorithm that leverages these characteristics to make storage migration much more efficient. We present the implementation of our scheduling algorithm on KVM in Section 5 and evaluate its performance in Section 6. In Section 7, we further present trace-based simulation results for the scheduling algorithm under two additional migration models not adopted by KVM. Finally, we summarize our findings in Section 8.

2. Background

A VM consists of virtual hardware devices such as CPU, memory and disk. Live migration of a VM within a data center is quite common. It involves the transfer of the memory and CPU state of the VM from one hypervisor to another. However, live migration across the wide area requires not only transferring the memory and CPU state, but also virtual disk storage and network connections associated with a VM. While wide-area memory and network connection migration have matured [5, 19, 22, 24], wide-area storage migration still faces significant performance challenges. The VM's disk is implemented as a (set of) file(s) stored on the physical disk. Because sharing storage across the wide area has unacceptable performance, storage must be migrated to the destination cloud. And because of the larger size storage has compared to memory and the limitations in wide-area network bandwidth, storage migration could negatively impact VM performance if not performed efficiently.

2.1 Storage Migration Models

Previous work in storage migration can be classified into three migration models: pre-copy, post-copy and pre+post-copy. In the pre-copy model, storage migration is performed *prior* to memory migration whereas in the post-copy model, the storage migration is performed *after* memory migration. The pre+post-copy model is a hybrid of the first two models.

Figure 1 depicts the three models on the left-hand side. In the pre-copy model as implemented by KVM [14] (a slightly different variant is also found in [5]), the entire virtual disk file is copied from beginning to end prior to memory migration. During the virtual disk copy, all write operations to the disk are logged. The dirty blocks are retransmitted, and new dirty blocks generated during this time are again logged and retransmitted. This dirty block retransmission process repeats until the number of dirty blocks falls below a threshold, then memory migration begins. During memory migration, dirty blocks are again logged and retransmitted iteratively.

The strength of the pre-copy model is that VM disk read operations at the destination have good performance because blocks are copied over prior to when the VM starts running at the destination. However, the pre-copy model has weaknesses. First, pre-copying may introduce extra traffic. If we had an oracle that told us when disk blocks are updated, we would send only the latest copy of disk blocks. In this case, the total number of bytes transferred over the network would be the minimum possible which is the total size of the virtual disk. Without an oracle, some transmitted blocks will become dirty and require retransmissions, resulting in *extra traffic* beyond the size of the virtual disk. Second, if the I/O workload on the VM is write-intensive, write-throttling is employed to slow down I/O operations so that iterative dirty block retransmission can converge. While throttling is useful, it can degrade application I/O performance.

In the post-copy model [11, 12], storage migration is executed after memory migration completes and the VM is running at the destination. Two mechanisms are used to copy disk blocks over: background copying and remote read. In background copying, the simplest strategy proposed by Hirofuchi et al. [12] is to copy blocks sequentially from the beginning of a virtual disk to the end. They also proposed an advanced background copy strategy which will be discussed later in Section 2.3. During this time if the VM issues an I/O request, it is handled immediately. If the VM issues a write operation, the blocks are directly updated at the destination storage. If the VM issues a read operation and the blocks have yet to arrive at the destination, then on-demand fetching is employed to request those blocks from the source. We call such operations *remote reads*. With the combination of background copying and remote reads, each block is transferred at most once ensuring that the total amount of data transferred for storage migration is minimized. However, remote reads incur extra wide-area delays, resulting in I/O performance degradation.

In the hybrid pre+post-copy model [15], the virtual disk is copied to the destination prior to memory migration. During disk copy and memory migration, a bit-map of dirty disk blocks is maintained. After memory migration completes, the bit-map is sent to the destination where a background copying and remote read model is employed for the dirty blocks. While this model still incurs extra traffic and remote read delays, the amount of extra traffic is smaller compared to the pre-copy model and the number of remote reads is smaller compared to the post-copy model. Table 1 summarizes these three models.

2.2 Performance Degradation from Migration

While migration is a powerful capability, any performance degradation caused by wide area migration could be damaging to users that are sensitive to latency. Anecdotally, every 100 ms of latency costs Amazon 1% in sales and an extra 500 ms page generation time dropped 20% of Google's traffic [9]. In our analysis (details in Section 7) of a 10 GB MySQL database server that has 160 clients migrating over a 100 Mbps wide area link using the post-copy model, over 25,000 read operations experience performance degradation during migration due to remote read. This I/O performance degradation can significantly impact application performance on the VM. Reducing this degradation is key to making live migration a practical mechanism for moving applications across clouds.

2.3 Our Solution

Our solution is called *workload-aware storage migration scheduling*. Rather than copying the storage from beginning to end, we deliberately compute a schedule to transfer storage at the appropriate granularity which we call *chunk* and *in the appropriate order* to minimize performance degradation. Our schedule is computed to take advantage of the particular I/O locality characteristics of

	Model	Pre-copy [5, 14]	Pre+post-copy [15]	Post-copy [11, 12]
Application Performance Impact	Write Operation Degradation	Yes	No	No
	Read Operation Degradation	No	Medium	Heavy
	Degradation Time	Long	Medium	Long
	I/O Operations Throttled	Yes	No	No
Total Migration Time		$\gg$ Best	$>$ Best	Best
Amount of Migrated Data		$\gg$ Best	$>$ Best	Best

Table 1. Comparison of VM storage migration methods.

the migrated workload and can be applied to improve any of the three storage migration models as depicted on the right-hand side of Figure 1. To reduce the extra migration traffic and throttling under the pre-copy model, our scheduling algorithm groups storage blocks into chunks and sends the chunks to the destination in an optimized order. Similarly, to reduce the number of remote reads under the post-copy model, scheduling is used to group and order storage blocks sent over during background copying. In the hybrid pre+post-copy model, scheduling is used for both the pre-copy phase and the post-copy phase to reducing extra migration traffic and remote reads.

Hirofuchi et al. [12] proposed an advanced strategy for background copying in the post-copy model by recording and transferring frequently accessed ext2/3 block groups first. While their proposal is similar in spirit to our solution, there are important differences. First, their proposal is dependent on the use of an ext2/3 file system in the VM. In contrast, our solution is general without any file system constraints, because we track I/O accesses at the raw disk block level which is beneath the file system. Second, the access recording and block copying in their proposal are based on a fixed granularity, i.e. an ext2/3 block group. However, our solution is adaptive to workloads. We propose algorithms to leverage the locality characteristics of workloads to decide the appropriate granularity. As our experiments show, using an incorrect granularity leads to a large loss of performance. Third, we show how our solution can be applied to all three storage migration models and experimentally quantify the storage I/O performance improvements.

To our knowledge, past explorations in memory migration [6, 10] leverage memory access patterns to decide which memory pages to transfer first to some extent. However, comparing to our technique, there are large differences.

In a pre-copy model proposed by Clark et al. [6], only during the iterative dirty page copying stage, the copying of pages that have been dirtied both in the previous iteration and the current iteration is postponed. In a post-copy model proposed by Hines and Gopalan [10], when a page that causes a page fault is copied, a set of pages surrounding the faulting page is copied together. This is done regardless of the actual popularity of the set of surrounding pages, and continues until the next page fault occurs.

In contrast, our scheduling technique for storage migration (1) is general for the three storage migration models as discussed above, (2) uses actual access frequencies, (3) computes fine-grained access-frequency-based schedules for migration throughout the disk image copying stage and the iterative dirty block copying stage, (4) automatically computes the appropriate chunk size for copying, and (5) proactively computes schedules based on a global view of the entire disk image and the access history, rather than reacting to each local event. Furthermore, under typical workloads, memory and storage access patterns are different, and the constraints in the memory and storage subsystems are different. Techniques that work well for one may not necessarily work well for the other. Our technique is tailored specifically for storage migration and storage access pattern.

Workload Name	VM Configuration	Server Application	Default # Clients
File Server (fs)	SLES 10 32-bit 1 CPU,256MB RAM,8GB disk	dbench	45
Mail Server (ms)	Windows 2003 32-bit 2 CPU,1GB RAM,24GB disk	Exchange 2003	1000
Java Server (js)	Windows 2003 64-bit 2 CPU,1GB RAM,8GB disk	SPECjbb @2005-based	8
Web Server (ws)	SLES 10 64-bit 2 CPU,512MB RAM,8GB disk	SPECweb @2005-based	100
Database Server (ds)	SLES 10 64-bit 2 CPU,2GB RAM,10GB disk	MySQL	16

Table 2. VMmark workload summary.

3. Workload Characteristics

To investigate storage migration scheduling, we collect and study a modest set of VMware VMmark virtualization benchmark [23] I/O traces. Our trace analysis explores several I/O characteristics at the time-scale relevant to storage migration to understand whether the history of I/O accesses prior to a migration is useful for optimizing storage migration. It is complementary to existing general studies of other storage workloads [2, 18, 21].

3.1 Trace Collection

VMmark includes servers, listed in Table 2, that are representative of the applications run by VMware users. We collect traces for multiple client workload intensities by varying the number of client threads. A trace is named according to the server type and the number of client threads. For example, "fs-45" refers to a file server I/O trace with 45 client threads. Two machines with a 3GHz Quad-core AMD Phenom II 945 processor and 8GB of DRAM are used. One machine runs the server application while the other runs the VMmark client. The server is run as a VM on a VMware ESXi 4.0 hypervisor. The configuration of the server VM and the client is as specified by VMmark. To collect the I/O trace, we run an NFS server as a VM on the application server physical machine and mount it on the ESXi hypervisor. The application server's virtual disk is then placed on the NFS storage as a VMDK flat format file. `tcpdump` is used on the virtual network interface to log the NFS requests that correspond to virtual disk I/O accesses. NFS-based tracing has been used in past studies of storage workload [3, 7] and requires no special OS instrumentation. We experimentally confirmed that the tracing framework introduces negligible application performance degradation compared to placing the virtual disk directly on the hypervisor's locally attached disk. We trace I/O operations at the disk sector granularity – 512 bytes. We call each 512 byte sector a block. However, this is generally not the file system block size. Each trace entry includes the access time, read or write, the offset in the VMDK file, and the data length. Each trace contains the I/O operations executed by a server over a 12 hour period.

3.2 History and Migration Periods

Let t denote the start time of a migration. Each I/O trace analysis is performed 20 times with different randomly selected migration start times $t \in [3000s, 5000s]$, where $0s$ represents the beginning of the trace. For simplicity, we use a fixed history period of 3000 seconds before t, and a fixed storage migration period of $(2 \times image\_size + memory\_size) / bandwidth$ seconds. The latter

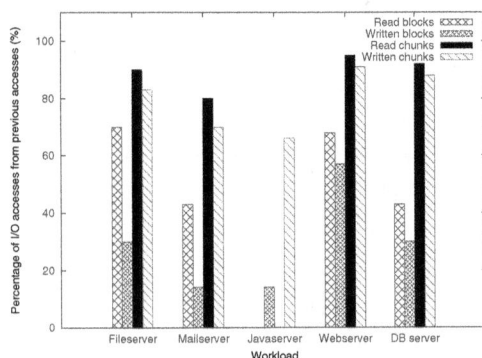

Figure 2. The temporal locality of I/O accesses as measured by the percentage of accesses in the migration that was also previously accessed in the history. The block size is 512B and the chunk size is 1MB. Temporal locality exists in all of the workloads, but is stronger at the chunk level. The Java server has very few read accesses resulting in no measurable locality.

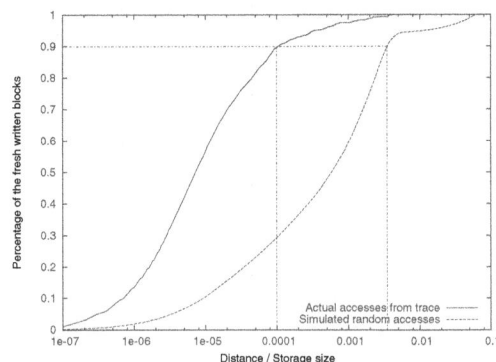

Figure 3. Spatial locality of file server writes and simulated random writes measured by normalized distance to closest block written in history. The 90th percentiles are 0.0001 and 0.0035.

corresponds to a pessimistic case that during the transfer of the disk image, all the blocks were written to by the VM and the entire image needs to be retransmitted. Other reasonable choices for these periods could be used, but the qualitative findings from our analysis are not expected to change. *image_size*, *memory_size*, and workload (i.e. # client threads) are as specified in Table 2, and *bandwidth* is 100 Mbps in the following analysis.

3.3 Temporal Locality Characteristics

Figure 2 shows that, across all workloads, blocks that are read during the migration are often also the blocks that were read in the history. Take the file server as an example, 72% of the blocks that are read in the migration were also read in the history. Among these blocks, 96% of them are blocks whose read access frequencies were ≥ 3 in the history. Thus, it is possible to predict which blocks are more likely to be read in the near future by analyzing the recent past history.

However, write accesses do not behave like the read accesses. Write operations tend to access new blocks that have not been written before. Again, take the file server as an example. Only 32% of the blocks that are written in the migration were written in history. Therefore, simply counting the write accesses in history will poorly predict the write accesses in migration.

Figure 2 also shows that both read and write temporal locality improves dramatically when 1MB chunk is used as the basic unit of counting accesses. This is explained next.

3.4 Spatial Locality Characteristics

We find strong spatial locality for write accesses. Take the file server as an example. For the 68% of the blocks that are freshly written in migration but not in history, we compute the distance between each of these blocks and its closest neighbor block that was written in history. The distance is defined as $(block\_id\_difference * blocksize)$. Figure 3 plots, for the file server, the cumulative percentage of the fresh written blocks versus the closest neighbor distance normalized by the storage size (8GB). For all the fresh written blocks, their closest neighbors can be found within a distance of 0.0045*8GB=36.8MB. For 90% of the cases, the closest neighbor can be found within a short distance of 0.0001*8GB=839KB. For comparison, we also plot the results for an equal number of simulated random write accesses, which confirm that the spatial locality found in the real trace is significant. Taken together, in the file server trace, $32\%+68\%*90\% = 93.2\%$

of the written blocks in the migration are found within a range of 839KB of the written blocks in history.

This explains why, across all workloads, the temporal locality of write accesses increases dramatically in Figure 2 when we consider 1MB chunk instead of 512B block as the basic unit of counting accesses. The temporal locality of read accesses also increases. The caveat is that as the chunk size increases, although the percentage of covered accessed blocks in migration will increase, each chunk will also cover more unaccessed blocks. Therefore, to provide useful read and write access prediction, a balanced chunk size is necessary and will depend on the workload (see Section 4).

3.5 Popularity Characteristics

Popular chunks in history are also likely to be popular in migration. We rank chunks by their read/write frequencies and compute the rank correlation between the ranking in history and the ranking in migration. Figure 4 shows that a positive correlation exists for all cases except for the Java server read accesses at 1MB and 4MB chunk sizes.[1] As the chunk size increases, the rank correlation increases. This increase is expected since if the chunk size is set to the size of the whole storage, the rank correlation will become 1 by definition. A balanced chunk size is required to exploit this popularity characteristic effectively (see Section 4).

4. Scheduling Algorithm

The main idea of the algorithm is to exploit locality to compute a more optimized storage migration schedule. We intercept and record a short history of the recent disk I/O operations of the VM, then use this history to predict the temporal locality, spatial locality, and popularity characteristics of the I/O workload during migration. Based on these predictions, we compute a storage transfer schedule that reduces the amount of extra migration traffic and throttling in the pre-copy model, the number of remote reads in the post-copy model, and reduces both extra migration traffic and remote reads in the pre+post-copy model. The net result is that storage I/O performance during migration is greatly improved. The algorithm presented below is conceptual. In Section 5, we present several implementation techniques.

4.1 History of I/O Accesses

To collect history, we record the most recent N I/O operations in a FIFO queue. We will show that the performance improvement is significant even with a small N in Section 6 and 7. Therefore the

---

[1] This is because the Java server has extremely few read accesses and little read locality

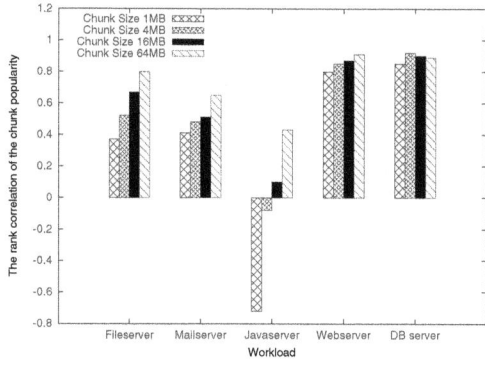

(a) Read Access

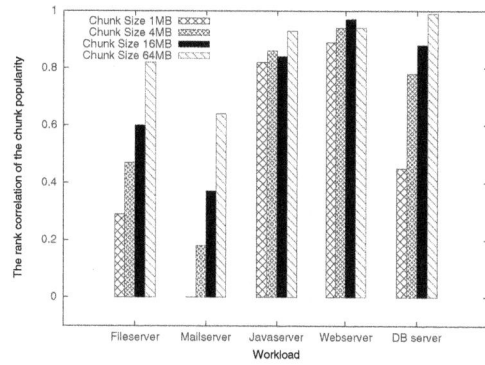

(b) Write Access

Figure 4. The rank correlation of the chunk popularity in history vs. in migration.

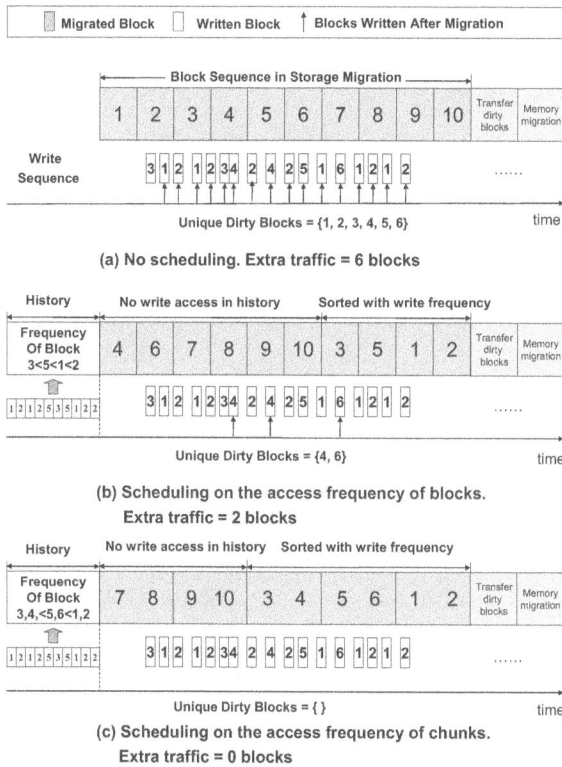

Figure 5. A simple example of the scheduling algorithm applied to the pre-copy model.

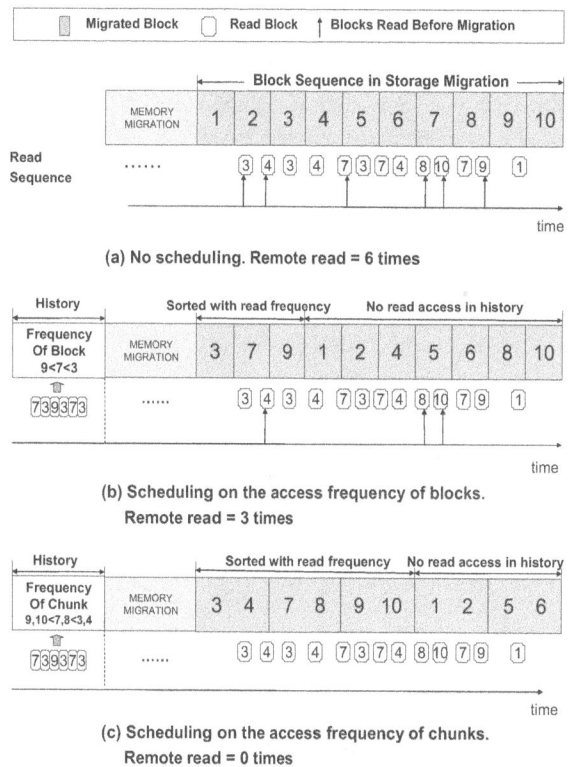

Figure 6. A simple example of the scheduling algorithm applied to the post-copy model.

memory overhead for maintaining this history is very small. Different migration models are sensitive to different types of I/O accesses as discussed in Section 2. This is related to the cause of the performance degradation. The extra migration traffic in the pre-copy model is caused by the write operations during the migration, while the remote reads in the post-copy model are caused by the read operations before certain blocks have been migrated. Therefore, when the pre-copy model is used, we collect only a history of write operations; when the post-copy model is used, we collect only a history of read operations; and when the pre+post-copy model is used, both read and write operations are collected. For each operation, a four-tuple, $< flag, offset, length, time >$, is recorded, where $flag$

indicates whether this is a read or write operation, $offset$ indicates the block number being accessed, $length$ indicates the size of the operation, and $time$ indicates the time the operation is performed.

4.2 Scheduling Based on Access Frequency of Chunks

In this section, we discuss how we use I/O access history to compute a storage transfer schedule. Figure 5 and 6 illustrate how the migration and the I/O access sequence interact to cause the extra migration traffic and remote reads for the pre-copy and post-copy models respectively. The pre+post-copy model combines these two scenarios but the problems are similar. Without scheduling, the migration controller will simply transfer the blocks of the virtual disk sequentially from the beginning to the end. In the examples, there are only 10 blocks for migration and several I/O accesses denoted as either the write or read sequence. With no scheduling, under pre-copy, a total of 6 blocks are dirtied after they have been transmitted and have to be resent. Similarly, under post-copy, there are 6 remote read operations where a block is needed before it is transferred to the destination.

Our scheduling algorithm exploits the temporal locality and popularity characteristics and uses the information in the history to perform predictions. That is, the block with a higher write frequency in history (i.e., more likely to be written to again) should be migrated later in the pre-copy model, and the block with a higher read frequency (i.e., more likely to be read again) should be migrated earlier in the post-copy model. In the illustrative example in Figures 5 and 6, when we schedule the blocks according to their access frequencies, the extra traffic and remote reads can be reduced from 6 to 2 and from 6 to 3 respectively.

In the example, blocks $\{4,6\}$ in the pre-copy model and blocks $\{4,8,10\}$ in the post-copy model are not found in the history, but they are accessed a lot during the migration due to spatial locality. The scheduling algorithm exploits spatial locality by scheduling the migration based on chunks. Each chunk is a cluster of contiguous blocks. The chunk size in the simple example is 2 blocks. We note that different workloads may have different effective chunk sizes and present a chunk size selection algorithm later in Section 4.3.

The access frequency of a chunk is defined as the sum of the access frequencies of the blocks in that chunk. The scheduling algorithm for the pre-copy model migrates the chunks that have not been written to in history first as those chunks are unlikely to be written to during migration and then followed by the written chunks. The written chunks are further sorted by their access frequencies to exploit the popularity characteristics. For the post-copy model, the read chunks are migrated in decreasing order of chunk read access frequencies, and then followed by the non-read chunks. The schedule ensures that chunks that have been read frequently in history are sent to the destination first as they are more likely to be accessed. In the example, by performing chunk scheduling, the extra traffic and remote reads are further reduced to 0.

The scheduling algorithm is summarized in pseudocode as Figure 7 shows. The time complexity is $O(n \cdot log(n))$, the space complexity is $O(n)$, where n is the number of blocks in the disk.

Note that α is an input value for the chunk size estimation algorithm and will be explained later. The pre+post-copy model is a special case which has two migration stages. The above algorithm works for its first stage. The second stage begins when the VM memory migration has finished. In this second stage, the remaining dirty blocks are scheduled from high to low read frequency. The time complexity is $O(n \cdot log(n))$, the space complexity is $O(n)$, where n is the number of dirty blocks.

The scheduling algorithm relies on the precondition that the access history can help predict the future accesses during migration, and our analysis has shown this to be the case for a wide range of workloads. However, an actual implementation might want to include certain safeguards to ensure that even in the rare case that the access characteristics are turned upside down during the migration, any negative impact is contained. First, a test can be performed on the history itself, to see if the first half of the history does provide good prediction for the second half. Second, during the migration, newly issued I/O operations can be tested against the expected access patterns to find out whether they are consistent. If either one of these tests fails, a simple solution is to revert to the basic non-scheduling migration approach.

4.3 Chunk Size Selection

The chunk size used in the scheduling algorithm needs to be judiciously selected. It needs to be sufficiently large to cover the

DATA STRUCTURE IN ALGORITHM:
-op_flag: the flag of operation to indicate it is a read or a write
-$Q_{history}$: the queue of access operations collected from history
-α: the fraction of simulated history.
-$L_b(op\_flag)$: A block access list of $< block_{id}, time >$
-$L_{cfreq}(op\_flag)$: A list of $< chunk_{id}, frequency >$
-$L_{schunk}(op\_flag)$: A list of $chunk_{id}$ sorted by frequency
-$L_{nchunk}(op\_flag)$: A list of $chunk_{id}$ not accessed in history

INPUT OF ALGORITHM: $Q_{history}, model\_flag$ and $\alpha \in [0. 1]$
OUTPUT OF ALGORITHM: migration schedule $S_{migration}$

$S_{migration} = \{ \}$;
IF (($model\_flag == PRE\_COPY$)
  $\|(model\_flag == PRE + POST\_COPY$))
    $S_{migration}$=GetSortedMigrationSequence(WRITE);
ELSE ($model\_flag == POST\_COPY$)
    $S_{migration}$=GetSortedMigrationSequence(READ);
RETURN $S_{migration}$;

FUNCTION GetSortedMigrationSequence(op_flag)
    $L_b(op\_flag)$ = Convert $\forall OP \in Q_{history}$
      whose $flag == op\_flag$ into $< block_{id}, time >$;
    $chunksize$=ChunkSizeEstimation($L_b(op\_flag),\alpha$);
    Divide the storage into chunks;
    $S_{all} = \{ All\ chunks \}$;
    FOR EACH $chunk_i \in S_{all}$
      $frequency_i = \sum frequency_{block_k}$
        where $block_k \in chunk_i$ and $block_k \in L_b(op\_flag)$;
      $frequency_{block_k}$ =# of times $block_k$ appearing in $L_b(op\_flag)$;
    END FOR
    $L_{cfreq}(op\_flag) = \{(chunk_i, frequency_i)|frequency_i > 0\}$;
    IF ($op\_flag == WRITE$)
      $L_{schunk}(op\_flag)$ =Sort $L_{cfreq}(op\_flag)$ by $freq$ low→high
    ELSE
      $L_{schunk}(op\_flag)$ =Sort $L_{cfreq}(op\_flag)$ by $freq$ high→low
      (chunks with the same frequency are sorted by id low→high)
    $L_{nchunk}(op\_flag) = S_{all} - L_{schunk}(op\_flag)$ with id low→high;
    IF $op\_flag == WRITE$
      return $\{L_{nchunk}(op\_flag), L_{schunk}(op\_flag)\}$;
    ELSE
      return $\{L_{schunk}(op\_flag), L_{nchunk}(op\_flag)\}$;

Figure 7. Scheduling algorithm.

likely future accesses near the previously accessed blocks, but not so large as to cover many irrelevant blocks that will not be accessed. To balance these factors, for a neighborhood size n, we define a metric called $balanced\_coverage = access\_coverage + (1 - storage\_coverage)$. Consider splitting the access history into two parts based on some reference point. Then, $access\_coverage$ is the percentage of the accessed blocks (either read or write) in the second part that are within the neighborhood size n around the accessed blocks in the first part. $storage\_coverage$ is simply the percentage of the overall storage within the neighborhood size n around the accessed blocks in the first part. The neighborhood size that maximizes $balanced\_coverage$ is then chosen as the chunk size by our algorithm.

Figure 8 shows the $balanced\_coverage$ metric for different neighborhood sizes for different server workloads. As can be seen, the best neighborhood size will depend on the workload itself.

In the scheduling algorithm, we divide the access list $L_b(op\_flag)$ in the history into two parts, S_{H1} consists of the accesses in the first α fraction of the history period, where α is a configurable parameter, and S_{H2} consists of the remaining accesses. We set the lower bound of the chunk size to 512B. The algorithm also bounds the maximum selected chunk size. In the evaluation, we set this bound to 1GB.

The algorithm pseudocode is shown in Figure 9. The time complexity of this algorithm is $O(n \cdot log(n))$ and the space complexity is $O(n)$, where n is the number of blocks in the disk.

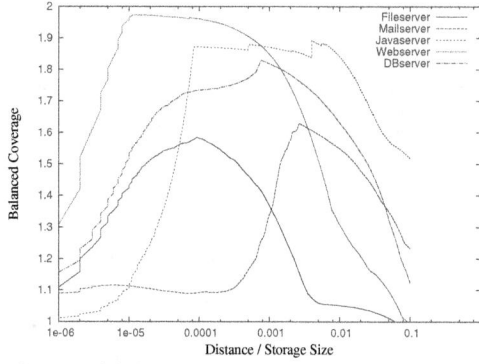

Figure 8. A peak in balanced coverage determines the appropriate chunk size for a given workload.

5. Implementation

We have implemented the scheduling algorithm on kernel-based virtual machine (KVM). KVM consists of a loadable kernel module that provides the core virtualization infrastructure and a processor specific module. It also requires a user-space program, a modified QEMU emulator, to set up the guest VM's address space, handle the VM's I/O requests and manage the VM. KVM employs the pre-copy model as described in Section 2. When a disk I/O request is issued by the guest VM, the KVM kernel module forwards the request to the QEMU block driver. The scheduling algorithm is therefore implemented mainly in the QEMU block driver. In addition, the storage migration code is slightly modified to copy blocks according to the computed schedule rather than sequentially.

Incremental schedule computation

A naive way to implement the scheduling algorithm is to add a history tracker that simply records the write operations. When migration starts, the history is used to compute, on-demand, the migration schedule. This on-demand approach works poorly in practice because the computations could take several minutes even for a history buffer of only 5,000 operations. During this period, other QEMU management functions must wait because they share the same thread. The resulting burst of high CPU utilization also affects the VM's performance. Moreover, storage migration is delayed until the scheduler finishes the computations.

Instead, we have implemented an efficient incremental scheduler. The main idea is to update the scheduled sequence incrementally when write requests are processed. The scheduled sequence is thus always ready and no extra computation is needed when migration starts. The two main problems are (1) how to efficiently sort the chunks based on access frequency and (2) how to efficiently select the optimal chunk size. We first describe our solution to problem (1) assuming a chunk size has been chosen; then we discuss our solution to problem (2).

Incremental and efficient sorting

We create an array and a set of doubly linked lists for storing access frequencies of chunks as shown in Figure 10. The index of the array is the chunk ID. Each element in the array (square) is an object that contains three pointers that point to an element in the frequency list (oval) and the previous and next chunks (square) that have the same frequency. An element in the frequency list (oval) contains the value of the access frequency, a pointer to the head of the doubly linked list containing chunks with that frequency and two pointers to its previous and next neighbors in the frequency list. The frequency list (oval) is sorted by frequency. Initially, the frequency list (oval) only has one element whose frequency is zero and it points to the head of a doubly linked list containing all chunks. When a write request arrives, the frequency of the accessed

DATA STRUCTURE IN ALGORITHM:
- $L_b(op\_flag)$: A block access list of $< block_{id}, time >$
- α: the fraction of simulated history.
- $total\_block$: the number of total blocks in the storage.
- $upper, low\_bound$: max & min allowed chunk size, e.g. 512B-1GB.
- S_{H1}, S_{H2}: the sets of blocks accessed in the first and second part.
- $distance$: The storage size between the locations of two blocks.
- ND: Normalized distance computed by $distance/storage\_size$.
- $S_{NormDistance}$: A set of normalized distances for blocks that are in S_{H2}.
- $S_{NormDistanceCDF}$: A set of pair $< ND, \% >$. The percentage is the cumulative distribution of ND in the set $S_{NormDistance}$.
- ES_{H1}: A set of blocks obtained by expanding every block in S_{H1} by covering its neighborhood range.
- $BalancedCoverage_{max}$: the maximum value of $balanced\_coverage$
- ND_{BCmax}: the neighborhood size (a normalized distance) that maximizes $balanced\_coverage$

INPUT OF ALGORITHM: $L_b(op\_flag)$ and $\alpha \in [0, 1]$
OUTPUT OF ALGORITHM: $chunk\_size$

FUNCTION ChunkSizeEstimation($L_b(op\_flag), \alpha$)
 max_time= the duration of $L_b(op\_flag)$;
 FOR EACH $< block_{id}, time > \in L_b(op\_flag)$
  IF $time < max\_time * \alpha$
   Add $block_{id}$ into S_{H1};
  ELSE ADD $block_{id}$ into S_{H2};
 END FOR
 FOR EACH $block_{id} \in S_{H2}$
  $NormDistance = \frac{\{min\ (|block_{id}-m|) \forall m \in S_{H1}\}}{total\_block}$;
  Add $NormDistance$ into $S_{NormDistance}$;
 END FOR
 $S_{NormDistanceCDF}$ = compute the cumulative distribution function of $S_{NormDistance}$;
 $BalancedCoverage_{max} = 0$;
 $ND_{BCmax} = 0$;
 ND_{min}= the minimal ND in $S_{NormDistanceCDF}$;
 ND_{max}= the maximal ND in $S_{NormDistanceCDF}$;
 $ND_{step} = \frac{ND_{max}-ND_{min}}{1000}$;
 FOR $ND = ND_{min}; ND \leq ND_{max}; ND+ = ND_{step}$
  $distance = ND * total\_block$;
  $ES_{H1} = \{\}$
  FOR EACH $m \in S_{H1}$
   add $block_{id}$ from $(m - distance)$ to $(m + distance)$ to ES_{H1};
  END FOR
  $storage\_coverage = \frac{\# of\ unique\ blocks\ in\ ES_{H1}}{total\_block}$;
  $access\_coverage$ =the percentage of ND in $S_{NormDistanceCDF}$;
  $balanced\_coverage = access\_coverage + (1 - storage\_coverage)$;
  IF $balanced\_coverage > BalancedCoverage_{max}$ {
   $BalancedCoverage_{max} = balanced\_coverage$;
   $ND_{BCmax} = ND$;
  }
 END FOR
 $chunk\ size = ND_{BCmax} * total\_block * block\_size$;
 IF $(chunk\_size == 0)$
  $chunk\_size = lower\_bound$;
 ELSE IF $chunk\_size > upper\ bound$
  $chunk\_size = upper\_bound$;
 RETURN $chunk\_size$;

Figure 9. Algorithm for chunk size selection.

chunk is increased by 1. The chunk is moved from the old chunk list to the head of the chunk list for the new frequency. A new frequency list element is added if necessary. The time complexity of this update is $O(1)$ and the space complexity is $O(n)$ where n is the number of chunks. The scheduling order is always available by simply traversing the frequency list in increasing order of frequency and the corresponding chunk lists. This same approach is used to maintain the schedule for dirty blocks that need to be retransmitted.

Incremental and efficient chunk size selection

To improve efficiency, we estimate the optimal chunk size periodically. The period is called a round and is defined as the duration of every N write operations. N is also the history buffer size. Only the latest two rounds of history are kept in the system, called the previous round and the current round. At the end of each round,

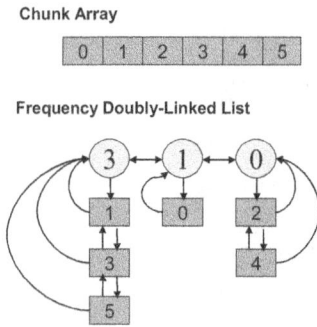

Figure 10. Data structures for maintaining the sorted access frequencies of chunks.

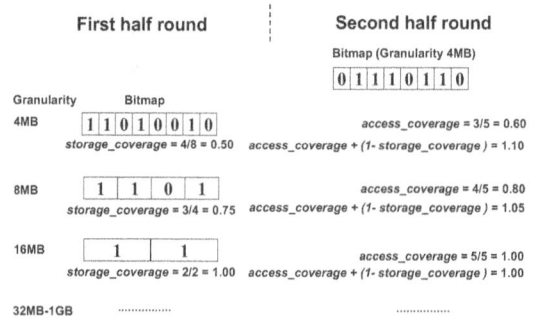

Figure 11. Data structures for chunk size selection.

the optimal chunk size is computed and it is used as the chunk size for tracking the access frequency in the next round using the aforementioned data structure. Initially, a default chunk size of 4MB is used.

It is not feasible to do a fine grained search for the optimal chunk size in reality. A trade-off between precision and efficiency must be made. We use a simple example to depict our idea in Figure 11. We pick 8 exponentially increasing candidate chunk sizes: 4MB, 8MB, 16MB, 32MB, 64MB, 128MB, 256MB, 512MB, and 1GB. Each round is subdivided into two halves. In the first half, each candidate chunk size is associated with a bitmap for logging which chunk is written to. When a chunk gets the first write access, the bit for that chunk is set to 1 and the storage coverage at that candidate chunk size is updated. Storage coverage is defined as $\frac{\# \ of \ set \ bits}{total \ bits}$. The storage coverage for the candidate chunk size 4MB is 0.5 in the example. In the second half, a new bitmap for the smallest candidate chunk size of 4MB is created to log the new accessed chunks in the second half. Moreover, for each candidate chunk size, we maintain the corresponding access coverage. When a 4MB chunk gets its first write access in the second half, the access bit is set to 1. Access coverage is defined as the percentage of bits set in the second half which are also set in the first half. The access coverage for each candidate chunk size is updated by checking whether the corresponding bit is also set in the previous bitmap in the first half. An update only occurs when a chunk is accessed for the first time. Each update operation is $O(1)$ time. At the end of each round, the storage coverage and access coverage for all candidate chunk sizes are available and we pick the chunk size that maximizes the $balanced\_coverage = access\_coverage + (1 - storage\_coverage)$. In Figure 11, the access coverage for chunk size 4MB is 0.6 and its balanced coverage is 1.1, which is the highest. Thus, 4MB is the selected chunk size for counting access frequencies in the next round.

When migration starts, the frequency list from the previous round is used for deciding the migration sequence and chunk size since the current round is incomplete.

We evaluate the impact of the scheduling algorithm on the latency and throughput of write operations in the file server. The history buffer size is set to 20,000 and we measure 100,000 write operations. With scheduling, the average write latency increases by only 0.97%. The application level write throughput reduces by only 1.2%. Therefore, the incremental scheduler is lightweight enough to be enabled at all time, or if desired, enabled manually only prior to migration.

6. Evaluation on KVM

The experimental platform consists of two machines as the source and destination for migration. Each of them is configured with a 3GHz Quad-core AMD Phenom II X4 945 processor, 8GB of DRAM, runs Ubuntu 9.10 with Linux kernel (with the KVM module) version 2.6.31 and QEMU version 0.12.50. The network is a 1Gbps Ethernet with varying rate-limits to emulate different network speeds.

During the initial transfer of the image file, we configure the migration process to read and copy image file data over the network at a relatively large granularity of 4MB to achieve high disk I/O throughput. Consequently, our scheduling algorithm chunk size is constrained to be a multiple of 4MB. In contrast, we configure QEMU to track dirty blocks at a much finer granularity of 128KB to keep unnecessary data retransmission down. When any bytes of a 128KB block is written to, the entire 128KB block is considered dirty and is retransmitted. We define the disk dirty rate as the number of dirty bytes per second. Setting the granularity to track dirty blocks larger (e.g. the QEMU default granularity of 1MB) will greatly increase the amount of unnecessary retransmissions. The history buffer size is set to 20,000. We run each experiment 3 times with randomly chosen migration start times in $[900s, 1800s]$. The average result across the 3 runs is reported. We present results for the mail server and the file server in VMmark, which have, respectively, a moderate and an intensive I/O workload (average write rate 2.5MB/s and 16.7MB/s). The disk dirty rate during migration could be much higher than the disk write rate because of the dirty block tracking granularity discussed above. Note that the benefit of scheduling is not pronounced when the I/O workload is light.

6.1 Benefits Under Pre-Copy

The following results show the benefits of scheduling under the pre-copy model since this model is employed by KVM. We measure the extra traffic and the time for the migration with and without scheduling. Migration time is defined as the duration from the migration command is received to the time when the VM resumes on the destination machine. Extra traffic is the total size of the retransmitted blocks.

QEMU provides a flow-control mechanism to control the available network bandwidth for migration. We vary the bandwidth from 224Mbps to 128Mbps. Figure 12 shows that when the bandwidth is 224Mbps, with scheduling, the extra traffic is reduced by 25%, and the migration time is reduced by 9 seconds for the mail server. When the network bandwidth decreases, we expect the extra traffic and the migration time to increase. With the scheduling algorithm, the rate at which extra traffic increases is much lower. At a network bandwidth of 128Mbps, the extra traffic is reduced by 41% from 3.16GB to 1.86GB. The migration time is reduced by 7% or 136s.

When the network bandwidth is 128Mbps, we find that the migration of the file server does not converge because its disk dirty rate is too high relative to the network bandwidth, and QEMU has no built-in mechanism to address this problem. There are two pos-

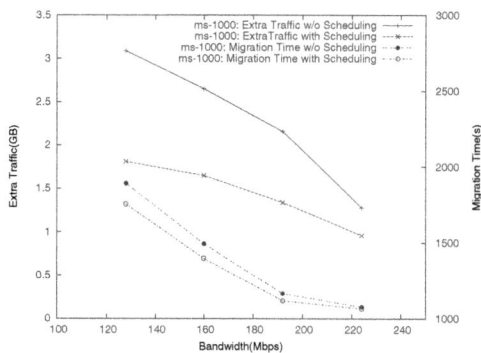

Figure 12. Improvement in extra traffic and migration time for the mail server.

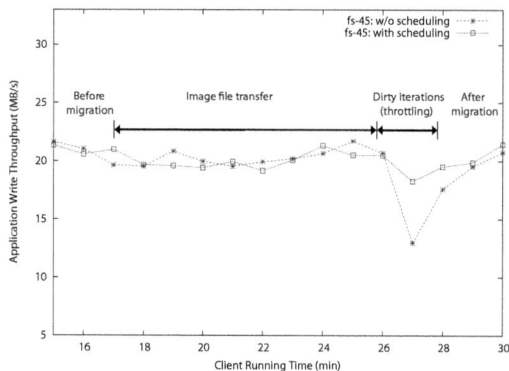

Figure 13. File server performance during migration.

		fs-30 no-schel	fs-30 schel	fs-45 no-schel	fs-45 schel	fs-60 no-schel	fs-60 schel
Soft-Throt	# of OP with Extra-latency	122	0	205	21	226	22
	Extra Traffic(GB)	1.08	0.82	1.62	1.45	2.01	1.53
	Migration Time(s)	585	575	642	625	694	665
Aggr-Throt	# of OP with Extra-latency	1369	1020	3075	2192	4328	3286
	Extra Traffic(GB)	0.84	0.80	1.51	1.33	1.93	1.38
	Migration Time(s)	582	574	628	613	674	641

Table 3. No scheduling vs. scheduling for file server with different number of clients (network bandwidth = 128Mbps).

sible solutions: stop the VM [26], or throttle disk writes (mentioned in [5]), with the latter achieving a more graceful performance degradation. However, there is no definitive throttling mechanism described in the literature. Thus, we have implemented our own simple throttling variants called aggressive throttling and soft throttling. During each dirty block retransmission iteration, the throttler limits the dirty rate to at most half of the migration speed. Whenever it receives a write request at time t_0, it checks the dirty block bitmap to compute the number of new dirty blocks generated and estimates the time t it takes to retransmit these new dirty blocks at the limited rate. If the next write operation comes before $t_0 + t$, aggressive throttling defers this write operation until time $t_0 + t$ by adding extra latency. In contrast, soft throttling maintains an average dirty rate from the beginning of the dirty iteration. It adds extra latency to a write operation only when the average dirty rate is larger than the limit. Aggressive throttling negatively impacts more write operations than soft throttling, but it can shorten the migration time and reduce extra traffic. We show results using both throttling variants.

We fix the network bandwidth at 128Mbps and vary the number of file server clients from 30 to 60 to achieve different I/O intensities. First, we evaluate the impact to I/O performance by measuring the number of operations penalized by extra latency due to throttling. Table 3 shows that when soft throttling is applied, scheduling can help to reduce the number of throttled operations from hundreds to a small number ($\leq$ 22). When aggressive throttling is applied, the number of throttled operations is in thousands. The scheduling algorithm can reduce the throttled operations by 25-28% across the three workloads. In order to know how this benefit is translated to application level improvement, Figure 13 shows the average write throughput as reported by the VMmark client before,

during and after migration under the fs-45 workload with aggressive throttling. Migration starts at the 17th minute. Before that, the average write throughput is around 21MB/s. When migration starts, the average write throughput drops by about 0.5-1MB/s because the migration competes with the application for I/O capacity. When the initial image file transfer finishes at around 25.7 minutes, the dirty iteration starts and throttling is enabled. The dirty iteration lasts for 2 minutes and 1 minute 43 seconds for no-scheduling and scheduling respectively. Without scheduling, the average write throughput during that time drops to 12.9MB/s. With scheduling, the write throughput only drops to 18.3MB/s. Under the fs-60 workload, the impact of throttling is more severe and scheduling provides more benefits. Specifically, throughput drops from 25MB/s to 10MB/s without scheduling, but only drops to 17MB/s with scheduling. Under the relatively light fs-30 workload, throughput drops from 14MB/s to 12.2MB/s without scheduling and to 13.5MB/s with scheduling.

Table 3 also shows that the extra traffic and migration time are reduced across the three workloads with the scheduling algorithm. Take the aggressive throttling scenario as an example, under fs-45, the extra traffic is reduced by 180MB and the migration time is reduced by 15s. Under fs-60, the I/O rate and the extra traffic both increase. The scheduling algorithm is able to reduce the extra traffic by 28% from 1.93GB to 1.38GB and reduce the migration time by 33s. The benefit of scheduling increases with I/O intensity.

We have also experimented with fs-45 under 64Mbps and 32Mbps of network bandwidth with aggressive throttling. At 64Mbps, scheduling reduces throttled operations by 2155. Extra traffic is reduced by 300MB and migration time is reduced by 56s. At 32Mbps, throttled operations is reduced by 3544. Extra traffic and migration time are reduced by 600MB and 223s respectively. The benefit of scheduling increases with decreasing network bandwidth.

7. Trace-Based Simulation

Since KVM only employs the pre-copy model, we perform trace-based simulations to evaluate the benefits of scheduling under the post-copy and pre+post-copy models. Although we cannot simulate all nuances of a fully implemented system, we believe our results can provide useful guidance to system designers.

We use the amount of extra traffic and the number of degraded operations that require remote reads as the performance metrics for evaluation. Extra traffic is used to evaluate the pre+post-copy model. It is the total size of retransmitted blocks. The number of degraded operations is used to evaluate both post-copy and pre+post-copy models. The performance of a read operation is degraded when it needs to remotely request some data from the source machine which incurs at least one network round trip delay. Therefore, a large number of degraded operations is detrimental to VM performance.

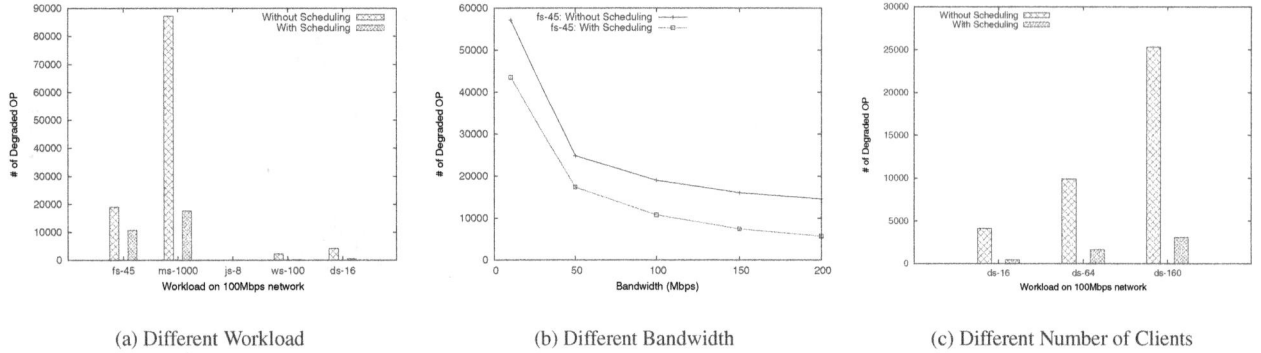

| (a) Different Workload | (b) Different Bandwidth | (c) Different Number of Clients |

Figure 14. The improvement of degraded operations under the post-copy model.

7.1 Simulation Methodology

We assume the network has a fixed bandwidth and a fixed delay. We assume there is no network congestion and no packet loss. Thus, once the migration of a piece of data is started at the source, the data arrives at the destination after $\frac{data\_size}{bandwidth} + delay$ seconds. In our experiments, we simulate a delay of 50ms and use different values of fixed bandwidths for different experiments.

For the following discussion, it may be helpful to refer to Figure 1. Each experiment is run 3 times using different random migration start times t chosen from $[3000, 5000]$ seconds. When the simulation begins at time t, we assume the scheduling algorithm has already produced a queue of block IDs ordered according to the computed chunk schedule to be migrated across the network in the specified order. Let us call this the primary queue. The schedule is computed based on using a portion of the trace prior to time t as history. The default history size is 50,000 operations. The default α for chunk size computation is 0.7. In addition, there is an auxiliary queue which serves different purposes for different migration models. As we simulate the storage and memory migrations, we also playback the I/O accesses in the trace starting at time t, simulating the continuing execution of the virtual machine in parallel. We assume each I/O access is independent. In other words, one delayed operation does not affect the issuance of the subsequent operations in the trace.

We do not simulate disk access performance characteristics such as seek time or read and write bandwidth. The reason is that, under the concurrent disk operations simulated from the trace, the block migration process, remote read requests, and operations issued by other virtual machines sharing the same physical disk, it is impossible to simulate the effects that disk characteristics will have in a convincing manner. Thus, disk read and write operations are treated to be instantaneous in all scenarios. However, under our scheduling approach, blocks might be migrated in an arbitrary order. To be conservative, we do add a performance penalty to our scheduling approach. Specifically, the start of the migration of a primary queue block is delayed by 10ms if the previous migrated block did not immediately precede this block.

In the post-copy model, the memory migration is simulated first and starts at time t. When it is completed, storage migration begins according to the order in the primary queue. Subsequently, when a read operation for a block that has not yet arrived at the destination is played back from the trace, the desired block ID is enqueued to the auxiliary queue after a network delay (unless the transfer of that block has already started), simulating the remote read request. The auxiliary queue is serviced with strict priority over the primary queue. When a block is migrated through the auxiliary queue, the corresponding block in the primary queue is removed. Note that

when a block is written to at the destination, we assume the source is not notified, so the corresponding block in the primary queue remains.

In the pre+post-copy model, in the pre-copy phase, the storage is migrated according to the primary queue; the auxiliary queue is not used in this phase. At the end of the memory migration, the dirty blocks' migration schedule is computed and stored in the primary queue. Subsequently, the simulation in the post-copy phase proceeds identically to the post-copy model.

Finally, when scheduling is not used, the simulation methodology is still the same, except that the blocks are ordered sequentially in the primary queue.

7.2 Benefits Under Post-Copy

Figure 14 shows the benefits of scheduling in terms of the number of degraded operations under the various server types, bandwidths, and workload intensities. The reductions in the number of degraded operations are 43%, 80%, 95% and 90% in the file server, mail server, web server and database server respectively when the network bandwidth is 100 Mbps. The traffic that is involved in remote reads is also reduced. For example, 172MB and 382MB are saved with the scheduling algorithm for the file server and mail server respectively. If the history size is reduced significantly from 50,000 operations to merely 1,000 operations, the corresponding benefits are reduced to 19%, 54%, 75%, and 83% respectively. Thus, even maintaining a short history could provide substantial benefits. The Java server performs very few read operations, so there is no remote read.

When the network bandwidth is low, the file server (fs-45) suffers from more degraded operations because the migration time is longer. At 10Mbps, 13,601 (or 24%) degraded operations are eliminated by scheduling in the file server. For the mail server, web server and database server, their degraded operations are reduced by 45%, 52% and 79% respectively when the network bandwidth is 10Mbps. The traffic involved in remote reads for the file server is reduced from 1.2GB to 0.9GB and for the mail server from 2.6GB to 1.4GB.

When the number of clients increases, the read rate becomes more intensive. For example, the ds-160 workload results in 25,334 degraded operations when scheduling is not used. With scheduling, the degraded operations is reduced by 84%-90% under the ds-16, ds-64, and ds-160 workloads. When the number of the clients in the file server is increased to 70, there are 23,011 degraded operations. With scheduling, it can be reduced by 47%.

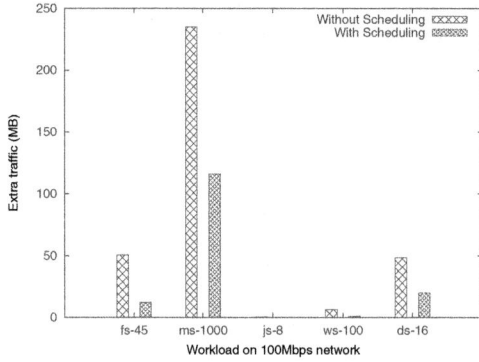

Figure 15. The improvement of extra traffic under the pre+post-copy model.

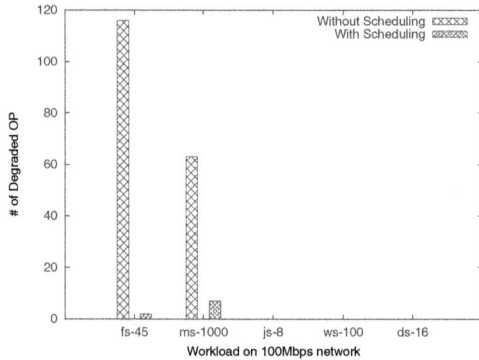

Figure 16. The improvement of degraded operations under the pre+post-copy model.

	fs-45	ms-1000	js-8	ws-100	ds-16
Worst chunk size performance gain	49%	43%	49%	74%	54%
Optimal chunk size performance gain	77%	70%	64%	90%	66%
Algorithm selected chunk size performance gain	76%	50%	58%	87%	64%

Table 4. Comparison between selected chunk size and measured optimal chunk size (extra traffic under pre+post-copy).

7.3 Benefits Under Pre+Post-Copy

In the pre+post copy model, the extra traffic consists of only the final dirty blocks at the end of memory migration. As Figure 15 shows, the scheduling algorithm reduces the extra traffic in the five workloads by 76%, 51%, 67%, 86% and 59% respectively.

In the pre+post copy model, the degraded operations exist only during the retransmission of the dirty blocks. Since the amount of dirty data is much smaller than the virtual disk size, the problem is not as serious as in the post-copy model. Figure 16 shows that the Java server, web server and database server have no degraded operations because their amount of dirty data is small. But the file server and mail server suffer from degraded operations, and applying scheduling can reduce them by 99% and 88% respectively.

7.4 Optimality of Chunk Size

In order to understand how optimal is the chunk size selected by the algorithm, we conduct experiments with various manually selected chunk sizes, ranging from 512KB to 1GB in factor of 2 increments,

to measure the performance gain achieved at these different chunk sizes. The chunk size that results in the biggest performance gain is considered the measured optimal chunk size. The one with the least gain is considered the measured worst chunk size. Table 4 compares the selected chunk size against the optimal and worst chunk sizes in terms of extra traffic under the pre+post-copy model. As can be seen, the gain achieved by the selected chunk size is greater than the measured worst chunk size across the 5 workloads. Most of them are very close to the measured optimal chunk size.

8. Summary

Migrating virtual machines between clouds is an emerging requirement to support open clouds and to enable better service availability. We demonstrate that existing migration solutions can have poor I/O performance during migration that could be mitigated by taking a *workload-aware approach* to storage migration. We develop our insight on workload characteristics by collecting I/O traces of five representative applications to validate the extent of temporal locality, spatial locality and access popularity that widely exists. We then design a *scheduling algorithm* that exploits the individual virtual machine's workload to compute an efficient ordering of *chunks* at an appropriate chunk size to schedule for transfer over the network. We demonstrate the improvements introduced by work-load aware scheduling on a fully implemented system for KVM and through a trace-driven simulation framework. Under a wide range of I/O workloads and network conditions, we show that workload-aware scheduling can effectively reduce the amount of extra traffic and I/O throttling for the pre-copy model and significantly reduce the number of remote reads to improve the performance of post-copy and pre+post-copy model. Furthermore, the overhead introduced by our scheduling algorithm in KVM is low.

Next, we discuss and summarize the benefits of *workload-aware scheduling* under different conditions and workloads using the pre-copy migration model as an example.

Network bandwidth: The benefits of scheduling increases as the amount of available network bandwidth for migration decreases. Given that lower bandwidth results in a longer pre-copy period, the opportunity for any content to become dirty (i.e., requiring a retransmission) is larger. However, with scheduling, content that is likely to be written is migrated towards the end of the pre-copy period thus reducing the amount of time and the opportunity for it to become dirty.

Image size: The benefits of scheduling increases as the image size (i.e., the used blocks in the file system) gets larger even if the active I/O working set remains the same. A larger image size results in a longer pre-copy period, thus the opportunity for any content to become dirty is bigger. However, with scheduling, the working set gets transferred last, reducing the probability that migrated content becomes dirty despite the longer migration time.

I/O rate: As the I/O rate becomes more intense, the benefits of scheduling increases. With higher I/O intensity, the probability that any previously migrated content becomes dirty is higher. Again, by transferring active content towards the end of the pre-copy period, we lower the probability that it would become dirty and has to be retransmitted.

I/O characteristics: As the extent of locality or popularity becomes less pronounced, the benefits of scheduling decreases. For example, when the popularity of accessed blocks is more uniformly distributed, it is more difficult to accurately predict the access pattern. In the extreme case where there is no locality or popularity pattern in the workload, scheduling provides similar performance to non-scheduling.

These characteristics indicate that our workload-aware scheduling algorithm can improve the performance of storage migration under a wide range of realistic environments and workloads.

References

[1] Michael Armbrust, Armando Fox, Rean Griffith, and et. al. Above the clouds: A berkeley view of cloud computing. Technical Report UCB/EECS-2009-28, EECS Department, University of California, Berkeley, Feb 2009.

[2] M.G. Baker, J.H. Hartman, M.D. Kupfer, K.W. Shirriff, and J.K. Ousterhout. Measurements of a distributed file system. *ACM SIGOPS Operating Systems Review*, 25(5):212, 1991.

[3] M. Blaze. NFS tracing by passive network monitoring. In *Proceedings of the USENIX Winter 1992 Technical Conference*, pages 333–343, 1992.

[4] "Amazon Web Services Blog". Animoto - Scaling Through Viral Growth. http://aws.typepad.com/aws/2008/04/animoto—scali.html, April 2008.

[5] Robert Bradford, Evangelos Kotsovinos, Anja Feldmann, and Harald Schioberg. Live wide-area migration of virtual machines including local persistent state. In *ACM/Usenix VEE*, June 2007.

[6] Christopher Clark, Keir Fraser, Steven Hand, Jacob Gorm Hansen, Eric Jul, Christian Limpach, Ian Pratt, and Andrew Warfield. Live migration of virtual machines. In *NSDI'05: Proceedings of the 2nd conference on Symposium on Networked Systems Design & Implementation*, pages 273–286, Berkeley, CA, USA, 2005. USENIX Association.

[7] M.D. Dahlin, C.J. Mather, R.Y. Wang, T.E. Anderson, and D.A. Patterson. A quantitative analysis of cache policies for scalable network file systems. *ACM SIGMETRICS Performance Evaluation Review*, 22(1):150–160, 1994.

[8] Derek Gottfrid. The New York Times Archives + Amazon Web Services = TimesMachine. http://open.blogs.nytimes.com/2008/05/21/the-new-york-times-archives-amazon-web-services-timesmachine/, May 2008.

[9] James Hamilton. The Cost of Latency. http://perspectives.mvdirona.com/2009/10/31/ TheCostOfLatency.aspx, October 2009.

[10] Michael R. Hines and Kartik Gopalan. Post-copy based live virtual machine migration using adaptive pre-paging and dynamic self-ballooning. In *VEE '09: Proceedings of the 2009 ACM SIGPLAN/SIGOPS international conference on Virtual execution environments*, 2009.

[11] Takahiro Hirofuchi, Hidemoto Nakada, Hirotaka Ogawa, Satoshi Itoh, and Satoshi Sekiguchi. A live storage migration mechanism over wan and its performance evaluation. In *VIDC'09: Proceedings of the 3rd International Workshop on Virtualization Technologies in Distributed Computing*, Barcelona, Spain, 2009. ACM.

[12] Takahiro Hirofuchi, Hirotaka Ogawa, Hidemoto Nakada, Satoshi Itoh, and Satoshi Sekiguchi. A live storage migration mechanism over wan for relocatable virtual machine services on clouds. In *CCGRID'09: Proceedings of the 2009 9th IEEE/ACM International Symposium on Cluster Computing and the Grid*, Shanghai, China, 2009. IEEE Computer Society.

[13] Hai Jin, Li Deng, Song Wu, and Xuanhua Shi. Live virtual machine migration integrating memory compression with precopy. In *IEEE International Conference on Cluster Computing*, 2009.

[14] KVM. QEMU-KVM code. http://sourceforge.net/projects/kvm/files, January 2010.

[15] Yingwei Luo, Binbin Zhang, Xiaolin Wang, Zhenlin Wang, Yifeng Sun, and Haogang Chen. Live and Incremental Whole-System Migration of Virtual Machines Using Block-Bitmap. In *IEEE International Conference on Cluster Computing*, 2008.

[16] Open Cloud Manifesto. Open Cloud Manifesto. http://www.opencloudmanifesto.org/, January 2010.

[17] Michael Nelson, Beng-Hong Lim, and Greg Hutchins. Fast transparent migration for virtual machines. In *USENIX'05: Proceedings of the 2005 Usenix Annual Technical Conference*, Berkeley, CA, USA, 2005. USENIX Association.

[18] J.K. Ousterhout, H. Da Costa, D. Harrison, J.A. Kunze, M. Kupfer, and J.G. Thompson. A trace-driven analysis of the UNIX 4.2 BSD file system. *ACM SIGOPS Operating Systems Review*, 19(5):24, 1985.

[19] K.K. Ramakrishnan, Prashant Shenoy, and Jacobus Van der Merwe. Live data center migration across wans: A robust cooperative context aware approach. In *ACM SIGCOMM Workshop on Internet Network Management (INM)*, Kyoto, Japan, aug 2007.

[20] IBM Redbooks. *IBM Powervm Live Partition Mobility IBM International Technical Support Organization*. Vervante, 2009.

[21] D. Roselli, J.R. Lorch, and T.E. Anderson. A comparison of file system workloads. In *Proceedings of the annual conference on USENIX Annual Technical Conference*, page 4. USENIX Association, 2000.

[22] Franco Travostino, Paul Daspit, Leon Gommans, Chetan Jog, Cees de Laat, Joe Mambretti, Inder Monga, Bas van Oudenaarde, Satish Raghunath, and Phil Yonghui Wang. Seamless live migration of virtual machines over the man/wan. *Future Gener. Comput. Syst.*, 22(8):901–907, 2006.

[23] VMWare. VMmark Virtualization Benchmarks. http://www.vmware.com/products/vmmark/, January 2010.

[24] Timothy Wood, Prashant Shenoy, Alexandre Gerber, K.K. Ramakrishnan, and Jacobus Van der Merwe. The Case for Enterprise-Ready Virtual Private Clouds. In *Proc. of HotCloud Workshop*, 2009.

[25] Timothy Wood, Prashant Shenoy, Arun Venkataramani, and Mazin Yousif. Black-box and gray-box strategies for virtual machine migration. In *NSDI*, 2007.

[26] XEN. XEN Project. http://www.xen.org, January 2009.

Patch Auditing in Infrastructure as a Service Clouds

Lionel Litty *

VMware, Inc.
llitty@vmware.com

David Lie

Department of Electrical and Computer Engineering
University of Toronto
lie@eecg.toronto.edu

Abstract

A basic requirement of a secure computer system is that it be up to date with regard to software security patches. Unfortunately, Infrastructure as a Service (IaaS) clouds make this difficult. They leverage virtualization, which provides functionality that causes traditional security patch update systems to fail. In addition, the diversity of operating systems and the distributed nature of administration in the cloud compound the problem of identifying unpatched machines.

In this work, we propose P2, a hypervisor-based patch audit solution. P2 audits VMs and detects the execution of unpatched binary and non-binary files in an accurate, continuous and OS-agnostic manner. Two key innovations make P2 possible. First, P2 uses efficient information flow tracking to identify the use of unpatched non-binary files in a vulnerable way. We performed a patch survey and discover that 64% of files modified by security updates do not contain binary code, making the audit of non-binary files crucial. Second, P2 implements a novel algorithm that identifies binaries in mid-execution to allow handling of VMs resumed from a checkpoint or migrated into the cloud.

We have implemented a prototype of P2 and and our experiments show that it accurately reports the execution of unpatched code while imposing performance overhead of 4%.

Categories and Subject Descriptors K.6.3 [*Software Management*]: Software maintenance

General Terms Algorithms, Design, Experimentation, Management, Measurement, Security

Keywords virtualization, cloud computing, infrastructure as a service, patch management, application discovery

1. Introduction

A large number of security vulnerabilities stem directly from software implementation flaws in critical code. To maintain the security of a system against attackers, it is critical that patches, which fix these flaws, be applied in a timely manner. As a result, many software packages and operating systems (OSs) contain support

---

* The majority of this work was done while Lionel Litty was at the University of Toronto

VEE'11 March 9–11, 2011, Newport Beach, California, USA.
Copyright © 2011 ACM 978-1-4503-0501-3/11/03...$10.00

for automatic patch installation. These systems are simple – they periodically check a central server for the existence of patches and apply any patches that have not yet been applied to the system they are running on.

However, automatic patch installation cannot always prevent the exploitation of known vulnerabilities and can reduce the stability of computer systems. Patches are not applied instantly as the patch installation system only checks for updates periodically. This creates an exploitable window of vulnerability between the time the patch is disclosed and the time it is applied [4]. In addition, automatic patch systems are unaware of which patches need to be applied, and proactively apply all available patches, even if the patched component is never used. Unfortunately, patches can have unintended side effects, so such unnecessary patches can needlessly cause system failures or performance degradation [2].

This problem is made more acute in a virtualized cloud environment. Public and private virtualized cloud environments offering Infrastructure as a Service (IaaS) have grown in popularity due to their ability to provide elasticity of resources and reduce user costs. These environments have two characteristics that make patch management even more complicated than in a unvirtualized environment. First, virtualization introduces new usage models that break standard automatic patch installation systems [10]. Patch installation systems rely on machines always being powered on so that they can check for updates and apply them. They also assume that time proceeds in a linear fashion so that patches are naturally applied in sequence. Unfortunately, virtual machines (VMs) can be archived and left powered off for long periods of time. They can be rolled back to a previous checkpoint in time, cloned, migrated, created and destroyed easily and frequently. These capabilities skew time in the VM and can cause automatic patch installation systems to fail.

Second, by separating the administration and maintenance of hardware from that of the software, IaaS clouds permit a larger number of administrative domains, resulting in a greater diversity of OSs and software environments. Whereas a single organization with a single IT department may have forced all users to conform to a homogeneous computing environment, a private cloud environment removes that restriction, giving users more freedom. Users may have any OS (i.e. Windows, Linux), any flavor of the OS (i.e. Vista, XP, Ubuntu, Red Hat), and any version level (i.e. Linux kernel version, Windows service pack). In a public cloud, such as those implemented by Amazon's EC2, GoGrid and Mosso, there are no restrictions at all on what OSs and software users may install. The de-federalization of administrative control and greater diversity in software make it difficult for a cloud provider to ascertain the patch level of VMs running on their infrastructure. Unfortunately, the insecurity of a single cloud user can negatively impact both their fellow cloud users and the cloud provider itself [18][26]. Thus, cloud providers are motivated to identify and protect themselves from VMs on their cloud that are vulnerable to attack.

In this paper, we demonstrate that virtualization can also solve the patch management problems it creates in cloud environments. We design and implement P2, a patch audit solution that leverages the hypervisor to detect and mitigate vulnerabilities in unpatched software in VMs. P2 has several advantages over existing solutions. First, P2 provides *continuous* protection, and does not fail if the machine is powered off or check-pointed and rolled back. Second, P2 is more *accurate* than existing solutions. P2 only reports unpatched software if it is actually executed, reducing the number of alerts and enabling administrators to apply only the minimal number of patches required. Finally, P2 is *OS-agnostic*, allowing it to work on any standard commodity OS. This allows the cloud provider to have a single patch audit solution, instead of having to support an OS-specific one for every OS their customers use.

P2 accomplishes this by relying on *architectural introspection* [18], which monitors virtual hardware to infer events within a VM. By restricting monitoring to only hardware state, P2 is able to detect unpatched software in VMs without having to rely on any detailed or implementation-specific information about the OS and software in the VM. P2 detects unpatched binary and non-binary software. Binary software denotes software that will execute natively on the underlying processor, such as executables or libraries. Non-binary software generally refers to scripts or byte-code, which will execute with the aid of an interpreter or just-in-time compiler (JIT). However, non-binary software can also include configuration files and other application resources.

To detect the execution of an unpatched binary, P2 monitors memory pages in a way similar to Patagonix [17]. However, Patagonix needs to be invoked before an application starts to identify it, meaning that it cannot be applied to VMs that have been resumed from checkpoints or migrated into a cloud. In contrast, P2 does not suffer from this restriction and can identify applications mid-execution. To detect scripts and byte code that are executed by an interpreter or JIT compiler, P2 uses lightweight, coarse-grain information flow tracking to determine if an unpatched file is read from disk into the address space of an interpreter or JIT compiler that is capable of executing the non-binary file. This allows P2 to detect the execution of unpatched non-binary code with low overhead and few false positives.

When P2 detects unpatched code it can take one of two actions depending on the mode it is used in. In *reporting mode*, it simply reports that a VM has executed unpatched code to the cloud administrator, who can then inform the VM administrator and take actions according to their service agreement (i.e. the VM administrator may have to patch the code or the cloud administrator could adjust firewall rules to prevent exploitation). In *prevention mode*, in addition to reporting the unpatched code, P2 actively prevents the exploitation of the unpatched code by injecting code into the vulnerable process that prevents it from executing any more instructions.

We make three contributions in this paper. First, we perform a study of patches on the Fedora Core 10 and 11 Linux distributions. We find that across both distributions, 102,819 files were updated, of which 23,711 are non-documentation files that may contain executable code or configuration resources. Among these files, only 36% are binary code files. This serves as a strong motivation for the ability to be able to detect the execution of unpatched non-binary code. Second, we describe P2, which uses architectural introspection to detect the execution of unpatched binary and non-binary code. We demonstrate the OS-agnostic property of P2 by running it on both Windows XP and Linux VMs. Finally, we evaluate the effectiveness and performance overhead of P2 by evaluating it on workloads that contain both patched and unpatched code. We find that P2 can accurately detect the execution of unpatched applications with minimal overhead.

We give a detailed motivation for P2 and state its assumptions and guarantees in Section 2. Then we describe our patch survey in Section 3, which illustrates and characterizes the need for monitoring of non-binary files. Section 4 describes the architecture of P2 and implementation details of our prototype are described in Section 5. We then evaluate P2's effectiveness and performance overhead in Section 6. Finally, Section 7 compares P2 to other related work and we conclude in Section 8.

2. Overview

2.1 Motivation

A survey conducted by Bellissimo et al. in 2006 [3] found that 69 out of 71 CERT Technical Cyber Security Alerts recommended applying updates or patches to fix vulnerabilities. This supports the conventional wisdom that many security attacks can be prevented by keeping a system patched. Software developers have come to the same conclusion and recent software systems now commonly incorporate automatic software update components. In this section, we motivate P2 by summarizing the existing state of the art in patch update systems and illustrating their deficiencies compared to P2 in terms of how accurate, continuous and OS-agnostic they are.

Automatic update systems can be provided by the OS, or built specifically into an application. OS-wide update systems, such as the ones built into Windows, Mac OS and Linux periodically check for patches and can be configured to automatically download and apply them. OS-wide automatic update systems may also be built into system administration tool suites, such as IBM's Tivoli system, which also performs various other security and compliance auditing tasks. Application-specific automatic update systems only handle patches for a specific application. Many popular applications, such as the Firefox and Chrome browsers, Acrobat Reader, and many games implement such solutions. Application-specific update systems usually execute when the application is run, when they will check for patches and if necessary, download and install them.

All automatic update systems are host-based: they execute as part of the software system, either as separate software agents or as software mechanisms built into applications. As a result, these systems are tied to a specific OS and are thus not OS-agnostic. In addition, the cloud provider must rely on the cloud user to properly install and configure host-based systems since the cloud provider does not have administrative access to the VMs. Automatic update systems can be accurate or continuous depending on whether they are OS-wide or application-specific. OS-wide updaters periodically compare a database of installed patches on the host with an online repository of patches to determine if patches need to be applied. They are unaware of whether the components they maintain are executed or not, making them inaccurate. In addition, because the check for patches is periodic, they are not continuous. Application-specific updaters that exist as separate applications from the application they maintain have the same properties as OS-wide updaters. However, many application-specific updaters are part of the application they maintain and only run when the application they are patching is run, making them accurate as a result. However, they are only partially continuous. These systems will check for patches when the application first starts up, and then periodically afterwards. Thus, if a patch exists at startup, they will apply it before the application actually runs. However, if a patch becomes available while the application is running, it will not be detected and applied until the next time the update system checks.

An alternative, OS-agnostic approach for detecting the presence of unpatched software is a network vulnerability scanner such as Nessus [21]. These scanners attempt to detect unpatched code by scanning all hosts and ports in a range of IP addresses and trying to identify the version of any network facing services installed on

Solution	Continuous	Accurate	OS-agnostic
OS-wide update	No	No	No
Application update	On startup	Yes	No
Network scanning	No	No	Yes
P2	**Yes**	**Yes**	**Yes**

Table 1. Comparison of P2 and current solutions.

those hosts. The identification of the software version can be done simplistically by examining the banner returned by the service, or in a more sophisticated way by sending requests to the hosts and observing the responses. After such scans, the network vulnerability scanner informs system administrators of the presence of software with known vulnerabilities on machines connected to the network. A network vulnerability scanner does not rely on any software agent being present on the host and thus is attractive in IaaS clouds where there is a diversity of OSs running and the cloud administrator has no administrative access to install and manage any host-based solution.

Unfortunately, a network-based approach has limited coverage. It can only be used to detect unpatched server software for which the version can be determined via network queries. As a result, it will not protect a user that uses an out-of-date browser to visit a malicious website. In addition, network scanning has limited precision and may not be able to definitively determine if a service is vulnerable or not. For example, if the network scanner relies on banners, it will fail if the server is configured not to return a banner. More sophisticated scanners that attempt exploits may fail if the exploit's success depends on random factors. Thus, network scanners have limited accuracy. Network scanning is also non-continuous since the scans only happen periodically. In a cloud environment, this problem is compounded by the fact that software executing on VMs that are only powered on occasionally could remain out-of-date for long periods of time.

In this work, we show how P2 takes advantage of a virtualized infrastructure to implement a patch audit system that has the combined advantages of existing systems. Table 1 summarizes the advantages of P2 over host-based automatic update systems and network-based vulnerability scanning. In a virtualized environment, a ubiquitous layer of software executes below OSs which now interact with virtualized hardware. Because it facilitates management and allows system administrators to retain some control over desktop machines, such a setup has become popular and is offered by VMware View [32] and Citrix XenClient [8], amongst others. This is also increasingly the architecture used in clouds, be they public or private.

2.2 Assumptions and Guarantees

We make several assumptions about the OS that will be installed in the VMs. First, we assume that an efficient, commodity OS is installed. P2 relies on the efficiency assumption because it uses information flow tracking to infer whether a non-binary file is read by an application that can interpret the non-binary file and expose the vulnerability. Specifically, we assume that when a process requests data from a file, data is copied directly from the disk into a buffer cache using Direct Memory Access (DMA), and then copied from there into the address space of the requesting process. If the OS inefficiently makes extra copies of the data before returning it, this will confuse the information flow tracking of P2. Similarly, DMA transfers are much faster than Programmed I/O (PIO) transfers. OSs will generally use DMA if it is available and only fall back to PIO if DMA is not available. We have confirmed that this assumption holds for all flavors of Linux and Windows. Memory copying is expensive and we believe that all OS implementations

that consider performance important will try to avoid unnecessary copying of disk data.

Second, P2 assumes that application code is stored on the local virtual disk of the VM. Applications that are executed over a web browser as JavaScript or stored on networked storage are not monitored by P2 because the files containing these applications are not read from the local disk. This assumption is reasonable for a cloud environment where VMs are usually self-contained, and contain all code necessary to execute.

Third, P2 assumes the system it is monitoring is not trying to covertly execute unpatched code. For example, for efficiency, P2 assumes that the flow of information from the disk to a process terminates at the process that reads the file. However, if the adversary wants to avoid detection, she can create a "scrubbing" application that reads an unpatched script, and then passes it to the `stdin` of the interpreter via a pipe. Thus, P2's patch auditing is restricted to VMs that are not under the control of a malicious adversary.

Finally, P2 inspects disk contents to identify blocks that correspond to unpatched files. Currently, if the disk or files on the disk are encrypted or compressed, P2 will not be able to monitor the content of these files. P2 can be extended to support encrypted or compressed files, by adding functionality that would allow it to decrypt or decompress files for analysis.

Given that these assumptions hold, P2 provides two guarantees. First, P2 will identify the execution of all unpatched applications, regardless of whether they are composed of native binary code, non-binary code, or some combination of the above. Non-binary code includes all forms of byte code or scripts, regardless of whether they are executed by an interpreter or a JIT compiler. P2 infers non-binary code execution anytime a script or byte code file is loaded into the memory of a matching interpreter or JIT compiler, i.e. if the Perl interpreter loads a valid Perl script or a JAVA virtual machine loads a JAVA class file. P2 can also detect unpatched resource and configuration files, provided that they match the unpatched, vulnerable version exactly – P2 does not identify vulnerabilities caused by custom configurations. Second, P2 works for any commodity OS. We have validated P2 on two widely used OS environments, Windows XP and Fedora Core Linux.

3. Patch Survey

To be OS-agnostic, P2 uses architectural introspection, which restricts hypervisor monitoring to the interaction between the guest VM and virtual hardware. As a result, P2 must make a distinction between applications implemented in native binary code and applications implemented in an interpreted language. On the one hand, binary code must execute directly on the processor and thus is observable through interactions with the memory management unit (MMU). On the other hand, interpreted code can only execute when it is read and executed by the appropriate interpreter or JIT, which itself is usually a native binary. To understand the importance of these two forms of monitoring, we conducted a survey of historical data to characterize the composition of security-sensitive patches.

We collected all security patches for Fedora Core 10 and 11 from the Fedora Project's admin website [1]. The Fedora Core 10 updates consist of security patches between its release date on November 25, 2008 until October 1, 2009 when we conducted the study. The Fedora 11 updates were for the same period starting from its release date on June 6, 2009. To identify which patches contain security fixes, we used the Fedora Project's update classification scheme, which classifies patches as pending, testing, stable or security. To be classified as security, the patch must contain at least one security critical fix.

---

[1] https://admin.fedoraproject.org/updates/

OS	Changed files	Documents	Binaries	Non-binaries	Top 10 non-binary file extensions
FC 10	73800	61037	4979	7784	pyo, pyc, php, js, tmpl, desktop, elc, info, inc, jar
FC 11	29019	24331	1307	3281	php, pyo, pyc, jar, js, inc, zip, gif, <none>, py

Table 2. Summary of Fedora Core security patch RPMs.

To characterize the types of files patched, we compared each security patch with the previous version of the application that the patch replaced. Fedora uses Red Hat's RPM package format to distribute patches. RPMs contain entire binaries, which will overwrite the binaries of the previous version when the patch is installed. In addition, patch RPMs can also be installed onto a system where no previous version of the application exists. Thus, patch RPMs also contain files that did not change from the previous version. Thus, to identify which files are patched, we compare the files in each patch RPM with the RPM of the previous version. From this, we can characterize the makeup of files that changed in response to a security vulnerability. We note that while a security patch must fix at least one security vulnerability, the patch may also contain fixes for non-security sensitive bugs. Unfortunately, neither the Fedora Project page nor the RPM package format contains sufficient information to remove files that contain non-security sensitive bug fixes from our study, so we assume that any file that changed due to a security patch contains a security fix.

Table 2 summarizes the data obtained from this survey, including the top 10 most common non-binary file types by extension. An extension of <none> denotes a file with no extension. We analyzed 446 out of the 495 security patches in Fedora Core 10 and 130 out of the 134 security patches in Fedora Core 11. Not all patches could be analyzed because we could no longer obtain the matching previous RPM packages in some cases. For each file in an RPM that was changed due to a security patch, we determined if it was a binary file or a non-binary file using the `file` utility, which classifies any ELF file as a shared object or as an executable, and any other file as a non-binary file. To get a fair assessment of the percentage of non-binary files that were modified by security updates, we filtered out `man` pages, document files stored in `/usr/share/doc`, `/usr/share/info`,... as well as `locale` files that contain localization data. We further classified the remaining non-binary files based on their extension. The results illustrate two important findings. First, 64% of the updates across both distributions were to non-binary files. This indicates that P2's ability to monitor the execution of non-binary code in an OS-agnostic way is critical to its success as a patch audit solution. Second, a significant number of the top 10 non-binary files are executable scripts and byte code: `pyo` and `pyc` are compiled python code, `php` and `inc` contain php code, which is often used to implement websites, `jar` and `js` are for JAVA and JavaScript respectively, and `elc` files contain Emacs Lisp code. The top 10 non-binary file types make up 77% and 84% of all non-binary, non-document files in Fedora Core 10 and 11 respectively, forming a significant portion of the patched non-binaries. Thus, many of the non-binary updates are to executables that are run with the aid of an interpreter or a JIT compiler. In particular, much of this code appears to be used to implement web applications. While P2 also has the ability to identify unpatched configuration or application resource files, patches to these types of files are not common in practice.

4. System Architecture

We now describe the design and architecture of P2, which provides accurate, continuous and OS-agnostic detection of unpatched code in a VM. P2 is most naturally implemented in the virtualization infrastructure that manages the cloud VMs or a company's VMs. As a result, its operation is administered by the cloud provider in the public cloud setting, or by the system administrators in charge of the computing infrastructure in an enterprise private cloud setting. The architecture of P2 is illustrated in Figure 1. While P2 leverages Patagonix as a component, all other components in the figure are new contributions of P2. We begin by describing the database of software information that P2 needs and then describe how P2 uses these databases to detect the execution of unpatched binary and non-binary software.

4.1 Software databases

To detect and report the execution of vulnerable, unpatched applications, P2 requires a database of information with which it can identify these applications. Such an *unpatched database* can be derived from the files that make up the application. A list of files that need to be patched can be easily obtained by monitoring the updates applied by automatic update systems, or manually monitoring security vulnerability distribution lists. P2 requires the files that each patch modifies, which can be obtained by comparing the files in the patch with the software version it was patching. The patch survey described in Section 3 was performed using scripts written over a course of 6 days by one of the authors of this paper. Based on this experience, we believe that building and maintaining a database of unpatched software would require only modest effort and time. P2 also requires an *interpreter database*, which lists applications that may load and interpret unpatched non-binary files. We use the term interpreter to denote all interpreters and JIT compilers on the system, as well as any application that can load unpatched configuration files. Each non-binary file in the unpatched database must be associated with at least one binary in the interpreter database, which can load the non-binary file and be subject to the vulnerability.

P2 also requires a *patched database* of files that do not need to be patched. Such a database would be considerably larger than the database of unpatched files since there are many more of such files. Maintaining such a database in a homogeneous enterprise setting where a single entity controls the software environment represents a tractable undertaking. In a more open setting, building a list of patched applications is a more difficult task, but not intractable. For example, anti-virus vendors already maintain large databases that keep track of information about malicious software. Some anti-virus vendors have suggested that it may actually be easier to maintain a white list of software instead of the current industry practice of maintaining a black list of malicious software [24]. The administrator can also leverage existing databases of software that currently exist. For example, NIST maintains a database of hashes for a large number of applications [23] and VersionTracker [31] keeps track of available software updates. Linux vendors also maintain large repositories of software and track updates to this software.

In a public cloud setting, the cost of the work required from the cloud provider can be spread amongst cloud customers. The task of maintaining the database can also be outsourced to third parties. The exact details of how such databases would be managed are

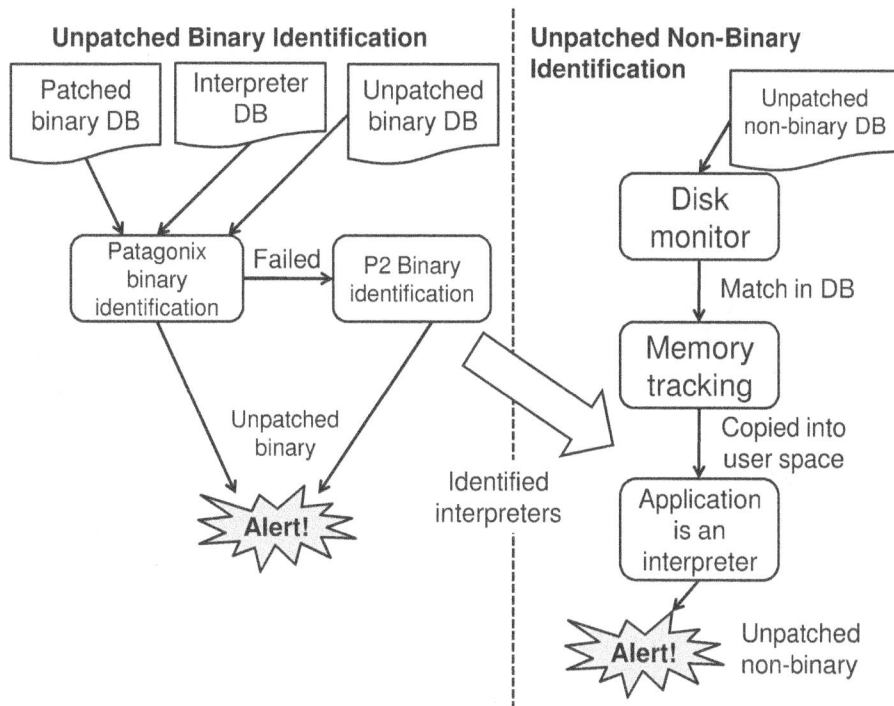

Figure 1. P2 architecture. P2's binary identification is only invoked if Patagonix's binary identification fails. P2's non-binary identification relies on information from the binary identification to find out which processes are running interpreter binaries.

outside the scope of this work. For the rest of this paper, we assume that the cloud provider has access to the files that correspond to the software that need to be monitored.

4.2 Monitoring

Patagonix [17] introduced a mechanism for identifying executing binaries that is accurate, continuous and OS-agnostic. However, Patagonix is not suitable for patch monitoring in a cloud environment for three reasons. First, Patagonix must be invoked before the application to be identified is run. Patagonix operates by tracking the mapping between regions in memory and binary files. For Windows PE binaries, this is problematic because these binaries may be modified at run time to relocate them to a different virtual address. To address this, Patagonix must observe the first instruction executed for any binary, which it uses to identify the binary using an entry point database. Second, Patagonix is only applicable to binaries and cannot identify interpreted or JIT-ed code. P2 extends Patagonix's binary monitoring so that it can identify applications in mid-execution. In addition, P2 adds a completely new monitoring mechanism for non-binary code based on coarse-grain information flow tracking.

The database of unpatched files is divided into two databases: one containing binary files and the other containing non-binary files. The database of unpatched binary files is then combined with a database of interpreters and the database of patched binaries. This combined database is then used for identifying executing binaries.

When P2 detects an executing binary, it first invokes Patagonix to identify the binary. If Patagonix is able to identify the binary it takes actions depending on which database the binary is identified in. If the binary is unpatched, P2 raises an alert and, if running in reporting mode, reports the alert to the cloud administrator. If P2 is running in prevention mode, it will also prevent the unpatched code from running using the technique described in Section 5.3. If

P2 matches the executing binary with an entry in the database of interpreters, then it notes the address space the interpreter occupies for use in detecting unpatched non-binary file use. If Patagonix fails to identify the binary, P2 uses the address inference based binary identification algorithm described in Section 5.1 to identify the binary.

P2's mechanism for identifying unpatched non-binary files starts with a virtual disk monitor that monitors disk blocks being read by the guest OS. Each block is compared with the database of unpatched non-binary files. If there is a match, P2 invokes a coarse-grain, page-based memory tracking mechanism to track the use of the data read from the file. Here, P2 leverages information from its binary execution tracking – if it detects that data from the unpatched non-binary file flows into the memory space of a matching interpreter for the file, then it raises an alert and takes action depending on its operating mode.

It is crucial that P2 detects that an unpatched non-binary file is actually loaded into the appropriate interpreter before raising an alert. For example, consider a simpler system where P2 does not track data flow through memory, but instead raises an alert whenever an unpatched file was read off disk. Such a naïve approach will raise alerts even when the file is accessed in a way that will not exercise the vulnerability in the unpatched file. Execution of a file by an interpreter or as a configuration file constitutes *vulnerable accesses*, as it has the potential to exercise the vulnerability in the file. On the other hand, access by applications such as anti-virus software performing a scan, desktop search software that is indexing the system, or backup applications constitute *non-vulnerable accesses* as the accessing applications do not interpret the file data in a way that can exercise the unpatched vulnerability. Without memory information flow tracking, P2 will lose accuracy and report non-vulnerable accesses as alerts. Unpatched files may be present on a system and accessed by such applications for a vari-

Instruction	Encoding
jnz 0x46	7544
push [ebp+0x8]	ff7508
call [0x76381004]	ff15**04103876**
push [0x76382018]	68**18203876**
mov [0x76382018],0x94	c705**1820387694**000000

(a) Example instruction sequence. Preferred address = 0x76380000.

Instruction	Encoding
jnz 0x46	7544
push [ebp+0x8]	ff7508
call [0x76382004]	ff15**04203876**
push [0x76383018]	68**18303876**
mov [0x76383018],0x94	c705**1830387694**000000

(b) Relocated instruction sequence at address = 0x76381000.

Figure 2. PE binary relocation.

ety of reasons. For example, Windows keeps copies of old libraries after an update to allow software rollback should the update fail or result in unforeseen problems.

5. Implementation

5.1 Binary file monitoring

5.1.1 Patagonix background

We use Patagonix [17] as a component to build P2. Patagonix is able to detect executing binary code and identify it using a database of known binaries. Patagonix detects code execution by manipulating page table entries in the hypervisor. Page table entries on x86 processors provide three permission bits for each memory page: a readable bit, a writable bit and a non-executable (NX) bit. Patagonix initially sets the NX bit on all memory pages in the guest VM. As a result, whenever the CPU executes code on a page for the first time, a trap is generated and control is transferred to Patagonix. Patagonix then suspends the guest VM and identifies the page that caused the fault. After identifying the binary, Patagonix enables execution on the page by clearing the NX bit and clearing the writable bit so that the page cannot be modified without its knowledge. If the page is subsequently modified, Patagonix makes the page writable and non-executable again. If the new page is executed, Patagonix is again invoked via a trap and will identify the new contents of the page.

To identify the binary from which a page originates, Patagonix uses *identity oracles*. Identity oracles are binary format specific. Patagonix contains oracles for the PE format [19], which is used by all versions of Windows since Windows NT 3.1 and an oracle for the ELF file format [30] used by many UNIX OSs, including Linux. In the PE case, dynamically loaded libraries (DLLs) may be *relocated* at load time, where the OS adjusts absolute addresses in the binary depending on the virtual address the library is loaded at. Consider the example instruction sequence in Figure 2(a). As we can see, the last 3 instructions have absolute addresses, which appear in the encoded format of the instructions (note that x86 byte order causes the bytes to appear in reverse order). Every DLL has a *preferred address*, which is the default address that all such absolute references assume the binary is loaded at. If it is loaded at any address other than the default address, the loader must adjust all absolute addresses in the binary by the difference. In Figure 2(b), the binary was loaded at address 0x76380000, which is 0x1000 more than the preferred address. As a result, all absolute addresses are also increased by 0x1000.

Since relocation causes the image of the binary in memory to be different from the image on disk, the Patagonix identity oracle must undo the relocations that were applied when the binary was loaded. To do this, Patagonix leverages the insight that all DLLs have a small number of entry points, which must be executed before any other code in the library. The offsets from the start of a memory page of these entry points are invariant under relocation and thus can be used to serve as identifier hints for the DLL. These hints enable Patagonix to narrow down the number of possible DLLs to just a small number, at which point Patagonix can identify the bytes in the page that correspond to relocated absolute addresses, undo the relocations and then check the true identity of the memory page.

Unfortunately, the entry point method only works if Patagonix is active at the time that the entry point is executed. If Patagonix is applied to a VM after resuming from a checkpoint, some applications will be in mid-execution. As a result, Patagonix will have missed the execution of the entry points for these applications and thus fail at identifying the binary. When Patagonix does fail in this way, P2 invokes its identification method based on *address inference* to identify the locations of absolute addresses in the page and undo the relocations on them, thus allowing the page to be identified.

5.1.2 P2 binary identification

To undo relocations in a page of binary code, P2 must infer which bytes in the page may be absolute addresses. To do this, we make the observation that absolute addresses used in a binary must fall within the binary itself. Let S be the size of the binary, and a, the address at which the code execution is detected. Since we know that a points to valid code and a is somewhere within a binary of size S, then all absolute addresses in the code segment of the binary must fall within the range $[a - S, a + S]$.

While we do not know S, we can use the size of the largest binary in the database, s, as an upper-bound for S (i.e. $S \leq s$). P2 then identifies any sequence of 4 bytes that fall within the range $[a - s, a + s]$ as a *candidate address*. When a RISC design is used, instructions are aligned and have fixed sized op-codes. However, there is no alignment restriction for x86 instructions, and instruction op-codes have a variable length. As a result, it is not possible to identify which part of the page consists of operands and which part of the page consists of instructions. Thus, P2 considers all overlapping 4-byte sequences on the page. For example, in the example in Figure 2(a), if s is 4MB, this would give a range of addresses from 0x75c00000 to 0x76400000. This would cause the three absolute addresses, as well as the first 4 bytes (0x75ff4475) to be identified as candidate addresses in the sequence of bytes. While the last three are true addresses, the first 4 bytes is a *false inference* because it just happens to fall within the right range, but is not really an address. To get an idea of the likelihood of such a false inference in general, assume that the byte values in the page are randomly distributed. The probability that a 4-byte candidate address will happen to fall within the range $[a - s, a + s]$ is given by:

$$p = \frac{2 * s}{2^{32}}$$

We remark that this probability increases linearly with s and that this is only an estimate, as code bytes are not randomly distributed. For example, if we use 4 MB for s, we get a 0.002 probability that a candidate address is not actually an absolute address.

To identify the binary from which the code originates, P2 makes a copy of the byte sequence and sets all candidate addresses to zero. A hash of this sequence is then computed and checked against the database of binaries, which contains hashes of sequences where the absolute addresses have also been set to zero. To address false

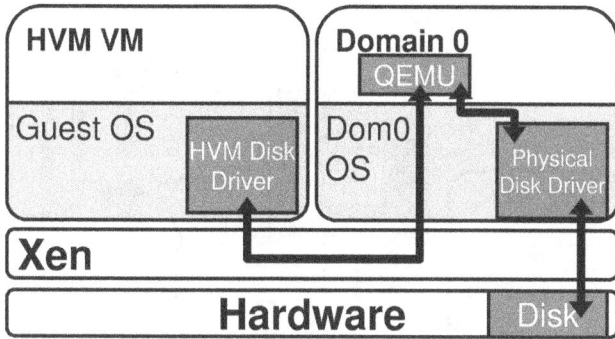

Figure 3. Basic virtual disk architecture for Xen HVM VMs.

inferences, P2 considers all subsets of the candidate addresses (i.e., the power set $\mathcal{P}$ of candidate addresses). This results in 2^k possibilities, where k is the number of candidate addresses. P2 starts by zeroing out all candidate addresses and searching for a match in the binary database. If no match occurs, it then tries all combinations where one candidate address is not zeroed out, then two candidate addresses and so on. The search stops as soon as the sequence is matched with a binary in the database. However, in the worst case, 2^k combinations need to be tested.

Since a page consists of 4096 bytes, k could be as large as 4096, causing 2^k to be extremely large. This would make the algorithm intractable. Rather than consider the entire page, P2 considers only substrings of length l within the page. Only considering substrings also enables P2 to handle pages that contain both code and data. l should be chosen so that strings will have a small number of candidates but be long enough to occur only in at most a few binaries. In our implementation of P2, we used l=64 bytes.

The l-length substrings should be taken at several offsets to provide a spread of offsets throughout the page so that at least one will fall in a code region should a page contain a mix of code and data. At the same time, none of the substrings should straddle a page boundary. In our implementation, we use offsets o in the following order: 0x3; 0x1000 - 0x3 - l; 0x103 + i*0x100, $i \in [0, 14]$. The code database is augmented with an index that contains hashes of the first l-length string at offset o in each binary. The database construction procedure searches for this string by trying different o's in the order given above.

During identification, all combinations of candidate addresses are searched. If a match occurs, then all relocations in the page are undone and a hash over the entire page is computed and checked to verify that the match is indeed correct. Because the hashes on the substrings are taken frequently, our implementation uses the non-cryptographic, fast murmur2 hash [1] for the hash on the substring and a sha256 hash on the whole page to verify the match. The complete process for trying the candidate addresses is summarized in Algorithm 1.

5.2 Non-binary file monitoring

P2's file execution monitor has two components. The first component is a disk monitor that listens on requests to the virtual disk and detects accesses to unpatched non-binary files. The second component is the memory tracking component, which tracks the flow of data from unpatched files through the guest OS. We give some background on Xen's virtual disk architecture and then describe the two components in turn.

Algorithm 1 The P2 binary identification algorithm.

> **function** identify_code(string *code*, int *a*, int *l*, int *s*)
> *offset_list* = [0x3, 0x1000 - 0x3 -l, 0x103, ..., 0xf03]
> **for** *offset* $\in$ *offset_list* **do**
>   *candidates* $\leftarrow \emptyset$
>   **for** $i \in [0, l + 3]$ **do**
>   *value* = integer value of 4-byte sequence of *code* from *offset*+i − 3 to *offset*+i
>   **if** *value* $\in [a - s, a + s]$ **then**
>   *candidates* $\leftarrow i$
>   **end if**
>   **end for**
>   **for** *candidate_set* $\in \mathcal{P}$(*candidates*) **do**
>   *candidate_string* $\leftarrow$ *code*[*offset..offset*+l[with sequences in *candidate_set* zeroed out
>   *hash* $\leftarrow$ hash of *candidate_string*
>   **if** *hash* is in database **then**
>   *candidate_pages* $\leftarrow$ pages in index that match *hash*
>   **for** *candidate_page* $\in$ *candidate_pages* **do**
>   *relocated_code* $\leftarrow$ *code* with relocations undone according to *candidate_page* relocation information.
>   **if** hash of *candidate_page* stored in database == hash of *relocated_code* **then**
>   **return** binary
>   **end if**
>   **end for**
>   **end if**
>   **end for**
> **end for**

5.2.1 Xen virtual disk background

In a virtualized environment, persistent storage is provided by virtual block devices. Figure 3 illustrates the Xen virtual disk architecture. In Xen Hardware Virtual Machines (HVM), virtual block devices are emulated using a user space QEMU process that runs in domain 0, which is a special VM that has access to the physical devices on the machine. The QEMU process faithfully emulates a physical disk in software. When the guest OS device driver sends DMA requests to the virtual disk, it is intercepted by Xen and forwarded to the QEMU disk emulator in domain 0. QEMU services the requests by accessing the physical disk and responding to the guest OS via Xen. It is possible to improve virtual I/O performance by inserting a custom paravirtualized (PV) disk driver into the guest OS. PV disk drivers are Xen-aware, thus saving domain 0 from having to emulate a physical disk and allowing direct communication between the guest OS driver and the Domain 0 physical disk driver. We could have implemented P2 to support both HVM and PV, but for simplicity, our prototype currently only supports HVM drivers.

The P2 disk monitor assumes that the file system block size is the same as the memory page size (4096 bytes), which is true for all major file systems today. Hard drives currently use a sector size of 512 bytes, which is the smallest addressable chunk of data that can be read from the disk. The memory page size for the x86 architecture is 4096 bytes. Since the sector size is smaller than the memory page size, it is possible that a single memory page could contain data from several different files. However, no file system we know of uses this capability. Instead, file systems match their minimum addressable block size with that of the CPU memory system for simplicity and efficiency. In response to this trend, hard drive manufacturers have agreed on a new standard [7], which specifies that all disks will eventually use a sector size of 4096 bytes instead of 512 bytes.

5.2.2 Disk monitor

The architecture of P2's file monitoring system is summarized in Figure 4, which shows the disk monitor, memory tracking component and binary file monitor from Section 5.1. The purpose of the disk monitor is to detect when an unpatched non-binary file is read and convey the address of the access, and the identity and associated interpreters of the file to the memory tracking component. As a result, the most natural place to implement disk monitoring is in the domain 0 QEMU disk emulator. The unpatched non-binary database contains the identity of each unpatched file and the associated interpreter(s) that can make vulnerable accesses to the file. These entries are indexed by hash values computed over each block-sized chunk of the file. On each disk access, the P2 disk monitor computes a hash of the block being read and searches the index in the unpatched non-binary database. If there is a hit, the disk monitor informs the memory tracking component of the physical address that the disk data will be read to. The disk monitor is able to get the destination address from the DMA request protocol, which includes this information. The disk monitor also conveys the identity of the file as well as the identity of the associated interpreters.

Two cases deserve special attention in the disk monitor: files may be smaller than a single 4096 block and some blocks appear in more than one file. For each unpatched non-binary file, the database stores a hash of a sub-block prefix of each block of the file along with the amount of space occupied by the file in this block in a *block prefix index*. The disk monitor first computes a non-cryptographic hash of this prefix and searches the block prefix index for a match. If there is a hit in the block prefix index, either a hash of the remainder of the block is taken if the file occupies the entire block, or a hash of the portion of the block that is occupied by the file is taken if the file does not occupy the entire block. This serves to verify that the file is indeed a match. If multiple files exist for a given prefix, then each candidate needs to be tested individually until a match is found. The length of the prefix is chosen to minimize the chances of a collision while retaining the ability to handle even very small files. P2 uses a prefix length of 64 bytes. As a result, only files smaller than 64 bytes cannot be handled. In our patch study, there were 32 files out of a combined 17351 files across both Fedora Core 10 and 11 that were less than 64 bytes. Due to their short length and simplicity, we also believe they are unlikely to contain security vulnerabilities. Use of the prefix index means that for the majority of blocks read from the disk which do not contain data from unpatched, non-binary files only a short prefix of the block needs to be hashed before P2 can establish that the block does not contain data that needs to be tracked.

To handle cases where a file block appears in multiple files, the disk monitor conveys the set of non-binary files that could have matched and the monitor component will apply the union of the associated interpreters in its checking. While rare, we have observed that different files do occasionally have exactly matching 4096 byte chunks.

5.2.3 Memory tracking component

The memory tracking component is implemented in the Xen hypervisor. When the memory tracking component is notified of an access to an unpatched non-binary file it clears the "present" bit of the corresponding page table entries in the shadow page tables, thus causing the processor to fault anytime the page containing unpatched file data is accessed. It also marks the page as *tracked* so that when a fault occurs on that page, the Xen hypervisor knows to invoke the P2 memory tracking component. In addition, if the guest OS creates new mappings to a tracked page, the Xen hypervisor will also clear the present bit on the new mappings in the shadow page table.

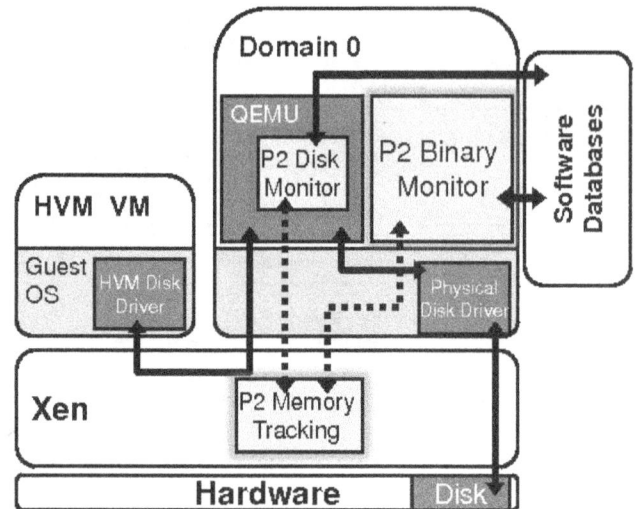

Figure 4. P2 non-binary file monitoring additions to Xen.

If and when a fault to a tracked page occurs, the P2 memory tracking component is invoked by Xen. P2 will inspect the instruction that caused the trap. The instruction can be either in the guest kernel or in a user space process in the guest VM. If the instruction is in the guest kernel, then the file data is being accessed by a process via a system call such as `read`. In this case, P2 inspects the instruction and verifies that the instruction is copying data from the tracked page into the user space process. If the trapping instruction is in a user-space process, then the file data has been mapped into the address space of the user space process. Thus, P2 can infer that the file data has flowed into the address space of a particular process. In either case, the memory tracking component has inferred that an unpatched non-binary file has been read into a user space process.

At this time, the memory tracking component queries the P2 binary file monitor, which tracks executing interpreters. If the current context (read from the `CR3 register`) matches that of a currently executing interpreter that can make a vulnerable access, P2 raises an alert. If running in reporting mode, P2 simply reports the vulnerable access to the cloud administrator. On the other hand, if P2 is running in prevention mode, then it will terminate the interpreter as described in Section 5.3.

If the accessing process is not a vulnerable interpreter, or is allowed to proceed because P2 is operating in reporting mode, then P2 allows the access to the tracked page to proceed by marking the page as present. It maintains this present marking until the content of the CR3 is changed by the guest OS, indicating a context switch. At this point, the memory tracking component must clear the present bit so that it can detect accesses by other processes. Since multiple traps may take place between two context switches, the tracking component maintains a list of page table entries that need to have their "present" bit cleared upon the next context switch.

In addition to detecting when a tracked page is being accessed, P2 needs to detect when the memory page no longer contains unpatched file data and no longer needs to be tracked. This may occur as a result of two events: the guest VM modified the content of the memory page, or it requested that a virtual device performs a DMA transfer to the memory page. To detect the first scenario, the tracking component clears the "writable" bit on any tracked page. As a result, when the page is written to, either because the page is being reused by the kernel for a different purpose or because the page content is being modified, a page fault will occur upon access. At this point, P2 clears the tracked flag from the page and stops tracking it.

To detect DMA transfers, we extend the disk monitor to inform the memory tracking component on every DMA transfer, not just the ones to unpatched files. DMA transfers of regular patched files are not tracked, but if they overwrite a tracked page, this will cause P2 to stop tracking the overwritten page.

5.3 Prevention mode

When running in prevention mode, P2 is in a position to prevent any unpatched code from executing. P2 does this with as few side-effects as possible. If the unpatched code is a binary, then P2 replaces the instruction at the faulting address with an illegal instruction. When the guest VM is resumed, the application will execute the illegal instruction causing an OS fault, and the guest OS will terminate the application cleanly.

If the unpatched code is a non-binary file, P2 must terminate the associated interpreter that is making a vulnerable access to the file. If the access occurred from user space because the file is mapped into the interpreter address space, P2 inserts an illegal instruction at the address that caused the trap and restarts the process just like above. However, if the accessed occurred from within the kernel, P2 cannot insert illegal instructions into the kernel as this would terminate the entire VM. Instead, P2 allows the access to complete but sets the entire user space address range to non-executable. When the guest OS returns to user space, a fault will be generated, at which time P2 can inject an illegal instruction and have the guest OS terminate the interpreter.

6. Evaluation

We evaluated P2's effectiveness at detecting unpatched applications and the performance overhead P2's monitoring introduces. All experiments were conducted on an AMD Athlon 64 X2 Dual Core 3800+ processor running at 2GHz, with 2GB of RAM. We used the Xen 3.3.0 VMM and allocated 512MB of RAM to the monitored VM and 1GB to the domain 0 VM. We pinned the domain 0 VM to the first core and the monitored VM to the second core to minimize VM scheduling effects. To demonstrate P2's OS-agnostic quality, unless otherwise stated, all tests were run on both Windows and Linux VMs. The Windows VM runs Windows XP SP2. The Linux VM is a Fedora Core 9 distribution with a 2.6.27.25 Linux kernel. Timing was recorded using an external time server to eliminate clock skew introduced by the hypervisor.

6.1 Effectiveness

We evaluated P2's ability to detect unpatched binary and non-binary code. To evaluate the ability of P2 to detect the execution of binary code, we ran P2 and compared the binaries it reports as running with that returned by the Task Manager. We also suspended and resumed the VMs several times and inspected the reported binaries. In all cases, P2 accurately listed the exact same executing binaries as the respective Linux and Windows tools. This shows that P2 can accurately identify the exact binary that is executing. We also installed both patched and unpatched versions of Apache in both Windows and Linux and executed both. P2 was able to differentiate the execution of the patched version from the unpatched one.

Next, we evaluated the effectiveness of P2 at detecting the execution of non-binary code. To do this, P2 must properly detect access to unpatched files and correctly attribute these accesses to the appropriate interpreter or JIT compiler. We placed a unique ruby script in each directory on the file system (4161 ruby scripts on Windows and 10268 ruby scripts on Linux). To see if P2 cor-

Setting	Vanilla	P2	P2, non-binary disabled
Linux	436.9s	455.8s (4.3%)	460.9s (5.5%)
Windows	581.3s	605.2s (4.1%)	617.7s (6.3%)

Table 3. Compilation time for Apache (overhead).

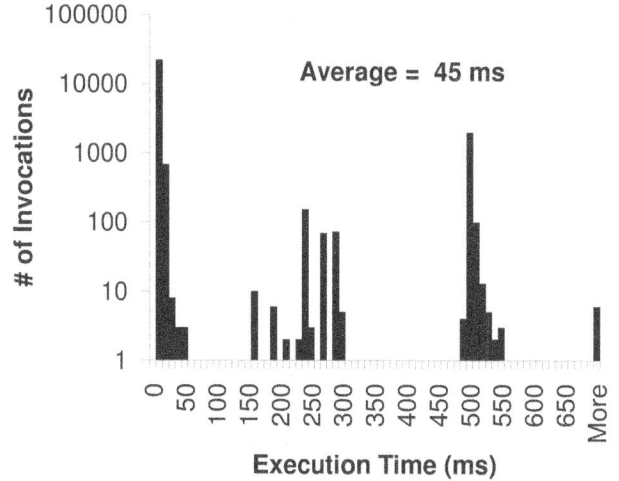

Figure 5. Histogram of P2 binary identification execution times.

rectly attributes the accesses to the correct application, we simultaneously run an anti-virus scanner (ClamAV 0.95.2 on Linux and Symantec 10.1.5 on Windows) and a specially crafted application that would randomly execute one of the ruby scripts every second. In both cases, P2 was able to identify exactly which scripts were accessed by which application and in what order, demonstrating its accuracy. In addition P2, does not miss any access, showing that it is continuous.

To test whether stress on the OS's buffer cache might affect P2's accuracy, we generated load on the system by creating an extension that would cause the Firefox web browser on our test system to randomly crawl websites, thus creating churn in its web cache. We did this at the same time as running the test above. Again, P2 attributed all accesses correctly. In addition, no access to any script was recorded for Firefox or any other application running on the system.

6.2 Performance

P2 is invoked when new code is executed, when data is read from disk into the OS buffer cache and when data in the buffer cache is read by a process. To evaluate the overall performance impact of P2, we measured the time required to compile the Apache web server on both Windows and Linux. In each case, we ran P2 with an unpatched database containing 20,532 entries and comprehensive patched and interpreter databases. We ran P2 twice, once auditing both unpatched binary and non-binary files and again with non-binary file auditing disabled. The results are tabulated in Table 3. In both the Linux and the Windows cases, the overall overhead of P2 was 4% (mean of 4 runs, standard deviation under 1% of the mean). Performance of P2 was actually slightly worse when monitoring only unpatched binaries, but the difference is comparable to measurement error in our system. Thus, we surmise that the majority of the overhead is imposed by the auditing and identification of executing binaries.

P2 binary identification is only invoked when the Patagonix identity oracle fails to identify an executing binary. To evaluate its overhead separately from the overhead of the Patagonix identity oracle, we instrumented the P2 binary identification component to measure both the number of times it is invoked after a VM resumes and the amount of time it takes to identify a binary each time it is invoked. We then perform the Apache compile and suspend the execution of a Windows VM compiling Apache at 1 minute and 2 minute intervals. We found that on average, the P2 algorithm was invoked an average of 46 times with a standard deviation of 2.5 when using a 1 minute interval, and an average of 48 times with a standard deviation of 3 when using a 2 minute interval. This illustrates that few invocations of the P2 algorithm are necessary when resuming a suspended machine. This is because at most one invocation is necessary per binary file that was in the process of being executed when the machine was suspended. The execution time of the P2 binary identification is essentially determined by the number of iterations of the two nested for loops in the algorithm, which are bounded by the number of candidate addresses that are wrongly inferred and the number of offsets that must be attempted. We graph a histogram of execution times in Figure 5. Note that the y-axis is logarithmic. While the execution times vary widely, there are two dominant cases, illustrated by the two peaks centered around 31 ms and 501 ms. The overall average execution time of the P2 binary identification algorithm is 45 ± 143 ms. As a result, combining the average run time of the P2 binary identification algorithm and the average number of times it needs to be invoked, we surmise that P2 adds an average of 3 seconds of overhead every time a VM is resumed.

To more accurately measure the overhead of non-binary file auditing, we evaluate it in isolation. We ran a micro-benchmark that sequentially read 2 GB of data from the disk to measure the disk transfer rate. The vanilla transfer rate was 79 MB/s (mean of 10 runs, standard deviation under 1% of mean) and 78 MB/s with auditing. To assess the impact of the software database size on the file monitoring overhead, we reran the benchmark with a larger database containing 1,252,977 entries. The transfer rate in this scenario dropped slightly to 63 MB/s since more time was required to query the database on each disk access. The modest overhead incurred by file monitoring on transfer rates explains why no noticeable overhead is introduced on a macro-benchmark such as compiling Apache.

7. Related Work

Virtual machine introspection is used to bridge the *semantic gap* [6], which exists between the hypervisor and software running in guest VMs. Many systems have used introspection in the past to bridge this gap. One of the first, Livewire [11], implements intrusion detection from the hypervisor, but required detailed, implementation-specific information on the location of code and data within the guest VM software. Introvirt [16] extends the concept to be able to detect intrusions that have occurred in the past. VMWatcher [14], uses introspection to enable standard anti-virus tools to be run on VMs from within the hypervisor. SBCFI [25] takes a different approach and uses hypervisor privileges to enforce control-flow integrity on the guest OS kernel. Finally, Patagonix [17], on which P2 is based, identifies covertly-executing binaries in guest VMs in a way that is OS-agnostic. P2 is different from these previous systems in two ways. First, all previous approaches are restricted to monitoring binary code, while P2 is capable of monitoring non-binary code as well. Second, all previous approaches focus on detecting intrusions or malicious code. P2 takes a pro-active approach and tries to detect and prevent unpatched software with known vulnerabilities from executing and exposing the system to attack.

Hypervisors have been used for security in general for a number of systems. Hypervisors offer a smaller trusted computing base,

and higher privileges, making them an attractive platform for implementing security. Terra [12] used a hypervisor to perform attestation for individual VMs, thus isolating attested high integrity code from unattested low-integrity code. Proxos [29], extended this idea to permit isolated applications to communicate with other VMs in a controlled way. There has also been recent research in using hypervisors to monitor and control what code executes in the kernel. SecVisor [27] is a small hypervisor with fewer than 2000 lines of code, which can verify the integrity of code executing in the kernel.

Dynamic information flow tracking (DIFT) and related taint tracking techniques have been extensively used to improve security. Suh et al. [28] and Taintcheck [22] both use taint tracking to detect corruption of critical pointers with external data. Suh's method requires specialized hardware but has low runtime overhead. Taintcheck uses a software-only method, but suffers from overheads of 30x or greater. Recently, Chang et al. [5] applied compiler analysis to optimize away some of the instrumentation required to perform taint tracking, achieving runtime overheads less than 13% without any specialized hardware. However, their compiler pass requires source code to perform the optimizations and instrument the program. Dalton et al. [9] introduce more complex security policies and a pointer identification algorithm to improve the accuracy of taint tracking. However, their technique requires specialized hardware to be added to the processor to be practical. P2 differs from previous uses of taint tracking for security in two respects. First, P2 uses taint tracking to determine if a non-binary file is accessed in an unsafe way while previous systems used taint tracking to detect attacks. Second, because P2's goals are different, P2 only needs to track taint at a page granularity, which allows it to leverage the processor MMU to monitor accesses to tainted data. This makes P2 far more efficient, allowing it to achieve low overheads without source code changes or special hardware.

Recently, information flow tracking was leveraged by Ho et al. [13] in a virtualization context to track data originating from the network in a virtualized environment. This allows the proposed system to determine if a VM ever attempts to execute data originating from the network. Like P2, page table manipulations are used to track tainted data at the page granularity. However, once tainted pages are accessed, the system switches to byte-level granularity and starts running VMs in an emulator, resulting in significant performance overhead. Because P2 uses coarse taint tracking, code can execute natively on the processor, resulting in modest performance overheads.

Finally, in a non-security context, others have also leveraged hypervisor virtualization of the MMU and disk to monitor systems. monitor the interaction between VMs and storage. Geiger [15] manipulates page table entries to detect evictions from the OS's buffer cache. This information allows optimizing memory allocations to VMs and helps implement a second-level buffer cache maintained by the VMM. Satori [20] hashes all disk content accessed by VMs to identify sharing opportunities between VMs to reduce memory consumption.

8. Conclusion

We have demonstrated that while virtualization has the potential to exacerbate the problem of patch management, it also offers capabilities to improve it. By monitoring only the virtual hardware interface, P2 is able to efficiently, accurately and continuously audit the use of unpatched code in both Linux and Windows systems. While previous systems that implement information flow tracking at the byte or word granularity have prohibitive overheads, P2 takes advantage of the fact that it does not need such fine-granularity. We find that by tracking information flow at a page-level granularity that matches that of the hardware MMU, P2 is able to infer the execution of non-binary code with very little overhead. This allows P2 to accurately detect unsafe uses of unpatched non-binary files.

We also find that to overcome Patagonix's inability to identify binaries in mid-execution, P2 must adopt a more expensive sampling-based approach to infer addresses. Our evaluation concludes that while P2's binary identification requires several milliseconds on average, it can have wide range of execution times. We are able to mitigate this shortcoming by combining P2 and Patagonix into a single system that achieves good performance equivalent to Patagonix, but does not suffer from the limitation of not being able to identify binaries that have already started execution. With its applicability across common commodity OSs, low overhead and high accuracy, we believe P2 is a practical solution to help IaaS cloud providers audit the patch level of VMs running on their infrastructure.

Acknowledgements

Support for the work in this paper was provided by the NSERC ISSNet Strategic Network and an Ontario MRI Early Researcher Award.

References

[1] A. Appleby. MurmurHash 2.0, 2010. http://murmurhash.googlepages.com/.

[2] S. Beattie, S. Arnold, C. Cowan, P. Wagle, C. Wright, and A. Shostack. Timing the application of security patches for optimal uptime. In *Proceedings of the 15th Large Installation Systems Administration Conference (LISA)*, pages 233–242, Nov. 2002.

[3] A. Bellissimo, J. Burgess, and K. Fu. Secure software updates: Disappointments and new challenges. In *Proceedings of the 1st Usenix Workshop on Hot Topics in Security (HOTSEC)*, July 2006.

[4] D. Brumley, P. Poosankam, D. Song, and J. Zheng. Automatic patch-based exploit generation is possible: Techniques and implications. In *Proceedings of the 2008 IEEE Symposium on Security and Privacy*, May 2008.

[5] W. Chang, B. Streiff, and C. Lin. Efficient and extensible security enforcement using dynamic data flow analysis. In *Proceedings of the 15th ACM Conference on Computer and Communications Security (CCS 2008)*, Oct. 2008.

[6] P. M. Chen and B. D. Noble. When virtual is better than real. In *The 8th Workshop on Hot Topics in Operating Systems (HotOS 2001)*, pages 133–138, May 2001.

[7] P. Chicoine, M. Hassner, M. Noblitt, G. Silvus, B. Weber, and E. Grochowski. Hard disk drive long data sector white paper. Technical report, The International Disk Drive Equipment and Materials Association (IDEMA), Apr. 2007.

[8] Citrix XenClient, 2010. http://www.citrix.com/xenclient.

[9] M. Dalton, H. Kannan, and C. Kozyrakis. Real-world buffer overflow protection for userspace and kernelspace. In *Proceedings of the 17th USENIX Security Symposium*, pages 395–410, July 2008.

[10] T. Garfinkel and M. Rosenblum. When virtual is harder than real: Security challenges in virtual machine based computing environments. In *The 10th Workshop on Hot Topics in Operating Systems (HotOS 2005)*, May 2005.

[11] T. Garfinkel and M. Rosenblum. A virtual machine introspection based architecture for intrusion detection. In *Proceedings of the 10th Symposium on Network and Distributed System Security (NDSS)*, pages 191–206, Feb. 2003.

[12] T. Garfinkel, B. Pfaff, J. Chow, M. Rosenblum, and D. Boneh. Terra: A virtual machine-based platform for trusted computing. In *Proceedings of the 19th ACM Symposium on Operating Systems Principles (SOSP)*, pages 193–206, Oct. 2003.

[13] A. Ho, M. Fetterman, C. Clark, A. Warfield, and S. Hand. Practical taint-based protection. In *Proceedings of the First European Conference on Systems (EuroSys)*, Apr. 2006.

[14] X. Jiang, X. Wang, and D. Xu. Stealthy malware detection through VMM-based "out-of-the-box" semantic view reconstruction. In *Proceedings of the 14th ACM Conference on Computer and Communications Security (CCS 2007)*, pages 128–138, Oct. 2007.

[15] S. T. Jones, A. C. Arpaci-Dusseau, and R. H. Arpaci-Dusseau. Geiger: Monitoring the buffer cache in a virtual machine environment. In *Proceedings of the 12th International Conference on Architectural Support for Programming Languages and Operating Systems (ASPLOS)*, pages 14–24, Oct. 2006.

[16] A. Joshi, S. T. King, G. W. Dunlap, and P. M. Chen. Detecting past and present intrusions through vulnerability-specific predicates. In *Proceedings of the 20th ACM Symposium on Operating Systems Principles (SOSP)*, pages 91–104, Oct. 2005.

[17] L. Litty, H. A. Lagar-Cavilla, and D. Lie. Hypervisor support for identifying covertly executing binaries. In *Proceedings of the 17th USENIX Security Symposium*, July 2008.

[18] L. Litty, H. A. Lagar-Cavilla, and D. Lie. Computer meteorology: Monitoring compute clouds. In *The 12th Workshop on Hot Topics in Operating Systems (HotOS 2009)*, May 2009.

[19] Microsoft. Visual Studio, Microsoft Portable Executable and Common Object File Format specification, May 2006. URL http://www.microsoft.com/whdc/system/platform/firmware/PECOFF.mspx. Rev. 8.0.

[20] G. Miłoś, D. G. Murray, S. Hand, and M. Fetterman. Satori: Enlightened page sharing. In *Proceedings of the 2009 Annual Usenix Technical Conference*, July 2009.

[21] Nessus, Tenable Network Security, 2010. http://www.nessus.org.

[22] J. Newsome and D. Song. Dynamic taint analysis: Automatic detection, analysis, and signature generation of exploit attacks on commodity software. In *Proceedings of the 12th Symposium on Network and Distributed System Security (NDSS)*, Feb. 2005.

[23] NIST. National software reference library, 2010. http://www.nsrl.nist.gov/.

[24] P. Nowak. Internet security moving toward "white list", Sept. 2007. Available at http://www.cbc.ca/news/background/tech/privacy/white-list.html.

[25] N. L. Petroni, Jr. and M. Hicks. Automated detection of persistent kernel control-flow attacks. In *Proceedings of the 14th ACM Conference on Computer and Communications Security (CCS 2007)*, pages 103–115, Oct. 2007.

[26] T. Ristenpart, E. Tromer, H. Shacham, and S. Savage. Hey, you, get off of my cloud: Exploring information leakage in third-party compute clouds. In *Proceedings of the 16th ACM Conference on Computer and Communications Security (CCS 2009)*, pages 199–212, Nov. 2009.

[27] A. Seshadri, M. Luk, N. Qu, and A. Perrig. SecVisor: A tiny hypervisor to provide lifetime kernel code integrity for commodity OSes. In *Proceedings of the 21st ACM Symposium on Operating Systems Principles (SOSP)*, Oct. 2007.

[28] G. E. Suh, J.-W. Lee, D. Zhang, and S. Devadas. Secure program execution via dynamic information flow tracking. In *Proceedings of the 11th International Conference on Architectural Support for Programming Languages and Operating Systems (ASPLOS)*, Oct. 2004.

[29] R. Ta-Min, L. Litty, and D. Lie. Splitting interfaces: Making trust between applications and operating systems configurable. In *Proceedings of the 7th Symposium on Operating Systems Design and Implementation (OSDI)*, pages 279–292, Nov. 2006.

[30] TIS Committee. Tool Interface Standard (TIS) Executable and Linking Format (ELF) specification, May 1995. V1.2.

[31] VersionTracker. VersionTracker, 2010. http://versiontracker.com/.

[32] VMware View, 2010. http://www.vmware.com/products/view.

Fine-Grained User-Space Security Through Virtualization

Mathias Payer

mathias.payer@inf.ethz.ch
ETH Zurich, Switzerland

Thomas R. Gross

trg@inf.ethz.ch
ETH Zurich, Switzerland

Abstract

This paper presents an approach to the safe execution of applications based on *software-based fault isolation* and *policy-based system call authorization*. A running application is encapsulated in an additional layer of protection using dynamic binary translation in user-space. This virtualization layer dynamically recompiles the machine code and adds multiple dynamic security guards that verify the running code to protect and contain the application.

The binary translation system redirects all system calls to a policy-based system call authorization framework. This interposition framework validates every system call based on the given arguments and the location of the system call. Depending on the user-loadable policy and an extensible handler mechanism the framework decides whether a system call is allowed, rejected, or redirect to a specific user-space handler in the virtualization layer.

This paper offers an in-depth analysis of the different security guarantees and a performance analysis of libdetox, a prototype of the full protection platform. The combination of *software-based fault isolation* and *policy-based system call authorization* imposes only low overhead and is therefore an attractive option to encapsulate and sandbox applications to improve host security.

Categories and Subject Descriptors D.4.6 [*Operating Systems*]: Security and Protection; D.3.4 [*Programming Languages*]: Processors — Run-time environments

General Terms Security, Performance

Keywords Security, Virtualization, Dynamic binary translation, Dynamic instrumentation, User-space software virtualization, Process sandboxing, Policy-based system call authorization, Optimization.

1. Introduction

The secure execution of unknown binary code is an important problem. As the complexity and diversity of the installed software base increases, more techniques are needed to guarantee the security of a system. Software patches in response to identified exploits or malware discovery tools are useful, yet both approaches are reactive (and solutions or workarounds for vulnerabilities may take time to develop) and are therefore of limited utility. A better solution is a step towards proactive security and fault detection by strictly limiting the potential damage that can be done.

To contain security problems in a practical system, it is important to encapsulate applications and to limit the data they can access. An application running in a user-space sandbox can access its data but cannot break out of the virtualization layer and access any other system data or escalate privileges.

User-space sandboxing builds an additional fine-grained layer of protection around an application. Binary translation enables fine-grained control of the executed instructions and enables additional security guards that can be added dynamically into the compiled code. These guards control all executed instructions inside the sandbox, and check all system calls that interact with the kernel inside the process itself. Instructions that change the control flow of the application are wrapped so that they comply with a tight security model and instructions that branch into the kernel are redirected to a policy-based interposition system. The system calls are checked depending on the name, supplied parameters, and call location. A per-application policy describes the set of system calls that a program can execute and specifies which parameter combinations are allowed for each system call.

The proposed sandbox is completely invisible to the running application. Applications see no functional difference to an untranslated run, so programs cannot detect or circumvent the sandbox.

This paper presents an approach to a fast, secure user-space sandbox that enforces security. The security concept is built on the following two principles:

1. *software-based fault isolation:* the binary translator uses special guards to ensure that only application and library code is translated, that code cannot escape the binary translator, that no injected code on the heap and on the stack is executed, and that all system calls are redirected to the interposition framework.

2. *policy-based system call interposition:* the system call interposition framework ensures that all system calls are checked and validated and that only authorized system calls are executed. A policy controls which arguments and which program locations are allowed for each individual system call.

The sandbox loads a policy file before an application is executed and enforces this policy at runtime. If the user-program executes an illegal system call, illegal code, or tries to execute an unchecked control transfer then the process is terminated by the sandbox.

The policies can contain both white-listing and black-listing of system calls based on system call numbers, locations and arguments. Wildcards can be used to specify groups of arguments. An additional extension are the *redirected system calls*. If a system call is blocked then a fake value can be returned to the user-space program. The user-space program is unable to detect if a real system call or a redirected system call was executed. This feature can be used to analyze untrusted software or to re-implement system calls in user-space. See Figure 1 for an overview of the fault isolation layer and the implementation of fake system calls in user-space.

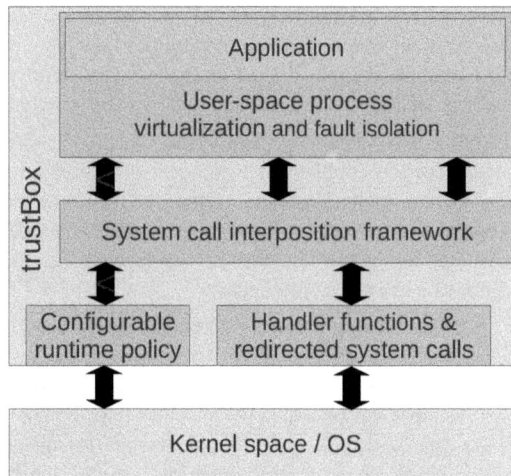

Figure 1. Sandbox overview with user-space fault isolation and delegation to redirected system calls.

The contributions of this paper are the combination of:

1. fine-grained *software-based fault isolation* using special guards that are implemented through binary translation to protect against code injections and the execution of unchecked code,

2. the additional guards that guarantee the fault isolation properties, and

3. flexible per-process user-defined *policy-based system call interposition* in user-space without the need for context switches to validate specific calls and without additional privileged code in the kernel. This paper also presents sample policies to guard the SPEC CPU2006 benchmarks and the nmap network security tool. A case study uses the Apache web-server to secure and benchmark a daemon process.

The presented approach is not limited to Linux or x86. libdetox, our implementation prototype for x86, supports the complete IA-32 ISA. libdetox is able to sandbox unmodified Linux binaries, dynamically add additional security guards, and redirect all system calls to the policy-based system call interposition framework.

Section 2 presents background information on a basic dynamic binary translator. Section 3 discusses security implications and covers process virtualization details as well as the specific guards and explains policy-based system call interposition. Important implementation details are highlighted in Section 4. The system is evalu-

ated in Section 5, followed by a discussion of related work and our conclusion.

2. Dynamic binary translation

This section describes the design of a basic dynamic binary translator that implements software-based fault isolation. The dynamic binary translator processes basic blocks of the original program and places the translated blocks in a code cache. The mapping between untranslated and translated blocks is recorded in a mapping table. Figure 2 illustrates the runtime layout of a basic table-based binary translator.

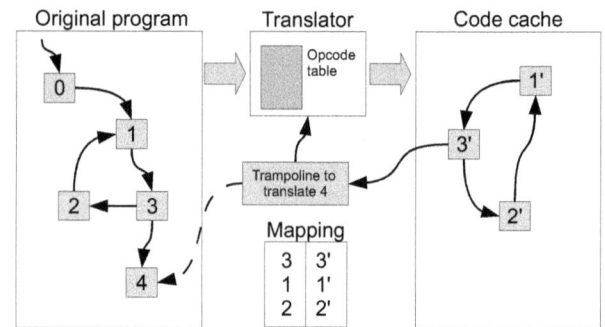

Figure 2. Runtime layout of a binary translator.

At the end of a basic block the translator checks if the outgoing edges are already translated and redirects control transfers to the translated counter parts in the code cache. If a target is not translated then the translator (i) constructs a trampoline that triggers the translation of the corresponding basic block and (ii) redirects control flow to that trampoline.

The translator processes one instruction at a time. Control instructions are translated using special handler functions, all other valid instructions are copied verbatim to the code cache. If the translator encounters an illegal instruction it aborts the program.

Control instructions are translated so that the execution of the translated program never leaves the code cache. For conditional control transfers, jump instructions, and call instructions the translator either constructs a trampoline if the target is not yet translated, or encodes a control transfer to the translated target in the code cache.

Indirect control transfers like indirect jumps, indirect calls, and function returns depend on runtime data and can change upon every execution. The targets of indirect control transfers point to untranslated code. The translator must replace these control transfers with a runtime lookup in the mapping table and a control transfer to the translated counterpart in the code cache. The runtime lookup for each indirect control transfer ensures that control flow is only transferred to well-known and translated locations.

These runtime lookups are responsible for most of the runtime overhead of dynamic binary translators, and most optimizations present in fast binary translators try to reduce this overhead.

3. Security guidelines

Software-based fault isolation is secure if programs are unable to escape the fault isolation sandbox and no code is executed that does not conform to a strict security policy. All executed code and all executed system calls must be checked and verified. If the executed code does not follow the security policy (e.g., due to programming bugs, potential exploits, or backdoors) then the sandbox detects these offenses and terminates the program.

The sandbox uses a layered security concept that builds on two principles, *software-based fault isolation*, and *policy-based system call interposition*. Each principle protects from specific attacks. Process sandboxing through dynamic binary translation is the first line of defense and ensures that (i) no injected code is translated or executed, (ii) application or library code cannot be overwritten, (iii) program code cannot escape or terminate the sandbox, and (iv) program code cannot overwrite any data structures owned by the sandbox. The binary translation framework translates all code before it is executed and uses special guards to ensure that the code conforms to the security specification and that, e.g., control transfers always target valid code. The first principle protects against all code based exploits (e.g., overflows and return to libc attacks).

Process sandboxing builds the foundation for the second security principle. The binary translation framework redirects all forms of system calls to the policy-based system call interposition framework. This framework checks every system call, the arguments of the system call, and the location of the system call. Only system calls that conform to the policy for the current application are allowed. Depending on the policy decision each system call can be:

1. rejected and the program is terminated,

2. rejected but a fake return value is returned,

3. redirected to an internal implementation (for special handling or additional checks),

4. allowed and the program continues.

Process sandboxing ensures that the translated code cannot escape the binary translator and the policy-based interposition framework limits the system calls that can be executed. The second principle protects against data based exploits (e.g., integer overflows and type errors) and builds a second line of defense at the coarse-grained system call level. This policy must be tight to avoid privilege escalation.

For performance reasons, target addresses of individual translated instructions are not checked. User-space software-based fault isolation and the system call interposition framework ensure that a program is unable to execute uncontrolled code and unspecified system calls and lays the power to control system calls and their allowed arguments into the hands of the policy writer.

3.1 Software-based fault isolation

Binary translation (BT) is a key component for user-space software-based fault isolation. A dynamic translation system translates and checks every machine code instruction *before* it is executed. Every direct control transfer is translated, and every indirect control transfer is intercepted and only translated branch targets are reached. The translator can change, adapt, or remove any invalid

instruction and is able to intercept system calls *before* they are executed. During the translation process code can be instrumented and augmented with additional security features. Security features like non-executable stack, stack guards, control flow evaluation, or argument checking for specific functions are added without the need to recompile the application. Even patches can be applied at runtime to fix bugs in running applications.

Fault isolation offers a very fine-grained control of security as all executed code must comply to a defined security policy, not just the executed system calls. Security frameworks that validate only bare system calls miss exploits that target the data integrity of the executed program because they only detect an intrusion if an invalid system call is executed but not when malicious code is executed in user-space; e.g., data can be written to open files or a memory mapped file can be changed without the need to execute a system call. Fault isolation detects code injections and terminates the program before the data structures are corrupted. Data-based exploits on the other hand are not detectable by fault isolation and are caught using policy-based system call interposition.

The binary translator is the foundation of the security guarantees of the presented sandbox. The binary translator should be modular and small to keep the trusted computing base small. This section presents design criteria for a modular and flexible binary translation fault isolation layer that is needed to implement the additional security guards and *system call authorization*. An important feature of the binary translator is that return addresses on the stack remain unchanged. This adds additional complexity when handling return instructions as they are translated to a lookup and an indirect control transfer. On the other hand an unchanged stack ensures that the original program can use the return instruction pointer on the stack for (i) exception management, (ii) debugging, and (iii) return trampolines. Additionally the user program does not know that it runs in a virtualized environment, and the address of the code cache is only known by the binary translator.

3.1.1 Translated code

Only translated application and library code is executed. This principle is enforced by the binary translator. By rewriting indirect control transfers into a runtime lookup and dispatch and adding trampolines to translate untranslated code on the fly, the translator ensures that execution of machine code is unable to escape the isolation layer. All outgoing edges of translated basic blocks either point to (i) trampolines that translate new code, (ii) translated code in the BT's code cache, or (iii) translated indirect control transfers that map untranslated targets to translated code and transfer execution flow accordingly. Only code in valid locations (e.g., imported library functions and application code) is translated. This principle ensures that no code injections on the heap or on the stack are possible.

3.1.2 Binary translation: static versus dynamic

The most important property of a binary translator is to ensure that all instructions are checked and translated prior to execution. Static binary translation is not able to cover all code. Hidden code in data sections could be reached through indirect jumps or a jump could target into an instruction. Such control transfers are hard to analyze statically, especially if malicious code targets a specific binary translator, but are handled naturally in dynamic binary translators that translate code on a basic block level before the basic block is executed the first time.

Dynamic binary translator are therefore well suited to implement user-space software-based fault isolation.

3.1.3 Additional security guards

Binary translation guarantees that only translated instructions will be executed but does not prevent individual instructions from overwriting memory regions or executing specific system calls. Dynamic binary translation enables the implementation of additional security guards by rewriting and encapsulating specific instructions.

An important feature of the binary translator is that no pointers to internal data structures are left on the stack. The binary translator uses the same stack as the translated user-program to dynamically translate new basic blocks and dispatch indirect control transfers. A custom tailored exploit could target the binary translator itself. If the program were able to locate the internal data structures of the binary translator (e.g., the code cache), it could modify the executed code by directly changing instructions in the code cache and so break out of the isolation layer. Therefore the stack is pruned of pointers to internal data structures before the execution returns to the translated user-program. Additionally the translator guarantees that application code that tries to access internal data structures is not translated by virtualizing, e.g., addresses or registers.

The basic binary translator is extended by the following security guards that harden the user-space isolation sandbox and to ensure that application code cannot escape out of the sandbox:

Executable space protection: implements a form of executable space protection for x86 on a section basis in user-space. This protection holds for regions defined in ELF headers of the programs and loaded libraries, even if they are smaller than a page. The guard checks if the target area is defined in the program or an imported library and if it actually contains code. If there is a violation then the program is terminated. This guard protects against the execution of code injected through stack-based and heap-based buffer overflows.

Executable bit removal: this guard marks the code of the untranslated program as *non-executable* (by using mprotect calls). The application does not know the location of the internal code cache and is therefore not able to overwrite parts of the code cache with injected code. This guard ensures that only code from the binary translator and translated code in the code cache can be executed.

Return address verification: This guard checks that the return address is not changed by implementing a shadow stack that is only accessible from internal code where the return address is verified for each return instruction. The shadow stack contains pairs of addresses, the original location and the translated counterpart. If the address on the original stack does not correspond to the address on the shadow stack then the program is terminated. This guard protects against stack based overflows and return to libc attacks and is orthogonal to solutions like StackGuard [14], Propolice [24], libverify [3], and Format-Guard [12].

Signal handling: the binary translator keeps a mask of installed signals on a per-thread basis. Whenever a new handler for a specific signal is installed the code of the handler is wrapped into a trampoline that guarantees the secure execution of the signal and ensures that the signal processing code cannot escape the binary translator. This guard protects against errors in the trap handling and enables the sandbox to catch memory accesses to unmapped memory regions (e.g., probing for the location of the code cache).

Secure context transfers: the control transfer from the binary translator to translated code uses an indirect control flow transfer to ensure that no pointers to any internal data structures of the binary translator are exposed on the stack. This guard hides the internal data structures of the sandbox from the application.

Randomized addresses: the binary translator allocates all internal data structures on random addresses using an internal mmap implementation. On IA-32 the instruction pointer cannot be read directly (e.g, through a register) and indirect control transfers (e.g., call instructions) are replaced by a secure sequence of virtualized instructions during the translation process. All translated indirect control flow transfers point into the original code region and are replaced with a lookup in the mapping table. The translated code is therefore unable to recover a pointer into the code cache or any other internal data structure of the binary translator. The internal mmap implementation uses the address space layout randomization feature that is available in the Linux kernel [7, 8, 30]. Address space layout randomization is exploitable if used in isolation [36] but all the exploits rely on some form of indirect control flow transfers and return to libc attacks. This guard relies on other guards to be secure. But the guard is nevertheless effective in raising the complexity for potential exploits.

The following security guards can be enabled on demand and are not part of the default configuration.

Section guard: only (direct and indirect) function calls and function returns are allowed to transfer control to a function in a different code region. All other control transfers (like jumps or indirect jumps) are verified to target the code of the same section. This guard prohibits unintended control flow transfers.

Call guard: call instructions are verified to transfer control to an existing function by checking the exported symbols of loaded objects. If the call does not target a symbol defined in any of the loaded libraries or the program itself then the call is not allowed. This guard prohibits arc attacks and the redirection of function pointers to unintended code.

Protection of internal data structures: adds an additional heavyweight guard that uses mprotect to disable write access to all internal data structures (e.g., mapping table, code cache, internal translator data) of the binary translator whenever translated code is executed. This way translated code is unable to change translated code or any other internal data structures of the binary translator. Even if this guard is not active all pointers to the internal data structures are pruned from the stack. An exploit is unable to detect the internal data structures due to the virtualization guarantees of the translator.

The current guard configuration does not allow applications with self-modifying code. An application with, e.g., a JIT compiler could be handled by specifying at exactly what regions the compiler will be emitting code and using an additional guard for these regions.

3.2 Policy-based system call interposition

All the potentially dangerous functionality of a program is performed by system calls (e.g., I/O, network sockets, privilege escalation). A mechanism that restricts a program's use of system calls is a useful and important extension to fault isolation. Code based exploits are handled by the software-based fault isolation. Data driven attacks where no malicious code is executed (e.g., integer overflows and type errors) are caught whenever a system call is executed that does not conform to the application's policy.

Policy-based system call interposition relies on *software-based fault isolation* and the rewriting and replacement of system calls. All system calls through both *sysenter*, and *int 80* instructions (Linux uses and supports both systems [21]) are rewritten by the binary translator to execute a validation function before they are allowed. The sandbox offers an extensible *system call interposition framework* that makes it possible to allow or disallow system calls based on the call stack, the system call number, and the parameters.

The sandbox validates system calls through handler functions and by a policy that is loadable at runtime. A policy has the advantage that combinations of allowed and disallowed parameters can be specified in a simple way. Handler functions on the other hand enable in-depth verification of arguments and can use state (e.g., a list of previous `mmap` calls, arguments, and call locations) to track application behavior throughout the execution of different system calls. The combination of a policy to handle simple and static combinations of system calls and handler functions for complex system calls enables an even tighter and more dynamic security model than policies alone.

3.2.1 Special handler functions

The privileges of a program can be managed by specific handler functions on a per system call basis. Every system call can use a different handler function that analyzes *call stack* and *arguments*. The handler functions are a part of the binary translator and have full control over the application. Handler functions may *allow* the system call, *abort* the program, or redirect the system call and return a *fake value*.

These redirected system calls can be used to implement different functionality in user-space. If a system call is redirected then a user-space function is executed whenever the system call is called. This function runs in the context of the binary translator and can execute arbitrary other system calls (redirected system calls can, e.g., emulate or isolate vulnerable system calls). More generally redirected system calls add additional validation of arguments that are passed to the kernel.

The sandbox uses additional handler functions to check all `mmap`, `mprotect`, `open`, and `openat` system calls. For `mmap` and `mprotect` the sandbox checks if the arguments overlap or touch any internal data structures that the binary translator uses. If there is a conflict then the application is terminated. For the `open` and `openat` system calls the sandbox uses `stat` to check

```
mode:whitelist /* deny unlisted syscalls */
open("/dev/arandom", O_RDONLY):allow
open("/dev/urandom", O_RDONLY):allow
time(null):allow
getuid32():return(0) /* return static uid=root */
close(*):allow /* close open files */
write(1,*,*):allow /* stdout */
access("/etc/*",*):allow
// implicit: access("*",*):deny
```

Figure 3. Example excerpt from a policy file that uses white listing as default policy. It allows two specific files to be opened, execution of the `time()`, `close()`, and `write()` system calls. `getuid()` returns 0 (root), and `access()` is restricted to /etc/* only.

if the file is in the black list or tries to access protected files like /prof/self/maps that would leak information about the sandbox.

The handler functions are used as an extension of the policy system. Handler functions enable additional control logic to guard and tighten the allowed actions of the application.

3.2.2 Policy-based system call authorization

The *system call authorization framework* for policy-based system call authorization builds on *process sandboxing* and extends the system call interposition framework. The sandbox loads a user-defined policy at startup to decide for each individual system call if it is allowed or not.

If a system call and its arguments do not match the policy (e.g., the configuration is not present in the policy for white-listing, or is present for black-listing), the isolation system assumes that there is an error, bug, or security problem and terminates the user process. Additionally it can signal the system operator that an authorization fault occurred.

The policy file contains a list of system calls and parameter-sets that are allowed or denied. This allows a combination of white-listing and black-listing of different argument combinations per system call. Arguments are encoded as integers, pointers, strings, null, or asterisk for an unspecified value that matches any input. Partial strings can be matched with an appended asterisk (e.g., "/etc/apache2/*"). Effective path arguments can additionally be evaluated using `stat` system calls. Possible actions for each combination are to allow the system call, to abort the program, or to return a predefined integer value. See Figure 3 for an excerpt from a policy file and Figure 4 for an overview of runtime data structures needed for the policy-based authorization.

The redirected system calls can be used to change and test the behavior of a program if certain system calls return special values (e.g., many programs behave differently if they are run as root, so returning a fake value for `getuid` is useful in some cases). The current policy is limited to returning a static fake value. But the system call interposition framework can be used to call any user supplied function to handle a specific system call. This functionality enables, e.g., additional stateful security checks, the emulation of (obsolete or unsafe) system calls, virtualization or reimplementation of specific system calls in user space, or can be used for whole kernel emulation in user-space.

Depending on the first line of the policy file either white-listing or black-listing is used. Black-listing can be used, e.g., for testing or implementation of new features. For security policies we assume that a white-listing approach is taken. An unmatched combination of parameters for a specific system call either aborts the program if white-listing is used, or is allowed if black-listing is used. White-listing specifically allows system calls and implicitly denies all other system calls. Black-listing denies or redirects specific system calls and implicitly allows all unspecified system calls.

3.2.3 TOCTTOU attacks

Time Of Check To Time Of Use (TOCTTOU) [40] attacks rely on the fact that a second thread can replace the arguments on the stack of another thread after they have been checked by the interposition framework but before the system call is executed.

Each thread of an application is guarded by a sandbox. The security guards inside each sandbox prohibit the execution of malicious code. A thread that tries to execute an illegal control flow transfer or illegal code terminates the application immediately. This setup prevents a second thread from using injected code to rewrite the system call arguments after they are checked by the policy-based system call interposition.

A hypothetical exploit could use a data-based exploit in one thread to corrupt a data-structure that is used in both threads after the system call interposition framework validated the arguments. To guard against such an exploit, we must restrict access to a thread's stack by other threads. The randomness introduced by the thread scheduler and random stack locations suffices in many scenarios to limit the risk of such an exploit.

The combination of the additional fine-grained checks of the additional security guards in the isolation layer and the policy-based system call interposition make TOCTTOU attacks based on code injection impossible.

4. Implementation

libdetox uses fastBT [31, 32], a generator for binary translators to generate a lean and efficient table-based user-space binary translator that follows the description in Section 2. The generated binary translator is extended by the security guards to enforce fine-grained

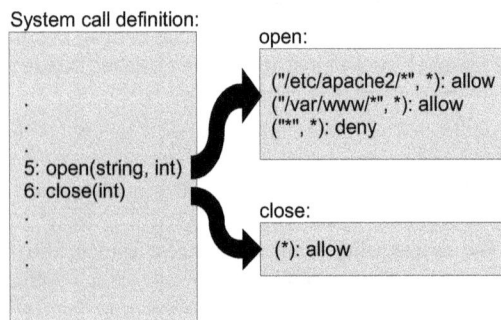

Figure 4. Runtime data structures for a given policy with examples for the open() and close() system calls.

user-space fault isolation and to implement the system call interposition framework.

This section discusses the implementation of the software-based fault isolation mechanism and highlights the changes needed to implement a secure binary translator. The policy-based authorization framework is then implemented on top of the software-based fault isolation.

4.1 Software-based fault isolation

The four binary translators that we evaluated for user-space fault isolation and the system call interposition framework are PIN [28], HDTrans [37, 38], DynamoRIO [9, 10, 23], and fastBT [31, 32]. These binary translators use different approaches to implement user-space binary instrumentation and isolation. HDTrans and fastBT use a table-based approach that translates instructions based on translation tables. DynamoRIO and PIN translate the machine code into a high level intermediate representation (IR) and compile the translated IR back to machine code.

Important features are that the binary translator must cover the complete IA-32 instruction set and that no pointers to thread local data structures are left on the stack if the binary translator uses the same stack as the user-program. To offer an attractive alternative to full system translation the overhead for the binary translation must be low, both for the translation of new instructions and for the execution of translated code.

libdetox uses fastBT because (i) the complete IA-32 instruction set is supported, (ii) the binary translator is very modular and extendable by new handler functions that control the low-level translation of control instructions, and (iii) the trusted computing base is small. libdetox consists of only a couple of thousand lines of code.

The binary translator framework translates all control flow instructions and ensures that the execution stays inside the code cache.

All internal data is allocated on a thread-local basis. Each thread has a private code cache and runs its own translator. This removes the need for inter-thread synchronization.

libdetox uses fastBT as a tool for software-based fault isolation. The security concepts presented in this paper are not specific to fastBT, but can be implemented in any table-based binary translator. Details of the implementation of the binary translator are available in [32]. The additional security guards that are discussed in 3.1.3 are an extension implemented on top of the binary translator and crucial to guarantee isolation.

The combination of fastBT with the additional security guards ensures the first security principle defined in Section 3. Illegal instructions and instructions that redirect control flow to malicious code lead to a direct abort of the program through the binary translator.

4.1.1 Thread and process handling

All system calls that create threads or new processes are handled in a special way. If the arguments are allowed according to the policy then the system call is instrumented such that the new thread or process is started in a new libdetox instance.

If a new thread is started then a trampoline is executed first that starts a new instance of the binary translator that controls the execution of the new thread. For each new process that is started the binary translator is injected with a LD_PRELOAD directive (if the started program supports dynamically shared libraries, otherwise the process creation is aborted).

4.1.2 Additional guards

libdetox reads all symbol and section information when the program or shared libraries are loaded. This information is imported into data structures of libdetox that are used at runtime to implement the additional security guards.

The guards from Section 3.1.3 are executed either when new code is translated or whenever the translated instruction is executed in the application. Executable space protection, executable bit removal, and signal handling are implemented using static implementations during the translation process. The section guard, call guard, and return address verification need both a check during the translation and an additional dynamic check. The check during the translation process is used for fixed or precomputed targets and the dynamic check is patched into the translated code for all dynamic control flow transfers.

Secure context transfers are implemented through changes in the binary translator. The optimizations for indirect control flow transfers are modified so that no pointers to the code cache are left on the stack of the user-program. For example a return instruction is translated into code that (i) executes a lookup in the mapping table, (ii) stores the translated target address in a local data structure, and (iii) uses an indirect jump through that data structure to redirect the control flow to the translated target. Using such trampolines guarantees that pointers to the code cache are never left on the application stack and there is no need to overwrite return addresses of the original application which would leak information about the sandbox.

4.2 Policy-based system call authorization

All system calls through interrupts and the sysenter instruction are rewritten by the binary translator. The system call interposition framework is implemented on top of the binary translator to wrap all system calls into individual evaluation functions. The system call interposition framework then checks the system call and its arguments against the loaded policy. libdetox loads the policy and parses it into an array of parameter lists. Per system call a parameter list is generated with combinations of valid parameters. If the user program wants to execute a system call then the list is checked. If a parameter-set matches then the system call is either executed or a fake value is returned. The process is terminated if no parameter-set matches. This enforces the second security principle. The combination of these two principles makes user-space isolation and encapsulation possible and secure.

5. Evaluation

This section evaluates the libdetox user-space virtual machine. Low overheads for isolation and sandboxing features show that the libdetox approach is highly attractive. The discussion about system call coverage shows that most programs execute a low number of specific system calls with a limited set of arguments.

The Apache case study in Section 5.3 shows that it is possible to isolate Apache in a user-space sandbox that implements a hard security policy with low overhead.

The benchmarks are run under Ubuntu 9.04 on an E6850 Intel Core2Duo CPU running at 3.00GHz, 2GB RAM, and GCC version 4.3.3. Averages are calculated by comparing overall execution time for all programs of untranslated runs against translated runs. The SPEC CPU2006 benchmarks are presented as a way to compare performance with other systems.

5.1 Isolation and sandboxing overhead

This section provides an analysis of the runtime overhead introduced through libdetox. The overhead is separated into (i) BT overhead alone, (ii) overhead for system call validation and executable space protection, and (iii) full protection using mprotect to guard the internal datastructures from attacks against the sandbox.

Table 1 displays overheads for all SPEC CPU2006 benchmarks compared to an untranslated run. The different configurations are:

BT: A configuration without additional security features, showing the overhead of the isolation and binary modification toolkit.

libdetox: This configuration shows libdetox's overhead with the default guards enabled.

libdetox+mprot: The last configuration shows full encapsulation including protection of internal data structures using explicit memory protection through mprotect.

Table 1 uses the standard SPEC CPU2006 benchmarks and shows the overhead for long running programs. The average slowdown for binary translation (and no other transformation) for the full SPEC CPU2006 benchmarks is 6.0%. The libdetox security extensions increase the overhead to 6.4%. The full protection mechanism results in an overhead of 8.2%. The overhead for binary translation and basic libdetox protection for most programs is between −3.5% and 4.0%; some benchmarks like 400.perlbench, 433.gcc, 453.sjeng, 483.xalancbr, 447.dealII, and 453.povray result in a higher overhead of 23% to 60% due to many indirect control flow transfers that cannot be optimized. The speedup of some programs is achieved by a better code layout through the translation process. libdetox adds static overhead per translated block and per system call. The SPEC CPU20006 benchmarks have a low number of system calls and high code reuse, which is typical for server applications. Therefore the libdetox extensions add no measurable overhead to these programs.

libdetox with full protection leads to more overhead (8.21% on average) because the number of system calls increases. But the overall overhead is low for these benchmarks, although the translation overhead is higher. The translation overhead is still small compared to the runtime of the translated program. As soon as all active code is translated, no further memory protection calls are necessary.

5.2 System call coverage

Figure 5 shows a policy that covers all SPEC CPU2006 benchmarks. This policy is not secure and only used to evaluate the over-

Benchmark	BT	libdetox	+mprot
400.perlbench	55.97%	59.88%	74.69%
401.bzip2	3.89%	5.39%	5.54%
403.gcc	20.86%	22.68%	55.56%
429.mcf	-0.49%	0.49%	0.25%
445.gobmk	18.17%	14.57%	16.69%
456.hmmer	4.64%	4.75%	5.72%
458.sjeng	24.62%	27.65%	31.22%
462.libquantum	0.98%	0.98%	0.98%
464.h264ref	6.17%	9.20%	9.20%
471.omnetpp	13.91%	14.11%	15.12%
473.astar	3.66%	3.83%	4.33%
483.xalancbmk	23.72%	27.22%	31.27%
410.bwaves	2.12%	2.68%	3.91%
416.gamess	-3.50%	-4.20%	-0.70%
433.milc	0.97%	2.18%	3.26%
434.zeusmp	-0.13%	-0.25%	0.13%
435.gromacs	0.00%	0.00%	0.00%
436.cactusADM	0.00%	-0.66%	0.00%
437.leslie3d	0.00%	0.00%	0.86%
444.namd	0.65%	0.65%	0.65%
447.dealII	44.20%	41.12%	43.66%
450.soplex	7.25%	5.02%	7.25%
453.povray	22.10%	25.14%	26.52%
454.calculix	-1.68%	-0.56%	-1.12%
459.GemsFDTD	1.79%	1.79%	2.68%
465.tonto	9.19%	10.27%	12.43%
470.lbm	0.00%	0.00%	-0.11%
482.sphinx3	2.36%	2.25%	1.89%
Average	**6.00%**	**6.39%**	**8.21%**

Table 1. Overhead for different configurations executing the SPEC CPU2006 benchmarks (relative to an untranslated run). +mprot: libdetox with full memory protection.

head of policy-based user-space software-based fault isolation. The policy is a summary of all individual policies for each SPEC benchmarks so that the overhead for all benchmarks can be evaluated in a single run of the SPEC benchmark script. Differences to real policies include the over-generalization of attributes and the lax handling of the `open`, `unlink`, `mmap2`, `unlink`, and `stat64` system calls. A production policy would tighten the policy for a single program and explicitly list all needed files and directories or restrict these system calls to specific directories. These system calls are used to access many data files in each individual benchmark and for each data size. The long list of explicit configurations was abbreviated through over-approximation to give a clearer picture. A safe policy for a single specific SPEC benchmark does not result in any measurable additional overhead.

Figure 5 shows that all SPEC CPU2006 benchmarks need no more than 38 different system calls with a few more individual parameter configurations.

The second case study shows *nmap*, which is a network exploration and security tool that checks and fingerprints running services of servers over the Internet. libdetox virtualizes and encapsulate version 4.53 of nmap into a secure sandbox. The policy shown in Figure 6 shows a set of rules that restricts nmap to a few different

```
mode:whitelist /* not listed: abort program */
brk(*):allow /* memory management */
mmap2(null,*, PROT_READ | PROT_WRITE, \
    MAP_ANONYMOUS | MAP_PRIVATE, -1,*):allow
mremap(*,*,*, MREMAP_MAYMOVE):allow
munmap(*,*):allow
execve("/bin/echo",*,*):allow /* allowed prog.s */
execve("/opt/cpu2006/bin/echo",*,*):allow
execve("/sbin/echo",*,*):allow
execve("/usr/bin/echo",*,*):allow
execve("/usr/local/bin/echo",*,*):allow
execve("/usr/local/sbin/echo",*,*):allow
execve("/usr/sbin/echo",*,*):allow
clone(*,null,0,null):allow /* allowed file I/O */
close(*):allow
dup(*):allow
fcntl64(*,*):allow
fstat64(*,*):allow
ftruncate64(*,*):allow
getcwd("*",*):allow
ioctl(*,*):allow
llseek(*,*,*,*, SEEK_SET):allow
llseek(*,*,*,*, SEEK_CUR):allow
lseek(*,*, SEEK_SET):allow
lseek(*,*, SEEK_CUR):allow
lstat64("/opt/cpu2006/benchspec/CPU2006/*", \
    *):allow
open("*",*):allow /* relaxed for spec */
pipe(*):allow
read(*,*,*):allow
stat64("*",*):allow
rmdir("foo"):allow /* remove foo directories */
unlink("*"):allow /* unlink relaxed for spec */
write(*,*,*):allow
writev(*,*,*):allow
futex(*, FUTEX_PRIVATE | FUTEX_WAKE, 0x7FFFFFFF, \
    null,*,*):allow /* process mgmt */
waitpid(*,*,0):allow
rt_sigprocmask(SIG_BLOCK,*,*):allow /* signals */
rt_sigprocmask(SIG_SETMASK,*,null):allow
getegid32():allow /* information retrieval*/
geteuid32():allow
getgid32():allow
getrusage(RUSAGE_SELF,*):allow
gettimeofday(*,null):allow
getuid32():allow
setrlimit(RLIMIT_DATA,*):allow
ugetrlimit(RLIMIT_DATA,*):allow
nanosleep(*,*):allow /* sleep and time */
time(null):allow
times(*):allow
```

Figure 5. A relaxed policy to measure the sandboxing overhead for the SPEC CPU2006 benchmarks. Some rules are relaxed to facilitate the run of the spec benchmark scripts.

system calls, e.g., opening any network connection. The nmap program uses 23 different system calls, individual parameters are used to `open` 15 different files, use `stat64` on 6 files, and use `access` for two files. This policy sandboxes the network scanner, and an attacker cannot escalate privileges if one of the many nmap detection modules contains exploitable code.

```
mode:whitelist /* not listed: abort program */
brk(*):allow /* memory management */
/* due to shared libraries all mmap calls must be
   additionally checked in a handler function for
   a set exec bit. */
mmap2(*,*,*,*,*,*):allow
munmap(*,*):allow
futex(*,*,*,*,*,*):allow /* thread futexes */
access("/etc/ld.so.nohwcap",*):allow /* limit I/O */
access("/usr/share/nmap/nmap-services",*):allow
close(*):allow
fcntl64(*, F_GETFL):allow
fcntl64(*, F_GETFD):allow
fcntl64(*, F_SETFL, O_RDWR | O_NONBLOCK):allow
fstat64(*,*):allow
ioctl(*, TIOCGPGRP, *):allow
llseek(*,*,*,*,*):allow
newselect(*,*,*,*,*):allow
open("/dev/arandom",*):allow
open("/dev/tty",*):allow
open("/dev/urandom",*):allow
open("/etc/host.conf",*):allow
open("/etc/hosts",*):allow
open("/etc/ld.so.cache",*):allow
open("/etc/localtime",*):allow
open("/etc/nsswitch.conf",*):allow
open("/etc/passwd",*):allow
open("/etc/resolv.conf",*):allow
open("/lib/i686/cmov/libnsl.so.1",*):allow
open("/lib/i686/cmov/libnss_compat.so.2",*):allow
open("/lib/i686/cmov/libnss_files.so.2",*):allow
open("/lib/i686/cmov/libnss_nis.so.2",*):allow
open("/usr/share/nmap/nmap-services",*):allow
read(*,*,*):allow
stat64("/etc/localtime",*):allow
stat64("/etc/resolv.conf",*):allow
stat64("/home/test/.nmap/nmap-services",*):allow
stat64("./nmap-services",*):allow
stat64("/usr/lib/nmap/nmap-services",*):allow
stat64("/usr/share/nmap/nmap-services",*):allow
write(*,*,*):allow
socketcall(PF_NETLINK, SOCK_RAW, 0):allow /* net */
socketcall(PF_INET, SOCK_STREAM, IPPROTO_TCP):allow
socketcall(PF_FILE, SOCK_STREAM | \
    SOCK_CLOEXEC | SOCK_NONBLOCK, 0):allow
geteuid32():allow /* system information */
gettimeofday(*,*):allow
getuid32():allow
time(*):allow
uname(*):allow
ugetrlimit(*,*):allow
setrlimit(RLIMIT_NOFILE, *):allow
```

Figure 6. Full policy covering and encapsulating the nmap network scanner and all additional detection modules. Network access is allowed as well as access to libraries and configuration files.

5.3 Apache isolation

The Apache 2.2.11 HTTP server is used to benchmark a daemon that needs both access to local files and is accessible over the network. libdetox encapsulates the Apache processes and threads and only allows few system calls with restrictive parameter con-

figurations. Like the nmap policy in Figure 6 Apache is only allowed to open specific files and access files in two directories (/etc/apache2, and /var/www) and is not allowed to execute other processes. On the other hand the daemon process is free to open connections over the network.

Benchmark	native	BT	libdetox
test.html	84.83s	97.47s	101.34s
	22.48Mb/s	19.57Mb/s	18.82Mb/s
phpinfo.php	84.40s	98.63s	101.34s
	3.28Mb/s	2.8Mb/s	2.73Mb/s
picture.png	249.87s	261.92s	266.98s
	945.18Mb/s	901.67Mb/s	884.6Mb/s
Avg. overhead	-	9.29%	12.06%

Table 2. The ab benchmark is used to compare a native run without isolation to fast binary translation only, and libdetox with user-space fault isolation and policy-based system call authorization.

The overhead for the Apache daemon was measured using the *ab* Apache benchmark which used 10 concurrent instances to receive each file 1'000'000 times. Table 2 shows the overheads using different configurations. The test uses the following files: (i) test.html, a static html file with 1.7kB, (ii) phpinfo.php, a small php file that issues the phpinfo call, and (iii) picture.png, a 242kB file.

The overhead to download a small file is 14.9% for binary translation because of the high number of system calls needed to open, read, and send the file. The overhead for libdetox is 19.5%. For larger files, as seen by the numbers for picture.png, the overhead of binary translation is 4.83% and 6.85% for libdetox.

An interesting feature is the throughput difference between small and large files. Throughput is increased from 22.48Mb/s to 945.18Mb/s for native runs and even more for libdetox, namely from 19.57Mb/s to 901.67Mb/s, which is more than 46 times faster compared to the small file.

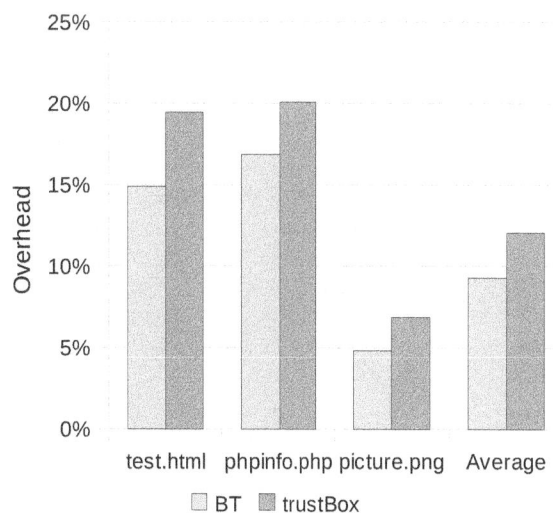

Figure 7. Overhead introduced through isolation, sandboxing, and policy-based authorization for the Apache benchmarks

Figure 7 shows the overhead introduced through isolation and sandboxing for the different Apache benchmarks. The numbers show that libdetox introduces a moderate overhead of about 20% for small static and small dynamic files. For larger files the overhead drops to below 7%. The SPEC CPU2006 benchmarks in Section 5.1 showed that the overhead for compute intensive programs is even lower. The average overhead of libdetox for the Apache web-server results is 12.06%, which makes user-space fault isolation attractive.

6. Related work

Related work to the presented approach combines ideas from different fields of research. An important area are systems that enforce some kind of security policy by either limiting the instruction set or relying on some kernel infrastructure. Security can be enforced on many levels. Some of them are limiting the system calls a program can use, others limit the instruction set inside the application, or use hardware extensions to limit the program.

An important characteristic of security systems is the granularity they work on. Some systems use full system translation to encapsulate and virtualize a complete running system. This offers strong security guarantees as hardware virtualization extensions can be used to separate different virtualized instances. A drawback of these solutions is data exchange between programs running on different virtualized instances and administrative overhead that is needed to configure and secure every single instance. Process encapsulation on the other hand limits the code and system calls a running process can execute.

This section discusses different alternate approaches to guarantee security. Full system translation offers the possibility to encapsulate complete systems and to guarantee security on a coarse-grained system level. System call interposition evaluates an application's system calls and offers coarse-grained interposition on the granularity of system calls. User-space isolation through dynamic binary translation offers a fine-grained level of control about all executed control flow transfers. Static binary translation limits the instruction set and uses a static checker that validates the application before it is run.

6.1 Full system translation

Full system translation virtualizes a complete system, including the operating system and all hardware. Complete system virtualization by QEMU [6] offers full encapsulation, but comes with high overhead. Other full system virtualization tools like VMware [11, 15] and Xen [4] rely on kernel or hardware support. Livewire [20] extends VMware to build an intrusion detection system around the virtual machine. Ho et al. [25] present a protection system that uses a Xen based virtualization approach that uses QEMU to emulate individual instructions based on taint information.

A disadvantage of full system virtualization is that every virtual machine is an independent system with its own configuration and support needs. Additionally only very coarse-grained events can be observed from such a high level of abstraction. From a security and safety perspective the encapsulation of such an approach is needed but without the complexity of administrating individual systems. Our sandbox offers user-space process isolation, combining encapsulation with fine-grained security on a single system.

6.2 System call interposition

System call interposition uses either a kernel module or ptrace support to implement a control mechanism on the level of system calls. These systems share several drawbacks. For one the protection mechanism is very coarse-grained and they do not detect the execution of malicious code until a system call that is not part of the policy is executed. These systems miss exploits that target opened files or use the policy's allowed system calls and are often prone to TOCTTOU attacks. These file changes evade detection of the security systems that validate purely on system calls. A second concern is the overhead introduced due to context switching. An expensive context switch has to be performed whenever a policy rule is checked. A third drawback is that these systems rely on trusted code in the kernel to stop the monitored program which poses an additional security risk.

Janus [22] is a system call interposition framework that uses the Solaris process tracing facility (ptrace) to allow one user mode process to filter the system calls of a second process. This framework builds on kernel support and has two drawbacks: (i) the traced application is already in the kernel when it is stopped, a situation that poses a potential security problem, and (ii) the overhead of switching between an inspecting process and the corresponding application is high. MAPbox [1], AppArmor [5], SubDomain [13], and Consh [2] extend the idea of a ptrace interposition framework by implementing policy-based authorization. Tal Garfinkel analyzed practical problems of system call interposition in [18].

The Linux kernel offers an API for security modules [41] that can be used to implement many kernel-based coarse-grained security extensions. Systrace [33] uses a kernel module to implement a system call policy. Some global system calls are validated in the kernel with low overhead, for all other system calls the program is stopped and a user-space daemon decides based on the parameters if the system call is allowed or not. Switchblade [16] enforces a system call policy using an in-kernel system call model and dynamic taint analysis. Ostia [19] prevents TOCTTOU attacks by using a proxy and a delegation model to delegate system calls to different processes or threads. Alcatraz [27] is a hybrid isolation approach that offers unrestricted read access to a sandboxed application but redirects all writes to a buffer which can be examined before it is committed. Unfortunately this approach does not protect against data leaked over the network or processes that use local root exploits to gain privileges.

Our sandbox uses a fine-grained level of control that checks individual instructions and makes it impossible to execute injected code. Each thread of an application runs in its own sandbox. Each sandbox is secured against the execution of malicious code, therefore a second thread cannot execute code that races between the system call argument check and the execution of the system call thereby removing the threat of TOCTTOU attacks.

6.3 User-space isolation through dynamic binary translation

Vx32 [17] implements a user-space sandbox built on BT that uses segmentation to hide the internal data structures. Due to the use of segmentation the Vx32 system is limited to 32-bit code. Interrupts, system calls, and illegal instructions are translated to traps that call special handler functions. The proposed BT results in a high overhead as there are no optimizations for indirect control transfers.

The traps for system calls offered by Vx32 are targeted towards a reimplementation of the system calls and are not intended for a policy-based system call authorization framework.

Strata [34, 35] is a safe virtual execution environment using software dynamic translation. It uses dynamic binary translation to isolate user-space programs and implements a basic system call interposition API. This API is used to instrument individual system calls. The translation framework is neither limited to a single system nor to a single architecture. Strata uses binary translation to enforce a non-executable stack but there are no additional security guards that limit return to libc attacks or heap based overflows.

Program shepherding [26] uses the DynamoRIO [9, 10, 23] framework to safeguard running applications. A single policy is hardcoded and enforced using binary translation. The binary translator adds additional checks to restrict code origins and to control the targets of indirect control transfers.

Our approach implements a user-space sandbox and extends this sandbox with additional security guards that check the execution of application code at runtime. System calls in our approach are not replaced by software traps but are validated through a policy-based system call authorization framework. Additionally libdetox does not depend on specific hardware features like segmentation, a feature that is not present on AMD64 and hinders portability. The policies used in the sandbox can be refined and changed without the need to recompile the safe execution platform.

6.4 Security through static binary translation

The Google Native Client [42] executes x86-code in a sandbox. The native client uses the same instruction padding techniques as presented in the software-based fault isolation [39] system by Wahbe et al.. The instruction set is limited to a safe subset of the IA-32 ISA, making illegal operations impossible. A verifier checks if the program is valid before the program is executed without any additional isolation. Such a system limits the possible range of used instructions, the programs must be linked statically, and no dynamic libraries can be used. Programs must be compiled with a custom-tailored compiler and special libraries.

PittSField [29] implements a static binary translation and checking tool used for software-based fault isolation. The static rewriting algorithm (i) aligns targets for control transfers on 16 byte boundaries, (ii) changes control transfer instructions so that targets are always 16 byte aligned, and (iii) separates data and code regions by adding additional instructions to force pointers to point to data or code. This static translation results in an overhead of 13% for instruction alignment and 21% for data verification as reported in [29].

The PittSFIeld approach only verifies that a program executes valid instructions and writes to the correct data regions. Our sandbox offers the executable space protection mechanism which write protects application and library code and implements full protection of the internal data structures using kernel memory protection. Additionally our sandbox approach offers a system call interposition framework which validates every single system call and its arguments.

The PittSFIeld approach validates that a return address on the stack is in the code region and not in the data region. But a carefully designed return to libc attack is possible. Our approach disables return to libc attacks by only allowing the execution of a safe subset of system calls that are defined by a custom-tailored policy, checking return addresses, and verifying all control transfers.

7. Conclusion

We present an approach to low overhead software-based fault isolation that implements fine-grained security in user-space. This approach limits programs in their use of system calls and execution of privileged instructions through flexible per-process policies and a configurable system call interposition framework.

An implementation prototype of our approach called libdetox uses dynamic binary translation to support the full IA-32 ISA without kernel support. Full binary translation adds security guards, detects code injections, guards dangerous instructions at runtime and interposes system calls with an authorization framework. System calls are validated based on individual handler functions for special system calls and a policy that allows to control the allowed parameters on a per system call basis.

The approach presented here is attractive for many scenarios that look for a low-cost and widely useable way to secure a system. Applications are isolated and encapsulated while using a shared system image with a single system configuration, and there is no need to virtualize a complete system. Our approach is the first virtual execution system that combines a fast and efficient software-based translator with additional guards and a policy-based system call interposition framework. This combination results in a low overhead software-based fault isolation and encapsulation system. Such a system then can guard daemon processes like the Apache web-server to prevent unwanted access to system resources.

As users (and system administrators) look for ways to deal with the wide range of security problems, libdetox presents a simple yet highly attractive approach to protect a system against a wide range of attacks.

References

[1] ACHARYA, A., AND RAJE, M. MAPbox: using parameterized behavior classes to confine untrusted applications. In *SSYM'00: Proceedings of the 9th conference on USENIX Security Symposium* (2000).

[2] ALEXANDROV, A., KMIEC, P., AND SCHAUSER, K. Consh: Confined execution environment for internet computations, 1999.

[3] BARATLOO, A., SINGH, N., AND TSAI, T. Transparent run-time defense against stack smashing attacks. In *ATEC '00: Proceedings of the annual conference on USENIX Annual Technical Conference* (2000).

[4] BARHAM, P., DRAGOVIC, B., FRASER, K., HAND, S., HARRIS, T., HO, A., NEUGEBAUER, R., PRATT, I., AND WARFIELD, A. Xen and the art of virtualization. In *SOSP '03* (New York, NY, USA, 2003), pp. 164–177.

[5] BAUER, M. Paranoid penguin: an introduction to novell apparmor. *Linux J. 2006*, 148 (2006), 13.

[6] BELLARD, F. QEMU, a fast and portable dynamic translator. In *ATEC '05* (Berkeley, CA, USA, 2005), pp. 41–41.

[7] BHATKAR, E., DUVARNEY, D. C., AND SEKAR, R. Address obfuscation: an efficient approach to combat a broad range of memory er-

The source code of the libdetox framework and additional examples can be downloaded at http://nebelwelt.net/projects/libdetox.

ror exploits. In *Proceedings of the 12th USENIX Security Symposium* (2003), pp. 105–120.

[8] BHATKAR, S., BHATKAR, E., SEKAR, R., AND DUVARNEY, D. C. Efficient techniques for comprehensive protection from memory error exploits. In *Proceedings of the 14th USENIX Security Symposium* (2005).

[9] BRUENING, D., DUESTERWALD, E., AND AMARASINGHE, S. Design and implementation of a dynamic optimization framework for Windows. In *ACM Workshop Feedback-directed Dyn. Opt. (FDDO-4)* (2001).

[10] BRUENING, D., GARNETT, T., AND AMARASINGHE, S. An infrastructure for adaptive dynamic optimization. In *CGO '03* (Washington, DC, USA, 2003), pp. 265–275.

[11] BUGNION, E. Dynamic binary translator with a system and method for updating and maintaining coherency of a translation cache. US Patent 6704925, March 2004.

[12] COWAN, C., BARRINGER, M., BEATTIE, S., KROAH-HARTMAN, G., FRANTZEN, M., AND LOKIER, J. Formatguard: automatic protection from printf format string vulnerabilities. In *SSYM'01: Proceedings of the 10th conference on USENIX Security Symposium* (2001).

[13] COWAN, C., BEATTIE, S., KROAH-HARTMAN, G., PU, C., WAGLE, P., AND GLIGOR, V. Subdomain: Parsimonious server security. In *LISA '00: Proceedings of the 14th USENIX conference on System administration* (2000).

[14] COWAN, C., PU, C., MAIER, D., HINTONY, H., WALPOLE, J., BAKKE, P., BEATTIE, S., GRIER, A., WAGLE, P., AND ZHANG, Q. Stackguard: automatic adaptive detection and prevention of buffer-overflow attacks. In *SSYM'98: Proceedings of the 7th conference on USENIX Security Symposium* (1998).

[15] DEVINE, S. W., BUGNION, E., AND ROSENBLUM, M. Virtualization system including a virtual machine monitor for a computer with a segmented architecture. US Patent 6397242.

[16] FETZER, C., AND SUESSKRAUT, M. Switchblade: enforcing dynamic personalized system call models. In *Eurosys '08: Proceedings of the 3rd ACM SIGOPS/EuroSys European Conference on Computer Systems 2008* (New York, NY, USA, 2008), ACM, pp. 273–286.

[17] FORD, B., AND COX, R. Vx32: lightweight user-level sandboxing on the x86. In *ATC'08: USENIX 2008 Annual Technical Conference on Annual Technical Conference* (Berkeley, CA, USA, 2008), USENIX Association, pp. 293–306.

[18] GARFINKEL, T. Traps and pitfalls: Practical problems in system call interposition based security tools. In *In Proc. Network and Distributed Systems Security Symposium* (2003), pp. 163–176.

[19] GARFINKEL, T., PFAFF, B., AND ROSENBLUM, M. Ostia: A delegating architecture for secure system call interposition. In *Proc. Network and Distributed Systems Security Symposium* (February 2004).

[20] GARFINKEL, T., AND ROSENBLUM, M. A virtual machine introspection based architecture for intrusion detection. In *Proc. Network and Distributed Systems Security Symposium* (February 2003).

[21] GARG, M. Sysenter based system call mechanism in linux 2.6 (http://manugarg.googlepages.com/systemcallinlinux2_6.html).

[22] GOLDBERG, I., WAGNER, D., THOMAS, R., AND BREWER, E. A. A secure environment for untrusted helper applications: Confining the wily hacker. In *Proceedings of the 6th Usenix Security Symposium* (1996).

[23] HAZELWOOD, K., AND SMITH, M. D. Managing bounded code caches in dynamic binary optimization systems. *TACO '06 3*, 3 (2006), 263–294.

[24] HIROAKI, E., AND KUNIKAZU, Y. propolice : Improved stack-smashing attack detection. *IPSJ SIG Notes 2001*, 75 (2001-07-25), 181–188.

[25] HO, A., FETTERMAN, M., CLARK, C., WARFIELD, A., AND HAND, S. Practical taint-based protection using demand emulation. vol. 40, pp. 29–41.

[26] KIRIANSKY, V., BRUENING, D., AND AMARASINGHE, S. P. Secure execution via program shepherding. In *Proceedings of the 11th USENIX Security Symposium* (Berkeley, CA, USA, 2002), USENIX Association, pp. 191–206.

[27] LIANG, Z., SUN, W., VENKATAKRISHNAN, V. N., AND SEKAR, R. Alcatraz: An isolated environment for experimenting with untrusted software. *ACM Trans. Inf. Syst. Secur. 12*, 3 (2009), 1–37.

[28] LUK, C.-K., COHN, R., MUTH, R., PATIL, H., KLAUSER, A., LOWNEY, G., WALLACE, S., REDDI, V. J., AND HAZELWOOD, K. Pin: building customized program analysis tools with dynamic instrumentation. In *PLDI '05* (New York, NY, USA, 2005), pp. 190–200.

[29] MCCAMANT, S., AND MORRISETT, G. Evaluating SFI for a CISC architecture. In *15th USENIX Security Symposium* (Vancouver, BC, Canada, August 2–4, 2006), pp. 209–224.

[30] PAX-TEAM. PaX ASLR (Address Space Layout Randomization). http://pax.grsecurity.net/docs/aslr.txt.

[31] PAYER, M., AND GROSS, T. Requirements for fast binary translation. In *2nd Workshop on Architectural and Microarchitectural Support for Binary Translation* (2009).

[32] PAYER, M., AND GROSS, T. R. Generating low-overhead dynamic binary translators. In *SYSTOR'10* (2010).

[33] PROVOS, N. Improving host security with system call policies. In *SSYM'03: Proceedings of the 12th conference on USENIX Security Symposium* (Berkeley, CA, USA, 2003), USENIX Association, pp. 18–18.

[34] SCOTT, K., AND DAVIDSON, J. Strata: A software dynamic translation infrastructure. Tech. rep., Charlottesville, VA, USA, 2001.

[35] SCOTT, K., AND DAVIDSON, J. Safe virtual execution using software dynamic translation. *Computer Security Applications Conference, Annual 0* (2002), 209.

[36] SHACHAM, H., PAGE, M., PFAFF, B., GOH, E.-J., MODADUGU, N., AND BONEH, D. On the effectiveness of address-space randomization. In *CCS'04* (2004), pp. 298–307.

[37] SRIDHAR, S., SHAPIRO, J. S., AND BUNGALE, P. P. HDTrans: a low-overhead dynamic translator. *SIGARCH Comput. Archit. News 35*, 1 (2007), 135–140.

[38] SRIDHAR, S., SHAPIRO, J. S., NORTHUP, E., AND BUNGALE, P. P. HDTrans: an open source, low-level dynamic instrumentation system. In *VEE '06* (New York, NY, USA, 2006), pp. 175–185.

[39] WAHBE, R., LUCCO, S., ANDERSON, T. E., AND GRAHAM, S. L. Efficient software-based fault isolation. In *SOSP'93* (New York, NY, USA, 1993), ACM, pp. 203–216.

[40] WATSON, R. N. M. Exploiting concurrency vulnerabilities in system call wrappers. In *WOOT '07: Proceedings of the first USENIX workshop on Offensive Technologies* (2007).

[41] WRIGHT, C., COWAN, C., SMALLEY, S., MORRIS, J., AND KROAH-HARTMAN, G. Linux security modules: General security support for the linux kernel. In *Proceedings of the 11th USENIX Security Symposium* (2002).

[42] YEE, B., SEHR, D., DARDYK, G., CHEN, J. B., MUTH, R., ORMANDY, T., OKASAKA, S., NARULA, N., AND FULLAGAR, N. Native client: A sandbox for portable, untrusted x86 native code. *IEEE Symposium on Security and Privacy* (2009), 79–93.

Minimal-overhead Virtualization of a Large Scale Supercomputer

John R. Lange
Department of Computer Science
University of Pittsburgh
Pittsburgh, PA 15260
jacklange@cs.pitt.edu

Kevin Pedretti
Scalable System Software Department
Sandia National Laboratories
Albuquerque, NM 87123
ktpedre@sandia.gov

Peter Dinda   Chang Bae
Department of Electrical Engineering
and Computer Science
Northwestern University
Evanston, IL 60208
{pdinda,changb}@northwestern.edu

Patrick G. Bridges   Philip Soltero
Department of Computer Science
University of New Mexico
Albuquerque, NM 87131
{bridges,psoltero}@cs.unm.edu

Alexander Merritt
College of Computing
Georgia Institute of Technology
Atlanta, GA 30332
merritt.alex@gatech.edu

Abstract

Virtualization has the potential to dramatically increase the usability and reliability of high performance computing (HPC) systems. However, this potential will remain unrealized unless overheads can be minimized. This is particularly challenging on large scale machines that run carefully crafted HPC OSes supporting tightly-coupled, parallel applications. In this paper, we show how careful use of hardware and VMM features enables the virtualization of a large-scale HPC system, specifically a Cray XT4 machine, with ≤5% overhead on key HPC applications, microbenchmarks, and guests at scales of up to 4096 nodes. We describe three techniques essential for achieving such low overhead: passthrough I/O, workload-sensitive selection of paging mechanisms, and carefully controlled preemption. These techniques are forms of symbiotic virtualization, an approach on which we elaborate.

Categories and Subject Descriptors D.4.7 [*Operating Systems*]: Organization and Design

General Terms Design, Experimentation, Measurement, Performance

This project is made possible by support from the National Science Foundation (NSF) via grants CNS-0709168 and CNS-0707365, and the Department of Energy (DOE) via grant DE-SC0005343. Patrick Bridges was partially supported by a faculty sabbatical appointment at Sandia National Labs. Alexander Merritt's work on this project was conducted as part of a student internship at Sandia National Laboratories. Sandia is a multiprogram laboratory managed and operated by Sandia Corporation, a wholly owned subsidiary of Lockheed Martin Corporation, for the U.S. Department of Energy's National Nuclear Security Administration under contract DE-AC04-94AL85000.

Keywords virtual machine monitors, parallel computing, high performance computing

1. Introduction

Virtualization has the potential to dramatically increase the usability and reliability of high performance computing (HPC) systems by maximizing system flexibility and utility to a wide range of users [11, 13, 23, 24]. Many of the motivations for virtualization in data centers apply also equally to HPC systems, for example allowing users to customize their OS environment (e.g. between full-featured OSes and lightweight OSes). Additionally, virtualization allows multiplexing of less-demanding users when appropriate. Finally, virtualization is relevant to a number of research areas for current petascale and future exascale systems, including reliability, fault-tolerance, and hardware-software co-design.

The adoption of virtualization in HPC systems can only occur, however, if it has minimal performance impact in the most demanding uses of the machines, specifically running the capability applications that motivate the acquisition of petascale and exascale systems. Virtualization cannot succeed in HPC systems unless the performance overheads are truly minimal and, importantly, that those overheads that do exist do not compound as the system and its applications scale up.

This challenge is amplified on high-end machines for several reasons. First, these machines frequently run carefully crafted custom HPC OSes that already minimize overheads and asynchronous OS interference (OS noise) [9, 25], as well as make the capabilities of the raw hardware readily available to the application developer. Second, the applications on these machines are intended to run at extremely large scales, involving thousands or tens of thousands of nodes. Finally, the applications are typically tightly coupled and communication intensive, making them very sensitive to performance overheads, particularly unpredictable overheads. For this reason, they often rely on the deterministic behavior of the HPC OSes on which they run.

In this paper, we show how scalable virtualization with ≤5% overhead for key HPC applications and guests can be achieved in a high-end message-passing parallel supercomputer, in this case a Cray XT4 supercomputer [2] at scales in excess of 4096 nodes. For guests, we examined the behavior of both the custom Catamount HPC OS [17] and the Cray CNL guest [16], an HPC OS derived from the Linux operating system. Our performance overheads are measured using three application benchmarks and a range of microbenchmarks.

The virtual machine monitor that we employ is Palacios, an open source, publicly available VMM designed to support the virtualization of HPC systems and other platforms. We have previously reported on the design, implementation, and evaluation of Palacios [20]. The evaluation included limited performance studies on 32–48 nodes of a Cray XT system. In addition to considering much larger scales, this paper focuses on the essential techniques needed to achieve scalable virtualization at that scale and how a range of different VMM and hardware virtualization techniques impact the scalability of virtualization.

The essential techniques needed to achieve low overhead virtualization at these scales are passthrough I/O, workload-sensitive selection of paging mechanisms, and carefully controlled preemption. Passthrough I/O provides direct guest / application access to the specialized communication hardware of the machine. This in turn enables not only high bandwidth communication, but also preserves the extremely low latency properties of this hardware, which is essential in scalable collective communication.

The second technique we have determined to be essential to low overhead virtualization at scale is the workload-sensitive selection of the paging mechanisms used to implement the guest physical to host physical address translation. Palacios supports a range of approaches, from those with significant hardware assistance (e.g. nested paging, which has several implementations across Intel and AMD hardware), and those that do not (e.g., shadow paging, which has numerous variants). There is no single best paging mechanism; the choice is workload dependent, primarily on guest context switching behavior and the memory reference pattern.

The final technique we found to be essential to low overhead virtualization at scale is carefully controlled preemption within the VMM. By preemption, we mean both interrupt handling and thread scheduling, specifically carefully controlling when interrupts are handled, and using cooperative threading in the VMM. This control mostly avoids introducing timing variation in the environment that the guest OS sees, in turn meaning that carefully tuned collective communication behavior in the application remains effective.

What these techniques effectively accomplish is to keep the virtual machine as true to the physical machine as possible in terms of its communication and timing properties. This in turn allows the guest OS's and the application's assumptions about the physical machine it is designed for to continue to apply to the virtual machine environment. In the virtualization of a commodity machine, such authenticity is not needed. However, if a machine is part of a scalable computer, disparities between guest OS and application assumptions and the behavior of the actual virtual environment can lead to performance impacts that grow with scale.

We generalize beyond the three specific techniques described above to argue that to truly provide scalable performance for virtualized HPC environments, the black box approach of commodity VMMs should be abandoned in favor of a symbiotic virtualization model. In the symbiotic virtualization model, the guest OS and VMM function cooperatively in order to function in a way that optimizes performance. Our specific techniques are examples of symbiotic techniques, and are, in fact, built on the SymSpy passive symbiotic information interface in Palacios.

Beyond supercomputers, our experiences with these symbiotic techniques are increasingly relevant to system software for general-purpose and enterprise computing systems. For example, the increasing scale of multicore desktop and enterprise systems has led OS designers to consider treating multicore systems like tightly-coupled distributed systems. As these systems continue to scale up toward hundreds or thousands of cores with distributed memory hierarchies and substantial inter-core communication delays, lessons learned in designing scalable system software for tightly-coupled distributed memory supercomputers will be increasingly relevant to them.

Our contributions are as follows:

- We demonstrate that it is possible to virtualize a high-end supercomputer at large scales (4096 nodes) with minimal performance overhead ($\leq 5\%$). As far as we are aware, our results represent the largest scale virtualization study to date.

- We describe the three techniques essential for achieving such low overheads at scale: passthrough I/O, workload-sensitive selection of paging mechanisms, and carefully controlled preemption.

- We generalize from the mechanisms to the concept of symbiotic virtualization, which we describe and argue will become of increasing importance as scalable systems become ubiquitous.

2. Virtualization system overview

Our contributions are made in the context of the Palacios VMM and Kitten lightweight kernel. For our experiments in this paper, Palacios is embedded into Kitten, making possible a system call for instantiating a VM from a guest OS image. A detailed description of these systems and their interaction is available elsewhere [20]. We now summarize these systems.

2.1 Palacios

Palacios is a publicly available, open source, OS-independent VMM designed and implemented as part of the V3VEE project (http://v3vee.org). developed from scratch that targets the x86 and x86_64 architectures (hosts and guests) with either AMD SVM [3] or Intel VT [14] extensions. It is designed to be embeddable into diverse host OSes, and we presently have embedded it into Kitten, GeekOS, Minix 3, and Linux. When embedded into Kitten, the combination acts as a type-I VMM—guest OSes do not require any modification to run. Palacios can run on generic PC hardware, in addition to specialized hardware such as Cray XT supercomputer systems.

Palacios creates a PC-compatible virtual environment for guest OSes by handling *exits* that are raised by the hardware on guest operations that the VMM defines as requiring interception. This is a common structure for a VMM, often referred to as "trap-and-emulate". For example, VM exits frequently occur on interrupts, reads and writes to I/O ports and specific areas of memory, and use of particular hardware instructions and registers (e.g. CPU control registers). These exits allow the VMM to intervene on key hardware operations when necessary, emulating or changing requested hardware behavior as needed. Because exit handling incurs overhead, carefully controlling what operations exit and what is done on each exit is essential to providing scalability and performance.

2.2 Kitten host OS

Kitten is a publicly available, GPL-licensed, open source OS designed specifically for high performance computing. The general philosophy being used to develop Kitten is to borrow heavily from the Linux kernel when doing so does not compromise scalability or performance (e.g., adapting the Linux bootstrap code). Performance critical subsystems, such as memory management and task scheduling, are replaced with code written from scratch.

Kitten's focus on HPC scalability makes it an ideal host OS for a VMM on HPC systems, and Palacios's design made it easy to embed it into Kitten. In particular, host OS/VMM integration was accomplished with a single interface file of less than 300 lines of code. The integration includes no internal changes in either the VMM or host OS, and the interface code is encapsulated together with the VMM library in an optional compile time module for the host OS.

The Kitten host OS exposes VMM control functions via a system call interface available from user space. This allows user level tasks to instantiate VM images directly. The result is that VMs can be loaded and controlled via processes received from the job loader. A VM image can thus be linked into a standard job that includes loading and control functionality.

3. Virtualization at scale

In our initial experiments, we conducted a detailed performance study of virtualizing a Cray XT 4 supercomputer. The study included both application and microbenchmarks, and was run at the largest scales possible on the machine (at least 4096 nodes, sometimes 6240 nodes). The upshot of our results is that it is possible to virtualize a large scale supercomputer with $\leq 5\%$ performance penalties in important HPC use-cases, even when running communication-intensive, tightly-coupled applications. In the subsequent sections, we explain how and present additional studies that provide insight into how different architectural and OS approaches to virtualization impact the performance of HPC applications and micro-benchmarks.

3.1 Hardware platform

Testing was performed during an eight hour window of dedicated system time on Red Storm, a Cray XT4 supercomputer made up of 12,960 single-socket compute nodes, each containing either a dual-core or quad-core processor. Because Palacios requires virtualization support not present in the older dual-core processors, testing was limited to the system's 6,240 quad-core nodes. These nodes each consist of a 2.2 GHz AMD Opteron Barcelona quad-core processor, 8 GB of DDR2 memory, and a Cray SeaStar 2.1 network interface. The nodes are arranged in a 13x20x24 3-D mesh topology with wrap-around connections in the Z dimension (i.e. the system is a torus in the Z-dimension only).

Red Storm was jointly developed by Sandia and Cray, and was the basis for Cray's successful line of Cray XT supercomputers. There are many Cray XT systems in operation throughout the world, the largest of which currently being the 18,688 node, 2.3 PetaFLOP peak "Jaguar" XT5-HE system at Oak Ridge National Laboratory. The experiments and results described in this paper are relevant to these systems and could be repeated on systems with quad-core or newer processors. We are in the process of negotiating time to repeat them on Jaguar.

3.2 Software environment

Each test was performed in at least three different system software configurations: native, guest with nested paging, and guest with shadow paging. In the native configuration, the test application or micro-benchmark is run using the Catamount HPC operating system [17] running on the bare hardware. This is the same environment that users normally use on Red Storm. Some tests were also run, at much smaller scales, using Cray's Linux-derived CNL [16] operating system.

The environment labeled "Guest, Nested Paging" in the figures consists of the VMM running on the bare hardware, managing an instance of Catamount running as a guest operating system in a virtual machine environment. In this mode, the AMD processor's nested paging memory management hardware is used to implement the guest physical address to host physical address mapping that

is chosen by Palacios. The guest's page tables and a second set of page tables managed by the VMM are used for translation. Palacios does not need to track guest page table manipulations in this case; however, every virtual address in the guest is translated using a "two dimensional" page walk involving both sets of page tables [6]. This expensive process is sped up through the use of a range of hardware-level TLB and page walk caching structures.

In contrast, the "Guest, Shadow Paging" mode uses software-based memory management which disables the processor's nested paging hardware. Shadow paging avoids the need for a two dimensional page walk, but requires that the VMM track guest page tables. Every update to the guest's page tables causes an exit to the VMM, which must then validate the request and commit it to a set of protected "shadow" page tables, which are the actual page tables used by the hardware. We elaborate on the choice of paging mechanism later in the paper.

Virtualizing I/O devices is critical to VM performance, and, here, the critical device is the SeaStar communications interface [7]. Palacios provides guest access to the SeaStar using passthrough I/O, an approach we elaborate on later. We consider two ways of using the SeaStar, the default way, which is unnamed in our figures, and an alternative approach called "Accelerated Portals." The default approach uses interrupt-driven I/O and host-based message matching[1], while accelerated portals performs message matching on the NIC and does not generally require interrupt delivery.

In the version of AMD SVM available on the Cray XT4, intercepting any interrupt requires that all interrupts be intercepted. Because a variety of non-SeaStar interrupts must be intercepted by the VMM, this adds a VM exit cost to SeaStar interrupts. Essentially, when the VMM detects an exit has occurred due to a SeaStar interrupt, it immediately re-enters the guest, re-injecting the SeaStar interrupt as a software interrupt. This process requires O(1000) cycles, resulting in interrupt-driven SeaStar performance having a higher latency under virtualization than natively. Because accelerated portals uses user-level polling instead, the interrupt exit cost described above does not occur when the guest is virtualized. As a result, virtualized accelerated portals performance is nearly identical to native accelerated portals performance.

It is important to point out that if future versions of AMD's SVM hardware (and of Intel's VT hardware) supported *selective* interrupt exiting, we would be able to use it to avoid exiting on SeaStar interrupts, which should make interrupt-driven SeaStar performance under virtualization identical to that without virtualization.

The guest Catamount OS image we used was based on the same Cray XT 2.0.62 Catamount image used for the native experiments. Minor changes were required to port Catamount to the PC-compatible virtual machine environment provided by Palacios (the native Cray XT environment is not fully PC-compatible). Additionally, the SeaStar portals driver was updated to allow passthrough operation as described in Section 4.

3.3 MPI microbenchmarks

The Intel MPI Benchmark Suite version 3.0 [15] was used to evaluate point-to-point messaging performance and scalability of collective operations.

3.3.1 Point-to-point performance

Figure 1 shows the results of a ping-pong test between two adjacent nodes. Small message latency, shown in Figure 1(a), is approxi-

---

[1] Many high-performance messaging systems *match* incoming large messages with pre-posted user buffers into which the data is directly received, avoiding unnecessary data copies.

(a) Latency

(b) Bandwidth

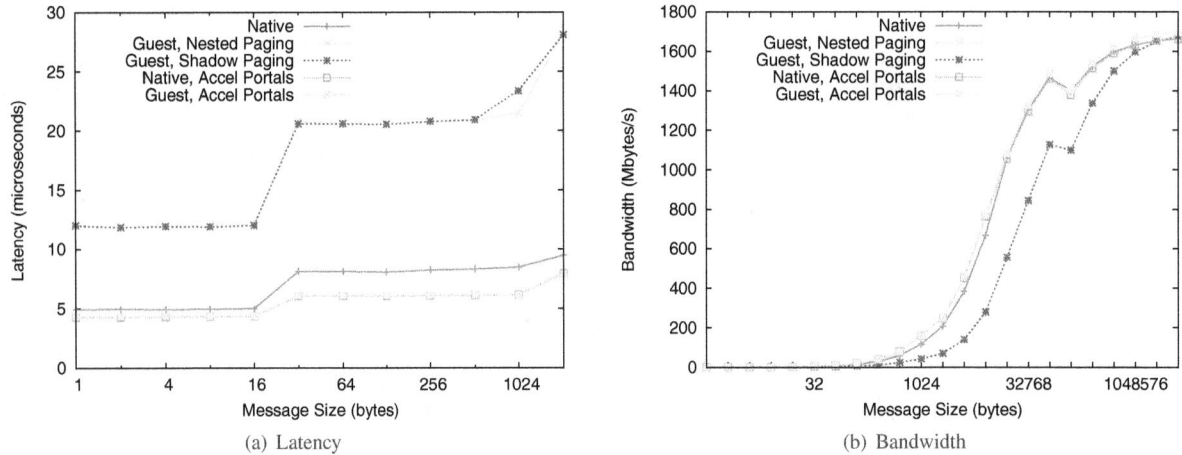

Figure 1. MPI PingPong microbenchmark (a) latency and (b) bandwidth for native and virtualized with both interrupt-driven message delivery and message processing offloaded to the Cray XT SeaStar NIC (accelerated portals). Note that with accelerated portals, guest and native performance are nearly identical due to the removal of interrupt virtualization overhead, resulting in overlapping lines on both graphs.

mately 2.5 times worse with nested or shadow guest environments compared to native, though choice of paging virtualization mode does not effect messaging latency. This is a result of the larger interrupt overhead in the virtualized environment. However, note that in absolute terms, for the smallest messages, the latency for the virtualized case is already a relatively low 12 μs, compared to the native 5 μs. Eliminating this virtualized interrupt overhead, as is the case with accelerated portals and would be the case with more recent AMD SVM hardware implementations, results in virtually identical performance in native and guest environments.

Figure 1(b) plots the same data but extends the domain of the x-axis to show the full bandwidth curves. The nested and shadow guest environments show essentially identical degraded performance for mid-range messages compared to native, but eventually reach the same asymptotic bandwidth once the higher interrupt cost is fully amortized. Bandwidth approaches 1.7 GByte/s. Avoiding the interrupt virtualization cost with accelerated portals results again in similar native and guest performance.

3.3.2 Collective performance

Figures 2, 3, 4, and 5 show the performance of the MPI Barrier, Allreduce, Broadcast, and Alltoall operations, respectively. The operations that have data associated with them, Allreduce and Alltoall, are plotted for the 16-byte message size since a common usage pattern in HPC applications is to perform an operation on a single double-precision number (8 bytes) or a complex double precision number (16 bytes).

Both Barrier. Allreduce, and Broadcast scale logarithmically with node count, with Allreduce having slightly higher latency at all points. In contrast, Alltoall scales quadratically and is therefore plotted with a log y-axis. In all cases, the choice of nested vs. shadow paging is not significant. What does matter, however, is the use of interrupt-driven versus polling-based communication in the guest environment. Similarly to what was observed in the point-to-point benchmarks, eliminating network interrupts by using the polling-based accelerated portals network stack results in near native performance. As noted previously, more recent AMD SVM implementations support selective interrupt exiting, which would make the virtualized interrupt-driven performance identical to the native or virtualized accelerated portals numbers. Still, even with this limitation, virtualized interrupt-driven communication is quite

fast in absolute terms, with a 6240 node barrier or all-reduce taking less than 275 μs to perform.

The Alltoall operation is interesting because the size of the messages exchanged between nodes increases with node count. This causes all of the configurations to converge at high node counts, since the operation becomes bandwidth limited, and the cost of interrupt virtualization is amortized.

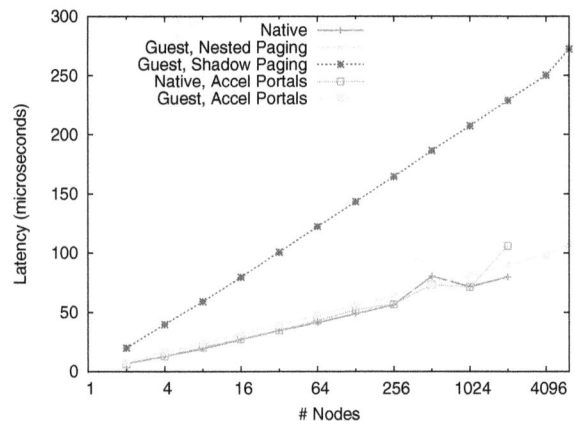

Figure 2. MPI barrier scaling microbenchmark results measuring the latency of a full barrier.

3.4 HPCCG application

HPCCG [12] is a simple conjugate gradient solver that is intended to mimic the characteristics of a broad class of HPC applications while at the same time is simple to understand and run. A large portion of its runtime is spent performing sparse matrix-vector multiplies, a memory bandwidth intensive operation.

HPCCG was used in weak-scaling mode with a "100x100x100" sub-problem on each node, using approximately 380 MB of memory per node. This configuration is representative of typical usage, and results in relatively few and relatively large messages being communicated between neighboring nodes. Every iteration of the CG algorithm performs an 8-byte Allreduce, and there are 149 iterations during the test problem's approximately 30 second runtime.

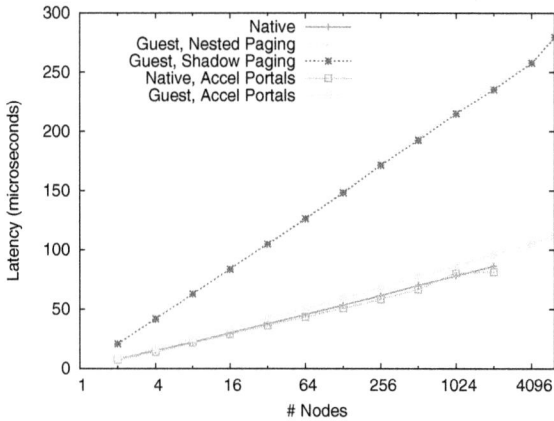

Figure 3. MPI all-reduce scaling microbenchmark results measuring the latency of a 16 byte all-reduce operation.

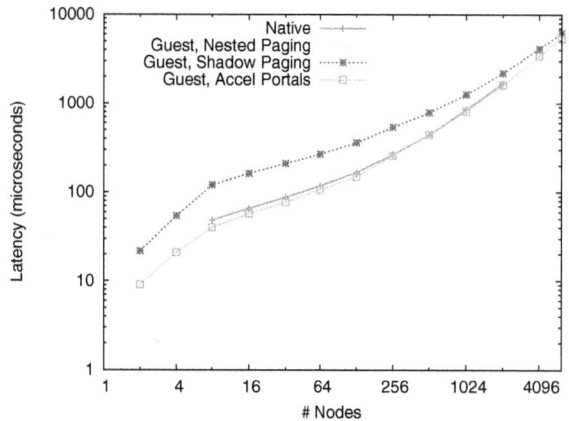

Figure 5. MPI all-to-all scaling microbenchmark results measuring the latency of a 16 byte all-to-all operation.

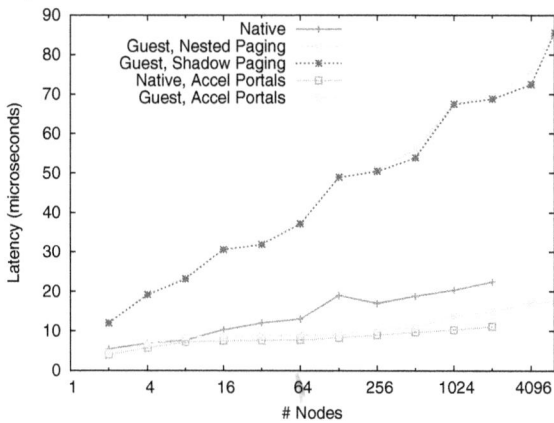

Figure 4. MPI broadcast scaling microbenchmark results measuring the latency of a broadcast of 16 bytes.

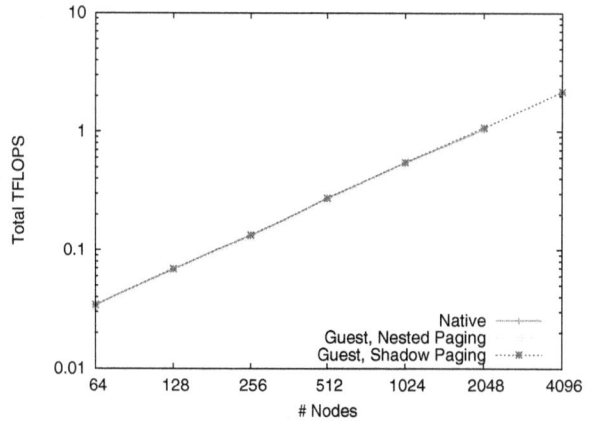

Figure 6. HPCCG application benchmark performance. Weak scaling is measured. Virtualized performance is within 5% of native.

The portion of runtime consumed by communication is reported by the benchmark to be less than 5% in all cases. Interrupt-driven communication was used for this and other application benchmarks. Recall that the microbenchmarks show virtualized interrupt-driven communication is the slower of the two options we considered.

As shown in Figure 6, HPCCG scales extremely well in both guest and native environments. Performance with shadow paging is essentially identical to native performance, while performance with nested paging is 2.5% worse at 2048 nodes.

3.5 CTH application

CTH [8] is a multi-material, large deformation, strong shock wave, solid mechanics code used for studying armor/anti-armor interactions, warhead design, high explosive initiation physics, and weapons safety issues. A shaped charge test problem was used to perform a weak scaling study in both native and guest environments. As reported in [9], which used the same test problem, at 512 nodes approximately 40% of the application's runtime is due to MPI communication, 30% of which is due to MPI_Allreduce operations with an average size of 32 bytes. The application performs significant point-to-point communication with nearest neighbors using large messages.

Figure 7 shows the results of the scaling study for native and guest environments. At 2048 nodes, the guest environment with

shadow paging is 3% slower than native, while the nested paging configuration is 5.5% slower. Since network performance is virtually identical with either shadow or nested paging, the performance advantage of shadow paging is likely due to the faster TLB miss processing that it provides.

3.6 SAGE application

SAGE (SAIC's Adaptive Grid Eulerian hydrocode) is a multidimensional hydrodynamics code with adaptive mesh refinement [18]. The timing_c input deck was used to perform a weak scaling study. As reported in [9], which used the same test problem, at 512 nodes approximately 45% of the application's runtime is due to MPI communication, of which roughly 50% is due to MPI_Allreduce operations with an average size of 8 bytes.

Figure 8 shows the results of executing the scaling study in the native and virtualized environments. At 2048 nodes, shadow paging is 2.4% slower compared to native while nested paging is 3.5% slower. As with CTH, the slightly better performance of shadow paging is due to its faster TLB miss processing.

4. Passthrough I/O

One of the principle goals in designing Palacios was to allow a large amount of configurability in order to target multiple diverse

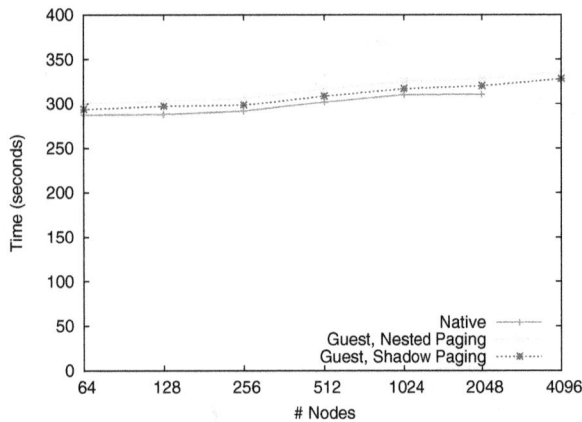

Figure 7. CTH application benchmark performance. Weak scaling is measured. Virtualized performance is within 5% of native.

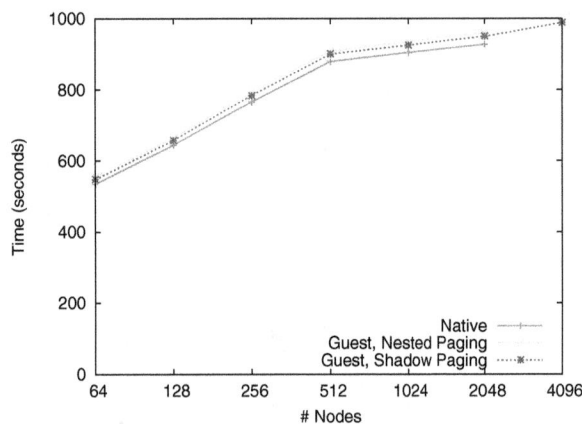

Figure 8. Sage application benchmark performance. Weak scaling is measured. Virtualized performance is within 5% of native.

environments. This allows us to use a number of configuration options specific to HPC environments to minimize virtualization overheads and maximize performance. The special HPC configuration of Palacios makes a number of fundamental choices in order to provide guest access to hardware devices with as little overhead as possible. These choices were reflected both in the architecture of Palacios as configured for HPC, as well as two assumptions about the environment Palacios executes in.

The first assumption we make for HPC environments is that only a single guest will be running on a node at any given time. Restricting each partition to run a single guest environment ensures that there is no resource contention between multiple VMs. This is the common case for large-scale supercomputers as each application requires dedicated access to the entirety of the system resources, and is also the common case for many smaller space-shared high performance systems. The restriction vastly simplifies device management because Palacios does not need to support sharing of physical devices between competing guests; Palacios can directly map an I/O device into a guest domain without having to manage the device itself.

The second assumption we make for HPC environments is that we can place considerable trust in the guest OS because HPC system operators typically have full control over the entire software stack. Under this assumption, the guest OS is unlikely to attempt to

compromise the VMM intentionally, and may even be designed to help protect the VMM from any errors.

4.1 Passthrough I/O implementation

In Palacios, passthrough I/O is based on a virtualized PCI bus. The virtual bus is implemented as an emulation layer inside Palacios, and has the capability of providing access to both virtual as well as physical (passthrough) PCI devices. When a guest is configured to use a passthrough device directly, Palacios scans the physical PCI bus searching for the appropriate device and then attaches a virtual instance of that device to the virtual PCI bus. Any changes that a guest makes to the device's configuration space are applied only to the virtualized version. These changes are exposed to the physical device via reconfigurations of the guest environment to map the virtual configuration space onto the physical one.

As an example, consider a PCI Base Address Register (BAR) that contains a memory region that is used for memory-mapped access to the device. Whenever a guest tries to change this setting by overwriting the BAR's contents, instead of updating the physical device's BAR, Palacios updates the virtual device's BAR and reconfigures the guest's physical memory layout so that the relevant guest physical memory addresses are redirected to the host physical memory addresses mapped by the real BAR register. In this way, Palacios virtualizes configuration operations but not the actual data transfer.

Most devices do not rely on the PCI BAR registers to define DMA regions for I/O. Instead the BAR registers typically point to additional, non-standard configuration spaces, that themselves contain locations of DMA descriptors. Palacios makes no attempt to virtualize these regions, and instead relies on the guest OS to supply valid DMA addresses for its own physical address space. While this requires that Palacios trust the guest OS to use correct DMA addresses as they appear in the host, it is designed such that there is a a high assurance that the DMA addresses used by the guest are valid.

The key design choice that provides high assurance of secure DMA address translation from the guest physical addresses to the host physical addresses is the shape of the guest's physical address space. A Palacios guest is initially configured with a physically contiguous block of memory that maps into the contiguous portion of the guest's physical address space that contains memory. This allows the guest to compute a host physical address from a guest physical address by simply adding an offset value. This means that a passthrough DMA address can be immediately calculated as long as the guest knows what offset the memory in its physical address space begins at. Furthermore, the guest can know definitively if the address is within the bounds of its memory by checking that it does not exceed the range of guest physical addresses that contain memory, information that is readily available to the guest via the e820 map and other standard mechanisms. Because guest physical to host physical address translation for actual physical memory is so simple, DMA addresses can be calculated and used with a high degree of certainty that they are correct and will not compromise the host or VMM.

It is also important to point out that as long as the guest uses physical addresses valid with respect to its memory map, it cannot affect the VMM or other passthrough or virtual devices with a DMA request on a passthrough device.

To allow the guest to determine when a DMA address needs to be translated (by offsetting) for passthrough access, Palacios uses a shared memory region to advertise which PCI devices are in fact configured as passthrough. Each PCI bus location tuple (bus ID, device ID, and function number) is combined to form an index into a bitmap. If a device is configured as passthrough the bit at its given index will be set by the VMM and read by the guest OS. This bitmap allows the guest OS to selectively offset DMA addresses, allowing for compatibility with both passthrough devices (which require offsetting) and virtual devices (which do not). Furthermore, when the guest is run without the VMM in place, this mechanism naturally turns off offsetting for all devices.

Comparison with other approaches to high performance virtualized I/O: Due to both the increased trust and control over the guest environments as well as the simplified mechanism for DMA address translation, Palacios can rely on the guest to correctly interact with the passthrough devices. The passthrough I/O technique allows direct interaction with hardware devices with as little overhead as possible. In contrast, other approaches designed to provide passthrough I/O access must add additional overhead. For example, VMM-Bypass [21], as designed for the Xen Hypervisor, does not provide the same guarantees in terms of address space contiguity. Furthermore, its usage model assumes that the guest environments are not fully trusted entities. The result is that the implementation complexity is much higher for VMM-Bypass, and further overheads are added due to the need for the VMM to validate the device configurations. Furthermore, this technique is highly device specific (specifically Infiniband) whereas our passthrough architecture is capable of working with any unmodified PCI device driver.

Self-Virtualization [26] is a technique to allow device sharing without the need for a separate virtual driver domain. While self virtualization permits direct guest interaction with hardware devices, it uses a simplified virtual interface which limits the usable capabilities of the device. It also requires specially architected hardware, while our passthrough implementation supports any existing PCI device.

Finally, recent work on assuring device driver safety in traditional operating systems [29] could also be used to supplement passthrough device virtualization. In particular, these techniques could be used to validate safety-critical guest device manipulations in virtual machines. This would enable the high performance of passthrough I/O while providing additional guest isolation in environments that where guest OSes are less trusted than in HPC environments.

4.2 Current implementations

We have currently implemented passthrough I/O for both a collection of HPC OSes, such as Catamount and Kitten, as well as for commodity Linux kernels. The Catamount OS specifically targets the Cray SeaStar as its only supported I/O device, so Catamount did not require a general passthrough framework. However, Kitten and Linux are designed for more diverse environments so we have implemented the full passthrough architecture in each of them. In each case, the implementation is approximately 300 lines of C and assembler built on the SymSpy guest implementation (Section 7). The actual DMA address offsetting and bounds checking implementation is about 20 lines of C.

Both Kitten and Linux include the concept of a DMA address space that is conceptually separate from the address space of core memory. This allows a large degree of compatibility between different architectures that might implement a separate DMA address space. The environment exposed by Palacios is such an architecture. Every time a device driver intends to perform a DMA operation it must first transform a memory address into a DMA address via a DMA mapping service. Our guest versions of both Linux and Kitten include a modified mapping service that selectively adds the address offset to each DMA address if the device requesting the DMA translation is configured for passthrough. Our modifications also sanity check the calculated DMA address, thus protecting the VMM from any malformed DMA operations. These modifications are small, easy to understand, and all-encompassing, meaning that

the VMM can have a high degree of confidence that even a complicated OS such as Linux will not compromise the VMM via malformed DMA operations.

4.3 Infiniband passthrough

To verify that Palacios's passthrough I/O approach also resulted in low-overhead communication on commodity NICs in addition to specialized hardware like the Cray SeaStar, we examined its performance on a small Linux cluster system built around the commodity Infiniband network interface. Specifically, we examined the performance both a low-level Infiniband communication microbenchmark (the OpenFabrics `ibv_rc_pingpong` test) and the HPCCG benchmark described earlier. Tests were run on a 4-node 2.4GHz AMD Barcelona cluster communicating over 64-bit PCI Express Mellanox MLX4 cards configured for passthrough in Linux. For ping-pong tests, the client system which performed the timings ran native Fedora 11 with Linux kernel 2.6.30, and the client machine ran a diskless Linux BusyBox image that also used Linux kernel 2.6.30 with symbiotic extensions either natively or virtualized in Palacios. For HPCCG tests, all nodes ran the Linux BusyBox image, and timings were taken using the underlying hardware cycle counter to guarantee accuracy.

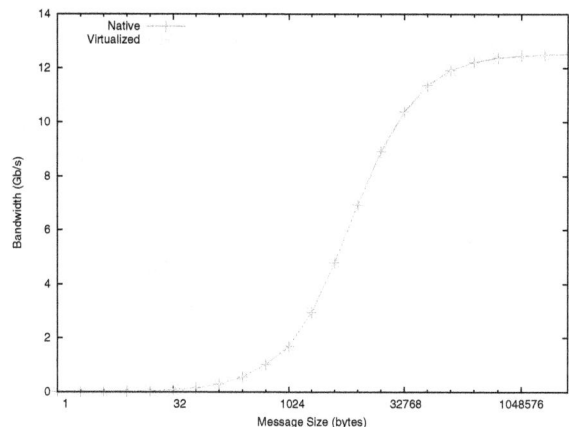

Figure 9. Infiniband bandwidth at message sizes from 1 byte to 4 megabytes averaged over 10000 iteration per sample. 1-byte round-trip latency for both native and virtualized environments was identical at 6.46 μsec, with peak bandwidth for 4 MB messages at 12.49 Gb/s on Linux virtualized with Palacios compared to 12.51 Gb/s for native Linux.

As Figure 9 shows, Palacios's pass-through virtualization imposes almost no overhead on Infiniband message passing. In particular, Palacios's passthrough PCI support enables virtualized Linux to almost perfectly match the bandwidth of native Linux on Infiniband, and because Infiniband does not use interrupts for high-speed message passing with reliable-connected channels, the 1-byte message latencies with and without virtualization are identical. Similarly, HPCCG ran an average of only 4% slower (43.1 seconds versus 41.4 seconds averaged over 5 runs) when virtualized using passthrough I/O and nested paging.

4.4 Future extensions

Future advances in hardware virtualization support may obviate the need for the passthrough techniques described above. For example, AMD's IOMMU adds hardware support for guest DMA translations. However, we should note that our approach includes a very minimal amount of overhead and it is not clear that hardware techniques will necessarily perform better. An IOMMU would introduce additional performance overhead in the form of page table lookups, something which our approach completely avoids. As we will show in the next section and as others have demonstrated [1], software approaches can often operate with demonstrably less overhead than hardware approaches.

5. Workload-sensitive paging mechanisms

In our scaling evaluations, we focused on the two standard techniques for virtualizing the paging hardware: shadow paging and nested paging as described in Section 3.2. These results demonstrate that while memory virtualization can scale, making it do so is non-trivial; we discuss the implications of these results in this section. Based on these results, we also present the results of several additional experiments that examine how more sophisticated architectural and VMM support for memory virtualization impacts HPC benchmark performance.

5.1 Scaling analysis

The basic scaling results presented earlier in Section 3 demonstrate that the best performing technique is dependent on the application workload as well as the architecture of the guest OS. As an example, Catamount performs a minimal number of page table operations, and never fully flushes the TLB or switches between different page tables. This means that very few operations are required to emulate the guest page tables with shadow paging. Because the overhead of shadow paging is so small, shadow paging performs better than nested paging due to the better use of the hardware TLB. In contrast, Compute Node Linux (CNL), another HPC OS, uses multiple sets of page tables to handle multitasking and so frequently flushes the TLB. For this OS, there is a great deal more overhead in emulating the page table operations and any improvement in TLB performance is masked by the frequent flush operations. As a result, nested paging is the superior choice in this case.

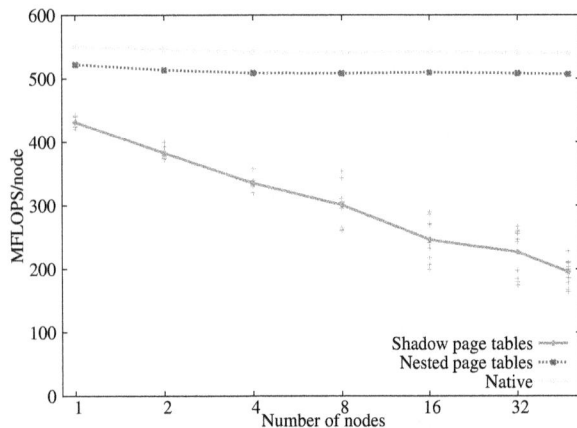

Figure 10. Strong scaling of HPCCG running on CNL. Nested paging is preferable, and the overhead of shadow paging compounds as we scale up. This is due to the relatively high context switch rate in CNL.

As these results demonstrate, behavior of the guest OS and applications have a critical impact on the performance of the virtualized paging implementation. We have found this to be true in the broader server consolidation context [5] as well as the HPC context we discuss here. Figures 10 and 11 (previously published elsewhere [20]) illustrate this point for HPC. Figure 10 shows the results of the HPCCG benchmark being run with a CNL guest environment as we scale from 1 to 48 nodes of a Cray XT. As the results

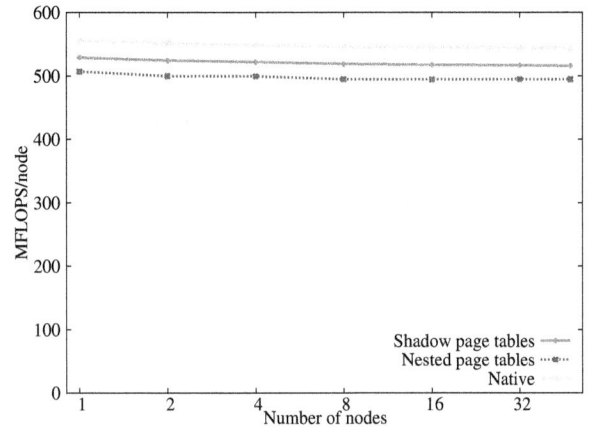

Figure 11. Strong scaling of HPCCG running on Catamount. Here shadow paging is preferable. This is due to the relatively low context switch rate in Catamount revealing shadow paging's better TLB behavior.

show, the overhead introduced with shadow paging is large enough to dramatically degrade scalability, while the nested paging configuration is able to still perform well as it scales up. Figure 11 shows the same benchmark run on the Catamount guest OS. Here, the situation is reversed. Shadow paging clearly performs better than nested paging due to the improved TLB behavior and lower overhead from page table manipulations.

5.2 Memory virtualization optimizations

In light of these results, we also examined the performance of key optimizations to nested and shadow paging. In particular, we studied the aggressive use of large pages in nested page tables and two different optimizations to shadow paging. For these evaluations, we used HPC Challenge 1.3 [22, 27], an HPC-oriented benchmark suite that tests system elements critical to HPC application performance.

5.2.1 2 MB nested page tables

Aggressively using large pages in nested page tables is an optimization that could dramatically improve the performance of nested paging on applications and benchmarks that are TLB-intensive. For example, using 2MB nested page tables on the x86_64 architecture reduces the length of full page table walks from 24 steps to 14 steps. Note that using large pages in shadow paging is also possible, but, like using large pages in a traditional operating system, can be quite challenging as the guest may make permission and mapping requests at smaller page granularities that could require the VMM to split large pages or merge smaller pages.

To evaluate the potential impact of using 2MB nested page tables on HPC applications, we implemented support for large-page nested page tables in Palacios. We then evaluated its performance when running the Catamount guest operating system, the guest on which nested paging performed comparatively worse in our scaling study. Because Catamount can make aggressive use of large pages, this also allowed us to study the impact of these different paging choices on guests that used 4KB pages versus guests like Catamount that make aggressive use of 2MB pages.

Our evaluation focused on the HPL, STREAM Triad, and RandomAccess benchmarks from HPC Challenge. HPL is a compute-intensive HPC benchmark commonly used to benchmark HPC systems [28], STREAM Triad is a memory bandwidth intensive benchmark, and RandomAccess is a simulated large-scale data analytics benchmark that randomly updates an array approximately the size of physical memory, resulting in a very high TLB miss rate.

Figure 12 shows the relative performance of nested paging with different nested and main page table sizes, with shadow paging and native paging numbers included for comparison. HPL performance shows little variability due to its regular memory access patterns in these tests, though 2MB nested page tables does improve nested paging performance to essentially native levels. Using large pages with nested paging makes a dramatic difference on the TLB miss-intensive RandomAccess benchmark. In particular, using large pages in the nested page tables reduces the penalty of nested paging from 64% to 31% for guests that use 4KB pages and from 68% to 19% for guests that use 2MB pages.

The RandomAccess results also show that nested paging is better able to support guests that aggressively use large pages compared to shadow paging. While nested paging performance is 19% worse than native, it is significantly better than shadow paging performance, which is limited by the performance of its underlying 4KB page-based page tables. With guests that use only 4KB pages, however, shadow paging achieves native-level performance while nested paging with 2MB pages is 30% slower than native.

5.2.2 Shadow paging optimizations

With stable guest page tables, shadow paging has the benefit of having shorter page walks on a TLB miss than nested paging. However, context switches in the guest ameliorate this advantage in a basic shadow paging implementation because they force a flush of the "virtual TLB" (the shadow page tables). Subsequent to this, a stream of exits occurs as page faults are used to rebuild the shadow page tables. We have considered two techniques in Palacios to reduce this cost: shadow page table caching and shadow page table prefetching.

In contrast to a basic shadow paging implementation, both caching and prefetching introduce a new overhead as they must monitor the guest page tables for changes so that the corresponding cached or prefetched shadow page table entries may be updated or flushed. While conceptually simple, preserving x86_64 page table consistency requirements is quite challenging, leading to considerably higher software complexity in the VMM. In particular, because portions of page tables may be shared across address spaces, page table updates in one address space may affect page tables mapping additional address spaces. Furthermore, a physical page containing a page table is allowed to appear at multiple levels in a page table hierarchy.

In a shadow page table caching implementation, when the guest switches from one context to another and the VMM already has the corresponding shadow context in its cache, the cost of the context switch is dramatically reduced. In the best case, where the guest makes frequent context switches but rarely edits its page tables, a context switch requires only that the VMM load the page table base register and continue. In the worse case, the guest frequently edits its page tables, but rarely performs context switches.

In a shadow page table prefetching implementation, a guest context switch acts as in a basic implementation, flushing the shadow page tables. However, on a single page fault, multiple guest page table entries are visited and reflected into the shadow page table. Our implementation prefetches an entire page's worth of entries on each page fault, so in the best case, where the guest makes frequent context switches but rarely edits its page tables, the overhead of a context switch is reduced by a factor of 512 (PAE) or 1024 (non-PAE). In the worst case, the guest frequently edits page tables but rarely performs context switches. In contrast to shadow page table caching, shadow page table prefetching requires no more space than basic shadow paging.

Approach	Run-time (s)
Native	15.7
Shadow	798.9
Shadow+Prefetching	1305.6
Shadow+Caching	32.9
Nested (4KB pages)	24.7

Figure 13. Performance of HPC Challenge benchmark suite in Palacios for different memory virtualization approaches.

To further evaluate the potential benefits of caching and prefetching, we studied their overall performance on the HPC Challenge benchmark suite. It is important to point out that this evaluation involved configuring HPC Challenge to emphasize the effects of address translation performance instead of to maximize overall benchmark performance. In particular, we configured the benchmarks to run with four processes per core, resulting in a significant context switch rate. The combination of context switches and memory reference behavior in the benchmark processes interacts differently with the different paging approaches, and represents a particular challenge for shadow paging. HPC Challenge includes seven benchmarks, with two, Random Access and HPL, accounting for almost all the variation among the different paging approaches. The experiments were run on a Dell PowerEdge SC1450 system with an AMD Opteron 2350 "Barcelona" processor with 2GB of RAM. The guest operating system was running Puppy Linux 3.01 (32-bit Linux kernel 2.6.18). The study is further described elsewhere [5].

Figure 13 shows the results. While shadow paging with prefetching is not an effective optimization for this workload, shadow paging with caching brings performance much closer to nested paging performance, although there remains a gap. We also evaluated shadow paging with caching using the more mature implementation in the KVM VMM. There, a run time of 24.3 s was measured, right on par with nested paging. Note that performance remains distant from native due to the Random Access benchmark.

5.3 Summary

These results show that the choice of virtual paging techniques is critically important to ensuring scalable performance in HPC environments and that the best technique varies across OSes, hardware, and applications. This suggests that an HPC VMM should provide a mechanism for specifying the initial paging technique as well as for switching between techniques during execution. Furthermore, an HPC VMM should provide a range of paging techniques to choose from. Palacios supports this through a modular architecture for paging techniques. New techniques can be created and linked into the VMM in a straightforward manner, with each guest being able to dynamically select among all the available techniques at runtime. We are also currently exploring adaptive runtime modification of guest paging virtualization strategies.

6. Controlled preemption

We now consider the third technique we found to be essential to low overhead virtualization at scale, controlled preemption.

6.1 Overview

It is well understood that background noise can have a serious performance impact on large scale parallel applications. This has led to much work in designing OSes such that the amount of noise they inject into the system is minimized and that the impact of necessary noise on application performance is minimized. Palacios is designed to support such efforts by minimizing the amount of overhead due to virtualization, placing necessary overheads and

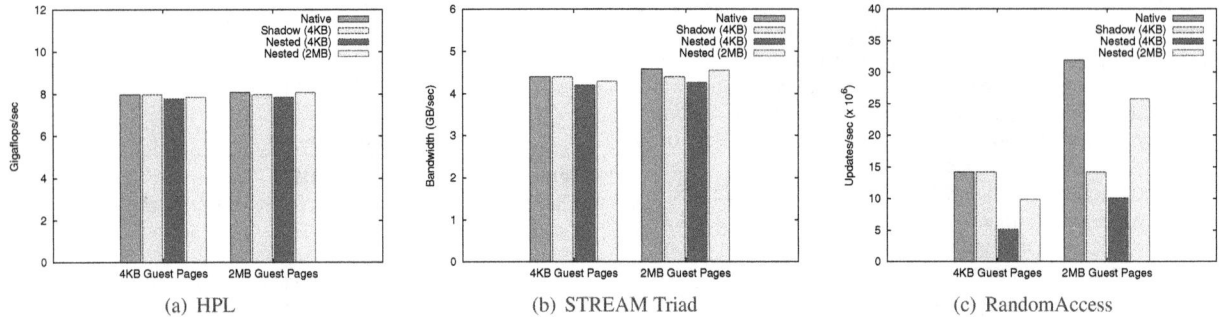

(a) HPL (b) STREAM Triad (c) RandomAccess

Figure 12. Performance of 2MB Nested Paging running HPC Challenge HPL, STREAM Triad, and RandomAccess benchmarks on a Cray XT4 node with a Catamount guest OS.

work into deterministic points in time in an effort to minimize the amount of noise added to the system by virtualization, and allowing system deployers control over when guests are preempted.

Palacios runs as a non-preemptable kernel thread in Kitten. Only interrupts and explicit yields by Palacios can change control flow. Palacios controls the global interrupt flag and guest interrupt exiting and uses this control to allow interrupts to happen only at specific points during exit handling. This allows Palacios to provide well-controlled availability of CPU resources to the guest. Background processes and deferred work are only allowed to proceed when their performance impact will be negligible.

When a guest is configured it is allowed to specify its execution quantum which determines the frequency at which it will yield the CPU to the Kitten scheduler. It is important to note that the quantum configured by Palacios is separate from the scheduling quantum used by Kitten for task scheduling. This separation allows each guest to override the host OS scheduler in order to prevent the host OS from introducing additional OS noise. Furthermore this quantum can be overridden at runtime such that a guest can specify critical sections where Palacios should not under any circumstances yield the CPU to another host process.

As a result of this, Palacios adds minimal additional noise to guests and applications that run on top of it, particularly compared to other VMMs not designed for use in HPC systems. To quantify this, we compiled the selfish noise measurement benchmark frequently used to measure OS interference in HPC systems into a minimal kernel with interrupts disabled to measure the amount of interference the VMM presents to guest operating systems. This benchmark spins the CPU while continually reading the timestamp counter, which is configured by the VMM to passthrough to hardware. We ran this guest kernel on a Cray XT4 node on both a minimal Linux/KVM VMM (`init`, `/bin/sh`, and `/sbin/sshd` were the only user-level processes running) and on Palacios.

In these tests, the Linux/KVM virtual machine used almost exactly 10 times as much CPU for management overhead as Palacios (0.22% for Linux/KVM versus 0.022% for Palacios). This is largely due to the increased timer and scheduler frequency of KVM's Linux host OS compared to the Kitten host OS, which can use a much larger scheduling quantum because of its focus on HPC systems. While these overheads both appear small in absolute terms, they are in addition to any overhead that the guest OS imposes on an application. Because past research has shown that even small asynchronous OS overheads can result in application slowdowns of orders of magnitude on large-scale systems [9, 25], minimizing these overheads is essential for virtualization to be viable in HPC systems.

6.2 Future extensions

An extant issue in HPC environments is the overhead induced via timer interrupts. An eventual goal of Kitten is to implement a system with no dependence on periodic interrupts, and instead rely entirely on on-demand one shot timers. However, periodic timers are occasionally necessary when running a guest environment with Palacios, in order to ensure that time advances in the guest OS. Because some guest OSes do require periodic timer interrupts at a specified frequency, the VMM needs to ensure that the interrupts can be delivered to the guest environment at the appropriate rate. We are developing a method in which the guest OS is capable of both enabling/disabling as well as altering the frequency of the host's periodic timer. This would allow a guest OS to specify its time sensitivity[2], which will allow Palacios and Kitten to adapt timer behavior to the current workload.

7. A symbiotic approach to virtualization

While our experiences have shown that it is indeed possible to virtualize large scale HPC systems with minimal overhead, we have found that doing so requires cooperation between the guest and VMM. Each of the three techniques we have described (Sections 4–6) relies on communication and trust across the VMM/guest interface for the mutual benefit of both entities. In other words, the relationship between the VMM and the guest is *symbiotic*. We have been working to generalize the interfaces involved in our techniques into a general purpose *symbiotic interface* that provides VMM↔guest information flow that can be leveraged in these and future techniques.

Our symbiotic interface allows for both passive, asynchronous and active, synchronous communication between guest and VMM. The symbiotic interface is *optional* for the guest, and a guest which does use it can also run on non-symbiotic VMMs or raw hardware without any changes. We focus here on the passive interface, *SymSpy*; the active interface, *SymCall*, is described elsewhere [19].

SymSpy builds on the widely used technique of a shared memory region that is accessible by both the VMM and guest. This shared memory is used by both the VMM and guest to expose semantically rich state information to each other, as well as to provide asynchronous communication channels. The data contained in the memory region is well structured and semantically rich, allowing it to be used for most general purpose cross layer communication. Each of the three techniques we have given in this paper are implemented on top of SymSpy. We have implemented SymSpy support in Catamount, Kitten, and in non-HPC guest OSes such as Linux.

---

[2] You can think of this as being loosely correlated to the guest's timer frequency setting

SymSpy is designed to be enabled and configured at run time without requiring any major structural changes to the guest OS. The discovery protocol is implemented using existing hardware features, such as CPUID values and Model Specific Registers (MSRs). When run on a symbiotic VMM, CPUID and MSR access is trapped and emulated, allowing the VMM to provide extended results. Through this, a guest can detect a SymSpy interface at boot time and selectively enable specific symbiotic features that it supports. Due to this hardware-like model, the discovery protocol will also work correctly if no symbiotic VMM is being used; the guest will simply not find a symbiotic interface.

After the guest has detected the presence of SymSpy it chooses an available guest physical memory address that is not currently in use for the shared memory region and notifies the VMM of this address through a write to a virtualized MSR. The precise semantics and layout of the data on the shared memory region depends on the symbiotic services that are discovered to be jointly available in the guest and the VMM. The structured data types and layout are enumerated during discovery. During normal operation, the guest can read and write this shared memory without causing an exit. The VMM can also directly access the page during its execution.

8. Conclusion

Our primary contribution has been to demonstrate that it is possible to virtualize the largest parallel supercomputers in the world[3] at very large scales with minimal performance overheads. In particular, tightly-coupled, communication-intensive applications running on specialized lightweight OSes that provide maximum hardware capabilities to them can run in a virtualized environment with $\leq 5\%$ performance overhead at scales in excess of 4096 nodes. In addition, other HPC applications and guest OSes can be supported with minimal overhead given appropriate hardware support.

These results suggest that HPC machines can reap the many benefits of virtualization that have been articulated before (e.g., [10, 13]). Another benefit that other researchers have noted [4] but that has not been widely discussed is that scalable HPC virtualization also opens the range of applications of the machines by making it possible to use commodity OSes on them in capacity modes when they are not needed for capability purposes.

We believe our results represent the largest scale study of HPC virtualization by at least two orders of magnitude, and we have described how such performance is possible. Scalable high performance rests on passthrough I/O, workload sensitive selection of paging mechanisms, and carefully controlled preemption. These techniques are made possible via a symbiotic interface between the VMM and the guest, an interface we have generalized with SymSpy. We are now working to further generalize this and other symbiotic interfaces, and apply them to further enhance virtualized performance of supercomputers, multicore nodes, and other platforms. Our techniques are publicly available from v3vee.org as parts of Palacios and Kitten.

References

[1] K. Adams and O. Agesen. A comparison of software and hardware techniques for x86 virtualization. In *Proceedings of the 12th International Conference on Architectural Support for Programming Languages and Operating Systems (ASPLOS)*, October 2006.

[2] S. R. Alam, J. A. Kuehn, R. F. Barrett, J. M. Larkin, M. R. Fahey, R. Sankaran, and P. H. Worley. Cray XT4: an early evaluation for petascale scientific simulation. In *SC '07: Proceedings of the 2007 ACM/IEEE conference on Supercomputing*, pages 1–12, New York, NY, USA, 2007. ACM. ISBN 978-1-59593-764-3. doi: http://doi.acm.org/10.1145/1362622.1362675.

[3] AMD Corporation. AMD64 virtualization codenamed "Pacifica" technology: Secure Virtual Machine Architecture reference manual, May 2005.

[4] J. Appavoo, V. Uhlig, and A. Waterland. Project kittyhawk: building a global-scale computer: Blue gene/p as a generic computing platform. *SIGOPS Oper. Syst. Rev.*, 42:77–84, January 2008. ISSN 0163-5980. doi: http://doi.acm.org/10.1145/1341312.1341326. URL http://doi.acm.org/10.1145/1341312.1341326.

[5] C. Bae, J. Lange, and P. Dinda. Comparing approaches to virtualized page translation in modern VMMs. Technical Report NWU-EECS-10-07, Department of Electrical Engineering and Computer Science, Northwestern University, April 2010.

[6] R. Bhargava, B. Serebrin, F. Spanini, and S. Manne. Accelerating two-dimensional page walks for virtualized systems. In *Proceedings of the 13th International Conference on Architectural Support for Programming Languages and Operating Systems (ASPLOS)*, March 2008.

[7] R. Brightwell, T. Hudson, K. T. Pedretti, and K. D. Underwood. SeaStar Interconnect: Balanced bandwidth for scalable performance. *IEEE Micro*, 26(3):41–57, May/June 2006.

[8] J. E.S. Hertel, R. Bell, M. Elrick, A. Farnsworth, G. Kerley, J. McGlaun, S. Petney, S. Silling, P. Taylor, and L. Yarrington. CTH: A Software Family for Multi-Dimensional Shock Physics Analysis. In *19th International Symposium on Shock Waves, held at Marseille, France*, pages 377–382, July 1993.

[9] K. B. Ferreira, R. Brightwell, and P. G. Bridges. Characterizing application sensitivity to OS interference using kernel-level noise injection. In *Proceedings of the 2008 ACM/IEEE Conference on Supercomputing*, November 2008.

[10] R. Figueiredo, P. A. Dinda, and J. Fortes. A case for grid computing on virtual machines. In *23rd IEEE Conference on Distributed Computing (ICDCS 2003*, pages 550–559, May 2003.

[11] A. Gavrilovska, S. Kumar, H. Raj, K. Schwan, V. Gupta, R. Nathuji, R. Niranjan, A. Ranadive, and P. Saraiya. High performance hypervisor architectures: Virtualization in HPC systems. In *1st Workshop on System-level Virtualization for High Performance Computing (HPCVirt)*, 2007.

[12] M. Heroux. HPCCG MicroApp. https://software.sandia.gov/mantevo/downloads/HPCCG-0.5.tar.gz, July 2007.

[13] W. Huang, J. Liu, B. Abali, and D. K. Panda. A case for high performance computing with virtual machines. In *20th Annual International Conference on Supercomputing (ICS)*, pages 125–134, 2006.

[14] Intel Corporation. Intel virtualization technology specification for the IA-32 Intel architecture, April 2005.

[15] Intel GmbH. Intel MPI benchmarks: Users guide and methodology description, 2004.

---

[3] The Red Storm machine we used is in the top-20.

[16] L. Kaplan. Cray CNL. In *FastOS PI Meeting and Workshop*, June 2007. URL `http://www.cs.unm.edu/~fastos/07meeting/CNL_FASTOS.pdf`.

[17] S. Kelly and R. Brightwell. Software architecture of the lightweight kernel, Catamount. In *2005 Cray Users' Group Annual Technical Conference*. Cray Users' Group, May 2005.

[18] D. Kerbyson, H. Alme, A. Hoisie, F. Petrini, H. Wasserman, and M. Gittings. Predictive performance and scalability modeling of a large-scale application. In *Proceedings of ACM/IEEE Supercomputing*, November 2001.

[19] J. Lange and P. Dinda. SymCall: Symbiotic virtualization through VMM-to-guest upcalls. In *Proceedings of the 2011 ACM SIGPLAN/SIGOPS International Conference on Virtual Execution Environments (VEE 2011)*, Newport Beach, CA, March 2011.

[20] J. Lange, K. Pedretti, T. Hudson, P. Dinda, Z. Cui, L. Xia, P. Bridges, A. Gocke, S. Jaconette, M. Levenhagen, and R. Brightwell. Palacios and kitten: New high performance operating systems for scalable virtualized and native supercomputing. In *Proceedings of the 24th IEEE International Parallel and Distributed Processing Symposium (IPDPS 2010)*, April 2010.

[21] J. Liu, W. Huang, B. Abali, and D. Panda. High Performance VMM-Bypass I/O in Virtual Machines. In *Proceedings of the USENIX Annual Technical Conference*, May 2006.

[22] P. Luszczek, J. Dongarra, and J. Kepner. Design and implementation of the HPCC benchmark suite. *CT Watch Quarterly*, 2(4A), Nov. 2006.

[23] M. F. Mergen, V. Uhlig, O. Krieger, and J. Xenidis. Virtualization for high-performance computing. *Operating Systems Review*, 40(2):8–11, 2006.

[24] H. Nishimura, N. Maruyama, and S. Matsuoka. Virtual clusters on the fly - fast, scalable, and flexible installation. In *7th IEEE International Symposium on Cluster Computing and the Grid (CCGRID)*, pages 549–556, 2007.

[25] F. Petrini, D. Kerbyson, and S. Pakin. The case of the missing supercomputer performance: Achieving optimal performance on the 8,192 processors of ASCI Q. In *Proceedings of SC'03*, 2003.

[26] H. Raj and K. Schwan. High performance and scalable I/O virtualization via self-virtualized devices. In *16th IEEE International Symposium on High Performance Distributed Computing*, July 2007.

[27] S. Song, R. Ge, X. Feng, and K. W. Cameron. Energy profiling and analysis of the HPC Challenge benchmarks. *International Journal of High Performance Computing Applications*, Vol. 23, No. 3:265–276, 2009.

[28] Top500. Top 500 Supercomputing Sites. URL `http://www.top500.org/`.

[29] D. Williams, P. Reynolds, K. Walsh, E. G. Sirer, and F. B. Schneider. Device driver safety through a reference validation mechanism. In *Proceedings of the 8th Symposium on Operating Systems Design and Implementation (OSDI'08)*, 2008.

Virtual WiFi: Bring Virtualization from Wired to Wireless

Lei Xia*, Sanjay Kumar§, Xue Yang§
Praveen Gopalakrishnan§, York Liu‡, Sebastian Schoenberg§, Xingang Guo§

* Northwestern University, Department of Electrical Engineering and Computer Science
lxia@northwestern.edu

§ Intel Labs, Hillsboro, OR
{sanjay.k.kumar, xue.yang, praveen.gopalakrishnan,sebastian.schoenberg, xingang.guo}@intel.com

‡ Intel Labs, Santa Clara, CA
yorkliu@hotmail.com

Abstract

As virtualization trend is moving towards "client virtualization", wireless virtualization remains to be one of the technology gaps that haven't been addressed satisfactorily. Today's approaches are mainly developed for wired network, and are not suitable for virtualizing wireless network interface due to the fundamental differences between wireless and wired LAN devices that we will elaborate in this paper. We propose a wireless LAN virtualization approach named *virtual WiFi* that addresses the technology gap. With our proposed solution, the full wireless LAN functionalities are supported inside virtual machines; each virtual machine can establish its own connection with self-supplied credentials; and multiple separate wireless LAN connections are supported through one physical wireless LAN network interface. We designed and implemented a prototype for our proposed *virtual WiFi* approach, and conducted detailed performance study. Our results show that with conventional virtualization overhead mitigation mechanisms, our proposed approach can support fully functional wireless functions inside VM, and achieve close to native performance of Wireless LAN with moderately increased CPU utilization.

Categories and Subject Descriptors D.4.4 [*Software*]: OPERATING SYSTEMS—Communications Management [Network communication]

Keywords Wireless, Virtualization, WiFi, Hypervisor, Performance

1. Introduction

Virtualization enables multiple operating systems to run simultaneously in isolated containers on a single physical machine and provides an abstraction layer to separate the underlying hardware from what the OS inside a Virtual Machine (VM) observes. Virtualization has already been widely adopted in data centers, where the technology has helped to consolidate servers and dynamically manage existing resources more efficiently.

The technology is moving towards "client virtualization", where a virtual machines run on end users' devices, from notebooks to smart phones, providing unification across a plethora of devices and securing disparate software environments. In particular, enterprise IT has been one of the driving forces behind this technology. The ability to provide strong separation between not only personal and enterprise data but also applications, the operating systems and the entire security configurations/managements, supports the emerging "bring your own device" trend without compromising necessary IT control. Imagine a user brings one's beloved device to the company where IT simply drops a corporate virtual machine onto it. On the device of the user's choice, IT gets the control necessary over all corporate data and applications while users retain the same control for their personal data and applications. The "client virtualization" trend is evidenced by the rapidly emerging desktop/mobile virtualization solutions on the market [16, 36, 37].

As compelling as client virtualization is, the variety of hardware technologies that are predominantly present in client systems make it much more complicated than creating server-based technology. Wireless virtualization represents one of such major technical obstacles. Today's client virtualization solutions typically map all network connections to a virtual wired 802.3 Ethernet card for simplicity. Using a legacy wired adapter works very well for data transfers but has a major downside for wireless connections: features of the underlying network infrastructure or the wireless adapter cannot be controlled from inside the VM and have to be configured and managed at the level of the Virtual Machine Monitor or the hosting OS. While such an approach is reasonable in server virtualization, it doesn't support mobile and ultra-mobile computing very well. In these environments, users have high mobility and often connect exclusively through wireless. They expect sophisticated software tools to manage their network connectivity based on location, availability, performance and cost. For example, only if the connection manager in the VM is aware of changes about wireless link conditions, it could handle the handover between cellular 3G connection and Wireless LAN connection whenever needed.

IT-managed security using IEEE 802.11 together with 802.1x certificate based authentication adds another perspective to consider. A network connection is established only if the certificate is valid and the device is permitted to access the network. The problem with current wireless virtualization approach is that the VMM is the only component aware of the wireless network and performing the authentication with the network. All VM network traffic is then bridged through the single connection, which gives all VMs access to the same network. As a result, maintaining a secured corporate environment has to rely on higher layer solutions such as VPN, which adds cost, connection overhead and increases power consumption.

In this paper, we propose a wireless LAN virtualization approach named *virtual WiFi* that addresses the above two issues. With our solution, the full wireless LAN functionalities are supported inside virtual machines; each virtual machine can establish its own connection with self-supplied credentials. Multiple separate wireless LAN connections are supported through one physical wireless LAN network interface. Our main contributions are as follows:

- We propose a new approach named *virtual WiFi* that is suitable for wireless LAN virtualization.

- We designed and implemented a prototype for our proposed virtual WiFi approach, and performed detailed performance study.

- We identified overhead sources for our approach and we show that with conventional virtualization overhead mitigation mechanisms, our proposed approach can support fully functional wireless functions inside VM, and achieve close to native performance of Wireless LAN with moderately increased CPU utilization.

The rest of the paper is organized as follows: Section 2 discusses the basics of the wireless LAN and contrasts them with wired networks. Section 3 presents our proposed virtual WiFi approach. Section 4 describes our prototype implementation based on the Linux Kernel Virtual Machine (KVM). We discuss the details of our performance study in Section 5 followed by the related work in Section 6. We conclude the paper and present our future work in Section 7.

2. Wireless LAN vs. Wired LAN

Wireless networks have fundamental characteristics that make them significantly different from traditional wired LANs. While a wired LAN device must be physically attached to the wire in order to communicate, wireless devices communicate with each other via electromagnetic wave that has no visible boundaries. Any conformant device with reasonable signal reception can share the air medium and establish its own communication link. In the design of wired LANs, it is implicitly assumed that an address is equivalent to a physical location. On the other hand, in wireless LAN, the addressable unit is a station (STA), where each STA indicates a message destination and is not associated with a particular location.

We describe Wireless LAN in more details below to facilitate deeper understanding of the differences between wireless LANs and wired LANs. IEEE 802.11 defines the wireless LAN (WLAN) standard. Throughout this paper, we use "WiFi", "WLAN" or "wireless LAN" interchangeably. The basic service set (BSS) is the basic building block of an IEEE 802.11 WLAN, where two types of BSS: the infrastructure BSS and the independent BSS (IBSS), are defined. Within an infrastructure BSS, member STAs communicate via a central Access Point, while within an IBSS, two STAs can communicate with each other directly. The widely deployed WLAN systems are primarily infrastructure BSS, which will be the focus of this paper. Figure 1 illustrates a WLAN system that can consist of multiple Basic Service Sets. Each Basic Service Set has a limited coverage since electromagnetic wave signal will be attenuated as it propagates through space, which constraints the

range a wireless device can directly communicate with. Multiple BSSs provide extended coverage.

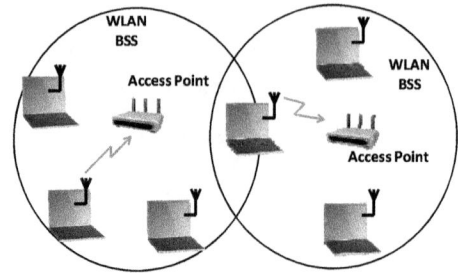

Figure 1. WLAN system with multiple BSSs

WLAN systems primarily operate in two unlicensed radio frequency bands: 2.4 GHz band and 5 GHz band. There are 14 channels designated in the 2.4 GHz band and 42 channels designated in the 5 GHz band[1]. When powered on, a WLAN STA will scan the available channels to discover active networks where Access Points are present. Once the STA has found an Access Point and decided to join its BSS, it will pursue becoming a member of the BSS.

A STA's membership in a BSS is dynamic as the STA turns on, turns off, moves within range, or moves out of range. To become a member of a BSS, a STA needs to authenticate itself, synchronize with the Access Point and become associated with the BSS. IEEE 802.11 Authentication and Association occur at the Access Point prior to any upper layer authentication (e.g., IEEE 802.1X link-layer network authentication). IEEE 802.11 Authentication requires that a STA establishes its identity before sending frames, where Open System Authentication uses the STA's MAC address as authentication identify, and Shared Key authentication supports several different shared key authentication mechanisms.

Once authentication has completed, stations can associate with an AP to access all services of the BSS. Association is logically analogous to plugging a cable into a wired network and it allows the AP to record each STA so that frames may be properly delivered. Only after the association process is completed, a station is capable of exchanging data frames with the access point.

A defining characteristic of the wireless channel is the variation of the channel condition over time and over frequency. In addition, a wireless device can experience significant interference from various sources. As a result, complex management functions have been used for WLAN radios in order to achieve efficient and reliable communication. Such management functions often involve the device driver[2] for control and configuration, which makes them important to consider when designing a solution for WiFi virtualization. Examples of such management functions include:

- Rate adaptation: Data streams at WLAN device are modulated and transmitted over the air at a certain rate. IEEE 802.11 mandates multiple transmission rates (e.g., 802.11g supports twelve rates from 1 to 54 Mbps). Higher data rates are commonly achieved by more efficient modulation schemes, which typically require a stronger signal to decode. In wireless networks, path loss, fading, and interference often cause variations in the received signal quality, which in turn, cause variations in the accuracy of decoding given a modulation scheme. A trade-off

---

[1] Depending on the regulations, the specific channels allowed in different countries may vary.

[2] The WLAN MAC software is typically divided into two entities: μCode run by a real-time micro controller on the WiFi device and a device driver that is part of the host operating system.

generally emerges: the higher the data rate, the higher the probability of receiving errors. Rate adaptation is the process of dynamically switching data rates to match the channel conditions with the goal of selecting the rate that will give the optimum throughput under the present channel conditions.

- Power management: Mobile devices with WLAN radio usually have a limited energy budget constrained by battery life. On the other hand, the shared channel access nature of IEEE 802.11 forces wireless STAs to continuously listen to the channel to determine its current status. As a result, a mobile device using WLAN radio would drain its battery very quickly. IEEE 802.11 standard provides power save modes to reduce the time required for a station to listen to the channel. The device driver can control how long and how often the radio needs to be on.

- Power control: Transmit power of WLAN devices affects many aspects of the underlying wireless network. It determines the range of a transmission, the quality of the signal received at the receiver as well as the magnitude of interference it causes to other receivers. The typical goal of power control is to set the transmit power of a WLAN device to the lowest possible level that is still compatible with the quality of the desired communication.

The above brief introduction of Wireless LAN provides a glimpse into the complexity of the Wireless LAN device, especially on the complexity of WLAN management functions. Compared with wired LAN devices that involve mainly data centric operations, their differences primarily lie in the following aspects:

1. There is a range of complex management functions that affect the fundamental functionalities of wireless LAN devices. The device driver is generally involved in many of those management decisions for the WLAN device to have acceptable performance. On the contrary, wired LAN devices are data centric and have very little management functions.

2. Wireless STA is not constrained by the physical location or the number of available network plugs. Inherently, multiple wireless links can be setup from one mobile device without the Access Point knowing that multiple wireless links originate from the same device.

3. Wireless LAN throughput is not bounded by the platform's I/O bandwidth. Rather, it is bounded by the wireless channel capacity. Additionally, due to the distributed channel access and dynamic nature of the wireless link, the channel utilization ratio is typically less than 50%. The achievable throughput to date is generally less than 20 Mbps for 802.11a/g (peak channel rate is 54 Mbps) and less than 200 Mbps for 802.11n (peak channel rate is 450 Mbps) [15].

3. Wireless LAN Virtualization

3.1 Limitations of current virtualization approaches

Today's network interface virtualization techniques can be categorized as either software or hardware based approaches. The software based approach is shown in Figure 2(a), where the VMM implements the virtualization functions in software [10, 35] to support virtual network interfaces for multiple guest VMs. The VMM establishes the actual network connection using the platform's physical NIC and then bridges the connection to multiple virtual machines. In many implementations, the selected virtual network card is a legacy ethernet card for simplicity, and the guest OS inside the VM uses the standard off-the-shelf ethernet device driver. In some other implementations, the para-virtualized driver will be used in the guest OS for function/performance enhancements.

The second approach focuses on providing hardware virtualization support on the NIC device itself. In particular, Single Root I/O Virtualization (SR-IOV) [29] provides a standard mechanism for devices to advertise their ability to be simultaneously shared among multiple virtual machines, and it allows for the partitioning of a PCI function into a set of virtual interfaces. As shown in Figure 2b, a SR-IOV enabled NIC device presents multiple virtual interfaces (VIF) and the VMM can directly assign a VIF to a specific virtual machine, hence drastically reducing the performance penalty of high-bandwidth network cards such as 10Gbit Ethernet.

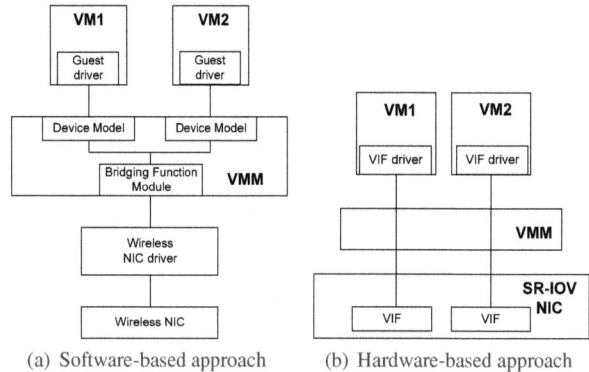

(a) Software-based approach   (b) Hardware-based approach

Figure 2. Existing network interface virtualization approaches

Existing approaches are primarily developed for wired network interface, and are not suitable for virtualizing wireless network interface due to the fundamental differences between wireless LAN and wired LAN devices we elaborated in Section 2. More specifically, the limitations of the 802.3-based emulation approach come from its difficulty to support Wireless LAN management functions inside the VM. IEEE 802.11 is required to appear to higher layers (logical link control (LLC)) as a wired IEEE 802 LAN. This requires IEEE 802.11 to incorporate functionality that is untraditional for MAC sublayers, in order to meet reliability assumptions and to handle QoS traffic in a manner comparable to wired LANs. In other words, IEEE 802.11 MAC functions is a super set of 802.3 MAC functions, and many management functions will get lost when emulating IEEE 802.11 device as 802.3 device.

Using a para-virtualization approach and have the VMM vendor supply the para-virtualized driver is technically possible. However, given the WLAN management functions are complex and the management interface between host driver and wireless LAN device is often proprietary, the reality is that VMM vendor would only provide the smallest common denominator of many wireless network cards. Any vendor specific feature or software component that provided additional benefits would not be possible inside the guest.

Hardware based virtualization approach provides virtualization support at NIC device, where the limitations mainly lie in the cost and complexity – validation and consolidation of management commands from multiple VMs have to be implemented on the device. Due to the wide range of management functions a WLAN device has to support, hardware based virtualization mechanism such as SR-IOV would significantly increase the complexity and cost of wireless NIC. As we mentioned before, wireless LAN throughput is not bounded by I/O bandwidth, given the best achievable wireless LAN throughput is less than 200 Mbps to date. As such, hardware based virtualization mechanisms do not add any additional value in boosting the data I/O bandwidth.

3.2 virtual WiFi: Proposed Wireless LAN Virtualization Architecture

In this paper, we propose a wireless LAN virtualization architecture shown in Figure 3 that takes a combined approach of software and hardware. The goal is to support native wireless LAN drivers inside guest VMs and allow each VM to establish its own wireless connection, all with minimum wireless LAN device changes. The desire to pass on the benefits of the various functions provided in a particular wireless network card leads to the approach of exposing to the guest VM the very same network card as the physical WiFi card. This is contrary to the desire to using Virtualization for a full abstraction of the underlying hardware. However, a similar approach has been taken with SR-IOV and we argue that such an approach is more suitable than the full device abstraction for wireless devices given their management-intensive nature.

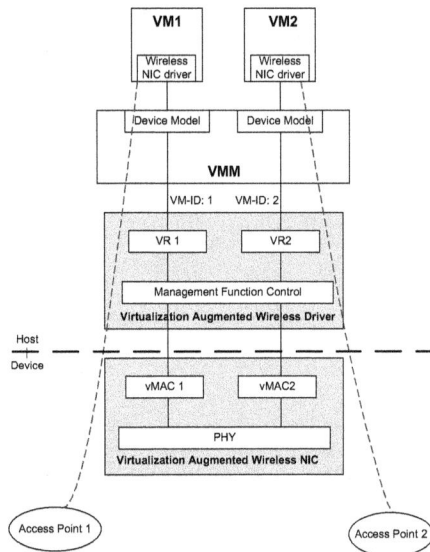

Figure 3. Proposed architecture for virtualizing WLAN network interface

We introduce the concept of *assisted driver direct execution* (ADDE), where an augmented wireless LAN host driver—residing either in a driver domain of a type I hypervisor or in the Host OS in case of a type II hypervisor—takes the primary role in supporting the management functions of the virtualized wireless interfaces. At the same time, some commands (e.g., TX command for data transmissions) will be directly passed on to wireless LAN device for execution. Since the virtual Wireless LAN devices exposed to the guest VMs are the same as the physical wireless LAN device, the commands issued by the guest VM drivers are understandable by the physical device. The augmented host driver can forward those commands to wireless LAN device without incurring any translation overhead.

Inside the virtualization augmented wireless NIC, virtual Wireless LAN interfaces are separated at MAC layer. As shown in Figure 3, multiple virtual MACs may be active and they share the common wireless physical layer via time domain multiplexing. As we mentioned previously, wireless STA is not constrained by the physical location. When multiple virtual MACs are running, each of them can initiate the authentication/association procedures, and setup its connection with an Access Point. From the view of the Access Point, it would not know that those wireless LAN connections are associated with virtual Wireless LAN interfaces located on the same device.

Given that the device-specific virtual wireless functions are provided by the augmented wireless driver and the wireless NIC, the VMM itself now only needs to emulate standard PCI config and MMIO space functions in its device model to expose a wireless network card into the guest. Such an architecture choice enables wireless vendors to provide their own wireless virtualization solutions and to show value differentiations, with minimum dependence on VMM software. Additionally, such an architecture choice allows the device model owned by VMM vendors to be agnostic to changes of the driver-μCode interfaces owned by WiFi device vendors.

Since the device model exposes the same device as the physical wireless interface to the VM, the guest OS inside the VM will load the card's native driver. Once the device model receives commands from the guest's driver, it will tag the commands with a *VM-ID* specific for each guest VM. Functional commands issued by a VM device driver will be forwarded by the device model to the augmented host driver. The device model is also responsible for injecting interrupts into the guest if needed.

3.3 Virtualization Augmented Wireless LAN Device

A typical Wireless LAN device consists of the RF transceiver that performs RF signal transmitting/receiving; the baseband section that operates at a lower frequency range and performs mainly digital signal processing; and the MAC portion that deals with link establishment, security, channel access mechanism, etc. Baseband and RF sections are generally referred to as physical layer (PHY) and the MAC layer runs on top of the PHY. The MAC portion often consists of a real-time controller on the device with associated μcode software, as well as the driver running on the host computer. As we mentioned previously, virtual wireless LAN interfaces are separated at the MAC layer.

The concept of having two MAC entities sharing the same PHY to function as two wireless interfaces in a non-virtualized environment has emerged in the wireless industry recently. It is driven by usage cases of supporting WiFi peer-to-peer connections while connecting to an infrastructure access point at the same time using a single WiFi radio. There, one MAC entity operates in the standard client wireless LAN (STA) mode to connect to an access point for Internet access, while the other operates as a software access point to manage a wireless personal area network (streaming video to a TV equipped with WiFi using the peer-to-peer connection, for example). Commercially available products include Intel My WiFi Technology [20], Atheros Direct Connect[9], and Marvell Mobile Hotspot [17]. Building upon such technology feasibility, we further expand it to support wireless virtualization in virtualized environments, where multiple MAC entities will operate in STA mode and will maintain their independent associations with corresponding access points.

The reason that multiple MAC entities sharing the same PHY can function as separate wireless interfaces is due to the broadcast nature of the wireless link. As long as the RF transceiver is tuned to a particular channel, it can transmit/receive packets on that channel. In the case where all virtual MACs operate on the same channel, the RF transceiver just need to stay on that channel and receive all packets. Irrelevant packets can be filtered out using MAC filters to save power and computing cycles. It is MAC layer's responsibility to identify a packet based on the BSS ID and source/destination MAC addresses. If different virtual MACs need to operate on different channels, then careful time-multiplexing scheduling across virtual MACs needs to be done to make sure each vMAC maintains synchronization with the corresponding access point, and it listens to the channel at the right time for intended traffic. Detailed scheduling algorithms specifically for multi-channel operations concern specific details of IEEE 802.11, which is out of scope of this paper.

Each virtual MAC will have a separate MAC address. The μCode on the network card will maintain information/state per connection associated with a VM-ID, which includes the access point MAC address, STA MAC address, data rates supported by the access point, operating channel, security credentials, rate scaling table, etc. More specifically, on the receiving path, with properly configured MAC filters, packets associated with all virtual MACs can reach the MAC layer. The μCode then determines the corresponding VM-ID based on destination MAC address, and program the hardware with appropriate parameters such as security method in use and corresponding security key to decrypt the received packet. The decrypted packet is then tagged with the appropriate VM-ID, and sent to the augmented host driver, which will in turn, route the packet to the corresponding VM.

On the transmission path, the augmented driver communicates directly with the card's μCode. Handling of the data transmission command is straightforward and the augmented driver passes the TX command that was tagged with the VM-ID by the device model directly to the card. The μCode then looks up the information/state associated with this VM-ID and applies the corresponding security key to encrypt the packet in case of an encrypted connection. The encrypted packet will then be transmitted over the air with the modulation rate, power and antenna configurations associated with this connection. Handling of management commands is more involving. As guest drivers from multiple VMs can issue independent commands, they can potentially conflict with each other (e.g., one VM likes to turn off the wireless LAN device while other VMs are still using it). To resolve such a conflict, μCode maintains per-VM data structures to keep VM specific states isolated from each other. A guest driver can modify its own state, but any command that affects the operation of the entire wireless NIC is carefully handled at the augmented driver to ensure consistent isolation among VMs. Several commonly used management commands are elaborated below.

Device initialization. Initialization command is used to bring up the PHY and set up all parameters needed for an association, such as band selection, channel selection, transceiver chain configurations, security method, BSS ID, etc. Each VM WiFi driver may independently issue device initialization commands. If one VM is actively using the WiFi device while another VM issues device initialization command, μCode needs to make sure that PHY setting of the active connection will not be affected. Additionally, the device initialization command should trigger μCode to start a new vMAC, and start maintaining state/information related to the new vMAC.

Scan request. Scan request command is issued by WiFi driver to request the WiFi device to search for all available channels to discover active networks where access points are present. Each VM WiFi driver can independently issue scan request commands. If one VM is actively using the WiFi device while another VM issues scan request, the augmented host driver needs to consolidate function requests from both VMs and set proper scan request for the μCode to execute. More specifically, the scan request is characterized by how often the WiFi device needs to switch to an unknown channel to search for available access points (i.e., Scan Interval), and how long it will stay on that channel for each scan attempt (i.e., Scan Duration). Depending on traffic amount of the active VM, the augmented host driver may need to set the Scan Interval and Scan Duration differently from what is requested by the guest VM. Alternatively, the augmented driver can also return the previously stored scan results directly to the VM without passing scan command to μCode, if the available scanning results were just recently obtained.

Power save command. Power save request is issued by WiFi driver to control how long and how often the WiFi radio needs to be on to save power consumption while maintaining the active connection. It sets sleep interval to allow the WiFi radio to go into low power mode. When different VMs issue power save commands, the augmented driver needs to consolidate these requests and determine a sleep schedule that satisfies the connection and traffic requirements of all VMs. Only one consolidated power save command will be passed down to the μCode for execution.

Rate control command. The WiFi driver can adaptively choose a set of suitable rates for the WiFi radio to be used, based on packet transmission/failure histories and based on channel feedbacks from the μCode. If a guest VM issues the rate control command, such a command should be passed down to μCode, where the μCode should only update the rate table associated with the specific VM-ID.

TX power control command. WiFi driver can specify TX power that should be used for a particular channel or modulation rate. When a guest VM issues the TX power control command, such a command should be passed down to μCode, where μCode should only update the TX power table associated with the specific VM-ID.

In some cases, μCode on the WiFi device needs to send management feedback up to the WiFi driver. Such management feedback may be delayed responses to a command that was originally issued by a VM, or it may be statistical information on packet error rate, the number of retransmissions performed for each packet, etc. The augmented host driver is responsible for routing those management feedbacks to the appropriate VM.

4. Prototype Implementation

We have implemented the *virtual WiFi* prototype in KVM (Kernel-based Virtual Machine). The core part of KVM [3, 21] is a Linux module that enables the Linux OS to function as a VMM. In KVM, VMs run as normal Linux processes. Since all physical pages of a VM are mapped into the process's user virtual memory space, the physical memory of the VM can be accessed easily when the VM process is in user mode. KVM takes advantages of hardware virtualization support such as Intel VT [6] or AMD-SVM [8] to achieve efficient virtualization of CPUs and memory.

The KVM can specify on which I/O ports the requests from VM need to be intercepted. Whenever an IO request to these ports happens in VM, a VM exit happens and processor switches control from guest to KVM. In KVM, the I/O request is redirected to a user mode device emulator called QEMU [11, 12], which is utilized by KVM to provide virtual device models to VMs.

Figure 4 shows the overall architecture of our virtual WiFi prototype implementation, which consists of three main components. The first is the *virtual WiFi device model*, which is implemented inside QEMU device model layer, responsible for exposing the virtual WiFi interface to the VMs. The second one is the *Virtualization augmented WiFi device driver* running in the host Linux kernel. The third one is the *Virtualization augmented WiFi NIC*, which involves only the μCode changes on the WiFi device. We will elaborate each of the three components in the virtual WiFi prototyping system in the following subsections.

4.1 Virtual WiFi Device Model

The prototype implements an Intel WiFi device model which works for both Intel's 5000 and 6000 series WiFi cards. Each VMM that supports virtualization of WiFi device through virtual WiFi approach will implement its own version of the virtual WiFi device model. The virtual WiFi device model virtualizes the PCI config and MMIO accesses itself, while forwarding all WiFi function commands to the augmented driver for processing. All IO requests

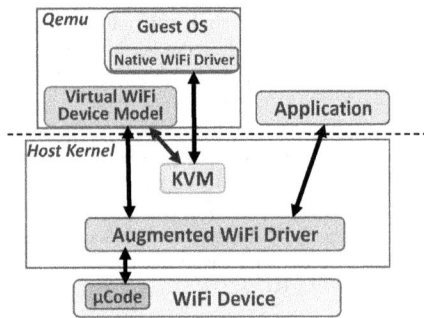

Figure 4. Virtual WiFi Prototype implementation based on KVM

from guest WiFi driver are intercepted by KVM and delivered to the virtual WiFi device model, which then hands these requests to the augmented host WiFi driver.

During initialization virtual WiFi device model establishes an ioctl interface to the augmented host driver, and uses this interface to allocate a new VM state inside the driver. For all commands/packets sent by guest WiFi driver, the device model tags them with host driver allocated VM-ID and deliver them to the augmented host driver via the ioctl interface. For received packet or incoming interrupt from physical WiFi NIC, the augmented host driver signals the device model about the availability of a packet or an interrupt. The device model retrieves the received packets/interrupts via an ioctl call. If the received packet is valid, device model enqueues it in the guest WiFi driver queue and injects an interrupt into the guest OS for further processing.

4.2 Virtualization Augmented Host Driver

The virtualization extension is added to the default "Intel Wireless WiFi" driver in Linux kernel release 2.6.33 [4] that works for both Intel's 5000 and 6000 series WiFi cards. The extension implements an IOCTL interface to interact with device model inside QEMU. On the transmission path, when the augmented driver receives a command from the device model, it either virtualizes the command locally, or validates the command and inserts it into the physical WiFi driver transmission queue (data or control queue). On the receiving path, when receiving a packet from wireless device, it examines the VM-ID associated with the packet to identify the intended receiver. It then signals the corresponding device model which wakes up from a waiting poll to pick up the packet.

4.3 Virtualization Augmented WiFi NIC

The μCode handles time critical MAC operations. The virtualization extension is added to WiFi μCode of both Intel's 5000 and 6000 series WiFi cards. Both Intel's 5000 and 6000 series WiFi cards have Intel My WiFi technology enabled, so the NIC hardware is capable of handling at least two virtual MACs. Configuration, connection status and state machine are maintained separately for each virtual MAC. Control/data messages to/from each vMAC will be tagged with different VM-ID so that they can be differentiated by the augmented host driver.

μCode changes made in our prototype are as follows. When a new virtual machine is initiated, a mapping table is created to map VM-ID with the virtual MAC, and configure the hardware filtering policy to allow packets targeted to this virtual MAC to be received. On the receiving path, VM-ID is identified based on the received packet's MAC addresses and the packet is tagged with the VM-

ID before sending it to the host driver. On the TX path, command response is generated after completing the command execution. The command response is also tagged with VM-ID before sending it to the host driver. The security keys are maintained in a unified security table, which is indexed by the combination of connecting access point and the virtual MAC address.

4.4 Address Translation

Typical device models copy TX packets from the VM's memory and send them to host networking stack for transmission. However, since virtual WiFi device model has a direct interface to host driver, it can avoid the extra copy for transmission packets. Once virtual WiFi device model receives a TX command from the VM that contains the guest physical address (GPA) of the packet buffer, the device model requests VMM to convert the GPA to host physical address (HPA) instead of copying the packet from the VM's memory. After the GPA in the TX command being replaced with the HPA, the TX command is sent to the wireless NIC by the host driver for actual transmission. The wireless NIC performs the DMA operation using the HPA, copying the packet directly from the VM's memory to avoid extra memory copy.

It was observed that address translation by the VMM in software causes significant CPU overhead. Thus one optimization is to exploit the address remapping hardware support present in the platform, such as Intel VT-d [6] or AMD IOMMU [8]. We implemented both software-based and hardware-assisted address translation in our virtual WiFi prototype for performance analysis. The hardware-assisted address translation is based on Intel VT-d in our implementation. VT-d hardware is typically used to support assignment of a single device to only one address domain (and hence only one VM). That is, only one VT-d context entry can be assigned for each PCI device. The GPAs used by a device in DMA requests are mapped to HPAs through the VT-d remapping table pointed by the device's VT-d context entry. On the other hand, in our virtual WiFi system, one physical wireless NIC has to be shared by multiple VMs, which will require one remapping table for each VM that shares the physical device. Virtual WiFi implements an approach that enables VT-d to support multiple address domains within a single VT-d context entry, by merging multiple VT-d tables into a single VT-d table.

The approach we implemented is based on the fact that current VT-d table has much larger physical address space than the physical memory available to each VM. Therefore a number of high order bits in GPAs will remain un-programmed in typical usages. We can partition the VT-d table into multiple chunks in a way that each chunk contains mappings for one VM. For example, if the VT-d hardware supports mapping up to 512 GB memory address space (39 bits long, 3-level page table), we can divide the address space into 16 chunks with each chunk supporting up to 32GB address space. In this way, VMM creates a merged VT-d table where each chunk represents the unique remapping sub-table for each VM.

During a VM's initialization, the virtual WiFi device model requests the VMM to add the VM's VT-d table into the merged VT-d table used by the device. The VMM selects the chunk location corresponding to the VM-ID and copies the top-level entries from the VM's table into the merged table. Using the same example as above, 32 top-level entries will be copied from the VM table to the merged VT-d table at chunk location 1 if the VM-ID is 1. When the virtual WiFi device model receives commands from guest driver, the device model integrates the VM-ID into the higher order bits (bits 35–38 in this example) of the GPA present in the command. When the command is sent to the wireless NIC, the device uses the VM-ID tagged GPA for DMA request, which will lead to GPA being translated to HPA using the correct chunk corresponding to the VM in the merged VT-d table.

5. Performance Evaluation

The goal of our performance analysis is to understand whether our proposed virtual WiFi architecture is an applicable approach for wireless virtualization. More specifically, we would like to understand, in comparison with native WiFi, is there any WiFi throughput or latency penalty; what is the CPU utilization by wireless virtualization; what are the major overhead sources for WiFi virtualization and what are the effective mitigation mechanisms.

To measure the UDP goodput, we used *IxChariot* [2] network benchmarking tool. The IxChariot tools contain both Console and Performance Endpoint programs. Performance Endpoints are installed at the source and destination points of a test to perform packet transmissions and receptions. The Console program configures the test, loads the test scripts to Endpoints and collects/processes test results. In our test setup, the Performance Endpoints run on the two test machines and the Console program runs on a separate management machine. The separation of management console from test machine allows us to isolate the CPU usage by Console program from the CPU usage due to WiFi traffic generated by the EndPoint [3].

To isolate the test management traffic (e.g., loading test scripts or gathering test results) from the testing traffic, the management network and the test network are separated into two different subnets. The primary test machine on which VM and virtual WiFi will be running connects with an access point via WiFi. The other end of the tested data connection is a machine running native Linux and connects to the access point via Ethernet. As such, a packet from the primary test machine will go through the WiFi link to reach the access point, which will then route the packet to the peer test node through Ethernet. As the WiFi link is the bottleneck link, the testing throughput reflects the throughput supported by the WiFi.

In our evaluation, Chariot 7.0 *UDP-Throughput* script is used to measure the end to end UDP goodput between the primary test machine and the peer test node. End to end TCP throughput is measured by *iPerf* [1]. To measure latency, we used the round-trip delay of an ICMP echo request/response pair (i.e., ping), by taking samples over hour-long intervals. All reported results are averaged over multiple measurements.

The primary test machine is a HP EliteBook 6930p laptop with Intel Core2 Duo CPU at 2.53GHz, 4 GB RAM, 80 GB HDD, and Intel WiFi 5300 AGN card. Both the host OS and guest OS are 32-bit Linux with kernel version 2.6.33.1. For the performance results below, we disabled one of the two CPU cores. The access point used is Cisco WAP410N. For our purpose of analysis, we performed the tests in several different scenarios:

- *Native:* Tests are performed in Linux with native WiFi driver. No virtual machine is running in this case. The original WiFi μCode is loaded onto the device. This is the baseline of the native WiFi performance. We refer to results in this scenario as *Native*.

- VM-Passthrough: Tests are performed in a Linux Guest OS, with the native WiFi driver running inside the guest VM. The VM is configured with 2G RAM and a single core CPU. The physical WiFi device is assigned directly to the VM with Intel VT-d support. In this case, the guest WiFi driver interacted directly with the physical device. The original WiFi μCode is loaded onto the device. Neither device model nor augmented host driver is involved. We use this configuration to capture the performance when there is hardware supported WiFi virtualization. We refer to the results in this configuration as *Passthrough*.

- Virtual WiFi: Tests are performed in a Linux Guest VM with the native WiFi driver running inside the guest VM. The augmented host driver runs in host Linux kernel, and the augmented μCode is loaded onto the device. The VM is configured with 2G RAM and a single core CPU. The virtual WiFi interface is exposed by virtual WiFi device model. This configuration follows our proposed approach as shown in Figure 4. The software-based address translation approach is applied unless VT-d is specifically mentioned. We refer to results in this configuration as *Virtual WiFi*.

To analyze virtual WiFi overhead contributing factors, we used the Oprofile [5] tool to analyze the performance behaviors on different components of the system. Oprofile can attain a system-wide statistical profiling results for Linux-based systems, which include codes executing at both user and kernel levels. In our profiling, we mainly focus on the CPU cycles (*UNHALTED_CPU_CYCLES* event) consumed by each of the major components of virtual WiFi prototype system. OProfile 0.9.6 is used in the tests. The profiling result is presented and analyzed in section 5.3.

5.1 Throughput

Throughput test results are shown in Figure 5, where TX/RX throughput is measured when the primary test machine transmits/receives to/from the peer test node respectively. UDP throughput is shown in Figure 5(a), where Chariot are configured to use 1450 byte packet size with traffic enough to saturate the WiFi link. Each test lasts for 60 seconds. The measured throughput has large variation across different runs due to the WiFi channel variation. The presented throughput is averaged over ten runs. As we can see, virtual WiFi achieves throughput comparable to the native case. In all testing scenarios, achieved WiFi UDP TX/RX throughput is around 22 Mbps/18 Mbps respectively using IEEE 802.11g WiFi mode. Similar observations can be made for TCP throughput tested using iPerf, as shown in Figure 5(b). In all testing scenarios, achieved WiFi TCP TX/RX throughput is around 20 Mbps/20 Mbps respectively using IEEE 802.11g WiFi mode. In the tests, iPerf is configured to use 1448 byte writes, the socket buffer size is maximized, and 4 million writes are made.

Both UDP and TCP throughput tests confirm that our proposed WiFi virtualization approach achieves throughput comparable to native WiFi case.

5.2 Latency

Latency test results are shown in Figure 5(c), where round-trip latency is measured when the primary test machine pings the peer test node. The latencies are the average of 15 measurements. The results show that the latency of virtual WiFi system is about 35% higher than the native case (7.87 ms vs. 5.74 ms). In the case of VM-Passthrough, the latency is 7% higher than native case (6.17 ms vs. 5.74 ms).

To understand where this extra latency comes from, we break down the latency of transmission path into various components. More specifically, we define the *virtualization extra path* as the additional path in the TX/RX critical path introduced by virtualization. In the virtual WiFi prototype system, the virtualization extra path on network transmit starts from the point when guest driver issues a packet sending (MMIO) request until the point the requests (packets) are sent to the TX queue of the physical WiFi device by the augmented host driver.

Our first instrumentation gauges the time spent on transmitting a packet by reading the processor's *Time Stamp Counter* (TSC) register at key points during the virtualization extra path on network transmit. The TSC allows a measurement of the total cycle count of the path and breakdown of interesting subsegments.

---

[3] Performance Endpoint itself is an unobtrusive software agent with light CPU load.

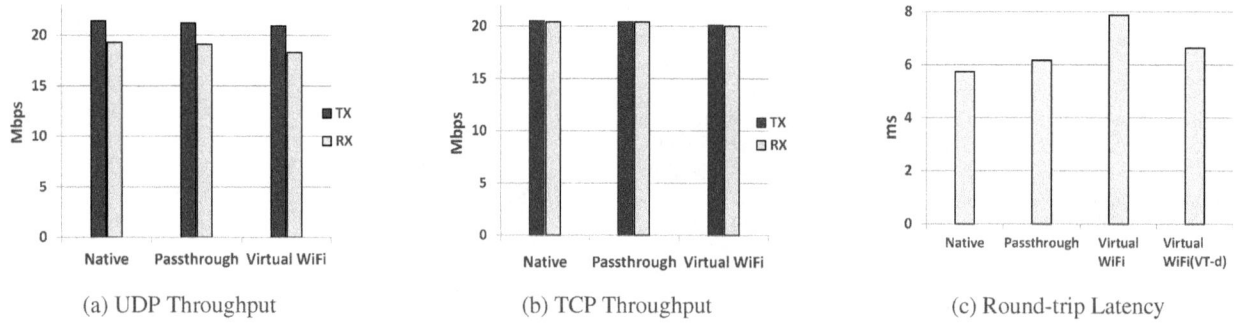

(a) UDP Throughput (b) TCP Throughput (c) Round-trip Latency

Figure 5. End-to-end Performance of Virtual WiFi (Throughputs and Latency)

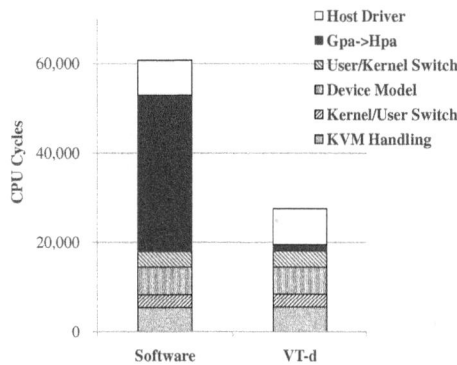

Figure 6. Cycle number spent on major components on virtualization extra path for single packet sending

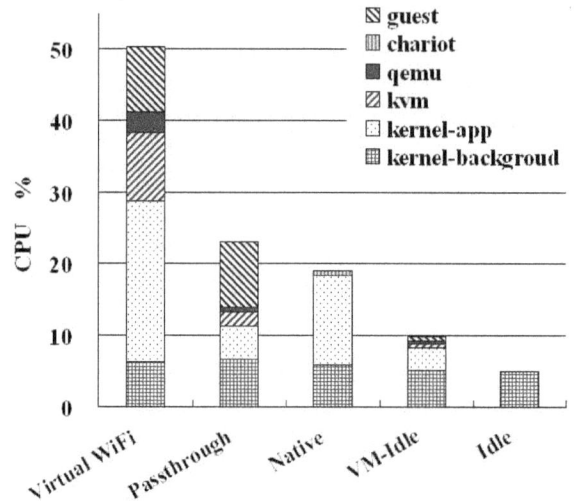

Figure 7. Overall CPU usage breakdown

Figure 6 presents the transmission latency break down involved along the instrumented virtualization extra path using virtual WiFi with software-based address translation mechanism and hardware translation support (VT-d). It takes a total of 60000 CPU cycles from the start of MMIO instruction from guest until packet is put in the TX queue of the physical WiFi device for software based address translation approach. The address translation (marked as "GPA → HPA" in Figure 6) in software-based approach is responsible for almost half of these cycles for network transmit.

With hardware IOMMU supports, we can reduce the latency caused by software address translation. Specifically, in our prototype system, we eliminated most of the latency caused from address translation by enabling VT-d support, and the round trip latency of virtual WiFi with VT-d is only 15% higher than the native case (6.63 ms vs. 5.74 ms in Figure 5(c)).

5.3 CPU Usage

Given that virtual WiFi achieves close to native WiFi throughput and latency, we are interested to see how much system resource is consumed by virtual WiFi. In particular, mobile devices such as smartphones and tablets typically have limited processing power, which may lead to CPU being a bottleneck. In this section, we dissect the CPU time consumed by each of the major components of virtual WiFi prototype system when the test machine is performing network transmission in maximal throughput. The goal is to understand what are the major overhead sources in terms of CPU consumption, as well as to identify effective mitigation mechanisms to reduce such overhead.

5.3.1 Overall System CPU Usage

Figure 7 shows the overall system CPU usage measured at the primary test machine in different test scenarios. In each non-idle test scenario, the primary test machine is performing UDP transmission in its maximal throughput. As we can see, when in system idle state without virtual environment running, the CPU usage is 5% due to background processes and Oprofile daemon itself. With one VM running idly, the system CPU usage is 10%. When Chariot test workload is running in host Linux and transmitting over native WiFi without any virtualization, the system CPU usage is 19.5%. When running Chariot in guest VM with passthrough WiFi device assigned, the system CPU usage is 23.6%. Finally, when Chariot is running in Linux guest VM using our proposed virtual WiFi approach without VT-d being enabled, the system CPU usage is 50.9%. Clearly, virtual WiFi consumes much more CPU time than the native WiFi case. In comparison, the CPU time consumed in VM-Passthrough case is much less.

To investigate the sources of overheads, we used Oprofile to determine where the CPU time is spent. Oprofile uses time-based sampling to profile the distribution of time spent in main components over the entire workload. The samples measure the percentage of time spent in code sections and the number of samples that hit a section. This gives a more comprehensive picture of the overheads present in transmitting packets and reveals some expensive functional components.

The CPU time consumption is broken down into percent of time spent in the major components of virtual WiFi system including:

- **Guest**: The guest VCPU thread, running guest OS and its applications.

- **Chariot**: The test workload. In native case, Chariot's CPU time is shown separately. However, in virtual WiFi and passthrough cases, Chariot is running in guest, thus its CPU time is included in the guest as OProfile cannot separate applications running inside VM.

- **QEMU**: The QEMU user process, which contains mainly the virtual WiFi device model.

- **KVM**: The KVM module running inside host kernel, this part is separated from the host Linux kernel for more analysis. However, some of KVM code calls routines in other part of kernel, the time spent by those routines is accounted to the host kernel.

- **Kernel-App**: The part of host Linux kernel time that runs on behalf of processing user requests, which includes host augmented driver and all kernel service for QEMU, KVM and other functions to support WiFi virtualization.

- **Kernel-Background**: The background routines running in kernel, including Oprofile daemon itself. This part consumes almost the same for all test scenarios, which we treat it as background CPU time unrelated to virtualization.

The overall CPU usage and distribution of CPU time on these major components described above is presented in Figure 7. We can observe that most of the extra CPU time are consumed by host kernel and KVM for virtual WiFi comparing with passthrough and native cases. It should be noted that in the passthrough case, the network stack is running inside Guest OS instead of Host OS, which is the reason why Figure 7 shows *Kernel-App* in passthrough case consumes less CPU time than the native case.

5.3.2 Host Kernel and KVM CPU Time

Table 1 further break down the CPU time distributed in KVM module and host Linux kernel (*Kernel-App* part in Figure 7), as we observed they are responsible for most of the extra CPU time consumption when running virtual WiFi. By comparing the CPU time distribution on host kernel and KVM for virtual WiFi with passthrough and native cases, we made the following observations:

Interrupt Handling. The WiFi driver in Linux kernel release 2.6.33 used in our prototype implementation sets interrupt coalescing timer to 2 ms [4]. However, it is observed that the μCode actually overrides the interrupt coalescing timer set by the driver and enables immediate interrupt for each TX command response. As a result, each transmitted packet results in a TX command response interrupt. This explains why in native WiFi case, the system CPU usage is relatively high (19.5%). In the case of virtual WiFi, when a physical interrupt arrived at the augmented host driver, the host driver will notify the device model running in QEMU, which in turn injects a virtual interrupt to the guest through KVM. As a result, one physical interrupt could trigger four components' involvements in series, which includes four times of kernel/user and VMM/VM switch. It obviously leads to much more CPU consumption if the interrupts happen in high frequency.

Address translation. In measures done for Figure 7 and Table 1, virtual WiFi uses the software-based address translation approach. Most of address translation work is done by KVM module, and it is another significant source of overhead. By applying hardware IOMMU support, this part of overhead is supposed to be eliminated or significantly reduced.

IO handling. Whenever guest driver issue a MMIO access, the control transits into KVM by VM exit. KVM is responsible for either handling the requests or forwarding it to the device models in QEMU. After the device model is done with MMIO handling, it returns to KVM, which resumes the guest VM. KVM IO handling takes a significant chunk of CPU time also. The I/O handled in KVM also includes accesses to the virtual interrupt controller. IO handling is also a major CPU cost in the host kernel. The I/O handling cost in host kernel corresponds to two parts: the primary one is due to handling *ioctl* system calls from the virtual WiFi device model and the other part is the I/O read/write to the physical wireless NIC by the augmented host driver.

Contention/Synchronization. In virtual WiFi case, threads synchronization/contention/scheduling cost is one of the major CPU overhead in host kernel. Recall that in KVM/QEMU architecture, guest VM run as separate threads from the device models. Any interactions between VMs and device models, such as MMIO accesses by guest OS to virtual devices, or virtual interrupts injected by device models into VMs, result in synchronization between VM threads and device model threads. The large CPU time spent in handling thread synchronization in host kernel indicates there are a large number of interactions between VMs and device models. Such interactions include MMIO accesses from guest and interrupt delivery/injection to guest, which further confirms our observations that I/O handling and interrupt handling are the major sources of overhead for our virtual WiFi prototype system.

Comparing with our virtual WiFi approach, the direct passthrough approach obviously needs much less kernel involvements. This is because every IO request from the guest VM is passed directly to physical device, and physical interrupt from physical device is delivered to guest by host kernel and KVM without the involvement of either host driver or device model.

5.3.3 Overhead Mitigation Mechanisms

The CPU time distribution breakdown results from above discussions indicate that interrupt handling and address translation consume large portions of CPU time in our prototype implementation, which can be mitigated using interrupt coalescing and the hardware-assisted address translation mechanism (e.g., VT-d), respectively.

Interrupt Coalescing The interrupt handling in the particular test case we analyzed mainly comes from TX command responses. After a TX command is sent to the WiFi device, a command response will be sent back by the device after the transmission attempt is completed. The command response can be sent to the augmented host driver by the device at various times through interrupt. The augmented host driver will then notify the device model running in QEMU, which then injects a virtual interrupt to the guest. Obviously, interrupts have a higher impact in such a virtualized environment due to additional involvements of the device model in QEMU and the augmented host driver. Most network devices today support *interrupt coalescing*, which is to delay generating the interrupt until either a specified number of packets is received or when the maximum specified delay is reached. The WiFi driver in Linux kernel release 2.6.33 used in our prototype implementation sets interrupt coalescing timer to 2 ms [4]. However, it is observed that the μCode actually overrides the interrupt coalescing timer set by the driver and enables immediate interrupt for TX command response. As a result, each transmitted packet results in a TX command response interrupt. With the average throughput of 22 Mbps and the payload size of 1450 bytes, we are observing close to 1900 interrupts per second. Without the interrupt coalescing at WiFi device, we implemented similar function at the device model, where the device model wait for 10 TX responses before it injects a virtual interrupt to the guest, in order to observe the mitigation effect

KVM Time		
Category	Percent of Total Time	
	Virtual WiFi	Passthrough
Delivering virtual IRQs	2.79%	0.34%
Address Translation	2.71%	0.15%
IN/OUTs handling and forwarding	2.06%	0.13%
Instruction Decoding	0.53%	0.33%
Managing guest shadow memory	0.69%	0.36%
Virtual CPU state updating	0.64%	0.44%

Host Kernel Time			
Category	Percent of Total Time		
	Virtual WiFi	Passthrough	Native
Interrupt handling/forwarding IRQs to device model	5.87%	1.22%	2.53%
IN/OUTs in driver/Handle IO requests from device model	4.95%	0.29%	2.56%
Locking/unlocking code section	4.72%	0.41%	1.08%
Scheduling user/kernel threads	2.06%	0.69%	0.30%
Packet memory copying	1.74%	0.35%	1.57%
Timer management/Timing service	1.15%	0.71%	0.10%
System call entry/return	1.78%	0.68%	0.56%
Other	0.50%	0.20%	0.34%
Network Stack			3.47%

Table 1. Distribution of CPU time spent in KVM and host kernel.

of interrupt coalescing. As we can see in Figure 8, with interrupt coalescing at the device model, CPU utilization is dropped from 50.4% to 34.2% while achieving the same throughput. We expect even less CPU utilization if the interrupt coalescing is enabled at the WiFi device, since the interrupt coalescing at the device will limit the number of physical and virtual interrupts, while the interrupt coalescing we implemented at the device model only limits the number of virtual interrupts.

Hardware-assisted Address Translation After enabling VT-d, we observed the CPU utilization is dropped from 50.4% to 44.2% as shown in Figure 8. With both interrupt coalescing and VT-d are enabled, the total CPU utilization is 28% while achieving the same throughput. Recall that the total CPU utilization is 19.3% in the native WiFi case with no virtual machine running.

The reduction of IO handling overhead cannot be achieved as long as the device model and host driver are involved in each guest I/O request. One of our future works is to further investigate the impact of *data passthrough* on wireless virtualization. More specifically, we are investigating an approach that can support data traffic passthrough between different guests and the physical device through separate queues. However, the management traffic will be intercepted by the hypervisor and forwarded to the augmented host driver for further handling. Such an approach can take advantage of the flexibility of software (i.e., augmented host driver) to support complex WiFi management functions. On the other hand, it has the potential of removing extra virtualization overhead from the critical path of data TX/RX.

In summary, with interrupt coalescing and hardware-assisted address translation, virtual WiFi achieves throughput comparable to the native WiFi case with relatively 45% more CPU utilization (28% vs. 19.3% CPU utilization).

6. Related Work

Virtualization The concept of virtualization has been widely studied in the context of operating system. Various optimizations have been proposed to improve the virtual machine monitors such as Xen, VMware, Palacios [10, 23, 38, 39]. In recent years, there

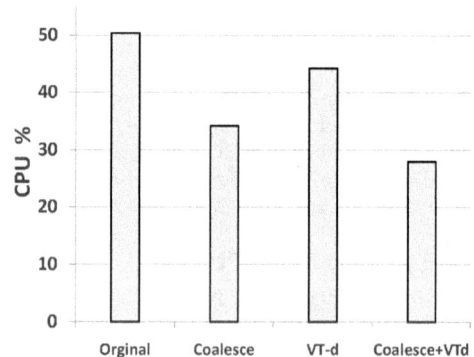

Figure 8. CPU usage with different optimizations

has been a fast growing interest in mobile/client virtualization [22]. Examples of client virtualization solutions on the market include XenClient [16], VMware desktop virtualization solutions [37] and VirtualLogix mobile virtualization solutions [36]. Existing research on I/O virtualization can be categorized into three approaches: Fully emulated I/O, para-virtualized I/O, and hardware-assisted virtualized I/O.

Full emulated I/O virtualization [35] provides virtualized views of devices by emulating real devices instead of providing physical devices. Device models (virtual devices) implement virtualized hardware devices completely in software within the VMM. Multiple virtual devices are then be multiplexed on a single physical device. In this approach, no guest software change is required. But there is significant performance overhead, due to large number of context switches between VM and hypervisor caused by guest's IO accesses. Para-virtualization I/O [10, 25, 27, 31] refers to modifying guest OS to run on the virtualized environment and exposing some details of the hardware for optimization. Xen I/O extends this concept by requiring guest changes and having the special driver talk to a special VM that has direct hardware access. Drivers can also be placed into separate driver VMs for better protection [24]. These techniques can often lead to significantly better I/O performance. Hardware-assisted virtualized I/O that exploits specialized hardware [7, 26, 29, 30, 32] has been proposed as an efficient I/O virtualization mechanism. With hardware assisted virtualization, the device presents multiple logical interfaces which can be securely accessed directly by guest OS. Close to native I/O performance can be achieved as a result of bypassing the hypervisor. However, hardware virtualization requires substantial investments in re-designing the device. In addition, hardware-assisted virtualized I/O breaks the device transparency, which is a benefit of using software-based device virtualization. Device transparency has the benefit of avoiding the need to maintain device-specific code in guest VMs, also simplifying live migration of guest VMs across physical machines that have different flavors of devices.

Our proposed virtual WiFi approach is similar to emulated I/O approach in that it supports unmodified WiFi device driver in guest OS. However, it is different from emulated I/O in that it requires device model emulate the same device as the physical device on the host and it passes many of the commands to the physical device without emulating it. Therefore, it can achieve better performance than emulated I/O approach. On the other hand, different from hardware-assisted virtualized I/O, virtual WiFi approach does not depend on any specific I/O virtualization support on device. Given WiFi devices available on the market[9, 17, 20] can already support more than one vMACs, only software (i.e., driver and μCode) upgrade is needed for supporting virtual WiFi solution. Essentially, virtual WiFi is a hybrid I/O virtualization approach that is more suitable for the purposes of exposing full wireless functionalities inside guest VM, providing WiFi link level isolation, simplifying hardware and software design and achieving appropriate performance/complexity tradeoff.

There also have been many existing works that study the performance overhead of different virtualization approaches on different hypervisors and platforms [14, 18, 19, 28, 32]. This paper analyzes the performance overhead of our proposed wireless virtualization approach. To our best knowledge, we are not aware of any existing work that addresses wireless virtualization and conducts associated performance study.

Wireless Network/Radio Virtualization Sachs *et al.* [33] proposed a radio resource sharing framework, which allow different virtual radio networks to operate on top of a common shared infrastructure and share the same radio resources without interfering with each other. Smith *et al.* [34] designed and implemented a virtualized 802.11 testbed system with the goal to allow multiple experiments to co-exist on a wireless experimental facility. Their key issues are to maintain the coherence of each wireless experiment (i.e., transmitter/receiver/potential interferers all need to operate on the same channel), and to keep different experiments isolated (i.e., one experiment will not affect results of another experiment). Miljanic *et al.* discussed virtual radio in the context of software defined radio. Their goal is to provide a common interface to layers above the link layer so that the radio resource scheduling/allocation is hidden from higher layers. A radio virtualization layer is introduced to handle the hardware resources responsible for managing communication bandwidth. MultiNet [13] proposes a driver based approach to facilitate simultaneous connections to multiple networks using a single wireless card. The "virtualization" of wireless card is implemented with intermediate driver, which continuously switches the card across multiple network. Microsoft Windows 7 has adopted this feature, which is not designed to support virtual machine environment.

7. Conclusion and Future Work

We proposed a hybrid wireless virtualization approach named *virtual WiFi*, which combines elements of software and hardware for virtualization support. The design goals of *virtual WiFi* are to expose full wireless functionalities inside guest VM, to provide WiFi link level isolation across different VMs, and to achieve appropriate performance/complexity tradeoff with architecture choices specifically suitable for wireless interface virtualization.

We have designed and implemented a prototype supporting the IEEE 802.11g compliant WiFi interfaces. Work is ongoing to extend the prototype to support IEEE 802.11n compliant WiFi interfaces that operate at higher speeds. We are also porting our virtual WiFi implementation to Xen and plan to understand virtual WiFi performance in the context of Xen.

We showed that with interrupt coalescing and hardware-assisted address translation, *virtual WiFi* achieves throughput comparable to the native WiFi case with relatively 45% more CPU utilization (28% vs. 19.3% CPU utilization). We also plan to further investigate the impact of *data passthrough* on wireless virtualization as we mentioned in Section 5.3.3.

References

[1] iperf homepage. http://iperf.sourceforge.net/.

[2] Ixchariot homepage. http://www.ixchariot.com/.

[3] Kvm homepage. http://www.linux-kvm.org/.

[4] Linux kernel 2.6.33, iwlwifi driver. http://lxr.linux.no/linux+v2.6.33/drivers/net/wireless/iwlwifi/.

[5] Oprofile homepage. http://oprofile.sourceforge.net/.

[6] ABRAMSON, D., JACKSON, J., MUTHRASANALLUR, S., NEIGER, G., REGNIER, G., SANKARAN, R., SCHOINAS, I., UHLIG, R., VEMBU, B., AND WIEGERT, J. Intel virtualization technology for directed I/O. *Intel Technology Journal 10*, 3 (2006), 179–192.

[7] ANWER, M. B., AND FEAMSTER, N. Building a fast, virtualized data plane with programmable hardware. In *ACM SIGCOMM Workshop on Virtualized Infastructure Systems and Architectures* (2009).

[8] APIKI, S. I/O Virtualization and AMD's IOMMU. Advanced Micro Devices, Inc. http://developer.amd.com/documentation/articles/pages/892006101.aspx.

[9] ATHEROS COMMUNICATIONS, INC. Direct connection. http://www.atheros.com.

[10] BARHAM, P., DRAGOVIC, B., FRASER, K., HAND, S., HARRIS, T., HO, A., NEUGEBAUER, R., PRATT, I., AND WARFIELD, A. Xen and the art of virtualization. In *ACM Symposium on Operating Systems Principles (SOSP)* (2003), pp. 164–177.

[11] BARTHOLOMEW, D. Qemu: a multihost, multitarget emulator. *Linux J. 2006*, 145 (2006), 3.

[12] BELLARD, F. Qemu, a fast and portable dynamic translator. In *ATEC '05: Proceedings of the annual conference on USENIX Annual Technical Conference* (Berkeley, CA, USA, 2005), USENIX Association, pp. 41–41.

[13] CHANDRA, R., BAHL, P., AND BAHL, P. Multinet: Connecting to multiple ieee 802.11 networks using a single wireless card. In *IEEE INFOCOM, Hong Kong* (2004).

[14] CHERKASOVA, L., CHERKASOVA, L., GARDNER, R., AND GARDNER, R. Measuring cpu overhead for I/O processing in the xen virtual machine monitor. In *USENIX Annual Technical Conference* (2005), pp. 387–390.

[15] CISCO SYSTEMS, INC. Enterprise wireless competitive performance test results. White Paper, 2010. http://www.cisco.com/.

[16] CITRIX SYSTEMS, INC. Xenclient virtual desktops. http://www.citrix.com/.

[17] GIORDANO, B. Transforming small mobile devices into full-featured wifi access points. Marvell Semiconductor, December 2009.

http://www.marvell.com/technologies/wireless/
marvell_wifi_mobile_hotspo%t_whitepaper.pdf.

[18] GUO, D., LIAO, G., AND BHUYAN, L. N. Performance characterization and cache-aware core scheduling in a virtualized multi-core server under 10gbe. *IEEE Workload Characterization Symposium 0* (2009), 168–177.

[19] GUO, D., LIAO, G., BHUYAN, L. N., LIU, B., AND DING, J. J. A scalable multithreaded l7-filter design for multi-core servers. In *Proceedings of the 4th ACM/IEEE Symposium on Architectures for Networking and Communications Systems* (New York, NY, USA, 2008), ANCS '08, ACM, pp. 60–68.

[20] INTEL CORP. Intel My WiFi Technology Tech Brief. http://www.intel.com/network/connectivity/products/wireless/mywifi.htm.

[21] KIVITY, A. kvm: the linux virtual machine monitor. In *OLS '07: The 2007 Ottawa Linux Symposium* (2007), pp. 225–230.

[22] LAMBERT, N. Demystifying client virtualization. Forrester Research, Inc., April 2008. http://www.vmware.com/files/pdf/analysts/Forrester_Demystifying-Client-%Virtualization.pdf.

[23] LANGE, J., PEDRETTI, K., HUDSON, T., DINDA, P., CUI, Z., XIA, L., BRIDGES, P., GOCKE, A., JACONETTE, S., LEVENHAGEN, M., AND BRIGHTWELL, R. Palacios and kitten: New high performance operating systems for scalable virtualized and native supercomputing. In *IEEE International Symposium on Parallel & Distributed Processing (IPDPS)* (2010).

[24] LEVASSEUR, J., UHLIG, V., STOESS, J., AND GTZ, S. Unmodified device driver reuse and improved system dependability via virtual machines. In *Proceedings of the 6th Symposium on Operating Systems Design and Implementation* (2004), pp. 17–30.

[25] LIAO, G., GUO, D., BHUYAN, L., AND KING, S. R. Software techniques to improve virtualized i/o performance on multi-core systems. In *Proceedings of the 4th ACM/IEEE Symposium on Architectures for Networking and Communications Systems* (New York, NY, USA, 2008), ANCS '08, ACM, pp. 161–170.

[26] LIU, J., HUANG, W., ABALI, B., AND PANDA, D. High performance vmm-bypass I/O in virtual machines. In *Proceedings of the USENIX Annual Technical Conference* (May 2006).

[27] MENON, A., COX, A. L., AND ZWAENEPOEL, W. Optimizing network virtualization in xen. In *Proceedings of the USENIX Annual Technical Conference* (2006), pp. 15–28.

[28] MENON, A., JOHN JANAKIRAMAN, G., SANTOS, J. R., AND ZWAENEPOEL, W. Diagnosing performance overheads in the xen virtual machine environment. In *VEE '05: Proc. 1st ACM/USENIX International Conference on Virtual Execution Environments* (2005), ACM Press, pp. 13–23.

[29] PCI-SIG. I/O virtualization. http://www.pcisig.com/specifications/iov/.

[30] RAJ, H., AND SCHWAN, K. High performance and scalable I/O virtualization via self-virtualized devices. In *Proc. of HPDC* (2007), pp. 179–188.

[31] RAM, K. K., SANTOS, J. R., TURNER, Y., COX, A. L., AND RIXNER, S. Achieving 10 gb/s using safe and transparent network interface virtualization. In *VEE '09: Proceedings of the 2009 ACM SIGPLAN/SIGOPS international conference on Virtual execution environments* (New York, NY, USA, 2009), ACM, pp. 61–70.

[32] RENATO, J., YOSHIO, S., JOHN, T. G., AND PRATT, J. I. Bridging the gap between software and hardware techniques for I/O virtualization. In *2008 USENIX Annual Technical Conference* (2008).

[33] SACHS, J., AND BAUCKE, S. Virtua radio – a framework for configurable radio networks. In *WICON '08: Proceedings of the Fourth International Wireless Internet Conference* (Maui, Hawaii, USA, November 2008), ACM.

[34] SMITH, G., CHATURVEDI, A., MISHRA, A., AND BANERJEE, S. Wireless virtualization on commodity 802.11 hardware. In *WiNTECH '07* (Montreal, Quebec, Canada, Sept 2007), ACM.

[35] SUGERMAN, J., VENKITACHALAN, G., AND LIM, B.-H. Virtualizing I/O devices on VMware workstation's hosted virtual machine monitor. In *Proceedings of the USENIX Annual Technical Conference* (June 2001).

[36] VIRTUALLOGIX INC. Virtuallogix vlx. http://www.virtuallogix.com/.

[37] VMWARE, INC. Vmware desktop virtualization products. http://www.vmware.com/products/desktop_virtualization.html.

[38] WALDSPURGER, C. A. Memory resource management in vmware esx server. In *OSDI '02: Proceedings of the 5th symposium on Operating systems design and implementation* (New York, NY, USA, 2002), ACM, pp. 181–194.

[39] XIA, L., LANGE, J., DINDA, P., AND BAE, C. Investigating virtual passthrough I/O on commodity devices. *SIGOPS Oper. Syst. Rev. 43*, 3 (2009), 83–94.

SymCall: Symbiotic Virtualization
Through VMM-to-Guest Upcalls

John R. Lange

Department of Computer Science
University of Pittsburgh
Pittsburgh, PA 15260
jacklange@cs.pitt.edu

Peter A. Dinda

Department of EECS
Northwestern University
Evanston, IL 60208
pdinda@northwestern.edu

Abstract

Symbiotic virtualization is a new approach to system virtualization in which a guest OS targets the native hardware interface as in full system virtualization, but also optionally exposes a software interface that can be used by a VMM, if present, to increase performance and functionality. Neither the VMM nor the OS needs to support the symbiotic virtualization interface to function together, but if both do, both benefit. We describe the design and implementation of the *SymCall* symbiotic virtualization interface in our publicly available Palacios VMM for modern x86 machines. SymCall makes it possible for Palacios to make clean synchronous upcalls into a symbiotic guest, much like system calls. One use of symcalls is to allow synchronous collection of semantically rich guest data during exit handling in order to enable new VMM features. We describe the implementation of *SwapBypass*, a VMM service based on SymCall that reconsiders swap decisions made by a symbiotic Linux guest. Finally, we present a detailed performance evaluation of both SwapBypass and SymCall.

Categories and Subject Descriptors   D.4.7 [*Operating Systems*]: Organization and Design

General Terms   Design, Experimentation, Measurement, Performance

Keywords   virtual machine monitors, operating systems

1. Introduction

Virtualization is rapidly becoming ubiquitous, especially in large-scale data centers. Significant inroads have also been made into high performance computing and adaptive systems [14]. The rapid adoption of virtualization in all of these areas is in no small part due to the ability of virtualization to adapt existing OSes to virtual environments with few or no OS implementation changes.

A consequence of this compatibility is that current virtualization interfaces are largely designed to be purely unidirectional. A guest OS is only able to interact with a VMM through a virtualized hardware interface (e.g., VMware [26], KVM [21]) or via paravirtualized hypercalls (e.g. Xen [3]). Conversely, the only way a VMM can signal a guest OS is through interrupts or interfaces built on top of a hardware device abstraction. Despite being easy to implement and widely compatible, such interfaces can be very restrictive.

This has resulted in the emergence of a substantial *semantic gap* [4] across the VMM/OS interface, which in turn has resulted in the creation of numerous techniques designed to bridge it [7, 10, 11]. While these efforts have the advantage of operating without guest modifications or cooperation, the information gleaned from such black-box or grey-box approaches is semantically poor. This restricts the kinds of decisions the VMM can make as well as the services it can offer. Furthermore, even when these tools can reconstruct needed guest state, the reconstruction effort can be a significant burden on the VMM and/or service developer, especially given that the desired information is probably already readily available inside the guest environment.

We propose *symbiotic virtualization*, a new approach to designing VMMs and guest OSes to work better together. In symbiotic virtualization, a cooperative symbiotic guest kernel can detect that it is running on a symbiotic VMM, synchronize with it, and then offer it access to semantically rich information, and, more generally, to what amounts to a system call interface that the VMM can use to interact with the guest kernel. This interface can then be used by the VMM and its associated services. If no symbiotic VMM (or even no VMM at all) is available, a symbiotic guest kernel behaves normally. Symbiotic virtualization preserves the benefits of full system virtualization, while providing a standard interface for VMM/OS interactions. A symbiotic interface is not a required mechanism for OS functionality, nor is a VMM required to use it if it is present.

In this paper, we focus on the SymCall symbiotic interface. SymCall allows the VMM to make upcalls into the guest kernel, making it possible for a guest to easily provide an efficient and safe system call interface to the VMM. These calls can then be used during the handling of a guest exit. That is, the VMM can invoke the guest directly *during the handling of a guest exit*. We describe the design and implementation of SymCall in Palacios in considerable detail, and we evaluate the latency of SymCall.

Using the SymCall interface, we designed, implemented, and evaluated a proof-of-concept symbiotic service in Palacios. This service, *SwapBypass*, uses shadow paging to reconsider swapping decisions made by a symbiotic Linux guest running in a VM. If the guest is experiencing high memory pressure relative to its memory partition, it may decide to swap a page out. However, if the VMM has available physical memory, this is unnecessary. Although a page may be swapped out and marked unavailable in the guest page table, SwapBypass can keep the page in memory and mark

This effort was funded by the United States National Science Foundation (NSF) via grant CNS-0709168, and the Department of Energy (DOE) via grant DE-SC0005343.

it available in the shadow page table. The effect is that access to the "swapped" page is at main memory speeds, and that the guest is using more physical memory than initially allotted, even if it is incapable of dynamically adapting to changing physical memory size.

Implementing SwapBypass requires information about the mapping of swap IDs to swap devices, which is readily provided via a SymCall, but extremely challenging to glean otherwise. We evaluate SwapBypass both through performance benchmarks, and through an examination of its implementation complexity.

The contributions of this paper include:

- The definition of symbiotic virtualization.

- The design and implementation of the SymCall framework to support symbiotic virtualization in the Palacios VMM.

- An evaluation of the performance of SymCall.

- The design and implementation of a proof-of-concept VMM feature that leverages SymCall: SwapBypass, a service that reconsiders Linux kernel swap decisions.

- An evaluation of SwapBypass, considering both performance and implementation complexity.

Palacios VMM: Our implementation is in the context of the Palacios VMM. Palacios is an OS-independent, open source, BSD-licensed, publicly available type-I VMM whose details can be found elsewhere [13, 14]. Palacios achieves full system virtualization for x86 and x86_64 hosts and guests using either the AMD SVM or Intel VT hardware virtualization extensions and either shadow or nested paging. The entire VMM, including the default set of virtual devices is on the order of 47 thousand lines of C and assembly. When embedded into Kitten, a lightweight kernel available from Sandia National Labs, as done in this work, the total code size is on the order of 108 thousand lines. Palacios is capable of running on environments ranging from commodity Ethernet-based servers to large scale supercomputers, specifically the Red Storm Cray XT supercomputer located at Sandia National Labs.

2. Symbiotic virtualization

Symbiotic virtualization is an approach to designing VMMs and OSes such that both support, but neither requires, the other. A symbiotic OS targets a native hardware interface, but also exposes a software interface, usable by a symbiotic VMM, if present, to optimize performance and increase functionality. The goal of symbiotic virtualization is to introduce a virtualization interface that provides access to high level semantic information while still retaining the universal compatibility of a virtual hardware interface. Symbiotic virtualization is neither full system virtualization nor paravirtualization, however it can be used with either approach.

A symbiotic OS exposes two types of interfaces. The first is a passive interface, called SymSpy, that allows a symbiotic VMM to simply read out structured information that the OS places in memory. This interface has extremely low overhead, as the VMM can readily read guest memory during an exit or from a different core. However, the information is necessarily provided asynchronously with respect to exits or other VMM events. Because of this, guest information that may be useful in handling the exit may not be available at the time of the exit.

The second is a functional interface, SymCall, that allows a symbiotic VMM to invoke the guest synchronously, during exit handling or from a separate core. However, these invocations have considerably higher costs compared to the passive interface. Furthermore, the implementation complexity may be much higher for two reasons. First, the VMM must be able to correctly support re-entry into the guest *in the process of handling a guest exit*. Second,

from the guest's perspective, the functional interface provides an additional source of concurrency *that is not under guest control.* The VMM and guest must be carefully designed so this concurrency does not cause surprise race conditions or deadlocks.

In addition to the functional and passive interfaces, symbiotic virtualization requires a discovery protocol that the guest and VMM can run to determine which, if any, of the interfaces are available, and what data forms and entry points are available.

3. Discovery and configuration

One of the principal goals of symbiotic virtualization is to provide an enhanced interface between a VMM and an OS while still allowing compatibility with real hardware. In contrast to paravirtualization, symbiotic virtualization is designed to be enabled and configured at run time without requiring any changes to the OS. As such, symbiotic upcalls are implemented using existing hardware features, such as CPUID values and Model Specific Registers (MSRs). A guest is able to detect a symbiotic VMM at boot time and selectively enable symbiotic features that it supports. The discovery and configuration process is shown in Figure 1.

In order to indicate the presence of a symbiotic VMM we have created a virtualized CPUID value. The virtualized CPUID returns a value denoting a symbiotic VMM, an interface version number, as well as machine specific interface values to specify hypercall parameters. This maintains hardware compatibility because on real hardware the CPUID instruction simply returns an empty value indicating the non-presence of a symbiotic OS which will cause the OS to abort further symbiotic configurations[1]. If the guest does detect a symbiotic VMM then it proceeds to configure the symbiotic environment using a set of virtualized MSRs.

4. SymSpy passive interface

The SymSpy interface provides a mechanism for the sharing of structured information between the VMM and the guest OS. This information is stored in a memory region that is mapped into the guest's physical address space. The guest indicates to the VMM a guest physical address at which to map the SymSpy page. After this is completed the guest can read/write to this memory location without an exit. The VMM can also directly access the page during its execution.

SymSpy is used to enumerate what structured data types are available as well as which symbiotic services, such as specific symcalls, are supported by the guest OS. The SymSpy interface is also useful for sharing VMM state information with the guest OS. For example, Palacios uses the interface to expose the identities of PCI devices that the guest has direct access to. This allows the guest to explicitly modify its DMA addresses to account for the location of guest memory inside physical memory.

Configuring SymSpy is the second step in the symbiotic configuration process shown in Figure 1. After a guest has detected the presence of a symbiotic VMM it chooses an available guest physical memory address that is not currently in use. This address does not have to be inside the guest's currently allocated memory, and can instead be mapped into any guest physical address range that the guest OS has available. Once an address has been found the guest writes it to the SymSpy MSR, which is a special virtual MSR implemented by the VMM. The symbiotic VMM intercepts this operation, allocates a new page, and maps it into the guest at the location specified in the MSR.

---

[1] We use CPUID instead of a virtual MSR because accesses to non-present MSRs generate a General Protection Fault

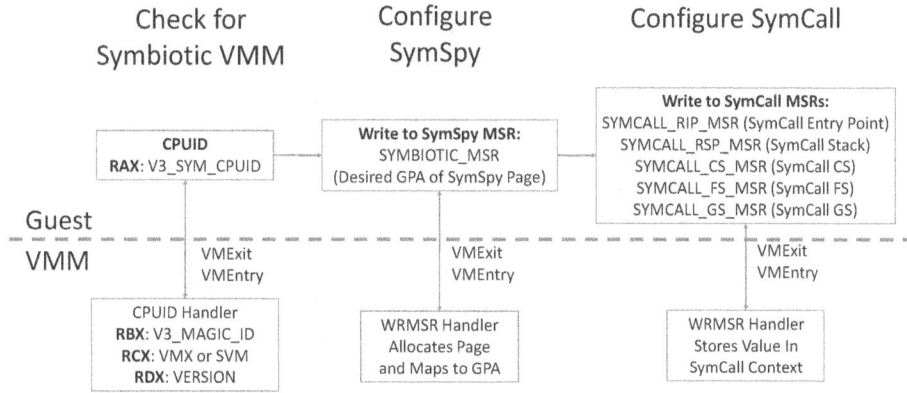

Figure 1. Symbiotic VMM discovery/configuration.

5. SymCall functional interface

SymCalls are a new VMM/guest interface by which a VMM can make synchronous upcalls into a running guest OS. In a guest OS, this interface is designed to resemble the existing system call interface as much as possible, both in terms of the hardware interface presented to the guest, as well as the internal upcall implementations. Based on the similarity to system calls we refer to symbiotic upcalls as symcalls.

5.1 Alternative upcall mechanisms

The utility of upcalls in layered architectures is well understood [6], and most existing virtualization architectures include interfaces that allow guest environments to react to requests made from the VMM layer. For example, balloon drivers are a common interface that allows a VMM to request that a guest release memory pages. These interfaces are built on top of the virtual device abstraction which is implemented using standard device I/O mechanisms: interrupts and DMA. As such, these interfaces are fundamentally different from upcalls as defined in [6], and instead rely on asynchronous signals (interrupts) to request that a VM take a guest defined action (I/O to/from a virtual device). In contrast, SymCall provides an interface that enables a VMM to directly execute a specific upcall synchronously as part of an exit handling operation.

This synchronous behavior allows a VMM to easily modify exit handler behavior based on complex information gleaned from internal guest state queries that are executed as upcalls inside the guest's context. This functionality is not possible when using a virtual device abstraction due to the asynchronous nature of the interface. Even if an exit handler were to raise an interrupt inside the guest context it would have no guarantee of when the associated interrupt handler would actually be executed. This prevents the virtual device interface from being used inside exit handlers or anywhere else where synchronous behavior is required.

5.2 SymCall architecture

The x86 architecture has a several well defined frameworks for supporting OS system calls. These interfaces allow a system call to be executed via a special instruction that instantiates a system call context defined at initialization time by the OS. When a system call instruction is executed, the context variables are copied out of a set of MSRs and instantiated on the hardware. When execution resumes the CPU is running a special OS code path that dispatches to the correct system call handler. When a system call returns it executes the corresponding exit instructions that reverse this procedure.

Due to the conceptual similarity between symcalls and system calls we designed our implementation to be architecturally similar as well. Just as with system calls, the guest OS is responsible for enabling and configuring the environment which the symcalls will execute in. It does this using a set of virtualized MSRs that are based on the actual MSRs used for the SYSCALL and SYSRET interface. When the VMM makes a symbiotic upcall, it configures the guest environment according to the values given by the guest OS. The next time the guest executes it will be running in the SymCall dispatch routine that invokes the handler for the specific symcall.

5.3 Virtual hardware support

The SymCall virtual hardware interface consists of a set of MSRs that are a union of the MSRs used for the SYSENTER and SYSCALL frameworks[2]. We combine both the MSR sets to provide a single interface that is compatible for both the Protected (32 bit) and Long (64 bit) operating modes. The set of symbiotic MSRs are:

- *SYMCALL_RIP:* The value to be loaded into the guest's RIP/EIP register. This is the address of the entry point for symcalls in the guest kernel

- *SYMCALL_RSP:* The value to be loaded into the guest's RSP/ESP register. This is the address of the top of the stack that will be used when entering a symcall.

- *SYMCALL_CS:* The location of the code segment to be loaded during a symcall. This is the code segment that will be used during the symcall. The stack segment is required to immediately follow the code segment, and so can be referenced via this MSR.

- *SYMCALL_GS:* The GS segment base address to be loaded during a symcall.

- *SYMCALL_FS:* The FS segment base address to be loaded during a symcall. The GS or FS segments are used to point to kernel-level context for the symcall.

The RIP, RSP, and CS(+SS) MSRs are needed to create the execution context for the symbiotic upcall. The FS and GS MSRs typically hold the address of the local storage on a given CPU core. FS or GS is typically used based on the operating mode of the processor.

---

[2] The execution model however more closely resembles the SYSCALL behavior

Figure 2 diagram (Guest / VMM execution path):

Convert Calling Convention → Dispatch SymCall via SymCall Table

SymCall Entry Point — Execute SymFunc(args...) — Symcall Exit Return code and values

Guest / VMM

VMExit — VMEntry — VMExits VMEntries — VMExits VMEntries — VMEntry

Save Guest Context

Invoke Exit Handler — Call SymFunc(ID,args...) (function call) — Marshall Arguments — Checkpoint Guest Context — Instantiate Symcall Context from MSRs (ARGS in GPRs)

Normal VMM Exit Handling (no nested SymCalls)

Unmarshall Return Values — Restore Guest Context From Original Exit — Return from SymFunc to Original Exit Handler — Finish Exit Handler — Restore Guest Context

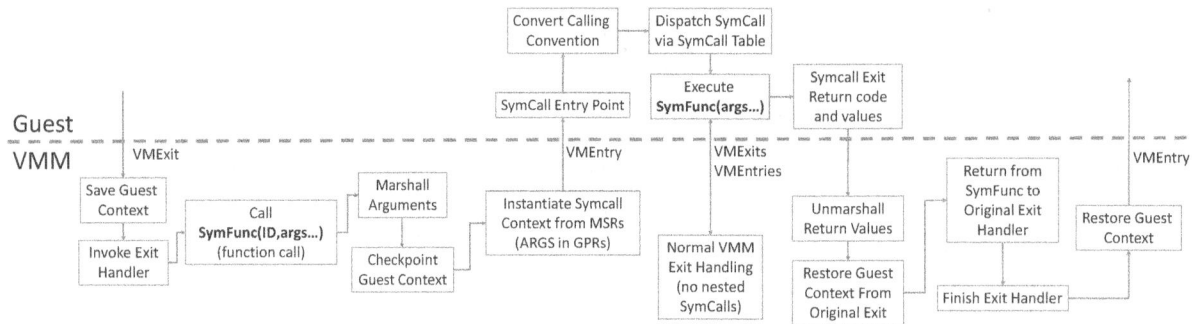

Figure 2. The execution path of the SymCall functional interface in the Palacios VMM. Symcalls execute synchronously with respect to VM exits, and allow exit handlers to optimize their behavior based on complex state information collected from queries executed inside the guest context.

Component	Lines of code
VMM infrastructure	300(C)
Guest infrastructure	211(C) + 129(ASM)
Total	511(C) + 129(ASM)

Figure 3. Lines of code needed to implement the SymCall infrastructure as measured by SLOCcount

As we stated earlier the execution model for a symbiotic upcall is based on system calls. The one notable difference is that symbiotic upcalls always store the guest state before the call is executed and reload it when the symcall returns. Furthermore the state is saved inside the VMM's address space and so is inaccessible to the guest OS. This is largely a safety precaution due to the fact that the guest OS has much less control over when a symbiotic call is executed. For example, a system call can only be executed when a process is running, but a symcall can also occur when the guest is executing in the kernel.

As we mentioned earlier, the system call return process copies back the context that existed before the system call was made (but possibly modified afterward). Returning from a symbiotic upcall is the same with the exception being that the symbiotic call always returns to the context immediately before the symcall was made. This is because the calling state is not saved in the guest environment, but instead stored by the VMM. Because there is no special instruction to return from a symcall the guest instead executes a special hypercall indicating a return from a symcall.

The virtual hardware interface we have developed follows the system call design to minimize the behavioral changes of a guest OS. Our other objective was to create an interface that would be implementable in physical hardware. Existing hardware implementations could be extended to provide hardware versions of the MSRs that would only be accessible while the CPU is executing in a VM context. A second type of VM entry could be defined which launches into the state defined by the MSRs and automatically saves the previous guest state in the virtual machine control structures. And finally a new instruction could be implemented to return from a symbiotic upcall and reload the saved guest state.

5.4 Symbiotic upcall interface

Using the virtual hardware support, we have implemented a symbiotic upcall facility in the Palacios VMM. Furthermore we have implemented symbiotic upcall support for two guest OSes: 32 bit Linux and the 64 bit Kitten OS. Our SymCall framework supports both the Intel VMX and AMD SVM virtualization architectures. The symcalls are designed to resemble the Linux system call interface as closely as possible. We will focus our description on the Linux implementation.

Implementing the SymCall interface required modifications to both the Palacios VMM as well as the Linux kernel running as a guest. The scale of the changes is shown in Figure 3. The modifications to the guest OS consisted of 211 lines of C and 129 lines of assembly as measured by SLOCcount. This code consisted of the generic SymCall infrastructure and did not include the implementation of any symcall handlers. The VMM infrastructure consisted of an additional 300 lines of C implemented as a compile time module.

5.4.1 Guest OS support

The Linux guest implementation of the symbiotic upcall interface shares much commonality with the system call infrastructure. Symbiotic upcalls are designed to be implemented in much the same manner as a normal system call. Each symbiotic upcall is associated with a given call index number that is used to look up the appropriate call handler inside a global array. The OS loads the *SYMCALL_RIP* MSR with a pointer to the SymCall handler, which uses the value of the *RAX* General Purpose Register (GPR) as the call number. The arguments to the symcall are supplied in the remaining GPRs, which limits each symbiotic upcall to at most 5 arguments. Our current implementation does not support any form of argument overflow, though there is no inherent reason why this would not be possible. The arguments are passed by value. Return values are passed in the same way, with the error code passed in *RAX* and additional return values in the remaining GPRs. Any kernel component can register a symbiotic upcall in exactly the same way as it would register a system call.

One notable difference between symcalls and normal system calls is the location of the stack during execution. Normal system calls execute on what is known as the kernel mode stack. Every process on the system has its own copy of a kernel mode stack to handle its own system calls and possibly also interrupts. Among other things this allows context switching and kernel preemption, because each execution path running in the kernel is guaranteed to have its own dedicated stack space. This assurance is possible because processes are unable to make multiple simultaneous system calls. Symbiotic upcalls on the other hand can occur at any time, and so cannot use the current process' kernel stack. In our implementation the guest OS allocates a symbiotic stack at initialization. Every symbiotic upcall that is made then begins its execution with *RSP* loaded with the last address of the stack frame. Furthermore we mandate that symbiotic upcalls cannot nest, that is the VMM cannot perform a symcall while another symcall is running. This also means that symbiotic upcalls are an independent thread of execution inside the OS. This decision has ramifications that place a number of restrictions on symcall behavior, which we will elaborate on in Section 5.5.

5.4.2 VMM support

From the VMM's perspective symbiotic upcalls are accessed as standard function calls, but are executed inside the guest context. This requires modifications to the standard behavior of a conventional VMM. The modifications to the Palacios VMM required not only additional functionality but also changes and new requirements to the low level guest entry/exit implementation.

As we stated earlier the VMM is responsible for saving and restoring the guest execution state before and after a symbiotic upcall is executed. Only a single instance of the guest state is saved, which means that only one symcall can be active at any given time. This means that symbiotic upcalls cannot nest. Our design does not perform a full checkpoint of the guest state but rather only saves the minimal amount of state needed. This allows symbiotic upcalls some leeway in modifying the current guest context. For example the guest OS is not prevented from modifying the contents of the control registers. In general the saved state corresponds to the state that is overwritten by values specified in the symcall MSRs.

The guest state that is saved by the VMM includes:

- *RIP:* The instruction pointer that the guest was executing before the exit that led to the symbiotic upcall.

- *Flags Register:* The system flags register

- *GPRs:* The full set of available General Purpose registers, including the Stack Pointer (*RSP*) used for argument passing.

- *Code Segment Descriptor/Selector:* The selector and cached descriptor of the code segment

- *Stack Segment Descriptor/Selector:* The selector and cached descriptor of the Stack segment

- *FS and GS Segment Bases:* The base addresses for both the FS and GS segments. These are used by the guest OS to store the address of the local processor data area.

- *CPU Privilege Level:* The AMD virtualization architecture requires the CPU Privilege level be saved as a separate entity, even though it is specified by the lower bits of the CS and SS segment selectors. For simplicity we save it separately when running on SVM.

Because symbiotic upcalls are executed in guest context we had to modify the VMM to perform a nested VM entry when a symcall is executed. VMM architectures are based on an event model. The VMM executes a guest in a special CPU operating mode until an exceptional event occurs, a special action is taken or an external event occurs. This causes the CPU to perform a VM exit that resumes inside the VMM context at a given instruction address. The VMM is then responsible for determining what caused the exit event and taking the appropriate action. This generally entails either emulating a certain instruction, handling an interrupt, modifying the guest state to address the exception, or servicing a request. This leads most VMMs to be implemented as event-dispatch loops where VM entries are made implicitly. That is a VM entry occurs automatically as part of a loop, and exit handlers do not need to be written to explicitly re-enter the guest.

For symbiotic upcalls we had to make VM entries available as an explicit function while also retaining their implicit nature. To do this we had to make the main event loop as well as the exit handlers reentrant. Reentrancy is necessary because it is not only possible but entirely likely that the guest will generate additional exits in the course of executing a symbiotic upcall. We found that it was fairly straightforward to modify the exit handlers to be reentrant, however the dispatch function was considerably more complicated.

Implementing reentrancy centered around ensuring safe access to two global data structures: The guest state structure which contains the state needed by the VMM to operate on a given guest environment and the virtualization control structures that store the hardware representation of the guest context. The guest state needed by the VMM is unserialized and serialized atomically before and after a VM entry/exit. This structure is reentrant because the VMM checkpoints the necessary state before and after a symbiotic call is made. This ensures that the guest will safely be able to re-enter the guest after the symbiotic upcall returns, because the guest state is copied back to the hardware structures before every entry. However it does not store the hardware state containing the exit information. In practice the exit information is small enough to store on the stack and pass as arguments to the dispatch function.

5.5 Current restrictions

In our design, symbiotic upcalls are meant to be used for relatively short synchronous state queries. Using symcalls to modify internal guest state is much more complicated and potentially dangerous. Since our current implementation is based on this fairly narrow focus, we made a number of design choices that limit the behavior of the symcall handler in the guest OS. These requirements ensure that only a single symcall will be executed at any given time and it will run to completion with no interruptions, i.e. it will not block.

The reasoning behind restricting the symcall behavior is to allow a simplified implementation as well as provide behavioral guarantees to the VMM executing a symbiotic upcall. If symbiotic upcalls were permitted to block the synchronous model would essentially be broken, because a guest OS would be able to defer the upcall's execution indefinitely. Furthermore it would increase the likelihood that when a symbiotic upcall did return, the original reasons for making the upcall would no longer be valid. This is in contrast to system calls where blocking is a necessary feature that allows the appearance of synchrony to applications.

In order to ensure this behavior, a symcall handler in the guest OS is not allowed to sleep, invoke the OS scheduler, or take any other action that results in a context switch. Furthermore while the guest is executing a symbiotic upcall the VMM actively prevents the injection of any external interrupts such as those generated by hardware clocks. Our implementation also blocks the injection of hardware exceptions, and mandates that symcall handlers do not take any action that generates a processor exception that must be handled by the guest OS. While this might seem restrictive, we note that, in general, exceptions generated in a kernel code path are considered fatal.

The requirement that symcall handlers not block has further ramifications in how they deal with atomic data structures. This is particularly true because, as we stated earlier, a VMM can execute a symbiotic upcall at any point in the guest's execution. This means that it is possible for a symcall to occur while other kernel code paths are holding locks. This, and the fact that symcalls cannot block, mean that symcalls must be very careful to avoid deadlocks. For example, if a kernel control path is holding a spinlock while it modifies internal state it can be pre-empted by a symbiotic upcall that tries to read that same state. If the symcall ignores the lock it will end up reading inconsistent state, however if it tries to acquire the spinlock it will deadlock the system. This is because the symcall will never complete which in turn means the process holding the lock will never run because symcalls must run to completion and cannot be interrupted.

In order to avoid deadlock scenarios while still ensuring data integrity, special care must be taken when dealing with protected data structures. Currently our implementation allows symbiotic upcalls to acquire locks, however they cannot wait on that lock if it is not available. If a symcall attempts to acquire a lock and detects that it is unavailable, it must immediately return an error code similar to the POSIX error *EWOULDBLOCK*. In multiprocessor environments we relax the locking requirements in that symbiotic upcall handlers can wait for a lock as long as it is held by a thread on another CPU.

6. SwapBypass example service

We will now show how symcalls make possible optimizations that would be intractable given existing approaches, by examining SwapBypass, a VMM extension designed to bypass the Linux swap subsystem. SwapBypass allows a VMM to give a VM direct access to memory that has been swapped out to disk, without requiring it be swapped in by the guest OS.

SwapBypass uses a modified disk cache that intercepts the I/O operations to a swap disk and caches swapped out pages in the VMM. SwapBypass then leverages a VM's shadow page tables to redirect swapped out guest virtual addresses to the versions in the VMM's cache. SwapBypass uses a single symcall to determine the internal state and permissions of a virtual memory address. The information returned by the symcall is necessary to correctly map the page and would be extremely difficult to gather with existing approaches.

We will now give a brief overview of the Linux swap architecture, and describe the SwapBypass architecture.

6.1 Swap operation

The Linux swap subsystem is responsible for reducing memory pressure by moving memory pages out of main memory and onto secondary storage that is generally on disk. The swap architecture is only designed to handle pages that are assigned to anonymous memory regions in the process address space, as opposed to memory used for memory mapped files. The swap architecture consists of a number of components such as the collection of swap disks, the swap cache, and a special page fault handler that is invoked by faults to a swapped out memory page. The swap subsystem is driven by two scenarios: low memory conditions that drive the system to swap out pages, and page faults that force pages to be swapped back into main memory.

6.1.1 Swap storage

The components that make up the swap storage architecture include the collection of swap devices as well as the swap cache. The swap devices consist of storage locations that are segmented into an array of page sized storage locations. This allows them to be accessed using a simple index value that specifies the location in the storage array where a given page is located. In Linux this index is called the *Swap Offset*. The swap devices themselves are registered as members of a global array, and are themselves identified by another index value, which Linux calls the *Swap Type*. This means that a tuple consisting of the *Swap Offset* and *Swap Type* is sufficient for determining the storage location for any swapped out page.

As pages are swapped out, the kernel writes them to available swap locations and records their location. As a side effect of swapping out the page, any virtual address that refers to that page is no longer valid and furthermore the physical memory location is most likely being used by something else. To prevent accesses to the old virtual address from operating on incorrect data, Linux marks the page table entries pointing to the swapped out page as not present. This is accomplished by clearing the *Present* bit in the page table entry (PTE). Because marking a page invalid only requires a single bit, the rest of the page table entry is ignored by the hardware. Linux takes advantage of this fact and stores the swap location tu-

ple into the available PTE bits. We refer to PTEs that are marked not present and store the swap location tuple as *Swapped PTEs*.

As a performance optimization Linux also incorporates a special cache that stores memory pages while they are waiting to be swapped out. Because anonymous memory is capable of being shared between processes and thus referenced by multiple virtual addresses, Linux must wait until all the PTEs that refer to the page are marked as swapped PTEs before it can safely move the page out of main memory and onto the appropriate swap device. Tracking down all the references to the page and changing them to Swapped PTEs is typically done in the background to minimize the impact swapping has on overall system performance. Thus it is possible for pages to remain resident in the cache for a relatively long period of time, and furthermore it is possible that one set of PTEs will point to a page in the swap cache while another set will be marked as Swapped PTEs. This means that just because a PTE is a Swapped PTE does not mean the page it refers to is actually located at the location indicated by the Swapped PTE. It is important to note that every page in the swap cache has a reserved location on a swap device, this means that every page in the swap cache can be referenced by its Swapped PTE. The swap cache itself is implemented as a special substructure in the kernel's general page cache, this is a complex internal kernel data structure organized as a radix tree.

6.1.2 Swapped page faults

As we mentioned earlier Linux marks the page table entries of swapped out pages as invalid and stores the swap location of the page into the remaining bits. This causes any attempted access to a swapped out virtual address to result in a page fault. Linux uses these page faults to determine when to swap pages back into main memory. When a page fault occurs the kernel exception handler checks if the faulting virtual address corresponds to a Swapped PTE. If so it first checks if the page is resident in the swap cache. If the page is found in the page cache then the handler simply updates the PTE with the physical memory address of the page in the swap cache and indicates that there is a new reference to the page. If the page is not found in the swap cache then the Swapped PTE contains the location of the page in the collection of swap devices. This triggers a swap in event, where the swap subsystem reads the page from the swap device and copies it to an available physical memory location. This operation could itself trigger additional swap out events in order to make a location in main memory available for the swapped in page. Once the page is copied into main memory it is added to the swap cache, because its possible that other Swapped PTEs reference that page and have not been updated with its new physical address. Once all references have been updated the page is removed from the swap cache.

Finally it should be noted that after a page has been swapped in a copy of the page remains on the swap device. This means that if a process swaps in a page only in order to read it, the page can simply be deleted from the swap cache without writing it to the swap device. The next time the page is referenced it will simply be copied back into the swap cache. Also note that a page can be swapped in from disk and written to while still in the swap cache, and then swapped out again. In this case the version in the swap cache must be written back to the swap device. This makes it possible for a swapped out page to be de-synchronized from its copy on the swap device. This behavior is important and has ramifications for SwapBypass that we will discuss later.

6.2 SwapBypass implementation

SwapBypass uses shadow page tables to redirect the swapped PTEs in a guest's page table to pages that are stored in a special cache located in the VMM. This allows a guest application to directly reference memory that has been swapped out to disk by its OS. An

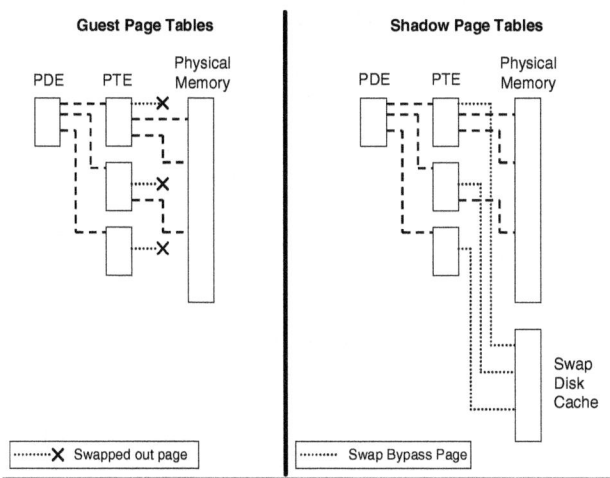

Figure 4. The guest and shadow page table configuration needed to provide a guest access to memory it has swapped out.

Component	Lines of Code
Swap disk cache	373(C)
Page fault handler	47(C)
SwapBypass core	182(C)
Guest SymCall functions	53(C)
Total	655(C)

Figure 5. Lines of code needed to implement SwapBypass as measured by SLOCcount

example set of page table hierarchies are shown in Figure 4. In this case the guest OS has swapped out 3 pages that are referenced by the current set of page tables. As we described earlier it has marked the Swapped PTEs as not present in order to force a page fault when they are accessed. However, when a VMM is using shadow paging all page faults cause VMExits, which allows a VMM to handle page faults before the guest OS. In many cases the VMM updates its shadow page tables to reflect the guest page tables and continues execution in the guest, other times the VMM must forward the page fault exception to the VM so it can be handled by the guest OS. Without SwapBypass the VMM would only see that the guest marked its page table entries as invalid, and thus forward the page fault to the guest OS. However when SwapBypass is active it is able to detect that the guest's PTE is in fact a Swapped PTE[3], and set the shadow PTE to point at the page in the cache. SwapBypass uses a special symcall to inspect the internal swap state of the guest Linux kernel as well as to determine the access permissions of the virtual address containing the swapped PTE.

SwapBypass is implemented with several components. A single symcall that returns the state of a guest virtual address, a special swap device cache that intercepts I/O operations to a swap disk, a new edge case that is added to the shadow page fault handler, and the SwapBypass core that provides the interface between the symcall, swap disk cache, and shadow page table hierarchy.

Figure 5 shows the implementation complexity of the different components in lines of code as measured by SLOCCount. All together SwapBypass consists of 655 lines of code.

---

[3] A Swapped PTE contains a set of flags to indicate a swapped page without any additional information

6.2.1 Swap disk cache

The first component of SwapBypass is a cache that is located inside the VMM between a guest and its swap disk. This cache intercepts all I/O operations and caches swapped out pages as they are written to disk. As swapped pages are written to disk they are first inserted into the cache, if the cache is full then victim pages are chosen and flushed to disk according to a Least Recently Used (LRU) policy. When pages are read from disk they are copied from cache if found, otherwise the pages are read directly from disk and not inserted into the cache.

During initialization the swap disk cache registers itself with SwapBypass, and supplies its *Swap Type* identifier as well as a special function that SwapBypass uses to query the cache contents. This function takes as an argument the *Swap Offset* of a page located on disk and returns the physical address of the page if it is present in the cache. In order for the swap disk cache to determine its *Swap Type* identifier we had to modify Linux to add the *Swap Type* to the swap header that is written to the first page entry of every swap device. The swap disk cache intercepts this write and parses the header to determine its *Swap Type*.

The swap disk cache is also responsible for notifying SwapBypass of disk reads which correspond to swap in events. These events drive invalidations that we will discuss in more detail later.

6.2.2 SwapBypass symcall

Implementing SwapBypass requires knowledge of the state of a swapped out page and the permissions that the current process has on the virtual address referring to that page. This information is extremely difficult to determine from outside the guest context. Furthermore this information cannot be collected asynchronously. The reason for this is that if the VMM does not immediately modify the shadow page tables to point to a page in the cache then it *must* inject a page fault into the guest. The page fault would then cause the guest to swap the page back into its memory space, and modify the Swapped PTE to point at the new location. By the time the asynchronous upcall completed the reason for calling it would no longer exist. Furthermore, because symcalls are executed synchronously they execute in the process context that existed when the exit leading to the symcall occurred. In the case of SwapBypass this means that the symcall executes as the process that generated the page fault on the swapped PTE. An asynchronous approach could not provide this guarantee, which would greatly complicate the implementation.

The symcall takes two arguments: a *guest virtual address* and a *Swapped PTE*. The guest virtual address is the virtual address that caused the page fault while the Swapped PTE is the guest PTE for that virtual address. The symcall returns a set of three flags that mirror the permission bits in the hardware PTEs (Present, Read/Write, and User/System). These bits indicate whether the virtual address is valid, whether the page is writable, and finally whether it can be accessed by user processes.

The first action taken by the symcall is to find the task descriptor of the process which generated the page fault. Linux stores the current task descriptor in a per-CPU data area whose location is stored in the FS segment selector. This means that the task descriptor is found by simply calling `get_current()`, because the FS segment is loaded as part of the symcall entry.

Next, the symcall determines if the page referenced by the Swapped PTE is in fact swapped out or if it is present in the kernel's swap cache. As we stated before, Linux does not immediately update all the Swapped PTEs referencing a given page, so it is possible for the PTEs to be out of date. In this case the guest's page fault handler would simply redirect the PTE to the page's location in the swap cache and return. Therefore, if the symcall detects that the page is present in the swap cache, it immediately returns with a value indicating that the VMM should not use the on disk version of the page. This will cause SwapBypass to abort and continue the normal VMM execution path by injecting a page fault into the guest, thus invoking the guest's swap subsystem. SwapBypass cannot operate on pages in the swap cache, even if they are available in the SwapBypass cache because of the synchronization issues mentioned earlier.

If the swapped PTE does not refer to a page in the swap cache, then it can be redirected by SwapBypass. In this case it is necessary to determine what access permissions the current process has for the virtual address used to access the page. Linux does not cache the page table access permissions for swapped out pages, so it is necessary to query the process' virtual memory map. The memory map is stored as a list of virtual memory areas that make up the process' address space. The symcall scans the memory map searching for a virtual memory area that contains the virtual address passed as an argument to the symcall. Once the region is located, it checks if the region is writable and if so sets the writable flag in the return value.

Finally the symcall checks if the virtual address is below the 3GB boundary, and if so sets the user flag in the return value.

6.2.3 Shadow page fault handler

Similar to the Linux swap subsystem, SwapBypass is driven by page faults that occur when a guest tries to access a swapped out page. When operating normally, the shadow page fault handler parses the guest page tables in order to create a shadow page table hierarchy. If the shadow handler determines that the guest page tables are invalid, then it simply injects a page fault into the guest.

For SwapBypass to function correctly the shadow page fault handler must be able to detect when a guest page fault was generated by a swapped PTE. This can be determined by simply checking several bits in the swapped PTE. If this check succeeds, then the shadow page fault handler invokes SwapBypass. Otherwise it continues normally and injects a page fault. The important take away here is that the shadow page fault handler can determine if a fault is caused by a swapped PTE by simply checking a couple of bits that are already available to it. This means that there is *essentially no additional overhead* added to the shadow paging system in the normal case.

When the shadow page fault handler invokes SwapBypass it supplies the virtual address and the swapped PTE from the guest page tables. SwapBypass returns to the shadow page fault handler the physical address where the swapped page is located and a set of page permissions. The shadow page fault handler then uses this information to construct a shadow PTE that points to the swapped out page. This allows the guest to continue execution and operate on the swapped out page as if it was resident in the guest's address space. If the swapped page is unavailable to SwapBypass then the shadow page fault handler falls back to the default operation and injects a page fault into the guest.

6.2.4 SwapBypass core

The SwapBypass core interfaces with the swap disk cache, the symcall, and the Shadow page fault handler and tracks the swapped PTEs that have been successfully redirected to the swap disk cache. SwapBypass is driven by two guest events: page faults to swapped PTEs and I/O read operations to the swap disk cache. Page faults create mappings of swapped pages in the shadow page tables, while read operations drive the invalidation of those mappings. The execution path resulting from a page fault is shown in Figure 6, and the execution path for disk reads is shown in Figure 7.

Page faults When a guest page fault occurs and the shadow page fault handler determines that it was caused by an access to a swapped PTE, SwapBypass is invoked and passed the faulting

virtual address and guest PTE. First SwapBypass determines which swap device the swapped PTE refers to and the location of the page on that device. Next, it queries the swap disk cache to determine if that page is present in the memory cache. If the page is present, SwapBypass makes a symcall into the guest passing in the virtual address and swapped PTE value. The symcall returns whether the swapped page is in fact located on disk, and the permissions of the virtual address.

If the page is present in the swap disk cache and the symcall indicates that the page on disk is valid, then SwapBypass adds the virtual address onto a linked list that is stored in a hash table keyed to the swapped PTE value. This allows SwapBypass to quickly determine all the shadow page table mappings currently active for a swapped page. Finally SwapBypass returns the permissions and physical address of the swapped page to the shadow page fault handler.

Disk reads Read operations from a swap disk result in the guest OS copying a page from the swap device and storing it in the swap cache. When this operation completes the OS will begin updating the swapped PTEs to reference the page in memory. When this occurs SwapBypass must remove any existing shadow page table entries that reference the page. If the shadow page table entries were not invalidated, then the guest could see two different versions of the same memory page. One version would be in the guest's swap cache and be referenced by any new page table entries created by the guest, while any old swapped PTEs would still only see the version on disk.

When the swap disk cache detects a read operation occurring, it combines its *Swap Type* with the page index being read to generate the swapped PTE that would be used to reference that page. The swap disk cache then notifies SwapBypass that the page referenced by the swapped PTE has been read. SwapBypass then locates the list of shadow page table mappings for that swapped PTE in the previously mentioned hash table. Each shadow page table entry is invalidated and the swapped PTE is deleted from the hash table. SwapBypass then returns to the swap disk cache which completes the I/O operation.

6.3 Alternatives

We believe that SwapBypass is a compelling example that argues for symbiotic virtualization in general, and SymCall in particular, when considered in comparison with the two current alternatives. The first alternative, the graybox/introspection approach, would require that the VMM read and parse the internal guest state to determine whether a page was capable of being remapped by SwapBypass. Even if the guest was modified to include the read/write and user/system bits in the swapped PTE format, the VMM would still have to access the swap cache directly. This would be a very complex procedure that would need to locate and access a number of nested data structures.

The second alternative approach would be to use the current upcall implementations that are based on hardware interrupts and guest device drivers. This approach has two problems: interrupts are asynchronous by nature and Linux uses a return from an interrupt handler as an opportunity to reschedule the current task. Asynchrony could potentially be handled within the VMM by first ensuring that the guest context was configured to immediately handle the interrupt if it was injected. However, this would be complex and might result in some upcalls being aborted. It would also require changes to the Linux interrupt handling architecture to forbid context switches for certain classes of interrupts.

Finally, a simple disk cache might be used in place of a SwapBypass-like service in order to speed up accesses to swapped pages. While this would indeed benefit performance, SwapBypass is further capable of *completely eliminating the overhead of the*

Page fault on a Swapped PTE

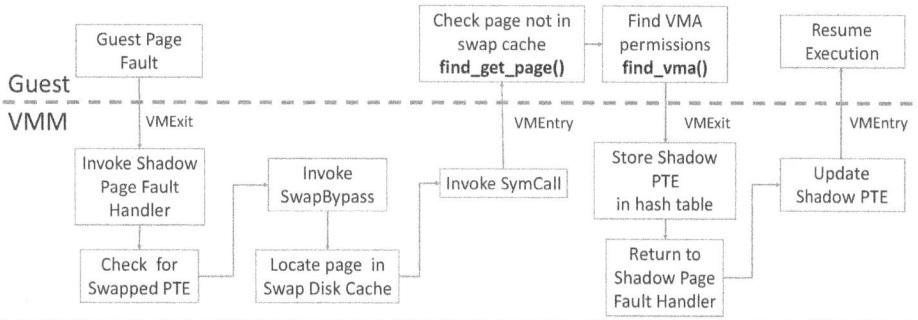

Guest / VMM

Guest Page Fault → VMExit → Invoke Shadow Page Fault Handler → Check for Swapped PTE → Invoke SwapBypass → Locate page in Swap Disk Cache → Invoke SymCall → VMEntry → Check page not in swap cache **find_get_page()** → Find VMA permissions **find_vma()** → VMExit → Store Shadow PTE in hash table → Return to Shadow Page Fault Handler → Update Shadow PTE → VMEntry → Resume Execution

Figure 6. The execution path of SwapBypass in response to a guest page fault on a swapped PTE

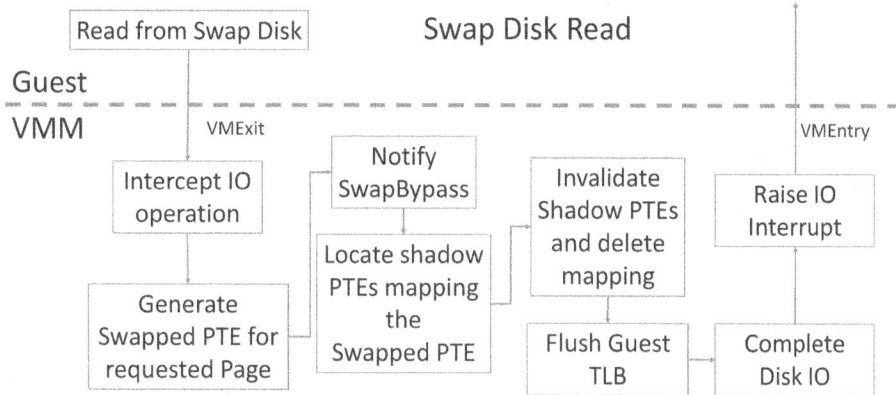

Swap Disk Read

Guest / VMM

Read from Swap Disk → VMExit → Intercept IO operation → Generate Swapped PTE for requested Page → Notify SwapBypass → Locate shadow PTEs mapping the Swapped PTE → Invalidate Shadow PTEs and delete mapping → Flush Guest TLB → Complete Disk IO → Raise IO Interrupt → VMEntry

Figure 7. The execution path of SwapBypass in response to an I/O read operation to a swap device

Latency for echo() SymCall			
First ("cold")	5 VMExits	63455 cycles	35 μs
Next ("warm")	0 VMExits	15771 cycles	9 μs

Figure 8. SymCall latency for a simple echo() symcall

swap system in the Linux kernel. As our evaluation shows, this dramatically improves performance, even over an ideal swap device with no I/O penalty.

7. Evaluation

We evaluated both the performance of our SymCall implementation as well as our implementation of SwapBypass. These tests were run on a Dell SC440 server with a 1.8GHz Intel Core 2 Duo Processor and 4GB of RAM. The guest OS implementation was based on Linux 2.6.30.4.

7.1 SymCall latency

The first test we ran measured the latency in making a symcall. For this test we implemented an echo() symcall, that simply returned the arguments as return values. First, we measured the latency of a symcall made for the first time. When a symcall is first executed, or "cold", it will access a number of locations in kernel memory that are not present in the shadow page tables. The guest will generate shadow page faults until all the memory locations are accessible. For a simple symcall with no external references this requires 5 shadow page faults. We also ran a second test of a symcall after

its memory regions have been added to the shadow page tables. In this "warm" case the symcall generated no exits. The results shown in Figure 8 are an average of 10 test calls. The latency for a "cold" symcall is 64 thousand CPU cycles, which on our test machine equates to around 35 microseconds. The "warm" symcall completed in ∼16 thousand cycles or 9 microseconds.

7.2 SwapBypass performance

We have evaluated the effectiveness of SwapBypass using a set of memory benchmarks that are implemented to use anonymous memory regions. These benchmarks include the microbenchmarks Stream [18] (small vector kernel) configured to use 300MB of memory and GUPS [20] (random access) configured to use 256MB of memory. Stream and GUPS are part of the HPC Challenge benchmark suite. We also used the ECT memperf benchmark [23] configured to use 256MB of memory. ECT memperf is designed to characterize a memory system as a function of working set size, and spatial and temporal locality. Each benchmark was run in a guest configured with 256MB of memory and a 512MB swap disk combined with a swap disk cache in the Palacios VMM. We measured the performance of each benchmark as a function of the size of the swap disk cache. The benchmarks were timed using an external time source.

For the Stream benchmark we ran tests using a hardware swap disk, a virtual swap disk implemented using a simple disk performance model, and a pure RAM disk implemented in VMM memory. The hardware disk was a 7200RPM SATA disk partitioned with a 512MB swap partition. Our hard disk model used a simple aver-

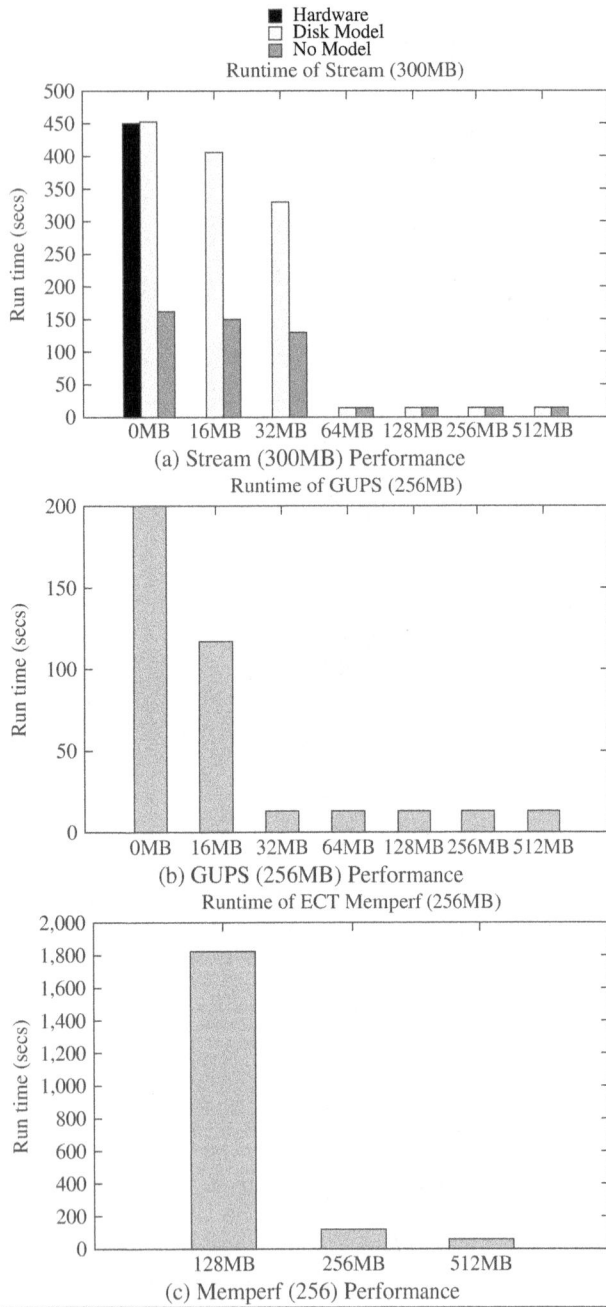

Figure 9. Performance results for Stream, GUPS, and ECT Memperf benchmarks. The benchmark run time was measured for variable sized swap disk caches.

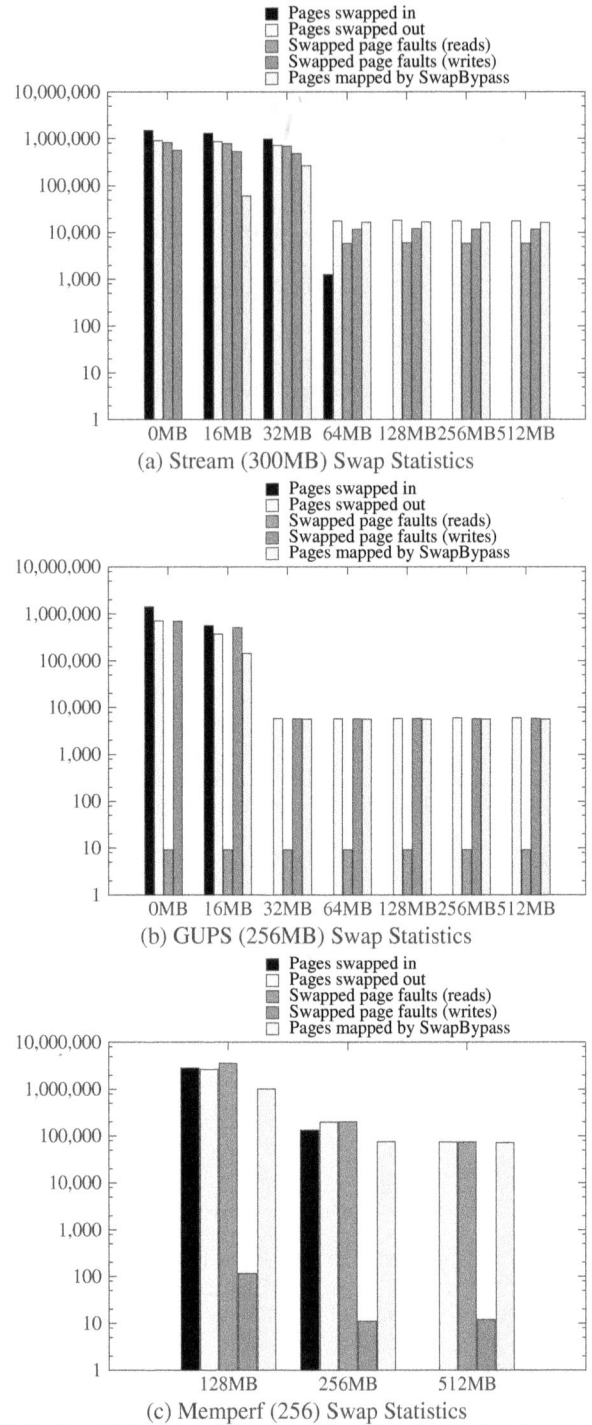

Figure 10. Hardware event statistics for Stream, GUPS, and ECT Memperf benchmarks. Events were counted for each benchmark run using variable sized swap disk caches.

age seek delay based on the hardware specifications of the SATA disk. For the other benchmarks we only used the RAM disk without a disk model. Our reason for concentrating our evaluation on a RAM-based swap disk is to generate ideal I/O conditions for the Linux swap system. With the RAM-based swap disk all disk I/O is eliminated and data is transferred at the speed of system memory. This means that the Linux swap architecture is the *sole* source of overhead, assuring that any performance benefits gained by Swap-Bypass are *not* simply the result of implementing a disk cache in RAM. Our inclusion of the hardware swap disk and disk model evaluations is to help illustrate the effects of SwapBypass with non-ideal I/O.

Stream Our initial benchmark is Stream, configured to use a 300MB region of memory. Figure 9(a) shows the run time of the Stream benchmark for exponentially increasing swap disk cache sizes. We first ran the benchmark using the hardware swap disk as well as with SwapBypass configured with no swap disk cache. Without a cache, SwapBypass flushes all swapped pages to disk and so cannot access them, meaning that SwapBypass will have no beneficial effect on the performance. As the figures show both the hardware and disk model configurations performed comparably with run times of around 450 seconds or 7.5 minutes. The configuration using the RAM disk swap device completed in only around 150 seconds or 2.5 minutes due to the lack of disk I/O.

We then began to scale up the size of the swap disk cache exponentially to determine the impact SwapBypass would have on performance. As the cache size increases the run time begins to decrease until the combined size of the cache and the VM's physical memory partition exceeds the working set size of the benchmark. As soon as this threshold is reached the run time drops off dramatically and the performance of both disk model and RAM disk configurations are essentially identical at 14 seconds. At this point and beyond, SwapBypass is able to satisfy every swapped page fault by mapping the shadow page tables to the page in the swap disk cache—the Linux swap system is completely bypassed and is essentially cut out of the guest's execution path.

The effectiveness of SwapBypass at bypassing the swap system is demonstrated in Figure 10(a), which provides a hardware level view of Linux swap system. For each benchmark run we collected the number of pages transferred to and from the swap device (*Pages swapped in* and *Pages swapped out*), the number of page faults generated by swapped out pages (*Swapped page faults (reads)* and *Swapped page faults (writes)*), and also the number of pages that SwapBypass was able to map into the guest from the swap disk cache (*Pages mapped by SwapBypass*). As the swap disk cache size initially increases the number of page faults and swap I/O operations does not change much but the number of pages mapped by SwapBypass increases substantially. However, when the cache size plus the guest memory partition size reaches the benchmark's working set size, all the measurements decrease dramatically. Also, the number of pages swapped in by the guest OS goes to 0.

GUPS GUPS exhibits behavior similar to that of Stream. The GUPS results are shown in Figures 9(b) & 10(b)

ECT Memperf ECT Memperf results are shown in Figures 9(c) & 10(c). The memperf results are limited to swap disk cache sizes of 128MB and greater because the execution time for lower cache sizes was too large to measure. The execution time for the 128MB cache size was around 1800 seconds or 30 minutes, and the test run for the 64MB cache size was terminated after 6 hours.

Summary of results

A summary of the speedups that SwapBypass can provide for the different benchmarks is shown in Figure 11. The reason for the dramatic increase in performance once the working set size

Benchmark	speedup
Stream (No model)	11.5
Stream (disk model)	32.4
GUPS	15.4
ECT Memperf	30.9

Figure 11. Performance Speedup factors of SwapBypass. The speedup of ECT memperf is measured over the 128MB swap disk cache configuration

threshold is reached is due to a compounding factor. When an OS is in a low memory situation, swapping in a page necessitates swapping another page out, which will need to be swapped in at a later time, which will in turn force a page to be swapped out, and so on. Therefore when SwapBypass is able to avoid a swap in operation, it is also avoiding a swap out that would be needed to make memory available for the swapped in page. SwapBypass is therefore able to prevent the guest from thrashing, which not surprisingly improves performance dramatically.

Our results show that it is possible to artificially and transparently expand a guest's physical memory space using a VMM service. Furthermore, the availability of a symbiotic interface makes implementing this feature relatively easy, while existing approaches would require deep guest introspection or substantial modifications to the guest OS. Being able to easily implement SwapBypass suggests that there are other extensions and optimizations that could be built using symbiotic interfaces.

8. Related work

There are currently two approaches taken by existing virtualization tools: full system virtualization [19, 25, 26] and paravirtualization [1, 3, 17, 27]. In fact it is quickly becoming the case that these approaches are no longer mutually exclusive. Despite the blurring of the boundaries between both of these methods there has not been a significant departure from either. Symbiotic virtualization is a new virtualization interface that introduces a high level guest interface accessible by a VMM. Furthermore, a guest OS can support a symbiotic interface without sacrificing hardware compatibility.

There has also been considerable effort put into better bridging the *semantic gap* of the VMM↔OS interface and leveraging the information that flows across it [8–10, 15, 16, 24]. One of the most compelling uses for this approach is virtual machine introspection, most commonly used in security applications [2, 5, 7, 11, 12, 22, 28]. However, the information gleaned from such black-box and gray-box approaches is still semantically poor, and thus constrains the decision making that the VMM can do. Further, it goes one way; the OS learns nothing from the VMM. Symbiotic virtualization allows explicit two way communication at a high semantic level. Using symbiotic interfaces a VMM can determine guest state by simply asking the guest for it, instead of reverse engineering the running OS.

While SymCall is a new interface for invoking upcalls into a running guest environment, providing upcall support for a guest OS is not a new concept. However the standard approaches are generally based on notification signals as opposed to true upcall interfaces [6]. These notifications usually take the form of hardware interrupts that are assigned to special vectors and injected by the VMM. Because interrupts can be masked by a guest OS, these upcall interfaces are typically asynchronous. Furthermore, existing upcalls consist of only a notification signal and rely on a virtual device or event queue to supply any arguments. Symcalls in contrast are always synchronous and do not need to be disabled with the same frequency as interrupts. Furthermore they allow argument passing directly into the upcall, which enables the VMM to expose them as normal function calls.

9. Conclusion

We have introduced symbiotic virtualization, a new approach to designing VMMs and OSes such that both support, but neither requires, the other. Furthermore we presented the design and implementation of a symbiotic framework consisting of the SymCall functional upcall interface. This framework was implemented in the Palacios VMM and a Linux guest kernel. Using the symbiotic interfaces we implemented SwapBypass, a new method of decreasing memory pressure on a guest OS. Furthermore we showed how SwapBypass is only possible when using a symbiotic interface. Finally, we evaluated SwapBypass showing it improved swap performance by avoiding thrashing scenarios resulting in 11–32x benchmark speedups.

References

[1] KVM: Kernel-based virtualization driver. White Paper.

[2] BAIARDI, F., AND SGANDURRA, D. Building trustworthy intrusion detection through vm introspection. In *IAS '07: Proceedings of the Third International Symposium on Information Assurance and Security* (Washington, DC, USA, 2007), IEEE Computer Society, pp. 209–214.

[3] BARHAM, P., DRAGOVIC, B., FRASER, K., HAND, S., HARRIS, T., HO, A., NEUGEBAUER, R., PRATT, I., AND WARFIELD, A. Xen and the art of virtualization. In *19th ACM Symposium on Operating Systems Principles (SOSP)* (October 2003).

[4] CHEN, P. M., AND NOBLE, B. D. When virtual is better than real. In *The 8th Workshop on Hot Topics in Operating Systems (HotOS-VIII)* (2001).

[5] CHEN, X., GARFINKEL, T., LEWIS, E. C., SUBRAHMANYAM, P., WALDSPURGER, C. A., BONEH, D., DWOSKIN, J., AND PORTS, D. R. K. Overshadow: A virtualization-based approach to retrofitting protection in commodity operating systems. In *Proceedings of the 13th International Conference on Architectural Support for Programming Languages and Operating Systems (ASPLOS '08)* (Seattle, WA, USA, Mar. 2008).

[6] CLARK, D. D. The structuring of systems using upcalls. In *Proceedings of the tenth ACM symposium on Operating systems principles (SOSP)* (1985).

[7] GARFINKEL, T., AND ROSENBLUM, M. A virtual machine introspection based architecture for intrusion detection. In *Proc. Network and Distributed Systems Security Symposium* (2003), pp. 191–206.

[8] GUPTA, A. *Black Box Methods for Inferring Parallel Applications Properties in Virtual Environments*. PhD thesis, Northwestern University, Department of Electrical Engineering and Computer Science, March 2008.

[9] JONES, S. T., ARPACI-DUSSEAU, A. C., AND ARPACI-DUSSEAU, R. H. Antfarm: tracking processes in a virtual machine environment. In *ATEC '06: Proceedings of the annual conference on USENIX '06 Annual Technical Conference* (Berkeley, CA, USA, 2006), USENIX Association, pp. 1–1.

[10] JONES, S. T., ARPACI-DUSSEAU, A. C., AND ARPACI-DUSSEAU, R. H. Geiger: monitoring the buffer cache in a virtual machine environment. In *ASPLOS-XII: Proceedings of the 12th international conference on Architectural support for programming languages and operating systems* (2006), pp. 14–24.

[11] JONES, S. T., ARPACI-DUSSEAU, A. C., AND ARPACI-DUSSEAU, R. H. Vmm-based hidden process detection and identification using lycosid. In *VEE '08: Proceedings of the fourth ACM SIGPLAN/SIGOPS international conference on Virtual execution environments* (2008), pp. 91–100.

[12] JOSHI, A., KING, S. T., DUNLAP, G. W., AND CHEN, P. M. Detecting past and present intrusions through vulnerability-specific predicates. In *SOSP '05: Proceedings of the twentieth ACM symposium on Operating systems principles* (New York, NY, USA, 2005), ACM, pp. 91–104.

[13] LANGE, J., PEDRETTI, K., DINDA, P., BRIDGES, P., BAE, C., SOLTERO, P., AND MERRITT, A. Minimal-overhead virtualization of a large scale supercomputer. In *Proceedings of the 2011 ACM SIGPLAN/SIGOPS International Conference on Virtual Execution Environments (VEE 2011)* (March 2011).

[14] LANGE, J., PEDRETTI, K., HUDSON, T., DINDA, P., CUI, Z., XIA, L., BRIDGES, P., GOCKE, A., JACONETTE, S., LEVENHAGEN, M., AND BRIGHTWELL, R. Palacios and Kitten: New high performance operating systems for scalable virtualized and native supercomputing. In *Proceedings of the 24th IEEE International Parallel and Distributed Processing Symposium (IPDPS 2010)* (April 2010).

[15] LANGE, J. R., AND DINDA, P. A. Transparent network services via a virtual traffic layer for virtual machines. In *In Proceedings of the 16th International Symposium on High Performance Distributed Computing (HPDC)* (2007).

[16] LANGE, J. R., SUNDARARAJ, A. I., AND DINDA, P. A. Automatic dynamic run-time optical network reservations. In *In Proceedings of the 14th IEEE International Symposium on High Performance Distributed Computing (HPDC)* (2005), pp. 255–264.

[17] LEVASSEUR, J., UHLIG, V., CHAPMAN, M., CHUBB, P., LESLIE, B., AND HEISER, G. Pre-virtualization: soft layering for virtual machines. Technical Report 2006-15, Fakultät für Informatik, Universität Karlsruhe (TH), July 2006.

[18] MCCALPIN, J. D. A survey of memory bandwidth and machine balance in current high performance computers. In *Newsletter of the IEEE Technical Committee on Computer Architecture (TCCA)* (December 1995).

[19] PARALLELS CORPORATION. http://www.parallels.com.

[20] PLIMPTON, S. J., BRIGHTWELL, R., VAUGHAN, C., UNDERWOOD, K., AND DAVIS, M. A simple synchronous distributed-memory algorithm for the hpcc randomaccess benchmark. In *Proceedngs of the IEEE International Conference on Cluster Computing (CLUSTER)* (September 2006).

[21] QUMRANET CORPORATION. Kvm - kernel-based virtual machine. Tech. rep., 2006. KVM has been incorporated into the mainline Linux kernel codebase.

[22] QUYNH, N. A., AND TAKEFUJI, Y. Towards a tamper-resistant kernel rootkit detector. In *SAC '07: Proceedings of the 2007 ACM symposium on Applied computing* (New York, NY, USA, 2007), ACM, pp. 276–283.

[23] STRICKER, T., AND GROSS, T. Optimizing memory system performance for communication in parallel computers. In *Proceedings of the 22nd annual international symposium on Computer architecture (ISCA)* (1995).

[24] SUNDARARAJ, A. I., GUPTA, A., AND DINDA, P. A. Increasing application performance in virtual environments through run-time inference and adaptation. In *In Proceedings of the 14th IEEE International Symposium on High Performance Distributed Computing (HPDC)* (2005).

[25] VIRTUALBOX. http://www.virtualbox.org.

[26] WALDSBURGER, C. Memory resource management in vmware esx server. In *Proceedings of the 2002 Symposium on Operating Systems Design and Implementation (OSDI)* (2002).

[27] WHITAKER, A., SHAW, M., AND GRIBBLE, S. D. Scale and performance in the denali isolation kernel. *SIGOPS Oper. Syst. Rev. 36*, SI (2002), 195–209.

[28] YU, Y., GUO, F., NANDA, S., LAM, L.-C., AND CHIUEH, T.-C. A feather-weight virtual machine for windows applications. In *VEE '06: Proceedings of the 2nd international conference on Virtual execution environments* (New York, NY, USA, 2006), ACM, pp. 24–34.

Overdriver: Handling Memory Overload in an Oversubscribed Cloud

Dan Williams *   Hakim Weatherspoon

Dept. of Computer Science
Cornell University, Ithaca, NY
{djwill, hweather}@cs.cornell.edu

Hani Jamjoom   Yew-Huey Liu

IBM T. J. Watson Research Center, Hawthorne, NY
{jamjoom,yhliu}@us.ibm.com

Abstract

With the intense competition between cloud providers, oversubscription is increasingly important to maintain profitability. Oversubscribing physical resources is not without consequences: it increases the likelihood of overload. Memory overload is particularly damaging. Contrary to traditional views, we analyze current data center logs and realistic Web workloads to show that overload is largely transient: up to 88.1% of overloads last for less than 2 minutes. Regarding overload as a continuum that includes both transient and sustained overloads of various durations points us to consider mitigation approaches also as a continuum, complete with tradeoffs with respect to application performance and data center overhead. In particular, heavyweight techniques, like VM migration, are better suited to sustained overloads, whereas lightweight approaches, like network memory, are better suited to transient overloads. We present *Overdriver*, a system that adaptively takes advantage of these tradeoffs, mitigating all overloads within 8% of well-provisioned performance. Furthermore, under reasonable oversubscription ratios, where transient overload constitutes the vast majority of overloads, Overdriver requires 15% of the excess space and generates a factor of four less network traffic than a migration-only approach.

Categories and Subject Descriptors D4.2 Operating Systems [*Storage Management*]: Main Memory

General Terms Performance, Design, Experimentation, Management

Keywords Cloud Computing, Virtualization, Resource Oversubcription, VM Migration, Network Memory

1. Introduction

Cloud computing is becoming increasingly competitive, with a growing list of large companies including Amazon, Microsoft, Google, and IBM, all investing in massive data centers [14]. Physical resources in these data centers are leased on an as-needed basis in the form of virtual machines. With this trend, effective usage of data center resources is becoming increasingly important. A cloud provider using the classical model of overprovisioning each VM with enough physical resources to support relatively rare peak load conditions will have trouble competing with one that can provide similar service guarantees using less resources. This suggests an opportunity for cloud providers to oversubscribe data center resources, placing multiple VMs on the same physical machine, while betting that the aggregate VM resource demands at any one point in time will not exceed the capacity of the physical machine. Unfortunately, without complete knowledge of all future VM resource usage, one or more VMs will likely experience *overload*. As oversubscription becomes increasingly popular, overload will become increasingly prevalent. The ability to manage overload is therefore a critical component of a next-generation, competitive cloud service.

While overload can happen with respect to any resource on a physical machine, we focus on memory overload. The availability of physical memory contributes to limits on VM density and consolidation and as such, is an attractive resource for oversubscription. In addition, recent pricing data for different configurations in Amazon's Elastic Compute Cloud (EC2) indicate that memory is twice as expensive as EC2 Compute Units.[1] However, memory is typically not oversubscribed in practice as much as other resources, like CPU, because memory overload is particularly devastating to application performance. Memory overload can be characterized by one or more VMs swapping its memory pages out to disk, resulting in severely degraded performance. Whereas overload on the CPU or disk result in the hardware operating at full speed with contention introducing some performance loss, memory overload includes large overheads, sometimes to the point of thrashing, in which no progress can be made. Unless a next-generation, oversubscribed cloud can manage memory overload, memory will be a bottleneck that limits the VM density that can be achieved.

Since the ability to manage overload is and will become increasingly critical, and overload of memory is particularly dangerous, we ask the question: *Can performance degradation due to memory overload under real workloads be effectively managed, reduced, or eliminated?*

---

* This work was performed while the first author was an intern at the IBM T. J. Watson Research Center in Hawthorne, NY

---

[1] We use Amazon's pricing data as input parameters for a series of linear equations of the form $p_m \times m_i + p_c \times c_i + p_s \times s_i = price_i$, where m_i, c_i, s_i, and $price_i$ are pricing data for configuration i for memory, EC2 Compute Units, storage, and hourly cost, respectively. Also, p_m, p_c, and p_s are the unknown unit cost of memory, EC2 Compute Units, and storage, respectively. Approximate solutions for the above equations consistently show that memory is twice as expensive as EC2 Compute Units. Particularly, the average hourly unit cost for memory is 0.019 cents/GB. This is in contrast with an average hourly unit cost of 0.008 cents/EC2 Compute Unit and 0.0002 cents/GB of storage.

In order to answer this question, it is essential to understand and characterize the types of memory overload a next-generation cloud provider should expect to mitigate. As we have mentioned, the cloud provider must address overload caused by oversubscription. Through analysis of data center logs from well-provisioned enterprise data centers, we conclude that there is ample opportunity for memory oversubscription to be employed: only 28% of machines experience any overload whatsoever, an average of 1.76 servers experience overload at the same time, and 71% of overloads last at most only long enough for one measurement period. Experimenting with higher degrees of oversubscription on a Web server under a realistic client load, we find, while the likelihood of overload can increase to 16% for a reasonably oversubscribed VM, the duration of overload varies. While overload occasionally consists of long, sustained periods of thrashing to the disk, this is not the common case: 88.1% of overloads are less than 2 minutes long. The fact that memory overload in an oversubscribed environment is a continuum, rather than entirely sustained or transient, suggests that different types of overload may be best addressed with a different mitigation strategy/technique.

Any overload mitigation strategy will have an effect on application performance and will introduce some overhead on the data center itself. Existing migration-based strategies [3, 15, 28, 34] address memory overload by reconfiguring the VM to physical machine mapping such that every VM has adequate memory and no VMs are overloaded. VM migration is a heavyweight process, best suited to handle predictable or sustained overloads. The overload continuum points to a class of transient overloads that are not covered by migration. Instead, we propose a new application of network memory [1, 2, 7, 8, 13, 19, 24] to manage overload, called *cooperative swap*. Cooperative swap sends swap pages from overloaded VMs to memory servers across the network. Unlike migration, cooperative swap is a lightweight process, best suited to handle unpredictable or transient overloads. Each technique carries different costs, and addresses a different section of the overload continuum, but neither technique can manage all types of overload.

We present *Overdriver*, a system that adaptively chooses between VM migration and cooperative swap to manage a full continuum of sustained and transient overloads. Overdriver uses a threshold-based mechanism that actively monitors the duration of overload in order to decide when to initiate VM migration. The thresholds are adjusted based on VM-specific probability overload profiles, which Overdriver learns dynamically. Overdriver's adaptation reduces potential application performance degradation, while ensuring the chance of unnecessary migration operations remains low.

For the mitigation techniques to work, excess space is required somewhere in the data center, whether it is as a target for migration or a page repository for cooperative swap. Overdriver aggregates the VM-specific probability overload profiles over a large number of VMs in order to provide insight into the amount and distribution of excess space in the data center. We have implemented Overdriver and evaluated it when compared to either technique on its own to show that Overdriver successfully takes advantage of the overload continuum, mitigating all overloads within 8% of well-provisioned performance. Furthermore, under reasonable oversubscription ratios, where transient overload constitutes the vast majority of overloads, Overdriver requires 15% of the excess space and generates a factor of four less network traffic than a migration-only approach.

To summarize, we make three main contributions:

- We observe the overload continuum: memory overloads encountered in a data center are, and will likely continue to include both transient and sustained bursts, although an overwhelming majority will be transient.

- We show there are tradeoffs between memory overload mitigation strategies that are impacted by the overload continuum, and propose a new application of network memory, called cooperative swap, to address transient overloads.

- We design, implement and evaluate Overdriver, a system that adapts to handle the entire memory overload continuum.

The rest of the paper is organized as follows. Section 2 examines the characteristics of overload to conclude that overload is and will likely continue to be overwhelmingly transient. Section 3 describes the tradeoffs between mitigation techniques under different types of memory overload. Section 4 describes the design and implementation of Overdriver and how it adaptively mitigates the damage of all types of memory overload. Section 5 quantifies Overdriver's effects on the application and the data center, comparing it to systems that do not adapt to the tradeoffs caused by the overload continuum. Finally, related work is presented in Section 6, and Section 7 concludes the paper.

2. The Overload Continuum

In this section we make three observations. First, we describe various causes of overload in an oversubscribed data center, with particular focus on overload due to oversubscription. Second, we justify the claim that an opportunity for memory oversubscription exists in today's data centers through analysis of data center logs from a large enterprise. Finally, we experimentally examine the characteristics of overload caused by oversubscription to conclude that overload is a continuum, with transient overloads being dominant.

2.1 Types of Overload

A VM is *overloaded* if the amount of physical memory allocated to the VM is insufficient to support the working set of the application component within the VM. In a cloud infrastructure that oversubscribes memory, overload can be caused by the cloud user or the cloud provider. The former occurs when the cloud user does not rent an instance configured with enough memory to handle its working set, or if a running application component has a memory leak. In this paper, we assume that the user should purchase a larger instance to eliminate this type of overload, which is in line with most (if not all) providers' policies.

We thus focus on mitigating overload caused by the cloud provider. We call the amount of memory that a cloud provider dedicates to a cloud user's VM the *memory allocation*. If the VM's memory allocation is less than requested, then we say the physical machine hosting the VM is *oversubscribed*. Oversubscribing memory while preserving performance is possible because application components running in VMs do not require a constant amount of memory, but experience application-specific fluctuations in memory needs (e.g. change in working set). In practice, memory oversubscription can be accomplished by taking machine memory away from one VM to give to another through memory ballooning [31], transparent page sharing [31], or other techniques [10]. If the aggregate memory demand of VMs sharing a physical machine exceed the amount of physical memory on the machine, it is the cloud provider's responsibility to manage overload such that a cloud user believes it has the amount of memory it requested.

2.2 Opportunities for Oversubscription

To justify the opportunity for memory oversubscription in today's data centers, we examine log data from a number of production enterprise data centers, which tend to be well-provisioned. The log data covers a number of performance metrics (including CPU, memory, and disk usage) for a large data center that hosts diverse applications, including Web, financial, accounting, CRM, etc. The collected performance data is typically used by the various data

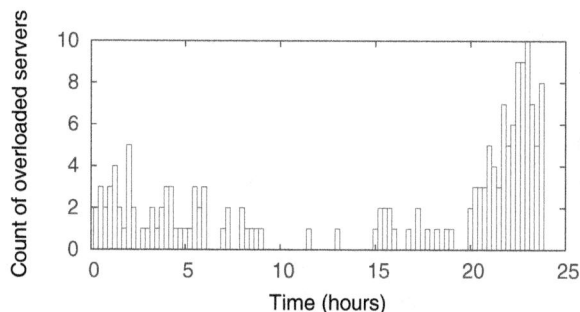

Figure 1. Count of simultaneously overloaded servers out of 100 randomly selected servers over a single representative day. Each point represents the number of overloaded servers during the corresponding 15 min. interval.

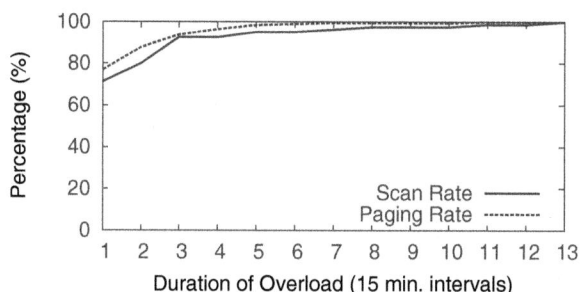

Figure 2. Memory overload distribution of 100 randomly selected servers over a single representative day.

centers to trend application resource usage to identify resource contention and assess the need for workload rebalancing.

There are generally two indicators used by the data center to identify if a server is having memory overload problems: page scan rate and paging rate. Paging rate is the primary indicator as it captures the operating system's success in finding free pages. In addition, a high rate of page scans provides an early indicator that memory utilization is becoming a bottleneck.

In well-provisioned data centers, overload is unpredictable, relatively rare, uncorrelated, and transient, indicating that an opportunity exists for memory oversubscription in today's data centers. To support this claim, we processed performance logs from 100 randomly selected servers. Each log is 24 hours long, while each point in the trace is the average paging rate over a fifteen-minute interval. This is the finest granularity of the log data; thus, sub-fifteen-minute information is not available to us without additional instrumentation of the servers. To capture transient overload bursts that may appear as very low paging rates when averaged over the entire fifteen minute interval, we define overload as an interval with a non-zero paging rate.

We analyzed the data in three different ways. First, we looked at the prevalence of overload (irrespective of its duration) across the 100 servers. We observed that overload is rare: only 28 of the servers experience some kind of memory overload. Second, we studied the frequency of simultaneous overload. Figure 1 shows a time series plot of the count of overloaded servers over the 24-hour measurement period. The figure shows that at most 10 servers were simultaneously overloaded. However, the average over the 24-hour period is 1.76 servers, suggesting that servers sharing physical machines are unlikely to experience correlated overload. Finally, we studied the duration of the overload. Figure 2 shows

the distribution of the duration of memory overload (using both metrics—page rate and scan rate). By definition, the figure only looks at the servers that experienced overload in one or more 15-minute intervals. The figure shows that 71% were overloaded for one interval, 80% (71% + 9%) up to two intervals, 92.5% (71% + 9% + 12.5%) up to 3 intervals (15 min, 30 min, 45 min respectively).

2.3 Overload Due to Oversubscription

If a cloud provider indeed takes advantage of memory oversubscription, we must understand the characteristics of overload as oversubscription is increased. We would like to analyze real data center logs again, however, we do not have access to traces from a data center that currently employs memory oversubscription.

Instead, we introduce a realistic application and workload in an environment within which we can experiment with different levels of oversubscription and gather fine-grained data at both application and system level. We use the SPECweb2009[2] banking benchmark to run on a LAMP[3] Web sever to provide a realistic client load. SPECweb2009 models each client with an on-off period [33], classified by bursts of activity and long stretches of inactivity. Each client accesses each Web page with a given probability, determined from analyzing trace data from a bank in Texas spanning a period of 2 weeks including 13+ million requests [29]. SPECweb2009 is intended to test server performance with a fixed client load, so, by default, client load is stable: whenever one client exits, another enters the system. This makes the benchmark act like a closed loop system. Real systems rarely experience a static number of clients, so, in order to better approximate real workloads, we use a Poisson process for client arrivals and departures. We choose Poisson processes for the clients as a conservative model; real systems would likely have more unpredictable (and transient) spikes.

We next examine the effect of oversubscription on the duration of overload. To do so, we varied the VM's memory allocation to simulate oversubscription and ran the SPECweb2009 Web server with Poisson processes for client arrivals and departure set so that the arrival rate is 80% of the service rate. Each experiment lasted for 10 minutes. Our measurement granularity within an experiment was set at 10 seconds. To ensure high confidence, each point in the graph is the average of 75 experiments.

From this experiment, we construct a probability profile for the application VM under the different memory allocations. As expected, Figure 3(a) shows an increase in the probability of overload as memory becomes constrained. However, in addition to the frequency of overload, we are also interested in the prevalence of each overload duration. Figure 3(b) shows a Cumulative Distribution Function (CDF) of the duration of overload. We see that even at high memory oversubscription ratios, most overload is transient: 88.1% of overloads are less than 2 minutes long, and 30.6% of overloads are 10 seconds or less for an allocation of 512 MB. If the VM memory is increased to 640 MB, 96.9% of overloads are less than 2 minutes long, and 58.9% of overloads are 10 seconds.

To conclude, we have confirmed that memory overload increases with memory oversubscription. In addition, overload is not solely sustained or transient, but covers a spectrum of durations. Finally, we have found that even at the high oversubscription levels that we expect to see in tomorrow's data centers, transient overloads dominate, which will be important to consider when designing Overdriver.

---

[2] http://www.spec.org/web2009/

[3] Linux, Apache, MySQL, PHP

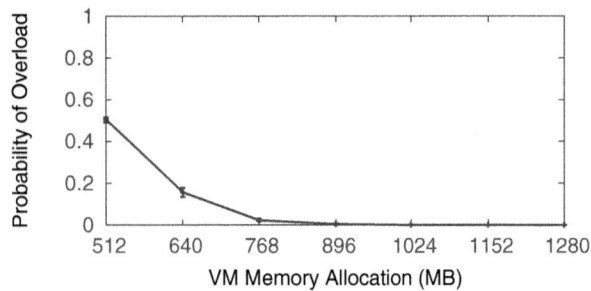

(a) Likelihood of overload.

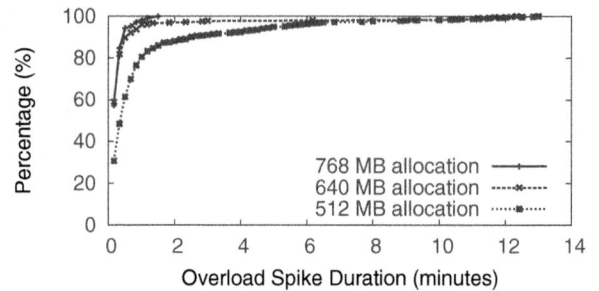

(b) CDF of overload duration

Figure 3. These two graphs form a memory overload probability profile for the web server component of the SPECweb2009 banking application under a variety of different oversubscription levels, including both the frequency and duration of overload.

3. Overload Mitigation

When considering an overload mitigation strategy, the cost of the strategy can be measured in two dimensions: the effect to the application that is experiencing overload and the effect to the data center caused by overhead intrinsic to the strategy.

Application effects refer to the performance of the application that is experiencing overload. Ideally, a mitigation strategy would sustain application response time, throughput, or other performance metrics throughout the overload, so that the cloud user is unaware that it even took place. Data center effects include the overhead or contention introduced by the overload and the mitigation strategy. Ideally, the resources used during the overload are no more than what would have been actively used if no oversubscription was in effect. In this section, we discuss the application and data center effects of two different mitigation techniques: VM migration and network memory.

3.1 Migration

Existing techniques to mitigate overload consist largely of VM migration techniques that address overload by reconfiguring the VM to physical machine mapping such that every VM has adequate memory and no VMs are overloaded [3, 15, 28, 34] (i.e. the VM memory allocation is increased, possibly up to the amount originally requested by the cloud user). VM migration is a relatively heavyweight solution: it incurs delays before it goes into effect, and has a high, fixed impact to the data center, regardless of the transience of the overload. For these reasons, migration strategies are usually designed to be proactive. Trending resource utilization, predicting overload, and placement strategies to minimize future overloads are key components of a migration strategy. Despite these challenges, VM migration strategies are popular because once migrations complete and hotspots are eliminated, all application components will have adequate memory to return to the performance they would have enjoyed without oversubscription.

While live migration boasts very low downtime, as low as 60ms for the migrating VM [5], in the best case, the time-until-completion of migration is dependent on the speed at which the entire memory footprint of the migrating VM can be sent over the network. In many settings, further migration delays are likely to arise from the complexity of migration decisions. In addition to computing VM placements for resource allocation, migration decisions may require analysis of new and old network patterns, hardware compatibility lists, licensing constraints, security policies and zoning issues in the data center. Even worse, a single application in a data center is typically made up of an elaborate VM deployment architecture, containing load balancers, worker replicas, and database backends, that may experience correlated load spikes.

[27] A migration decision, in such case, has to consider the whole application ecosystem, rather than individual VMs. This complexity can be reason enough to require sign off by a human operator. Finally, in the worst case, the infrastructure required for efficient VM migration may not be available, including a shared storage infrastructure, such as a SAN, and a networking infrastructure that is migration aware.

The effect that a migration strategy has on the data center is mostly measured in terms of network impact. Typically, VM migration involves sending the entire memory footprint of the VM or more in the case of live migration. This cost is fixed, regardless of the characteristics of the overload that may be occurring[4]. A fixed cost is not necessarily a bad thing, especially when considering long, sustained overloads, in which the fixed cost acts as an upper bound to the data center overhead. Migration also requires a high, fixed amount of resources to be available at the target physical machine. The target must have enough resources to support a full VM, including CPU and enough memory to support the desired allocation for the migrating VM.

Coupled with the unbeatable performance of local memory available to a VM after a migration strategy completes, the fixed cost to the data center makes migration an attractive strategy to handle both predictable load increases, as well as sustained overloads.

3.2 Network Memory

Two important results from Section 2 highlight a gap in the solution space that existing migration-based solutions do not address. First, overload follows unpredictable patterns. This indicates that, unless oversubscription policies are extremely conservative, reactive strategies are necessary. Second, transient overload is, and will likely continue to be, the most common type of overload. As described above, migration, when used reactively, has high delays, and high network overhead due to relatively short lived transient overloads. There is an opportunity to consider reactive strategies that focus on transient overloads.

Network memory is known to perform much faster than disk [1, 2, 7, 8, 13, 19, 24], especially on fast data center networks, and has been applied to nearly every level of a system. We propose *cooperative swap*, an application of network memory as an overload mitigation solution in which VM swap pages are written to and read from page repositories across the network to supplement the

---

[4] Live VM migration will send more than the few hundred megabytes to tens of gigabytes of data comprising the VM's memory footprint because it must re-transmit the written working set in iterations. However, the network cost of live migration strategies is still relatively fixed because live migration strategies impose a limit on the number of iterations.

	Tput (MB/s)		Latency (μs)	
	Read	Write	Read	Write
Network Mem	118	43.3	119 ± 51	$25.45 \pm .04$
Local Disk	54.56	4.66	451 ± 95	$24.85 \pm .05$

Table 1. Network memory vs local disk performance.

memory allocation of an overloaded VM. Cooperative swap is entirely reactive, and begins to mitigate overload when the very first swap page is written out by the overloaded VM[5]. Its impact on the network is dependent on the duration of overload. However, using cooperative swap does not match the performance of local memory over the long term.

Table 1 shows the relative throughput of disk I/O vs. network memory. These numbers were computed from running a disk dump between the system (/dev/zero or /dev/null) and a hard disk (/dev/sda1) versus a Linux network block device (/dev/nbd0) attached to a ramdisk across the network. The network connecting physical machines is 1 Gbps so can sustain a maximum rate of 125 MB/s. Both are block devices and so should be affected by Linux equally in terms of overhead[6]. Each result is the average of 20 runs of writing or reading 1 GB for the throughput test and one 4 KB page for the latency test. In our setup, network memory is significantly faster than disk. Using cooperative swap, short bursts of paging complete faster, allowing it to maintain application performance through transient bursts of overload. However, cooperative swap does not restore local memory and so cannot restore application performance to where a cloud user would expect if oversubscription was not taking place.

Cooperative swap affects the data center by spewing memory pages across the network. The amount of memory pages read or written from the network is dependent on the length of the overload. This means that cooperative swap is relatively cheap in terms of network overhead for transient overloads, but could generate unbounded amounts of network traffic for very sustained overloads. The amount of pages that must be available from the remote page repositories is also dependent on the duration of overload, however, this number is bounded by the size of the VM's originally requested memory size.

Reactivity, proportional network overhead to overload duration, and long-term performance issues make cooperative swap an attractive solution for unpredictable overloads and transient overloads, filling the gap in the solution space left by existing migration strategies.

4. Overdriver

As seen in Section 3, the overload continuum leads to tradeoffs between mitigation strategies. We design a system, called *Overdriver* to manage overload while being aware of these tradeoffs, adaptively deciding to use cooperative swap for transient overloads and migration for sustained overloads.

Figure 4 shows the high level components in Overdriver. Each physical machine is running a hypervisor and supporting some number of guest VMs. It also runs an *Overdriver agent* in its control domain (Domain 0), that monitors the memory overload behavior of the local guest VMs in terms of paging rate. Within the Overdriver agent, the *workload profiler* locally learns a memory

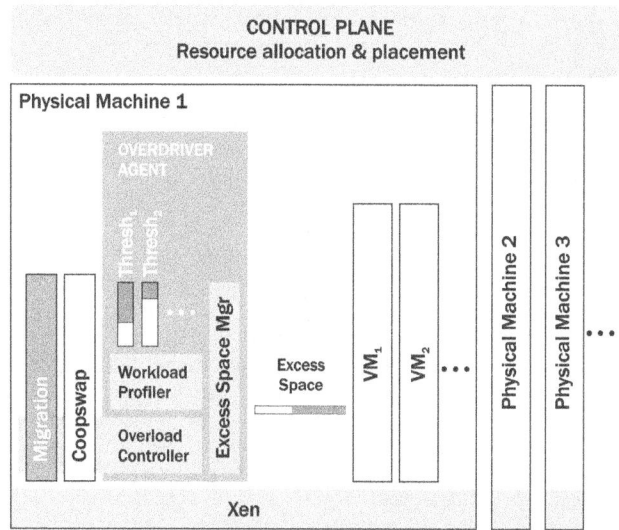

Figure 4. The memory resources in the data center are split into space for VMs and excess space to mitigate overload, of which there are two types: cooperative swap page repositories, and future migration targets. Resource allocation and placement of all resources is performed by the control plane.

overload probability profile for each VM similar to that in Figure 3, which it then uses to set adaptive thresholds on the length at which the overload is classified as sustained. Using these thresholds, the *overload controller* decides which mitigation strategy to employ for a given overload. A transient overload, defined as an overload whose duration has not yet passed the threshold, is mitigated by redirecting the overloaded VM's swap pages to cooperative swap page repositories, rather than to the local disk. If the transient overload becomes sustained, characterized when the duration of the overload exceeds the threshold, the overload controller initiates a migration operation, wherein one or more VMs on the physical machine, are migrated to perform an increase of the memory allocation of the overloaded VM.

For either mitigation strategy to be useful, there must be some *excess space* in the data center. The *excess space manager* on each physical machine is responsible for dedicating some of the local excess space to act as a target for migration, and some to act as a page repository for cooperative swap from overloaded VMs throughout the data center. The actual allocation and placement of VMs and excess space, including page repositories, throughout the data center is performed by the *control plane*, which is similar to the one in [34]. The control plane may run a proactive migration algorithm to avoid hotspots [34] or to consolidate VMs [15], however its design is out of the scope of this paper.

4.1 Deciding to Migrate

As described above, Overdriver uses a threshold on the duration of overload to determine when to classify an overload as sustained and employ migration. Choosing an appropriate threshold is difficult, and a good choice depends on the overload characteristics of the application VM. At one extreme, a very low threshold approaches a solely migration-based overload mitigation strategy, with good application performance, but high data center cost. On the other hand, setting the threshold to be too large approaches a network memory-based strategy, with lower application performance but also lower data center cost. Intuitively, a good choice for the threshold would be high enough that a vast majority of the overloads do not require migration while being low enough that performance does not suffer

---

[5] We do not use cooperative swap unless the VM has a reduced memory allocation due to oversubscription. Otherwise, overload is the responsibility of the cloud user.

[6] Care was taken to eliminate caching effects as much as possible for the latency tests, dropping the caches and writing 500 MB to the device between each latency test.

too much. A profile of the application VMs, including the probabilities of each duration of overload, can help determine a reasonable value for the threshold.

In reality, an application VM profile that describes the probability of overload having a particular duration is not available. However, rather than selecting a single threshold for all VMs, the overload manager starts with a fixed threshold, then relies on the workload profiler to learn the probabilities of various duration overloads to give a basis for reducing the threshold.

There are two challenges in learning a probability profile. First, in the case of sustained overload where migration is employed, the overloaded VM will be granted additional resources that will fundamentally change its overload behavior. In particular, the probability profile of the application VM will change, requiring the learning process to start anew. Second, the learned probability profile takes some time to converge. For example, we attempted to learn the probability profile for a VM allocated 640 MB from the SPECweb2009 experiments in Section 2. For this scenario, at least 25 sustained overloads must be witnessed before the learned profile becomes reasonable. Since the local profile is useless after a migration takes place, the 25 sustained overloads must be endured using only cooperative swap in order to learn a complete profile.

Despite these challenges, focusing only on the different durations of transient overloads, the workload profiler learns enough to reduce the threshold without resorting to excessive migration. The workload profiler maintains a list of buckets for each VM, corresponding to possible transient overload durations. As the paging rates of a VM are monitored, the profiler maintains a count for the number of times an overload of a specified duration is encountered in the appropriate bucket. Once the number of measurements exceeds a base amount, we begin to estimate a tighter bound on the migration threshold by computing the distance from the mean in which transient overload is unlikely to occur. For example, as a heuristic, we assume the distribution of transient overloads is normal, then compute $\mu + 3\sigma$ to be a new threshold. If the new threshold is lower than the original threshold, we adopt the tighter bound to reduce the time until migration is triggered for sustained overload.

4.2 Capacity Planning

Despite the limitations of the learned probability profiles, they can be sent to the control plane, where they can be aggregated over a large number of VMs over time. This can give insight into the quantity of excess space in the data center needed to handle overload and how to partition it between space for migration and space for cooperative swap. The control plane, in return, informs each excess space manager how to subdivide its resources.

To demonstrate how the probability profiles inform the subdivision of excess space, consider a VM running the webserver component of the SPECweb2009 application described in Section 2, when allocated only 640 MB of memory. According to its probability profile (Figure 3) this application VM has a 16% chance of experiencing overload where 96% of the overloads are less than 1 minute in duration. In order for migration to handle sustained overload, we assume that there must be enough excess capacity to have room to migrate a full VM. Similarly, in order for cooperative swap to handle transient overload, we conservatively assume that the sum of the overloaded VM's current memory allocation and the excess space that is required for cooperative swap is equal to the non-oversubscribed allocation, regardless of how short the burst is.

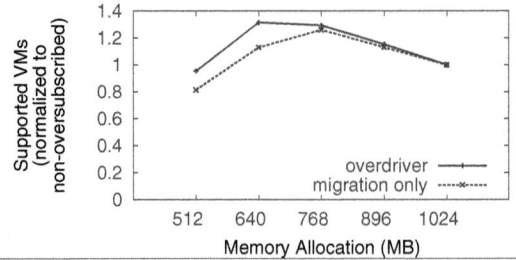

Figure 5. Overdriver allows more VMs to be supported by balancing the amount of excess space needed for sustained and transient overloads.

Assuming the overload characteristics of all VMs are independent[7], if p is the probability of the most likely VM to have overload, we can compute a bound on the probability that at most k VMs will experience simultaneous overload:

$$P \{\text{\# overloaded VMs} \leq k\} = \sum_{i=0}^{k} \binom{n}{i} \cdot p^i \cdot (1-p)^{n-i},$$

where n is the number of VMs in the data center. For example, consider an oversubscribed data center supporting 150 VMs, all running the SPECweb2009 configuration described above. Even if each VM is allocated 640 MB, rather than the 1024 MB they would have requested, we would expect—with probability 0.97—that no more than 3 VMs experience simultaneous sustained overload and no more than 31 VMs experience simultaneous transient overload. This, along with our assumptions about how much excess space is required to satisfy a single overload of either type, allows us to compute—with high probability—the amount of each type of excess space needed to handle all overloads in the entire data center.

Recognizing the overload continuum exists, and selecting the correct amount of each type of excess space can allow an increase in the number of VMs supported in the data center. Assuming that migration and cooperative swap can handle overload longer and shorter than one minute respectively while preserving application performance, we numerically compute the total number of VMs that can be run in the data center under different oversubscription levels. We fix the total amount of memory in the data center as a constant just under 100 GB. For each memory allocation, we input the likelihood of overload and the likelihood that the overload is transient or sustained from Figure 3. The analysis iteratively increases the number of VMs and calculates the amount of excess needed to handle the expected number of simultaneous overloads, in order to find the maximum number of VMs that can be safely supported.

Figure 5 shows the number of VMs that can be supported with high probability using Overdriver or a migration-only strategy. As memory becomes more oversubscribed, more VMs can be run, but more excess space must be maintained to endure overload. Since cooperative swap consumes space proportional to the overload duration, it allows more room for VMs than an approach that uses migration to address all types of overload, including transient overload. To make this point clear, Figure 6 shows the breakdown of memory in the data center, with Overdriver saving 12% more of the data center resources for VMs in the 640 MB case. If the physical machines are oversubscribed too much, corresponding to VM allocations of only 512 MB in this case, the excess space required

---

[7] VMs that make up a single application can experience correlated overload; however the enterprise data in Section 2 indicates that overload is not highly correlated across all VMs in a well provisioned data center.

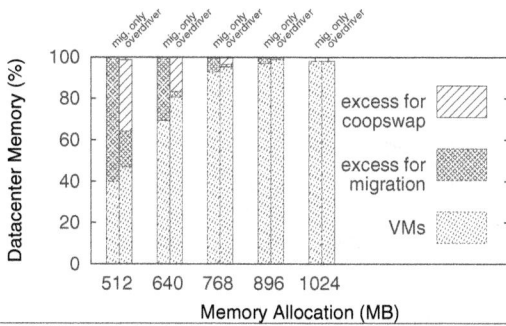

Figure 6. The breakdown of data center resources in terms of space for VMs, excess space for migrations, and excess space for cooperative swap.

to handle sustained overload through migration begins to dominate, reducing the available memory to support additional VMs.

4.3 Discussion

The maintenance of excess space is a key issue when designing a system to handle overload in the data center. Where the various types of excess space are placed throughout the data center, when and how excess space is reclaimed after an overload, and how to combat fragmentation within excess space, are all important questions to consider.

Each mitigation strategy imposes different constraints on how its portion of excess space can be placed throughout the data center. Excess space saved for cooperative swap in the form of page repositories has very few constraints on placement: there is no requirement that swap pages are stored on the same physical machine, nor do the page repositories need many other resources, like CPU. On the other hand, excess space saved for migration has more constraints: there must be enough resources to support a full VM co-located on a single physical machine, including memory and CPU. Another mitigation strategy that we have not discussed is memory ballooning, or modifying the memory allocation on the local machine. Excess space saved for ballooning has very limiting constraints, namely that it must reside on the same physical machine as the VM that is experiencing overload. Resource allocation and placement algorithms must adhere to each of these various constraints.

Overload occurs in a continuum of durations, but when it finally subsides, the excess space that was being used for the overload must be reclaimed. The reclaiming process can be proactive, in which excess space is pre-allocated before overload occurs, or reactive, in which resources are dynamically carved out of the data center on an as-needed basis. Regardless, policies for reclaiming resources are tightly integrated into VM placement and resource allocation, located in the control plane.

Reclaiming memory resources for future migration operations may require squeezing the memory allocations of VMs which may or may not have experienced an overload, and care must be taken to ensure that the reclaiming process does not trigger more overloads in a cascading effect. Reclaiming space in a cooperative swap page repository, on the other hand, can be straightforward—if the VM reads a swap page after overload subsides, that swap page can most likely be deleted from network memory. Otherwise, if the swap page has not been read, the swap page will remain outside of the VM. However, the swap page can be copied to local disk

and removed from network memory at any time,[8] although the performance of a future read of the page will suffer.

Resource reclaiming may also need to consider the fragmentation that occurs within excess space. For example, after a migration completes, some resources are allocated to the overloaded VM. The amount of resources awarded need not be the original requested amount nor must they include all of the available resources on the physical machine. More likely, there will be some resources remaining that are insufficient to host a new VM, but not needed by any of the running VMs. Filling the unused resources with cooperative swap page repositories is one option to combat fragmentation, but ultimately, some consolidation process involving migration will be necessary, once again tightly integrated with VM placement and resource allocation.

4.4 Implementation

We have implemented Overdriver to run on Xen. We leverage Xen's built-in support for live migration and implement cooperative swap clients and page repositories from scratch. The Overdriver agent, written in Python, locally monitors the paging rate of the VMs on its physical machine to detect and react to overload. Probability profiles are maintained in a straightforward manner, which updates the migration threshold. Page repositories implementing excess space for cooperative swap exist as C programs, executed in Xen's Domain 0, that pin memory to ensure that pages written and read do not encounter additional delays. While much of the implementation is straightforward, given space constraints, we focus on some interesting implementation considerations for the overload controller and the cooperative swap subsystem.

4.4.1 Overload Controller

As described above, the overload controller within the agent initiates a migration operation after overload has been sustained past an adaptive threshold. However, the implementation must be able to identify overload from normal behavior. Based on our observations of VMs that are using the paging system, a very low paging rate tends to be innocuous, done occasionally by the operating system even if there is no visible performance degradation. While any paging may be a good indication of future overload, Overdriver uses a threshold on paging rate to determine whether overload is occurring.

Furthermore, the implementation must differentiate between a series of transient overloads and a sustained overload which has some oscillatory behavior. From our experiments inducing sustained overload, we observe oscillations that can last almost a minute long. In order to correctly classify periods of oscillation as sustained overload, Overdriver includes a sliding window, where a configurable number of time intervals within the window must have experienced overload.

4.4.2 Cooperative Swap

A key factor in the performance of cooperative swap is where the client is implemented. In order to remain guest agnostic, we only consider implementations within the VMM or the control domain (Domain 0) of the hypervisor. We have experimented with two different architectures. In the first, we leverage the Xen block tap drivers [32] (`blktap`) as an easy way to implement cooperative swap clients in user-space of Domain 0. When a VM begins to swap, Xen forwards the page requests into userspace, where the block tap device can either read or write the pages to the network or the disk. We noticed that swapping to disk, using a `blktap` driver in Domain 0 for the disk, was significantly outperforming

---

[8] Depending on the fault tolerance policy, a swap page may already be on local disk (see Section 4.4.2).

cooperative swap. The reason for this unexpected result was that pages being written by the user-space disk driver were being passed into the kernel of Domain 0, where they would enter the Linux buffer cache, and wait to be written asynchronously. Asynchrony is especially well suited to cooperative swap, because, unlike writes to file systems or databases, the pages written out have no value in the case of a client failure. Furthermore, the buffer cache may be able to service some reads. In order to take advantage of the buffer cache, in addition to reducing context switch overhead, we decided to implement cooperative swap in the kernel underneath the buffer cache, similar to a network block device (`nbd`).

Regardless of the location of the cooperative swap client, the implementation must provide some additional functionality to reading and writing pages to and from page repositories across the network. We highlight two interesting aspects of the implementation. First, cooperative swap clients must be able to locate pages, which may or may not be on the same page repository, even after a VM has migrated. In-memory state consists mainly of a per-VM hash table, indexed by the sector number of the virtual swap device. Each entry includes the address of the page repository the page is stored at, a capability to access the page, and the location of the page on disk. Both the data structure and the swap pages on disk must be migrated with a VM. This is currently done during the stop-and-copy portion of live migration, although a pre-copy or post-copy live migration technique could be implemented for both the data structure and disk pages. Second, it is important to ensure that failure of a remote machine in the data center does not cause failure of a VM that may have stored a swap page there. Fortunately, there are several accepted mechanisms for reliability in a system that uses network memory. By far the simplest is to treat the page repositories across the network like a write-through cache [7, 8]. Since every page is available on the disk as well as to the network, the dependency on other machines is eliminated, and garbage collection policies are simplified. Reads enjoy the speed of network memory, while writes can be done efficiently through asynchrony. Alternative approaches exist, such as using full replication of swap pages or a RAID-like mirroring or parity scheme [19, 22], but they add considerable complexity to failure recovery as well as garbage collection.

5. Evaluation

We have argued that in order to enable high data center utilization using aggressive memory oversubscription, it is necessary to *react* to overload, both transient or sustained. In this section, we quantify the tradeoffs described in Section 3 in terms of the impact of each strategy on application performance, and in terms of overhead to the data center, most notably network and excess space overhead. We also show that Overdriver successfully navigates this tradeoff, maintaining application throughput to within 8% of a non-oversubscribed system, while using at most 150 MB of excess space for transient overloads.

At a high level we want to answer the following questions:

- Does Overdriver maintain application performance despite memory overloads?

- Does Overdriver generate low overhead for the data center despite memory overloads?

The answers to these questions clearly depend on the application, its traffic, and the level of oversubscription employed. Ideally, we would like to deploy Overdriver in a production data center and experiment with varying oversubscription levels to answer these questions. Unfortunately, we do not have access to a production data center, so we once again experiment with SPECweb2009. Instead of simulating a realistic client workload as described in Section 2, we run a steady base load of clients and inject bursts of

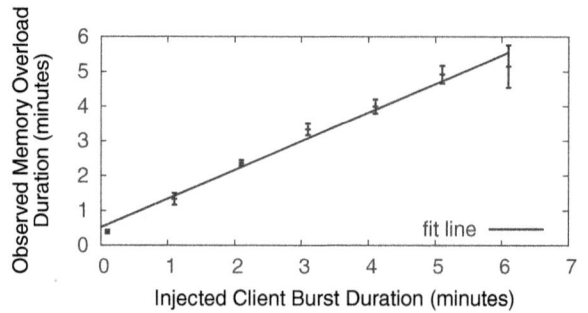

Figure 7. Observed memory overload duration roughly matches the duration of the injected client burst.

various duration in order to evaluate the performance of Overdriver in the face of different types of memory overload.

To be more precise, each SPECweb2009 experiment consists of a steady client load of 250 simultaneous sessions being imposed upon a web server VM. The VM, which initially requested 1024 MB, has only been allocated 512 MB of memory because of oversubscription, achieved by inflating the VM's memory balloon. The experiment lasts for 10 minutes. After waiting for 1 minute at the steady state, a client burst is injected, increasing the number of simultaneous sessions by 350 for a total of 600 sessions during bursts. The burst is sustained for a configurable amount of time before the simultaneous sessions return to 250 for the remainder of the experiment. A longer client burst roughly corresponds to a longer memory overload, as shown in Figure 7. The physical machines used in the experiments have 4 GB of memory each, while the memory allocation of Domain 0 is set at 700 MB.

Through the experiments we compare how Overdriver handles overload (identified as `overdriver` in each graph) to several other techniques. First, as a best-case, we measure the performance of the application, had its VM been well-provisioned. Then, the option of simply swapping pages out to disk (called `disk swap`) is provided as a worst case for application performance, and a baseline for data center overhead. In between these two extremes we run a solely cooperative swap approach (`coopswap`) and a solely migration-based approach (`migration`). The migration approach has a number of factors, discussed earlier, that make it difficult to compare against. Resource allocation and placement are central to migration strategies, as is some sort of migration trigger. To avoid these issues, we compare against an idealized migration scenario involving a different VM co-located on the same physical machine as the overloaded VM. On the first sign of overload, this other VM, which has a memory allocation of 1024 MB, is migrated to another physical machine, releasing its memory for use by the overloaded VM. In reality, VM allocations can be much larger than 1024 MB, resulting in longer delays before migration can complete and more impact to the network. So, in some sense, the migration strategy we compare against is a best-case scenario in terms of application impact and data center overhead.

Throughout the experiments, we configure Overdriver to monitor the VM every 10 seconds, and consider time intervals where the paging rate is above 200 operations per second as periods of overload. The threshold used to trigger migration is initially set at 120 seconds, with a sliding window parameter requiring 8 out of the 12 measurements to be overloads (i.e. 120 seconds comes from twelve 10 second monitoring periods and requires at least 80 seconds out of a window of 120 seconds to trigger a migration).

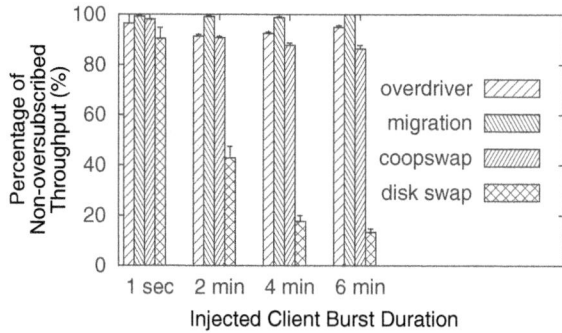

(a) Throughput

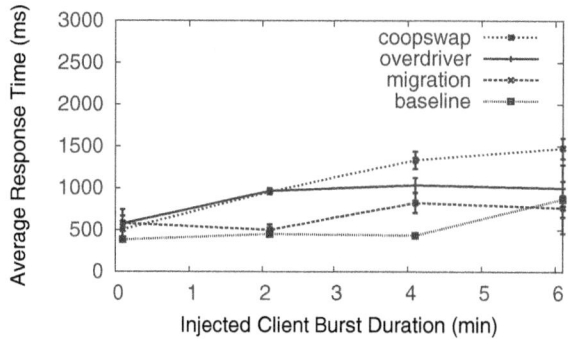

(b) Average response time

Figure 8. The effects of each mitigation technique on the SPECweb2009 application. Overdriver maintains application throughput within 8% of that of a non-oversubscribed VM and an average response time under 1 second for any length overload.

Threshold(s)	Tput(%)	Response Time (ms)
100	94.97	946
120	92.47	1249
150	93.76	1291
170	84.52	1189
200	84.85	1344

Table 2. As the threshold for migration increases, more performance loss is experienced. This table shows the lowest percentage of throughput achieved, and highest average response time, out of all durations of overload.

5.1 Application Effects

Figure 8 shows the performance degradation experienced by the application under various overload mitigation strategies in terms of lost throughput and increase in average response time. First, we examine the aggregate throughput over the 10 minute experiment. The experiment was run on a well-provisioned VM to get a baseline for how many connections should have been handled if no overload occurred, which was between 23 and 38 thousand connections, depending on the length of the injected client burst. Figure 8(a) shows the percentage of that ideal throughput for each strategy. The first thing to notice is that the throughput while using disk swap drops off dramatically, whereas degradation is much more graceful using cooperative swap. Migration, on the other hand, completes with nearly full performance, except for very small spikes resulting in reductions in throughput performance for short periods of time, until migration completes and benefits of migration can be seen. A less aggressive solely migration-based strategy would degrade with disk swap until migration was triggered. Overdriver, on the other hand, begins to degrade gracefully along with cooperative swap, but then improves for longer overload as it switches to rely on migration. A similar pattern can be seen with application response time, shown in Figure 8(b). While longer overload periods cause cooperative swap to increase the average response time, Overdriver levels off when migration is used. Disk swap is not shown on Figure 8(b) because it performs significantly worse than other strategies; the average response time varies between 2.5 s and 16 s, depending on the overload duration. Overall, Overdriver achieves a throughput within 8% of a well-provisioned, non-oversubscribed VM, and an average response time under 1 second.

In terms of application throughput, we see that Overdriver degrades gracefully to a point, at which overload is sustained and warrants migration. The cost of Overdriver to the application, while fairly low, is higher than a very aggressive migration strategy, be-

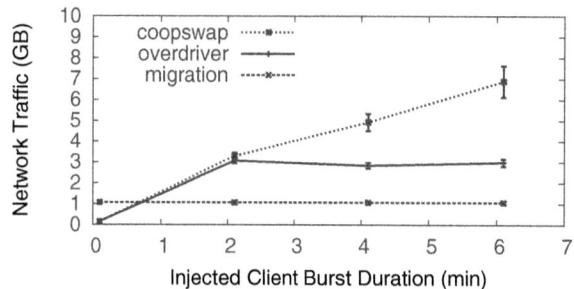

Figure 9. Network traffic induced by various length load spikes using cooperative swap versus disk swap.

cause Overdriver pays for the time spent deciding whether the spike will be sustained. Cooperative swap drastically improves performance while making this decision. As discussed earlier, especially given the prevalence of transient overload, the number of migration operations required is also drastically reduced, affecting both the amount of excess space required, and ultimately the number of VMs that can be supported in the data center.

The choice of threshold has an effect on the application performance, because a higher threshold translates into an increased reliance on cooperative swap. Table 2 shows application performance experienced by Overdriver as the migration threshold due to sustained overload varies. As the threshold increases above 120 seconds performance degrades. This performance degradation gives an idea of the performance that can be gained by adaptively learning a tighter threshold.

5.2 Data Center Effects

The most immediately quantifiable impact to the data center of the overload mitigation techniques we have described is in terms of the amount of traffic induced on the network, and in terms of the amount of excess space required for migration or cooperative swap. We show that Overdriver can handle transient overloads with a fraction of the cost of a purely migration-based solution. However, we also show that Overdriver incurs additional costs for sustained overloads.

Figure 9 shows the amount of traffic sent and received during the experiments described above for various length client bursts. The number of pages written to the cooperative swap page repositories increases fairly linearly as the length of the overload increases. However, cooperative swap also reads from the page repositories,

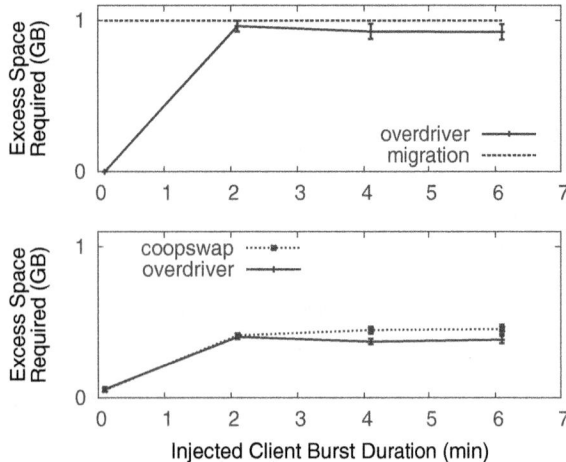

Figure 10. Amount of excess space required for migration and cooperative swap using Overdriver.

Threshold(s)	Traffic(GB)	Space(MB)
100	2.1	424
120	3.6	549
150	4.4	554
170	5.6	568
200	6.1	590

Table 3. For sustained overloads, as the threshold for migration increases, more overhead is accumulated while waiting for migration to happen. This table shows the maximum overhead for cooperative swap in terms of traffic generated and excess space required for a sustained overload.

which results in a further increase in network traffic. Migration, on the other hand, exerts a fixed constant, which is almost entirely written, regardless of the duration of overload. The fact that the value on the graph is fixed at 1 GB is because that is the memory allocation of the VM that is being migrated in this experiment. If a larger, 2 GB VM was migrated, we would see the migration line at 2 GB instead. Overdriver follows the cooperative swap line until the duration of overload exceeds its threshold, and it resorts to migration. This causes a sharp increase by the memory allocation of the VM (1 GB in this case) in the amount of data written to the network by Overdriver for sustained overload. In other words, to get the benefit for transient overloads, Overdriver pays a cost for sustained overloads that is proportional to the amount of time it used cooperative swap.

The amount of traffic over the network does not necessarily show the amount of excess space that is required for cooperative swap. For example, some pages may be written, read, then overwritten, without consuming more space at the page repository. Figure 10 quantifies the amount of excess space required for migration and cooperative swap. Even though cooperative swap may generate a virtually unbounded amount of network traffic for sustained overload, the amount of space that is required remains reasonable. In particular, the amount of space required does not increase above the amount of memory that was withheld because of oversubscription. For transient overloads, Overdriver must only use the modest amount of excess space for cooperative swap. For sustained overloads, however, Overdriver uses both.

Similarly to application performance, data center impact is also affected by the threshold that Overdriver uses. Table 3 quantifies the

increases in overhead for a sustained overload that can be reduced by adaptively shrinking the threshold.

Finally, while Figures 9 and 10 quantify a tradeoff, and show how Overdriver navigates the tradeoff for a single overload, they only provide a glimpse into the tradeoffs that would appear if done at a data center scale. In particular, transient overloads are dominant, and so the modest savings that Overdriver achieves in this graph must be multiplied by the number of transient overloads, which should far outweigh the overhead incurred for the relatively rare sustained overloads; namely, Overdriver saves over a factor of four network bandwidth when compared to migration only. Furthermore, as discussed in Section 4, the differences in terms of how excess space is being used has far-reaching implications in terms of additional costs related to maintaining excess space.

6. Related Work

Overdriver uses aggressive memory oversubscription to achieve high data center utilization. This section describes some related work on memory oversubscription in a virtualized environment, VM migration, and network memory.

6.1 Memory Oversubscription

The ability to oversubscribe memory is common in modern virtual machine monitors. VMWare ESX server [31] was the first to describe memory balloon drivers which provided a mechanism to remove pages from a guest OS by installing a guest-specific driver. Xen [4] also contains a balloon driver. Balloon sizing can be done automatically with an idle memory tax [31] or as a more sophisticated driver inside the guest OS[12]. While ballooning allows changes to the allocation of machine pages, memory usage can also be reduced through page sharing techniques: mapping a single page in a copy-on-write fashion to multiple VMs. This technique was first described in VMWare ESX server [31] and has subsequently been extended to similarity detection and compression in Difference Engine [10]. Memory Buddies [35] is a migration-based strategy that tries to place VMs to optimize for page sharing. Satori [21] is examining new mechanisms to detect sharing opportunities from within the guest OS. These systems are great mechanisms for oversubscribing memory; however, a robust system to reactively handle and mitigate overload, like Overdriver, is necessary to maintain performance.

6.2 Migration

VM migration has become very popular and is touted as a solution free of residual dependency problems that have plagued process migration systems for years [20]. Stop-and-copy VM migration appeared in Internet suspend/resume [17]. Compression has been noted as a technique to improve the performance of migration, especially if the image contains lots of zeroes [26]. However, these techniques all impose significant downtimes for VMs. Live migration techniques, on the other hand, allow VMs to be migrated with minimal downtime. Push-based live migration techniques are the most popular; implementations include VMWare's VMotion [23], Xen [5], and KVM [16]. Pull-based live migration [12] has been evaluated and a similar mechanism underlies the fast cloning technique in SnowFlock [18].

We do not discuss addressing memory overload by spawning VMs. If a hosted service is structured to be trivially parallelizable, such that a newly initialized VM can handle new requests and share the load, spawning may be another viable mechanism to alleviate memory overload. Work has been done to maintain a synchronized hot spare [6] and to speed up cloning delays [18, 25].

There are many migration-based approaches that try to achieve various placement objectives, but they do not discuss maintaining excess space to handle overload. Khanna et al. [15], use heuristics to try to consolidate VMs on the fewest physical machines, while other approaches Entropy [11] and Van et al. [30] aim for an optimal consolidation with the fewest migrations. Sandpiper [34] uses migration to alleviate hotspots in consolidated data centers. In an effort to eliminate needless migrations, Andreolini et al. [3] use a trend analysis instead of triggering migration with a utilization threshold. Stage and Setzer [28] advocate long-term migration plans involving migrations of varying priority in order to avoid network link saturation.

6.3 Network Memory

Overdriver uses cooperative swap to address the paging bottleneck of overloaded VMs. Accessing remote memory on machines across a fast network has been recognized to perform better than disk for some time [2], and this concept has been applied to almost every level of a system. memcached [1] leverages network memory at the application level. Cooperative caching [7] gains an extra cache level in a file system from remote client memory. The Global Memory System [8] uses a remote memory cache deep in the virtual memory subsystem of the OS, naturally incorporating all memory usage including file systems and paging. Nswap [24] and the reliable remote paging system [19] focus specifically on sending swap pages across the network. Cellular Disco [9] is a hypervisor that uses network memory to borrow memory between fault-containment units called cells. Most similar to cooperative swap, MemX [13] implements swapping to the network for a guest VM from within the hypervisor. MemX is focused on extremely large working sets that do not fit in a physical machine's memory, whereas cooperative swap is designed to react quickly to overload bursts, many of which are transient. Other techniques to increase the performance of paging include the use of SSDs. However, addressing the paging bottleneck is not enough to handle the entire overload continuum, particularly sustained overloads.

7. Conclusion

As interest grows in oversubscribing resources in the cloud, effective overload management is needed to ensure that application performance remains comparable to performance on a non-oversubscribed cloud. Through analysis of traces from an enterprise data center and using controlled experiments with a realistic Web server workload confirmed that overload appears as a spectrum containing both transient and sustained overloads. More importantly, the vast majority of overload is transient, lasting for 2 minutes or less.

The existence of the overload continuum creates tradeoffs, in which various mitigation techniques are better suited to some overloads than others. The most popular approach, VM migration-based strategies, are well suited to sustained overload, because of the eventual performance that can be achieved. Cooperative swap applies to transient overloads, where it can maintain reasonable performance at a low cost.

We have presented Overdriver, a system that handles all durations of memory overload. Overdriver adapts its mitigation strategy to balance the tradeoffs between migration and cooperative swap. Overdriver also maintains application VM workload profiles which it uses to adjust its migration threshold and to estimate how much excess space is required in the data center to safely manage overload. We show, through experimentation, that Overdriver has a reasonably small impact on application performance, completing within 8% of the connections that a well-provisioned VM can complete under the continuum of overload, while requiring (under reasonable oversubscription ratios) only 15% of the excess space that a migration-based solution would need. Overdriver shows that safe oversubscription is possible, opening the door for new systems that

effectively manage excess space in the data center for the purpose of handling overload, ultimately leading to a new class of highly efficient, oversubscribed data centers.

The Overdriver project webpage is available at: http://overdriver.cs.cornell.edu.

Acknowledgments

This work was partially funded and supported by an IBM Faculty Award received by Hakim Weatherspoon and NSF TRUST. Also, this work was performed while Dan Williams was an intern at IBM T. J. Research Center in Hawthorne, NY.

References

[1] memcached. http://www.danga.com/memcached/, May 2003.

[2] T. E. Anderson, D. E. Culler, D. A. Patterson, and the NOW team. A case for NOW (Networks of Workstations). *IEEE Micro*, 15(1):54–64, Feb. 1995.

[3] M. Andreolini, S. Casolari, M. Colajanni, and M. Messori. Dynamic load management of virtual machines in a cloud architecture. In *Proc. of ICST CLOUDCOMP*, Munich, Germany, Oct. 2009.

[4] P. Barham, B. Dragovic, K. Fraser, S. Hand, T. Harris, A. Ho, R. Neugebauer, I. Pratt, and A. Warfield. Xen and the art of virtualization. In *Proc. of ACM SOSP*, Bolton Landing, NY, Oct. 2003.

[5] C. Clark, K. Fraser, S. Hand, J. G. Hansen, E. Jul, C. Limpach, I. Pratt, and A. Warfield. Live migration of virtual machines. In *Proc. of USENIX NSDI*, Boston, MA, May 2005.

[6] B. Cully, G. Lefebvre, D. Meyer, M. Feeley, N. Hutchinson, and A. Warfield. Remus: high availability via asynchronous virtual machine replication. In *Proc. of USENIX NSDI*, San Francisco, CA, Apr. 2008.

[7] M. D. Dahlin, R. Y. Wang, T. E. Anderson, and D. A. Patterson. Cooperative caching: Using remote client memory to improve file system performance. In *Proc. of USENIX OSDI*, Monterey, CA, Nov. 1994.

[8] M. J. Feeley, W. E. Morgan, E. P. Pighin, A. R. Karlin, H. M. Levy, and C. A. Thekkath. Implementing global memory management in a workstation cluster. In *Proc. of ACM SOSP*, Copper Mountain, CO, Dec. 1995.

[9] K. Govil, D. Teodosiu, Y. Huang, and M. Rosenblum. Cellular Disco: Resource management using virtual clusters on shared-memory multiprocessors. In *Proc. of ACM SOSP*, Charleston, SC, Dec. 1999.

[10] D. Gupta, S. Lee, M. Vrable, S. Savage, A. C. Snoeren, G. Varghese, G. M. Voelker, and A. Vahdat. Difference engine: Harnessing memory redundancy in virtual machines. In *Proc. of USENIX OSDI*, San Diego, CA, Dec. 2008.

[11] F. Hermenier, X. Lorca, J.-M. Menaud, G. Muller, and J. Lawall. Entropy: a consolidation manager for clusters. In *Proc. of ACM VEE*, Washington, DC, Mar. 2009.

[12] M. Hines and K. Gopalan. Post-copy based live virtual machine migration using adaptive pre-paging and dynamic self-ballooning. In *Proc. of ACM VEE*, Washington, DC, Mar. 2009.

[13] M. R. Hines and K. Gopalan. MemX: supporting large memory workloads in Xen virtual machines. In *Proc. of IEEE VTDC*, Reno, NV, Nov. 2007.

[14] R. H. Katz. Tech Titans Building Boom. http://www.spectrum.ieee.org/feb09/7327, Feb. 2009.

[15] G. Khanna, K. Beaty, G. Kar, and A. Kochut. Application performace management in virtualized server environments. In *Proc. of IEEE/IFIP NOMS*, Vancouver, Canada, Apr. 2006.

[16] A. Kivity, Y. Kamay, and D. Laor. KVM: The kernel-based virtual machine for Linux. In *Proc. of Ottawa Linux Symposium*, Ottawa, Canada, June 2007.

[17] M. Kozuch and M. Satyanarayanan. Internet suspend/resume. In *Proc. of IEEE WMCSA*, Calicoon, NY, June 2002.

[18] H. A. Lagar-Cavilla, J. Whitney, A. Scannell, P. Patchin, S. M. Rumble, E. de Lara, M. Brudno, and M. Satyanarayanan. SnowFlock: Rapid virtual machine cloning for cloud computing. In *Proc. of ACM EuroSys*, Nuremberg, Germany, Apr. 2009.

[19] E. P. Markatos and G. Dramitinos. Implementation of a reliable remote memory pager. In *Proc. of USENIX Annual Technical Conf.*, San Diego, CA, Jan. 1996.

[20] D. S. Milojicic, F. Douglis, Y. Paindaveine, and S. Zhou. Process migration. *ACM Computing Surveys*, 32(3):241–299, Sept. 2000.

[21] G. Miłoś, D. G. Murray, S. Hand, and M. A. Fetterman. Satori: Enlightened page sharing. In *Proc. of USENIX Annual Technical Conf.*, San Diego, CA, June 2009.

[22] B. Mitchell, J. Rosse, and T. Newhall. Reliability algorithms for network swapping systems with page migration. In *Proc. of IEEE CLUSTER*, San Diego, CA, Sept. 2004.

[23] M. Nelson, B.-H. Lim, and G. Hutchins. Fast transparent migration for virtual machines. In *Proc. of USENIX Annual Technical Conf.*, Anaheim, CA, Apr. 2005.

[24] T. Newhall, S. Finney, K. Ganchev, and M. Spiegel. Nswap: A Network Swapping Module for Linux Clusters. In *Proc. of Euro-Par*, Klagenfurt, Austria, Aug. 2003.

[25] H. Qian, E. Miller, W. Zhang, M. Rabinovich, and C. E. Wills. Agility in virtualized utility computing. In *Proc. of IEEE VTDC*, Reno, NV, Nov. 2007.

[26] C. P. Sapuntzakis, R. Chandra, B. Pfaff, J. Chow, M. S. Lam, and M. Rosenblum. Optimizing the migration of virtual computers. In *Proc. of USENIX OSDI*, Boston, MA, Dec. 2002.

[27] V. Shrivastava, P. Zerfos, K. won Lee, H. Jamjoom, Y.-H. Liu, and S. Banerjee. Application-aware virtual machine migration in data centers (to appear). In *Proc. of IEEE INFOCOM Mini-conference*, Shanghai, China, Apr. 2011.

[28] A. Stage and T. Setzer. Network-aware migration control and scheduling of differentiated virtual machine workloads. In *Proc. of ICSE Workshop on Software Engineering Challenges of Cloud Computing*, Vancouver, Canada, May 2009.

[29] Standard Performance Evaluation Corporation. Specweb2009 release 1.10 banking workload design document. http://www.spec.org/web2009/docs/design/BankingDesign.html, Apr. 2009.

[30] H. N. Van, F. D. Tran, and J.-M. Menaud. Autonomic virtual resource management for service hosting platforms. In *Proc. of ICSE Workshop on Software Engineering Challenges of Cloud Computing*, Vancouver, Canada, May 2009.

[31] C. A. Waldspurger. Memory resource management in VMware ESX server. In *Proc. of USENIX OSDI*, Boston, MA, Dec. 2002.

[32] A. Warfield, S. Hand, K. Fraser, and T. Deegan. Facilitating the development of soft devices. In *Proc. of USENIX Annual Technical Conf.*, Anaheim, CA, Apr. 2005.

[33] S. Weber and R. Hariharan. A new synthetic web server trace generation methodology. In *Proc. of IEEE ISPASS*, Austin, TX, Mar. 2003.

[34] T. Wood, P. Shenoy, and A. Venkataramani. Black-box and gray-box strategies for virtual machine migration. In *Proc. of USENIX NSDI*, Cambridge, MA, Apr. 2007.

[35] T. Wood, G. Tarasuk-Levin, P. Shenoy, P. Desnoyers, E. Cecchet, and M. D. Corner. Memory buddies: Exploiting page sharing for smart colocation in virtualized data centers. In *Proc. of ACM VEE*, Washington, DC, Mar. 2009.

Selective Hardware/Software Memory Virtualization

Xiaolin Wang

Dept. of Computer
Science and Technology,
Peking University,
Beijing, China, 100871
wxl@pku.edu.cn

Jiarui Zang

Dept. of Computer
Science and Technology,
Peking University,
Beijing, China, 100871
zjr@pku.edu.cn

Zhenlin Wang

Dept. of Computer Science,
Michigan Technological
University
Houghton, MI 49931, USA
zlwang@mtu.edu

Yingwei Luo

Dept. of Computer
Science and Technology,
Peking University,
Beijing, China, 100871
lyw@pku.edu.cn

Xiaoming Li

Dept. of Computer
Science and Technology,
Peking University,
Beijing, China, 100871
lxm@pku.edu.cn

Abstract

As virtualization becomes a key technique for supporting cloud computing, much effort has been made to reduce virtualization overhead, so a virtualized system can match its native performance. One major overhead is due to memory or page table virtualization. Conventional virtual machines rely on a shadow mechanism to manage page tables, where a shadow page table maintained by the VMM (Virtual Machine Monitor) maps virtual addresses to machine addresses while a guest maintains its own virtual to physical page table. This shadow mechanism will result in expensive VM exits whenever there is a page fault that requires synchronization between the two page tables. To avoid this cost, both Intel and AMD provide hardware assists, EPT (extended page table) and NPT (nested page table), to facilitate address translation. With the hardware assists, the MMU (Memory Management Unit) maintains an ordinary guest page table that translates virtual addresses to guest physical addresses. In addition, the extended page table as provided by EPT translates from guest physical addresses to host physical or machine addresses. NPT works in a similar style. With EPT or NPT, a guest page fault can be handled by the guest itself without triggering VM exits. However, the hardware assists do have their disadvantage compared to the conventional shadow mechanism – the page walk yields more memory accesses and thus longer latency. Our experimental results show that neither hardware-assisted paging (HAP) nor shadow paging (SP) can be a definite winner. Despite the fact that in over half of the cases, there is no noticeable gap between the two mechanisms, an up to 34% performance gap exists for a few benchmarks. We propose a dynamic switching mechanism that monitors TLB misses and guest page faults on the fly, and dynamically switches between the two paging modes. Our experiments show that this new mechanism can match and, sometimes, even beat the better performance of HAP and SP.

Categories and Subject Descriptors D.4.2 [**Operating Systems**]: Storage Management – main memory, virtual memory.

General Terms Algorithms, Management, Measurement, Performance, Design, Experimentation, Verification.

Keywords virtual machine; hardware-assisted virtualization; shadow paging; dynamic switching; hardware assisted paging

1. Introduction

System virtualization has regained its popularity in the recent decade and has become an indispensable technique for supporting cloud computing. Virtualization provides server consolidation and creates an illusion of a real machine for an end user. To make a virtual machine (VM) acceptable for the end user, it is critical for it to match the performance of a native system with the same resource subscription. However, virtualization brings an additional layer of abstraction and causes some unavoidable overhead. The performance of a VM is often much inferior to the underlying native machine performance. Much effort has been made recently to reduce virtualization overhead in both software and hardware sides [1, 4, 11, 13]. This paper focuses on one major overhead caused by memory or page table virtualization.

Most operating systems (OSes) support virtual memory so an application can bear a view of the whole address space. The OS maintains a group of page tables, which map virtual memory addresses to physical memory addresses for each process. The hardware memory management unit (MMU) translates virtual memory addresses to physical memory addresses according to these page tables. With virtualization, the physical memory is virtualized and the virtual machine monitor (VMM) needs to support physical to machine address translation.

In a system with paging enabled, the VMM can realize memory virtualization on a per-page basis and enforce isolation among multiple VMs. There exist three address spaces in a virtualized system: 1) machine address, the address which appears on the system bus; 2) guest physical address, the pseudo-physical address as seen from VMs; and 3) guest virtual address, the conventional linear address that the guest OS presents to its applications. As illustrated in Figure 1, we denote the mapping from guest physical address to machine address as *p2m*, and the mapping from guest virtual address to guest physical address as *v2p*.

Figure 1. Machine, physical and virtual address

Since there is an additional layer of address translation in a virtualized system, a common scheme to accelerate this two-layer address translation is to generate a composition of *v2p* and *p2m*, denoted as *v2m*, and then load it directly into the hardware Memory Management Unit (MMU). The VMM controls mapping *p2m* and it can retrieve mapping *v2p* by querying the guest page tables. As illustrated in Figure 2, all three existing memory virtualization techniques, para-virtualization, shadow paging-based full virtualization and hardware-assisted full virtualization, take this approach. They differ in hardware support and/or the way the VMM synchronizes *v2m* and *v2p*. Note that full virtualization does not require modification to the guest OS while para-virtualization does. This paper focuses on a combination of the two full virtualization techniques.

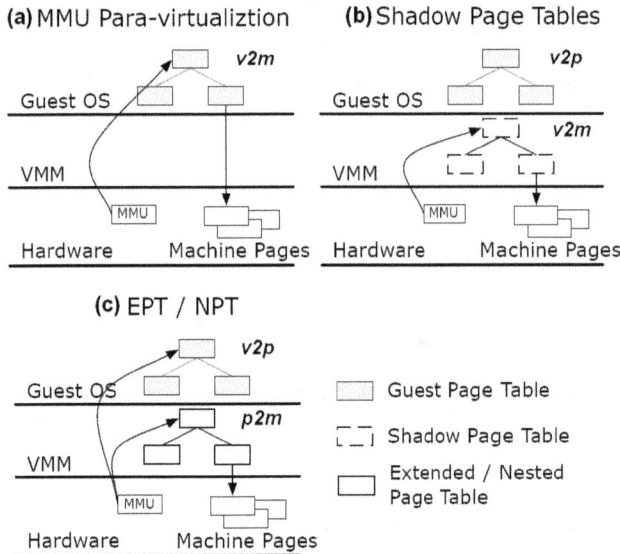

Figure 2. Comparison of memory virtualization architectures

At the cost of compatibility, para-virtualization can achieve better performance than full virtualization, as well as reduce the complexity of the VMM. As shown in Figure 2(a), the VMM simply replaces the mapping *v2p* stored in a guest page table with the composite mapping *v2m*. To ensure that the guest OS functions properly after the replacement, it requires some modification to the source code of the guest OS, which leads to the compatibility issue. For safety, the VMM needs to validate any updates to the page table by the guest OS. By taking back write permission on those memory pages used as the page table , the VMM prevents the guest OS from writing to any guest page table directly. The guest OS has to invoke hypercalls to the VMM to apply changes to its page table. XEN provides a representative hypervisor following this design [2].

A software solution to support full virtualization relies on a shadow paging (SP) mechanism for address translation, where a shadow page table maintained by the VMM maps virtual addresses directly to machine addresses while a guest maintains its own virtual to physical page table [5]. The VMM links the shadow page table to the MMU so most address translations can be done effectively. Figure 2(b) illustrates this implementation. The VMM has to ensure that the content in the shadow page table is consistent with what in the guest page table. Since the guest OS does not know the existence of the shadow page table and will change its guest page table independently, the VMM should perform all the synchronization work to make the shadow page table keep up with the guest page table. Any updates to the shadow page table need also to be reflected in the guest page table. All these synchronizations will result in expensive VM exits and context switches. Moreover, the source code structure for the SP mechanism is quite complex. VMWare Workstation,VMWare ESX Server, KVM, and XEN all implement shadow paging [2, 8, 12].

To avoid the synchronization cost in the SP mechanism, both Intel and AMD provide hardware assists, EPT (extended page

table) and NPT (nested page table), to facilitate hardware-assisted address translation as illustrated by Figure 2(c) [4, 10]. We call the paging mechanism using EPT or NPT *hardware assisted paging* (HAP). With the hardware assists, the MMU maintains ordinary guest page tables that translate virtual addresses to guest physical addresses. In addition, the extended page table as provided by EPT translates from guest physical addresses to host physical or machine addresses. The function of NPT is similar to EPT. All evaluation in this paper is based on EPT on an Intel machine. However, we expect our design to work on an AMD machine with NPT support. With EPT or NPT, a guest page fault can be handled by the guest itself without triggering VM exits. However, the hardware assists do have their disadvantages compared to the conventional shadow mechanism. With HAP, an address translation from virtual to host physical needs to go through both the guest table and the extended table. This page walk yields more memory accesses and thus longer latency. The problem becomes more prominent in 64-bit systems compared to 32-bit systems since the page walk length is doubled in 64-bit systems.

Both HAP and SP have their own advantages and disadvantages. Our experimental results on SPEC CPU2006 [9] in Figures 3 and 4 show that neither HAP nor SP can be a definite winner. Both figures show the normalized execution time with respect to HAP. In eight of the twenty-nine benchmarks there is a 3% or more performance gap between the two mechanisms. Notably, SP is 34% slower than HAP for *gcc*. There is a 13%, 15%, and 22% performance gap, respectively, for *mcf*, *catusADM* and *tonto*.

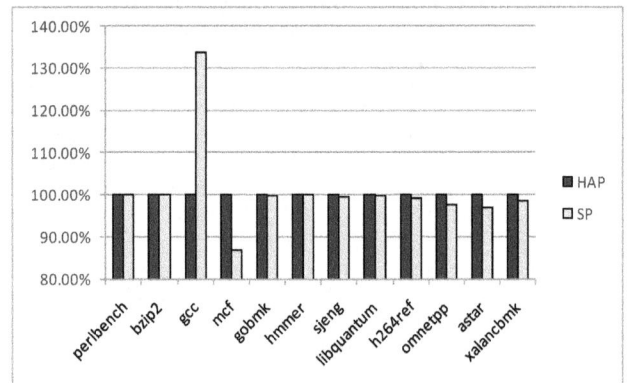

Figure 3. Normalized execution time (SPEC Int).

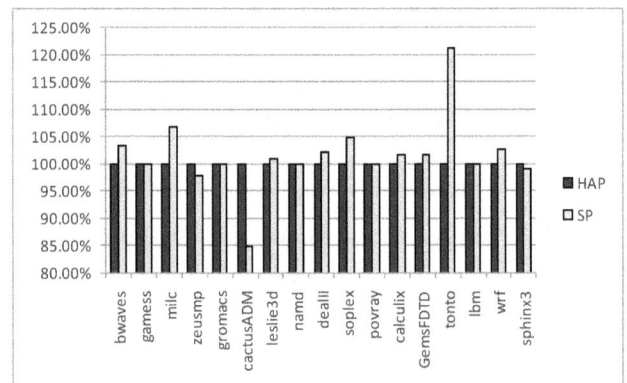

Figure 4. Normalized execution time (SPEC FP)

Since neither HAP nor SP performs better all the time, we can lose performance no matter which one we pick as the default. An intelligent mechanism should be able to exploit the advantages of both HAP and SP based on the VM behavior. So we propose a dynamic switching mechanism that can switch the paging mode between HAP and SP based on the runtime behavior of the current applications. We name this mechanism *Dynamic Switching Paging* (DSP). DSP relies on online sampling of TLB misses and page faults to make decisions on paging mode switching. We develop a set of heuristics to assist the decision making. Our results show that DSP is able to match or even beat the better performance of SP and HAP for all benchmarks, either in a 32-bit system or a 64-bit system. In the meantime, the overhead of DSP is negligible.

The remainder of this paper is structured as follows. In Section 2 we describe the design of DSP. Section 3 details an implementation of this mechanism based on XEN [2, 14]. Section 4 evaluates DSP using some industry standard benchmarks and compares it with HAP and SP. Section 5 discusses related work. We finally conclude and discuss future work in Section 6.

2. DSP Design

2.1 DSP Functionality

HAP is controlled by the CPU control register. By setting or resetting the corresponding control bit, we can choose whether or not to use HAP on a machine where HAP is supported. Take Intel's EPT as an example. There is a Secondary Processor-Based VM-execution Control Register in the CPU. Bit 1 of this register, defined as "Enable EPT", controls EPT. If this bit is set, EPT is enabled. Otherwise, it is disabled.

To switch to HAP mode, the VMM should prepare a group of page tables as the extended page tables, which map guest physical addresses to host machine addresses. In Section 1, we name this guest physical address to host machine address map the *p2m* map. For the extended tables to take effect, the VMM needs to transfer the root address of the top-level page directory to the hardware virtual machine control structure (VMCS). For most VMM implementations, the *p2m* map is fixed. Therefore, the content of EPT is often fixed as well. When the extended tables are ready, we can enable EPT by setting the control bit.

To switch to SP mode, we need a shadow page table. Because the guest page table is available in both SP mode and HAP mode, the shadow page table can be constructed based on the guest page table and the *p2m* map. The switching thus requires reconstruction of the shadow page table and resetting the EPT control bit.

Since both modes need the *p2m* map, we keep this map intact in both modes. When switching from HAP mode to SP mode, we store the root address of EPT temporarily and restore it to the designed register in VMCS at the time when switching back. In SP mode, the shadow page table should be synchronized with the guest page table, while we do not need a shadow page table in HAP mode. To facilitate quick switching, one approach is to maintain a shadow page table in HAP mode so we do not need to reconstruct it when switching to SP mode. We find that this approach damages the independence of HAP mode and also results in high overhead. We instead rebuild a new shadow page table every time we switch to SP mode. The table is destroyed when leaving SP mode for HAP mode.

To summarize, when switching from HAP mode to SP mode, store the root address of the top level page directory of the *p2m* map, rebuild the shadow page table, and then disable the "Enable EPT" control bit in the Secondary Processor-Based VM-execution Control Register; when switching from SP mode to HAP mode, destroy the shadow page table, restore the root address of the top level page directory of the *p2m* map, and then turn on the "Enable EPT" control bit in the Secondary Processor-Based VM-execution Control Register.

2.2 DSP Tradeoff Analysis

To find out when is a good time to switch between the two paging modes, we need to understand the advantages and disadvantages of each mode. HAP mode eliminates the expensive VM exits and context switches from SP mode when there are needs to synchronize the shadow page table and the guest page table. SP mode enables quicker address translation because it only needs to walk through the shadow page table while HAP mode needs to walk both the guest page table and the *p2m* map, which doubles the number of memory accesses. An ideal switching policy would require predicting the number of VM exits saved by HAP mode and the number of memory accesses saved by SP mode. With an estimation of VM exit penalty and memory access latency, one can design a cost model to determine when to switch between the two modes. Unfortunately, it is difficult to predict either of the two metrics. In HAP mode, there is no shadow page table and thus no VM exits due to shadow-guest synchronization. Although we can monitor the TLB misses and estimate the number of page walks, the MMU cache available in both NPT and EPT eliminates this direct correlation. A TLB miss can hit the MMU cache and thus does not need to walk the page table. Both NPT and EPT come with effective MMU translation caches [3, 4]. Nevertheless, we find that TLB misses are still closely correlated to HAP and SP performance. Rather than estimate the number of VM exits, we take the guest OS page fault statistic as a replacement metric. We observe that HAP mode performs better than SP mode in the applications with a large number of page faults, such as *gcc* and *tonto*, while HAP performs worse in those applications with a small number of page faults but intensive memory accessing and a large number of TLB misses, such as *mcf* and *cactusADM*. Based on the analysis above, DSP switches to HAP mode when we expect frequent page faults in the next period and to SP mode when we foresee frequent TLB misses. To fulfill dynamic switching, we rely on historic TLB miss and page fault information to predict the future trend and make a switching decision.

2.3 DSP Switching Strategy

Both TLB miss and page fault penalties are hardware and system dependent. To estimate the trend, in our implementation, we instead measure page fault frequency and TLB miss frequency, which is the number of page faults and the number of TLB misses, respectively, per thousand retired instructions. To make a decision in DSP, we need a pair of system-dependent thresholds that guard page fault and TLB miss frequencies, respectively. If neither the page fault frequency nor the TLB miss frequency goes beyond its threshold, there would be little difference between HAP and SP mode. DSP should stay in the current mode to avoid the switching cost. If one metric is beyond the threshold and the other is low, DSP needs to take action and switch to the other mode. If both frequencies are high, we need to weigh the relative penalty of each. We introduce a third metric, *P-to-T* ratio, as an estimation of this relative penalty. The P-to-T ratio is the page fault frequency divided by the TLB miss frequency. A third threshold is used to guard the P-to-T ratio.

We manually take a simple machine learning approach to learn the thresholds that determine DSP switching. By training the decision model through the SPEC INT benchmarks on a 32-bit guest, we obtain a heuristic DSP switching algorithm as follows.

1. If the TLB miss frequency is higher than the TLB miss upper-bound threshold and the page fault frequency is lower than 80 percent of the page fault upper-bound threshold, switch from HAP mode to SP mode or stay in SP mode.

2. If the page fault frequency is higher than the page fault upper-bound threshold and the TLB miss frequency is lower than 80 percent of the TLB miss upper-bound threshold, switch from SP mode to HAP mode or stay in HAP mode.

3. If both the TLB miss frequency and the page fault frequency are lower than their lower-bound thresholds, stay in the current paging mode.

For the remaining cases, we will need to use the P-to-T ratio. We notice that the P-to-T ratios show a large range of fluctuations from period to period. We use both a running average of recent P-to-T ratios, called *historic P-to-T ratio*, and the P-to-T ratio in the current monitoring period to help make decision. Below is our policy where step 4 helps avoid divide by 0 exceptions.

4. If either the historic TLB miss frequency or the current TLB miss frequency is zero, switch from SP to HAP or stay in HAP mode.

5. If both the historic average P-to-T ratio and the current P-to-T ratio are bigger than the P-to-T ratio upper-bound threshold, the page fault penalty is more significant than the TLB miss penalty and DSP decides to switch from SP mode to HAP mode or stay in HAP mode.

6. If both the historic average P-to-T ratio and the current P-to-T ratio are lower than the P-to-T ratio lower-bound threshold, the TLB miss penalty is more significant than the page fault penalty. Now DSP switches from HAP mode to SP mode or stays in SP mode.

7. If both the historic average P-to-T ratio and the current P-to-T ratio are between the lower-bound and upper-bound thresholds, neither is significant and there would be little difference between the two paging modes. In this case, the system stays in the current mode.

8. Otherwise, the historic average P-to-T ratio and the current P-to-T ratio fit into different threshold intervals. We cannot decide the trend and the system stays in the current mode.

Figure 5 summarizes the eight policies and shows the workflow of the DSP decision algorithm where the acronyms are listed below.

- FTLB: Frequency of TLB misses
- FPF: Frequency of Page Faults
- HTLB: Historic TLB miss frequency
- HPT: Historic average P-to-T ratio
- CPT: Current P-to-T ratio
- TLBU: TLB miss Upper-bound threshold
- TLBL: TLB miss Lower-bound threshold
- PFU: Page Fault Upper-bound threshold
- PFL: Page Fault Lower-bound threshold
- PTU: P-to-T ratio Upper-bound threshold
- PTL: P-to-T ratio Lower-bound threshold

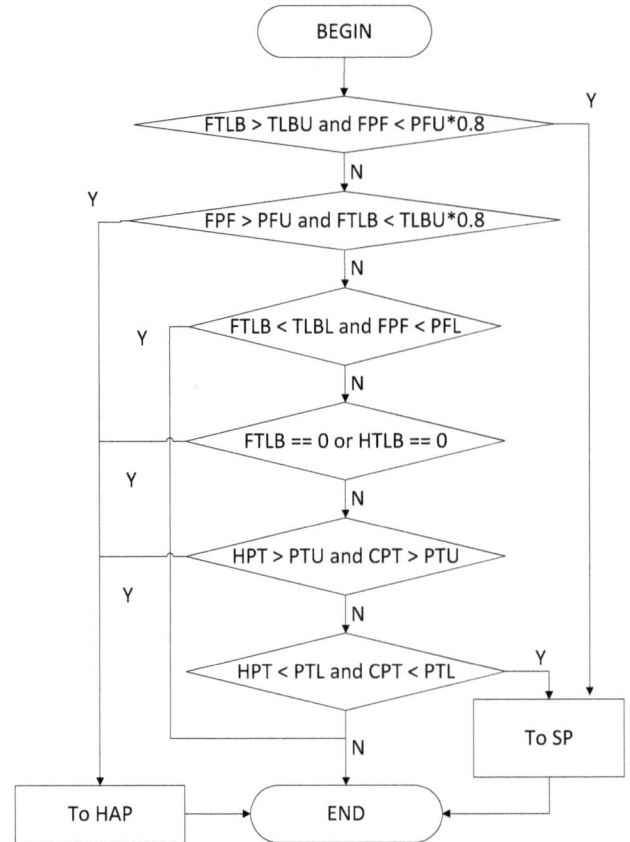

Figure 5. DSP decision diagram

3. DSP Implementation on XEN

We have implemented DSP in XEN 3.3.1. Domain 0 operating system is CentOS 5.4 x86_64 with Linux kernel 2.6.18. Domain U operating system is CentOS 5.4 x86_32 with Linux kernel 2.6.18.

3.1 DSP Design in XEN

Figure 6 illustrates our implementation of DSP in the XEN system. Since most management operations of XEN are integrated in the *xm* tools in Domain0, we add two sub-commands in the *xm* tools, *dsp* and *undsp* to enable or disable DSP.

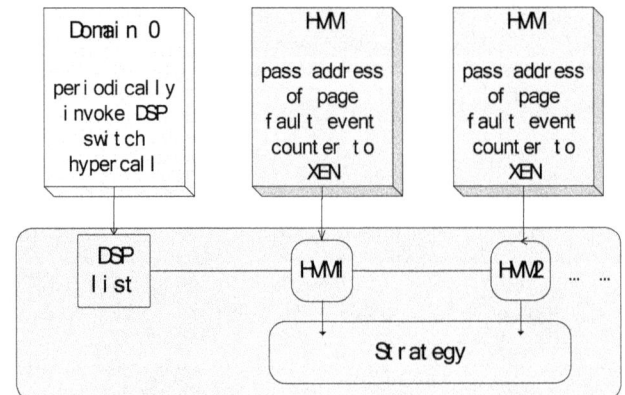

Figure 6. DSP implementation on XEN

We take advantage of the existing timer in XEN to sample a guest OS. In order to count the number of page faults, TLB misses, and retired instructions in the recent period of T seconds, we start a timer in the *xend* service process when executing the *xm dsp* command. The timer will invoke the corresponding XEN *hypercall* every T seconds, request the XEN hypervisor to collect those statistics and decide whether to change paging mode or not.

We get the number of TLB misses and retired instructions from the processor performance monitor unit (PMU) in the XEN hypervisor. To get the number of page faults, we add a kernel module in each guest OS of interest. When the guest OS starts up, the kernel module will notify the XEN hypervisor of the memory address of the variable that records the number of page faults in the guest OS. The XEN hypervisor can read the variable directly and get the number of page faults efficiently.

All virtual machines using DSP are organized as a list in the hypervisor. Whenever the timer invokes the *hypercall*, the XEN hypervisor will only collect samples for the virtual machines in the DSP list. A virtual machine will be removed from the list when it is destroyed, or when the command *xm undsp* is executed. If the list becomes empty, the timer in the *xend* process will be terminated. This implementation allows enabling or disabling DSP on each virtual machine independently.

The effectiveness of DSP is greatly dependent on the thresholds of page faults, TLB misses, and P-to-T ratios. The thresholds might be quite different on different hardware platforms. Our current approach relies on machine learning and profiling to locate appropriate thresholds for a specific machine. All thresholds can be customized by executing the *xm dsp* command with corresponding parameters. Thus, a user or a system administrator can choose a set of thresholds that fit his/her hardware platform.

3.2 Major Interface Functions

In our implementation, we extend an existing hypercall, *do_hvm_op,* with a new operation, *hvmop_dsp*. Both the kernel module in a guest OS and the DSP timer in the *xend* service process invoke *do_hvm_op* to interact with the XEN hypervisor.

The operation, *hvmop_dsp*, is called on the *hvmop_dsp* branch in the *do_hvm_op* hypercall. According to the parameters, *hvmop_dsp* will perform the following actions respectively.

1. Accept the memory address of the page fault event variable (counter) in a guest OS, and translate the memory address to the corresponding virtual memory address in the VMM.

2. Enable DSP on the target virtual machine and add it to the DSP list.

3. Retrieve the number of page faults, TLB misses, and retired instructions in the current sampling period, and calculate the corresponding frequencies. Call *process_dsp* to make a decision as to whether to change the paging mode according to the strategy introduced in Section 2.3.

4. Disable DSP on the target virtual machine by calling *paging_stop_switch*, and remove the virtual machine from the DSP list; and if the DSP list becomes empty, stop the DSP timer in the *xend* service process. *Paging_stop_switch* will also switch the VM back to the former paging mode before DSP is enabled.

Two functions, *paging_switchto_hap* and *paging_switchto_sp*, are implemented to fulfill paging mode switching. The function *paging_switchto_hap* performs switching from SP mode to HAP mode. In order to complete the switching, it destroys the existing shadow page table, loads the root address of the *p2m* map to the

proper register in VMCS, and modifies the Secondary Processor-Based VM-execution Control Register to enable EPT. The function simply returns when the virtual machine is already in HAP mode.

The function, *paging_switchto_sp*, conducts switching from HAP mode to SP mode. In order to complete the switching, it saves the root address of the *p2m* map, rebuilds shadow page tables by constructing an initially empty shadow page tables, and modifies the Secondary Processor-Based VM-execution Control Register to disable EPT. When SP mode starts, the shadow page table will be filled by demand during execution. If the virtual machine is already in SP mode, the function simply returns.

4. Evaluation

In this section, we first run a set of experiments to learn the thresholds for DSP decisions. We then validate the thresholds with a different set of benchmarks or a different guest OS.

4.1 Experimental Environment

We conduct our experiments on a PC with an Intel i7-860 processor, 8GB of memory, and a 1TB SATA hard disk. All 4 cores of the i7-860 processor are enabled while disabling hyperthreading. The hypervisor we use is XEN 3.3.1. We patch our DSP implementation onto it.

Domain0 runs a 64-bit Linux OS, CentOS 5.4 x86_64, and is configured with 3 GB of memory and 2 CPU cores. We install two guest domains, Dom32 and Dom64, running a 32-bit and a 64-bit OS, respectively. Dom32 runs CentOS 5.4 i863 with 3 GB of memory and 1 CPU core. Dom64 runs CentOS 5.4 x86_64 with 3GB of memory and 1 CPU core.

We choose SPEC CPU2006, since the 29 benchmarks in the suite show a variety of memory behavior and DSP is intended to optimize memory virtualization. A memory and CPU intensive benchmark is more suitable than an I/O intensive benchmark to evaluate the effectiveness of DSP.

Table 1. 32-bit VM SPEC INT statistics

PF per 1K inst * 10^7	TLB miss per 1K inst	PF*10^7/TLB (col. 1/col. 2)	Winner
40	0.5	80	SP
125	0.5	250	HAP
0	< 0.5	0	Draw
> 150000	< 1	> 230000	HAP
10000	2.4	4500	HAP
4700	0.3	15000	Draw
1600	16	100	SP
90000	2.7	50000	HAP
0, sometimes 100	0.02	0, sometimes 40000	Draw
0 or 10000	0.3	0 or 30000	HAP
Sometimes>10000	frequently>10		SP
< 50	> 3.9	< 10	SP
> 150000	< 1	> 230000	HAP

4.2 Threshold Selection

In order to find out proper thresholds, we run SPEC INT2006 on Dom32 both in SP mode and in HAP mode. We collect the sample page fault frequency, TLB miss frequency, and historical P-to-T ratio every five seconds. For each benchmark, we select a typical sample value that dominates the whole benchmark. Table 1 lists these samples. Based on this table, we generate thresholds that will result in a correct decision for DSP in most cases. The final thresholds we pick are listed in Table 2.

For all samples values that can help select between HAP and SP, we take their average as the final threshold, expecting it will best fit other programs. We pick the most recent three samples to calculate the historical average ratios. We observe that the three sample points, which denote a 15-second interval, are sufficient to smooth a short-term change in a program. Due to the switching overhead, it is not worth performing switching when there is a short burst of page faults or TLB misses. However, a longer than 15 second interval may result in longer turnaround time. In other words, the system may stay in one mode for too long.

Table 2. Thresholds for DSP decision

	Upper-bound	Lower-bound
Page fault threshold	5000×10^{-7}	100×10^{-7}
TLB miss threshold	10	0.1
P-to-T ratio threshold	200×10^{-7}	150×10^{-7}
Interval for recent history	15 seconds (3 sample points)	

4.3 Sampling Interval Selection

Table 3 shows total TLB misses, page faults and execution times of *mcf* and *gcc* under HAP or SP only. Based on these statistics, we can estimate that the overhead of one TLB miss in HAP mode compared with SP mode is approximately 4 nanoseconds (roughly 12 cycles), and the overhead of one page fault in SP mode compared with HAP mode is around 10 microseconds. Based on the total execution times of the two benchmarks, switching from HAP to SP can save about 100 milliseconds per second on *mcf*, and switching from SP to HAP can save about 300 milliseconds per second on *gcc*. If switching can bring *mcf* or *gcc* to the best paging mode for more than one second, the benefit would overcome the overhead. As both *mcf* and *gcc* are the best cases that benefit most from proper switching, other benchmarks would have to stay in the best paging mode for a longer time to overcome the overhead of paging switching. Based the above analysis, we thus choose an interval at the granularity between one and 10 seconds in our experiments.

Table 3. Total TLB misses and page faults of *mcf* and *gcc*

	TLB miss	page fault	exec time
mcf in HAP mode	12539673680	243491	383
mcf in SP mode	12752691972	346439	329
gcc in HAP mode	1082065972	13320141	403
gcc in SP mode	3198642850	13302782	534

4.4 Overhead

Overhead of paging switching falls in two categories. One is the overhead of switching from SP mode to HAP mode, and the other is the overhead of switching from HAP mode to SP mode. To switch from SP to HAP, we simply load the EPT base address. To switch from HAP to SP, the shadow page table has to be rebuilt, and thus its overhead is larger than switching from SP to HAP.

In order to measure the overhead of switching from SP to HAP, we let the VM initially run in HAP mode. For every second, we invoke a hypercall operation (H-S-H), which will switch the VM from HAP to SP, and then, before returning back to the VM from the hypercall, immediately switch back from SP to HAP. Though the VM has been once in SP mode, but no instruction of the VM has been executed in SP mode. Therefore the shadow page table has never been actually used and it remains empty before switching back to HAP mode. The overhead of H-S-H would be larger than the overhead of single switching from SP to HAP.

Similarly, to measure the overhead of switching from HAP to SP, we let the VM initially run in SP mode. For every second, we invoke another hypercall operation (S-H-S), which will switch the VM from SP to HAP, and then switch immediately from HAP back to SP before returning to the VM. Since the shadow page table is completely destroyed when switching from SP to HAP, after switching back from HAP to SP, the shadow page table has to be rebuilt. The overhead of S-H-S would be larger than the overhead of switching from HAP to SP.

Table 4. Switching overhead of H-S-H

benchmark	Conf. Interval HAP	Conf. Interval H-S-H	#switches	ovhd (%)
perlbench	487.95 ± 0.40	488.62 ± 0.46	489	0.14
bzip2	859.54 ± 0.05	858.70 ± 0.11	859	-0.10
gcc	402.56 ± 3.37	406.38 ± 4.34	406	0.95
mcf	383.00 ± 1.98	380.23 ± 1.59	380	-0.72
gobmk	636.53 ± 0.23	636.38 ± 0.15	636	-0.02
hmmer	1240.70 ± 0.08	1240.06 ± 0.06	1240	-0.05
sjeng	727.12 ± 0.15	729.74 ± 0.18	730	0.36
libquantum	812.87 ± 0.79	813.00 ± 0.93	813	0.02
h264ref	1045.03 ± 0.35	1045.88 ± 1.01	1046	0.08
omnetpp	379.24 ± 0.29	378.86 ± 0.20	379	-0.10
astar	664.04 ± 0.58	663.30 ± 0.32	663	-0.11
xalancbmk	341.54 ± 0.60	341.46 ± 0.17	341	-0.02
bwaves	773.29 ± 1.55	771.44 ± 1.38	771	-0.24
gamess	1431.17 ± 0.56	1429.26 ± 0.68	1429	-0.13
milc	511.27 ± 0.84	511.02 ± 1.25	511	-0.05
zeusmp	839.16 ± 0.96	838.16 ± 1.29	838	-0.12
gromacs	1050.90 ± 0.85	1049.80 ± 0.62	1050	-0.11
cactusADM	1589.21 ± 3.80	1581.87 ± 3.57	1582	-0.46
leslie3d	891.25 ± 0.39	891.03 ± 0.85	891	-0.03
namd	640.94 ± 0.38	640.07 ± 0.17	640	-0.13
dealII	606.92 ± 0.09	605.67 ± 0.25	606	-0.21
soplex	354.31 ± 0.55	354.27 ± 0.36	364	-0.01
povray	332.41 ± 0.35	333.26 ± 1.25	333	0.26
calculix	1764.04 ± 0.83	1762.44 ± 0.33	1762	-0.09
GemsFDTD	836.53 ± 1.26	834.75 ± 0.83	835	-0.21
tonto	941.64 ± 0.46	940.91 ± 0.46	941	-0.08
lbm	405.74 ± 0.33	405.23 ± 0.50	405	-0.13
wrf	1145.45 ± 0.24	1144.22 ± 0.76	1144	-0.11
sphinx3	708.50 ± 2.13	709.11 ± 1.45	709	0.09

We run each benchmark seven times, respectively, at HAP, SP, H-S-H, and S-H-S modes. To avoid measurement noise and to report measurement errors, we pick the top 6 execution times and calculate the confidence intervals. Columns 2 and 3 in Tables 4 and 5 show the confidence intervals of execution times. The number of switches (column 4) is from the run with median execution time which is roughly equal to the mean execution time since switching is performed every second. The percentage overhead (column 5) for H-S-H is measured as (mean$_{H-S-H}$ − mean$_{HAP}$) / mean$_{HAP}$ *100%. The overhead calculation for S-H-S is similar.

As shown in Table 4, the average overheads of H-S-H on most benchmarks are negative although they are all within one percent. Benchmark *gcc* yields the largest overhead which is still less than 1%. We notice that the confidence intervals of HAP and H-S-H overlap for a majority of benchmarks where the overheads are shown in grey. So we can conclude that the overhead of H-S-H is statistically negligible. However, since the overheads are dominantly negative, we suspect H-S-H may have some slightly positive impact on cache or TLB, which calls for further investigation.

Table 5. Switching overhead of S-H-S

benchmark	Conf. Interval SP	Conf. Interval S-H-S	#switch	ovhd (%)
perlbench	488.29 ± 0.52	494.32 ± 0.58	494	1.23
bzip2	858.05 ± 0.07	861.11 ± 0.19	861	0.36
gcc	534.16 ± 0.19	539.27 ± 0.30	539	0.96
mcf	329.11 ± 0.70	345.03 ± 0.86	345	4.84
gobmk	634.04 ± 0.04	636.94 ± 0.12	637	0.46
hmmer	1237.54 ± 0.10	1240.29 ± 0.08	1240	0.22
sjeng	723.47 ± 0.24	736.44 ± 0.17	736	1.79
libquantum	806.05 ± 0.80	811.21 ± 0.35	811	0.64
h264ref	1043.31 ± 0.68	1046.59 ± 0.61	1047	0.31
omnetpp	371.01 ± 0.25	374.06 ± 0.13	374	0.82
astar	648.26 ± 2.89	649.83 ± 0.12	650	0.24
xalancbmk	336.47 ± 0.19	341.78 ± 0.38	342	1.58
bwaves	790.95 ± 2.60	813.52 ± 3.93	814	2.85
gamess	1427.78 ± 0.50	1430.66 ± 0.83	1430	0.20
milc	547.50 ± 0.91	566.16 ± 1.16	566	3.41
zeusmp	816.55 ± 0.20	836.19 ± 0.83	836	2.40
gromacs	1047.90 ± 0.49	1049.94 ± 0.56	1050	0.19
cactusADM	1343.24 ± 4.64	1370.80 ± 3.14	1371	2.05
leslie3d	900.24 ± 0.39	907.33 ± 0.45	907	0.79
namd	639.34 ± 0.31	640.83 ± 0.22	641	0.23
dealII	614.32 ± 0.55	618.65 ± 0.49	619	0.70
soplex	368.44 ± 0.30	376.07 ± 0.46	376	2.07
povray	332.02 ± 0.11	332.87 ± 0.19	333	0.26
calculix	1790.88 ± 0.67	1799.67 ± 0.69	1800	0.49
GemsFDTD	845.10 ± 0.83	904.73 ± 0.83	905	7.06
tonto	1129.54 ± 0.81	1137.89 ± 1.50	1138	0.74
lbm	404.75 ± 2.11	417.98 ± 0.40	418	3.27
wrf	1181.33 ± 0.18	1198.07 ± 0.66	1198	1.42
sphinx3	701.91 ± 0.91	705.42 ± 1.67	705	0.50

S-H-S causes more noticeable overhead as destroying and restoring the shadow page tables definitely cost time. Particularly, for the benchmarks with large working set and thus likely large page table, the overhead is more prominent. So it is not a surprise for *GemsFDTD* and *mcf*, the two benchmarks with the largest working set sizes in SPEC CPU2006, to take the top two spots on overhead [7]. For all other benchmarks, the overheads are all below 5% and most of them are within 1%.

Note that we report an extreme upper bound on overhead here. Our actual implementation suggests a 5-second interval and, for all benchmarks, DSP performs only a couple of dozens of switching at most. Compared to hundreds of switching in Tables 4 and 5, the actual overhead would be negligible.

4.5 Validation Using SPEC INT

We apply the thresholds picked in Section 4.2 back to SPEC INT2006. Figure 7 shows the results where the bars are normalized execution times. The performance of DSP can almost always reach the better case of HAP and SP. For each individual benchmark, the performance difference between DSP and the higher one of HAP and SP is within 1%. For *gcc*, the performance of DSP is 34% better than SP, and for *mcf*, the performance of DSP is 13% better than HAP. The "total" bars in Figure 7 show the normalized total execution time of all integer benchmarks. DSP shows a slight improvement over both HAP and SP.

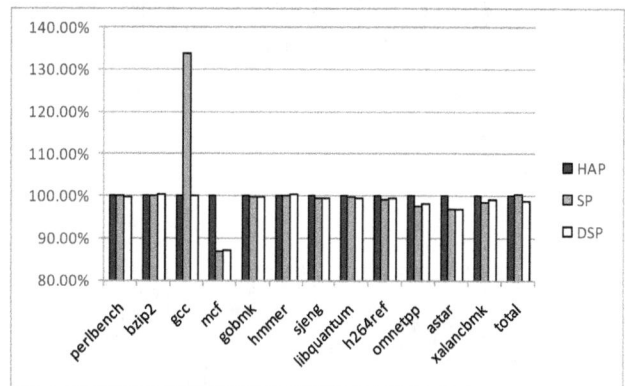

Figure 7. SPEC INT on 32-bit VM.

Figure 8 shows the distribution of execution time of each SPEC CPU2006 benchmark in HAP mode and in SP mode, when DSP is enabled. We also report the floating pointing benchmarks here for comparison purpose. The numbers over the bars are the number of times of paging switching. Note that, for most benchmarks, one mode dominates the execution time. Often there are no or only a few switches. As discussed in Section 4.4, the overhead of switching is very small, thus, the overhead of the DSP mechanism itself is negligible. Once a proper paging mode is selected, the performance gain comes directly from the mode itself.

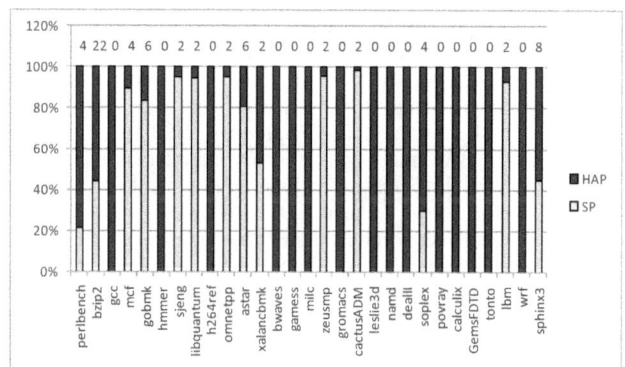

Figure 8. Time distribution of each benchmark in different paging mode (5s interval)

All experimental results in this section so far are based on a 5-second sampling interval. We further compare the performance of

DSP under three different intervals, 2 seconds, 5 seconds and 10 seconds. As shown in Figure 9, the differences among 2-second, 5-second and 10-second intervals are not significant. Note that the number of page faults and TLB misses are measured on a per thousand instruction basis. They do not vary remarkably for most benchmarks among these three intervals. Moreover, most SPEC CPU2006 benchmarks have distinct phases that are longer than 10 seconds, DSP would make the same decision under different timer intervals.

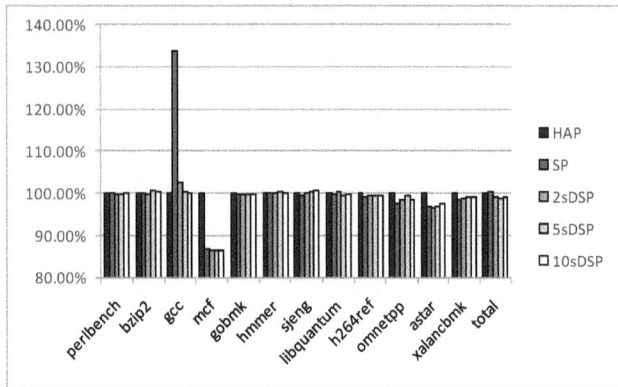

Figure 9. Effects of length of sample intervals

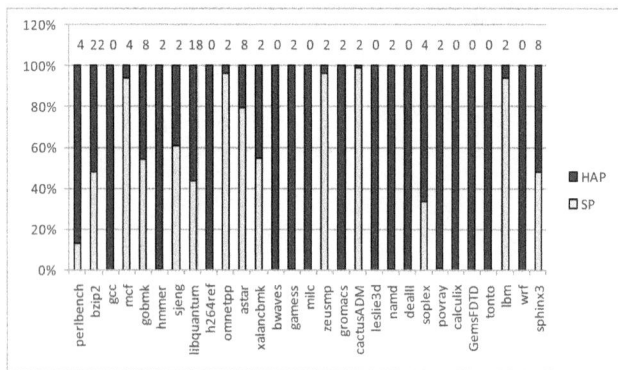

Figure 10. Time distribution of each benchmark in different paging mode (2s interval)

Figures 10 and 11 show that the distribution of execution time and the number of mode switches under the 2-second and 10-second intervals, respectively. Comparing Figure 8 with Figures 10 and 11, we can see that the distribution is almost the same for each benchmark except for *libquantum*, and the number of switches can slightly vary. For *libquantum*, DSP spends over a half of time in HAP mode with the 2-second interval, while only 6% of time with the 5-second or 10-second interval. We observe that *libquantum* shows frequent yet short bursts of page faults. DSP under the 2-second interval switches to HAP when encountering a burst and switches back to SP in the next interval. While under the 5-second and 10-second intervals, DSP stays in SP mode most of time because the bursts are smoothed in a longer interval.

In general, the 2-second interval typically causes the most mode switching while the 10-second interval the least. So we observe some slight performance difference among the three intervals. It is basically a tradeoff between switching overhead and performance gain due to paging switching. As shown in Figure 9, *bzip2*, *sjeng*, *astar* and *xalancbm* perform slightly better under the

2-second interval while *gcc* and *libquantum* prefer the 5-second interval.

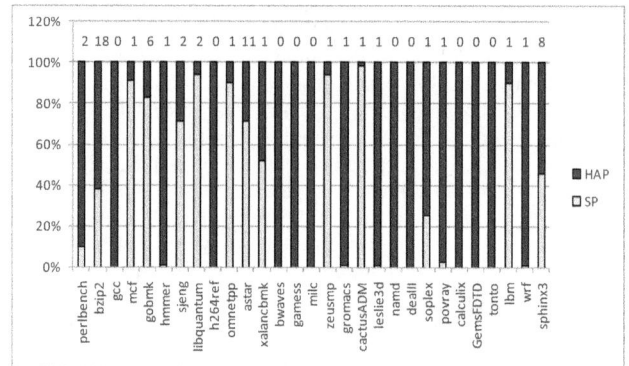

Figure 11. Time distribution of each benchmark in different paging mode (10s interval)

4.6 Validation Using SPEC FP and 64-bit System

This section first validates the same set of thresholds using SPEC FP2006 in Dom32 with DSP enabled and then using a 64-bit guest for all SPEC CPU2006 benchmarks.

Figure 12 shows the results for SPEC FP under a 32-bit guest. Again, DSP always matches the better performance of HAP and SP. DSP achieves a 2% improvement over SP and HAP for SPEC FP. It obtains both the 15% performance gain by SP for *cactusADM* and the 22% gain for *tonto* by HAP.

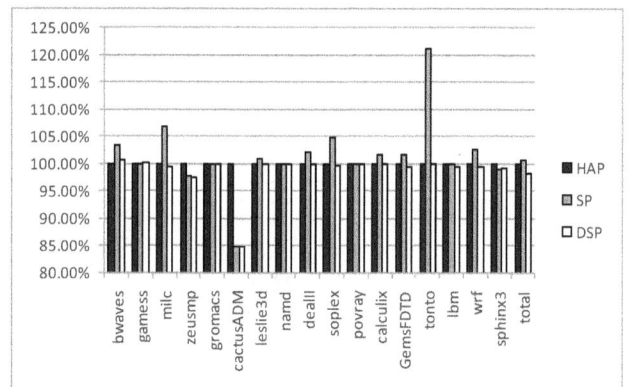

Figure 12. SPEC FP on 32-bit VM

Figures 13 and 14 show the results on the 64-bit guest. Although HAP loses it advantage for most benchmarks, DSP is still able to catch the better performance of the two modes. For the two benchmarks, *gcc* and *milc*, where HAP shows a notable performance advantage over SP, DSP is able to keep the system in HAP mode. For the benchmarks where SP shows significant advantages, DSP switches to SP mode for a majority of time. For *cactusADM*, DSP indeed shows a slight improvement over SP, which performs 14% better than HAP. Benchmark *wrf* cannot be compiled on the 64-bit OS and thus is not reported here.

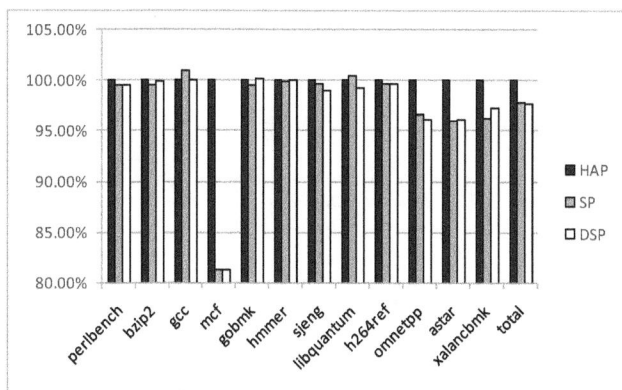

Figure 13. SPEC INT on 64-bit VM

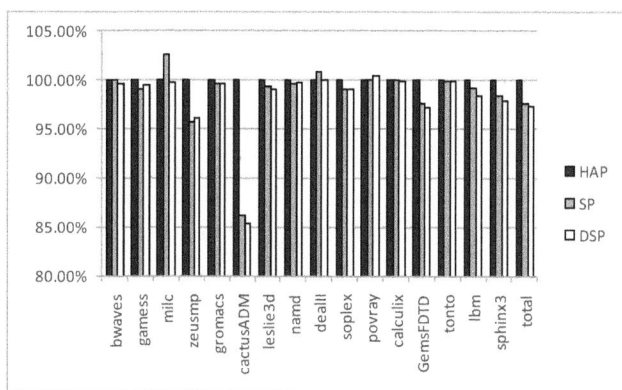

Figure 14. SPEC FP on 64-bit VM

5. Related Work

Keith Adams and Ole Agesen describe an implementation of a software VMM that employs Binary Translation (BT) for x86 guest execution [1]. Their experimental results show that BT outperforms traditional shadow paging with a previous generation of hardware-assisted virtualization available at the point of their research. They also survey software and hardware opportunities on virtualization, pointing out the potential problem of page walk for hardware MMU support such as AMD's "nested paging" and Intel's EPT, and mention several ways to optimize. One solution proposed by VMware is to reduce the overhead of page walking by applying only large pages both in Guest OS and in VMM, and therefore, TLB misses will be reduced dramatically [10, 11]. However, large pages can cause memory pressure and fragments. Gillespie also provides a comparison between EPT and shadow paging but offers no design and implementation details [6].

Ravi Bhargava *et al.* present an in-depth examination of the 2D page table walk of AMD's "nested paging" and options for decreasing the page walk penalty [4]. They use the processor's *page walk cache* to exploit the strong reuse of page entry references. By applying large pages with *page walk cache*, the hypervisor can improve the guest performance by 3%-22%. Barr *et al.* later explore the design space of MMU caches [3].

Hardware assisted virtualization has become more mature nowadays than its initial version. Neither software virtualization nor hardware assisted virtualization will win in all cases. Our solution is based on two mature techniques, shadow paging mode and hardware assisted paging mode, and involves no compatibility issue. It can also work orthogonally with large page mode for more performance improvement.

As another attempt, Wang *et al.* propose *Dynamic Memory Para-virtualization* (DMP) to improve the performance of memory virtualization in [13]. For a VM in SP mode, DMP instruments the VMM to dynamically modify the Guest OS kernel binary code, so as to make use of the guest page table to find machine addresses. Host machine addresses are filled in the page table entries instead of guest physical memory addresses. When the guest OS reads or writes these page table entries, the modified kernel code is executed to translate host machine addresses back to guest physical addresses for the guest to use. DMP can achieve close to native performance. However, DMP introduces security issues, which prevents it from being applied in a security-sensitive public service environment. Our DSP solution brings the benefits in performance without any security risks.

6. Discussion and Conclusion

To reduce the overhead of memory virtualization, both Intel and AMD have provided hardware virtualization support. Unfortunately, hardware assisted virtualization does not always bring performance benefit. In this paper, we compare the performance of hardware-assisted paging and conventional shadow paging, and show that either of them can significantly outperform the other in certain benchmarks. We design and implement an effective paging scheme that dynamically switches between the two page modes and thus exploits the advantages of both. Based on online sampling of TLB misses and guest page faults, we emulate a machine learning process to pick a set of thresholds to help DSP make choices in paging modes. We implement this system in the open source XEN environment and share our patch with the research community. The code patch is now available at http://www.cs.mtu.edu/~zlwang/dsp.tar.gz. We plan to automate the threshold selection using support vector machines and compare it with our manual selection results. Our experimental results show that HAP is not as effective in the 64-bit system as in the 32-bit system. It is not a surprise as the 64-bit system doubles the levels of the page table and thus the penalty of page walk. It is worth a further study in effective hardware support for 64-bit systems.

Acknowledgments

This work is supported by the National Grand Fundamental Research 973 Program of China under Grant No. 2007CB310900, National Science Foundation of China under Grant No.90718028 and No.60873052, National High Technology Research 863 Program of China under Grant No.2008AA01Z112, and MOE-Intel Information Technology Foundation under Grant No.MOE-INTEL-10-06. Zhenlin Wang is also supported by NSF Career CCF0643664. We also owe thanks to the anonymous reviewers and Steve Carr for their valuable comments and suggestions.

References

[1] K. Adams and O. Agesen. A Comparison of Software and Hardware Techniques for x86 Virtualization. In *ASPLOS '06: Proceeding of International Conference on Architectural Support for Programming Languages and Operating Systems*, 2006 .

[2] P. Barham, B. Dragovic, K. Fraser, *et al*. Xen and the art of virtualization. In *SOSP '03: Proceedings of the Nineteenth ACM Symposium on Operating Systems Principles*. p. 177, 2003.

[3] T. W. Barr, A. L. Cox, and S. Rixner. Translation Caching: Skip, Don't Walk the Page Table. In *ISCA '10: Proceedings of International Symposium on Computer Architecture*, 2010.

[4] R. Bhargava, B. Serebrin, F. Spadini, and S. Manne. Accelerating Two-Dimensional Page Walks for Virtualized Systems. In *ASPLOS*

'08: *Proceeding of International Conference on Architectural Support for Programming Languages and Operating Systems*, 2008.

[5] S. Devine, E. Bugnion, and M. Rosenblum. Virtualization system including a virtual machine monitor for a computer with a segmented architecture. *US Patent*, 6397242, Oct. 1998.

[6] M. Gillespie. Best Practices for Paravirtualization Enhancements from Intel® Virtualization Technology: EPT and VT-d. June 1, 2009. http://software.intel.com/en-us/articles/best-practices-for-paravirtualization-enhancements-from-intel-virtualization-technology-ept-and-vt-d/.

[7] D. Gove. CPU2006 working set size. In *SIGARCH Comput. Archit. News*, 35(1):90–96, 2007.

[8] A. Kivity, Y. Kamay, D. Laor, U. Lublin and A. Liguori. kvm: the Linux virtual machine monitor. In *Linux Symposium*. Jan, 2007.

[9] SPEC. http://www.spec.org.

[10] VMware. Performance Evaluation of Intel EPT Hardware Assist. Copyright® VMware. Inc.

[11] VMware. Large Page Performance: ESX Server 3.5 and ESX Server 3i v3.5, Copyright® 2008 VMware. Inc.

[12] C. Waldspurger. Memory resource management in VMware ESX serve. In *OSDI '02: Proceedings of the 5th Symposium on Operating Systems Design and Implementation*. Dec, 2002.

[13] X. Wang, Y. Sun, Y. Luo *et al*. Dynamic memory paravirtualization transparent to guest OS. In *Science China Information Sciences*, January 2010, 53(1): 77-88.

[14] Xen. http://www.xen.org.

Hybrid Binary Rewriting for Memory Access Instrumentation

Amitabha Roy
University of Cambridge
amitabha.roy@cl.cam.ac.uk

Steven Hand
University of Cambridge
steven.hand@cl.cam.ac.uk

Tim Harris
Microsoft Research, Cambridge
tharris@microsoft.com

Abstract

Memory access instrumentation is fundamental to many applications such as software transactional memory systems, profiling tools and race detectors. We examine the problem of efficiently instrumenting memory accesses in x86 machine code to support software transactional memory and profiling. We aim to automatically instrument all shared memory accesses in critical sections of x86 *binaries*, while achieving overhead close to that obtained when performing manual instrumentation at the source code level.

The two primary options in building such an instrumentation system are static and dynamic binary rewriting: the former instruments binaries at link time before execution, while the latter binary rewriting instruments binaries at runtime. Static binary rewriting offers extremely low overhead but is hampered by the limits of static analysis. Dynamic binary rewriting is able to use runtime information but typically incurs higher overhead. This paper proposes an alternative: hybrid binary rewriting. Hybrid binary rewriting is built around the idea of a persistent instrumentation cache (PIC) that is associated with a binary and contains instrumented code from it. It supports two execution modes when using instrumentation: active and passive modes. In the active execution mode, a dynamic binary rewriting engine (PIN) is used to intercept execution, and generate instrumentation into the PIC, which is an on-disk file. This execution mode can take full advantage of runtime information. Later, passive execution can be used where instrumented code is executed out of the PIC. This allows us to attain overheads similar to those incurred with static binary rewriting.

This instrumentation methodology enables a variety of static and dynamic techniques to be applied. For example, in passive mode, execution occurs directly from the original executable save for regions that require instrumentation. This has allowed us to build a low-overhead transactional memory profiler. We also demonstrate how we can use the combination of static and dynamic techniques to eliminate instrumentation for accesses to locations that are thread-private.

Categories and Subject Descriptors D.3.4 [*Software*]: Programming Languages Processors

General Terms Design, Performance, Algorithms

Keywords Binary Rewriting, Transactional Memory

1. Introduction

The recent shift towards multicores has led to a large body of research that deals with shared memory multithreaded applications. The focus areas range across improved safety through race detection [14], to profiling [22], to improved scalability using software transactional memory [12]. In each of these cases, researchers have used runtime methods leveraging existing dynamic binary rewriting engines for instrumentation. Two of these applications – software transactional memory and profiling – form the motivation for the x86 binary instrumentation system in this paper.

Dynamic binary rewriting is attractive for these applications since it does not require source code availability or modification. Unfortunately, dynamic binary rewriting traditionally incurs large overheads. An alternative, that also operates at machine code level is static binary rewriting. Static binary rewriting does not suffer from the runtime overheads of dynamic binary rewriting. Unfortunately, static binary rewriting achieves only limited insight into executed code paths; for example it is difficult to determine the targets of indirect branches in binaries with static techniques alone. This in turn limits the effectiveness of static analysis in determining instrumentation points or optimisations.

In this paper, we describe an instrumentation infrastructure that combines some of the best ideas from static and dynamic binary rewriting into an instrumentation technique we call *hybrid binary rewriting*. Hybrid binary rewriting generates instrumentation at runtime. However, instead of discarding generated instrumentation at the end of execution, it is placed in an on-disk file called the persistent instrumentation cache (PIC). This "active" mode of instrumented execution discovers and instruments code as it is run, thereby providing all the benefits of dynamic binary rewriting. In addition to "active" mode, our instrumentation system also allows execution in "passive" mode. In this mode execution proceeds out of the native binary unless an instrumented version is available in the PIC. If so, it executes the instrumented version. If the PIC contains all the necessary instrumentation then "passive" mode approximates the low overhead that is obtained from the static pre-instrumentation of binaries.

The instrumentation system in this paper automatically instruments shared memory accesses in critical sections — i.e. we only wish to instrument code in critical sections delimited by lock acquire and release calls. For example, consider the fragment of source code in Figure 1. It shows a portion of code from the SSCA2 benchmark in the STAMP suite [5]. We are interested in the critical section delimited by the TM_BEGIN() and TM_END() calls. There are two shared memory accesses in that region that have been annotated using TM_SHARED_READ and TM_SHARED_WRITE calls. The STAMP benchmark already contains instrumentation for shared memory accesses within transactions (critical sections protected by a single global lock). Clearly, inserting such instrumentation is cumbersome and error prone. Our instrumentation infrastructure automatically

```
void
computeGraph (void* argPtr)
{
  ...
  ULONGINT_T j;
  ULONGINT_T maxNumVertices = 0;
  ULONGINT_T numEdgesPlaced = SDGdataPtr->numEdgesPlaced;
  ...
  TM_BEGIN();
    long tmp_maxNumVertices =
      (long)TM_SHARED_READ(global_maxNumVertices);
    long new_maxNumVertices =
      MAX(tmp_maxNumVertices, maxNumVertices) + 1;
    TM_SHARED_WRITE(global_maxNumVertices, new_maxNumVertices);
  TM_END();
  ...
```

Figure 1. Annotated fragment from the SSCA2 benchmark

places the same instrumentation at very little extra overhead (on average 26%).

The rest of this paper is organised as follows. In Section 2 we discuss the relevant merits of the two binary rewriting approaches. Next, in Section 3 we discuss how hybrid binary rewriting works, in particular the difference between running in active and passive instrumentation modes. We then cover the operation of active instrumentation mode (§3.1) and the operation of passive instrumentation mode (§3.2). In Section 4 we focus on two applications for the instrumentation system: a profiler for critical sections (§4.1) that combines memory access traces with lock contention data to produce useful transactional memory related profiles for the binary; and a system for automatically eliding locks in x86 binaries to execute critical sections using software transactional memory (§4.2). Finally, we focus on how hybrid binary rewriting can enable interesting instrumentation features that are normally not possible with either static or dynamic binary rewriting alone. The first is a technique to dramatically increase the rate at which the PIC reaches completion i.e. to ensure it contains instrumented versions of all basic blocks in all critical sections (Section 5). The second is a technique to automatically filter out thread-private locations in the instrumentation (Section 6). This is critical to approaching the performance of manual instrumentation, where the programmer is aware of – and exploits – the fact that locations that are thread private need not be instrumented when using software transactional memory.

2. Binary Rewriting Approaches

Research in the area of instrumenting machine code has been driven both by the need to build profiling tools that operate at the binary level (such as [16]), as well as for tools that actively modify execution by eliminating dead code [3] or even automatically applying software transactional memory [12]. Given x86 machine code contained in a program, there are two prevalent approaches to rewrite binary code into an instrumented form: one is purely static, while the other is purely dynamic. We next discuss each of these approaches, focusing on their strengths and weaknesses with regard to our intended applications.

2.1 Static Binary Rewriting

Static binary rewriting modifies binaries before execution to produce an instrumented version. An early example of static binary rewriting is the binary rewriting tool Atom [8]. Other examples are Diablo [21] and PLTO [17]. Static binary rewriting operates by reading an executable file (or object file), disassembling it, and rewriting instructions as desired (e.g. to insert profiling code).

```
if(AnalysisOpaqueCondition()) {
  pthread_mutex_lock(&lock);
}
pthread_mutex_lock(&possibly_nested_lock);
...
pthread_mutex_unlock(&possibly_nested_lock);
// Should the following be instrumented ?
...
if(AnalysisOpaqueCondition()) {
  pthread_mutex_unlock(&lock);
}
```

Figure 2. Possibly Nested Locking

Static binary rewriting has one major advantage over dynamic binary rewriting: there is no runtime overhead incurred to insert the instrumentation, since the process occurs before the binary is executed. However, from the perspective of our intended applications there are two key difficulties with using static binary rewriting.

The first problem arises due to indirect branches. Static binary rewriting needs to analyse the control flow graph to decide which basic blocks[1] in the binary need to be instrumented. For example, in the case of software transactional memory, the critical section comprises all basic blocks reachable from the basic block containing the lock call, but without encountering an unlock call. This cannot, in general, be determined a priori with static binary rewriting[2].

The second problem is demarcating critical sections in the presence of nested locking. Consider the example code fragment shown in Figure 2. A purely static approach cannot determine whether the portion of code after the first unlock call should be instrumented since its inclusion in a critical section depends on a dynamically evaluated condition. Runtime information is critical to being able to make such decisions correctly.

2.2 Dynamic Binary Rewriting

Dynamic binary rewriting modifies binaries at execution time to insert instrumentation. Dynamic binary rewriting has gained popularity since it enables extremely useful program analysis and optimisation tools to be built. A number of dynamic binary rewriting engines have been built such as PIN [10], FastBT [13], Dynamo [2] and Valgrind [11]. They have formed the basis for useful program analysis tools such as Memcheck [18], and for program optimisation, for example using Dynamo. Since instrumentation is inserted dynamically, it does not suffer from the limitations of static rewriting mentioned above. However, dynamic binary rewriting can suffer from high overhead. There are two primary sources of this overhead.

The first is the cost of inserting instrumentation. Code execution must be stopped in order to rewrite it with instrumentation inserted. This happens every time new instrumentation is inserted. This cost is particularly high for short programs, or for those with little locality.

Another source of high overhead is maintenance of the *code cache*. Since the dynamic binary rewriting engine cannot at any point guarantee that no new code requiring instrumentation will be executed, it executes all code out of a code cache. The code cache contains all encountered basic blocks, even those which have not been instrumented; this ensures that the dynamic binary rewriting engine

---

[1] A single-entry single-exit sequence of machine code

[2] Atom used a "grey box" approach of understanding the manner in which case statements are complied (by a C complier) to work out possible targets of indirect branches; however such approaches are fragile in the face of language or compiler changes.

Benchmark	Description	Basic Blocks Executed (static)		
		Overall	*Within CS*	
Bayes	Learn a Bayesian network	5641	763	(13.6%)
Genome	Gene Sequencing	4243	220	(5.2%)
Intruder	Intrusion Detection	4556	476	(10.4%)
Kmeans	Clustering	4902	101	(2.1%)
Labyrinth	Routing in a maze	4894	342	(7.0%)
SSCA2	Efficient graph representation	4630	105	(2.3%)
Vacation	Scaled down SpecJBB	4866	622	(12.8%)
Yada	Delaunay mesh refinement	6403	1006	(15.7%)

Table 1. STAMP: Basic Block Profile from Execution

maintains control of code execution and is able to see all newly executed code. Unfortunately the code cache imposes significant overhead even for un-instrumented code. This stems from the cost of maintaining the finitely sized cache, and hence taking care of events such as evictions, as well as linkage between basic blocks.

From our perspective, the code cache is a completely unnecessary source of overhead. There is no need to instrument code outside critical sections, and thus no need to put it into the code cache, possibly displacing more useful instrumented blocks. This is illustrated in the profile of basic blocks from the STAMP benchmark suite shown in Table 1. For each benchmark, this shows the number of (static) blocks in the binary that were actually executed while the next column shows the number of those that were within a critical section (CS). It is clear that only a small fraction of basic blocks need be executed with instrumentation, and thus it is desirable to avoid any overhead (in terms of both code cache space and execution time) for the others.

3. Hybrid Binary Instrumentation

The x86 binary instrumentation system in this paper aims to combine the benefits of static and dynamic binary rewriting while side-stepping their problems. At the heart of this hybrid instrumentation system lies the Persistent Instrumentation Cache (PIC).

A PIC contains instrumented versions of basic blocks within critical sections of its originating binary. It is persistent, i.e. held in an on-disk file. In form it thus resembles instrumentation that would have been added by a static binary rewriting engine. A *complete* PIC contains instrumented versions of *every* reachable basic block within *every* possible critical section of the binary. The completeness of a PIC is clearly undecidable in the presence of indirect branches in the binary. We return to the problem of tolerating incomplete PICs later in the paper.

The PIC is generated dynamically, and we depend on execution to look past indirect branches. We also depend on execution to properly handle nested critical sections (such as the example in Figure 2) by dynamically counting held locks. The PIC is thus generated by operating in a dynamic instrumentation mode.

The process of generation of the PIC is shown in Figure 3. The "Backend Runtime System" consumes instrumentation and contains callbacks for the instrumentation hooks. The instrumentation flow starts with a number of iterations of *active* execution (top half of figure). In this mode, we depend on a dynamic binary rewriting engine to intercept all executed code in the binary. Basic blocks in critical sections are instrumented and placed in the PIC.

Once the PIC obtains sufficient coverage, we can execute in *passive* mode (bottom half of the figure). In this mode a low cost "dispatcher" loads the PIC into memory and intercepts lock calls. Within a critical section, instrumented versions of basic blocks are

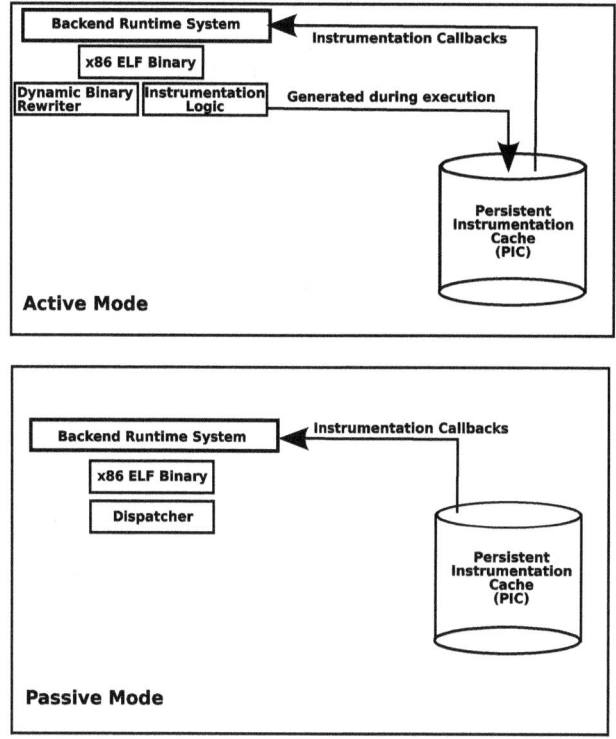

Figure 3. Instrumentation Flow

executed *if available*. Passive mode provides best-effort instrumentation but cannot itself add new instrumentation to the PIC. If the PIC is incomplete and execution enters a basic block that has no instrumented version in the PIC, a special instrumentation hook informs the consumer of the instrumentation of this event in order that it may take appropriate action. Execution then switches to the *un-instrumented* version of the critical section.

We now describe in detail the operation of each of these modes of instrumentation.

3.1 Active Instrumentation Mode

Active mode uses a dynamic binary rewriting engine to intercept execution and instrument basic blocks in critical sections. Dynamic binary rewriting engines are fairly complex to build and maintain. We thus chose to leverage an existing dynamic binary rewriting engine for this part of the instrumentation system. We use PIN [10], a widely used and stable dynamic binary rewriting engine for x86 binaries. Our decision to use PIN was guided by two factors.

First, although the source code for the core modules of PIN are not publicly available, it provides a high level API through which it can be controlled and extended. The user provides a "pintool" written in C++ that uses this API to inspect and manipulate x86 code. The API can operate at various levels of abstraction: from whole images, down to functions, basic blocks and individual instructions. PIN also includes a lower level (and not so widely used) API to directly decode, manipulate and re-encode x86 instructions (complex due to their CISC nature) from and to machine code called the X86 Encoder Decoder (XED). We made extensive use of XED to build the instrumentation system in this paper.

Second, PIN has a large community of users and is actively maintained. This is important because the x86 ISA is actively changing

```
...
strcpy(dst1, src1, size1);
...
// enter critical section
pthread_mutex_lock(&lock);
...
   strcpy(dst2, src2, size2);
...
pthread_mutex_unlock(&lock);
```

Figure 4. The same function in multiple contexts

(e.g. the addition of SSE4 instructions), and it is important that the binary rewriting engine keep up with these additions to be useful for our applications now and in the future.

3.1.1 Critical Sections

There are two subtle problems in determining critical section boundaries and intercepting all executed code within them.

The first is that of accurately delimiting critical sections (a problem already mentioned in §2.1). We require the backend runtime system to maintain per-thread counters to determine when critical sections are begun, and when they end. On a critical section begin, we require a call to a specially named function in the backend runtime (cs_begin); similarly, on encountering the end of a critical section, we require a call to another specially named function (cs_end). The instrumentation infrastructure looks for execution of these functions (which can be empty "no-ops") in order to learn when critical sections begin and end.

The second problem is ensuring that any code that is executed both within and outside critical sections is properly instrumented. Consider Figure 4. The string copy function is first called outside critical section context. We thus do not generate an instrumented version. Later it is called within a critical section context. This time, however, PIN does not present us with the basic blocks in strcpy since it has already added them to its code cache (unmodified since we did not see them in critical section context).

PIN allows basic blocks to be annotated with a version that can be propagated through branches out of a basic block to their target basic blocks. The same basic block with a different version is treated differently and presented individually for instrumentation. We hence annotate basic blocks within a critical section with a special tag, ensuring that, for example, the strcpy function in Figure 4 is presented again for instrumentation on the subsequent execution because it has a different tag.

3.1.2 Instrumentation

We generate instrumentation for critical section begin/end calls and for each shared memory access within a critical section. The instrumentation for critical section begin/end calls are tailored to provide a variety of information to the backend runtime system. For our STM application, that replaces locks with transactions in the binary, the region begin call provides information such as the actual lock acquired, the type of lock (pthreads mutex, openmp nested lock, etc.); information about the current top of stack (before the call to the instrumentation routine); and the size of the function frame where the lock call is encountered. The last two pieces of information are used by the STM runtime system to construct a precise checkpoint (together with a setjmp call) that can be used to rollback execution in the event that it encounters a conflict (through a longjmp call followed by a copy to restore the stack frame). The instrumentation can thus be tailored to suit the particular backend runtime system being used.

The second type of instrumentation generated is for shared memory accesses within a region. Figure 5 shows the example of a basic block in a shared memory region from one of the benchmarks we used. The numbered instructions on the right correspond to the numbered instructions on the left. For example, the first instruction accesses memory. This is converted into an instruction that first loads the target address into the eax register. The next few instruction load the size of the access into the edx register, and set a flag – stored in ecx – which indicates whether or not this instruction is a read-modify-write (both a read and a write) instruction. The size and read-modify-write flag are encoded such that the most common values (4 bytes, false) map to zero. This means the registers can be set up with a two byte instruction (exclusive or-ing the register with itself), keeping the size of instrumentation and hence instruction cache pressure down. The call to the instrumentation hook returns the (possibly different) address to use for the memory access in eax, which is then used in the instrumented version of the basic block.

The first notable feature of the instrumentation is CPU flag and register management. Since the call to the instrumentation hooks is expected to destroy the eax, edx and ecx registers as well as the flags, these need to be saved and restored as appropriate. This is accomplished by the un-numbered instructions in the instrumented version of the basic block. The save area is setup on stack (the PIC is shared between threads) by the first instruction. We perform liveness analysis at the level of the basic block to optimise away unnecessary save restores — for example, the fourth instruction overwrites the x86 flags and thus the flags are not saved.

The second notable feature of the instrumentation is the treatment of memory accessed through the stack pointer (register esp). The stack is usually thread private and (due to the limited number of registers on the x86) heavily accessed. Assuming accesses to the stack to be thread private means that they can be performed directly in our applications. However, stack accesses need to be adjusted to account for the save area we create on stack. In the example this can be observed in instruction 5, where the offset is adjusted upward by 16 bytes.

The final notable feature about the instrumentation is the handling of the call instruction that terminates the basic block. The instrumented version pushes the return address before jumping to the target. This is standard practise for binary rewriting engines and originates from the need to leave return addresses unmodified on stack. In the example, the rebalance_insert function would see the original native address rather than the address from the PIC were it to query the return address of the function. A common occurrence of this kind of behaviour is in position independent code, where a call is made to the immediately following instruction, which then queries the top of stack to discover the current instruction pointer. This is done as there is no direct way on 32-bit x86 to materialise the instruction pointer in a general purpose register.

Memory access instrumentation is also complicated by the fact that the x86 Instruction Set Architecture permits complex instructions. Some instructions allow accessing more than one location (such as a push of the contents of a memory location). Another complication arises from string operations where the length of the access cannot be determined statically (it usually depends on the contents of the ecx register). We handle such cases by breaking them down into simpler RISC style operations that are then instrumented.

3.1.3 PIC Operations

There are four basic operations performed on the PIC in active mode. These are *(i)* loading the PIC into memory; *(ii)* appending

```
// Note: AT&T format-> operation src, dst            lea      0xfffffff0(%esp),%esp
1. subl    $0x1,0x8(%eax) # Memory[8 + Reg[eax]] -= 1;    mov      %eax,0x0(%esp)
                                                    1.1 lea      0x8(%eax),%eax
                                                        mov      %ecx,0x4(%esp)
                                                        mov      %edx,0x8(%esp)
                                                    1.2 xor      %edx,%edx
                                                    1.3 xor      %ecx,%ecx
                                                    1.4 inc      %ecx
                                                    1.5 call     0xff6a4730 # Instrumentation
                                                    1.6 subl     $0x1,(%eax)
                                                        mov      0x0(%esp),%eax
2. mov     %esi,0xc(%eax) # Memory[12 + Reg[eax]] = Reg[esi];  2.1 lea      0xc(%eax),%eax
                                                    2.2 xor      %edx,%edx
                                                    2.3 xor      %ecx,%ecx
                                                    2.4 call     0xff6a4730
                                                    2.5 mov      %esi,(%eax)
                                                        mov      0x0(%esp),%eax
3. mov     %eax,0x4(%esp) # Memory[4 + Reg[esp]] = Reg[eax];  3.  mov      %eax,0x14(%esp)
4. xor     %ebx,%ebx # Reg[ebx] = 0;               4.  xor      %ebx,%ebx
5. mov     %edi,(%esp) # Memory[Reg[esp]] = Reg[edi];  5.  mov      %edi,0x10(%esp)
                                                        mov      0x8(%esp),%edx
                                                        mov      0x4(%esp),%ecx
                                                        lea      0x10(%esp),%esp
6. call    8048ba0 <rebalance_insert>              6.1 push     $0x8048e12
                                                    6.2 jmp      0x123c4ba0
```

Figure 5. Shared memory instrumentation for a basic block

instrumented basic blocks to the PIC; *(iii)* executing from the PIC; and finally *(iv)* querying the PIC.

We load the PIC into memory by doing a memory map (Unix `mmap`) from the disk file containing it. This ensures that the disk file is up-to-date with any additions to the PIC. Appending basic blocks to the PIC simply consists of writing out instrumented versions of basic blocks to the end of the PIC.

Executing from the PIC presents a problem due to the special handling of self-modifying code implemented by PIN. In order to detect self-modifying code, PIN looks for pages that are being executed from while being marked writable. It then marks these pages as read-only and traps writes to them in order to detect any self-modifying code. This causes large slowdowns when executing instrumented code out of PIC pages. To work around this problem, we map the same PIC page twice, once as executable but read-only and once as read-write but not executable. Appending to the PIC is done through the writable mapping while actual execution uses the executable read-only mapping.

The final operation that needs to be supported by the PIC is queries to map executable native addresses to instrumented basic block addresses in the PIC, if present. The core of the logic that handles queries is a map:

$$f : \text{native address} \rightarrow \text{PIC offset}$$

Such a map is easy to setup and maintain for a single run but difficult to persist across runs. The reason is that the native executable address originating the instrumented basic block in the PIC can change across runs. For example, the native address might originate in a shared library that can change its load address on each active execution. To solve this problem, the map is persisted as:

$$f : (\text{native address relative to base}, \text{image name}) \rightarrow \text{PIC offset}$$

It is loaded and turned into the required form by querying the base of each loaded image (main binary or shared library). A similar technique is used by dynamic binary rewriting engines that persist instrumentation across runs [15].

3.2 Passive Instrumentation Mode

We now discuss instrumented execution in passive mode. In this mode, we use the Unix `LD_PRELOAD` mechanism to accompany the x86 binary with the instrumentation system and the backend, both of which are implemented as shared libraries. The critical feature of execution in passive mode is simplicity and low overhead. There is zero overhead to add instrumentation and, as we shortly show, zero overhead when executing code outside an instrumented critical section.

3.2.1 Preparation

As Figure 3 shows, the PIC prepared during active instrumentation can be used in passive mode. An offline tool needs to be run on the PIC before any passive execution that follows an active execution. The job of this offline tool is effectively to "stitch" together basic blocks in the PIC by patching branches across them, to target instrumented basic blocks in the PIC rather than in the native binary. As an example, consider the call instruction at the end of Figure 5. During active execution it targets the native binary and is intercepted and redirected via PIN. The offline patching step patches the branch to point to the instrumented version of the target. Note that on the x86, direct branches are instruction pointer relative and thus the patching is unaffected by PIC relocation across different runs. The patching step is fast — for example, it takes barely a few seconds for a 5MB PIC.

3.2.2 Intercept and Dispatch

The heart of passive execution is the intercept and dispatch logic. The first step is to intercept all lock calls. This is done through the unix `LD_PRELOAD` mechanism by the intercept logic, and is specific to the type and functionality of the locking in use. When a lock call is intercepted, any instrumentation hooks related to lock acquisition are invoked, and then control is transferred to the dispatcher.

The dispatcher queries the PIC to determine the instrumented version of the basic block pointed to by the return address of the original lock call. It then *modifies* the return address on the stack to

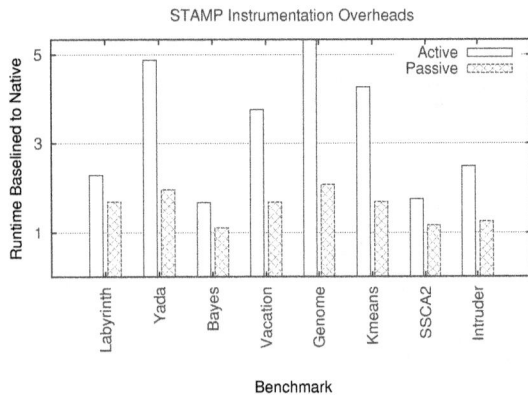

Figure 6. Instrumentation Overhead

point to the instrumented version of the basic block (the PIC having been mapped into memory). On exit from the dispatcher, control transfers into the PIC and executes the instrumented version of the critical section. The unlock call is replaced with a call into the instrumentation hook, which indicates on return if any locks are held. If no locks are held, control returns to the native binary. Otherwise control returns to the dispatcher which decides the appropriate basic block to branch to in the PIC.

The result of this scheme is that, when executing in passive mode, there is no overhead for inserting instrumentation (as it has already been inserted during the active phase). Nor is there any overhead when executing *un-instrumented code* outside any critical section, as in such cases execution proceeds directly from the native binary.

The dispatcher is also used to resolve indirect branches by looking up the PIC. Finally, if a query into the PIC fails due to the PIC not being complete, an exception is raised to the backend. The default behaviour on an unhandled exception is to switch to executing un-instrumented code out of the native binary.

3.2.3 Passive Instrumentation Overheads

In this section, we evaluate the difference in overhead between running in active and passive modes. We use a specially constructed "no-op" backend in this section, that simply acquires and releases necessary locks at critical section boundaries (substituting the original lock and unlock calls) and directly returns the address passed in for shared memory references. The only overheads left are thus the instrumentation call overhead, and that due to PIN (in active mode) or the dispatcher (in passive mode). Other backends illustrating various case studies follow later in the paper.

We use the STAMP benchmarks to demonstrate how the dispatcher lowers overheads. We use a single global lock to implement the transactions in STAMP and thus the TM_BEGIN and TM_END calls (such as in Figure 1) are compiled to pthread lock acquire and release calls. We use macros to turn the manual instrumentation of shared memory accesses (such as shown in Figure 1) into direct memory accesses. We then use the instrumentation system presented thus far to instrument these automatically in the binary. Our baseline is the x86 binary running *without any instrumentation*.

Figure 6 shows the performance overhead with this no-op backend for the STAMP benchmarks (running with 16 threads). We measure the execution time running with instrumentation baselined to (divided by) the execution time of the binary running without instrumentation. Using the dispatcher instead of PIN is faster in all

cases, with benefits ranging from 26% for labyrinth to as much as 61% in the case of genome.

A key limitation of the dispatcher is that it depends on critical sections being delimited by shared library calls (in order to use the LD_PRELOAD mechanism). In future work, we intend to remove this restriction by providing a means to redirect function execution within the loaded binary. This can be done, for example, by placing an appropriate branch instruction at the first few bytes of the function after the binary is loaded into memory.

4. Case Studies

In the following we describe two case studies (backend runtime systems) that make use of the PIC through more complex backends We demonstrate both of them using STAMP, starting with a prebuilt PIC, running in passive mode. Note that we use the same binaries and the *same PIC* for both the case studies, since the backend is decoupled from the instrumentation.

4.1 STM Profiler

The profiler uses ideas from a similar profiler we have built earlier to predict transactional memory performance [16]. That work used PIN to trace memory accesses in a critical section as well as to measure lock contention. Unfortunately PIN added significant overhead, making it extremely difficult to measure the time spent waiting for a lock accurately. This instrumentation system allows a simple remedy to that problem by using passive execution mode.

An example output from the profiler for the vacation benchmark of STAMP is shown in Figure 7. For each critical section (source line number is optionally obtained from debug information for the binary), the profiling tool prints the fraction of total execution time spent waiting for and executing the critical section followed by the average number of waiters seen for the lock. It then prints properties of the critical section: number of shared memory reads and writes instrumented, the number of locations reads from and written to and, finally, the *dependence density*. This last metric [22] is the probability that, were the critical sections scheduled in parallel, there would be a data flow dependence seen by a dynamic instance of this critical section. It essence it estimates the conflict probability were the binary to be run with transactional memory.

The crucial point about the profiler output is that the first two metrics depend on accurate timing information about locks and minimum instrumentation overhead. The last five metrics depend on tracing all memory accesses in a critical section (the log files are post-processed later) and thus impose significant overhead. In order to satisfy both these goals in a single run of the binary, the dispatcher for profiling implements four phases of execution, shown in the state machine of Figure 8. Lock timing and waiters-related information is collected in the timing phase. Critical section tracing is done in the tracing phases. No information is collected during the silent phases. Tuning the length of the four phases changes the sampling rate (fraction of critical sections instrumented for either timing or tracing). The dispatcher switches to the instrumented version of the critical section in the PIC only in the tracing phase, thus eliminating any tracing overhead when it is not needed. This flexibility in applying instrumentation is essential for building an efficient and accurate profiler.

Finally, the profiler ignores exceptions raised in passive instrumentation mode, since un-instrumented execution in a critical section only affects the accuracy of the profiled data and does not affect correct execution of the binary.

CS	cs_frac(%)	wait_frac(%)	avg_waiters	rd_ops	rd_locs	wr_ops	wr_locs	dep_dens
client.c:247	0.120	0.811	6.870	447.585	203.204	20.510	14.076	0.440
client.c:267	0.041	0.882	6.868	126.768	74.950	4.363	4.307	0.016
client.c:196	8.037	82.849	6.871	447.412	127.811	12.094	11.601	0.007

Figure 7. Profiling the vacation benchmark in STAMP

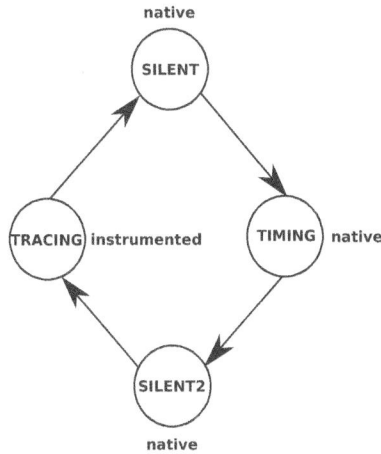

Figure 8. Profiler Phases

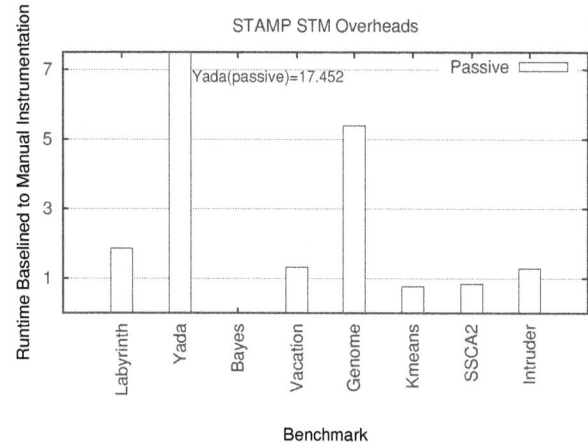

Figure 9. Instrumentation Overhead over Manual

4.2 Software Lock Elision

The second case study we discuss is software lock elision: the automatic transformation of a lock-based binary into one which uses software transactional memory. The instrumentation for shared memory accesses allows indirection of reads and writes to STM buffers. We apply the well known two-phase commit protocol that most STMs use [6] to atomically apply changes to shared memory at the end of the critical section. In order to judge the efficiency of our automatic shared memory access instrumentation, we compared against manually inserted instrumentation at the source code level. The STAMP benchmarks are already available with this instrumentation. We kept the backend runtime system (the STM implementation) the same. Figure 9 shows the overhead (running time with automatic instrumentation divided by running time with manual instrumentation) of the automatic instrumentation over the manual one, when running with 16 threads. The goal is to achieve overheads equal to that of the manual instrumentation using a purely automatic technique. Most of the benchmarks are at a ratio close to 1.0, meaning our automatic instrumentation is as efficient as the manual one.

However, Yada and Genome however show extremely high overheads (17X, 5X), and in the case of Bayes the amount of instrumented accesses is so large that it overflows the STM buffers. When we compared the data provided by the profiler (previous section) with statistics obtained from the manual instrumentation, we realised that the instrumentation infrastructure inserted far more instrumentation calls than the manual one for these three benchmarks.

To understand why this is the case, consider Figure 10, which shows a fragment of code from the genome benchmark. It includes a transaction, that subsequently makes a call to insert an entry into a hash table that uses the hash function at the bottom. The hash function includes no (manual) instrumentation of the string being hashed. This reflects the knowledge of the programmer that, al-

```
TM_BEGIN(); { // stamp/genome/sequencer.c:290
 long ii_stop = MIN(i_stop, (i+CHUNK_STEP1));
 for (long ii = i; ii < ii_stop; ii++) {
  void* segment = vector_at(segmentsContentsPtr, ii);
  TMHASHTABLE_INSERT(uniqueSegmentsPtr, segment,
                     segment);
 } /* ii */
} TM_END();

ulong_t hash_sdbm (char* str) {
  ulong_t hash = 0;
  ulong_t c;
  while ((c = *str++) != '\0') {
    hash = c + (hash << 6) + (hash << 16) - hash;
  }
  return hash;
}
```

Figure 10. A fragment of code from the genome benchmark

though the string is shared between threads, the organisation of the program is such that past the initialisation point the string is shared read-only. A program-specific optimisation has thus been made by the programmer to remove any instrumentation in the hash_sdbm function. Unfortunately our instrumentation infrastructure cannot incorporate such knowledge and ends up adding a far larger number of instrumentation calls. In Section 6 we show how a combination of static and runtime techniques can be used to *safely* incorporate these optimisations automatically.

Finally, the STM needs to handle exceptions raised in passive mode correctly. This is done through the standard STM practise of *irrevocability* [23], where only one transaction is allowed to run at a time, and hence can operate without any instrumentation. Note that this only occurs for any critical sections not discovered when generating the PIC. In the next section we describe how we ensure good coverage of basic blocks by applying an on-demand static discovery technique.

5. Static Basic Block Discovery

Passive mode should ideally execute with every basic block reachable in a critical section instrumented and placed in the PIC. The instrumentation system presented thus far depends on PIN to discover basic blocks for us. PIN allows instrumentation of code at the granularity of a trace: a contiguous sequence of basic blocks terminated by an unconditional branch. Crucially, traces are presented for instrumentation only when they are about to be executed. This leaves the process of generating a complete PIC dependent on program inputs and, in the case of the multithreaded programs we are interested in, timing.

Deciding if the PIC is complete is undecidable in the presence of indirect branches. However, it is entirely decidable given only direct branches. Hence, we use proactive basic block discovery by *statically* traversing the control flow graph at *runtime*. This allows us to discover reachable basic blocks even before they are executed. We do this using a depth-first search of the control flow graph in the binary using Algorithm 1. The basic block at the root (the starting block in the trace that needs instrumenting) is added to the basic block stack, which is then passed to the algorithm. The traversal is terminated on either finding an indirect branch or a call that terminates a critical section.

Algorithm 1 Depth-First Search of Control Flow Graph

```
 1: while BasicBlockStack is not empty do
 2:     bb = BasicBlockStack.pop()
 3:     Instrument bb and add to persistent instrumentation cache
 4:     ins = bb.LastInstruction()
 5:     /* ins must be a branch */
 6:     if ins ends a critical section (unlock call) then
 7:         continue
 8:     else
 9:         if ins is a direct branch then
10:             bb = BasicBlockAt(ins.target())
11:             BasicBlockStack.push(bb)
12:         end if
13:         if ins is a conditional branch then
14:             /* has a basic block at fall-through */
15:             bb = BasicBlockAt(ins.next())
16:             goto line 3
17:         end if
18:     end if
19: end while
```

Using static traversal improves the rate at which the PIC approaches completion but we still depend on dynamic execution to discover starting points of critical sections, and to look past indirect branches. Another limitation in practise is PIN's capability to locate basic block boundaries. An interesting example we encountered when instrumenting the standard C library was an instruction sequence that checked the thread count and, if it was zero, jumped into a locked instruction at a point just past the lock prefix, effectively removing the overhead of the lock when there is only one thread. PIN does not make the target of the jump available in its list of instructions until actual execution discovers it. Note that the implementation of proactive basic block discovery pushes PIN's APIs into uses that were likely not envisaged by the developers.

Proactive basic block discovery borrows some of the best features from static and dynamic binary rewriting techniques. Practically, we found it extremely effective in quickly building the PIC. For example, we used this infrastructure extensively on the STAMP benchmarks.

Benchmark	Static + Dynamic			Dynamic		
	1	*2*	*3*	*1*	*2*	*3*
Bayes	1435	0	0	723	2	0
Genome	383	0	0	221	0	4
Intruder	629	0	0	452	2	4
Kmeans	178	0	0	91	4	0
Labyrinth	443	0	0	340	2	0
SSCA2	394	0	0	111	0	0
Vacation	853	0	0	464	0	0
Yada	1113	0	0	899	1	0

Table 2. The number of basic blocks added to the PIC for each successive iteration of instrumented execution. The combination of dynamic execution with static basic block discovery (*lhs*) enables much faster convergence than with just dynamic execution (*rhs*).

Benchmark	Executable(bytes)	CS Count	PIC size/Binary size
Bayes	181603	18	0.34
Genome	118334	8	0.16
Intruder	153089	6	0.20
Kmeans	52821	6	0.17
Labyrinth	116384	6	0.18
SSCA2	140156	13	0.14
Vacation	143772	6	0.28
Yada	196715	9	0.29

Table 3. Persistent Instrumentation Cache Space Costs

As Table 2 shows, with static walking of the control flow graph the PIC converges within one iteration. On the other hand, without static walking of the CFG, the PIC does not converge even after three iterations. Another advantage of proactive code discovery is that we were able to run STAMP with reduced inputs sets in order to build the PIC. Thus, even with the overhead of interception using PIN, building the PIC for all the benchmarks took only a minute and 18 seconds. On the other hand, running with the STM backend took 18 minutes. Proactive basic block discovery proved to be an invaluable time saving tool for much of our research.

In spite of proactive basic block discovery, the PIC is space efficient since it usually holds only a fraction of the actual executable, unlike a dynamic binary rewriting engine that would ultimately hold all executed code in its code cache. Table 3 shows the original executable size, the number of critical sections and the size of the fully generated PIC as a fraction of the executable size. Bayes has the largest relative size of the PIC at 34%. In reality the relative size of the PIC is even smaller since the static executable size does not take into account shared library code that may be called. In the case of Bayes, for example, the PIC includes an instrumented version of the glibc `quicksort` function.

6. Private Data Tracking

Making automatic shared memory access instrumentation practical requires some way to distinguish data that is thread-private from that which is not. This is a problem for data on the heap, as there is no clear way to distinguish these (unlike either global thread private variables – which are usually accessed through a special segment base – or auto variables on the stack).

The Genome, Bayes and Yada benchmarks in STAMP represent three cases where this is problematic, as was seen in Figure 9. One way to get around this issue is to expose an annotation that indicates thread-private variables to the instrumentation methodology. For example, some compilers that automatically instrument STAMP [20] choose to make such annotation visible to the com-

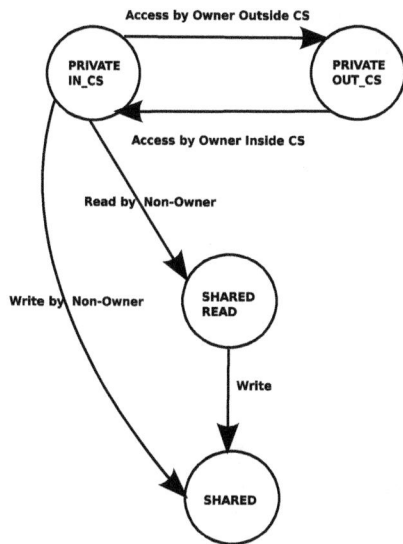

Figure 11. State machine for allocation pools

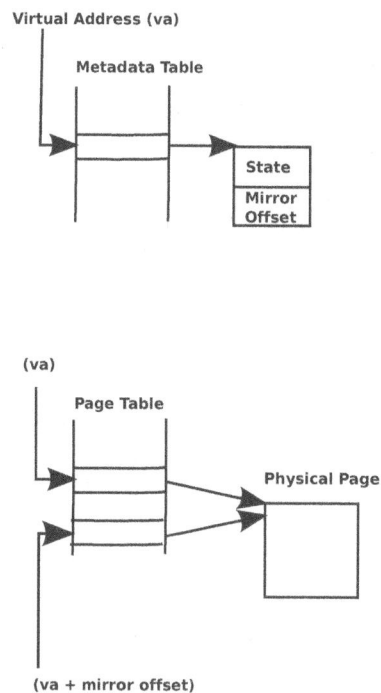

Figure 12. Memory mapping for allocation pools

piler as a language extension. This is not possible in our case since we operate at the binary level where source code information is not available. Hence we wanted to come up with an automatic technique that can reduce the impact of these extra barriers. In this section we present a private data tracking (PDT) scheme that safely reduces the cost of instrumentation for thread-private locations without using any source code information.

6.1 Allocation Pools

Our solution starts with the observation that it is usually possible to discriminate thread-private heap data from that which is not by considering their allocation sites. In the STAMP benchmarks, for example, thread private data is allocated at different physical call sites in the binary from data that is shared. However, it is not possible to statically know which allocation site allocates thread-private data. Instead we start with the assumption that all allocation sites allocate thread-private data and then dynamically detect when an allocation site has allocated data that turns out to be shared between threads.

A complication with this approach is that it is not possible to intercept memory accesses outside critical sections (access to shared data can happen outside critical sections using other methods of synchronisation). A key design cornerstone for us was to allow direct execution from the native binary for any code outside a critical section. Hence we make use of hardware memory protection to detect when memory regions are shared among threads.

Our solution intercepts all memory allocation and free calls in the binary (using the LD_PRELOAD mechanism) and uses a separate per-thread, per-allocation site allocation pool. The pages for each allocation pool can thus be independently protected using the standard mprotect call in Linux.

Figure 11 shows the states that each allocation pool can be in and the possible transitions between them. The states PRIVATE IN_CS and PRIVATE OUT_CS correspond to cases where the allocation pool (and its associated pages) are owned by a single thread (private). The state SHARED READ represents read-only access to the entire allocation pool. Finally the SHARED state represents shared read-write access to the allocation pool.

We use a different privilege protection for pages in each state. Faulting accesses trap into a fault handler that changes page state to reflect sharing (transitions in Figure 11). In the read-only state only read access is permitted to the pages. In the shared state all access is permitted to the pages.

Setting page permissions for the owned (private) states is tricky. We want to be able to detect when other threads access the page while still allowing access by the owner. Unfortunately, the page tables in Linux are shared among threads and thus one cannot expose different protections for the same page to different threads. The solution we use is to separate accesses by the owner within a critical section from those outside of any critical section.

The PRIVATE OUT_CS state represents the case where access is only allowed outside critical sections. In this state we use the *most permissive* page protection settings, allowing all access. This might seem strange, but only results in us being unable to detect sharing when in the PRIVATE OUT_CS state. On the positive side however, it means that the owning thread can freely access pages from its owned allocation pools.

The PRIVATE IN_CS state represents the case where access is only allowed inside critical sections. In this state *all* access to the page is withdrawn. Thus any access by a non-owning thread faults resulting in a state transition. This however means that there must remain some way for the owning thread to access these pages. We accomplish this by a *mirror* mapping (Figure 12). Each page in an allocation pool is mapped twice (from a backing file on an in-memory filesystem). In addition to the virtual address visible to the application, we map it at a known mirror offset. The mapping at the mirror offset is always accessible and is used by the owner for any accesses within the instrumentation callbacks.

The two private states capture thread-private patterns where allocations made and initialised outside a transaction are used within transactions. They also capture patterns where allocations are made, used, and discarded exclusively within transactions [7].

```
b4: nop
b5: nop
b6: nop
b7: jmp    0xf1 #patched jump
bc: mov    $0x55cf7000,%edx
c2: mov    %eax,%ecx
c4: shr    $0xc,%ecx
c7: mov    (%edx,%ecx,4),%ecx
ca: test   %ecx,%ecx
cc: je     0xdc
d2: mov    (%ecx),%edx
d4: test   %edx,%edx
d6: je     0xf8
dc: push   %eax
de: mov    $0xb8,%ecx
e4: mov    $0x35,%edx
ea: call   0xfe06abb0 #patching routine
ef: pop    %eax
f1: xor    %edx,%edx
f3: call   0xfe067400 #instrumentation callback
f8: mov    (%eax),%edx
```

Figure 13. Self-Modifying Instrumentation

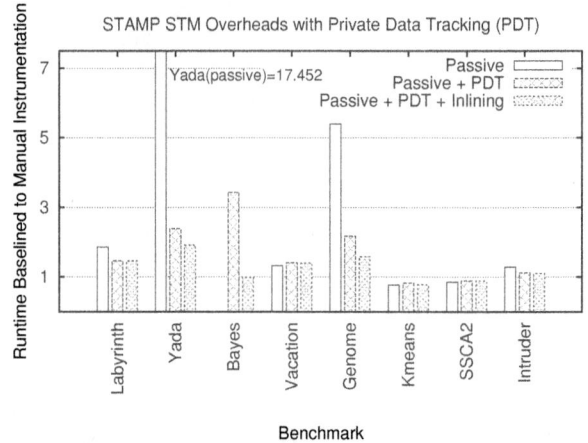

Figure 14. STAMP + Private Data Tracking

However if a thread-private allocation is used frequently both within and outside a transaction, it leads to excessive state changes with the corresponding mprotect calls becoming a performance bottleneck. We currently limit the occurrence of such cases by placing a threshold on the number of times an allocation pool can transition between the two private states: if this threshold is exceeded, we permanently place the pool in the shared state. In future work, we intend to explore solutions where we give each thread its own private page table, thereby simplifying the state machine and removing this case.

Finally, changing states for an allocation pool requires ensuring that no other thread can speculatively use the old state. We accomplish this through a quiescing mechanism whereby we ensure that no thread is executing out of the PIC before changing the allocation pool state.

6.2 Per-Page Metadata

In the shared read-only state, all reads simply use the original pointer for the access, since the location is shared read-only. For the PRIVATE IN_CS state, all reads and writes use the corresponding mirror pointer. To maintain the current state of a page, we allocate a global array whose elements are pointers for each page in the system: the metadata table in Figure 12. The entry points to a per allocation pool structure recording the current state for the pool. The instrumentation callbacks for shared memory access perform a lookup and a check to determine the correct mode of access and whether a state change needs to be performed.

Our data structures are designed to add a space overhead of under 2% to each physically accessed page. Virtual address space is also at a premium on the 32-bit machines we used for our experiments: with some benchmarks allocating as much as 1.5 GB of space, doubling the virtual address space required to 3GB for mirror maps was not feasible. Instead we make the observation that the mirror map is never required once we transition out of the two private states. We can therefore unmap the mirror space when we reach either of the non-private states.

6.3 Optimising Instrumentation

To fully realise the benefits of private data tracking, it is desirable to eliminate the call from the PIC altogether, at least for reads to thread-private memory. We do this through a combination of

inlining checks within the PIC and using self-modifying code. First, we place a jump to the next instruction that begins the PDT checks. If the PDT checks succeed, we jump over the call to the instrumentation routine. On the other hand, if the PDT check fails, we call back to special patching function that patches the initial jump to the next instruction. This will directly branch to the call to the instrumentation routine, removing the inlined PDT checks.

A example of this "self-modifying instrumentation" is shown in Figure 13. The jmp is placed (via padding through nops) such that the branch offset is aligned to a 4 byte boundary (to avoid x86 self modifying code related quirks). The jump (in this disassembled fragment from the PIC) has been patched to jump to the callback (at 0xf3) meaning the inlined PDT checks right afterwards must have failed during execution. If the PDT checks were to succeed, the conditional jump at 0xd6 would have moved directly to using the original pointer at 0xf8.

This form of self modifying instrumentation works on the assumption that instructions that access thread-private locations can be statically partitioned from those that do not, and hence a single run is usually sufficient to set up the PIC appropriately to eliminate callbacks for accesses to thread-private locations. Note that if this assumption does not hold it simply means that all accesses are modified to call into the backend runtime system, which can then dynamically filter out thread-private accesses.

In Figure 14 we demonstrate the effects of private data tracking. It adds little overhead to most benchmarks but in the case of Genome and Yada it significantly reduces the overheads of automatic instrumentation. In the case of Bayes it brings the amount of shared memory access within reach of STM buffering. The average overhead for automatic instrumentation over the manual one is 26% with private data tracking and inlining enabled.

6.4 Special Case: OpenMP Thread-private Data

A special case for the PDT infrastructure is when one can statically identify allocations sites that allocate thread private data. In this case, we can relinquish memory protection while placing such data in the PRIVATE_IN_CS mode. Mirror maps are no longer necessary and accesses can be made directly.

An example of this is OpenMP thread private data. The OpenMP specification prohibits thread-private data from being shared between threads. Furthermore, compilers often use dynamic data al-

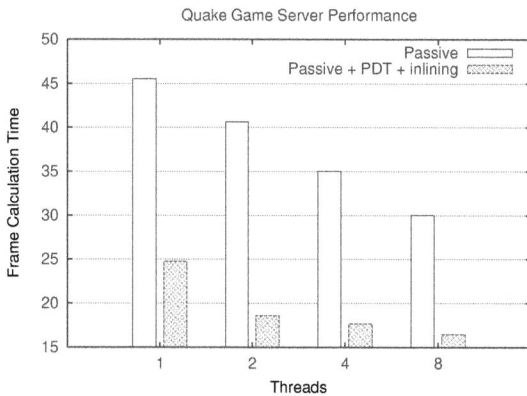

Figure 15. Quake

location for OpenMP thread-private data — for example, the Intel compilers use a specific call (`_kmpc_threadprivate_cached`) in order to allocate any thread-private data. By hooking this call we can place all such allocated thread-private data in a specially marked pool that does not require instrumentation.

We used this kind of filtering in conjunction with our instrumentation infrastructure on a multithreaded version of the Quake game server [9]. It uses OpenMP for multithreading and coarse grained OpenMP locks for synchronisation. We compiled the code using the Intel 3.0 C compiler. Figure 15 shows the benefits of filtering such accesses when applying software transactional memory to an executing game server. We report on the frame calculation time, which represents the parallel portion of the benchmark. Private data tracking significantly lowers the overhead of shared memory instrumentation for Quake.

7. Related Work

There has been significant work on instrumenting execution using dynamic binary rewriting engines in general [3, 10, 11, 19], as well as some which applies dynamic binary rewriting to critical sections in particular [12]. A key distinguishing characteristic of our work from these solutions is that we execute directly out of the native binary outside critical sections, thus paying no overhead when there is no instrumentation. We obtain these benefits by exploiting our specific use-case: instrumentation is only necessary inside critical sections. Our instrumentation methodology also bears resemblance to static instrumentation tools [8] since we operate out of a static persistent instrumentation cache. However we sidestep the problem of static instrumentation tools in looking past indirect branches and locating regions to instrument by depending on dynamic execution. We thus implement a hybrid instrumentation scheme.

Bruening et al. [4] implemented a scheme to share and persist code caches across processes, reducing code cache space overheads for common code such as shared libraries. Reddi et al. [15] implemented a scheme to persist the code cache of PIN across multiple runs. This allowed lowering the overhead of using dynamic binary rewriting, particularly for short programs since there was no overhead to re-generate instrumentation. However neither of them consider the possibility of eliminating the dynamic binary rewriting engine altogether as we do for passive instrumentation mode.

Another key aspect of our work is elimination of instrumentation for thread-private locations. We use multiple memory maps to allow access by the owning the thread while preventing accesses by

other threads; a similar idea has been explored in work on providing STM with strong atomicity [1]. However, that work required the capability to generate instrumentation for accesses outside transactions at runtime. They also placed the mirror map at a constant offset from the actual page, thus assuming a limit to the size of the heap. We add a level or indirection and in return obtain the capability to dynamically size the heap and unmap mirror mappings that are not needed, thus conserving virtual memory.

8. Conclusion

We have presented a system for instrumenting shared memory accesses that uses a combination of static and dynamic instrumentation, persistence and a custom dispatcher to provide low overhead pay-to-use instrumentation. It has proven particularly efficient for our applications and we believe that it can be extended to more general purpose instrumentation such as instrumenting functions or entire libraries. The low overhead of using a static persistent instrumentation cache would make binary rewriting for program optimisation far more feasible. A persistent instrumentation cache can also be pre-generated and distributed with binaries for useful applications such as on-demand profiling and tracing. We intend to make our infrastructure available to other researchers for use and possible extensions.

We also believe that the techniques in this work can be used to improve existing binary rewriting engines. PIN for example, already provides a mechanism to dynamically attach to and detach from running binaries. A more fine-grained version of this capability where it attaches past a marker function (like a lock acquire) and detaches past another marker function (like a lock release) would bring much of the pay-to-use instrumentation benefits that we have aimed for in this work to PIN.

References

[1] M. Abadi, T. Harris, and M. Mehrara. Transactional memory with strong atomicity using off-the-shelf memory protection hardware. In *Proceedings of the 14th ACM SIGPLAN symposium on Principles and practice of parallel programming*, pages 185–196, 2009.

[2] V. Bala, E. Duesterwald, and S. Banerjia. Dynamo: a transparent dynamic optimization system. In *Proceedings of the ACM SIGPLAN 2000 conference on Programming language design and implementation*, pages 1–12, 2000.

[3] D. Bruening, E. Duesterwald, and S. Amarasinghe. Design and implementation of a dynamic optimization framework for windows. In *4th ACM Workshop on Feedback-Directed and Dynamic Optimization*, 2000.

[4] D. Bruening and V. Kiriansky. Process-shared and persistent code caches. In *VEE '08: Proceedings of the fourth ACM SIGPLAN/SIGOPS international conference on Virtual execution environments*, pages 61–70, 2008.

[5] C. Cao Minh, J. Chung, C. Kozyrakis, and K. Olukotun. STAMP: Stanford transactional applications for multi-processing. In *Proceedings of the IEEE International Symposium on Workload Characterization*, pages 35–46, 2008.

[6] D. Dice, O. Shalev, and N. Shavit. Transactional locking II. In *Proceedings of the 20th International Symposium on Distributed Computing*, pages 194–208, 2006.

[7] A. Dragojevic, Y. Ni, and A.-R. Adl-Tabatabai. Optimizing transactions for captured memory. In *Proceedings of the twenty-first annual symposium on Parallelism in algorithms and architectures*, pages 214–222, 2009.

[8] A. Eustace and A. Srivastava. Atom: a flexible interface for building high performance program analysis tools. In *Proceedings of the USENIX 1995 Technical Conference Proceedings*, pages 303–314, 1995.

[9] V. Gajinov, F. Zyulkyarov, O. S. Unsal, A. Cristal, E. Ayguade, T. Harris, and M. Valero. QuakeTM: parallelizing a complex sequential application using transactional memory. In *Proceedings of the 23rd international conference on Supercomputing*, pages 126–135, 2009.

[10] C.-K. Luk, R. Cohn, R. Muth, H. Patil, A. Klauser, G. Lowney, S. Wallace, V. J. Reddi, and K. Hazelwood. Pin: building customized program analysis tools with dynamic instrumentation. In *Proceedings of the 2005 ACM SIGPLAN conference on Programming language design and implementation*, pages 190–200, 2005.

[11] N. Nethercote and J. Seward. Valgrind: a framework for heavyweight dynamic binary instrumentation. In *Proceedings of the 2007 ACM SIGPLAN conference on Programming language design and implementation*, pages 89–100, 2007.

[12] M. Olszewski, J. Cutler, and J. G. Steffan. Judostm: A dynamic binary-rewriting approach to software transactional memory. In *Proceedings of the 16th International Conference on Parallel Architecture and Compilation Techniques*, pages 365–375, 2007.

[13] M. Payer and T. R. Gross. Generating low-overhead dynamic binary translators. In *Proceedings of the 3rd Annual Haifa Experimental Systems Conference*, pages 22:1–22:14, 2010.

[14] P. Ratanaworabhan, M. Burtscher, D. Kirovski, B. Zorn, R. Nagpal, and K. Pattabiraman. Detecting and tolerating asymmetric races. In *Proceedings of the 14th ACM SIGPLAN symposium on Principles and practice of parallel programming*, pages 173–184, 2009.

[15] V. J. Reddi, D. Connors, R. Cohn, and M. D. Smith. Persistent code caching: Exploiting code reuse across executions and applications. In *Proceedings of the International Symposium on Code Generation and Optimization*, pages 74–88, 2007.

[16] A. Roy, S. Hand, and T. Harris. Exploring the limits of disjoint access parallelism. In *Proceedings of the First USENIX conference on Hot topics in parallelism*, 2009.

[17] B. Schwarz, S. Debray, G. Andrews, and M. Legendre. PLTO: A link-time optimizer for the Intel IA-32 architecture. In *Proceedings of the 2001 Workshop on Binary Translation*, 2001.

[18] J. Seward and N. Nethercote. Using valgrind to detect undefined value errors with bit-precision. In *Proceedings of the annual conference on USENIX Annual Technical Conference*, 2005.

[19] S. Sridhar, J. S. Shapiro, and P. P. Bungale. HDTrans: a low-overhead dynamic translator. *SIGARCH Computer Architecture News*, 35(1):135–140, 2007.

[20] T. Usui, R. Behrends, J. Evans, and Y. Smaragdakis. Adaptive locks: Combining transactions and locks for efficient concurrency. In *Proceedings of the 2009 18th International Conference on Parallel Architectures and Compilation Techniques*, pages 3–14, 2009.

[21] L. Van Put, D. Chanet, B. De Bus, B. De Sutter, and K. De Bosschere. DIABLO: a reliable, retargetable and extensible link-time rewriting framework. In *Proceedings of the 2005 IEEE International Symposium On Signal Processing And Information Technology*, pages 7–12, 2005.

[22] C. von Praun, R. Bordawekar, and C. Cascaval. Modeling optimistic concurrency using quantitative dependence analysis. In *Proceedings of the 13th ACM SIGPLAN symposium on Principles and practice of parallel programming*, pages 185–196, 2008.

[23] A. Welc, B. Saha, and A.-R. Adl-Tabatabai. Irrevocable transactions and their applications. In *Proceedings of the twentieth annual symposium on Parallelism in algorithms and architectures*, pages 285–296, 2008.

Author Index

www.ingramcontent.com/pod-product-compliance
Lightning Source LLC
Chambersburg PA
CBHW061405210326
41598CB00035B/6109